The Soviet Union

by T. M. Oberlander

Syracuse University / Department of Geography

Scale

Miles

The Moscow Kremlin   Courtesy of the Foreign Languages Publishing House, Moscow

Geography of the U.S.S.R.

Geography of the U.S.S.R.

Third Edition

PAUL E. LYDOLPH

Professor of Geography
University of Wisconsin—Milwaukee

Cartographers:
Don and Denise Temple

John Wiley & Sons
New York / Santa Barbara / London / Sydney / Toronto

Text and cover design by Eileen Thaxton

Library of Congress Cataloging in Publication Data:

Lydolph, Paul E
  Geography of the U.S.S.R.

  Includes bibliographies.
  1. Russia—Description and travel—1970-
I. Title.

DK29.L9 1977   914.7   76-26657
ISBN 0-471-55724-2

Printed in the United States of America

10 9 8 7 6 5 4 3 2

preface

The information on the U.S.S.R. has become so voluminous that it is no longer possible to cover adequately the entire geography of the Soviet Union in a book of reasonable length that can be studied in a one-semester course. Therefore, the present edition will concentrate on only the regional analysis of the country. The regional breakdown is based on the official Soviet economic regions used for the purposes of planning and statistical reporting (18 economic regions plus Moldavia). In many cases these do not make very good general geographical regions, but any regional scheme is going to have drawbacks, and any regional scheme that might be devised for the Soviet Union is going to be based more on convenience than on any intrinsic value. Use of standard economic regions will at least facilitate year-to-year comparisons and allow for updating of the book in subsequent years by means of standard Soviet statistical literature such as the various *Narodnoye Khozyaystvo*. Although the statistical reporting regions have changed occasionally, the 19 regions used here have been fairly consistent since the early 1960s, except for a few shifts of political units from one region to another.

Although the regional breakdown is based on official economic regions, the discussion within regions is by no means limited to economic geography. In fact, the discussions of landform and climate within each region have been considerably strengthened in comparison to previous editions. In addition,

V

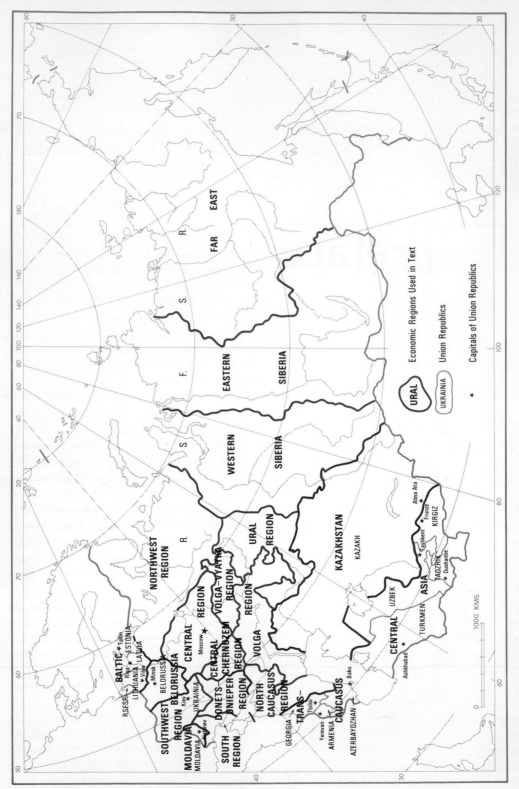

Figure 0-1 Nineteen economic regions for planning and statistical reporting.

historical perspectives and ethnology, where they are appropriate, have been dealt with in some detail. Thus, the book is more than a simple revision of the regional chapters from the second edition. It attempts to cover the entire geography of the Soviet Union, region by region. Each region is developed as a functioning whole, and its interactions with other regions are revealed. It is hoped that by the time students finish reading the book they will have a unified understanding of the intricate people-land relations that take place within the Soviet Union.

In all cases except one (Moldavia) the economic regions are subdivided into political administrative units. The political makeup of each region is shown in a table at the beginning of each chapter, along with its territorial extent and population characteristics. The statistics in the tables date from January 1, 1973, the latest available at the time of their compilation. Although there are frequent changes in the political units, most of the changes are minor and do not greatly affect the overall impression conveyed by the tables. These political units are the result of a mixture of two systems of units, one based on administrative convenience, the other on nationality groups. These relate to one another as shown in the schematic diagram in Fig. 0–2.

The U.S.S.R. is divided into 15 Soviet Socialist Republics, which supposedly are based on the 15 most populous and most advanced nationality groups in the country. There are some exceptions to this; it is deemed necessary for an S.S.R. to border on the periphery of the country, because the constitution says that a union republic has the right to secede at any time. Therefore, some major nationality groups, such as the Tatars in the Volga Bend region, have not been accorded union republic status, because theoretically their secession from the Soviet Union would leave a hole in the middle of the country. They, and some other major groups, have been accorded the status of Autonomous Soviet Socialist Republic, which is the second highest nationality-based political unit.

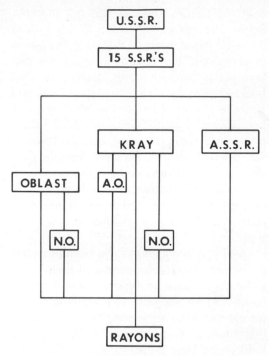

Figure 0-2 Organizational structure of political administrative units in the U.S.S.R.

At the same general level of political jurisdiction as the A.S.S.R. are the oblast and the kray. The oblast is a unit without any nationality overtones. It has been created purely for administrative convenience. The kray combines the characteristics of both the oblast and the A.S.S.R. It usually covers a fairly large territory, most of which is not based on any nationality, but within which is situated a lesser administrative unit based on some nationality group. The kray can contain either autonomous oblasts or national okrugs or both, while the oblast can contain only a national okrug. The lowest of the political units based on nationality, the national okrug, is usually a large, remote, sparsely settled area, which might be likened to some of the Indian reservations in the United States of America. But okrugs do have representation in the House of Nationalities in the bicameral legislature of the Soviet Union. At the bottom of the political administrative structure, all these units are divided into rayons, which in the United States countryside might compare to the township and in the city to the ward or borough.

In most cases statistics are not reported below the oblast-kray-A.S.S.R. level, and therefore it is at this level that most discussion of economic and cultural phenomena will take place. In many cases statistics are not broken below the economic region level, and in some cases not below the S.S.R. level. A breakdown of statistics into only the S.S.R.s is relatively useless, of course, because the Russian Soviet Federated Socialist Republic covers more than three-fourths of the territory of the entire country and contains more than 53 percent of the entire population. Therefore, its statistics generally dwarf those of any other republic.

Specific reference lists have been provided at the ends of chapters, some of them quite extensive. However, many general works were used for reference in compiling the information for the book, and the main ones are listed below. Some general bibliographical works have been added for the convenience of readers who might want to pursue information further. The single greatest source of information on up-to-date economic geography has been the translation journal *Soviet Geography: Review & Translation,* which is listed below with the rest of the serials. Particularly valuable have been the News Notes at the end of each issue, compiled by Theodore Shabad. Shabad's book, *Basic Industrial Resources of the USSR,* has been of great help in writing this book, and he has been kind enough to read and comment on the entire manuscript. Without his great fund of knowledge on factual information on the Soviet Union, a book such as this could never have been written.

Bibliographies

1. *The American Bibliography of Slavic and East European Studies,* yearly. American Association for the Advancement of Slavic Studies, Columbus, Ohio.

2. Harris, Chauncy D., *Guide to Geographical Bibliographies and Reference Works in Russian or on the Soviet Union,* University of Chicago, Geography Research Paper No. 164, 1975, 478 pp.

3. *Referativnyy Zhurnal* (published in the U.S.S.R. in Russian). The section on geography is one of the most complete abstract journals in the world. It lists titles and summaries of periodical articles and monographs published all over the world.

Atlases

1. *Atlas SSSR* (Atlas of the U.S.S.R.), Moscow, 1969, 2nd ed., 199 pp. (in Russian). The best and most recent general atlas on the U.S.S.R. Pages 6–64 are general regional maps showing great detail of landform and location. Pages 66–123 are maps of the entire country showing many aspects of the physical and economic geography of the area. Pages 124–147 are regional economic maps. The remainder of the atlas is primarily an exhaustive gazetteer of place names.

2. *Atlas razvitiya khozyaystva i kultury SSSR: 1917–1967* (Atlas of the Growth of the Economy and Culture of the U.S.S.R.: 1917–1967), Moscow, 1967, 172 pp. (in Russian). Excellent maps of all aspects of economy and culture. Map symbols are generally divided into time periods to illustrate the growth of the economy.

3. *Atlas selskogo khozyaystva SSSR* (Atlas of Agriculture of the U.S.S.R.), Moscow, 1960, 309 pp. (in Russian). The last word on agricultural distributions in the country as of about 1957. In addition, there are many maps on the physical geography of the country, many aspects of climate as it pertains to agriculture, and political and population maps. Although the agricultural data are becoming obsolete, nothing more recent matches this monumental mapping job.

4. *Fiziko-Geograficheskiy Atlas Mira* (Physical Geographical Atlas of the World), Moscow, 1964, 298 pp. (in Russian). All printed material has been translated by Theodore Shabad and published in *Soviet Geography: Review & Translation,* May–June 1965. One of the best world atlases available.

5. *Atlas avtomobilnykh dorog SSSR* (Atlas of Highways of the U.S.S.R.), Moscow (in Russian). This atlas is revised frequently and contains many regional maps at fairly large scales. Thus, it is useful for detailed location purposes.

6. *Atlas obrazovaniye i razvitie Soyuza SSR* (Atlas of the Formation and Development of the U.S.S.R.), Moscow, 1972, 116 pp. (in Russian).

7. *Atlas SSSR v devyatoy pyatiletke* (Atlas of the U.S.S.R. for the Ninth Five-Year Plan), Glavnoye upravleniye geodezii i kartografii, Moscow, 1972, 40 pp.

8. Plummer, Thomas F., Jr., William G. Hanne, Edward F. Bruner, and Christian C. Thudium, Jr., *Landscape Atlas of the USSR*, Department of Earth, Space, and Graphic Sciences, United States Military Academy, West Point, New York, 1971, 197 pp. An excellent selection of topographic maps combined with interesting textual materials.

9. *USSR Agriculture Atlas*, Central Intelligence Agency. U.S. Government Printing Office, Washington, D.C., 1974, 59 pp. An excellently conceived compilation on all aspects of the rural scene in the U.S.S.R.

Encyclopedias

1. Florinsky, Michael T., ed., *Encyclopedia of Russia and the Soviet Union*, McGraw-Hill, New York, 1961, 624 pp.

2. Karger, Adolf, *Europaische Sowjetunion*, Westermanns Lexikon der Geographie, Wolf Tietze, ed., George Westermann Verlag, Braunschweig, 1968, 206 pp. (in German).

3. *Kratkaya geograficheskaya entsiklopediya* (Short Geographical Encyclopedia), Moscow, 1960, 5 volumes (in Russian).

4. Maxwell, Robert, ed., *Information U.S.S.R.* (Translation of most of Volume 50 of the *Great Soviet Encyclopedia*), Pergamon Press, New York, 1962, 982 pp.

5. Plaschka, O., *Sowjetunion (Asiatischer Teil)*, Westermanns Lexikon der Geog-

raphie, Wolf Tietze, ed., George Westermann Verlag, Braunschweig, 1968, 121 pp. (in German).

6. Utechin, S.V., *Everyman's Concise Encyclopedia of Russia*, Dutton, New York, 1961, 623 pp.

Serials

Among English-language periodicals the following are the most useful for geographic information on the U.S.S.R.:

1. *Soviet Geography: Review & Translation*, published ten times per year by Scripta Publishing Company in cooperation with the American Geographical Society, edited by Theodore Shabad. An indispensable publication of translated articles from professional geographical journals in the Soviet Union. In addition Shabad compiles several pages of "News Notes" at the end of each issue. Materials from this journal have been used extensively throughout the book.

2. *Soviet Studies*, published by the University of Glasgow, Scotland. A scholarly journal with occasional articles pertinent to geography.

3. *The Annals of the Association of American Geographers*. A few articles pertaining to the Soviet Union.

4. *The Geographical Review*. A few articles pertaining to the Soviet Union.

5. *Economic Geography*. A few articles pertaining to the Soviet Union.

6. *The Geographical Journal*. A few articles pertaining to the Soviet Union.

7. *The Current Digest of the Soviet Press* (weekly since 1949) and *Current Abstracts of the Soviet Press* (monthly, except July and August, since April 1968). Translations of key news items from Soviet newspapers and magazines, published by the Joint Committee on Slavic Studies of the American Council of Learned Societies and the Social Science Research Council. Many news items of interest, especially full texts of plan goals,

plan fulfillments, international agreements, and so forth. Human-interest items give pungent insight into the domestic situation.

8. *Slavic Review*. The professional journal of the American Association for the Advancement of Slavic Studies. Articles predominantly dealing with literature, political science, history, and economics.

Russian language serials of a geographical nature are:

9. *Akademiya nauk SSSR, izvestiya, seriya geograficheskaya* (Bulletin of the Academy of Sciences of the U.S.S.R., Series in Geography).

10. *Vsesoyuznoye geograficheskoye obshchestvo, izvestiya* (Bulletin of the All-Union Geographical Society).

11. *Voprosy geografii* (Problems of geography). A monograph series published by the University of Moscow.

12. *Leningrad Universitet, Vestnik, Seriya geologii i geografii* (Leningrad University, Bulletin, Series in Geology and Geography).

13. *Moskva Universitet, Vestnik, Seriya geografiya* (Moscow University, Bulletin, Series in Geography).

Books and Statistical Series

1. Domanitskiy, A.P., R.G. Dubrovina, and A.I. Isayeva, *Reki i ozera Sovetskogo Soyuza* (Rivers and Lakes of the Soviet Union). Statistical Handbook, Gidrometeoizdat, Leningrad, 1971, 104 pp.

2. Gerasimov, I.P., et al., eds., *Prirodnye usloviya i estestvennye resursy SSSR* (Natural Conditions and Natural Resources of the U.S.S.R.), Nauka, Moscow, 1963–1972, 15 volumes.

3. Harris, Chauncy D., *The Cities of the Soviet Union,* Rand McNally, Chicago, 1970, 484 pp.

4. Lydolph, Paul E., *Climates of the Soviet Union,* Vol. 7 of *World Survey of Climatology* under the general editorship

of H.E. Landsberg, Elsevier, Amsterdam, to be published in 1976.

5. Meshcheryakov, Yu. A., *Relyef SSSR* (Relief of the U.S.S.R.), Mysl, Moscow, 1972 (in Russian).

6. *Narodnoye khozyaystvo* (National Economy). Annual statistical abstracts of U.S.S.R. and regions. Listed in the January issues of *Soviet Studies* beginning in 1959 (in Russian).

7. Nikitin, N.P., E.D. Prozorov, and B.A. Tutykhin, *Ekonomicheskaya geografiya SSSR, Obshchiy Obzor* (Economic Geography of the U.S.S.R., General), Prosveshcheniye, Moscow, 1973, 367 pp. *Soyuznye respubliki (krome RSFSR)* (The Union Republics without the R.S.F.S.R.), 1974, 319 pp.

8. *Pochvenno-geograficheskoe raionirovanie SSSR,* Nauka, Moscow, 1962. Translated by Israel Program for Scientific Translations and published in English by Daniel Davey & Co. as *Soil-Geographical Zoning of the USSR,* New York, 1963, 480 pp. & fold maps.

9. Pokshishevsky, V., *Geography of the Soviet Union,* Progress Publishers, Moscow, 1974, 279 pp.

10. Saushkin, Yu. G., I.V. Nikolsky, and V.P. Korovitsyn, *Ekonomicheskaya geografiya SSSR, Chast II, ekonomicheskiye rayony* (Economic Geography of the USSR, Part II, Economic Regions), Izd. Moskovskogo universiteta, Moscow, 1973, 380 pp.

11. Shabad, T., *Basic Industrial Resources of the USSR,* Columbia University Press, New York, 1969, 393 pp.

12. *Soviet Economic Prospects for the Seventies,* Joint Economic Committee, Congress of the United States, Washington, 1973, 776 pp.

13. *Sovetskiy Soyuz* (Soviet Union), 22 volumes, Izdatelstvo Mysl, Moscow, 1966–1972 (in Russian). Regional monographs covering physical landscape, history, ethnography, culture, economy, and regional subdivisions.

14. *SSSR: Administrativno-territorialnoye deleniye soyuznykh respublik,* Moscow, yearly (in Russian). A statistical compilation of all political administrative units of the country with their areas, populations, and subdivisions.

15. Tushinskiy, G.K., ed., *Fizicheskaya Geografiya SSSR,* Prosveshcheniye, Moscow, 1966. Translated by U.S. Dept. of the Army as *Physical Geography of the USSR,* J6585, 1970, 657 pp.

16. *USSR 75,* Novosti Press Agency Yearbook, Moscow, annually. About 300 pp.

Regional Studies

1. Bandera, V.N., and Z.L. Melnyk, *The Soviet Economy in Regional Perspective,* Praeger, New York, 1973, 368 pp.

2. Dienes, Leslie, "Investment Priorities in Soviet Regions," *Annals of the Association of American Geographers,* September 1972, pp. 437–454.

3. Dienes, Leslie, "Issues in Soviet Energy Policy and Conflicts Over Fuel Costs in Regional Development," *Soviet Studies,* 23, No. 1, July 1971, pp. 26–58.

4. Dienes, Leslie, "Regional Variations of Capital and Labor Productivity in Soviet Industry," *Journal of Regional Science,* No. 3, 1972, pp. 401–406.

5. Hooson, David, "The Outlook for Regional Development in the Soviet Union," *Slavic Review,* September 1972, pp. 535–554. See also Vardys, Stanley V., "Geography and Nationalities in the USSR: A Commentary," pp. 564–570, and Hooson, "Reply," pp. 571–573.

6. Kopylov, N.V., *Krupnye ekonomicheskie rayony SSSR* (Main Economic Regions of the U.S.S.R.), Vysshaya shkola, Moscow, 1974, 280 pp.

7. Mazanova, M.B., *Territorialnye proportsii narodnogo khozyaystva SSSR* (Territorial Proportions of the National Economy of the U.S.S.R.), Nauka, Moscow, 1974, 205 pp.

8. Mints, A.A., *Prirodnaya sreda kak faktor regional'nogo ekonomicheskogo razvitiya (na primer SSSR)* (The Natural Environment as a Factor in Regional Economic Development with Particular Reference to the U.S.S.R.), *Izvestiya Akademii Nauk SSSR, seriya geograficheskaya,* 1972, No. 3, pp. 50–54 (in Russian).

9. North, Robert N., "Centralization and the Soviet Regional Economy," *Occasional Papers in Geography,* Vancouver, 1972, pp. 103–110.

acknowledgments

I wish to express my thanks to my wife, Mary, who typed most of the material several times and helped with many other tedious aspects of the work; to Don and Denise Temple, who drafted the illustrations; to my student, Kay Reynolds, who did all sorts of work involving both Russian and English language materials; and to my good sister-in-law, Lynn Klahn, who bailed out my wife when she became swamped with typing. Our departmental secretaries, Laurie Schultz, Darlene Anderson, and Holly Moss, helped in many ways.

Paul E. Lydolph

Elkhart Lake, Wisconsin
December 1975

contents

Central Economic Region

	Area (km²)	Population	Persons/km²	Percent Urban
Bryansk Oblast	35,000	1,554,000	44.5	52
Vladimir Oblast	29,000	1,531,000	52.8	70
Ivanovo Oblast	24,000	1,329,000	55.6	78
Kalinin Oblast	84,000	1,701,000	20.2	61
Kaluga Oblast	30,000	989,000	33.1	56
Kostroma Oblast	60,000	825,000	13.7	59
Moscow City ⎤	47,000	7,410,000 ⎤	284.3	100
Moscow Oblast ⎦		5,952,000 ⎦		70
Orel Oblast	25,000	906,000	36.7	45
Ryazan Oblast	40,000	1,387,000	35.0	52
Smolensk Oblast	50,000	1,095,000	22.0	53
Tula Oblast	26,000	1,943,000	75.6	75
Yaroslavl Oblast	36,000	1,402,000	38.5	74
Total	485,000	28,024,000	57.8	74

chapter 1

the central economic region

Our discussion of the Soviet Union begins in the heart of the country, the Central Economic Region around Moscow. As can be seen in the table on the preceding page, this region politically consists of Moscow City and Moscow Oblast in the center, Vladimir, Ivanovo, Yaroslavl, and Kostroma Oblasts in the northeast, Ryazan Oblast in the southeast, Tula and Orel Oblasts in the south, Kaluga and Bryansk Oblasts in the southwest, Smolensk Oblast in the west, and Kalinin Oblast in the northwest. On January 1, 1973 these political units constituted an area of 485,000 square kilometers and a population of 28,024,000 people.

In spite of its relatively small area, the Central Region is the most populous economic region in the country. It contains about 11.4 percent of the population of the U.S.S.R. in 2.2 percent of the country's area. The region is highly industrialized and urbanized; almost three-fourths of its population is classified as urban, and the greatest part of the rural population works not in agriculture but in industry, transport, and so forth, commuting daily to jobs from home villages. The region contains 234 cities and 345 urban settlements (these urban areas account for 10.5 percent of all such settlements in the country).

Not all parts of the region are equally urbanized. Although the Central Economic Region is often referred to synonymously as the Central Industrial Region, the Central

1

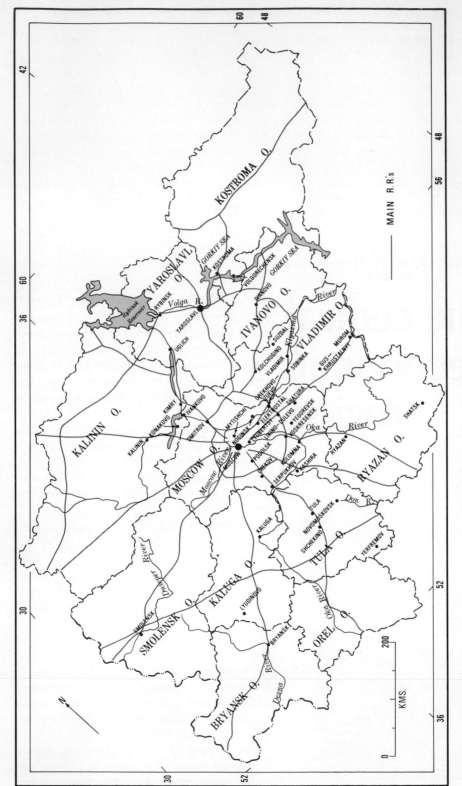

Figure 1-1   The Central Region. Large city dot indicates > 500,000 population; small dot < 500,000.

Economic Region contains extensive areas of only moderate or little city development. This is particularly true in the southern oblasts, where agriculture is more important, and it is also true in the northeastern and northwestern extremities of the region, where neither agriculture nor industry is highly developed. Kostroma Oblast in the northeast, for instance, has a population density of only 13.7 people per square kilometer, and 59 percent is classified as urban; Kalinin Oblast in the northwest has only 20.2 people per square kilometer, and 61 percent of the population is classified as urban. The least urbanized oblast is Orel at the southern extremity of the region, where 55 percent of the population is classified as rural. Thus, in spite of its relatively high average density of population, the Cen-

tral Region shows a great deal of variance within it, from 13.7 people per square kilometer in Kostroma Oblast to 284.3 people per square kilometer in the combined units of Moscow Oblast and Moscow City. Looking only at the rural population, the density varies from less than 10 people per square kilometer throughout much of Kostroma Oblast, the northwestern parts of Yaroslavl and Kalinin Oblasts, and the eastern part of Smolensk Oblast to more than 130 people per square kilometer in the immediate surroundings of the city of Moscow.

In spite of its relatively high overall population density, the region contains extensive areas of little development, usually due to poor drainage or sterile sandy soils. Over 36 percent of the entire area of the Central Re-

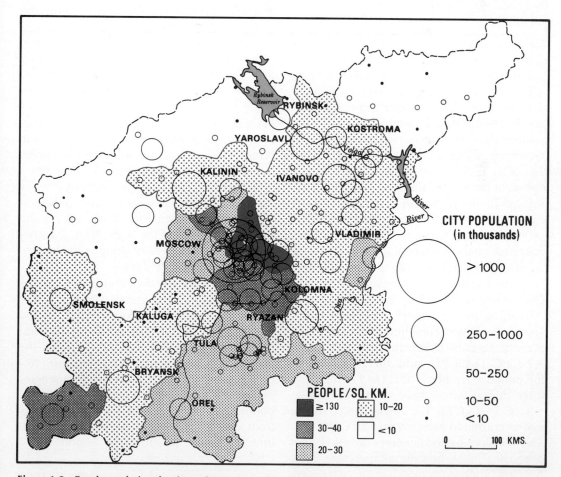

Figure 1-2 Rural population density and city sizes. From *Tsentralnyy ekonomicheskiy rayon,* p. 28.

gion is still forested. In Kostroma Oblast forests still cover 68 percent of the territory. Even in heavily populated Moscow Oblast, forests still cover 38 percent of the territory. Forests are less extensive in the oblasts farther south where originally there were more areas of grass and where better soils and a more amenable climate have provided a greater basis for agriculture. Thus, some of the less densely populated southern oblasts are more continuously settled than are the more urbanized oblasts farther north where networks of large cities are often interspersed with sparsely populated, little-used open spaces.

PHYSICAL SETTING AND NATURAL RESOURCES

Climate

The natural resource base for the central Region is limited, both for agriculture and for industry. First, the climate is relatively severe; winters are cold and long, and summers are short and cool. The region stretches from 52° to 59° north latitude, which puts even the southern boundary of the region well north of Winnipeg, Canada. Moscow, at a latitude of 55°45′N, lies far north of the limit of effective settlement in central Canada. This part of the Russian plain can sustain settlement only because of the considerable ameliorating effect of the Atlantic Ocean on the climate. Temperatures on the Russian plain in winter show significant positive deviations from latitudinal normals, but it must be remembered that the Central Region lies at high latitudes, and there is nothing in the United States that corresponds to climatic conditions in Moscow. The average January temperature in Moscow is −10.3°C (13.50°F), and the average July temperature is only 17.8°C (64°F). Temperatures during winter have dipped as low as −42°C (−45.6°F). The highest temperature ever recorded in Moscow was 37°C (98.6°F). The frost-free period averages only 141 days per year. Below-freezing temperatures have been recorded every month of the year except July and August.

The broad expanse of the Russian plain is relatively open to air movement on all sides and provides ready access to a variety of air masses coming from different directions. Since the latitudinal belt lies within the westerlies, the greatest influence comes from that direction. Air intrusions are least significant from the south, where they are blocked to a great extent by the Caucasus, the Crimean Mountains, the Balkans, and the Carpathians. Of course, there is no fresh source of maritime tropical air in the south because the large land masses of Africa, Arabia, and the Middle East interrupt.

There is no real source of continental polar air either, because the European continent tapers westward and, except for Scandinavia, there is only water to the northwest of European Russia. The continental polar air that reaches European Russia moves in from the east — from southern Siberia, Mongolia, and northern China — particularly in winter, when the Asiatic High spreads over much of the continent north of the southern mountains. A western protrusion of this high generally occupies the southern half of the east European plain during winter, and air circulating slowly around it in a clockwise fashion brings cold easterly winds into the region along its southern perimeter. This air has a long trajectory around the southern edge of the high and often reaches the Central Region after it has recurved northeastward around the western nose of the high. Thus, it comes into the Central Region along with the prevailing southwesterly flow.

When air from any direction comes into the Central Region, it is greatly modified over large expanses of land before it arrives, so any classification of air masses in the Central Region shows a predominance of what the Soviets call continental temperate air. According to Borisov,[1] air-mass frequencies during the year in Moscow are as follows: continental temperate air derived locally from various air masses, 52.6 percent; maritime temperate air from the Atlantic, 20.7

[1]A. A. Borisov, Climates of the USSR, Aldine, Chicago, 1965, p. 93.

percent; maritime arctic air from the Barents and Kara Seas, 12.1 percent; continental arctic air from the northeast, 8.7 percent; continental tropical air from the south (summer only), 5.4 percent; and maritime tropical air from the southwest, 0.5 percent.

Thus, many different air masses affect the region, but they do not differ as much as those in, say, eastern North America between the continental polar air from the north and the maritime tropical air from the south. Fronts and weather in general are not as extreme in the Central Region as they are in eastern North America because air mass contrasts are generally somewhat weaker. However, this does not mean that the weather is less complex on the east European plain. In fact, this is one of the most complex meeting places of air masses in the world. The subtle differences between air masses make for hard-to-distinguish fronts that may slope in different directions in different seasons and often develop into grotesque systems of fronts as storms swing in from various directions. During winter a major storm track goes from the Baltic eastward across the northern part of the plain and another goes from the Black Sea area northeastward across the southern part of the plain. Storms moving along these two tracks often coalesce somewhere in the Central Region to form complicated fronts that cause a great deal of cloudiness and frequent, though generally light, precipitation. Fronts are less frequent and even less distinguishable during summer, but they do penetrate the area from various directions, and they combine with convectional activity to bring a fairly pronounced summer maximum of precipitation to the area.

Winters in the Central Region are marked by days on end of featureless stratus clouds and light snow flurries. Moscow during December averages more than 23 days with sky cover between eight and ten tenths. This type of weather is so common in the east European plain that the inhabitants have a word for it, *"pasmurnaya,"* which is translated as something such as "dull, dreary weather." Throughout the year Moscow experiences 171 days of such weather. July has only 7.5

such days on the average; clouds are more of the cumulus type and precipitation is less frequent but more in amount. In December there are 19 days of at least 0.1 millimeter of precipitation, totaling an average of 36 millimeters. In July there are only 16 days of precipitation, totaling 74 millimeters. During winter, of course, the air is usually too cold to hold much moisture, and even though the air is near saturation much of the time, the absolute humidity is rather low. During summer, when the air is warmer, the absolute humidity is somewhat higher, but even in summer the average air mass is relatively cool in Moscow and precipitation amounts are not great. The precipitation total for the year averages 575 millimeters (23 inches), which is usually sufficient to produce humid conditions in this cool region. However, there can be periods during summer when drought is experienced.

While it is fortunate for agriculture that precipitation reaches a maximum during summer, the distribution during the summer is not the best for crops, since the maximum precipitation falls during middle and late summer when many crops are being harvested, rather than during early summer when the crops are undergoing their most rapid growth. It is a fairly reliable rule of thumb that in continental interiors there is a pronounced tendency for the precipitation maximum to occur during summer when convective activity is greatest, and toward the pole this summer maximum lags later and later into summer as surface heating, and hence convective activity, also gets later. Nearer the pole the snow cover melts later, and as long as there is snow to be melted the temperature of the surface air does not rise much above freezing. The heat gained from maximum insolation during the summer solstice, as well as from advection of warm air masses from the south, is used up in the latent heat of melting the snow, and little heat is left over to cause a sensible temperature rise. Hence, higher latitudes experience considerable asymmetry in seasons with respect to both temperature and precipitation. The coming of spring is delayed by the melting of snow, and by the time all the snow is gone the summer solstice is at hand and the large amounts of insolation during the almost 24-hour days cause temperatures to shoot up very rapidly to summer heights. In the fall, when there is no snow cover, the transition is much more gradual, although it is certainly more abrupt than it is at lower latitudes.

Moscow, at 55°45'N, does not illustrate this principle in classic form, but it does show some tendency toward it — the maximum precipitation falls during July and August. Farther south in the Ukraine the maximum shifts to July and even June along the Black Sea coast, while northward it lags into August and even September in places along the Arctic Coast. Thus, the higher latitudes are hampered not only by a short growing season but also by a poor distribution of precipitation during the growing season, which makes the harvest period hazardous. The often rainy harvest season, often terminated abruptly by

early winter snows, combines with poor organization and inadequate equipment and storage facilities to cause losses during the harvest of as much as a fourth of the crop, either through the inability to get the crops out of the field or through the rotting of the grain and other crops temporarily stored in the open exposed to the elements.

Although the winter precipitation is rather light, snow accumulates in the Moscow region to an average maximum depth of 52 centimeters (20 inches). A persistent snow cover remains on the ground an average of 146 days per year. The snow cover is usually adequate to protect wintering crops such as clover and alfalfa, and it generally provides ample melt water during spring to moisten the soil for crops.

The climatic conditions described for Moscow vary significantly from south to north

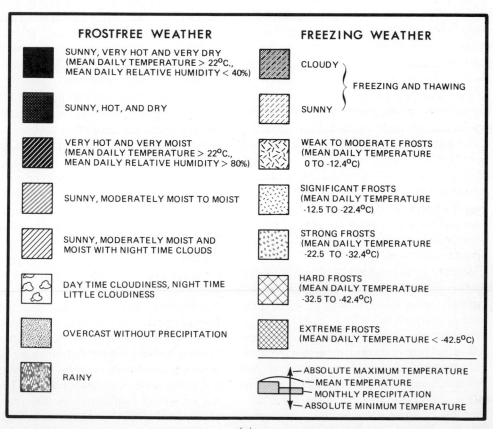

(a)

across the Central Region, which spans a distance of about 550 kilometers. The growing season is significantly warmer and longer in the south in Bryansk and Orel Oblasts and shorter and cooler in the north in Yaroslavl and Kostroma Oblasts. Also, the humidity conditions diminish from north to south so that the southern extremities of the region become subhumid. In fact, only recently Bryansk (1961) and Orel (1962) Oblasts were transferred for statistical and planning purposes to the Central Region from the Central Chernozem Region to the south, which is characterized by its droughty climate, natural grass vegetation, and fertile black soil.

Vegetation

The cool, humid climate of much of the Central Region has been conducive to the growth of a mixed forest vegetation over much of the area, except for the drier southern fringe where the so-called forest-steppe begins to extend southward out of the region. Originally in this southern area broad expanses of grasses were interspersed with clumps of trees, particularly in river valleys where a source of ground water was constantly available. But dense forests originally covered the bulk of the Central Region. These consisted of mixtures of broadleaf deciduous hardwoods and coniferous evergreen softwoods. Generally the broadleaf deciduous trees predominated in the south and the coniferous evergreens in the north. Much of the region represents a transition between the two.

Small elevation and drainage differences cause variations in vegetation over short distances. Uplands tend to have mixtures of spruce, oak, maple, linden, birch, and aspen, with occasional ash, elm, and crabapple. Low, ill-drained areas are generally occupied by birch thickets and some aspen underlain with brushy growths of spirea, hazelnut, and so forth. Black alder with some mixtures of aspen and birch are generally found on the floodplains of the streams. On gravelly morainic hillocks the forest growth tends toward pure spruce, which adapts well to droughty soils. Pine may also be found in such areas. These are particularly prevalent on the ancient alluvial sands of the Oka River Valley,

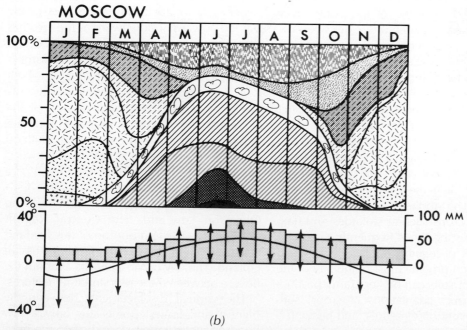

(b)

Figure 1-3   Weather types, temperature, and precipitation at Moscow.

where thin pine stands mixed with broom grass present a steppelike character to the landscape. In the sandy, ill-drained glacial plain of the Meshchera Lowland in eastern Moscow Oblast, a pine-marsh region prevails with some admixtures of spruce.

The forests of the Central Region have been cut over again and again. The original stands contained some prime lumber trees, particularly oaks, which have been extensively cut for shipbuilding since the time of Peter the Great. Secondary growths have been important for firewood and paper pulp, and some of the better trees have yielded lumber as well. But in spite of the heavy cutting, a significant portion of the area is still in forest, primarily because of drainage conditions. Wherever there is poor drainage, cultivation has not taken over and the forests remain, albeit in a much modified state from original stands.

Soils

The cool, humid climatic conditions and forest vegetation over much of the Central Region have been conducive to the formation of podzolic soils. The soils throughout much of the region have been badly leached of plant minerals, and on some of the hillier river breaks they have undergone extensive erosion. The forest cover has provided some organic material to the soil, but not as much as grass would have. In the marshier areas, bog soils have developed that are high in humus but low in basic minerals. The best soils of the region are probably the alluvia on river floodplains, but these locations are subject to frequent floods. Therefore, the soil resources of the area are not very good. The soils are relatively fertile in the south, but are less so in the north. The northern acidic soils can be adapted to crops such as potatoes and flax, but they must be limed frequently to sustain good stands of legumes such as clover and alfalfa, which provide most of the hay of the region. Such soils can be kept fairly productive by correct adaptations of crops, soil-erosion prevention measures, and heavy fertilization.

Landform

The Central Region is in the middle of the broad east European plain where relief features are minimal. Significant variations in landscape do occur, generally related either to bedrock or to glacial materials. The east European plain sits on a Precambrian base of complex igneous and metamorphic rocks, overlain by a veneer of sedimentary strata laid down in broad shallow seas during certain periods of the Paleozoic and Mesozoic.

The gross structural configuration of the east European plain is that of a great basin, so the sedimentary strata are thicker in the center than on the sides. Particularly to the north and south of the center the Precambrian basement complex rises. It reaches the surface north of Leningrad and continues as the surface rock throughout the Karelian and Scandinavian region. In the south it generally does not reach the surface except in incised river valleys, such as the Dnieper, where the outcropping of the harder crystalline rocks has produced significant rapids in the stream. In the center around Moscow the Precambrian foundation lies at a depth of about 1650 meters (about 5000 feet).

In most places the sedimentary strata do not lie perfectly horizontally but have been gently warped upward or downward as the area has undergone minor vertical movements in and out of the sea. One of the primary upwarps is the so-called Central Russian Upland, which is a broad swell that trends northwest-southeast across the central portion of the plain just to the west of Moscow. Another significant upwarp is oriented north-south on the western side of the Volga River between Kazan and Volgograd, the so-called Volga Heights. In between these two upwarps lies a broad synclinal basin generally known as the Oka-Don Lowland. The Central Region straddles the western portion of this lowland and the eastern flank of the Central Russian Upland. The city of Moscow sits at about the flexure between these two structural features.

The vertical displacements between the highest and lowest points are only a few hundred meters at most, and since the hori-

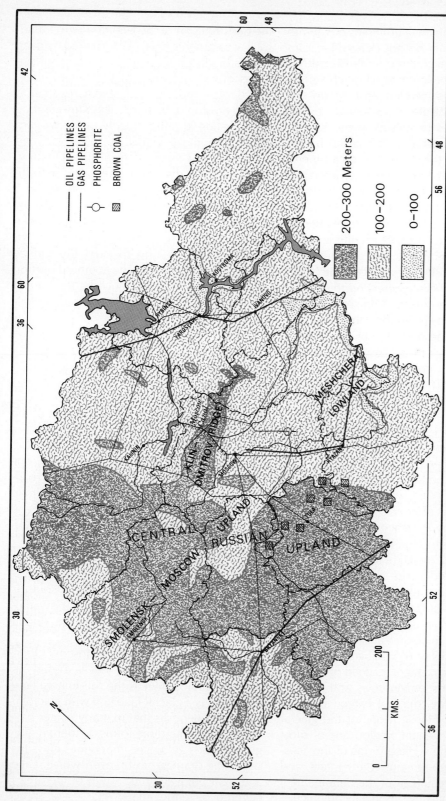

Figure 1-4 Landform, hydrology, minerals, and pipelines of the Central Region.

zontal distances involve hundreds of kilometers, the rock strata do not deviate far from horizontal. However, these subtle departures from horizontal have imparted much variety to the landscape. Stream erosion on the slightly tilted strata of varying resistances has produced a series of cuestas whose escarpments form fairly prominent features in various segments of the plain. The escarpments face outward from the downwarped areas and inward toward the uplifted areas. In the more humid central and northern parts of the plain, myriads of small streams have eroded the escarpments into broad zones of complex hills. In the Central Region one such cuesta zone is the so-called Klin-Dmitrov Ridge, which runs west-east 50 to 70 kilometers north of Moscow. Here a hilly strip of land separates the rolling upland on the south from the broad, flat lowland to the north through which the Volga River flows in an easterly direction. Many water gaps breach the ridge in a north-south direction. The one at Klin is occupied by the Moscow-Leningrad railroad, and the one at Dmitrov is occupied by the Moscow Canal built from 1933–1937.

The surface landform to the north of Moscow is complicated by recent deposits of glacial till over the bedrock features. The northern part of the plain was affected by four primary advances of ice out of a Scandinavian center during the Pleistocene, much as was the case in eastern North America. The two older glaciations, the Likhvin or Oka and the Dnieper, extended across the Central Region. The Dnieper stage advanced farthest south, with separate lobes extending down the Dnieper Valley to approximately Kremenchug and down the Don Valley to about 170 kilometers northwest of Volgograd. The third stage, the Moscow stage, reached only to the northern outskirts of Moscow, and the last stage, the Valday, did not extend into the Central Region. Hence, none of the glacial features in the Central Region are of most recent origin; the surface forms of the Moscow glacial stage remain largely intact, and poor drainage results from the derangement of stream channels by this glacial advance.

Swamps and lakes cover extensive areas in the northern part of the Central Region. Bedrock escarpments have been masked by deep covers of glacial till, and the present surface forms along such rises as the Klin-Dmitrov Ridge relate more to glacial features than to stream erosion of bedrock. The Klin-Dmitrov Ridge is buried rather deeply in the western portion, but the glacial till thins eastward and is only about 3 meters deep around Dmitrov. Kames, kettles, disrupted eskers, and so forth, are typical of the topography of this region.

In the older glacial areas south of Moscow the glacial surface forms have largely been obliterated by subsequent stream erosion, but the glacial till remains to mask the surface expression of bedrock. The southern portion of the Central Region is much better drained than the north, and the surface forms are typical stream erosion features.

The elevation of the Klin-Dmitrov Ridge continues west-southwestward across the upwarp of the Central Russian Upland as a broad irregular zone of terminal moraine features known as the Smolensk-Moscow Upland. This marks the southerly margin of the Moscow stage of glaciation and presents a somewhat higher elevation than the land to either the north or the south. Thus, it is a zone where better drainage has provided the roadbeds for a major highway and a major railroad that runs from Moscow through Smolensk and Minsk to Warsaw. It is along this better-drained upland that Napoleon's and Hitler's armies advanced eastward toward Moscow. To the north lies the poorly drained area of more recent glaciation, and to the south in southern Belorussia lies the very flat, swampy proglacial lake bed known as the Pripyat Marshes.

In the southeastern part of Moscow Oblast north of the Oka River lies a broad flat swampy area known as the Meshchera Lowland. This is a glacial lake bed with glaciofluvial sandy deposits that in many places have been blown into dune forms. Underlying the glacial sands are water-impervious clays that cause the drainage to be even worse. Lakes and peat bogs abound. Much of the area is covered by either marsh grasses or spruce forests.

Mineral Resources

The mineral resources of the Central Region are very limited. Most significant is the Moscow coal basin, which underlies much of the southern and western parts of the Central Region and extends northward into the Northwest Region. Although it covers quite a large area, the coal is all low grade and can be used only for heating and electrical generation. However, since it is so close to the huge urban markets of the Central Region, it is one of the more productive coal fields of the country. Some small local iron deposits in the southern part of the region early provided the impetus for the development of an iron and steel industry in such towns as Bryansk and Tula. These early steel industries were fueled by charcoal manufactured from the local forests. Sand deposits in several areas provided the early development of glass industries in such cities as Gus-Khrustalny. In more recent years the mining of phosphorite has become important at Yegoryevsk and Polpino. In addition, abundant building materials such as sands and gravels are available for the great amount of construction taking place in the region, and there are some gypsum and lime resources for the manufacture of cement. However, all of these mineral resources are minor compared to similar resources in other parts of the country, and they have provided only for local development. There are no mineral resources of national significance in the region.

SETTLEMENT

With such a meager supply of resources, both for agriculture and for industry, one might wonder why this region has become the most populous and most industrialized area in the country. Historical analysts do not agree on the causes for this development. They do agree that it was not due to the natural resource base. Some environmental determinists point out that Moscow was situated in an advantageous position among the headwaters of the Volga River, which before the development of other forms of transportation provided it with ideal water connections with much of the European plain. However, one might logically question why Moscow prospered rather than some of the other cities around it, since Moscow is located on the Moscow River, which flows into the Oka, which eventually flows into the Volga far downstream at Nizhniy Novgorod (Gorkiy). The Moscow River is a poor stream for navigation. Why was it not Tver (Kalinin), Yaroslavl, Nizhniy Novgorod, or some other city along the Volga itself that prospered and became the primary center?

The original Slavic state had been centered far to the south at Kiev on the Dnieper in the Ukraine where the potentials for agriculture were much greater and the climate was less severe. But after Kiev was destroyed by the Tatars in 1240 A.D., the Central Region gradually emerged as the core of what was eventually to become the Russian Empire. For more than two centuries there was bloody rivalry for supremacy within the Central Region between such city states as Muscovy, Tver (Kalinin), Vladimir, and Rostov-Suzdal, as well as competition with the older, more established center of Novgorod outside the region to the northwest. Eventually Muscovy gained supremacy over the others (perhaps because of more crafty, unscrupulous rulers) and united the Slavic principalities to repulse the Tatars in the southeast and the Germans, Swedes, Poles, and Lithuanians in the northwest.

During this early period of state formation, the land in the Central Region became partially cleared and settled by agriculturalists wherever cultivation was possible. Naturally open areas (opolye) were the first to be occupied, but these natural clearings did not occupy much of the total area, and the early Slavic settlements were primarily characterized by slash-and-burn agriculture. Most of the land was held in large estates by noblemen, by the crown, or by the orthodox church. The peasants who lived in villages on these landed estates worked various small parcels of land and frequently shifted their fields about as soil fertility became depleted by continuous cropping. This shifting agriculture eventually evolved into the "perelog" (infield-outfield) system. Permanent settlements were established, often line villages along a stream bank or a pathway, which controlled small fields nearby manured and cultivated each year, and shifting fields beyond. The peasants in the villages gained the rights from landowners to cultivate parcels of land either in return for payments in cash or kind (share of the crop), which was known as *obrok,* or in return for labor performed on the manor fields, *barschchina.* The common standard under the barshchina system was two days work per week on the manor arable. The peasants had to supply their own oxen and work from sunrise to sunset with three half-hour breaks during the day or three one-hour breaks with animals. As this system became more entrenched, it led to complete serfdom of the peasants who were denied the right to shift from one estate to another. The two-day work week requirement was often expanded to include much of the daytime period of the week. Many peasants could work their own small holdings only at night. Some village residents who had particular skills to offer satisfied rental requirements on their peasant holdings by serving as smiths, carpenters, coopers, priests, or soldiers.

The development of service trades, coupled with the development of commodity trading around storehouses that were used for tribute collection, led to the establishment of towns at river confluences and portages. In some instances the settlements were no more than rows of tradesmen, known as *ryads,* which were generally bigger than peasant villages but smaller than bona fide towns. Sometimes a ryad consisted entirely of one type of tradesman. Tradesmen usually engaged in agriculture as well as offering their services as carpenters, smiths, coopers, and so forth, and agriculture frequently predominated over trade.

The larger towns generally were laid out and founded by the landowners in order to increase revenues. Tax moratoriums were often offered by the state. Due to these incentives, hundreds of towns were founded during the sixteenth century by both private landowners and the church. During the late sixteenth and early seventeenth centuries, most of these towns became the property of the crown, although some large landowners and monasteries held on to their towns. Most towns held weekly markets for local peasant trade and one to four fairs per year according to their charters. Towns were granted monopolies on their respective trading areas.

Towns often began as fortified refuges surrounded by embankments and moats, *gorodishchi.* Many of these originally were not permanent settlements but provided only temporary refuge from marauders. A town would often begin with a fortified monastery. Frequently a prince's castle and a cathedral were built on a promontory and surrounded by a wall. This was the *vyshgorod* (upper city), sometimes called *gora* (mountain), which finally became known as *kreml* (kremlin). On the low ground at the foot of the kremlin, settlements of tradesmen and craftsmen often emerged and eventually also became walled for protection. These were known as *posad,* or *podol* (low ground at the foot of), the kremlin. Thus, many towns began with twin centers, the vyshgorod, which was the seat of governmental control and religion, and the posad, which was the site for business. These two centers grew together in the larger towns and became surrounded with residential sections that often were contained within one great wall enclosing everything.

In the case of Moscow, for instance, the Kremlin was built on high ground to the east of the Moscow River and the posad, "Kitay-Gorod," developed to the east of the Kremlin. Red Square originally was the large market square. The first wall around the Moscow Kremlin was constructed of high wooden posts embanked with earth. This was replaced by a stone wall, and then during the period 1485–1495 the present brick wall was built. It is estimated that by 1500 Moscow had a population of about 30,000. The city first grew toward the north in what is known as Belyy Gorod (White City), which eventually prompted the building of a new wall, the "White Wall," which surrounded the entire city in 1500. Then the city expanded southward and all around Belyy Gorod into what became known as Zemlyanoy Gorod (Earthen City), around which was constructed during the 1590s the so-called Earthen Wall. It is estimated that by 1600 the population of Moscow was about 40,000. The Earthen Wall included within its confines a ring of four or five fortified monasteries that had served as a protection to Moscow on the southern flank from raids by the Tatars and other marauding groups from the southeast. Moscow continued to grow beyond the Earthen Wall, and by 1800 it is estimated that the population was at least 200,000. However, after 1600, with the gradual demise of the Tatar horde, the necessity for the entire city to be within walls lessened, and no more walls were built.

In addition to walled settlements, defense measures were taken against the nomads of the steppes to the southeast in the form of a series of fortified lines that included not only the walled settlements but also forest belts, earth embankments, and trenches. Within the Central Region, the Tula Line along its southern fringe became famous. Here a forest belt had been retained in the foremost frontier position while the land behind it had been cleared for agriculture. Trees were felled, their branches facing southeastward with the portions of the trunks still attached to the stumps to form what was known as an *abattis,* which presented quite an obstacle to the horsemen from the steppes. A little later, in the Central Chernozem Region farther south, the Belgorod Line extended all the way from the city of Belgorod northeastward to Simbirsk (Ulyanovsk) on the Volga.

Although city walls and fortified lines have long since disappeared, they are still reflected in many of the city and rural patterns. Most of the larger old cities still retain their kremlins, which usually have been reconstructed and opened as tourist attractions, and annular and radial streets occupy the positions of old walls and intercity highways. Cities terminate abruptly at the ends of long rows of apartment buildings with nothing but open fields

Figure 1-5 An abattis, felled trees to form a barrier against the steppe horsemen from the southeast.

and forests beyond. In the Soviet Union there is no such thing as a lowering skyline in a broad zone of suburban sprawl.

Rural villages in the forest zone still consist almost entirely of log cabins, either in long lines along roads or helter-skelter in river valleys. Picket fences line the roadsides, and wells with windlasses to draw water are spaced one for every seven cabins between the picket fences and the roads. The government would like to reconstruct and consolidate all the villages and house all the peasants in *agrogorods,* agricultural cities composed of blocks of apartment houses, but so far there has not been the wherewithall to do it. A few of the more "progressive" farms have begun such a conversion of dwelling units, but most have not, and the peasants are still living in their log cabin *izbas* as they always have. Electricity may have been added recently, but running water and sewers have not. Outdoor toilets are the rule. Each cabin is heated separately by a huge brick and concrete stove that takes up much of the room in the cabin and provides a warm surface in winter where aged members of the family can sleep.

Many peasants prefer to remain in individual cabins, and many peasant groups are constantly extending their line villages by building new cabins exactly like the old, using logs from forests on the collective farm property that has been made available to them. Unable to effect a major conversion in rural housing at this time, the state has taken the position that it is politically wiser to allow, and even help and encourage, groups of people to construct new housing by means of their own devices rather than cause them to become seriously discontented by the absence of no new housing at all. But government officials warn that if the peasants ever want the conveniences of central heating, running water, bathrooms, and cooking by natural gas they will have to consolidate their dwellings into apartment houses because it is too costly and inefficient to supply all these amenities to scattered groups of single-family dwellings. But some of the more idealistic people reply, "America has been able to do it; why can't we?"

AGRICULTURE

The cool, short summers and acidic forest soils of the Central Region limit the choices of crops that can be grown. Most adapted to this natural environment are potatoes, flax, oats, hay, and some of the other small grains, particularly winter rye and barley. In this general farming region, much of the crop production is geared to the livestock industry, which is the basis for most of the cash income of the farms, although flax has long been an impor-

Figure 1-6   Log cabins in line village south of Moscow.

tant cash crop in this area and potatoes have been considered an industrial crop as well as a food crop. Everything from vodka to synthetic tires has been made from potato alcohol in the Soviet Union. Potatoes are also used as fodder for livestock.

Because of the spotty nature of drainage, soil, and topographic conditions in the Central Region, individual fields have remained relatively small and interspersed between nonagricultural land. In 1970 less than half of the land in the region was classified as agricultural, and only one-third was classified as arable. Of the 13,732,000 hectares of arable land, in 1970 the various grains occupied 48.7 percent, hay crops 37.1 percent, potatoes 8.9 percent, flax 2.9 percent, sugar beets 1.1 percent, and vegetables 0.9 percent. Among the grains, barley accounts for the greatest production in the Central Region, with oats and rye nearly equal seconds. However, within the perspective of the entire country, the Central Region is much more important for oat production than for barley, which is much more heavily produced farther south and east in the country. The Central Region produces more oats than any other region in the country. Oats are well adapted to the cool, moist conditions of the Central Region, and they serve as an excellent cover crop for the establishment of clover and alfalfa, which are the chief hay crops of the region. Oats are also excellent high-protein livestock feed. Thus, they integrate nicely into both the livestock economy of the area and the crop rotation scheme. Both winter and spring wheat are grown in the Central Region, and together they constitute the single greatest production of any grain in that area, but relative to the rest of the country the Central Region's wheat production is negligible.

The Central Region is most distinctive in its flax production. It raises much more flax than any other single economic region, and normally accounts for about one-third of all U.S.S.R. production.

As can be seen in Figure 1-7, crop complexes vary significantly from one part of the region to another. These variations relate to both environmental and marketing condi-

tions. Much of the flax is grown in the northern and western portions of the region where the climate is cooler and moister and the soil is more acidic, while grain is concentrated in the southeast where soils are more fertile and the climate is warmer and drier. Some sugar beets are grown in the far south in Orel, Tula, Ryazan, and Bryansk Oblasts.

Because the Central Region was already densely settled before the Bolshevik Revolution, the reorganization of agriculture during the late 1920s and early 1930s primarily took the form of collective farms rather than state farms, since the peasants had a great vested interest in specific parcels of land. However, during the last couple of decades there has been a concerted drive to establish large state farms in close proximity to large cities to specialize in vegetables, fruit, and livestock products to serve the large urban markets. Because this is the most urbanized region of the country, there has been a significant conversion from collective farms to state farms in this area in recent years. Also, particularly in this area, where there is such a density of industrial working population, private plot farming is exceedingly important. Besides the peasants on the collective and state farms, many of the industrial workers who live in semirural settlements are also allotted parcels of land to use as they wish. These small bits of land produce disproportionately great amounts of livestock products, vegetables, and fruits, both for personal consumption and for sale in the collective farm markets in the cities where farmers are free to market their own produce.

During the next 15 years, 1975-1990, the Central Region is destined to participate in a general program to revamp the nonchernozem agricultural zone of European Russia. This is one of the main projects specified as being of national significance in the 15-year plan for the period. It will mean large investments of government capital to improve the land by drainage, clearing of brushy growth, grading of steep slopes, consolidation of small fields into larger units for mechanization, and large applications of mineral fertilizers, lime, and peat and manure composts. In addition, it

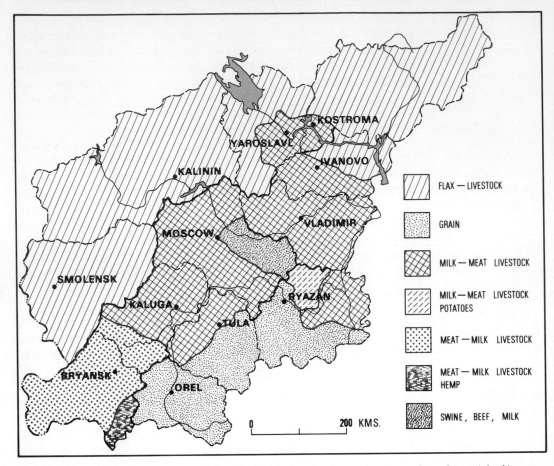

FLAX — LIVESTOCK

GRAIN

MILK — MEAT LIVESTOCK

MILK — MEAT LIVESTOCK POTATOES

MEAT — MILK LIVESTOCK

MEAT — MILK LIVESTOCK HEMP

SWINE, BEEF, MILK

0   200 KMS.

Figure 1-7   Agricultural regions. From *Tsentralnyy ekonomicheskiy rayon,* p. 172.

will mean building roads, supplying electricity, reconstructing rural dwellings, and supplying a whole range of amenities to rural areas, which in this region have lagged somewhat behind the better farming areas of the south. Hence, the 15-year plan envisages not only an improvement of agricultural yields in this region, but also a significant improvement in living standards for the rural dwellers.

This region has long suffered from rural poverty and dislocation of rural labor. With a burgeoning urbanization in the area there has been a prolonged stream of people moving from farm to city, usually the younger more able-bodied males, and during World War II this area suffered further depopulation of its young men. From 1939 to 1970 the rural population in this area declined by exactly half. This was by far the largest decline of any of the economic regions in the entire country. During World War II when many of the men were absent, farm women, unable to cope with all the work, abandoned many fields to their natural state. Many of the fields became overgrown with brush and have never been reclaimed. Shortly after World War II Soviet sociologists reported the presence of rural villages in this region in which there were no able-bodied males at all. The farming was being done by older women and young children. Their skills were low, particularly in the operation of machinery, their production was low, and their demands for living standards were low. Now that the economy in the entire country has improved to the point that the government feels it can invest some money to improve these conditions, the Central Region, along with other parts of the nonchernozem farming zone of European Russia, may be brought into greater use to provide stable production in an area relatively unhampered by droughts that cause such large swings in annual production in the better farming areas of the south.

INDUSTRIALIZATION AND URBANIZATION

Although limited, agricultural resources make up most of the natural resources of the Central Region. According to a recent study, 73.9 percent of the natural resources of the Central Region are accounted for by its arable land, 10.6 percent by its timber, 10.6 percent by its pastures, 3.1 percent by its coal, 1.4 percent by its waterways, and 0.4 percent by its iron ore.[1] Thus, the urban growth and industrialization in the Central Region cannot be accounted for by the resource base of the region. We must examine the economic considerations of market, labor, early start, central position, and the like for an explanation of this industrialization.

Located in the forest zone among the headwaters of the great Volga River system, the Central Region was in a strategic position with regard to water routes and to defense from the Tatar horders to the south. It thereby got an early start as a center of relatively dense population, which in the seventeenth and eighteenth centuries provided the basis for the beginning of industrialization in the form of home industry. Thus, the emergence of this region as the most important industrial area in the country was prompted by an early concentration of people that provided both labor and market and accumulated capital for the basis of a growing economy.

Larger towns grew up early on the main river routes along the headwaters of the Vol-

[1]A.A. Mints, and T.G. Kakhanovskaya, "An Attempt at a Quantitative Evaluation of the Natural Resource Potential of Regions in the USSR," *Soviet Geography: Review & Translation*, November 1974, p. 560.

ga. Northwest of Moscow, at the head of navigation on the Volga, the old city of Tver, now named Kalinin, during the thirteenth and fourteenth centuries challenged the position of Moscow for supremacy over the central part of the Russian plain. About 150 miles northeast of Moscow a string of cities along the Volga River early grew into a major manufacturing district. Here are situated the old cities of Yaroslavl, Kostroma, Ivanovo, and many smaller towns. A string of lesser cities grew up along the Oka River, the major right-bank tributary of the upper Volga. Cities such as Ryazan and Kolomna date back to medieval times. Today they are important to industry, commerce, and government, but none of them has reached the size or eminence of the cities along the Volga.

The greatest urban development has taken place between the Volga and the Oka. Cities grouped around Moscow extend in two lines eastward along two minor streams, the Moscow River, which flows through the city of Moscow and joins the Oka at Kolomna, and the Klyazma River, which flows eastward north of the city of Moscow. A smaller concentration of urban settlements has developed in the iron and phosphate ore district about 100 miles south of Moscow around the city of Tula. The Dutchman Vinius established the Tula ironworks as early as 1632.

The urbanization of the area proceeded from several positions: from the city of Kalinin in the northwest, from the concentration of cities along the Volga in the northeast, from a central position along minor streams around Moscow, and from Tula in the south. Gradually the area between these centers filled in with urban settlements, and today there is a close concentration of cities throughout the region that distinguishes it from its surroundings.

Industrialization began during the first quarter of the eighteenth century during the reign of Peter the Great, when 233 industrial establishments were constructed. The process took a major leap forward in the latter half of the eighteenth century during the reign of Catherine the Great, when the number of industrial establishments increased to more than 2000. Initially industries were concentrated on textiles, primarily in Moscow and in cities to the northeast along the Volga. Very early the city of Ivanovo became the main center of cheap cotton textiles. At first this industry in Russia was largely dependent on imports of raw cotton. As late as 1928, more than half the raw cotton used in the Soviet Union was supplied by imports from Egypt, India, and the United States. Since then cotton growing in Soviet Central Asia and Transcaucasia has been expanded to meet almost the entire needs of the country. Although there has been some effort to establish textile plants in the cotton-growing areas, the Central Region still produces about two-thirds of the cotton textiles in the U.S.S.R. This is the largest cotton-textile-producing region in the world; it produces more than twice as much as Japan.

The manufacture of linen, based on locally grown flax, also became important in this region, particularly in the city of Kostroma. Russia has always led the world in flax production, and Kalinin Oblast northwest of Moscow now raises more flax than any other political unit in the Soviet Union. The Central Region still produces around 60 percent of the country's linen.

Woolens and synthetic fabrics have also become concentrated in this region. At present the Central Region produces about 50 percent of the woolen goods and 55 percent of the synthetic fabrics in the country. Wool factories are concentrated in Moscow and in Moscow Oblast as well as in Bryansk Oblast. Synthetic fabrics are concentrated in Kalinin, Klin, Ryazan, Serpukhov, and Shuya. Although the clothing industry is less concentrated than is the textile materials industry, the Central Region does have a disproportionate share of the clothing industry of the country, as well as leather working and shoe manufacturing.

With the development of the iron and steel industry around Tula, then in the Urals, and finally in the eastern Ukraine, the machine-building industry started in the Central Region. Moscow became the primary center for this industry, but many other cities shared in

it, and some of them came to concentrate heavily on one particular item. Machine tool construction works have developed in Moscow, Kolomna, Ryazan, and other cities. Diesel locomotives are manufactured in Kolomna, Murom, and Lyudinovo. Railroad cars are manufactured in Bryansk and Kalinin. Subway cars are manufactured in Mytishchi, a northern suburb of Moscow. Riverboats are manufactured in Moscow, Rybinsk, and Kostroma. Motor vehicles and parts are manufactured in Moscow, Yaroslavl, Likino, and Bryansk. Motorcycles are manufactured in Tula and Serpukhov. Road construction machines are manufactured in Rybinsk, Smolensk, and Kostroma. Airplanes are manufactured in Moscow. In addition, industrial machines for textile, chemical, and many other industries, and a wide range of fine instruments, watches, photo apparatus, and so forth, are manufactured in other cities of the Central Region, as is agricultural machinery.

Some of the machine construction enterprises produce their own steel at small plants in Moscow, Elektrostal, Tula, and Bryansk. In 1970 the Central Region produced 2.6 million tons of pig iron, 1.9 million tons of steel, and 0.9 million tons of rolled steel—only about 1.5 percent of the country's iron and steel production, but important to some of the industries of the region. The iron industry began in the seventeenth century using low-grade iron ores in the Tula area and charcoal from the local forests. The old steel-producing plant in Tula is still operative. The new plant, Novo Tula, produces pig iron, steel, and rolled steel. Steel-rolling mills also exist in Órel, Shchelkovo, and Moscow. Today the steel in the Central Region is produced from iron ores brought in from the Kursk Magnetic Anomaly in the Central Chernozem Region to the south and from Krivoy Rog in the southern Ukraine, Coal comes from the Donets Basin in the eastern Ukraine. Light metals are produced primarily from metallurgical scrap, in the Central Region, particularly in Moscow, Kolchugino, and Rybinsk.

As the textile and machine-building industries were developing, many food-processing factories were growing to serve the large urban markets. These have been dispersed throughout most of the cities, but are concentrated in intermediate-size cities in the better farming regions of the south.

At present the fastest-growing group of industries in the Central Region are the chemical industries, which until recently have been based primarily on long-haul coke and potato and grain alcohol. In the last few years a rapid shift to the utilization of natural gas, which is piped into the area from the south, east, and northeast in ever-increasing quantities, has greatly speeded their development. Oil is piped into the area from the Volga-Urals fields and from Western Siberia, and oil refineries have been established in Yaroslavl, Ryazan, and Moscow. Gas pipelines have been constructed into the area from the eastern Ukraine and North Caucasian fields, the Central Asian fields, the northeast European fields, and most recently from the huge gas fields near the Arctic coast of Western Siberia. The availability of these gas supplies has formed the basis for many petrochemical industries. Synthetic rubber is made at Yaroslavl and Yefremov. Plastics are manufactured in Moscow, Vladimir, and Orekhovo-Zuevo. Chemical fibers are manufactured in Ryazan, Kalinin, Klin, and Serpukhov. Nitrogen fertilizers are manufactured from natural gas (formerly coking gases) in Novomoskovsk and Shchekino.

Oil and gas now have a much greater effect on the raw materials base for chemistry in the Moscow area than does the Moscow coal basin, which provided the original raw material for the development of synthetic industries in this region. Underground gasification of coal to be used for chemicals takes place at Shatsk. However, most of the Moscow coal is used for electrical generating stations and heating. Heat from thermal electric stations is often used to heat many buildings in cities. But even in the heating and power-generation industries, coal has lost its predominance in the region. Gas now supplies about 50 percent of all the heating fuel in the Central Region. Coal provides only about one-fourth, while fuel oil, peat, firewood, and other minor fuels supply the rest.

Many of the thermal power plants in the Central Region have been switched from coal to gas and fuel oil. In this power-hungry area of many industries, thermal plants must produce most of the electricity. Recently some monster thermal stations have been built to utilize the new fluid fuels. The Konakovo plant, with a 2.4-million-kilowatt capacity, transmits power from its site in Kalinin Oblast over an experimental 750-kilovolt ac power transmission line to Moscow. A similar line is now being constructed to Leningrad. Construction began in 1965 on what has been advertised as the world's largest thermal complex at the new town of Volgorechensk 25 miles southeast of Kostroma. This has a designed capacity of 4.8 million kilowatts, about equal to both the Kuybyshev and Volgograd hydroelectric plants on the Volga River. A 500-kilovolt power transmission line links this with Moscow. This new line is the fourth extra-high voltage line to feed the Moscow region. Other lines come in from the Volgograd and Kuybyshev hydroelectric stations, as well as the Konakovo thermal electric station. A major new thermal power plant went into operation near Ryazan in 1973, burning local brown coal. Oil-fired units are to be added to it for an eventual total capacity of 3.6 million kilowatts. These and other thermal power plants in the Central Region provide most of the electricity to the region and also about 25 percent of all the domestic heating in the area.

The continuing high demand for power in this heavily industrialized region has prompted plans for new sources of power, such as nuclear power plants that are to be constructed near Smolensk and Kalinin and a pumped power storage station to be built northeast of Moscow on the small Kunya River, where reversible turbines will raise water to an elevated 300-hectare reservoir during periods of low power loads at night and generate power during peak-demand periods during the day. There are still important peat-fired power plants in cities such as Shatura just to the east of Moscow and Kashira. These are under a continual program of expansion.

Four smaller cities have become very important in the production of phosphate and nitrogenous materials. In Shchekino south of Tula is a large nitrogenous chemical complex. It was a small coal-mining and chemical center before the Revolution and used to generate gas from coal. With the arrival of natural gas pipelines from the Stavropol area in the North Caucasus, Shchekino began to develop into a major chemical complex using natural gas as the raw material for ammonia synthesis. Most recently a kapron tire cord unit has been added. To the southeast of Tula, Novomoskovsk is another large nitrogenous chemical complex. It began operations in 1933, and for a long time used metallurgical coke from the Urals to derive hydrogen for the ammonia synthesis, but with the arrival of natural gas from the North Caucasus after 1958, the plant shifted increasingly to more concentrated nitrogenous fertilizers such as urea.

In southeastern Moscow Oblast two chemical complexes are based on local phosphorite ores. The Voskresensk plant went into operation in 1931 and produced superphosphate from local low-grade phosphate rock deposits. In 1935 its production shifted to the use of apatite concentrate from the Kola Peninsula, and the operation has developed into the production of double superphosphate and boron. A new ammonia unit derives the necessary hydrogen from natural gas transmitted from Central Asia and other gas-producing regions into the central Russian pipeline system. The nearby town of Yegoryevsk processes local phosphorite deposits to produce defluorized feed phosphate.

Producing industrial construction materials is a huge industry in the Central Region. Glacial sands and gravels are used extensively for building and road construction, and cement is manufactured at Voskresensk, Bryansk, and Podolsk. Glass is manufactured at Gus-Khrustalnyy, which has long been a famous glass-making center. Its products include cut glass, decorative objects, and souvenirs, which are exported throughout the world and displayed at world exhibitions and international fairs.

The wood industries are important in the Central Region. About one-third of the woodworking in the Central Region is in Kostroma Oblast, which uses some local wood, but gets most of its supplies from the Volga-Vyatka Region just to the east. Furniture is manufactured in Moscow, Chekhov, Yaroslavl, and Rybinsk. Paper and cartons are manufactured mainly in Moscow and Kalinin.

The textile industries still occupy first place in the Central Region in terms of workers employed. The various textile and clothing industries employed 24.1 percent of the total labor force of the Central Region in 1970. Chemical and metallurgical industries usually require far fewer workers for a given value added by manufacture than do such industries as textiles and food processing. Thus, when industries are ranked according to number of workers, the role of heavy industries is minimized in comparison to light industries. Textiles are most dominant in some of the intermediate and smaller cities.

CITIES

The Central Economic Region contains 24 cities with over 100,000 people each. Among all the economic regions of the country, this ranks second behind only the Donets-Dnieper Region in the eastern Ukraine for the greatest number of large urban centers. Of course, it contains the largest city in the country, which serves as the capital of both the U.S.S.R. and the R.S.F.S.R., as well as the seat of government for Moscow Oblast. But there is a tremendous drop between Moscow, population 7,528,000 and the next largest city in the Central Region, Yaroslavl, which has a population of only 558,000. Thus, the Central Economic Region is not so much a region of very large cities as it is a region of one very large city, Moscow, which apparently is fourth ranking in the world, and then a large number of intermediate and smaller cities, often occurring in clusters, a number of which are in close juxtaposition to Moscow. Because there are only two cities with populations of more than 500,000, Moscow and

Yaroslavl, the Central Region ranks behind the Volga Region, the Donets-Dnieper Region, and the Urals in this category.

Since a large city is a phenomenon of itself on the landscape, not always readily identifiable with respect to specific industries or other characteristics, a brief rundown on the largest cities of the region will be summarized here. Many of the cities have already been mentioned for one thing or another, but some of them have not, and those which have should be viewed in their entirety rather than according to one or two of their functions.

Moscow

Moscow is the metropolis of the Soviet Union. On January 1, 1974, it had a population of 7,528,000. Besides serving as the governmental and cultural center of the U.S.S.R. and the R.S.F.S.R., it is the country's largest industrial center, normally producing about 10 percent of all the industrial output of the U.S.S.R. Because Moscow is the nerve center of the entire country, it is described in detail, as an example of both the prototype and the ultimate in city planning and development in the Soviet Union.

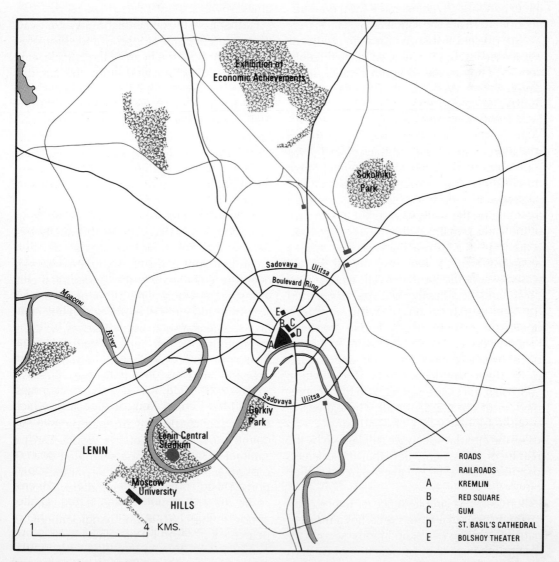

Figure 1-8   The city of Moscow.

The city of Moscow is roughly circular, with streets and railways radiating outward in all directions from the center, crossing circular boulevards and railways in an ever-widening pattern. Its form reflects the historical process of city building throughout much of old Russia. The Kremlin, or citadel, erected in 1147, was a construction of high walls along the bank of the Moscow River surrounding an area of perhaps three or four blocks that contained all the important governmental and religious buildings as well as most of the individual dwellings. As the city grew, walls were constructed around successive peripheries of the expanding city to defend it from marauding nomads from the southeast.

The present Moscow Kremlin walls of weathered red brick date back to the fifteenth century. Early in the sixteenth century, a so-called White Wall was constructed around the boundaries of the city at that time, and later in the sixteenth century, after Tatar attacks, another rampart of wood and earth, the so-called Earthen Wall, or Garden Wall, was built around the periphery of the city. Since then the city has far outgrown the area enclosed within these walls and has outgrown the function the walls served, but the imprint of the walls remains in the present street patterns. In 1943 a 10-year plan was launched to revamp the city of Moscow, and all the old walls, except the Kremlin Wall, were pulled down, and the areas they occupied were used for the construction of wide, circular boulevards. About one-half mile from the Kremlin, Boulevard Ring occupies what was once the site of the White Wall, and about a mile from the Kremlin is the 12-lane Sadovaya, or Garden, Ring, which occupies the site of the Garden Wall. The expansive squares formed where the radiating streets cross the circular streets are still known by the names of gates, reminders that these streets previously passed through gates in the walled city.

Between this simple lattice of intersecting radial and circular main streets lies a maze of narrow, crooked, discontinuous secondary streets reminiscent of the old cities of western Europe. They stand in great contrast to boulevards such as Sadovaya Ring, whose broad expanse of unmarked lanes is bewildering in its immensity to the drivers of buses, trucks, and taxis using it, not to mention the pedestrians who must plan their crossings to avoid wildly careening vehicles. To add to the confusion, both small and large streets typically change names every block or so. To facilitate pedestrian crossing of some of the vast squares in Moscow, pedestrian tunnels have been built under the squares with walls and ceilings lined with photo mosaics of the above surface features so that the pedestrian in the tunnel can ascertain where he is at all times.

Farther from the center of the city, a railway completely encircles Moscow and eliminates train traffic from the heart of the city. Several train stations are located along the circular railway at the ends of 11 trunk railways that come from various parts of the country. Train traffic terminates at these stations, and connection with the central part of the city is done by subway, which now is a well-developed system of branching lines diametrically crossing under the city and intersecting with a line that encircles the city.

A dual-belt highway 109 kilometers long has been completed around the newly expanded city limits. Beyond this a so-called green belt approximately six miles wide has been preserved from further agricultural and industrial development. Primarily wooded with pine and birch trees, this green belt contains residential suburbs and *dachas,* or summer homes, of people living in Moscow. More than a million people live within its confines.

Beyond the green belt lie four airports, Vnukovo, Bykovo, Sheremetyevo, and Domodedovo, which serve the great amounts of air traffic to Moscow from all parts of the country and the rest of the world. During summer 600 Aeroflot liners carrying 80,000 passengers land or take off daily at these airports. The newest one is Domodedovo, south of the city, completed in 1965. It is the largest airport in the U.S.S.R. and handles about 10 percent of all Aeroflot passenger and freight traffic.

In addition to highways, railroads, and air-

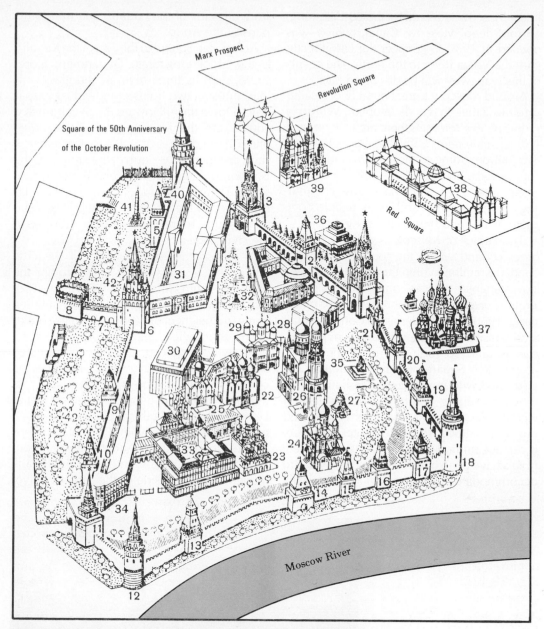

Figure 1-9 The Moscow kremlin. From *USSR 75,* p. 124; 1-Saviours Tower;
2-Tower of the Senate; 3-St. Nicholas Tower; 4-Corner Arsenal Tower;
5-Intermediate Arsenal Tower; 6-Trinity Tower; 7-Trinity Bridge; 8-Kutafya Tower;
9-Commandant's Tower; 10-Armory Tower; 11-Borovitsky Tower; 12-Water
Tower; 13-Tower of the Annunciation; 14-Tower of Secrets; 15-1st Nameless
Tower; 16-2nd Nameless Tower; 17-St. Peter Tower; 18-Beklemeshevsky
(Moskvoretsky) Tower; 19-Constantine and Helen Tower; 20-Nabatnaya Tower;
21-Tsar's Tower; 22-Cathedral of the Assumption; 23-Cathedral of the
Annunciation; 24-Archangel Cathedral; 25-Faceted Hall; 26-Belfry of Ivan the
Great; 27-Tsar Bell; 28-Tsar Cannon; 29-Cathedral of the Twelve Apostles;
30-Palace of Congresses; 31-Former Arsenal; 32-Obelisk to the Officers and Cadets
of the Kremlin Military School; 33-Grand Kremlin Palace; 34-Armory;
35-Monument to Lenin; 36-Lenin Mausoleum; 37-Cathedral of the Intercession (St.
Basil's); 38-State Department Store (GUM); 39-Museum of History; 40-Grave of
Unknown Soldier; 41-Obelisk to Revolutionary Thinkers; 42-Alexander Garden

lines, Moscow is served by the 80-mile-long, 18-foot-deep Moscow Canal, which was opened in 1937 to connect the city directly with the Volga River to the north. The details of this waterway will be discussed later.

Around Moscow a great number of smaller satellite cities have developed. Within a radius of 50 kilometers there are 65 cities and worker settlements with a total population of 1.6 million. Some of these towns are dormitory suburbs and others are satellite cities or resort areas. All of them have close commuting ties to Moscow, and many people commute by bus and train to the central city.

The center of Moscow is occupied by 64 acres of land within the roughly triangular-shaped Kremlin. Within the Kremlin Wall are governmental palaces, onion-domed cathedrals, museums, and monuments. During the early 1960s the modernistic Congress Hall was constructed to house large congresses, operas, and so forth. Many of the streets around Red Square outside the Kremlin are also lined with governmental buildings, historical museums, and hotels. In this general vicinity the Hotel Rossiya was constructed during the 1960s. The largest hotel in Europe, it can accommodate 6000 guests. Many new hotels have been built throughout Moscow to accommodate the visitors that arrive daily from all parts of the country and from other parts of the world.

Across Red Square to the east of the Kremlin is the block-long State Department Store, GUM, with its three high arched glass ceilings, housing two floors of individual bazaar stalls. Down the hill toward the river from Red Square are the brightly painted, baroque, onion-domed spires of St. Basil's Cathedral. A short distance to the north of the Kremlin is the Bolshoi, or large, Theater, and the Malyy, or small, Theater. Not far away is the Lenin Library, one of the largest in the world. Several art museums round out the major buildings in the civic center.

In the southwestern portion of the city, where the Moscow River cuts through the so-called Lenin Hills, stands the University of Moscow with its magnificent central building rising to a height of 32 stories, the tallest building in the Soviet Union. Together with six other widely spaced, similarly constructed skyscrapers of varying functions, it pierces the otherwise squat skyline of the flat city. Across the river from the university is the Central Lenin Stadium and other facilities that form a complete sports area within one of the loops of the Moscow River. About the only topographic feature of any note is the high bank along the western side of the Moscow River

Figure 1-10   Red Square, looking north from Saint Basil's Cathedral. Statue to Minin and Pozharsky in foreground, Historical Museum in background, Kremlin on left, GUM on right.

Figure 1-11   Inside GUM (State Department Store).
Courtesy of Virgil Petty.

rising perhaps 200 feet above the level of the water. Eventually many of the embassies of foreign countries, now scattered about the central portion of the city, will be relocated in new buildings in this area.

Beginning about a mile and a half south of the Kremlin and stretching for another mile and half along the river is Gorkiy Park, which at present is the most highly developed park within the city. It has all sorts of sports facilities, theaters, outdoor bandshells, areas for chess and other games, a huge ferris wheel, and many other features. As in all parks in the Soviet Union, many billboards and banners proclaim the goals and ideals of the Soviet system and loud speakers add to the din, exhorting people to produce to their utmost.

In the north-northeast part of the city lies Sokolniki Park, site of many trade exhibitions, and to the northwest of that, the Exhibition of Economic Achievements, a 490-acre permanent exhibition of agricultural and industrial products of the Soviet Union. Each sector of the economy has a large pavilion in which to show its wares. Other pavilions house dis-

Figure 1-12   Main building of the University of Moscow.

Figure 1-13 View from top of Moscow University. Formal gardens in foreground and Central Lenin Stadium across Moscow River in background.

plays of new scientific achievements such as space travel.

All the parks are minutely landscaped and neatly kept. Formal gardens seem to be a fetish with the Russians. They are found not only in parks but also around many public buildings. The formal gardens surrounding the University of Moscow are outstanding. Many old or unskilled people are kept busy digging at the flowers in these parks, and thus the Soviets are able to say there is no unemployment. The Soviets pride themselves on the establishment of broad expanses of greenery in all cities. Trees, shrubbery, and flowers cover about one-sixth of the city of Moscow.

The newer and heavier industries of Moscow are found in the east and southeast portions of the city, where factories have pushed southeastward into formerly vacant marshy land. The wide variety of industrial plants in Moscow has already been mentioned. Moscow contains two automotive plants, the Moskvich Motor Vehicle Plant (AZLK), which until 1971 was the largest producer of small passenger cars in the country, and the Moscow Motor Vehicle Plant named Likachev (ZIL), which now concentrates on the production of medium road trucks of 2.5–5-ton

capacities. At present the Moscow Motor Vehicle Plant and the Gorkiy Motor Vehicle Plant produce 80 percent of the trucks in the U.S.S.R., all the gasoline engines for all the truck plants in the country, and all the chassis and engines for all the bus plants in the country. A newer assembly plant in the satellite city of Likino now turns out 6000 city transit buses per year and is one of the four largest bus assembly plants in the country. A small petroleum refinery was established in 1938 in the southeastern suburb of Lyubertsy.

The Moscow subways are truly outstanding among the subways of the world in splendor, cleanliness, and service. The Soviets seem to have put their hearts and souls into the construction of a monumental showpiece in the form of a labyrinth of passages and stations deep beneath the city. Extensive use has been made of statuary, chandeliers, mosaics, marble, porcelain, bronze, and stainless steel to express the motif of each station. The escalators leading down to the subways are awe inspiring. Plunging at inclines of 45 degrees, they are so long that one cannot see one end from the other. In 1974 Moscow contained 94 miles of subways and 96 stations. These subways carried over 5 million people daily. Trolley buses carried over 2 million people daily,

Figure 1-14 Entrance to Exhibition of Economic Achievements.

buses 4 million, streetcars 1.5 million, and taxis 700,000, for a grand total of about 13 million passenger trips per day.

People in most Soviet cities seem to be on the move constantly when they are not working. Living quarters are very confined, and there is no opportunity to engage in economically gainful endeavors outside of one's regular job, so most people simply wander the streets when they are not either working or sleeping. This is encouraged by very cheap mass transportation fares. The subway and surface buses cost only 5 kopeks (approximately 7 cents) to go any distance in the city; trolley buses charge only 4 kopeks and streetcars only 3. Therefore, public transportation facilities are usually jammed at any time of day.

With the great demand for public transportation, the system can afford to run its routes very frequently. The time interval in subway stations averages 60 seconds. Buses, streetcars, and trolley buses run at 2–5-minute intervals. Thus, public transportation is very convenient. There are few private automobiles on the streets, and most of these are officially assigned. But there are a surprising number of taxis, some of which run regular routes to augment the other forms of public transportation. In order to rationalize rush-hour traffic, the Soviets stagger the working day at various enterprises and institutions so that the city is hit by several waves of traffic during the day.

Moscow, as well as the rest of the Soviet Union, is still struggling to provide adequate housing and communication for its citizens. Although housing construction is going on at

Arbatskaya Station, Moscow Subway.

a furious rate, new apartments are small by most standards, and many families in old apartments still share kitchen and bathroom facilities. Although rent usually amounts to only 5 percent or less of a family's total budget, one cannot simply rent an apartment as he pleases. It is allocated by the city, usually after a long waiting period. And not all dwellings are supplied with individual telephones. The Moscow city government is presently attempting to achieve a ratio of two telephones per three apartments in the city.

In 1971 another general plan for the development of the city of Moscow was laid out for a period up to the year 2000. This plan includes the reconstruction of the 14 radial highways focusing on Moscow and the conversion of the entire city center enclosed by Garden Ring into business, cultural, and educational areas. Rows of new apartment houses will have no less than 12 floors and no more than 25, in contrast to the standard five-floor apartment complex that has generally been built in the past. Away from the city center the height of buildings will rise first to 30 floors and farther out to 40–60 floors and perhaps higher. Thus, Moscovites envision their city eventually will look much like a huge saucer with lower buildings in the center surrounding the Kremlin and higher buildings around the periphery. A more prominent skyline will then be visible. At present the skyline is pierced only by seven rather grotesque buildings of the Stalin era, similar to the main building of Moscow University, and the more recent Ostankino television tower, which soars to a height of more than 1100 feet and contains a rotating restaurant. Studios, conference halls, editorial offices, and so forth, are in a low television building nearby.

Yaroslavl

The second most populous city in the Central Region is Yaroslavl, with a 1974 population of 558,000. It was founded in 950 as the major settlement within a group of settlements established very early along the Volga northeast of Moscow. It has maintained its supremacy among this group of cities concentrated on the textile industries, and in recent years it has grown steadily under the impetus of the machine-building and chemical industries. From the very beginning of the automobile age Yaroslavl has figured very importantly in the production of a wide array of automobile parts including engines of various sorts. In the 1930s it was a leader in the development of synthetic rubber, and soon became the leading tire manufacturing center of the country. Originally the synthetic industry was based on potato alcohol, but now it has shifted to by-product gases derived from the oil refinery that has been constructed in Yaroslavl to utilize oil piped in from the Volga-Urals fields, and now from Western Siberia. Yaroslavl is one of the most intensively industrialized cities in the Soviet Union, with approximately 60 percent of its gainfully employed actually working in factories.

Tula

Third in size in the Central Region is Tula, which in 1974 had a population of 494,000. It was founded in 1146 south of Moscow on the border between the forest and forest-steppe. Thus, it sits in a fairly good agricultural region. Because it was located among some minor iron ore deposits, it became the first center for ironworks in 1632. It later developed as one of the major centers for mining the low-grade coal of the extensive Moscow coal basin that underlies the region. It has continued to be a center for heavy metallurgy, although it is not of first-rank importance at present. It has also developed an important machine-building industry, and it now functions as the metropolitan center for a cluster of smaller cities in the area — notably Novomoskovsk to the southeast and Shchekino to the south, which concentrate on the chemical industries, primarily the nitrogenous fertilizer industries that now utilize natural gas from the pipeline coming northward from the eastern Ukraine and the North Caucasus. With the opening of extensive iron ore mining in the Kursk Magnetic Anomaly to the south, the Tula iron and steel industry has been revitalized, and during the last 15 years the city's relative population has increased more than other cities in the Central Region.

Ivanovo

Fourth in size in the Central Region is Ivanovo, which in 1974 had a population of 447,000. Ivanovo early became the main center of the cheap cotton textile industry and it has maintained that position ever since. It has been accorded some prominence by the Bolsheviks as the site of the establishment of the first city soviet during the abortive 1905 revolution.

Ryazan

Fifth in size is Ryazan, which in 1974 had a population of 405,000. Founded in 1095 as Pereyaslav, it is one of the old centers on the Oka River southeast of Moscow that was on the frontier of settlement during the time of the Tatar hordes. Many times it withstood the first onslaughts of the Tatars in their punitive expeditions northward from the Tatar capital of Sarai to Moscow. It is a city with diversified industries, emphasizing forging equipment, heavy machine tools, and calculating machines. It has recently constructed a rayon plant using the viscose process and an oil refinery to process crude oil piped in from the Volga-Urals and Western Siberian fields. Two oil-product pipelines have been laid from Ryazan to Moscow, where the Ryazan refinery now markets one-third of its output. The refinery was put into operation in 1960 and underwent an expansion program in 1968. Its throughput capacity is now on the order of 12 million tons per year. During the last 15 years, with the establishment of the oil refinery and other industries in Ryazan, the city has become revitalized and has been improving its position among the cities of the Central Region.

Kalinin

Sixth in size, on the upper Volga northwest of Moscow is Kalinin, which in 1974 had a population of 383,000. It was founded in 1180 at the head of navigation on the Volga as the city of Tver, and during the thirteenth–fifteenth centuries was one of the main contenders with Moscow for supremacy over the central Russian plain. It early became an important center for the textile industry, and more recently an important center for the manufacture of railroad rolling stock. During the Soviet period its population has been surpassed by some of the other cities in the region as most of the urban growth has proceeded eastward and southward from Moscow. It is now the northwestern outpost of the Central Region. However, its industries continue to expand, and a nuclear power plant with two million kilowatts capacity is being built in the northern part of its oblast. In 1931 it was renamed Kalinin after Mikhail Kalinin, a party revolutionary and one-time president of the U.S.S.R.

Bryansk

Seventh in size is Bryansk, which in 1974 had a population of 358,000. Situated in the far southwestern part of the Central Region, it lies in one of the best farming areas of the region. Only since 1961 has this area been considered a part of the Central Region as industries in Bryansk have developed. It has become an important machine-building center with special emphasis on railroad locomotives and railroad rolling stock. A complex plant was started in 1873 as a rail rolling plant and was later converted to produce locomotives and rolling stock such as refrigerator cars, tank cars, and freight cars of other configurations. The manufacture of locomotives was suspended in the middle 1950s, and the production of other types of rolling stock was added. Recently a steel foundry dating from the 1930s has been converted into an assembly plant to produce tractors and off-highway trucks for heavy construction work. The industrial expansion of Bryansk in the 1960s has spurred the population growth in Bryansk from 207,000 in 1959 to 358,000 in 1974.

Orel

Eighth in size is Orel, with a 1974 population of 265,000. Like Bryansk, it lies in the southern part of the Central Region and only recently has been attached to it. It is in a good agricultural area and recently has been growing as a machine-construction city with some rolled-steel industry. Its machine-construction industries specialize in road-building machinery.

Vladimir

Ninth in size is the old city of Vladimir northeast of Moscow, which in 1974 had a population of 263,000. Founded in 1108, it was one of the princely states that rivaled Moscow. For a brief time during the twelfth century it was the center of the orthodox Slavic area and the central seat of government as well. After its takeover by Muscovy it faded from prominence, and now it is experiencing only modest growth along with the rest of the Central Region. Its industries are varied — machine construction, chemicals, and textiles, with some specialization in tractors, plastics, and cotton cloth.

Smolensk

Tenth in size is the old city of Smolensk in the western part of the region with a 1974 population of 242,000. Founded in 882, it is one of the oldest cities in the country along with Kiev and Novgorod. It occupied the head of navigation on the Dnieper River and gained its early preeminence from its position in the midsection of the Baltic-to-Black Sea trade route. It also occupies a major west-east trade route along the higher ground on the terminal moraine that leads from Warsaw to Moscow. In this strategic position it has suffered most heavily from invasions from the west, most recently Hitler's in the early 1940s. It has thus had repeated setbacks in its development, but

since World War II it has been reconstructed and developed into a significant machine-construction and textile center specializing in road-building equipment, instruments, automation equipment, and linen textiles. At present the largest nuclear power plant in the Central Region is being constructed 170 kilometers southeast of Smolensk at a new settlement named Desnogorsk on the Desna River, a tributary of the Dnieper. It is to have a capacity of two million kilowatts. This will become known as the Smolensk Station. It should further enhance the industrial development of the city.

Kaluga

Southwest of Moscow, the city of Kaluga had a 1974 population of 240,000. It is primarily a machine-building center specializing in diesel locomotives, turbines, and electrical equipment. It also produces such things as plywood and matches.

Kostroma

Kostroma, with a 1974 population of 240,000, is an old Volga River city in the far northeastern part of the Central Region. It gained early preeminence as the largest producer of linen textiles in the country. It also has machine construction industries and specializes in excavators and industrial equipment. It is now the same size as Kaluga, but it is growing more slowly.

Rybinsk

Thirteenth in size in the Central Region is Rybinsk, with a 1974 population of 230,000. It sits at the site of the dam that forms the Rybinsk Reservoir north of Moscow. It is specially known as a shipbuilding and woodworking center.

Except for Rybinsk, all the cities over the 200,000 class in the Central Region are oblast centers. Thus, it is obvious, as will be apparent in all the other regions of the country as well, that the governmental function is the primary determinant of the growth of cities in the Soviet Union. Most of these cities became seats of government in their respective *guberniya* at the time of their establishment during the reign of Catherine the Great in the later half of the eighteenth century, and they have served as regional centers ever since. As industrialization has come into the regions, these cities are the ones that have primarily attracted much of the industry and developed well-rounded economies, providing the critical mass for continued growth.

Besides these cities of 200,000 or more population, there are eleven cities in the Central Economic Region with populations between 100,000 and 200,000. In order of size they are: Podolsk, an old satellite city 20 miles south of Moscow; Lyubertsy, an industrial suburb southeast of Moscow; Novomoskovsk, a satellite city of Tula; Kolomna, an old city southeast of Moscow at the juncture of the Moscow and Oka Rivers; Kovrov, on the lower Klyazma River east of Moscow; Serpukhov, an industrial center south of Moscow; Elektrostal, the site of an electric steel plant in an eastern suburb of Moscow; Mytishchi, the subway car manufacturing suburb to the north of Moscow; Orekhovo-Zuyevo, a chemical center east of Moscow; and Kaliningrad and Noginsk, industrial satellites of Moscow. Many smaller cities are important for particular industries and have been mentioned in connection with those industries.

TRANSPORTATION AND MOVEMENT OF COMMODITIES

Since both the industry and the concentrated population of the Central Region depend on large imports of raw materials and foodstuffs from other parts of the country, the transportation system is vital to the area. It focuses on Moscow in a radial pattern from all other parts of the country. Many of the finished products of manufacturing are shipped to all parts of the country from this area, which has fostered a close network of transportation lines.

The Central Region sits among the headwaters of three major river systems — the Volga, the Dnieper, and the Western Dvina (Daugava), as well as some minor systems. Although the rivers were the primary means of transport when the area was emerging in the Middle Ages, today the 11 trunk railroads have greatly superseded the streams in total traffic. In 1970 the railroads handled 85 percent of the traffic and the rivers only 8 percent. Rapid conversion to electrical traction is further enhancing the position of the railroads.

The Volga River is the most heavily traveled river in the Soviet Union, but in the Moscow area it is closed by ice at least five months of the year. Also, river traffic is slow and is economical only with regard to the handling of bulky, low-cost goods. Lumber, coal, petroleum, and grain make up the bulk of water shipments — and most of these commodities are brought in by rail. The railways must bring in cotton and wool from the southeast; grain, meat, butter, and milk from the east; timber and fish from the north; machine tools and finished products from the Baltic Republics in the northwest; and sugar, grain, meat, coal, and steel from the Ukraine in the south. Railways must carry a great variety of finished products to all directions from the Central Region.

Since much of the incoming freight is bulky raw materials and the outgoing freight is more compact finished goods, import tonnages are considerably larger than export tonnages. In 1970 the Central Region imported 259.3 million tons of freight from other parts of the country and exported 226 million tons. Moscow Oblast alone imported 107.5 million tons and exported 59.2 million.

Highways serve primarily to supplement the role of the railroads; intercity truck traffic is not well developed in the Soviet Union. In 1970 trucks carried only 5 percent of the freight in this region. The average length of truck hauls in the U.S.S.R. is about 20 kilometers, which indicates that trucks serve only to distribute produce once it is brought into cities by rail.

Pipelines to carry oil and gas from the Caucasus, the Ukraine, Central Asia, the Volga Region, and Western Siberia have been constructed into the Central Region and are continually being added to. As the fuel balance shifts from predominantly coal to predominantly oil and gas, pipelines are increasingly important. In 1970 they carried 2 percent of the freight of the Central Region.

WATER CONSTRUCTION PROJECTS

Although its share of total traffic has been decreasing, river traffic has increased through the years, and during the Soviet period improvements to navigation, which also serve other functions, have been made on the Volga and its tributary streams. The main obstacle to navigation on the Volga, other than ice, was its large seasonal fluctuation in flow, with floods in spring and shoals in late summer and fall. The small Moscow River was not navigable for boats of appreciable size.

To provide Moscow with a navigable waterway, the 130-kilometer-long Moscow Canal was completed in 1937. It joins the Moscow River in Moscow, through a system of eight locks, with the Volga 128 kilometers to the north. A dam with a hydroelectric power plant of 30,000 kilowatts capacity was constructed on the Volga River near Ivankovo, which raised the water level on the Volga as far as 100 kilometers above the city of Kalinin to form the Volga Reservoir. One-third of the water collected in the reservoir is used to feed the Moscow Canal, and the rest goes down the Volga into the Uglich Reservoir. The Uglich dam and power plant, with a capacity of 110,000 kilowatts, was put in operation in 1940. In 1941 the Rybinsk Reservoir was formed by two dams on the Volga and its tributary, the Sheksna. With a surface area of 4550 square kilometers, it was the largest man-made body of water in the world at the time. The power plant at Rybinsk, with a capacity of 330,000 kilowatts, provides electricity to Moscow, Yaroslavl, and Kalinin Oblasts.

These reservoirs have regulated the flow of the upper Volga and have supplied additional water to the Moscow River via the Moscow

Canal to provide a 6-meter-deep water route for navigation from the city of Moscow to the Volga River. The reservoirs and the canal also have assured recreational facilities and a domestic water supply for the city of Moscow, whose population previously drank about half of the Moscow River. Moscow's expanding industries and population today use more than half of all the additional water being dumped into the canalized river. The function of supplying water to Moscow has transcended the Moscow Canal's importance as a transportation artery.

The deepened channel of the Moscow River meanders through Moscow between granite-lined embankments and landscaped parks. Pleasure craft make regular runs between river stations, which in most cases consist of old double-deck riverboats that have been lashed securely to the riverbank and converted into combination restaurants and dance halls. One can spend a weekend making a trip up the Moscow Canal to Kimry and back. The locks along the way have been constructed to blend aesthetically with the landscape.

During the 1950s and 1960s many other large dams and reservoirs have been constructed on the Volga downstream from Rybinsk, and the Volga-Don Canal was built to connect the lower Volga with the Don River and the Sea of Azov, and hence the open seas. In addition, the old Mariinsk Canal system leading north from the Rybinsk Reservoir to the Baltic and White Seas has been revamped, so that Moscow is now known as the port of five seas, the Baltic, the White, the Caspian, the Azov, and the Black. Long-term plans envision a shipping canal that will skirt Moscow on the east. Also planned is an Oka-Moscow Canal, for the Oka River in the vicinity of Serpukhov has an even greater flow of water than does the upper Volga.

To improve river transport in this region, and throughout the rest of the country for that matter, construction of docking facilities and expansion of appropriate types of rivercraft are needed. Many large factories situated on the Moscow River in Moscow have no docking facilities whatsoever and are making no use of the river as a transportation artery. Planners ruefully joke that industrial plant managers have hydrophobia.

CURRENT TRENDS AND PROSPECTS FOR THE FUTURE

The Central Region is the most populous, most highly industrialized region in the country and is in the most mature stage of economic and social development. Therefore, its rates of change have leveled off, and its growth is not as spectacular as in some regions with lower bases for computing percentage changes of population and economic development. The Central Region has the lowest average birth rate in the country, the second highest death rate (after the Baltic Region), and the lowest natural population increase, amounting to no more than 0.3 percent per year. Except for Moscow Oblast, the Central Economic Region has been primarily a region of out-migration for quite a number of years, so that most of the area has been undergoing an absolute decline in population. The population decline has not been as drastic as it is farther east in the Volga-Vyatka Region, but it is widespread throughout the area. Ultimately the decline has taken place in the rural areas, since almost all the cities have shown absolute growth.

Since Moscow Oblast is so highly urbanized, this region has shown a rapid increase in population, in contrast to its immediate surroundings. In terms of population increase per area, Moscow Oblast ranks among some of the most intensively growing regions in the country. The migration into Moscow Oblast more than equals the out-migration from the other oblasts of the Central Economic Region, so that the region as a whole from the 1959 census to the 1970 census showed a population increase of 8 percent. This was only half the rate of increase of the country as a whole, but was higher than such regions as the Volga-Vyatka Region to the east, the Central Chernozem Region to the south, and the Urals farther east.

Between the 1939 and 1970 censuses, the Central Region showed the greatest decrease in its rural population of any of the economic regions (50 percent) and the second lowest increase in its urban population (only 80 percent, as compared to a U.S.S.R. average of 125 percent). Only the Northwest Region showed a lower urban increase.

The same trend is seen in the growth of industrial production. Between 1940 and 1972, according to Soviet statistics, industrial production in the Central Region increased by 8.4 times, whereas in the country as a whole it increased 13.6 times. Again, the Central Region started with a very high base figure, so that low percentage increases could still mean very great absolute increases. The same thing is reflected in the heavily industrialized Donets-Dnieper Region of the eastern Ukraine, which increased its industrial production during the 1940-1972 period by only 7.8 percent. However these two regions, which are the most highly industrialized in the country, had much higher absolute growths than most of the other regions of the country. Thus, the gap is not really being narrowed between these advanced regions and the more lagging ones. The Central Region undoubtedly will continue to be the leading manufacturing region of the country for a long, long time, and it will continue its function as industrial innovator for the rest of the country.

Government policies to limit the growth of big cities and to spread industries evenly across the country for the most part have been unsuccessful, and economic realities have worked in favor of already established industrial centers, just as they do in any country. Moscow grew from a population of 5,046,000 at the time of the 1959 census to 7,061,000 at the time of the 1970 census. Part of this growth was the result of the incorporation of some surrounding territories, but even discounting this, the city grew by one million. Since the 1970 census it has continued to grow by more than 100,000 people per year, and the same is true of many of the other larger cities in the region. Not only are these large cities gaining population at a disproportionate rate, but they are also gaining some of the better elements of the population. In-migrants consist mainly of the more highly trained young people who look upon the Central Region in general and Moscow in particular as the ultimate in modern living. This exodus of the better-trained young people has left many of the rural areas in the Central Region populated mainly by old women and younger children. This has led to a tendency for higher birth rates in cities than in the surrounding countrysides. But both urban and rural areas in the Central Region generally have low birth rates. Few families have more than one child, if that.

The Central Region might even grow in importance in relation to the rest of the country in the immediate future now that the Soviet leaders have largely abandoned ideological policies that were in conflict with economic realities. The allocation of large shares of capital investment to the location of industries in small and medium-sized cities in the European part of the country, in order to utilize surplus pools of labor and the advantages of concentration, should tend to fill in the Central Region even more. The growth of large cities might slow down, but the filling in of spaces between large cities should accelerate. Also, the newly found mobility of the fluid fuels has largely erased one of the traditional industrial ailments of the region. Most of the new oil refineries of the country are being built in consuming areas rather than in producing regions. Thus, large consuming areas are suddenly on the threshold of another leap forward for a whole range of industries, particularly the chemical industries based on by-products of oil refining and natural gas. Recently a program for the recovery of production in the Moscow brown coal basin has been announced. This had been on the decline since a production peak of 47 million tons in 1958. The Soviets hope to stabilize production around 35 million tons per year. This is in response to the rapidly growing needs of electric power in the Central Region, which cannot be served entirely by the importation of gas and fuel oil to fuel the thermal power stations.

The grandiose plan for the next 15 years to revitalize the agriculture of the noncher-nozem zone should greatly improve production and living conditions on the farms in the Central Region as well as in surrounding areas to the north. Large areas are to be drained and cleared of brush, small fields are to be consolidated for mechanization, and large amounts of commercial fertilizer are to be made available to improve production. The further development of state farms next to large cities for urban supply purposes, coupled with the "conveyor belt" principle to intermingle early- and late-maturing fruits and vegetables to provide a continuum of fresh produce on the market for the longest possible season, should solve some of the marketing problems in the cities as well as provide higher cash returns to the farms of the area. If living conditions and social amenities improve enough on the farms, some of the more able youths might find it advantageous to remain there, which should help agriculture considerably.

READING LIST

- Alaev, E.B., *Tsentralnyy ekonomicheskiy rayon* (Central Economic Region), Moscow, 1973, 269 pp. (in Russian).
- Fuchs, Roland J., "Moscow," *Focus*, American Geographical Society, New York, January 1966, 6 pp.
- Lappo, G.M., "Trends in the Evolution of Settlement Patterns in the Moscow Region," *Soviet Geography: Review & Translation*, January 1973, pp. 13–24.
- Mints, A.A., *Podmoskovye* (The Moscow region), Moscow, 1961 (in Russian).
- Mishchenko, G. Ye., "Satellite Cities and Towns of Moscow," *Soviet Geography: Review & Translation,* March 1962, pp. 35–42.
- Morris, A.S., "The Medieval Emergence of the Volga-Oka Region," *Annals of the Association of American Geographers,* December 1971, pp. 697–710.
- "Moskva i podmoskovnye rayony" (Moscow and the Moscow region), *Voprosy geografii*, No. 51, Moscow, 1961, 220 pp. (in Russian).

- Peretokin, A.A., "Tsentralnyy ekonomicheskiy rayon v devyatoy pyatiletka" (The Central Economic Region in the Ninth Five-Year Plan), *Geografiya v shkole* (Geography in School), No. 5, Moscow, 1973, pp. 4–8 (in Russian).

- *Priroda kostromskoy oblasti i yeye okhrana* (The Natural Environment of Kostroma Oblast and Its Conservation), Yaroslavl', 1973 (in Russian).

- Rodoman, B.B., "Gorod, priroda, turizm v Podmoskovye — prognozy i predlozheniya" (City, Nature, and Tourism in the Moscow Region — Forecasts and Suggestions), *Vestnik Moskovskogo Universiteta, seriya geografiya,* No. 3, Moscow, 1972, pp. 87–90 (in Russian).

- Saushkin, Yu. G., *Moskva* (Moscow), Mysl, Moscow, 1964, 240 pp. (in Russian).

- Starikov, V.N., "The Formation of the Network of Places in Moscow's Suburban Zone," *Voprosy geografii,* 1971, No. 87, pp. 71–77; translated in *Soviet Geography: Review & Translation,* January 1973, pp. 7–12.

- "Toponimiya tsentralnoy Rossii" (Place Names of Central Russia), *Voprosy geografii,* No. 94, 1974, 204 pp. (in Russian).

- "Tsentralno-promyshlennyy rayon" (Central Industrial Region), *Voprosy geografii,* No. 49, Moscow, 1960, 157 pp. (in Russian).

- "Tsentralnyy ekonomicheskiy rayon" (Central Economic Region), *Razvitiye i razmeshcheniye proizvoditelnykh sil SSSR,* Nauka, Moscow, 1973, 269 pp. (in Russian).

- *Tsentralnyy rayon: Ekonomiko-geograficheskaya kharakteristika* (Central Region: Economic-Geographic Characteristics), Akademiya Nauk SSSR, Institut Geografii, Moscow, 1962, 800 pp. (in Russian).

Volga-Vyatka Economic Region

	Area (km²)	Population	Persons/km²	Percent Urban
Gorky Oblast	75,000	3,665,000	49.0	68
Kirov Oblast	121,000	1,675,000	13.9	60
Mari A.S.S.R.	23,000	691,000	29.8	45
Mordvinian A.S.S.R.	26,000	1,014,000	38.7	40
Chuvash A.S.S.R.	18,000	1,251,000	68.4	39
Total	263,000	8,296,000	31.5	56

chapter 2

the volga-vyatka economic region

To the east of the Central Region lies the Volga-Vyatka Economic Region, which stretches in a southwest-northeast direction across the middle Volga and the drainage basin of the Vyatka River that flows southeastward into the Kama just to the east of the Volga Bend. Politically the region includes two Russian oblasts and three Autonomous Soviet Socialist Republics based on the western three groups of a variety of remnant non-Russian nationalities occupying the Volga Bend area and the adjacent western slopes of the Urals in a region that is often called an ethnological museum.

TERRITORY AND POPULATION

This general area from the Volga Bend to the Urals has been a meeting place for Finno-Ugric groups migrating southeastward from the Scandinavian region and Turkic groups migrating northwestward from the Central Asian area. In this region there is a great intermingling of various branches of these two great families of nationalities and the Russians. Within the Volga-Vyatka Economic Region lie Gorkiy and Kirov Oblasts, which are peopled primarily by Russians, the Mari and Mordvinian A.S.S.R.'s, which are political units based on Finno-Ugric nationality groups, and the Chuvash A.S.S.R., which is a

37

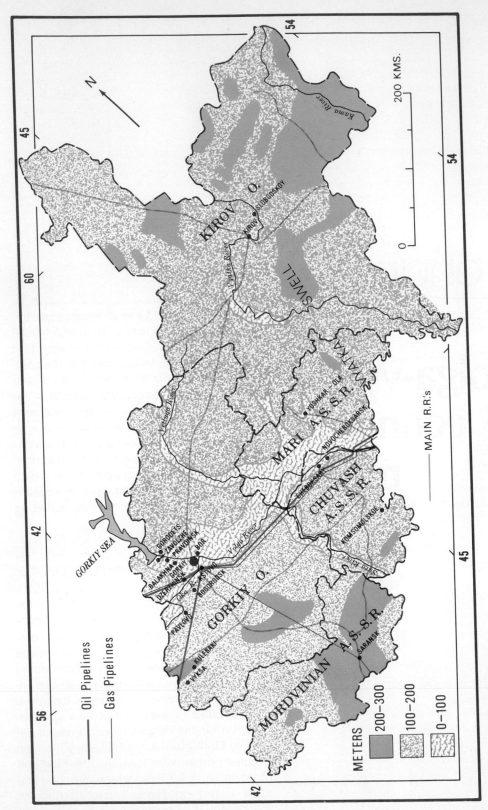

Figure 2-1 The Volga-Vyatka Region.

political unit based on a Turkic nationality group.

Although the three A.S.S.R.s are based on non-Russian nationality groups, the Russians are represented heavily in these republics. In fact, only the Chuvash A.S.S.R. is peopled by a majority of Chuvash, who constitute 70 percent of the total population of their region, while Russians constitute only 25 percent. In the Mari A.S.S.R. the Mari people are only a bare plurality, constituting 44 percent of the total population, while Russians constitute 43 percent; in the Mordvinian A.S.S.R. the Mordvinians are a minority group, constituting only 35 percent of the population, while Russians constitute 59 percent.

The steady erosion of the titular groups in the A.S.S.R.s is not unique to this area; it is a common occurrence throughout the country. As governmental capital is invested in these regions to establish industries and boost their economies, it is often found necessary to move in Slavic groups, particularly Russians, to man these new industries, since very often indigenous nationality groups do not take well to factory work. Therefore, there is often a large influx of Russians into these regions while simultanously there is an outflow of the native groups to other areas of the country. The native groups of the Volga-Vyatka Region have been particularly mobile in this respect.

If this region has been characterized by any one feature it has been the high level of out-migration for many years. Although the Volga-Vyatka Region has a little higher birth rate and a little lower death rate, and hence a little higher natural population increase, than the Central Region does, the greater out-migration has reduced its rate of population growth to a lower level than that of the Central Region and, in fact, to the lowest of any region in the entire country. During the 1959–1970 intercensal period, the Volga-Vyatka Region increased its population by only 1 percent, while the country as a whole increased 16 percent. The next lowest increases were 3 percent in the Central Chernozem Region south of the Central Region, and the Central Region itself with an increase of 8 percent. The somewhat higher birth rates of the non-

Russian groups in the Volga-Vyatka Region have counterbalanced the migration trends in the region, and thus the ratio of non-Russians to Russians has remained essentially the same during the past couple of decades. During the 1959–1970 intercensal period the Chuvash remained at exactly the same percentage level in the total population of their republic, the Mari improved their position by 1 percent, and the Mordvinians decreased by 1 percent.

The five political units of the Volga-Vyatka Region total an area of 263,000 square kilometers and contained a population in 1973 of 8,296,000 for an average population density of 31.5 people per square kilometer, 56 percent of whom were classified as urban, an urban ratio that was slightly below the 59 percent for the average of the entire country. Population density and urbanization vary considerably from one part of the region to another, because of both the physical environment and the nationality traits. In the northeast, where agricultural potentials are lowest and where cities have not been well developed, the average population density in Kirov Oblast is only 13.9 people per square kilometer and the urbanization is 60 percent. In adjacent Gorkiy Oblast to the west, which contains the large city of Gorkiy, the population density is 49 people per square kilometer and the urbanization is 68 percent. In the southeast the Chuvash A.S.S.R. has a population density of 68.4 per square kilometer and an urbanization of only 39 percent. The Chuvash and Mordvinians remain quite rural, and the Mari A.S.S.R. is only 45 percent urbanized.

The Volga-Vyatka Region is one of the least well-endowed, least distinctive economic regions in the country. If it were not for the large metropolitan area of Gorkiy it would not have a very viable economy, and there would be little reason for considering it as a separate region. However, it has been a traditional region in the minds of the Russians, one that perhaps has vaguely brought to mind a region of peasant poverty and outmigration. This was particularly true during the early part of the Soviet period, when the region was constituted as the Vyatka-Vetluga Region, named after the two rivers in the area, with the seat of government at Vyatka (named Kirov in 1934). At this time Gorkiy was not part of the region. Probably the large city of Gorkiy should be included as the eastern extremity of the Central Region, because its urban industrial complex has intimate relations with cities to the west.

PHYSICAL SETTING, RESOURCES, AND AGRICULTURE

Climate, Vegetation, and Soils

The Volga-Vyatka Region extends the physical characteristics of the Central Region eastward with the addition of increasing continentality. Since the moisture gradient across the east European plain runs in a southeastly direction, the moisture, vegetation, and soil zones run across the plain from west-southwest to east-northeast, and therefore the northern part of the Volga-Vyatka Region is most like the Central Region to the west. The southern part of the Volga-Vyatka Region, to the south of the Volga River, displays climatic, vegetation, and soil characteristics more like those of the Central Chernozem Region to the southwest.

The increasing continentality eastward causes a greater swing in seasons in the Volga-Vyatka Region than in the Central Region. For instance, Kirov, which lies about 170 kilometers farther north than Moscow and has winters that average about 4°C colder, has summers that average slightly warmer than Moscow. Thus, although the winters are longer and colder, and more consistently cold, than the Central Region, the shorter summers are warmer.

Because the Volga-Vyatka Region is greatly extended in a north-northeast, south-southwest direction, there are considerable changes in climate, vegetation, and soil characteristics from the northern extremities to the southern. The area to the south of the Volga River lies primarily within the wooded steppe zone and displays gray forest and degraded chernozem soils similar to those of the northern part of the Central Chernozem Re-

gion to the southwest. This is particularly true of the Mordvinian A.S.S.R., which lies farther south and which until 1960 was considered as the northeastern extremity of the Central Chernozem Region. Only since 1960 has it been included in the Volga-Vyatka Region. Therefore, the Mordvinian and Chuvash A.S.S.R.s and the southern part of Gorkiy Oblast have greater agricultural potentials than anything in the Central Region, except perhaps Orel and Bryansk Oblasts in the southern part of the Central Region, which until 1962 were also included in the Central Chernozem Region. The northern part of Gorkiy Oblast and the Mari A.S.S.R. have agricultural potential commensurate with Moscow Oblast, and Kirov Oblast has limited agricultural potential similar to that of Kostroma Oblast in the northeastern extremity of the Central Region.

Precipitation in the Volga-Vyatka Region is a little less than in the Central Region, but the longer, colder winters with fewer thaws allow for a thicker snow accumulation, and snow lies on the ground somewhat longer — an average of 172 days of the year in Kirov. Like the Central Region, the Volga-Vyatka Region displays a pronounced summer maximum of precipitation, with June and July maxima in the southern part and July and August maxima in the northern part. Hence, again, the summer distribution of rainfall is less satisfactory in the north. Because the harvest season is limited more by early frosts in this region than it is in the Central Region, the late summer rainfall is even more detrimental to harvests. At Kirov the frost-free period averages only 122 days per year, as contrasted with 141 in Moscow.

The natural vegetation varies from taiga forests in the northern part of Kirov Oblast to broadleaf forests in the vicinity of the Volga and forest-steppe south of the Volga. The taiga in the north is composed primarily of spruce and fir forests, and pine is also widespread. The fir occurs in combination with spruce or linden with frequent mixtures of pine. There are some pure spruce stands on uplands and pure pine stands on the terraces of the Vyatka and other streams. Small-leaved forests of

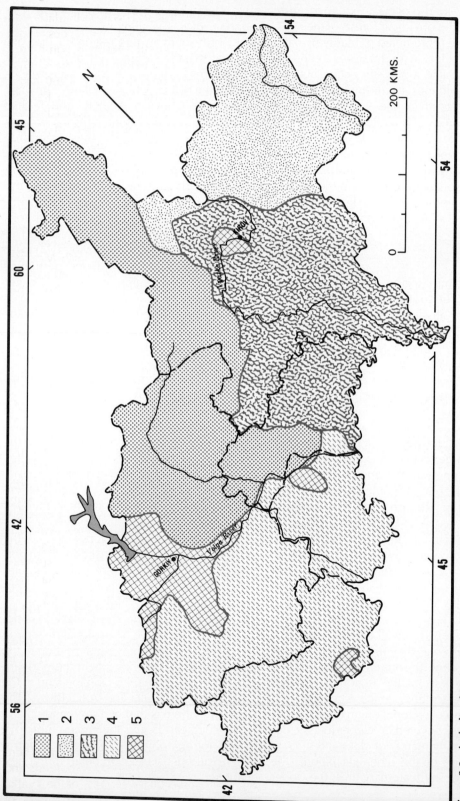

Figure 2-2 Agricultural Regions. From Saushkin, p. 60.; 1-Flax growing and dairying, with some potato growing and meat livestock; 2-Grain growing and dairying; 3-Grain growing and general livestock; 4-Grain and hemp growing with dairying, swine, and sheep; 5-Urban oriented vegetable growing and dairying.

birch and aspen also occupy extensive areas in the north. The broadleaf forests of the middle section are represented primarily by oak, linden, and elm, with mixtures of other species. Birch and aspen still occur, but are not so conspicuous as farther north. The forest-steppe south of the Volga is characterized by clumps of broadleaf trees within a predominance of grasses. On some of the steeper riverbanks there are mixtures of pines.

Soils vary from podsols in the north, through podsolized forest soils in the center, to degraded chernozems in the far south of the region.

Landform

Like the Central Region, the Volga-Vyatka Region is underlain by sedimentary strata of various ages, all lying on the Precambrian crystalline foundation of the Russian platform. Upper Permian deposits, consisting of variegated clays, marls, limestones, dolomites, and gypsums, are the most commonly encountered rocks. In some places Permian deposits are covered with Triassic and Upper Jurassic rocks. The Permian rocks all dip toward the west; they exhibit a number of both small and large tectonic flexures, which are the western edges of the ripples of the Urals geosynclinal zone. The major swell in the Volga-Vyatka Region runs north-south through the center of the region and passes through the vicinity of the city of Kirov. This is the so-called Vyatka Swell. It is a northern extension of the Volga Heights, which extend south of the Volga through the eastern part of the Chuvash A.S.S.R. The highest parts of the Vyatka Swell lie between 250 and 300 meters above sea level. The swell exhibits a number of local warpings that run parallel to one another in a north-south direction. In the northeastern part of the region begins the Upper Kama Upland, which is a somewhat higher upland of tectonic origin composed of Permian rocks covered by Upper Jurassic deposits consisting mainly of clays and sand.

During one of the older glaciations, the Dnieper stage in Quaternary time, the Upper Kama Upland was covered by glaciers. The boundary of this glaciation was oriented almost north-south in this region so that old morainal materials composed of loams and sandy loams form a north-south zone reaching from the center of Kirov Oblast southward through the Chuvash A.S.S.R. and farther southward out of the region almost to Volgograd on the lower Volga. These morainal materials still contain some fragments of rock that were transported from as far away as the Kola Peninsula and the polar Urals, but the long period of postglacial weathering and erosion has destroyed any morainal topography that might have existed in the area. The next-to-last glacial stage, the Moscow stage, barely reached into the northwest portion of the Volga-Vyatka Region, and the last stage, the Valday stage, did not enter the region at all. However, Quaternary deposits of glaciofluvial materials appear in many of the river valleys of the region.

The surface of the Vyatka Swell is dissected by many small streams into a number of complicated ravines, divides, and watershed plateaus. In some places the region is quite hilly, and the river valleys are deep and narrow with precipitous rocky slopes. Where the Vyatka River cuts through the swell, its valley assumes almost the character of a canyon. The river valleys are typically asymmetrical with steep right banks and gently sloping left banks. Karst processes have played a great role in shaping the present topography of the Vyatka Swell, particularly in the southern portion. In this southern area are found sinkholes up to 15–20 meters in depth as well as numerous lakes up to 2–5 kilometers long.

East and west of the swell, elevations decrease and the degree of erosional dissection diminishes. In the very western portion of the region the city of Gorkiy sits in the northern part of the estensive Oka-Don lowland at the confluence of the Oka and Volga Rivers. The topography here is that of a low sandy plain. To the southeast begins the higher, more dissected topography of the Volga Heights, which will be discussed in detail in the next chapter.

Agriculture

The agriculture of the Volga-Vyatka Region is some of the most poorly developed in the country, partially due to the natural environment and partially due to poor organization. Some of the lowest yields in the country are found in both crops and livestock products. Over the region as a whole only 6.5 million hectares are cultivated. Of this 60 percent is in grains, 30 percent in hay and other fodder crops, and the remainder in potatoes, vegetables, flax, sugar beets, buckwheat, peas, makhorka (low-grade tobacco), hemp, and hops.

The crop complex and yield vary greatly from south to north because of the deteriorating climate and soils toward the north. South of the Volga River the climate is warmer and drier and the soils are much better. This region is essentially a northeastward extension of the Central Chernozem Region, which is the best farming area in the Russian Republic. Here more of the specialty crops are raised. Most of the sugar beets are grown in the very southern part of the region in Mordvinian A.S.S.R., as are the hemp and the traditional foodcrop, millet. Agriculture is particularly intensive in the Chuvash A.S.S.R., where the population pressure is greatest on the land and the people have a great attachment to it. The foodcrops — buckwheat and peas — occupy large areas here, and the Chuvash A.S.S.R. accounts for more than 40 percent of all the hops grown in the country. But these specialty crops do not occupy a great deal of area, and most of the cultivated land even in the south is taken up by grains and fodder crops. Potatoes are a main crop throughout the area. The grains are primarily oats, winter rye, and spring wheat.

To the north of the Volga River the specialty crops disappear, and grain, fodder crops, and potatoes and other vegetables become the main crops, and flax becomes the cash crop in the coolest and moistest part of the region in the northwest.

In the southern part of the region much of the land is under cultivation. Only the steeper riverbanks where erosion is most severe have been left to low-grade forests. But northward

in the region the forest becomes more and more prevalent and the fields smaller and more scattered. North of Kirov there are only isolated patches of cultivation within the forest.

Because the region has such a limited endowment for cropping, animal husbandry is highly developed. Dairy farming is carried on throughout the region and is the mainstay of agriculture in the north. Meat animals, particularly swine and sheep, are raised toward the south. Relatively low yields of crops in this area would be expected because of the limitations of the physical environment, but also the diary industry in this region produces the least milk per cow of any region in the country. Therefore, something must be wrong with the organization of the farm economy.

Forest and Mineral Resources

Although the potential for agriculture is limited in this region, it constitutes the greatest natural resouce of the area. This region is even less well endowed than the Central Region. Probably the next most important resource is the forests, which provide the basis for a significant lumber and paper industry, some of the best in the country. However, the forest supply here is definitely limited, and resources are steadily diminishing as cutting exceeds annual growth. Timber felling diminished from 38.2 million cubic meters in 1960 to 30 million cubic meters in 1970. At the present rate of use, the forest supply will not last more than 10 years.

Mineral resources are limited to some phosphorites in the Upper Kama region, where it is estimated that more than 2 billion tons of reserves exist, peat, oil shale, and mineral construction materials, particularly gypsum for the making of cement. Recently there has been increasing mention of the possibility of oil in the Volga-Vyatka Region, but so far no deposits have been confirmed and no idea has been given as to exactly where they might exist. However, the Soviets continue to anticipate that as oil reserves become depleted in the Volga-Urals Region, more will be found in a northwesterly extension into the Volga-Vyatka Region.

Water Resources

Because the Volga River runs through the middle of this region, there are considerable possibilities for the use of water for power and transportation. Two major construction projects have taken place on the Volga in this region. The Gorodets Dam 55 kilometers upstream from Gorkiy was completed in 1955, which created the Gorkiy Sea (420 kilometers long) and backed up water all the way to Yaroslavl. The hydroelectric plant at Gorodets has a capacity of 520,000 kilowatts. Recently it has been reported that important shipyards have been established in Gorodets. Among rivercraft produced is a new innovation, a "floating motel," which provides mooring for 200 motorboats and offers the services of a restaurant, a library, and a repair shop.

A second dam, at Cheboksary, was planned in the 1960s, and a workers' settlement, Novocheboksarsk, was established at the site. The population of the settlement at the time of the 1970 census was reported to be 39,000 people, and a chemical plant producing aniline dyes had been established. Construction on the dam was to have started in 1969, but was postponed during the ninth five-year plan (1971–1975). The hydroelectric station has a designed capacity of 1.4 million kilowatts. When this dam is finished, it will complete the conversion of the Volga into a giant stairway of reservoirs.

INDUSTRIES AND CITIES

The industries of the Volga-Vyatka Region are concentrated primarily on machine construction and metalworking, particularly construction of riverboats, automobiles and trucks, and industrial lathes. Also important are the wood and paper industries and chemical industries, which are now based primarily on the importation of oil and gas from other regions. Leather-working, textiles, instructional

materials, and food industries are also important. Since so many of the industries are concentrated in the large city of Gorkiy and its suburbs and satellite cities, it will be most expedient to discuss industries as individual cities are discussed.

By far the greatest part of the industry of the entire region is located in the huge metropolitan area of Gorkiy. The second most important node is Kirov with its satellite city of Slobodskoy in the northern part of the region, but this in no way compares to the Gorkiy area. There has been some attempt since World War II to establish industries in some of the other towns of the region, particularly the capitals of the three A.S.S.R.s. During the war some industries were relocated in the cities from the west. But none of them have grown to the industrial importance of even Kirov, let alone Gorkiy.

Since the region started with a low industrial base, it has shown a respectable rate of industrial growth during the Soviet period. From 1940 to 1972, according to Soviet figures, industrial production in the Volga-Vyatka Region increased by 16.5 times, which was somewhat higher than the 13.6 average for the entire country and about twice as high as the 8.4 average for the Central Region. But this region still remains one of the least industrialized and least urbanized regions of the European part of the country. If the city of Gorkiy were removed from the region, the industrialization and urbanization would be low indeed. As has already been mentioned, it is questionable whether the city of Gorkiy should be included in this region or not, since its economic ties are much closer to those of the Central Region than to the rest of the Volga-Vyatka Region.

Gorkiy

The largest city in the region by far is Gorkiy, which in 1974 had a population of 1,260,000. This makes it the seventh largest city in the Soviet Union, although if all the suburbs and satellite cities were included, the Gorkiy metropolitan area would probably be the third largest in the country after Moscow and Leningrad. Gorkiy was founded in 1219 as the fortress of Nizhniy Novgorod in defense against the Volga Bulgars and Mordvinians on a triangular promontory overlooking the confluence of the Oka with the Volga. During the later Russian Empire, days, Nizhniy Novgorod became famous for its annual trade fairs that attracted business people from all over Russia and much of the rest of the world. Since the death of the writer Maxim Gorkiy, the city has been renamed after him, its most famous native son.

Approximately half the industrial production in Gorkiy is in the machine-building industries, which include shipbuilding, automobile and truck manufacture, aircraft industries, and many others. Gorkiy early became the major automotive center in the country. The first major Soviet truck plant was established in Gorkiy in 1932 using the architectural drawings of the Ford River Rouge plant, technical advice of Ford engineers, and machinery and equipment for producing Ford Model A trucks, which by then were obsolete. The Gorkiy Motor Vehicle Plant (GAZ) is still the largest truck producer in the Soviet Union. In 1972 it built 262,000 trucks, which was 44 percent of the U.S.S.R. total. The GAZ-51 cargo truck has been in continuous production without major modification for 24 years. Although the GAZ plant is undergoing modernization, there are no plans for a major expansion in the near future. GAZ also produces the Volga car, which is the most expensive of the four mass-produced passenger cars in the country. GAZ used to be the largest car producer in the country, accounting for 50,200, or 38 percent of all cars, in 1960. But in recent years, with the dispersion of the industry into other cities, especially the big plant in Togliattia, the Gorkiy plant has dropped to fifth in car assembly in the country, and in 1972 its production of 60,000 was only 8 percent of Soviet car output.

GAZ has also been the leading bus assembly plant in the country. The Gorkiy and Moscow truck plants used to produce all the buses in the country, and they still build all the chassis and engines for all bus plants in the

country. However, there has always been intense competition in the plants between truck production and bus production, with trucks generally taking the higher priority, and therefore the Soviets have attempted to locate new bus assembly plants in different cities of the country. Apparently the largest bus assembly plant at present is at Pavlovo, one of the satellite cities just to the southwest of Gorkiy. A new plant for the production of engines for jeeps has been established at Arzamas a little further south, and the production of heavy-duty off-highway trucks has been shifted to a new plant at Saransk in the Mordvinian A.S.S.R. A tire factory has been established at Kirov. Automobile engines are also produced in the new city of Zavolzhe on the northwest side of Gorkiy.

The Sormovo shipbuilding yards in Gorkiy are famous throughout the country for the construction of many of the riverboats and also larger vessels for use on some of the larger lakes of the country, such as Lakes Onega and Ladoga in the north and the Caspian Sea in the south.

Many of the smaller cities around the Gorkiy metropolitan area specialize in parts and radio and electrical equipment for the automotive and shipbuilding industries. This is especially true of the city of Bor on the northeast side of Gorkiy, which turns out various parts for riverboats, glass for automobile windshields, and so forth. The automotive and shipbuilding industries have also spawned a number of steel mills, with a combined steel output of 2 million tons, for production of sheet metal stamped into various forms at Gorkiy, Vyksa, and Kulebaki, southwest of Gorkiy. With the large program of oil and gas pipeline construction into European Russia from other parts of the country during the last couple of decades, these plants have also turned out steel pipe.

Piping oil into the Central Region through the Gorkiy area stimulated the establishment of a large refinery in 1958 at Kstovo, a suburb on the east side of Gorkiy. The Kstovo plant has undergone continual expansion and modernization and in 1973 became the site for the first major petroleum-based protein plant in the country, producing protein concentrates from petroleum paraffins for use in animal feed.

In addition to the industries mentioned in the Gorkiy industrial node, the suburbs of Balakhna and Pravdinsk, on the northwest side of Gorkiy, make up a major newsprint and paperboard complex, producing among other things all the paper for the newspaper *Pravda*. Other types of woodworking and furniture manufacture are important, as are textile, leather-working, and food industries. The textile industries are not as well established in this region as they are in the Central Region, but the leather-working industries are more established, and they are particularly concentrated in the suburb of Bogorodsk.

The largest satellite city in the Gorkiy area is the chemical city of Dzerzhinsk west of Gorkiy. It will be discussed separately below.

Kirov

The second largest city in the Volga-Vyatka Region is Kirov, just about at the northern limits of agriculture. In 1974 it had grown to a population of 364,000. Together with the smaller city of Slobodskoy on its east, this forms the second most important industrial node in the Volga-Vyatka Region. Kirov was founded as Khlynov in 1174 and became known as Vyatka in 1781, after the Vyatka River on which it sits — a tributary of the Kama. In 1934 it was renamed Kirov after Sergey Kirov, Bolshevik revolutionary and Leningrad party boss, who had been born in the Vyatka region and was assassinated in 1934. Situated in the forest zone, it has become one of the most important centers for wood processing in the country. It is particularly known for its manufacture of teaching aids, which are used all over the country, and it produces such things as matches, prefabricated houses, and furniture made from local wood supplies. In addition to the wood industries, leather working, fur processing, and shoe manufacturing are important. As mentioned before, a tire plant recently has been established in Kirov.

Cheboksary

The third largest city is Cheboksary with a 1974 population of 251,000. It is the capital city of the Chuvash A.S.S.R. and an important port on the Volga River. It is the site for the construction of the Cheboksary Dam and hydroelectric plant, which is still not completed. The city contains half the urban population of the Chuvash A.S.S.R. It specializes in electrical equipment and cotton textiles. Industrial capital has been invested in Cheboksary in recent years in line with the policy to build up industry in the autonomous republics of the Volga Bend area. The biggest plant under construction at present is a heavy-duty tractor plant scheduled to go into operation sometime in the middle 1970s. It will turn out several thousand tractors per year for use in pipelaying, earthmoving, and land reclamation work. It appears that Cheboksary has been singled out as one of the main centers from which heavy equipment will operate to bring about the transformation of the rural areas of the nonchernozem zone during the next 15-year plan. The power station satellite of Novocheboksarsk has already been mentioned in conjunction with the building of the hydroelectric plant. In 1974 this new town had already reached a population of 58,000 and contained a chemical plant producing aniline dyes.

Dzerzhinsk

The fourth largest city of the region is a satellite of Gorkiy, the chemical center of Dzerzhinsk, which is located about 30 kilometers west of Gorkiy. It was a small town until 1929, when it was renamed Dzerzhinsk, after Stalin's chief of secret police and revitalized by the establishment of some important chemical industries. Since then it has grown into one of the main chemical centers in the country and in 1974 had a population of 235,000. It receives apatite ores from the Khibiny Mountains in the Kola Peninsula, coke from the Urals, salt from the lower Volga, and so forth, and turns out sulfuric acid, caustic soda, mineral fertilizer, plastics, and synthetics. It also manufactures gypsum board and silicate bricks for the construction materials industry.

Saransk

Fifth in size is Saransk, capital city of the Mordvinian A.S.S.R., which in 1974 had a population of 223,000. It contains about half the urban population of the Mordvinian Republic. Like Cheboksary in the Chuvash Republic, it has recently received considerable capital investment to improve the economy, although on a somewhat smaller scale than Cheboksary. It has become one of the Soviet Union's leading producers of electronic and electrical goods. Other plants turn out off-highway trucks for heavy construction purposes and large earth-excavating machinery. Its satellite town of Ruzayevka, to the south, makes chemical equipment. Nearby, at the small workers' settlement of Komsomolskiy, the Alekseyevka cement plant was established in 1955 and has since been expanded to an annual capacity of about 3 million tons. An asbestos-cement sheet mill was inaugurated next to the cement mill in 1960. This Alekseyevka complex is the only cement producer in the Volga-Vyatka Economic Region.

Yoshkar-Ola

The sixth city in size, and the final one above 100,000 population in the Volga-Vyatka Region, is Yoshkar-Ola, the capital of the Mari A.S.S.R., which in 1974 had a population of 195,000. The city contains about 60 percent of all the urban population in the republic. Yoshkar-Ola is a regional center in an area that is not very well developed. Its light industries are diversified, specializing in precision machinery and automation equipment.

TRANSPORT

Transport is not very highly developed in the Volga-Vyatka Region, which has one of the lower freight turnovers in the country. In 1970 it imported 66.1 million tons of freight from other parts of the country and exported 58.5 million tons. Of this, 76.2 percent was carried on railroads, 13.5 percent on rivers, 7 percent by pipelines, and 3.3 percent by trucks. River transport is important to the region and utilizes not only the Volga and the Oka but also the Vyatka, Vetluga, and Sura Rivers. Pipelines coming in from the east-southeast focus on the Gorkiy region and continue westward and northwestward into the Central and Northwest Regions of the country. The primary trade of the region is with the Central Region, the Central Chernozem Region, and the Donets-Dnieper Region to the west and southwest. Main exports from the Volga-Vyatka area to these regions are wood and wood products and main imports from these regions are coal, heavy metals, and cement.

PROSPECTS FOR THE FUTURE

It appears that the Volga-Vyatka Region will remain one of the lesser developed areas of the country. Although some investment is being poured into the capital cities of the autonomous republics, and although the Gorkiy industrial node continues to develop, there are no major plans for any crash development of this area. It will probably retain its role as one of the main exporters of population to the rest of the country, since job opportunities are limited. Because of the continuing increase in the use of steel for the automotive and shipbuilding industries in the region, there has been some talk that in the near future a metallurgical works with an annual output of perhaps 8–12 million tons should be established somewhere in the area to use iron ore from the Kursk Magnetic Anomaly to the southwest and coal from the Pechora Basin to the northeast. However, no definite plans have yet been made. Because of the lowering birth rate in the region and the continued outmigration, some of the smaller towns that have recently become industrialized are beginning to experience considerable labor deficits. Therefore, what plans have been made for the industrialization of this area are being looked at carefully a second time. The region is also part of the development program of the agriculture of the nonchernozem zone, aimed at halting the flight from the countryside.

READING LIST

• Duz, P.D., "Volga-Vyatka ekonomicheskiy rayon" (The Volga-Vyatka Economic Region), *Nauchnye Trudy, Tsentralnyy Nauchno-Issledovatelskiy Ekon,* Institut, No. 1, 1969, pp. 267–281 (in Russian).

Volga Economic Region

	Area (km²)	Population	Persons/km²	Percent Urban
Astrakhan Oblast	44,000	890,000	20.2	62
Volgograd Oblast	114,000	2,380,000	20.9	68
Kuybyshev Oblast	54,000	2,915,000	54.4	75
Penza Oblast	43,000	1,513,000	35.0	48
Saratov Oblast	100,000	2,487,000	24.8	68
Ulyanovsk Oblast	37,000	1,232,000	33.0	57
Bashkir A.S.S.R.	144,000	3,831,000	26.7	52
Kalmyk A.S.S.R.	76,000	267,000	3.5	39
Tatar A.S.S.R.	68,000	3,232,000	47.5	56
Total	680,000	18,747,000	27.6	61

chapter 3

the volga economic region

The remainder of the Volga Valley is constituted as the Volga Economic Region. This contains two more non-Russian nationality-based political units in the Volga Bend area adjacent to those in the Volga-Vyatka region to the west, one nationality-based political unit in the far southwest of the Volga delta, and six Russian oblasts in between. In the north are the Tatar and Bashkir A.S.S.R.s, and in the south the Kalmyk A.S.S.R. Only recently has the Bashkir A.S.S.R. been added to the Volga Region. For a long time it had been considered a part of the Urals Economic Region, but apparently with the high development of the petroleum industry in the Volga-Urals area, the Soviets finally decided to include the Bashkir A.S.S.R. with the rest of the major petroleum-producing area. Its economic ties are no doubt more oriented toward the Volga Valley than toward the Urals. Also, Penza Oblast has recently been added to the western part of the region. It previously had been considered a northeastern extension of the Central Chernozem Region, and physically and agriculturally it is most like that area. But its oblast center, the city of Penza, and much of the rest of the urban economy of the region is oriented more toward the Volga than toward the west.

Thus, the extended Volga Economic Region from north to south consists of the following political units: Tatar and Bashkir A.S.S.R.s, Penza, Ulyanovsk, and Kuybyshev

51

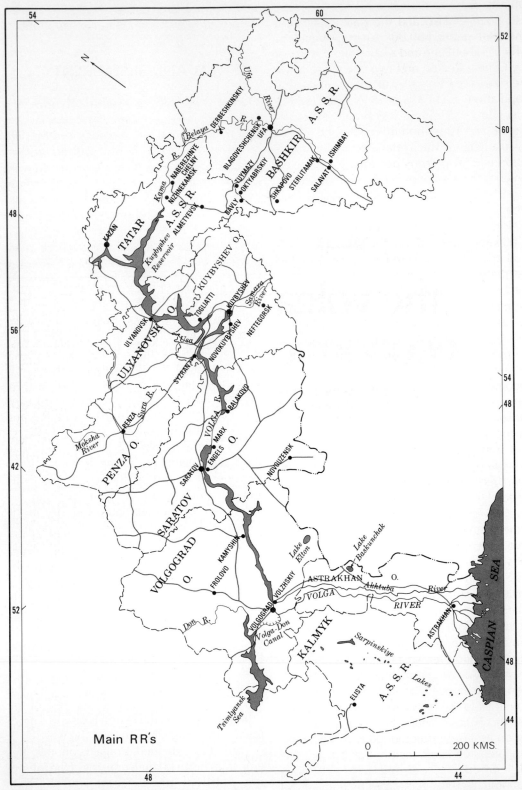

Figure 3-1 The Volga Region.

Oblasts, Saratov Oblast, Volgograd Oblast, Astrakhan Oblast, and the Kalmyk A.S.S.R. The total area is 680,000 square kilometers, which is about one and a half times the size of the Central Region and two and a half times the size of the Volga-Vyatka Region. Its total population in 1973 was 18,747,000, which was about 10 million less than the Central Region and 10 million more than the Volga-Vyatka Region. The average density of population is 27.6 persons per square kilometer, which is the least dense region studied so far, and 61 percent of the population is classified urban.

North-south the region extends for nearly 1700 kilometers and thus the natural and cultural conditions vary greatly from one end of the region to the other. Population density reaches as much as 54.4 people per square kilometer in Kuybyshev Oblast, where 75 percent of the people are urbanized, and is only 3.5 people per square kilometer in the Kalmyk A.S.S.R., where only 39 percent of the people are urbanized. This elongated area has become known as a traditional region because a great quantity of commodities are transported up and down the river. Originally the main function of most of the cities was the river traffic. But as the economy has grown, particularly since World War II, the cities have become industrialized and have transcended the transport function. Economic ties have developed across the river, particularly in the north with the development of oil, that have severed traditional north-south connections. The recent additions of the Bashkir A.S.S.R. and Penza Oblast to this region are further indication of this trend to develop and enlarge the economic region in the north somewhat independently from the south. Construction of the Volga-Don Canal in the early 1950s further isolated the lower part of the river by providing an alternate outlet to the open ocean through the Azov and Black Seas, as well as to the heavy industry areas of the eastern Ukraine. Thus, the Volga Economic Region as it is constituted today is not a very integrated economic region. But statistics are still compiled according to the official economic regions recognized by the Soviets,

and until a better regionalization is offered, the Volga Region will be treated as a unit.

HISTORY AND SETTLEMENT

During the ninth to twelfth centuries, the Volga Bend area was settled by Bulgar farmers and traders, Turkic in language and Moslem in religion. They had subdued earlier Finnish-speaking settlers, and all in turn were overwhelmed in the early thirteenth century by the Tatars. As the Golden Horde disintegrated into three groups, one of the groups established itself in the center of Kazan around 1438. Another established itself in Astrakhan at the mouth of the Volga. The Kazan khanate lasted little more than a century when it was conquered and incorporated into Russia by Ivan the Terrible in 1552. Four years later Ivan's armies moved down the Volga and captured the khanate at Astrakhan, and the entire Volga Valley came under the control of the Russian Empire where it has remained ever since.

For more than two centuries the Volga Valley represented a strip of Russian-controlled land along which trade could move from south to north through alien territory on either side. During this period the primary functions of the region were trade and defense. A string of settlements such as Samara (Kuybyshev), Saratov, Tsaritsyn (Volgograd), and Astrakhan were established as fortresses overlooking the steppes to the southeast. During the seventeenth century the Mongol Kalmyks established themselves in the semidesert west of the Volga delta, and later, primarily during the reign of Catherine the Great, German colonists formed a large farming community in the middle Trans Volga across the river from Saratov.

As the Russian Empire expanded southward to the west of the river and eventually to the east, security became less of a problem, and the defense function of the cities along the Volga ceased to exist. During the nineteenth century trade was their primary function as many of them became transfer points between the river and the rail system that was beginning to develop. Particularly around the turn of the century, when Baku oil was becoming all important and the eastern Ukraine began to develop heavy metallurgy, the Volga became a major carrier of freight moving northward to the Central Industrial Region. But testaments to the early defense function of the Volga cities remain to this day in the form of kremlins in most of the towns and such things as remnants of the wall that extended northwest from the city of Volgograd, which was part of Peter the Great's so-called security line connecting fortifications between Tsaritsyn and the Don River, built in 1718 to strengthen further this flank of Russia against the Tatars and the Kalmyks.

After the Bolshevik Revolution most of the non-Russian peoples in the Volga area were given political recognition in autonomous oblasts or autonomous republics within the middle Volga Kray that eventually were elevated to the status of A.S.S.R. The Tatar A.S.S.R. formed in 1920 was one of the first autonomous republics in the country. In short order the Bashkir, Volga-German, and Kalmyk A.S.S.R.s were also established. During World War II the Volga-German and Kalmyk A.S.S.R.s were abrogated to prevent collaboration with the Germans, and their peoples were scattered throughout the Russian, Kazakh, and Central Asian Republics. This involved the movement of nearly one-half million Germans into Siberia and Central Asia. Although after Stalin's death in 1953 the Volga-Germans were officially absolved of any collaboration with the enemy, they have not been reestablished in the middle Volga. In 1956 the Kalmyks were reinstated as an autonomous oblast in Stavropol Kray, and very soon thereafter as an A.S.S.R.

As the economy in the Volga Valley has developed, the cities have outgrown the trade function and have become important industrial centers in their own rights, and Russians have moved into the area in large numbers. As a consequence the Tatars have been reduced to only 49 percent of the population of their republic, the Bashkirs only 23 percent of their republic, and the Kalmyks 41 percent, as of the 1970 census.

THE NATURAL LANDSCAPE

Climate

Stretching 1000 miles north-south, the Volga Region and its climate obviously change drastically from one end to the other. The climate also changes significantly in a west-east direction as it becomes more continental and drier eastward. The general southwest-northeast trend of climatic zones across the East European Plain is accentuated along the middle Volga between Kuybyshev and Volgograd by the major break in topography that takes place from the high west bluff to the low flat eastern bank of the river. Thus, precipitation amounts diminish rapidly both southward and eastward through the Volga Region. Kazan in the north receives 435 millimeters of precipitation per year, while Astrakhan in the south receives only 190. Penza in the west gets 559 millimeters per year, and Kuybyshev at the same latitude farther east receives only 449. Farther northeast Ufa receives only 419.

None of the region is abundantly humid. Even in the northwest the potential evaporation somewhat exceeds the precipitation, and as the precipitation diminishes southeastward the potential evaporation increases, so that at Astrakhan it exceeds precipitation by about five times. The entire region is subject to some drought, and the southeast is subject to consistent drought every year. The North Caspian Lowland has the aspects of a desert. Summers are hot and sunny. In Astrakhan only two or three days per month have overcast skies from June to September. In Kazan this increases to seven or eight days per month. Frequent incursions of the desiccating *sukhovey* occur as far north as Kuybyshev. During spring and early summer they are particularly hazardous to agriculture. Most of the region receives a fairly pronounced middle and late summer maximum of precipitation, which is not the best summer distribution of rainfall for growth and harvesting conditions.

Midsummer temperatures in the Volga Region range from a July average of 20°C at Kazan to 25°C at Astrakhan. Thus, the entire area is warm during the summer, and the

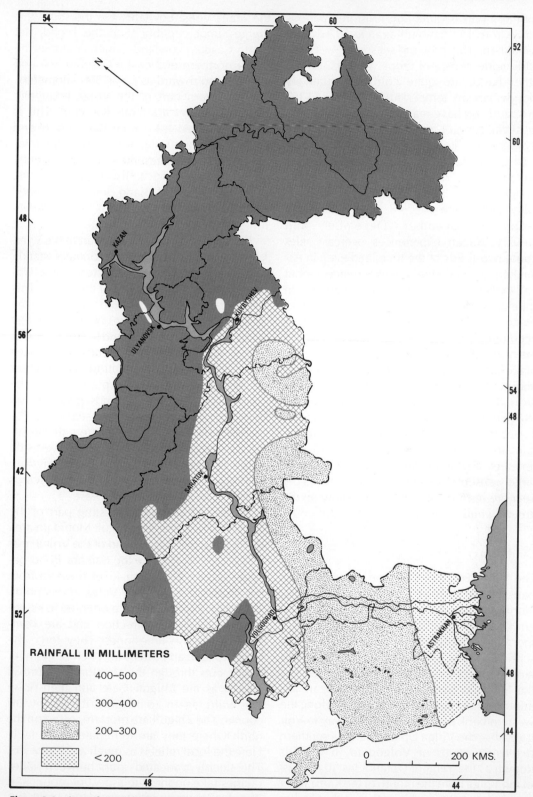

RAINFALL IN MILLIMETERS

	400–500
	300–400
	200–300
	< 200

0   200 KMS.

Figure 3-2 Annual precipitation in the Volga Region.

southern part is quite hot. Frost-free periods range from 151 days at Kazan to 187 days at Astrakhan. This growing season allows for a fairly wide choice of crops. Winters, on the other hand, are quite cold and relatively cloudy. January temperatures average −13°C in Kazan and have reached as low as −44°C. In Astrakhan January averages −7°C and the temperature here has fallen to as low as −34°C. Winter temperatures decrease more rapidly eastward than northward. Over the Volga Upland, January isotherms run essentially north-south.

During November, December, and January, Kazan experiences overcast skies about two-thirds of the time, and even in Astrakhan overcast skies are experienced about half the time in December and January. But in spite of the large amount of cloudiness, winter precipitation is quite light. Therefore, snow accumulation is relatively thin, but it stays on the ground a long period of time. Yearly maximum snow cover in Kazan averages about 52 centimeters and remains on the ground 154 days of the year. As far south as Volgograd snow stays on the ground an average of 101 days per year, but there it accumulates to a maximum depth of only 15 centimeters. Farther south the snow cover is largely absent. At Astrakhan only 12 days per year are reported as having any snow on the ground at all.

Landform

The Volga Economic Region contains all or parts of five distinct geomorphic provinces. North of the Volga and Kama Rivers in northern Tatar A.S.S.R. is the southern extension of the Vyatka-Kama Upland, which was described in the Volga-Vyatka Economic Region. South of the eastward-flowing stretch of the Volga between Gorkiy and Kazan lies another major upland that stretches along the western bank of the Volga all the way to Volgograd — the Volga Upland. It has a southern extension south of Volgograd in what is known as the Yergeni Upland. Just to the east of the Volga from the mouth of the Kama River in the north to Kamyshin in the south stretches

the Trans Volga Lowland. On the south this merges imperceptibly with the broad, flat North Caspian Lowland, which encircles the entire northern end of the Caspian Sea and stretches northward as far as 500 kilometers. In the eastern part of the Volga Economic Region stretches the Urals Foreland. This is usually divided into three parts north and south, but in the Volga Region only the middle section is represented by the recently added Bashkir A.S.S.R. This is known as the Bugulma-Belebey Upland, which is drained by the Belaya and Ufa Rivers, and is sometimes known as the Ufa Plateau.

The gently rolling southern part of the Vyatka Upland north of Kazan contrasts starkly with the higher, more dissected Volga Uplands to the south and west of the Volga. This is one of the great north-south upwarps on the east European plain that has been deeply dissected by the Volga River and its tributaries. In places the flexures of the rock strata have been accentuated by faulting. The highest elevations of the Volga Upland are in the southeast where the summits generally lie more than 300 meters above sea level. The highest point of all is 367 meters in the so-called Khvalynsk Mountains on the west side of the Volga between Saratov and Kamyshin. Here are some of the most imposing scarps overlooking the Volga to the east.

Probably the most interesting part of the upland is the so-called Zhiguli Mountain area in the great horseshoe bend of the Volga near Kuybyshev, known as the Samara Bend because the small Samara River flows in from the southeast to join the Volga at this point. The Zhiguli Mountains are oriented in essentially an east-west direction and are composed of dense limestones. They force the Volga to take an eastern turn before the river finally cuts through the structure in narrows known as the Zhiguli Gate and then flows westward again to resume its southward course. The Zhiguli are most imposing on the north where they are terminated by a fault. Here the local relief is as much as 300 meters. The steeply truncated spurs between valley ravines take on the true aspect of mountains. The dense stands of forests, dark evergreens

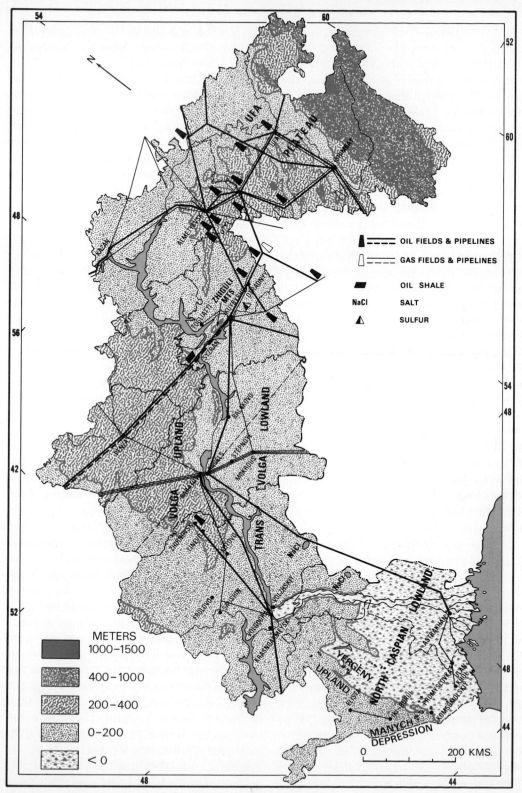

Figure 3-3 Landform, hydrology, minerals, and pipelines of the Volga Region.

on the uplands and lighter deciduous trees in the valleys, contrast with the farmland on the flat floodplains north of the Volga and add to the mountainous aspect of the Zhiguli. The slopes of the Zhiguli that face the Volga in many places are so steep that forests have not been able to take hold. Here naked limestone and sandstone cliffs with talus slopes at their bases peak out of the forest cover to form enormous scars on the landscape.

Much of the Zhiguli is underlain by fissured limestones and dolomites that have been conducive to the formation of many karst forms, including broad, elongated, enclosed valleys formed from the coalescence of large cave-ins. The most extensive of these valleys is traversed by the small Usa River, which flows eastward near the west-flowing Volga on the south side of the Zhiguli and then suddenly cuts northward through the Zhiguli to join the Volga on the north. Before this valley was flooded by the Kuybyshev Reservoir it was a favorite trip of young people to leave Kuybyshev by rowboat, float downstream on the Volga to the point opposite the headwater of the Usa, carry their small boat up over the hills for a distance of about 1.5 kilometers, and then embark down the Usa back to the Volga and down the Volga again to Kuybyshev. This jaunt took about a fortnight and was known as "the round-the-world cruise."

Although the Volga Uplands are complicated by transverse structures such as the Zhiguli and other minor deviations from the general pattern, the overall structure is one of a broad upwarp along a north-south axis that is breached by the Volga and its tributaries. The Volga River over a long period of time has adjusted to the structure and worked its way slowly westward down the dip of the strata, maintaining a high right bank and a low left bank along the strike of one of the hard rock layers. In general the upland is supported by sandstone or some such insoluble rock, while the weak layer underneath is usually limestone. In places the bases of the cliffs are underlain by clays with water-bearing interbeds of sand providing slick surfaces that cause many landslides along the high western escarpment. Especially in the vicinity of Ulyanovsk there are many cirque-shaped scars of landslides.

In the midsection of the Volga Upland lies the valley of the north-flowing Sura River. To the west of this during Quaternary times the ice cover scattered a thin veneer of boulder loam that in some of the preglacial valleys reaches thicknesses of as much as ten meters. Northward-flowing streams such as the Sura, the Alatyr, the Tsna, and the Moksha were for a time ponded by the glacial ice and accumulated thick glaciofluvial deposits in their valleys that formed broad valley floors. In places these easily eroded deposits are being attacked by the wind, which has blown the sand into dune forms on some of the river floodplains. East of the Sura there are no glacial deposits, and bedrock outcrops are frequent. Loess-like loams are found on the slopes of many of the watersheds.

The Volga Uplands pinch into a narrow ridge no more than 800 meters wide west of the city of Volgograd, and then south of the Volga-Don Canal they rise again in a southern extension known as the Yergeni Upland in the southern part of Volgograd Oblast and the western part of the Kalmyk A.S.S.R. The Yergeni Upland extends north-south for a distance of about 350 kilometers roughly from the city of Krasnoarmeysk in the north to the Manych Depression in the south. Its mean elevation is only 140–160 meters above sea level, with a maximum elevation of 222 meters in the southern portion of the region to the west of Elista, the capital city of the Kalmyk A.S.S.R. However, the general surface of the North Caspian Lowland east of the Yergeni is below sea level and the area is very dry, so the eastern escarpment is quite imposing. It overlooks an old course of the Volga River that runs southward from Volgograd, now occupied by a string of shallow brackish bodies of water known as the Sarpa Lakes. Here the steep spurs cut by the jagged ravines of short intermittent streams reach heights of 70–80 meters, and from the lowland of the Sarpinsk-Davansk Rill give the impression of the beginning of a mountain range. Everywhere along the eastern slopes of the Yergeni can be traced three terraces with above-sea-level elevations of 15–20 meters, 25–35 meters, and 40–55 meters. These mark old levels of the Caspian during various stages of the Pleistocene when the water filled up the basin and overflowed northwestward through the Manych Depression to the head of the Sea of Azov. On the west the Yergeni slopes gently downward to join the steppes of the lower Don.

The third geomorphic region, the Trans Volga Alluvial Plain, lies between the steep scarp of the Volga Upland on the west and the more gentle slopes of the Bugulma-Belebey Upland on the east. This depression represents primarily the slip-off slope of the Volga that has worked its way westward down the dip slope of the rock structure. It is separated into northern and southern parts by the transverse Zhiguli Range, which produces high cliffs on both sides of the Volga just to the north of Kuybyshev. In most places on this lowland three distinct terraces can be traced above the present floodplain. The present floodplain lies 5–10 meters above the water level of the Volga and in places reaches widths of as much as 10 kilometers. It is cut by side channels and oxbow lakes that in most cases have become marshy. Wind has whipped some of the floodplain sand into dune forms. The first terrace rises 5–10 meters above the floodplain. It is not continuous, and its average width is only 500–1000 meters, but in places the width can increase to as much as 10 kilometers. The construction of the Kuybyshev Reservoir flooded both the present floodplain and the first terrace in the northern part of the Trans Volga Lowland. The second terrace lies 20–30 meters above the water level of the Volga, and its width varies from 1–30 kilometers. This terrace dates from the time of the Dnieper glaciation. Dunes are common in the sandy areas. The second terrace in places merges with the third terrace, and in other places there is a discontinuity between the two with the third terrace lying 40–50 meters above the Volga.

To the east of the Trans Volga Lowland, primarily in the Bashkir A.S.S.R., is the area of the High Trans Volga Upland, more specifi-

cally in this region the Bugulma-Belebey Upland or the Ufa Plateau. The surface here is underlain primarily by limestones, marls, and dolomites of Devonian and Carboniferous ages, everywhere covered by Permian deposits. These are the oil-bearing strata of the Bashkir A.S.S.R. The Ufa Plateau is deeply incised by river valleys to depths of 150–200 meters that form canyonlike valleys between flat interfluves. The interfluves exhibit two distinct denudation levels. The upper level, lying at elevations of 240–320 meters, is not really continuous but is represented by isolated massifs, known in Bashkiria as *shikhany* (monadnocks derived from ancient limestone reefs), that stand 60–80 meters above the lower erosion level. This level lies generally at 180–250 meters above sea level and represents the basic surface of the region. It comprises the present watersheds, the highest points of which reach 400 meters above sea level. Along the slopes of the interfluves, structural terraces have formed under the process of differential erosion in hard and soft rock layers. Because of the dense nature of much of the bedrock and the subhumid nature of the climate, the erosion texture is rather coarse. In the eastern part of the region the sedimentary strata are interbedded with a number of gypsums whose outcrops are marked by karst forms of relief.

The fifth geomorphic region is the large North Caspian Lowland, which not only occupies the southern third of the Volga Region but also extends far eastward around the northeastern end of the Caspian into the Kazakh Republic. It is the northern part of the large geosynclinal structure that is occupied by the Caspian Sea. Here the sediments have accumulated to a thickness of about 3000 meters over the basement crystalline rock. Some of the sediments are of land origin, but others indicate a large marine transgression, known as the Akchagyl Basin, which probably occurred around the end of the Paleocene. At its greatest extent this transgression of the sea might have reached as far north as Kuybyshev.

Earlier transgressions laid down nearly horizontal older strata, many of which contain gypsum and rock salt, that subsequently have been forced by lateral pressures into dome structures. In places these form a broadly arched surface relief of as much as 100–150 meters in height. On the surface of many of these are autoprecipitating salt lakes that gain their salts from brines working upward from below. Some of these lakes, such as Baskunchak and Elton southeast of Volgograd, provide the basis for a thriving salt industry. In other areas the salt plugs have provided dome structures in the overlying strata that have created pools of oil and gas, most of which lie east of the Volga Region in western Kazakhstan, but a few of which are found in the southwestern part of the Kalmyk A.S.S.R. in the Volga Region.

The northern part of the plain consists of monotonously flat surfaces marked here and there by shallow sinkholes no more than 2 meters in depth and 10–100 meters in diameter. They are made obvious by fresh green vegetation growing within them while the surrounding surfaces are covered by sagebrush and other xerophytic vegetation. In the north the elevation is at approximately sea level. The flat surface slopes gently southward to the Caspian, where it declines to about 27 meters below sea level. The main erosional features on this flattish surface are the so-called rills that run from north to south and apparently represent old shallow drainage channels that formed as the sea shrank from the region. Most of them run no more than a few kilometers in length and vary from 100–1000 meters in width. They carry water during rains, particularly in the spring when melt waters are available, and end in stagnant lagoons before reaching the Caspian. They are particularly well developed in the western part of the region where the so-called Sarpinsk-Davansk Rill runs southward through a series of stagnant pools of water along the eastern edge of the Yergeni. As mentioned earlier, this represents an earlier channel of the Volga.

In the southern part of the region large areas are occupied by drifting sand, and the surface has been sculptured by the wind into barkhan dunes that commonly reach heights of 5–6 meters and sometimes as much as 15 meters. These are interspersed with oval-shaped deflation hollows that may reach diameters of as much as 1–2 kilometers. The prevailingly southeasterly winds of the area have blown up hummocks of sand along the western and northwestern sides of these depressions.

Immediately along the shores of the Caspian, all the way from the Emba River in the northeast to the mouth of the Kuma in the southwest, are the so-called Ber's hummocks, 7–10 meters in height and 0.5–8 kilometers in length running almost due east-west. The depressions between these ridges are 400–500 meters in width, and when the Volga is at flood stage these depressions are filled with water. Therefore, all the towns in the region, including the large city of Astrakhan, are built on these hummocks. They are so named from a study by Karl M. Ber, the Russian naturalist, who in 1856 attributed their formation to a catastrophic flood caused by a sudden rise in the Caspian Sea. However, there are many theories regarding their origin, and the most logical one relates to long-term wind action around the southern edge of the Asiatic High during winter when strong winds blow persistently from east to west.

The lower Volga Valley slices through the North Caspian Lowland in a northwest-southeast direction and divides the region into two separate parts. After leaving the city of Volgograd, the Volga enters the flat lowland and breaks into a myriad of distributary channels that together form a broad floodplain 10–20 kilometers wide occupied by intertwining channels, abandoned meander loops, and stagnant lagoons. The main channel of the Volga River itself occupies the western edge of this floodplain, and the main distributary channel, the Akhtuba, occupies the eastern edge of the floodplain. In between are many short, discontinuous, interconnecting channels. The entire floodplain is well watered and supports a verdant growth of black poplar, white poplar, and elm, standing out starkly as an oasis within the desert landscape on either side. In the drier parts of the floodplain most of the land has been cleared and put into intensive cultivation under irrigation. Approaching the delta toward the southeast, the river breaks up into more distributaries and spreads over a wider area. Water comes to the surface in many places so that nothing more than a lush growth of a watery mass of reeds can be sustained. This provides the habitat for an exceedingly rich population of fish and waterfowl. Shortly after the Bolshevik Revolution, Lenin set aside a large part of the delta as the Astrakhan Reservation, one of the richest birdlife regions in the country. The reservation is on the flyway from arctic Siberia to South Africa, and annually the region is visited by about 10 million birds of more than 260 species.

Natural Vegetation and Soils

The vegetation and soil zones follow the moisture zones in a southwest-northeast orientation across the region. North of Kazan much of the area was originally forested by a mixture of deciduous and evergreen trees. Pines predominated, and in some places pine-spruce combinations acquired the character of taiga. But in most places there was a wide admixture of broadleaf species, particularly oak, linden, maple, and elm. The small-leaf trees, birch and aspen, were also well represented. Soils beneath these forests were podsolized types. Although considerable clearing has taken place over the centuries for cultivation, a great deal of the area is still covered by such forests.

The mixed forest continues to cover much of the region southward on the Volga Upland west of the river as far as Ulyanovsk, after which it narrows to a strip that just includes the higher parts of the upland. This continues south almost as far as Saratov. Pines continue to occupy some of the sandier soil areas and even some of the limestone uplands, which have little soil on them. More and more expanses of steppe grasses are interspersed with the forest farther south, and south of Ulyanovsk the wooded steppe becomes the predominant vegetative type. East of the Volga the forest does not continue very far south of Kazan before it becomes a wooded steppe, and by the time the Samara River is reached at Kuybyshev the trees have almost disappeared entirely and the open steppe is at hand.

The wooded steppe zone is characterized by gray forest soils and degraded chernozems. These occupy much of Penza and Ulyanovsk Oblasts, the north central portion of Saratov Oblast on the west side of the Volga, the southern half of the Tatar A.S.S.R., and the northern half of Kuybyshev Oblast to the east of the Volga. They continue northeastward to cover much of the Bashkir A.S.S.R., although elevations rise in the Urals Foreland, and the topography is much more dissected than it is to the west, so that considerable variation in vegetation and soil types occurs between the dryish uplands, which often have carbonate rocks outcropping to form stony, scrubby steppe lands and deeply incised river valleys.

The forest steppe gives way toward the southeast to the true steppe with typical chernozem soils occupying a southwest-northeast zone stretching from the northwestern portion of Volgograd Oblast northeastward through much of Saratov Oblast west of the Volga, the northern third of Saratov Oblast, and the southern half of Kuybyshev Oblast east of the Volga. This zone contains the best soils of the region but is more subject to drought than the wooded steppe to the northwest.

South of Balakovo the territory east of the Volga becomes dry steppe land with chestnut-colored soils. This landscape crosses to the west side of the river about halfway between Saratov and Kamyshin and occupies the whole width of the Volga Region southward to Volgograd, beyond which it merges into semidesert and eventually desert conditions near the Volga Delta. From Volgograd southward the vegetation is typified as sparse sagebrush and bunch grass as well as other drought-resistant species of low plants interspersed with broad areas of takyrs (playa lake beds) with clay and salt incrustations. As the Caspian is approached the soils become very sandy, and much of the sand is on the move under the action of the wind.

AGRICULTURE

The Volga Region is an important agricultural area. Although it is not the best-endowed region in the country, because of its size and its great north-south extent it is one of the leading agricultural regions in terms of sown acreage and variety of crops. Normally the region contains about 10 percent of the cultivated area of the country.

Since all but the northern extremity of the Volga Region is rather dry, the region specializes in grains, particularly spring wheat, which occupies by far the largest area of any single crop. Grains of all kinds occupy about two-thirds of the sown territory, but a wide range of other things are also grown. These vary considerably from one end of the region to another, which stretches from the cool, humid north to the hot, dry south.

In the cool forest lands north of Kazan, with their somewhat podsolized soils, scattered fields are planted with potatoes, flax, hay crops, and some of the small grains. The legume crops, primarily alfalfa and clover, are an important part of the rotation scheme in both the forest and the wooded steppe to the south. The Volga Region devotes more acreage to these crops than does any other region in the country. The Volga Economic Region annually accounts for about one-sixth of all the legume crops in the U.S.S.R.

Farther south in the wooded steppe some of the northern crops are still prominant, but other crops enter the complex, some of which belong to what the Soviets call the "industrial crops" category. Sugar beets have been introduced in Penza and Kuybyshev Oblasts and in the Tatar and Bashkir A.S.S.R.s, and hemp is an important crop in Penza and Ulyanovsk Oblasts. Buckwheat, although it occupies little acreage, is a basic foodcrop throughout this zone as well as the forest zone to the north. Millet also becomes an important foodcrop, and it increases in importance farther south in the droughty steppe area

where it is well adapted. Wheat and sunflowers are also important in the wooded steppe, but not as important as they are farther south in the true steppe, because they are drought resistant.

In the steppe zone, stretching from Volgograd northeastward to Saratov and beyond, wheat, sunflowers, and corn grown for dry grain are the major crops. The Volga Region ranks third in the country in sunflower production, after the Ukraine and the North Caucasus. The Volga Region normally accounts for about one-sixth of all the area in the country sown with sunflowers. The steppe zone also grows considerable amounts of makhorka and mustard.

South of Volgograd the area becomes too dry for cultivation without irrigation. Most of the area away from the river is utilized only for extensive grazing, particularly sheep. The Yergeni Upland is known for its good pastures. But the Volga oasis between the main stream of the Volga and its main distributary channel, the Akhtuba, contains intensive irrigation agriculture of vegetables, melons, and rice. The lower Volga floodplain is particularly known for its tomatoes and watermelons, which are marketed throughout the country. A significant number of vineyards have also been developed in the irrigated Volga-Akhtuba floodplain near Astrakhan, as well as in the Don Valley where the river passes through the western part of Volgograd Oblast.

Some of the flattest land and the richest soils of the entire Volga Region lie in the Trans Volga Lowland east of Saratov. This was the area of the development of the German agricultural colony during the eighteenth century under the auspices of Catherine the Great. After the Bolshevik Revolution the Volga-German A.S.S.R. was formed in this area with its capital city at Engels. But during World War II the A.S.S.R. was abolished and the Germans were scattered eastward. The Soviets would like to use these lands more intensively, but drought is a constant hazard. There are plans to irrigate much of the Trans Volga Lowland, primarily from the Kuybyshev Reservoir, and more recently from

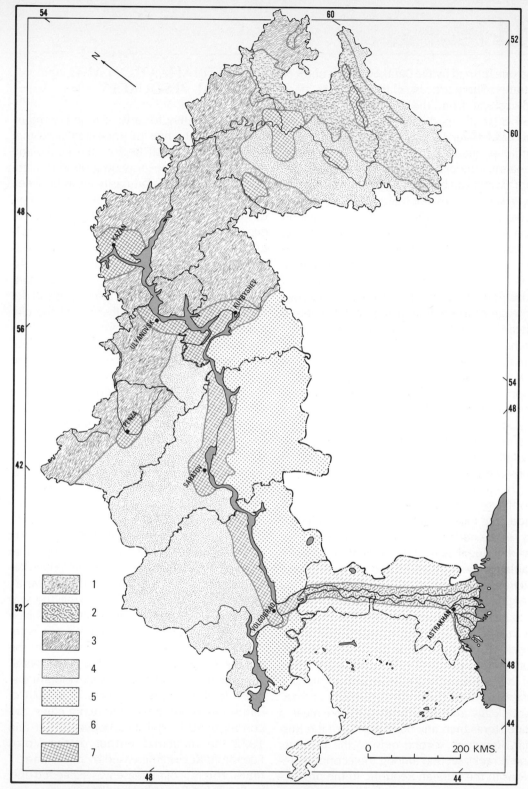

Figure 3-4 Agricultural regions. From Saushkin, p. 106.; 1-Orchards, berries, hunting; 2-Irrigated vegetables, melons, truck gardens, and rice; 3-Grain, flax, sugar beets, livestock for meat and milk; 4-Grain, sunflowers, dairying, meat livestock; 5-Spring wheat, sunflowers, mustard, cattle for meat and milk, sheep for meat and wool; 6-Sheep and cattle; 7-Urban oriented agriculture.

the one formed by the Balakovo Dam north of Saratov. There are also plans to irrigate areas downslope from the Volgograd Reservoir farther south, particularly eastward toward the Ural River in western Kazakhstan. The initial segments of some of these irrigation canals are under construction. However, until more water can be diverted into the Volga, the river simply does not have enough water to serve all these purposes. Therefore, irrigation from these reservoirs has been minimal, and most of the irrigated land of the Volga Region is limited to the Volga-Akhtuba floodplain. The irrigated acreage in the Volga Region constitutes only about 2 percent of the sown acreage of the region. If the Soviets ever go ahead with plans to divert waters from some of the northern streams in northeast European Russia southward to the Volga system, then the Volga Economic Region might find itself supplied with sufficient water to irrigate much of the dry Trans Volga and greatly increase its yields. However, in the southern part of the North Caspian Lowland, the expansion of irrigation will eventually be limited by saline soils and drifting sand.

The wide sowing of legume crops in the north and central parts of the region has provided the basis for a thriving livestock industry. In the north this is concentrated primarily on dairying, but as one proceeds southward cattle for meat purposes and swine enter the picture. In the far south, particularly in the Yergeni Upland south of Volgograd, sheep grazing is the primary activity. The Volga Region accounts for about 7 percent of the livestock in the entire Soviet Union. It accounts for about 10 percent of all the sheep and goats of the country. The Volga Region is thus one of the major producers in the country of meat, wool, eggs, and milk. It delivers more meat to state stores than any other region in the Russian Republic, second only to the Ukraine, and it ranks second among the economic regions in the Russian Republic in the production of milk, eggs, and wool. The region turns out about 10 percent of the woolen textiles of the country.

INDUSTRIALIZATION AND NATURAL RESOURCES

The Volga Valley for a long time lay industrially dormant while the three giant industrial nodes in the Central Region, the Urals, and the eastern Ukraine grew up around it. Until World War II it was primarily an in-between area crisscrossed by traffic from the three industrial nodes. What factories existed were engaged primarily in processing local agricultural produce, flour milling, distilling, soap-making, tanning, leather-working, fur processing, and some shipbuilding, cement manufacturing, and lumbering. Lime kilns still dot the narrow floodplain at the foot of the cliff along the west side of the Volga where limestone outcrops at the base of the escarpment. The processed lime and cement are loaded directly on riverboats for distribution.

The Soviet industrialization drive of the 1930s did establish some agricultural-machine-building industries in the region, but the Volga Valley still had virtually no power supply of its own. The Volga River had not yet been harnessed, and although the Volga-Urals oil-bearing region had been discovered, its extent was not yet known and it was only being exploited at scattered points.

World War II, with its attendant evacuation of industries eastward, was the catalyst that triggered the development of the Volga Region that has continued since the war at an unabated pace. For a time during the war when Moscow was under heavy siege, even parts of the central government were relocated largely in Kuybyshev. Since 1940 the Middle Volga and adjacent Ural Foreland have been the most rapidly developing regions in the country in terms of growth of industrial output, trade, and major cities. According to Soviet statistics, between 1940 and 1972 the industrial output of the Volga Economic Region increased by more than 27 times. This rate of increase was exceeded only by the Baltic Republics and Moldavia.

This industrial growth probably was inevitable in the long run because of the intermediate position of the region between the three industrial nodes and the great amount of traffic crossing it, but the industrialization has been greatly speeded up by the sudden explosion of the region into a large powerhouse, due to the rapid development of its large oil and gas deposits and hydroelectric power.

Oil, Gas, and Petrochemicals

Commercial production of petroleum began in the Volga Region in 1932 at Ishimbay in the Bashkir Republic, and in 1936–1937 it spread into Kuybyshev Oblast. During World War II it expanded into eastern Tatar A.S.S.R. and Saratov Oblast. After the war it continued to expand southward into Volgograd and Astrakhan Oblasts and to a small extent into the Kalmyk Republic. During the 1950s the Volga Region rapidly expanded into the biggest oil-producing area in the country, although at that time the Bashkir Republic, which ranked second only to the Tatar Republic in production, was considered to be part of the Urals Region. By 1960 the Volga-Urals area was credited with about two-thirds of the country's oil reserves, and it accounted for about two-thirds of the country's annual petroleum production.

The Tatar A.S.S.R. rapidly became the leading single political unit in the country in oil production. Although Tatar oil was first struck at Bavly in 1946, the discovery of the great Romashkino oil pool at Almetyevsk put the Tatar Republic over the top. By 1970 the Tatar Republic alone was producing 100 million tons per year. In early 1971 it produced its billionth ton of oil. It appears that the Tatar production has stabilized at about 100 million tons per year and that probably some of the fields are approaching depletion.

The Bashkir Republic reached its peak production in 1967 when it produced 45.3 million tons. By 1970 it had declined to 39.2 million tons. As the Volga production has leveled off, Western Siberian oil production has expanded rapidly during the last decade,

so that the portion of total U.S.S.R. production in the Volga area has declined significantly. However, in the mid-1970s the Volga Region was still producing more than half the country's oil, and it appears that it will remain a major producer for a number of years.

The great expansion of petroleum production in the Volga Region has prompted the construction of many pipelines, refineries, and petrochemical plants in the region. Oil pipelines radiate from Almetyevsk in the Tatar Republic northwestward through Kazan and Gorkiy to the Central Region and the Northwest Region, southwestward to Kuybyshev and surrounding cities, westward as the Druzhba ("friendship") pipeline through the Central Chernozem Region and Belorussia into the East European satellites, and eastward through the southern Urals to Siberia as far east as Irkutsk. Originally oil radiated outward from Almetyevsk to all the other regions. Now, with the great production in Western Siberia, the oil flow on the eastern line has been reversed, and Western Siberian oil comes into the Almetyevsk area from where it is disseminated to other regions in the west including the Friendship Pipeline to the satellite countries. In 1975 a pipeline was completed all the way from Kuybyshev southwest to Novorossiysk on the northeastern Black Sea coast to provide a southern outlet for Western Siberian oil.

Oil refineries have been built in the cities of Kuybyshev, Novokuybyshevsk, and Syzran, all in the Kuybyshev area, and at Saratov and Volgograd, as well as at Ufa, Ishimbay, and Salavat in the center of the Bashkir A.S.S.R. The Volga Region is now the largest oil-refining region in the entire country. Kuybyshev has become the refining and financial center for the entire oil region of the Volga-Urals, and Ufa has acted as the center for a cluster of smaller cities to its south and west that concentrate on oil refining and petrochemicals. The Tatar A.S.S.R., which is the largest producer of oil in the Volga Region, has not shared in the buildup of refining capacity, although it has developed petrochemical industries based on feedstocks from other refining centers.

Natural gas production began in the Volga Region in 1942, first in northeastern Kuybyshev Oblast and then in western Saratov and Volgograd Oblasts and south-western Astrakhan Oblast. The Saratov fields early became the major producer in the country, and the first major gas pipeline in the U.S.S.R. was constructed in 1946 from Saratov to Moscow. However, no great reserves have been found in the Volga Region, and as the gas industry rapidly expanded in other parts of the country after 1955, the Volga area quickly receded into a minor producing region. Very few of the great deposits of oil in the Volga Region have gas associated with them. By 1970 the Volga Region (without the Bashkir A.S.S.R.) produced about 15 billion cubic meters of natural gas, which amounted to about 7.5 percent of the total production of the U.S.S.R. Almost half of this production took place in Saratov Oblast, a little more than half in Volgograd Oblast, and very small amounts in Astrakhan and Kuybyshev Oblasts and the Kalmyk Republic.

The utilization of oil well gas in the Volga Region was delayed for years by the lack of gas-processing plants. Now a number of large plants have been built in the area, and the production of gas condensates has improved considerably. In 1954 a gas plant was built at Tuymazy, Bashkir A.S.S.R., and it now has a capacity of 730 million cubic meters. A second plant was built in Bashkiria at Shkapovo in 1959 with a capacity of 876 million cubic meters. In the Tatar A.S.S.R. the Minnibayevo gas plant was opened in 1956 near Almetyevsk. This plant has a capacity of 3.7 billion cubic meters, which makes it the largest Soviet processing installation, pending completion of large plants in Western Siberia with individual capacities of 5 to 6 billion cubic meters. During the mid-1960s this plant alone accounted for as much as 45 percent of all the Soviet natural gas liquids. Two pipelines have been built to carry ethane from Minnibayevo to the petrochemical complex at Kazan that began operations in 1963. In Kuybyshev Oblast gas plants went into opera-

tion in 1962 at Otradnyy (1.1 billion cubic meters) and in 1968 at Neftegorsk. A gas plant opened in 1966 at Kstovo in Volgograd Oblast.

The tremendous buildup of gas and petroleum production and petroleum refining in the Volga Region during the past three decades has spurred the development of many petrochemical industries in the Volga Region. Main petrochemical complexes exist in Kuybyshev and the Togliatti-Zhigulevsk urban area in Kuybyshev Oblast; in Ufa, the capital of the Bashkir A.S.S.R., and in the three-city metropolitan area to the south of Ufa consisting of Sterlitamak, Ishimbay, and Salavat; in Kazan; in the Saratov-Engels area; and in the Volgograd-Volzhskiy area. Many of these plants turn out the base products for the production of synthetic rubber and automobile tires to supplement the automobile industry being developed in Togliatti and Naberezhnyye Chelny in the Volga Region, as well as in other parts of the country. Petrochemicals are the basis for many of the large mineral fertilizer industries that are being established in the Volga Region. Synthetic fibers, various plastics, and paints and dyes are also being derived from petrochemical products.

Synthetic rubber is being produced in Togliatti, Volzhskiy, Kazan, Nizhnekamsk, and Sterlitamak. The Sterlitamak plant is one of the largest synthetic rubber producers in the Soviet Union. It opened in 1960, and has since developed into one of the four major polyisoprene rubber-producing plants in the country. The other three are at Togliatti, Volzhskiy, and Nizhnekamsk, all in the Volga Region. The Nizhnekamsk rubber plant began operating in 1970. When it is fully operative it will be one of the biggest synthetic rubber plants in the world. A tire plant also has been completed at Nizhnekamsk to utilize the locally produced polyisoprene rubber for the manufacture of automobile tires to be used primarily in the Zhiguli passenger car plant at Togliatti and in the truck plant at Naberezhnyye Chelny. There is also a tire plant in Volzhskiy.

The Salavat petrochemical complex includes a large nitrogenous fertilizer unit. Nearby, the city of Sterlitamak, in addition to the synthetic rubber operation, has an alkali-chlorine plant based on local salt and limestone deposits and a chemical plant producing carbon-based acetalene and chlorine derivatives. A phosphate fertilizer plant opened in Balakovo in 1973 and one opened earlier in Togliatti. Mineral fertilizers are also produced at Chapayevsk. The mineral fertilizer complex in the Togliatti area is to be expanded in an exchange agreement between the Soviet Union and the Occidental Petroleum Corporation in the United States.

Other Minerals

In addition to the oil and gas in the Volga Region, there are deposits of oil shale, brown coal, and peat. Of these, perhaps the oil shale is the most important. It occurs primarily in the southwestern part of Kuybyshev Oblast near the settlement of Kashpirovka, a southern suburb of Syzran. But there are also minor deposits in Saratov and Volgograd Oblasts and in the Tatar A.S.S.R. Small amounts are mined in Kuybyshev Oblast for the production of various chemical products. These are processed in Syzran. Annual production amounts to about 1.2 million tons, which is a very poor second to the oil shale industry in Estonia. Most of the brown coal occurs in eastern Tatar A.S.S.R. and is used only locally for heating and power-production purposes. The peat occurs in the north of the Tatar A.S.S.R. and is used locally for fuel.

Other industries based on mineral deposits relate to various salts and sulfur deposits. Sodium chloride is found in great quantities in salt lakes in the southeastern part of Volgograd Oblast, southeastern Kuybyshev Oblast, and in the Kalmyk A.S.S.R. The primary deposits are in Lake Baskunchak and Elton southeast of the city of Volgograd. Rock salt deposits are also found underground in Kuybyshev Oblast. Lake Baskunchak produced 37 percent of all the Soviet salt in 1970, or 4.6 million tons. The salt industry of southeastern Volgograd Oblast is well situated to serve the needs of the large fish-processing industry in Astrakhan and other port cities around the northern Caspian.

Natural sulfur deposits occur in Kuybyshev Oblast and are utilized in the sulfur combine to produce sulfuric acid, which is a basic ingredient for many chemical industries, including the large superphosphate industry in the area.

Machine Construction and Metalworking

Because of its intermediate position between the industrial nodes of the Central Region, the Donbas, and the Urals, the Volga Region has become an important machine-building center, and to support these industries some metalworking has also developed. These industries occupy 47 percent of all the factory workers in the region and are more important than the petrochemical industries in value of output and employment. The Volga Region concentrates primarily on transport equipment, agricultural machinery, machine tools, bearings, and some diversified machinery for mining, chemical industries, textiles, and other light industries.

In the transport industry, the two complexes that have attracted the most attention during the last five years are the Volga Automobile Plant at Togliatti and the Kama Truck Plant at Naberezhnyye Chelny. However, there are many older industries turning out transport equipment in the Volga cities. Some of the earliest of these industries concentrated on equipment for river and marine shipping. For a long time the city of Astrakhan at the mouth of the Volga has been one of the main centers in the country for the construction and repair of fishing vessels, not only for the Volga-Caspian system, but also for many other fishing regions of the country. The Krasnoarmeysk shipyards in Volgograd construct self-propelled freight barges and other craft for the Volga system. Astrakhan also contains the main railroad repair shops in southeastern European U.S.S.R.

For a number of years the city of Ulyanovsk has been one of the main producers in the country of buses and light trucks, particularly panel trucks. In 1972 the plant built 16,000 new-model panel trucks mounted on jeep chassis. It is supposed to reach an output of 60,000 of these trucks in 1975, and ultimate plans are to build 150,000 per year. Ulyanovsk is to become the country's major producer of light trucks. Also, in 1966 the Ulyanovsk plant took over the building of military jeeps from the Gorkiy plant. These are counted as passenger cars in the Soviet statistics. The city of Engels has become the primary trolley bus producer in the country, annually turning out about 90 percent of all the trolley buses manufactured in the Soviet Union.

The biggest construction project in the U.S.S.R. during the eighth five-year plan (1966–1970) was the Volga Motor Vehicle Plant at Togliatti. This was designed by Fiat of Italy and built with the help of Fiat and other Western technology and equipment. About 10 percent of the foreign expenditures were made in the United States for technology, licenses, and equipment. The plant began production in late 1970 and reached its full capacity of 660,000 cars per year in late 1973. Over 50,000 people are employed in two shifts. There are plans eventually to expand the plant to double its present size. The plant turns out a variant of the Fiat 124, which has been modified to withstand the rough roads and cold climate of the East European Plain. The domestic model is named the "Zhiguli" after the Zhiguli Hills area in the Samara Bend of the Volga nearby. This five-passenger, four-cylinder, 60-horsepower car sells for about $6600 in the Soviet Union, the equivalent of about five years' wages of the average Russian factory worker. A similar model named the "Lada" has been designed for foreign export for a price of $1200.

The Togliatti facility is a highly integrated plant that combines all basic production processes at one site. Since no support facilities existed in the Soviet Union, the plant had to incorporate foundry, forging, stamping, pressing, engine production, assembly, and tooling sections. In addition, a number of supplier plants have been built in other towns of the region. Some of these have already been mentioned under the section on synthetic rubber and tires.

The largest construction project in the Soviet Union during the ninth five-year plan (1971–1975) has been the Kama River Truck Plant at Naberezhnyye Chelny. It consists of six major facilities integrated into one huge complex. About three-forths of all the machinery, equipment, and technology is being purchased from Western suppliers. Renault in France has the largest contract, which is for the engine plant. Another very large contract is held by a United States engineering firm for the foundry. West German plants are providing machinery for transmissions and forging presses, Italian plants for conveyor systems, and Japanese plants for press lines and transfer presses. Upon completion, this plant will be by far the largest truck complex in the world. It has a designed capacity of 150,000 three-axle trucks per year and 250,000 diesel engines. By comparison, the United States in 1971 built 93,000 trucks with three or more axles. Three basic variants of trucks will be built: standard body platform and stake trucks that can also pull trailers with a combined capacity of up to 16 tons, truck tractors for pulling semitrailers up to 20 tons capacity, and dumptrucks with 7 tons capacity. Because the Soviets could not get as much cooperation from foreign firms as they wished, production has lagged somewhat, and the opening of the first section of the plant is now scheduled for 1976.

Among the agricultural machine-building plants in the Volga Region, several are outstanding. The Volgograd caterpillar tractor plant was established during the first five-year plan (1929–1932). Although tractor production has been dispersed throughout the country, and the Volgograd plant is no longer the largest plant in the country, it is still one of the main plants. Volgograd also contains the Red October Metallurgical Works, which is the main steel-producing plant in the Volga Region. This also was established during the first five-year plan to produce the steel for the tractor plant as well as for other machine plants. It uses local scrap and pig iron from the Donets Basin in the eastern Ukraine just to the west. Major agricultural machine-construction combines in Saratov and Syzran turn out self-propelled combines and silage choppers, potato diggers, ditching apparatus, self-feeders for livestock production, and so forth.

Syzran and Saratov also turn out machinery for the petrochemical industries, as do Kuybyshev, Kazan, Penza, and Kuznetsk. Oil and gas pipe mills have been built in Volzhskiy and Kuybyshev. Four bearings plants — in Kuybyshev, Saratov, and Volzhskiy — produce 40 percent of all the roller bearings in the Soviet Union.

Figure 3-5   Log rafting near Volgograd. A cabin is built on each raft to house the workmen who accompany the rafts to their destinations where both rafts and cabins are sold.

Other Industries

Although the petrochemical and machine-building industries are by far the most important groups in the Volga Region, some of the other industries are well developed. The textile industries are distributed rather widely; Kamyshin is the largest center outside the Central Region. Leather-working and fur processing have been important for centuries in such cities as Kazan. Although the Volga Region does not possess much commercial timber, the region does a lot of woodworking because of the great numbers of logs that are floated down the Kama-Volga system from the northern part of the European U.S.S.R. and the western slopes of the Urals, some of the best logging regions in the country. Typical scenes on the lower Volga are large rafts, each with a log cabin set on it to house the workmen, moving down the river for eventual sale in the treeless steppes of the south. Rafts and cabins are sold in the south, and the workers return to their places of origin by rail. Many of the log cabins are set up incongruously in the southern steppe and desert to be used as dwellings by the Kalmyk herdsmen.

The construction-materials industries have developed highly in the Volga Region because of the large amounts of construction going on there. The region now produces about 12 percent of all the cement in the country. Most of the raw materials are derived from the limestone outcrops at the bases of the cliffs along the high right bank of the Volga.

Fishing has always been an important industry on the lower Volga. Including the shallow northern end of the Caspian, this is one of the major fishing grounds in the Soviet Union. For many years during both the Russian Empire and the Soviet period, the Caspian was the major fishing ground in the country. But since World War II, with the worldwide expansion of the fishing effort by the Soviets, the Barents Sea in the north and the Okhotsk Sea in the east have surpassed the Caspian in total fish catch. Also, fishing on the high seas has become of prime importance to the Soviets. Nevertheless, the Caspian and lower Volga area remains one of the major fishing grounds of the country. It provides some specialties, the outstanding one being beluga caviar, the eggs from the Caspian sturgeon. These huge fish can grow to weigh 3000 pounds, reach as much as 24 feet in length, and live to be 200–300 years of age. The Caspian provides 95 percent of the beluga caviar in the world. One single female sturgeon can yield 100 pounds or more of fresh roe, and the best grade may bring as much as $100 per pound in foreign markets. Astrakhan is the main processing center for the caviar, although many other Caspian ports also deal in it, and

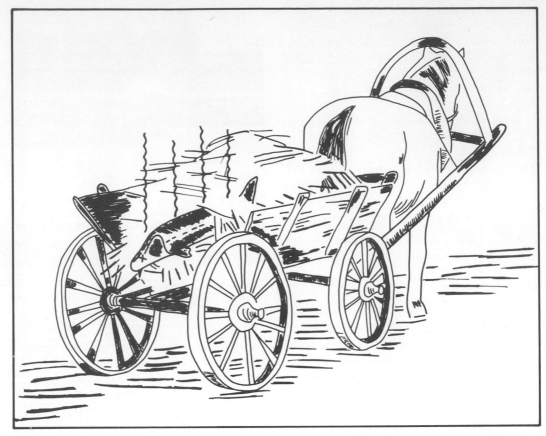

Figure 3-6   Drunk but alive sturgeon arriving by drozhky.

along the southern shore of the Caspian, Iran is a major producer. Most people think of the sturgeon for its caviar, but the flesh is also prized. During Tsarist times the royal family and the nobility often had Volga beluga shipped to Moscow by troika or drozhky packed in wet hay and tranquilized with vodka. After a month's travel the fish arrived drunk but alive. Because of overfishing, pollution, and the lowering level of the Caspian, the sturgeon catch has decreased by more than half in the last 35 years. This drastic reduction in the sturgeon catch, as well as in the catch of many other types of fish and sea animals in the Caspian, has become of major concern to the Soviets and will be discussed along with the general Caspian Sea problem in the next section.

THE VOLGA-CASPIAN WATERWAY

The unity of the Volga Region depends on the Volga River, because the river and the traffic on it have historically bound together the ends of the region and induced the establishment of the towns along its banks. Now the towns have transcended their original functions and grown into great industrial cities, and the river traffic has been eclipsed by rail traffic. Although the trade function of the cities and the water transport of freight both have increased greatly during the Soviet period, they have been relegated to minor roles. Although the Volga now carries three to four times the freight that it did at the time of the Bolshevik Revolution, its percent of all freight traffic in the Volga Region has dropped to around 10, while railroads carry around 70 percent and pipelines account for almost 20 percent of the freight of the region.

Historically, wheat, coal, and pig iron from the Ukraine, fish from the Caspian, salt from the lower Volga, and oil from Baku have gone up the river in great quantities to supply the population concentrations in the Central, Northwest, and Urals Regions, while timber and finished products have moved downriver to the lower Volga and the Ukraine. The wheat trade has diminished as the wheat base has shifted from the Ukraine to Western Siberia and northern Kazakhstan; the oil traffic has diminished somewhat and shifted its direction as the Baku fields have faded in importance and the Volga-Urals and Western Siberian fields have become the dominant suppliers. Timber has remained the primary freight on the river. The most significant change in the freight makeup in recent years has been the rapid growth of short-distance hauling of mineral construction materials. As the large cities along the Volga have grown at very rapid rates, great quantities of cement and other construction materials, generally derived locally within the region, have been hauled to many construction sites. The construction of the system of large dams and associated facilities on the river itself has necessitated the movement of incredible quantities of bulky construction materials. Such materials recently have averaged about 25 percent of all Volga freight handled, although they account for a smaller percentage of total traffic because of the short distances hauled. Timber has retained its number-one position, while oil has declined a little. Thus, timber, petroleum, and mineral construction materials now comprise much of the Volga tonnage and traffic on the river.

The Great Volga Scheme

The continued growth of traffic on the Volga has prompted a grand scheme to control the flow of the river completely by constructing a stairway of huge reservoirs, each of which would reach upstream to the dam forming the next reservoir. This would assure complete navigability during the six or seven months when the river is free of ice and incidentally would provide large amounts of hydroelectric power and some water for irrigation in the steppes from Kuybyshev southward. The construction projects on the upper Volga have already been discussed within the chapters on the Central Region and the Volga-Vyatka Region.

The first project to be completed on the lower Volga was the Volga-Don Canal, which in 1952 connected the Volga with the Don at the point where they bend most closely toward each other and provided an outlet for the Volga traffic to the sea. The canal starts along the west bank of the Volga a few miles below Volgograd and follows a looping course for 62 miles across the lowest part of the divide to the Don River. Thirteen locks, each with a lift of about 30 feet, raise the water 145 feet above the Don and drop it 290 feet to the Volga. The Volga at Volgograd is just about at sea level. To provide water for the canal and to improve the channel on the lower Don, an earthen dam was strung for more than seven miles across the broad, shallow valley of the Don River at the town of Tsimlyansk in Rostov Oblast. The Tsimlyansk Dam raised the water 85 feet and backed it up the Don Valley 216 miles to form the Tsimlyansk Sea, most of which lies within Volgograd Oblast. At the time it was built this was the largest man-made body of water in the world.

From the vantage point of a steamer in the middle of the reservoir, the Tsimlyansk Sea appears as vast as the Great Lakes of North America, but it is quite shallow. In most places, boats are forced to follow the submerged channel of the Don River in order to stay afloat. Navigation aids in the form of large signboards along the banks enable navigators to keep the boats in channel. The signs consist of white-painted billboards about 10 feet high with broad black stripes painted vertically down their middles. To keep on course the navigator must keep two of these striped boards in alignment. Traffic on the canal has been somewhat disappointing. Railroads have proved to be much more efficient movers of bulky goods, and even this far south, the Volga-Don Canal system is closed by ice five months of the year, from December to May. The water supply to the canal, all of which comes from the Don, is not very adequate, and small amounts of water from the Tsimlyansk Reservoir have been led off in canals to irrigate some land to the southeast.

The Tsimlyansk Sea had enjoyed its reputation as the worlds largest artificial body of water for only four years when it was surpassed in size by the Kuybyshev Sea, which was filled in 1956. The earth and concrete spillway dam upstream from Kuybyshev raises the Volga water 80 feet and backs up the reservoir some 380 miles up the Volga and its tributaries, the Kama River, and others. The city of Kazan, which formerly was two miles east of the Volga up the small Kazanka River, now sits on the shore of the Kuybyshev Sea. The dock facilities at Kazan had to be relocated, and a 20-mile earthen dike was built to protect the city. Some 280 villages containing more than 40,000 houses had to be moved to prepare for the flooding of the reservoir. With a capacity of 2.3 million kilowatts, the hydroelectric plant is somewhat larger than that of Grand Coulee Dam in the United States, and at the time of its dedication in 1957 it was the largest hydroelectric plant in the world. High-voltage transmission lines carry power west to Moscow and east through the Tatar and Bashkir oilfields to the Urals. A double canal and lock system bypass the dam and allow for simultaneous passage of boats in both directions. Also, a three-kilometer stretch in the bypass canal provides a winter harbor with repair docks. It is planned that eventually one million hectares of land southeast of Kuybyshev will be irrigated from this reservoir, but so far little of that has been accomplished.

Since 1957 the Kuybyshev Dam and Reservoir have been surpassed in size by those at Volgograd. The reservoir extends about 400 miles upstream. The capacity of the hydroelectric plant at Volgograd is more than 2.6 million kilowatts. About 40 percent of the power is transmitted all the way to Moscow over 500,000-volt transmission lines. The power is also transmitted 300 miles west to the Donets Basin over an experimental 800,000-volt dc line. In the 1960s the Volga Region transmitted about one-fifth of the power produced to other regions over these high-voltage lines. It is planned to irrigate some land on both sides of the Volga downstream from Volgograd, but so far little has been done in this respect. However, there have been recent reports of revival of the Volga-Ural Canal project. This is the long-dreamed plan to lead off water from the Volgograd Reservoir 464 kilometers eastward to the Ural River to provide the basis for irrigating much of the North Caspian Lowland. Three pumping stations would be needed to raise the water 44 meters during the first part of the canal to the town of Novouzensk, after which the water would run freely under gravity to the Ural River. Branch canals would lead southward carrying water by gravity flow down the gentle slope of the North Caspian Lowland. Numerous small river channels already exist in the lowland oriented from north to south that could provide channels for the feeder canals. It is planned that eventually as much as 200,000 square kilometers of fertile land could be irrigated in this way. Although it appears that there would be a deficit in the Volga River to provide water for such a canal system, in 1973 the Soviets announced that they were going ahead with the first section of the project, which was to be completed in 1979 and the second section by 1985. A proposed third section of the system would have to wait for additional water that might be dumped into the Volga from rivers to the north. It is planned now that even before the discharge of northern rivers into the Volga, the Ural River system will receive 220 billion gallons of water from the Volga every year. This water not only will help farmers and livestock breeders improve crops and pastures, but will also bring back to life some of the stagnant pools of water along the Ural River floodplain and in the west Kazakh area in general, providing the habitat for a rich fish and bird population. According to a report in 1973, construction was to have started on this canal system in 1974. However, no reports have since been made regarding this project.

The Saratov hydroelectric plant went into operation in 1967 and became fully operative in 1969. The plant is situated at Balakovo upstream from Saratov where the Volgograd Reservoir ends. The Saratov Dam raises the water level 13 meters and extends the reservoir upstream all around the east side of the Zhiguli Bend past Kuybyshev to the Kuybyshev Dam site. The hydroelectric plant has a capacity of 1.3 million kilowatts. An 80-mile irrigation canal has been built into the dry steppe on the east bank of the river from the Saratov Reservoir to raise yields in this very fertile part of the Transvolga Lowland. No information is available yet on how much land has been irrigated or how successful the project has been.

In north central Tatar A.S.S.R. the Nizhnekamsk dam and hydroelectric plant with a planned capacity of 1,248,000 kilowatts is under construction on the Kama River near the new industrial town of Naberezhnyye Chelny. This project will complete the transformation of the Kama River into a stairway of three giant reservoirs. The Nizhnekamsk Reservoir will reach upstream nearly to the Votkinsk Dam and flood valleys of many streams in the oil-bearing region of the north Tatar and adjacent Bashkir A.S.S.R.s. Many of the oil rigs now being constructed in this region are being built on stilts so that they will be above the water level when the reservoir is eventually filled. The Kama truck plant now under construction will eventually find itself along the shore of the Nizhnekamsk Reservoir. The old town of Derbeshkinskiy at the mouth of the Belaya River will be flooded, and the small manufacturing town of Blagoveshchensk, north of the Bashkir capital of Ufa, is being expanded to succeed Derbeshkinskiy as the major ship-repair center on the Belaya River.

Although the water-construction projects on the Volga are multipurpose systems, the original purpose for building them was to improve navigation along the stream. The sys-

tem of dams regulates the highly seasonal flow of the Volga and maintains a minimum navigational depth of 3 meters. However, the construction projects have not been entirely beneficial. The reservoirs have flooded much fertile farmland, and the transformation of the flowing stream into a staircase of extremely large quiet bodies of water has rendered timber-rafting virtually impossible. Log rafts must be towed through the reservoirs, and even that is not very satisfactory. Storm waves on these "inland seas" break up the rafts and cause hazards to life and property, and the intricate system of locks between reservoirs necessitates delays that have lengthened the transport time of logs from the upper Volga to Astrakhan from 30–40 days to 60–80 days. Also, the reservoirs stay frozen longer in spring than the river used to. These difficulties are, among other things, inducing a shift in the lumber-milling industry from traditional market areas in the larger cities of the south to smaller towns in the logging areas of the north, where the logs can be sawed into lumber and the lumber loaded onto river barges or railroad cars for shipment southward.

Increased evaporation from the large reservoirs on the Volga and the utilization of some of the water for irrigation of land has severely curtailed the limited flow of the Volga, which provides about three-fourths of the water for the Caspian Sea. This reduced flow in the Volga has exacerbated the general problem of the lowering level of the Caspian, and has made navigation increasingly difficult in the northern end of the sea, as the Caspian shoreline recedes southward and the Volga delta builds farther and farther into the sea.

The Caspian Sea Problem

The maintenance of the level of the Caspian Sea has been deemed such an important problem in the Soviet Union that since 1960 several national conferences have been called to discuss the problem. The water level of the Caspian has dropped more than 8 feet since 1929 and is currently dropping about 2½ inches every year. It appears that the water level is lower now than it has been for 1500 years.

In the shallower parts of the Caspian, particularly in the north, this reduction in water level has shifted the shoreline many miles (Fig. 3-7). The shallowing water and shifting shoreline necessitate the constant relocation of shoreline facilities, hamper navigation, severely limit the fish population found mainly in the shallow northern end, and affect the salt industry on the eastern side of the Caspian around Kara-Bogaz-Gol. Not only has the receding shoreline in the northern end of the Caspian provided for a smaller area of fish growth, but the spawning grounds upstream in the Volga and Ural Rivers have become polluted and the large dam at Volgograd on the Volga has blocked about 90 percent of the sturgeon from going upstream to their traditional spawning grounds, even though a specially designed elevator has been provided at the big dam. The installation of powerful pumps to provide irrigation water along the lower Volga has caused many of the tiny fish trying to make their way back to the Caspian to be sucked up through the pumps into the irrigation systems. At the same time the Caspian has become more and more polluted by the oil activity on it. There is steady spillage of oil from underwater wells east of Baku and from oil tankers crossing the sea. During 1973 it was estimated that about a half-million sturgeon were killed by this pollution.

Several elaborate schemes have been devised to restore and stabilize the water level of the Caspian, but all of these have their drawbacks, and none of them have been started. When concern first began to be discussed, it was tacitly assumed that the restoration of the sea to its 1929 level was the desired thing to do. However, as discussions on how to provide more fresh water for the Volga have continued, they have shifted more and more toward what to do with this fresh water once it is available. It has been pointed out that it would be rather foolish to dump it into the salty Caspian, that a better use of it would be to irrigate the North Caspian Lowland, where the added crops would be much more valuable than the improved fishing that might be provided by raising the Caspian level. Also, it has been pointed out by Soviet economists

that to raise the water level back up to where it had been would simply require on more relocation of all the shoreline facilities, and this would be very expensive. It is thought that perhaps it should be attempted to stabilize the water at some level below the present level rather than to try to raise it back up.

Plans to stabilize the water level range from schemes for construction projects within the Caspian itself to schemes involving huge construction projects far outside the region to dump extra water into the Volga River system. A grand scheme to regulate the water level within the Caspian has been proposed, whereby a series of dams would be built across the northern Caspian. They would total about 460 kilometers in length with an average height of about 6 meters and would separate the shallow northern end from the rest of the Caspian. The dams would allow the water level in the north to be maintained about 3 meters above that of the south. This would provide adequate fishing grounds and a dependable navigation depth in the northern part of the Caspian. There would also be several fringe benefits, such as generation of power along the dams and the exposure of more oil-bearing strata by an additional drop in the water in the south.

However, such a dam system would be very expensive. It would be more feasible to bring additional water into the Caspian drainage basin. Tentative plans have been laid out to provide for bringing in large quantities of water from either or both of two sources. One is the northeast European Russia area, primarily the Pechora and Northern Dvina River systems, part of whose volumes could be diverted southward into the upper Kama River, which eventually flows into the Volga and southward to the Caspian. The other source of water would be from Western Siberia, primarily the Ob River system, which theoretically would be diverted southward into Central Asia toward the Aral Sea and subsequently southwestward to the Caspian. Of the two, the North European project seems much more feasible, and at times in the past it appeared that this project definitely had been placed on the drawing boards. However, each time new

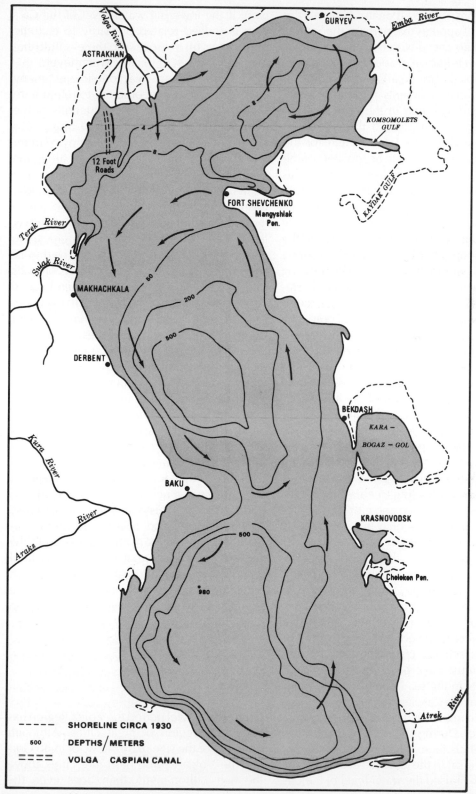

Figure 3-7 Old shorelines and depths of the Caspian. After Micklin.

considerations shelved it again. Now, in the mid-1970s, it appears that perhaps the Soviets will indeed go ahead with this project. However, as far as is known, no definite plans have been laid for it. The details of this proposal and the counterarguments regarding its effects on the local area in the north will be discussed in the chapter on the Northwest Economic Region. The latest design for the diversion of water from the headwaters of the Pechora and Vychegda Rivers would ultimately allow for approximately 37 cubic kilometers of additional water to flow down the Volga annually, an amount approximately equal to one-sixth the present flow of the Volga. Among other beneficial effects along the Volga, it would increase the water flowing through the turbines of the hydroelectric stations already constructed on the Volga, thereby increasing their annual electrical output by an amount approximately equal to the present output of the Kuybyshev hydroelectric station. It has been estimated that the cost of the Pechora-Vychegda diversion project would be only about half the cost of the Kuybyshev dam and power station, and therefore the additional electrical generation would quickly pay for the entire project.

A smaller project within the Caspian that is quite feasible is a plan to build a dam across the narrow strait leading to Kara-Bogaz-Gol. Metal gates would open and close to regulate the inflow of water, which now amounts to about two cubic miles per year. In this way a significant amount of the evaporation loss from the Caspian system could be eliminated.

During the 1960s a well-known seismologist pointed out that during the 1956–1958 period, a slight rise in the Caspian level was not accompanied by a significant increase in discharge of tributary streams and therefore must have been related to crustal movements in the sea floor. The deep southern basin of the Caspian lies in a very tectonically active region that is undergoing general subsidence. During this two-year period in the late 1950s there might have been a temporary reversal in the general subsidence that significantly raised the water level of the Cas-

pian. If the lowering water level of the Caspian is indeed related primarily to tectonic movements on the sea floor, there is little that man can do to stabilize the water level.

Since this theory was publicized, many other scientists have come out to refute it, to support the idea that the fluctuations of the Caspian have been related primarily to climatic changes in the Volga Basin and more recently to the man-made changes along the Volga. However, a wealth of geological and archeological evidence indicates that the Caspian Sea level has fluctuated drastically in the past and that at times it was at much lower levels than it is at present. Therefore, there have been both ups and downs during the last several thousand years. Foundations of walls of drowned ancient cities have been located beneath the waters of the Caspian in a number of shore areas, and skin divers have brought up many pieces of glazed dishes, jugs, coins, and small ornaments. Also, ancient sea terraces in many places lie beneath the present water surface. All this indicates that in the not too distant past, Caspian water levels were considerably lower than now. On the other hand, the North Caspian Lowland with its various shoreline features stretching as far northward as Saratov and beyond attest irrefutably to the fact that the Caspian level at one time was much higher and that indeed during the late Pleistocene the Caspian rose above sea level and overflowed northwestward through the Manych Depression to the Sea of Azov. Therefore, it appears that natural forces operative in the past have been of such magnitude that any present attempts by the Soviets to regulate the level of the Caspian might be in vain.

CITIES

During the Soviet period the Volga Region has become a region of great cities. Although none are of the size of Moscow, or even Gorkiy, the Volga Region has more cities above the half-million mark than does even the

Central Region. Five cities have more than 500,000 people each, seven cities more than 400,000 each, and nine cities more than 300,000 each. In all these categories, the Volga Region is tied with the Donets-Dnieper Region for first rank in the country. There are a total of 16 cities with more than 100,000 population each.

Kuybyshev

During the Soviet period Kuybyshev has grown into the biggest city in the Volga Region. Before the Revolution it was smaller than both Kazan and Saratov. In 1974 it had 1,140,000 people. Together with some of its suburbs and satellite towns, the Kuybyshev area has become the focal center for the entire Volga Region. The largest of these satellite towns is Syzran, about 80 kilometers around the Samara Bend to the west on the other side of the river. Together, Kuybyshev and Syzran are the chief refining centers of the Volga-Urals oil fields. A long railroad bridge crosses the river between Syzran and Kuybyshev, and the line continues eastward to join with the Trans Siberian Railroad.

Kuybyshev is the old city of Samara, which was established in 1596 as a fortress at the mouth of the small Samara River which flows into the Volga from the southeast. Samara early distinguished itself as the financial capital of the Volga wheat trade during the days of the Russian Empire. The wheat barons constructed bank buildings along the main streets facing the river, and farther out in the countryside they established large estates. Many of the bank buildings and mansions still stand, but they now serve as government buildings, rest homes, children's homes, and so forth. In 1935 the city was renamed after the Bolshevik leader V. V. Kuybyshev. During World War II, when Moscow was threatened by the Germans, much of the central government for a time moved to Kuybyshev. Today Kuybyshev is a great industrial city concentrating on machine building, oil refining, and chemicals. It is also an important river port and rail focal point.

Kazan

The second largest city in the Volga Region is Kazan, the old center of the Tatars that now serves as the capital of the Tatar A.S.S.R. Founded in 1437 by the Tatars, it was captured by Muscovy in 1552 when its kremlin was undermined and blown up. In 1974 Kazan had a population of 931,000. It is being industrialized much the same as is Kuybyshev to the south. It also lies within the Volga-Urals oil fields, and it has developed a chemical complex based on oil products. Kazan is also known for its machine-building industries, particularly some of the lighter ones manufacturing business machines, typewriters, calculators, and so forth. It early became a center for the buying and tanning of cattle hides, fur processing, shoemaking, and soap processing. These industries are still concentrated in Kazan. The university at Kazan is one of the oldest in the country. For a time Lenin studied law there. Like Kuybyshev, Kazan is an important river port and rail focal point. It is also very important for its air routes between Moscow and the east.

Volgograd

Third in size is Volgograd, with a 1974 population of 885,000. It is the old city of Tsaritsyn, which was founded in 1589 as a Russian fort overlooking the steppes to the southeast. It occupies a strategic position on the high right bank of the Volga where the river makes its major bend toward the southeast. During the late nineteenth century the city became a main transshipping point between rail and water for oil, lumber, coal, and fish. Stalin distinguished himself here as a leader in the Red Army during the civil war following the Bolshevik Revolution, and the name *Tsaritsyn* was changed to Stalingrad. With the posthumous purge of Stalin in 1961, the name was changed once more to Volgograd. Now the Soviets seldom mention the name *Stalingrad*. In some official lists of city name changes the original name of Volgograd is shown as Tsaritsyn. But the world still remembers the battle of Stalingrad as the turning point in World War II.

During World War II the city suffered much damage, and it has been designated as one of the hero cities of the Soviet Union. The rubble has been cleared away since the war and most of the city has been reconstructed, but near the center of town overlooking the Volga a large bombed-out shell of a building has been left standing as a war memorial. A tall, graceful obelisk dominates the central square of the city, on the base of which are commemorated the fallen heroes of World War II. The Soviet people keep this monument smothered in flowers. Their remembrances are much too vivid for them to view the war with any sort of objectivity.

The city now stretches in a crescent-shaped arc for about 60 kilometers along the west side of the river. A low, narrow floodplain exists between the high right bank and the river, and on this floodplain much of the industry of the city is located. Situated just to the east of the heavy industrial area in eastern Ukraine, Volgograd has become the recipient of some heavy metallurgy and much machine-building based on the iron and steel of the Ukraine. Particularly well known are the Red October metallurgical works and the tractor factory. For a long time Volgograd, along with Chelyabinsk in the Urals, produced all the tractors in the Soviet Union.

The building of the dam about 15 kilometers north of the city has assured the area of an abundance of electric power. With a capacity of 2.6 million kilowatts, the Volgograd power plant is the largest on the river. The workers settlement of Volzhskiy near the east end of the dam has grown into an industrial city in its own right and will be discussed separately below. An aluminum industry has been located in Volgograd to make use of some of the hydroelectric power for the conversion of alumina from the Urals and Hungary.

An oil refinery has been built in Volgograd, and petrochemical industries have become important in the city. An important gas field lies near Frolovo about 80 kilometers northwest of Volgograd, and a gas pipeline connecting the two centers has existed for some years. Volgograd has always been an important center for woodworking and food processing as well as many other light industries.

Ufa

Fourth in size in the Volga Region is Ufa, the capital, industrial, transport, and cultural center of the Bashkir Republic, with a 1974 population of 871,000. After Kuybyshev it is the most important node of the oil industry in the Volga-Urals area, with a complex of oil refining and petrochemicals. It is also an important machine-building center and has woodworking, food, and other light industries. With its satellite cities of Sterlitamak, Salavat, and Ishimbay to the south and Tuymazy and Oktyabrskiy to the west, the Ufa region in central Bashkiria is perhaps the biggest petrochemical region in the U.S.S.R.

Saratov

Fifth in size is Saratov, with a 1974 population of 820,000. It sits on the high west bluff of the river halfway between Volgograd and Kuybyshev, and it is the site of one of the major rail crossings of the Volga. It sits in the center of the earliest developed gas fields in the Volga Region. Its industries are concerned with machine-building, chemicals, and food. Across the river from Saratov are the towns of Marx and Engels, which were situated in the Volga German A.S.S.R. before World War II.

Astrakhan

Sixth in size is Astrakhan, with a 1974 population of 445,000. The city was founded as a fortress in 1558 at the mouth of the Volga and has been growing at a somewhat slower rate than many of the other cities on the river. It lies on the dead-end branch of the waterway off the main stream of products going down the Volga-Don Canal to the Ukraine and the open sea. Its function remains primarily that of a port city handling products of the local water area: fish, oil, and salts. It has the largest fish-processing plant in the country.

Penza

Seventh in size is Penza, with a 1974 population of 414,000. This is the central city of Penza Oblast, which has recently been added to the Volga Region from the Central Chernozem Region. The city has various machine-building, paper, and food industries.

Ulyanovsk

Eighth in size is Ulyanovsk, with a 1974 population of 410,000. The city was founded in 1648 as the fortress of Simbirsk and was renamed Ulyanovsk in 1924 after Lenin (whose original family name was Ulyanov), because it was his birthplace. Its industries are concentrated on machine-building and food processing. The light truck factory has already been mentioned.

Togliatti

One of the fastest-growing cities in the entire U.S.S.R. during the last 15 years has been the new chemical and automobile center of Togliatti on the Volga upstream from Kuybyshev. The city had its origins in the old Volga river town of Stavropol, which had a population of only about 15,000. The original site of Stavropol was flooded when the Kuybyshev Reservoir was filled in the mid-1950s, and a new town of Stavropol was relocated to the east beyond a wooded area on higher ground. This new site began to be developed as an industrial center, first with cement kilns and mercury rectifiers and then with a synthetic rubber plant in 1961, a phosphorus chemical plant in 1963, and a nitrogen fertilizer plant in 1965. With the planning of the new Fiat automobile plant, in 1964 the new town of Stavropol was renamed Togliatti after the Italian communist leader Palmiro Togliatti, and a new civic center arose farther north near the site of construction for the automobile plant. As was mentioned earlier, Togliatti is now by far the largest car manufacturer in the U.S.S.R. It has added an ammonia-based synthetic plant turning out a type of nylon and other chemical industries, and its growth is still continuing at a rapid pace. In 1974 it had a population of 403,000. A branch pipeline has been built into Togliatti to tap off natural gas from the pipeline running from Central Asia to the Central Region of European Russia and supply the Togliatti chemical complex with a natural gas base.

Sterlitamak

Sterlitamak is one of the oil refining and chemical centers to the south of Ufa in the center of the Bashkir A.S.S.R. In 1974 it had a population of 205,000.

Syzran

Syzran is the satellite city of Kuybyshev around the bend to the west of the Volga. It concentrates on oil refining, chemicals, shale processing, and railroad transport. In 1974 it had a population of 181,000.

Volzhskiy

Volzhskiy is the workers' settlement that was established at the time of the building of the Volgograd Dam on the east side of the river across from Volgograd. After the dam was built the town was retained and turned into a major chemical center. It produces synthetic fiber, rubber, and plastics. In 1969 a large-diameter steel pipe plant was put into production. This plant produces 40-inch pipe for long-distance oil and gas transmission lines. The pipe diameter will ultimately be increased to 56 inches. In 1974 Volzhskiy had a population of 178,000.

Engels

Engels has been mentioned as a satellite city of Saratov on the east side of the Volga. For a time before World War II it was the capital city of the Volga-German A.S.S.R. It is primarily a commercial center for a rich farming area. But it also is the main trolley bus manufacturing center in the U.S.S.R. In 1974 it had a population of 148,000.

Salavat

Salavat is another oil refining and chemical center next to Sterlitamak south of Ufa in the Bashkir Republic. In 1974 it had a population of 126,000.

Balakovo

Balakovo north of Saratov is the site of the Saratov Dam on the Volga River. In 1974 it had a population of 123,000.

Novokuybyshevsk

Novokuybyshevsk is another of the satellite cities in the Kuybyshev area which recently has grown above the 100,000 mark. In 1974 it had a population of 111,000.

Prospects for the Future

Since World War II the Volga Region has seen a tremendous spurt in its industrialization and urbanization because of its huge power base and its intermediate location between the three great industrial nodes of the country. Now the impetus from the power base is tapering off, and the Volga oil region ultimately is to be overshadowed by oil production in Western Siberia. But the intermediate position between the Urals, the Ukraine, and the Central Industrial Region remains, and this portends a continued growth for the future. The Volga Valley is now an integral part of the industrial complex of the country.

Recently Yulian Saushkin, one of the leading geographers at Moscow State University specializing in the economic geography of the Soviet Union, underscored this point when he advocated that the Volga Valley between Gorkiy and Volgograd seems best suited to the concentrated location of additional iron and steel capacity in the country, which may eventually amount to four or five times the present capacity of the country. He pointed out that the area east of the Urals does not warrant any major expansion in iron and steel plants, and any increase there should be limited to the use of available scrap metal. On the other hand, the European territory of the country needs all the steel it can get for its great concentration of machine-building and other steel-using industries. The European territory contains all the iron ore, manpower, water, and markets it needs for the new iron and steel plants projected. The only problem is the supply of coking coal. Therefore, some of the new iron and steel capacities should be shifted eastward toward the coking coal of the Kuznetsk Basin in Western Siberia. The Volga-Kama River region seems to be optimally located to make use of iron ore from the Kursk Magnetic Anomaly in the Central Chernozem Region and from the Krivoy Rog Basin in the east central Ukraine as well as coking coal from the four major producing basins: the Donets Basin in the eastern Ukraine, the Pechora Basin in northeast European Russia, the Kuznetsk Basin in Western Siberia, and the Karaganda Basin in north central Kazakhstan. Coal can be delivered from any of these four major producing fields to the Volga Valley at roughly equal delivery prices. Therefore, one might expect heavy metallurgy to enter the scene in the middle Volga Valley much more importantly than it has so far. This should greatly expand the whole machine-building industry of the area. It appears, then, that for the forseeable future the Volga Valley will remain one of the most rapidly industrializing regions in the country.

READING LIST

- Adamesku, A.A., "Povolzhskiy ekonomicheskiy rayon v devyatoy pyatiletke" (The Volga Economic Region in the Ninth Five-Year Plan), *Geografiya v shkole* (Geography in School), Moscow, No. 1, 1973, pp. 12–16 (in Russian).
- Aristarkhova, L.B., "Deshifirovaniye regionalnykh lineynykh morfostruktur prikaspiyskoy vpadiny na orbitalnykh snimkakh" (Interpretation of Regional Linear Morphostructures in the Caspian Depression on the Basis of Orbital Photographs), *Vestnik Moskovskogo Univer-*

siteta, seriya geografiya, No. 2, 1974, pp. 93–96 (in Russian).

• Bobrov, S.N., "The Transformation of the Caspian Sea," *Soviet Geography: Review & Translation,* September 1961, pp. 47–59.

• "Conference on the Multipurpose Use and Conservation of Water Resources in the Volga Basin (Perm, August 1975)," *Vodnyye Resursy,* No. 1, 1975, pp. 199–200.

• Dolgolopav, K.V., and E.F. Fedorova, *Povolzhye: ekonomiko-geograficheskiy ocherk* (Volga Region: Economic-Geographic Study), Prosveshcheniye, Moscow, 1967, 206 pp. (in Russian).

• Dubrovskiy, A.G., "KamAZ-glavnaya stroyka pyatiletki" (The Kama Truck Plant, Main Construction Project of the Five-Year Plan), *Geografiya v shkole,* No. 1, 1973, pp. 17–20 (in Russian).

• Dzhimbinov, B., *Sovetskaya Kalmikiya* (Soviet Kalmyk), Moscow, 1960, 144 pp. (in Russian).

• Geller, S. Yu., "On the Question of Regulating the Level of the Caspian Sea," *Soviet Geography: Review & Translation,* January 1962, pp. 59–66.

• Glazovskiy, N.F., and B.N. Golubov, "K probleme regulirovaniya rezhima Kaspiyskogo morya" (On the Problem of Regulating the Regime of the Caspian Sea), *Izvestiya Akademii Nauk SSSR, seriya geograficheskaya,* No. 6, 1973, pp. 49–52; translated in *Soviet Geography: Review & Translation,* January 1975, pp. 41–45.

• Goremykin, V. Ya., "Prirost kraya delty Volgi za period zaregulirovaniya stoka v Volgograda" (Growth of the Edge of the Volga Delta since the Regulation of Stream Flow at Volgograd), *Izvestiya vsesoyuznogo geograficheskogo obshchestva,* No. 2, 1970, pp. 166–189 (in Russian).

• Hooson, David, J.M., "The Middle Volga — An Emerging Focal Region in the Soviet Union," *The Geographical Journal,* June 1960, pp. 182–190.

• Hooson, David, J.M., *A New Soviet Heartland?* Van Nostrand, New York, 1964, 132 pp.

• Karamysheva, N.I., "Factors Shaping the Hierarchical Structure of the System of Fishery Settlements in the Northern Caspian," *Soviet Geography: Review & Translation,* December 1974, pp. 619–624.

• Kompaniyets, Yu. I., "Narastanie morskogo kraya delty r. Volgi" (The Growth of the Seaward Margins of the Volga River Delta), *Izvestiya Akademii Nauk SSSR, Seriya geograficheskaya,* No. 5, 1974, pp. 94–97 (in Russian).

• Micklin, Philip P., "Dimensions of the Caspian Sea Problem," *Soviet Geography: Review & Translation,* November 1972, pp. 589–603.

• Micklin, Philip P., *An Inquiry into the Caspian Sea Problem and Proposals for its Alleviation,* Dissertation, University of Washington, Seattle, 1971, 338 pp.

• Mironova, N. Ia., *Stok v zaliv Kara-Bogaz-Gol i izmenenie gidrologicheskogo rezhima proliva i zaliva* (Discharge into the Kara Bogaz Gol and Change in the Hydrologic Regime of Bays and Sounds), Akademii Nauk SSSR, Okeanograficheskaya Komissiya, Trudy, 5 (Academy of Science of the USSR, Oceanographical Commission, Work No. 5), 1959, pp. 146–150 (in Russian).

• Muckleston, Keith W., "The Volga in the Pre-revolutionary Industrialization of Russia," *Yearbook of the Association of Pacific Coast Geographers,* 1965, pp. 67–76.

• Muckleston, Keith W., and Fred E. Dohrs, "The Relative Importance of Transport on the Volga Before and After the Communist Revolution," *Professional Geographer,* March 1965, pp. 22–25.

• Padick, Clement, "Reorientation in Power Generation in the Volga Basin, USSR," *Yearbook of the Association of Pacific Coast Geographers,* 1965, pp. 27–37.

• *Povolzhye: Ekonomiko-geograficheskaya kharakteristika* (Volga Region: Economic-Geographic Characteristics), Akademiya Nauk SSSR, Institut geografii, Moscow, 1957, 464 pp. (in Russian).

• *Problemy Kaspiyskogo morya* (Problems of the Caspian Sea), USSR Academy of Sciences, Moscow, 1959 (in Russian).

• Prociuk, Stephan G., "The Territorial Pattern of Industrialization in the USSR: A Case Study in Location of Industry," *Soviet Studies,* July 1961, pp. 69–95.

• Ratkovich, D. Ya., "On the Possible Regulation of Caspian Level Fluctuations by Means of a Dividing Dam," *Vodnyye Resursy,* No. 2, 1975, pp. 5–17.

• Rikhter, V.G., "Vertical Movements of the Earth Crust and the Fluctuations in the Level of the

Caspian Sea," *Soviet Geography: Review & Translation,* September 1961, pp. 59–64.

- Shaposhnikov, A.S., "Problemy razvitiya selskogo khozyaystva Povolzhya v svyazi s orosheniem i obvodneniem" (Problems of Development of Agriculture in the Volga Region in Connection with Irrigation and Waterspreading), *Geografiya v shkole,* Moscow, No. 5, 1973, pp. 15–17 (in Russian).

- *Soviet Geography: Review & Translation,* February 1967; entire issue is devoted to the Volga Region.

- *Soviet Geography: Review & Translation,* November 1972; entire issue is devoted to the Caspian problem.

- Taaffe, Robert N., "Volga River Transportation: Problems and Prospects," in Richard S. Thoman, and Donald J. Patton, *Focus on Geographic Activity,* McGraw-Hill, New York, 1964, pp. 185–193.

- Taskin, George A., "The Falling Level of the Caspian Sea in Relation to Soviet Economy," *Geographical Review,* October 1954, pp. 508–527.

- Vendrov, S.L., G.G. Gangardt, S. Yu. Geller, L.V. Korenistov, and G.L. Sarukhanov, "The Problem of Transformation and Utilization of the Water Resources of the Volga River and the Caspian Sea," *Soviet Geography: Review & Translation,* September 1964, pp. 23–34.

- Zalogin, B.S., and A.N. Kosarev, "Nekotorye prirodno — khozyaystvennye problemy Kaspiyskogo morya" (Some Physical and Economic Problems of the Caspian Sea), *Geografiya v shkole,* No. 5, 1973, pp. 18–20 (in Russian).

- Zepster, I.S., and A.N. Meskheteli, "O podzemnoy sostavlyayushchey vodnogo balansa Kaspiyskogo morya" (About the Geological Aspects of the Water Balance of the Caspian Sea), *Izvestiya vsesoyuznoye geograficheskoye obshchestvo,* No. 2, 1972, pp. 88–94 (in Russian).

Central Chernozem Economic Region

	Area (km²)	Population	Persons/km²	Percent Urban
Belgorod Oblast	27,000	1,260,000	46.5	42
Voronezh Oblast	52,000	2,511,000	47.9	49
Kursk Oblast	30,000	1,438,000	48.2	39
Lipetsk Oblast	24,000	1,223,000	50.7	48
Tambov Oblast	34,000	1,457,000	42.5	43
Total	168,000	7,889,000	47.0	45

chapter 4

the central chernozem economic region

West of the middle Volga and south of the Central Region lies the so-called Central Chernozem (or Black Earth) Region. It is not a very distinctive region, but it is a traditional region. It is understood to be the Russian part of the very fertile soil area that extends southwestward into the Ukraine. In the south it is arbitrarily cut off at the Ukrainian border, so it is an all-Russian region. Since it has no well-defined boundaries other than the political one to the south, peripheral parts of it have been designated as parts of surrounding regions as city development and urbanization has taken place. During the last 15 years Bryansk and Orel Oblasts have been severed and put into the Central Region, the Mordvinian A.S.S.R. has been included in the Volga-Vyatka Region, and Penza Oblast has been included in the Volga Region. Thus, at present all that is left of the Central Chernozem Region are five medium-sized Russian oblasts: Belgorod, Voronezh, Kursk, Lipetsk, and Tambov. Together they constitute an area of 168,000 square kilometers and a population of 7,889,000. This makes the Central Chernozem Region the smallest economic region within the R.S.F.S.R. Within the entire country only the South Region and Moldavia are smaller.

Although this region is noted for its agricultural potential, historically it has always been an area of peasant poverty because of over-

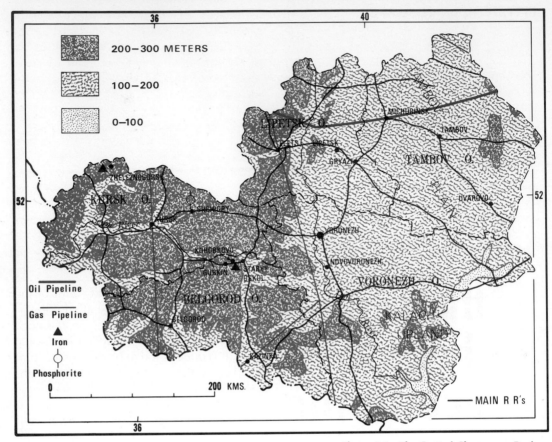

Figure 4-1   The Central Chernozem Region.

population, poor land tenure, and poor farming methods that have led to severe erosion,
particularly in the hillier western part of the
region. It is still one of the more rural regions
of the country. According to the 1970 census
only 45 percent of the population was urban
dwelling. Thus, there has not been the urban-
industrial buildup commensurate with surrounding regions to provide the means for
draining off excess population from the land.
Therefore, it has been a region of heavy out-
migration. At present it is a region of low
natural population increase, high out-
migration, and approximately zero population growth. Next to the Central Region, the
Central Chernozem Region has the lowest

natural increase of any economic region in
the country, and next to the Volga-Vyatka
Region and Western Siberia, it has the highest
net out-migration per thousand population.
Next to the Volga-Vyatka Region it has the
highest ratio of net out-migration to total
population increase. The southwestern portion of the Central Chernozem Region actually showed an absolute population decline
during the 1959–1970 intercensal period, but
the rest of the region showed a modest increase. With an average population density of
47 people per square kilometer, it is considerably more densely populated than either the
Volga or the Volga-Vyatka Regions but somewhat less dense than the Central Region.

PHYSICAL LANDSCAPE

Landform

The Central Chernozem Region straddles two geomorphic provinces that run north-south through the area. In the western half of the region is the southern extension of the Central Russian Upland, which also occupied the western half of the Central Economic Region to the north. This is a strongly eroded upland that averages 200 meters above sea level. The highest portion lies between Kursk and Yefremov where elevations reach 290–300 meters. The upland in Kursk, Voronezh, and Orel Oblasts is underlain by the Voronezh anticline, which is composed of Precambrian rocks that in this area do not lie far below the surface. The Kursk Magnetic Anomaly owes its existence to the Precambrian formation. The zone of magnetic anomalies extends along the line Kursk-Tim-Shchigry and is due to a belt of quartzites containing 35–45 percent iron. The thickness of the sedimentary rocks covering the Precambrian formations at this point is not greater than 120–200 meters. On the sides of the anticline the Precambrian rocks descend to great depths, and the thickness of sedimentary layers increases.

On the south the Voronezh anticline descends toward the Dnieper-Donets syncline. Here in places Cretaceous strata are very thick and include layers of white writing chalk, processed around Belgorod. These chalk strata form picturesque cliffs and tall erosion columns, the so-called divas around Belgorod. The chalk is covered by chalky sands and loess-like loams that have been eroded into deep gullies with vertical walls.

To the east of the Don River in southeastern Voronezh Oblast is a particularly dissected extension of the upland known as the Kalach Upland. Here valleys and gullies may reach depths of 125–150 meters and a network density of 1–2 kilometers of stream per square kilometer of territory.

The other geomorphic province contrasts greatly with the upland in the west. This is the so-called Oka-Don Lowland, which stretches north-south through the eastern part of the region. This is a downwarp between the Central Russian Upland to the west and the Volga Upland to the east. The northern end of the lowland was discussed in the chapter on the Central Region, where the territory along the Oka River was known as the Meshchera Meadows. Within the Central Chernozem Region the lowland is generally known as the Tambov Plain, after the city of Tambov in its center. Elevation in the Tambov Plain averages about 150–180 meters, and nowhere is it greater than 200 meters. The streams within the plain have weakly developed valleys, *ploskomesti*, which sometimes are bordered by broad terraces. The valley of the Don is the best developed in the region. It has three terraces in addition to its present floodplain, which is a well-developed structure reaching 20 kilometers in width in some places.

The breadth of the valleys in this area is incongruous with the present streams flowing through them, signifying an earlier time when they were occupied by more water. This testifies to the influences of glaciation. During the Dnieper stage the Don glacial tongue extended southward as far as the eastward-flowing section of the Don River in Volgograd Oblast. The glacial border looped sharply northward over the Central Russian Uplands and did not reach the Central Chernozem Region in that area. To the west of the upland, out of the region, a glacial tongue extended southward again down the Dnieper Valley. The valleys of the Tambov Plain are choked with glaciofluvial deposits that form the present broad floodplains of the streams. Wind deflation in many places has reworked the sands into an udulating or hummocky surface. The finer materials have been blown up on the watershed areas to form thick mantles of loess.

Climate, Vegetation, and Soils

The Central Chernozem Region lies between the cool humid north and the warm, dry south. It is neither very hot nor very cold and neither very wet nor very dry. July averages about 20°C (68°F), which would be comparable to northern Wisconsin. The highest temperatures ever reached have been around 40°C (104°F), but these are not experienced every year. The coldest month is usually February, which averages around −10°C (14°F). Absolute minimum temperatures are around −40°C (−40°F). Annual precipitation averages around 500–550 millimeters, which is about equal to the potential evaporation in the area, and therefore the region is sub-humid. The northwest is significantly more humid than the southeast, which begins to be semiarid. Summer generally has about 50 percent more precipitation than winter, with the latter half of summer being somewhat wetter than the first half. Therefore, the distribution of summer precipitation is not the best for harvesting. Snow lies on the ground about 120–130 days per year with maximum snow cover reaching about 30 centimeters (1 foot) in February. There is much drifting of snow during frequent blizzards in the winter.

Much of the Central Chernozem Region lies within the wooded steppe zone that runs southwest-northeast across south-central European U.S.S.R. Native trees are oak, ash, maple, and linden. Most of the natural forest has been destroyed on the uplands where cultivation has taken over almost all the territory. What trees remain are generally on the steeper slopes of the river valleys. In the southeastern part of Voronezh Oblast, the original vegetation was open steppe with practically no trees. Almost 100 percent of the steppe areas has been put under cultivation except for a few small plots that have been retained as virgin study areas. The Voronezh Reserve is known throughout the country.

Throughout the region soils are primarily chernozem. In the northwest they may be somewhat degraded because of slight leaching under original forests, but in the southeast they are typical chernozems with very high humus content. In most places the soils have a significant admixture of loess. On the steeper slopes, particularly in the western part of the region in the Central Russian Upland, the soils have been badly damaged by gully erosion. Much of this took place during the centuries of occupancy under Tsarist rule when the land was frequently reapportioned among peasant families by controlling villages. The uncertainty of the land tenure was conducive to maximum exploitation for the short run and little thought of conservation for the long run.

SETTLEMENT AND AGRICULTURE

During the Tatar dominance on the Russian plain much of the Central Chernozem Region was a no-man's-land between the Russian-dominated area around Moscow and the Tatar strongholds at Sarai on the lower Volga and in the Crimea. As the Tatar hold began to weaken, particularly in the fifteenth to sixteenth centuries, some of the bolder Russians escaped from the oppression of the Russian princes and migrated southward into what was then known as the "wild field" either to settle and cultivate the land or to band into seminomadic groups of horsemen to carry on forays against the Tatars, against Moscow, against the Turks to the south, and against the settlers in the area.

These mounted bands became known as Cossacks, and although they derived from the same origins as the more sedentary settlers of the region, they were the more rebellious, more adventurous element that had run away from serfdom in the north, and they tended to live separate existences from the rest of the people in the region. Often they were the forerunners of settlement, pushing the frontier ever southward as the land was taken up behind them. Often they derived their livelihoods by serving as military arms to the Tsar in Moscow, from whose rule they had previously escaped, to bring some order to outlying regions where men lived by their own laws. They helped to establish defense lines consisting of earthen embankments, trenches, and felled trees, such as the famous Belgorod Line in the southern part of the region that was established to protect the settlers to the north from the nomadic steppe peoples in the south and east. They worked hard, fought hard, and were ready for any adventure. In attitudes and actions they much resembled the cowboys of the early days of the American West. During the eighteenth century the wild field disappeared; the Central Chernozem Region became a completely settled integral part of the Russian Empire, and the frontier moved southward, the Cossacks with it, to the steppes of the Black Sea and the lower Don.

During the eighteenth and nineteenth centuries the Central Chernozem Region, being nearer to the populous center around Moscow than was the Ukraine to the southwest, became one of the most productive agricultural areas in the country with one of the densest rural populations. The peasants, as was the case throughout the Russian Empire, were serfs in a feudal system of land holding, a system that led to the neglect of the fertile soils, excessive erosion, and the ultimate near collapse of the rural economy. Thus, owing to overpopulation and a feudal land tenure system, one of the richest naturally endowed agricultural regions in the country remained an area of underdevelopment and rural poverty.

Although the land is now held in large collective farms, most of the people have not been consolidated into larger villages or cities; they still live in their haphazardly scattered villages along muddy stream valleys.

The typical rural dwelling in the forests of the north is the log cabin *izba* and in the steppes of the south the adobe *khata*. Although many of the rural villages now have been supplied with electricity, few have running water or sewage disposal facilities. The typical waterworks is the village well from which the water can be drawn by a windlass.

The Central Chernozem Region is an area of general farming, transitional between the potato-, small grain-, flax-growing area of the Central Region to the north and the commercial wheat and sunflower fields of the steppes to the southeast. The region each year sows about 11 million hectares of land. This is twice as much as the Central Region to the north, which is three times the size. Of these 11 million hectares of sown land, 5.6 million are sown with grains, particularly wheat, 3.4 million with fodder crops, about 1.5 million with technical crops (sugar beets, hemp, sunflowers, and so forth), and 0.5 million with potatoes and vegetables.

Sugar beets generally occupy about 722,000 hectares in the Central Chernozem Region, which is more than 20 percent of all the sugar beet acreage in the country. Most of them are grown in the southwest and central part of the region as a northeasterly extension of the main sugar beet belt in the Ukraine to the southwest. Sunflowers occupy about

Figure 4-2 The village "waterworks." A well with a windlass serves a row of seven cabins. Courtesy of Clara Dundas Taylor.

503,000 hectares, which is more than 10 percent of all the land sown with sunflowers in the U.S.S.R. These are found primarily in the droughty southeastern part of the region. The northern part of the Central Chernozem Region is known for its hemp, makhorka (a type of tobacco), and other technical cultures, as well as potatoes. Here is grown most of the hemp in the country. Lipetsk Oblast is the traditional makhorka-growing region of Russia, and Tambov Oblast is the principal producer of millet.

In spite of severe soil erosion and little application of mineral fertilizers, the Central Chernozem Region achieves fairly high crop yields. The average yield for grain is somewhat higher than the average for the country as a whole, but the yield of sugar beets is a little lower than the average for the country. Sugar beets are more suited to the natural conditions in the Ukraine to the southwest, and very high yields of sugar beets are obtained in certain regions of Central Asia under irrigation.

Livestock production is very important in the Central Chernozem Region. Dairy cattle and hogs are the primary emphasis. More milk is produced here than in the traditional milk regions of the Northwest and Volga-Vyatka. As a consequence of the rich agricultural base, food processing has become a very important industry in the region. Sugar refining is of first-order importance, as is the manufacture of oleomargarine from sunflower oil.

Recently corn has been added to the crop complex, both for grain and for silage. The expansion of sugar beet and corn growing is the most important trend taking place in the agriculture of the region at present. With renewed emphasis on agricultural investment, greatly improved farming methods, heavy application of mineral fertilizers, and the introduction of soil conservation methods, the potential of the area is greatly improving. At the same time, alternate work is being provided for the surplus of labor on the farms in the form of a great variety of small industries that are being established in many of the towns of the region. Thus, it appears that at long last the region may be moving into the industrialization-urbanization stream.

For the time being the Soviets have not deemed it economically feasible to try to house all the new factory workers in urban places. Therefore, there is a growing tendency to truck young people into nearby towns each day to work in small factories and then truck them home at night to their villages on the farms. These are high school graduates who are not involved in the operations of their farms but are still living at home where they have been reared. Such a daily "transhumance" is not the policy of the government, but it is the system that has grown up naturally in response to job opportunities and lack of

Figure 4-3   Hemp field. Courtesy of O. A. Davidson.

housing. In some cases it is beginning to generate a situation that is somewhat the reverse of that in metropolitan areas of the West where people often work in central cities and live in suburbs. Here they derive their livelihoods in the cities but do not pay their fair share of city taxes. The suburbs where they live derive the most benefit from their incomes. In the Soviet case, it is just the opposite. The younger generation often lives on the farms but neither engages in their work nor proportionally contributes to their upkeep. Since these young people are living with their farmer parents, no one complains much, but eventually even parents may get tired of sponging children.

RESOURCES AND INDUSTRIES

The Central Chernozem Region is another "in-between" area that has not shared significantly in the industrialization-urbanization drive that has been taking place during the Soviet period on either side. But its position between the two main industrial nodes of the country, the Central Region to the north and the eastern Ukraine to the south, makes it almost inevitable that eventually this area will fill in with industries. A tremendous amount of freight traffic crosses it on the several main trunk railroads running between the eastern Ukraine and the Central Region. Therefore, convenient transportation lines could be utilized at various points along the way. In addition, during the last couple of decades, the area has become crossed with some of the most important pipeline systems in the country, both for oil and natural gas. The Friendship oil pipeline that runs from the Volga-Urals to the East European satellites runs right through the heart of the region from east to west, and three gas pipelines carrying natural gas from the North Caucasus and the eastern Ukraine to the Central Region run through the region from south to north. Gas pipelines from Central Asia to the Central Region skirt the northeastern border of the region. Thus, any industries located in the Central Chernozem Region can easily tap off

whatever necessary fluid fuels they need, and therefore the region no longer is power starved.

In addition to this convenient in-between location, the Central Chernozem Region has one of the highest density reserves of unused labor on the farms. This is becoming a significant industrial location factor in the Soviet Union, as labor becomes in short supply in many parts of the country.

The primary mineral resource in the area, and the only one of national significance, is the iron ore of the Kursk Magnetic Anomaly (KMA). It is now estimated that these reserves are 10 times those of the famous Krivoy Rog Basin in the east central Ukraine, which thus far has supplied most of the iron ore to the country. The KMA is now credited with about 50 billion tons of high-grade iron ore averaging 56–66 percent-iron content and about 10 trillion tons of lower-grade quartzites averaging 35–37 percent iron. This represents about one-fourth of all the industrial reserves of iron ore in the country. The rich ores of the KMA alone could supply all the iron ore needs of the country for 150 years.

The existence of a huge deposit of iron ore was first suspected in 1783 by the Russian academician Pyotr Inokhodtsev, who recognized the importance of the striking anomaly of terrestrial magnetism that threw off all the compasses in the area. Shortly after the Bolshevik Revolution, Lenin sent a geological survey team into the area headed by Ivan M. Gubkin, and in June 1923 a drilling team found iron ore at a depth of 175 meters near the town of Shchigry in Kursk Oblast. During the next decade many separate ore deposits were discovered that together outlined an ore-bearing region consisting of two subparallel zones, the "west wing" and the "east wing," that stretched 850 kilometers in a northwest-southeast direction all the way from Smolensk to Rostov. The zone was 220 kilometers wide and covered an area of 200,000 square kilometers.

The rich ores lie on top of the quartzites and are the residuals of the silica leaching of the top layers of the quartzites. In general the depth of the ore bodies increases toward the south. In the west wing (Orel, Kursk, and Belgorod Oblasts), which contains four-fifths of the deposits, the trend is for reserves to increase and for quartzites to be totally replaced by rich ores toward the south. Thus, Belgorod Oblast in the south has the largest reserves and the richest ores, but at the greatest depths. Belgorod Oblast is now credited with possessing more than half of the total reserves and more than 90 percent of the rich ores of the entire KMA.

Development finally got underway in 1932 in northern Belgorod Oblast with the establishment of the new town of Gubkin and the drilling of an experimental shaft mine near the small town of Korobkovo just to the north of Gubkin. Production of iron ore began in the spring of 1933. Several other mines were being tunneled in the area when drilling teams ran into insurmountable problems of flooding from saturated aquifers that overlay the iron quartzites. Then the Nazis invaded in June 1941 and interrupted the program, and production did not resume until the 1950s. The second underground quartzite mine was opened at South Korobkovo in 1959. The combined output of the two underground mines was converted by the Gubkin concentrator into about 1.5 million tons of 60 percent concentrate. In 1959 the Lebedi open-pit mine of high-grade (56 percent) ore opened with a capacity of 6 million tons of direct shipping ore. Since then two other open-pit mines have been developed in the Gubkin area of Belgorod Oblast, the largest of which is the Stoyla mine. In Kursk Oblast the open-pit Mikhaylovka mine near Zheleznogorsk (iron mountain) began producing high-grade ore in 1962.

The underground mining operation at Korobkovo was considered to be uneconomical, and although that mine continued to operate, after the early 1960s development efforts concentrated on open-pit mining of great depth to work both the near-surface rich ores and the deeper, lower-grade quartzites. Most of the development so far has taken place in the Lebedi mine of the Gubkin area and the Mikhaylovka mine of the Zheleznogorsk area. At present the Lebedi quarry is a vast bowl

hollowed out of the earth with a radius of about two miles. It contains tiers of worked rock spiralling down from the rim to the bottom that provide for roads and train tracks to haul ore up out of the mine. Only from a helicopter can one view the whole panorama. In 1973 the KMA produced 24.6 million tons of usable iron ore and concentrates, which accounted for 11.5 percent of the U.S.S.R.'s production. Of this total, 14.1 million tons came from the Gubkin district; the Lebedi mine produced 9.6 million tons, mostly high-grade direct-shipping ore, although some were low-grade concentrates. The Stoyla open-pit mine in the Gubkin area produced 3 million tons, and the Korobkovo underground mine produced 1.5 million tons. In Kursk Oblast the Zheleznogorsk area produced 10.5 million tons. The KMA should have produced 38 million tons in 1975. This would constitute about 16 percent of the U.S.S.R. production. It is envisioned that eventually the KMA might become the major producer in the country.

Interest in underground mining has been renewed by the discovery of the huge, rich deposit at Yakovlevo 20 miles north of the city of Belgorod. It lies at a depth of around 500 meters (1475–1650 feet). The average iron content of the ore is 60.5 percent, and about 80 percent of it can be used directly in steelmaking, bypassing the blast furnace process. Reserves have been estimated at 11 billion tons, which alone is four times as much as the rich ore reserves of the Krivoy Rog Basin. Unfortunately the ore lies at great depths and is overlain by six or seven large waterlogged aquifers. However, construction on the shaft mine is continuing, and it appears that perhaps the water problem has been solved by injecting substances, such as liquid nitrogen at a temperature of −196°C, into the aquifers to freeze the rocks.

Although open-pit mining appears to be considerably more economical than shaft mining, concern has been expressed regarding the damage that open-pit mining does. It disturbs thousands of hectares of rich chernozem soil cover and lowers the water table in an area that is already somewhat deficient in soil moisture and domestic and industrial water resources. Already more than 15,000 hectares of fertile land have been despoiled by open pits, spoil banks, and tailing piles of concentrators. Even under the best conservation methods, only the spoil banks, which constitute about 40 percent of the despoiled area, can be rehabilitated for farming. It has been pointed out that each new quartzite-concentrating complex will cover about 4000 hectares of land, and over an estimated period of operation of 60 years this would cause a loss of 300 million rubles in agricultural products. Thus, it may be that much of the future development will be in underground mines in spite of the additional cost.

KMA ore is being shipped primarily to Lipetsk in the immediate region, to Tula in the Central Region, to Cherepovets in the Northwest Region, and to Chelyabinsk and Magnitogorsk in the Urals. Some may also be moving to Novotroitsk in the southern Urals and even to some of the steel mills of the eastern Ukraine. At present Lipetsk and Tula take about 60 percent of the ore, and the Urals take about 25 percent. As production expands in the KMA more ore will probably go to the Urals and also for export to some of the East European satellites. Several Soviet economists recently have written articles calling for greater shipments of KMA ores to the Urals using railroad cars that are now returning empty in an east-west traffic shuttle from Western Siberia to European U.S.S.R. that at present is heavily overbalanced by westward moving freight. There have also been suggestions that some intermediate positions in the Volga-Kama River area might provide ideal locations for future iron and steel plants based on KMA iron ore and coal from the east.

For a number of years there has been much discussion concerning the need for the construction of one or two large iron and steel plants within the area of the KMA itself. Much of the controversy has centered on the need for greater amounts of water than are available in the area. A steel plant uses huge amounts of water, and the development that has already taken place has produced urban settlements that are taxing local water supplies. For instance, the settlement of Gubkin has grown to about 60,000 population. Just to the east the old town of Staryy Oskol has expanded to about the same size. However, despite this drawback, the Soviet Union signed an agreement in March 1974 with a consortium of four West German firms to build a steel plant during the late 1970s using the direct-reduction process bypassing the blast furnace stage. The first stage of the plant, with a capacity of about 2 million tons of semifinished steel and 1.5 million tons of finished products, is now under construction in the Staryy Oskol area. A second stage is to be completed by 1980. Staryy Oskol is to become the most rapidly growing city in the U.S.S.R. during the late 1970s. Plans are for its population ultimately to grow to about 500,000. It is planned to be one of the biggest Soviet steel centers. The Soviets talk about damming three small streams in the area to provide water, but these will soon become inadequate, and therefore there are also plans for a canal to be built from the Oka River to the upper Don and eventually to Staryy Oskol. Conversation continues on the need for a larger conventional iron and steel plant in the KMA area. The Soviets are hopeful that the other Comecon countries will join in the effort to build a huge complex that will produce about 12 million tons of steel annually for export to these countries as well as for use within the Soviet Union. It has been suggested that such a plant might use Polish coking coal.

The KMA ores average 1.2–1.7 percent alumina, as well as the iron, and it has been advocated that a significant aluminum industry be established in the area. Also, considerable cement is derived from the chalk overburden that is being removed in huge quantities from the open-pit mines. The largest cement plant has been constructed at Staryy Oskol. It now has an annual output of about 2.4 million tons of portland cement. Thus, cement production in the area has been considerably expanded beyond the traditional production that has been going on in Belgorod for years. The city of Belgorod has long been one of the major producers of cement in the country utilizing raw materials from the prominent chalk escarpment running east-west near the city. Belgorod means "white city," a name that undoubtedly relates to the chalk escarpment in the vicinity. In addition to cement production, Belgorod also produces large quantities of writing chalk.

A superphosphate plant began operations in 1968 in the town of Uvarovo in Tambov Oblast to provide needed fertilizers for the rich agriculture of the Tambov Plain. Much of its raw materials come from the apatite mines in the Kola Peninsula in the far northern part of European Russia.

The greatest drawback for industrialization in the Central Chernozem Region has always been the almost total lack of power. There are no coal deposits, and there are no rivers of any significant size. Of course, with the crossing of the region by the oil and gas pipelines already mentioned, much of this problem has been resolved. However, the Soviets look to nuclear power as the solution to the electrical needs of the region. The third nuclear plant to be built in the country was built at Novovoronezh on the Voronezh River 50 kilometers south of the city of Voronezh. Electrical production began there in 1964, and capacity has since been expanded to 1.5 million kilowatts. There are tentative plans to expand production here with as many as three more 1-million-kilowatt reactors, which would give the plant eventually a total capacity of 4.5 million kilowatts. The plant in Novovoronezh is presently the largest nuclear power plant in the country.

A second plant is under construction at Kursk. The first 1-million-kilowatt capacity stage is to be completed in 1975. Definite plans call for a capacity of 2 million kilowatts, and tentative plans for as much as 4 million kilowatts. The Kursk station is situated near the new town of Kurchatov 50 kilometers west of the city of Kursk on the left bank of the Seym River, which has been dammed to form a small reservoir of water to supply the plant with its cooling needs. The town of Kurchatov was founded initially in 1971 and has a population of around 5000 people.

CITIES

The largest cities of the Central Chernozem Region are the capitals of the respective oblasts, and they serve primarily as regional centers providing governmental and commercial services. However, some of the cities are now becoming highly industrialized, and as the KMA development continues and new steel plants are established, new industrial centers are bound to arise.

Voronezh

Voronezh is the metropolis of the Central Chernozem Region. In 1974 it had a population of 729,000. Half of its industry is concerned with the production of many types of machines such as ore-concentration equipment, excavators, forge and press equipment, machine tools, grain-cleaning machines, small electric motors, radio and television sets, and machines and equipment for the food industry and the production of building materials. Its aircraft factory is the producer of the supersonic TU-144 airliner which is to fly at about double the speed of sound, 2100 kilometers per hour. However, the city is better known for its chemical industries. The synthetic rubber industry was established here early, along with that in Yaroslavl in the Central Region. The original industry was based on potato alcohol in Yaroslavl and on grain alcohol in Voronezh. Now it has been converted to the use of natural gas in both areas. There is also an automobile tire factory in Voronezh. The highly developed food industries are based on local raw materials: grain, sunflower seeds, and sugar beets. Industries producing building materials also are important.

Lipetsk

Lipetsk has been the most rapidly growing city in the Central Chernozem Region for the last 20 years. By 1974 it had grown to a population of 339,000 and had tied with Kursk for second place among cities in the Central Chernozem Region. The Lipetsk industrial node, which encompases the city of Lipetsk, the city of Gryazi, and the workers' settlements of Syrskiy and Kazinka, accounts for three-fourths of the gross value of industrial production of the entire Central Chernozem Region. Most of this industrial production comes from the two iron and steel plants. An old plant, Svobodnyy Sokol ("free falcon"), was established in 1899 to produce high-phosphorus foundry iron from small local iron ore deposits. The plant has been in continuous operation ever since and has been expanded a little as time has gone on. It specializes in cast-iron pipe 50 millimeters in diameter.

The first five-year plan, 1928–1932, called for the transformation of Lipetsk into one of the main iron and steel centers of the Soviet Union. In addition to the expansion of the Svobodnyy Sokol plant, work began on a new large plant, the Novo-Lipetsk iron and steel plant, which was finally inaugurated in 1934. With the opening of the KMA mining district in the 1950s, the Novo-Lipetsk plant began a major expansion program that is still continuing. By 1975 both pig iron and steel annual capacities were increased to 7 million tons

and should be 15 million tons in the early 1980s and perhaps more than 20 million tons sometime in the future. Thus, Lipetsk is to become the heavy industry giant of the Central Chernozem Region, as well as much of central European Russia. It is destined to be one of the three leading Soviet steel producers, together with Magnitogorsk in the Urals and Krivoy Rog in the Ukraine.

The Novo-Lipetsk plant is one of the most modern in the country. It has no open-hearth furnaces. Steel is smelted in oxygen converters and electric furnaces. This plant produces 80 percent of all the electrotechnical steel in the country. It is a fully integrated plant that includes a coke-chemical shop, an agglomeration factory, a blast furnace department, a steel smelting and electric furnace department, hot and cold rolling mills for carbon steels and electrical engineering steels, nitrate fertilizer production, and slag processing. The plant specializes in the production of steel shapes, cold-rolled auto sheet, zinc-coated and aluminum-coated sheet, as well as plastic coating sheet. It is scheduled to receive a pipe rolling mill to produce large-diameter pipe.

The Novo-Lipetsk plant receives almost 100 percent of its iron ore from various mines of the KMA. About 0.4 percent comes from

Figure 4-4 Novolipetsk metallurgical works. Courtesy of *Soviet Life.*

Krivoy Rog in the Ukraine. The smaller Svobodnyy Sokol plant receives about one-third of its ore from Krivoy Rog and the other two-thirds from the KMA. All the manganese for both plants comes from Chiatura in Georgia in the Transcaucasus. All the coking coal comes from the Donets Basin, although a considerable amount of coke is shipped in from the various plants of the Donets Basin and the plant in Cherepovets in the north, which uses a mix of Pechora and Kuznetsk coal. At present about one-fourth of the coke needs of Lipetsk is being provided by the so-called Cherepovets mix. In the near future the coking plant at Novo-Lipetsk is supposed to be expanded enough to take care of all the coke needs at Lipetsk as well as in some of the surrounding regions. When this takes place, it is planned that considerable amounts of Kuznetsk coal will be brought into the coking process in Lipetsk. Limestone and dolomite fluxing materials are provided from within the Central Chernozem Region, some of them within a radius of 10 kilometers from Lipetsk.

The local availability of many of the ingredients going into the steel-making industry at Lipetsk, as well as modern technology and large-scale production, has made it possible to reduce the cost of pig iron below the established levels of costs for the iron and steel industry in the U.S.S.R. Production is now more efficient than it is at either the Krivoy Rog plant or the Zhdanov plant in the Ukraine. This, plus the fact that Lipetsk is closer to the huge markets of the Central Region, places Lipetsk in a very advantageous position in the steel industry. Undoubtedly the large buildup of the iron and steel industry in the Central Chernozem Region will provide a great impetus for the establishment of machine-building industries in the region. The fact that the city lies on the Friendship oil pipeline leading to the west and on a short branch pipe leading off from the main gas line coming up from the North Caucasus, as well as on the 500-kilovolt electrical transmission line running from Volgograd to Moscow, provides Lipetsk with all the energy needs that can be envisioned for the future.

In addition to the iron and steel industries, Lipetsk contains important chemical industries, building materials industries, and machine industries. Among the machine industries it is particularly known for its tractor plant. Among its chemical industries, an ethyl-benzene plant has been built to extract ethylene and benzene from coke gas. These gases are used chiefly in the manufacture of styrene, a basic ingredient of the synthetic rubber industry. Lipetsk ethyl-benzene is being shipped to nearby snythetic rubber plants in Voronezh and Yefremov.

Kursk

Tied for second in population among the cities of the Central Chernozem Region is Kursk, with a 1974 population of 338,000. However, it is not growing as fast as Lipetsk and is not undergoing the same industrialization. It serves as the governmental and commercial center of Kursk Oblast, including the mining region around Zheleznogorsk. Just to the east of Kursk is the smaller city of Shchigry, whose industries are concentrated totally on ground phosphate derived from phosphate deposits in the vicinity. The industry in Kursk is primarily machine-building and chemical groups, with synthetic fibers being one of the more important products. During World War II Kursk distinguished itself as the site of perhaps the greatest tank battle ever fought anywhere in the world.

Tambov

Fourth in size in the Central Chernozem Region is Tambov, the center of Tambov Oblast and a rich agricultural area of the Tambov Plain. In 1974 it had a population of 252,000. Its main industries are machine-building and chemicals, concentrated in the satellite city of Kotovsk (population 36,000) to the south. To the west of Tambov, about halfway from Tambov to Lipetsk, lies the smaller city of Michurinsk, which in 1974 had a population of 99,000. It is primarily known as the home of Michurin, the Soviet "Luther Burbank." His experimental nurseries developed special strains of plums, peaches, apples, and other fruits and vegetables.

Belgorod

Belgorod is the oblast center in the south. It has long been an important cement-producing center utilizing the chalky limestone from the cuesta escarpment in the area. It appears to be deriving considerable growth recently from the activity taking place in the various iron ore mines in Belgorod Oblast. In 1974 it had a population of 198,000.

Yelets

The sixth and last city above the 100,000 class in the Central Chernozem Region is Yelets, a short distance west of Lipetsk. In 1974 it had a population of 108,000. Its industries concentrate on machine construction and electrical apparatus.

PROSPECTS FOR THE FUTURE

It appears that at long last the Central Chernozem Region may be awakening from its rural background and beginning to be developed as the connecting industrial corridor between the Central Region to the north and the eastern Ukraine to the south. With the development of the Kursk Magnetic Anomaly and the large iron and steel plant at Lipetsk and the new steel center of Staryy Oskol, the coming of natural gas and oil pipelines to the region, and the utilization of the region's advantageous location and abundant labor supply, the region can hardly help but develop in spite of the fact that so far there has been no grand scheme laid out to accomplish this. At the same time it will continue to be one of the most productive farming regions in the country. With proper soil erosion control, fertilization, and crop adaptation, the region can further intensify its agriculture while reducing its agricultural labor force. For the immediate future it will probably remain one of the main regions of significant out-migration in the country.

READING LIST

- *Atlas Kurskoi oblasti* (Atlas of Kursk Oblast), Gugk, Moscow, 1968 (in Russian).
- Kapitonov, Ye. I., "The Kursk Magnetic Anomaly and Its Development," *Soviet Geography: Review & Translation,* May 1963, pp. 10–15.
- Khrushchev, A. T., "The Formation of the Industrial Complex of the Kursk Magnetic Anomaly," *Soviet Geography: Review & Translation,* April 1975, pp. 239–249.
- Kirillova, T.B., and V.A. Ovchinnifov, "Prognozirovaniye rekultivatsii zemel pri otkrytoy dobychye v tsentralnochernozemnom rayonye" (Predicting the Rehabilitation of Land after Strip Mining in the Central Chernozem Region), *Vestnik Moskovskogo Universiteta, seriya geografiya,* No. 2, 1974, pp. 40–48 (in Russian).
- Nikitina, S.A., "The Iron and Steel Industry of the Lipetsk Industrial Node," *Soviet Geography: Review & Translation,* March 1974, pp. 128–134.
- Novikov, V.P., "The Kursk Magnetic Anomaly — A Promising Iron-Ore Base for the Iron and Steel Industry of the Urals," *Soviet Geography: Review & Translation,* February 1969, pp. 43–86.
- Turkin, A.V., "Tsentralnochernozemnyy ekonomicheskiy rayon v devyatoy pyatiletkye" (The Central Chernozem Economic Region in the Ninth Five-Year Plan), *Geografiya v shkole,* No. 1, Moscow, 1974, pp. 5–10 (in Russian).

Donets-Dnieper Economic Region

	Area (km²)	Population	Persons/km²	Percent Urban
Voroshilovgrad Oblast	27,000	2,794,000	104.6	84
Donetsk Oblast	27,000	5,018,000	189.4	88
Kharkov Oblast	31,000	2,907,000	92.6	72
Sumy Oblast	24,000	1,478,000	62.1	46
Poltava Oblast	29,000	1,730,000	60.1	45
Zaporozhye Oblast	27,000	1,847,000	67.9	68
Dnepropetrovsk Oblast	32,000	3,471,000	108.8	78
Kirovograd Oblast	25,000	1,267,000	51.5	46
Total	221,000	20,512,000	92.8	

chapter 5

the donets-dnieper economic region

Let us now leave the Russian Republic temporarily and consider the next contiguous region that lies to the south of the Central Chernozem Region and to the west of the lower Volga Region. This is the Donets-Dnieper Economic Region of the eastern Ukraine. It is distinguished from its predominantly agricultural surroundings by its heavy industrial buildup due to the coal of the Donets Basin in the eastern part of Ukraine and the iron ore of the Dnieper Bend area about 300 kilometers to the west.

The region consists administratively of eight oblasts, all in the Ukraine S.S.R. In the east, Donetsk and Voroshilovgrad Oblasts constitute much of the coal-mining region; in the west, Zaporozhye, Dnepropetrovsk, and Kirovograd Oblasts constitute the iron-mining district of the Dnieper Bend region; in the north, Kharkov, Sumy, and Poltava Oblasts round out the region although they are not yet very industrialized. Altogether the region contains 221,000 square kilometers and 20,512,000 people.

Thus, it contains about 45 percent as much territory as the Central Region around Moscow and about 73 percent as many people. Therefore, although in terms of territory and numbers of people it is not quite as big an industrial complex as the Central Region, it is a region of denser population settlement, of greater concentration of industries, particu-

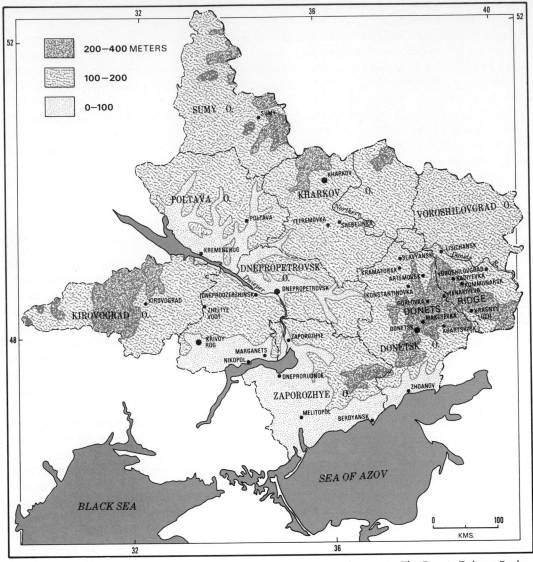

Figure 5-1 The Donets-Dnieper Region.

larly heavy metallurgical industries based on local resources, and of more large cities than the Central Region in spite of the fact that it does not have one huge city, such as Moscow. It contains three cities with more than 900,000 population each, which ties it with the Urals for first place in the country in that category. It has five cities with more than 500,000 population, seven with more than 400,000, and nine with more than 300,000, which ties it with the Volga Region for first place in the country in those categories. It has

25 cities of more than 100,000 population each, one more than the Central Region, which puts it in first place in that category. It contains some of the most highly urbanized oblasts in the country. The population of Donetsk Oblast is 88 percent urban, Voroshilovgrad is 84 percent urban, and Dnepropetrovsk 78 percent. On the other hand, Poltava, Sumy, and Kirovograd Oblasts are only 45–46 percent urban.

The Donets-Dnieper Region is without a doubt the second most important industrial region in the U.S.S.R. after the Central Region around Moscow. Because it has mostly basic industries, while the Central Region has many diversified finished-goods industries that depend on such basic industries, it could be argued that perhaps the Donets-Dnieper Region is even more important to the total economy of the U.S.S.R. than the Central Region. Like the Central Region, industrial growth rates in the Donets-Dnieper Region have not been spectacular compared to some of the other less-developed areas of the country, because of the high production base to begin with, but absolute growth continues here at an unabated pace, and it is destined to do so for the forseeable future.

When considering the great significance of the industrial complex of this area, one must not lose sight of the fact that it is also a very important agricultural region. The agriculture, of course, is based on climate and soil resources. Therefore, both the industrial and agricultural economies of the region are based on local natural resources. As a basis for understanding these economies, let us first consider physical landscape.

THE PHYSICAL LANDSCAPE

Geological Structure and Landform

Topographically the Donets-Dnieper Region consists of three segments. The first is the so-called Donets Ridge, a broad, hilly, dissected upland that runs for a distance of about 300 kilometers from west-northwest to east-southeast between the Northern Donets River Valley on its northern edge and the Black Sea Steppes on the south. Elevations of this hilly tableland average 200–250 meters, but elevations of as much as 367 meters above sea level are attained. The second geomorphic region is the Dnieper Lowland, around the great bend of the Dnieper River in Dnepropetrovsk and Zaporozhye Oblasts, that separates the Donets Ridge to the east from the higher, more extensive Podolian Upland to the west. The third region is the flat-to-undulating plain in Poltava, Kharkov, and Sumy Oblasts,

which is broken occasionally by cuesta escarpments that have been somewhat dissected by streams.

The relatively simple topographic expressions in the Donets Ridge belie a very complex rock structure and geological history in the eastern Ukraine. At times the region was one of geosynclinal activity that accumulated great thicknesses of sedimentary materials. During other geological periods the region was intensely warped, folded, and faulted, peneplaned by erosion, and then uplifted and eroded again and again. In places the massive Precambrian crystalline rocks come close to the surface and are exposed in some of the more deeply incised river valleys, particularly that of the Dnieper. At other places this old Precambrian basement is thousands of meters below the surface, and sedimentary strata are very thick. The thickest of all the deposits are the carboniferous strata that reach thicknesses of as much as 10,000–12,000 meters. These consist primarily of shaley limestones containing thick seams of coal.

At present the region is a strongly denuded fold structure complicated by faults. Small streams running north to the Northern Donets River or south to the Sea of Azov cross the structure and cut gorges and ravines as deep as 150–200 meters. The erosion texture is dense, and the interfluve areas are narrow. None of the streams have much flow, and many of them dry up in late summer. In places rock outcrops along river valleys form cliffs that resemble mountain gorges. Remnants of cuesta formations primarily in limestones and sandstones locally produce unusual forms that stand out starkly on the landscape, such as the so-called tombstones on the Northern Donets-Mius Divide, where monoliths rise as high as 100 meters above the surrounding countryside. In some of the limestone areas karst forms of relief are found — sinks and caverns. Bases of cuestas are generally underlain by shales.

The Dnieper Lowland in general has more subdued relief, although in the Dnieper Bend area between Dnepropetrovsk and Zaporozhye, where the crystalline rock outcrops in the riverbed, the river has formed a

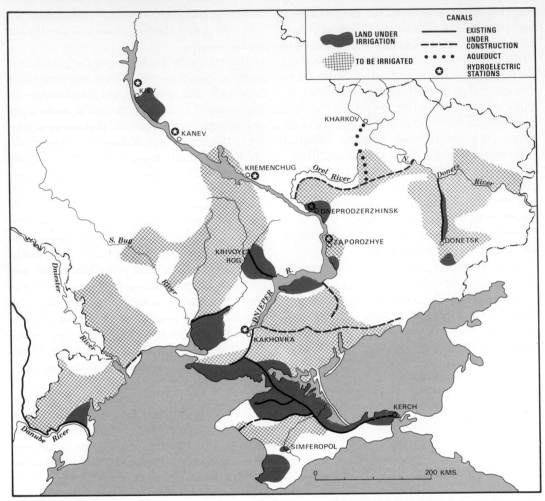

Figure 5-2 Hydrology and irrigation in the Ukraine. Modified from Nikitin, p. 36.

narrow gorge between fairly steep rocky banks. The hard crystalline rock has retarded erosion and created a steepened gradient in the river with many barren gray-black rocky islands in the stream. The valley widens greatly both to the northwest of Dneprope-trovsk and to the southwest of Zaporozhye. To the northwest of Dnepropetrovsk the stream valley takes on its characteristic high right bank–low left bank aspect, which continues northwestward through the central Ukraine to Kiev and beyond. Southwest of Zaporozhye the stream simply flows down the gentle dip slope of the rocks through the dryish Black Sea Steppes and does not form very distinct banks on either side.

During the Dnieper glacial stage a tongue of ice extended down the Dnieper Valley as far as Dnepropetrovsk. Although in this southern extension no very distinct glacial forms were produced, the melt waters provided great quantities of alluvial sands and clays that washed down the streams and formed broad alluvial terraces, which have since been reworked by the wind. Therefore, much of the Donets-Dnieper Region is covered with loess, and the floodplains of the streams are generally sandy with dune forms.

Loess deposits are also a product of the present era, originating from deflation, primarily in the lower Volga-Don region during winter when the prevailing winds are from the southeast.

Climate, Vegetation, and Soils

The climate of the Donets-Dnieper Region is one of the mildest in the east European plain, but by most standards it is still quite severe. January temperatures in the Donbas (Donets Basin) average around −6°C (21°F). The temperature has dropped as low as −34°C at Zaporozhye and −36°C farther north at Kharkov. Summers are mildly warm, with July temperatures averaging around 22°C (72°F) in the Donbas and the Dnieper Bend area and around 20°C (68°F) farther north at Kharkov. Absolute maximum temperatures range from 39°C at Kharkov to 41°C at Zaporozhye. The frost-free period ranges from 173 days at Kharkov to 187 days at Zaporozhye. Thus, the growing season amounts to about half the year, which is sufficient for a considerable variety of crops, but often rather risky for ripening of the long-growing crops such as corn.

Precipitation is only modest throughout the region and is generally deficient in the southeast. Kharkov averages 519 millimeters (about 20 inches) per year, and Zaporozhye averages only 443 millimeters. Because of its slight elevation, the Donets Ridge has a little moister climate than the surrounding plain. Here precipitation amounts to about 450–500 millimeters.

June is generally the rainiest month in the southern part of the region and July in the northern part. The summer maximum of precipitation is characterized by thunderstorms and brief hard showers that cause considerable runoff and erosion and are not very effective in moistening the soil. Skies are generally sunny in the summer, averaging no more than three- to five-tenths sky cover, and evaporation rates are high. During winter the skies are relatively cloudy, averaging more than eight-tenths sky cover from November through February. Snow is a fairly common occurrence during winter, but the total snowfall is not great, and snow does not accumulate to very great depths on the ground. At Kharkov snow lies on the ground about 105 days per year, and the greatest depth reached is around 26 centimeters. Farther south at Zaporozhye snow is on the ground only 58 days per year and reaches a depth of only 8 centimeters.

The most dangerous snowstorms during winter are associated with the forward edges of northeastward-moving Black Sea cyclones. These cyclones either have formed over the Mediterranean and moved northeastward across the Black Sea or have formed locally in the Black Sea and continued their northeastward movement across the southern Ukraine and southeast European Russia across the southern Urals and into the Ob Basin where they finally move into the Arctic near the Ob Gulf. As they move across the southeastern Ukraine, the northeastern quadrant of these storms ahead of the warm fronts strengthens the easterly circulation around the western end of the Asiatic High and brings cold surface air into the region from the east which is overridden by warmer, moister air coming from the southwest off the Black Sea. Such situations are conducive to the formation of ground fog, freezing drizzle, and glaze ice over the Donets Ridge. This region experiences some of the most frequent occurrences of fog and glaze-ice during winter of any region in the country. Some fog forms about every other day over some portion of the Donets Ridge during winter. Donetsk experiences 115 days per year with fog. Glaze ice is experienced 20–40 days per year and reaches thicknesses of as much as 60–80 millimeters.

During winter this region generally finds itself along the western edge of the westerly extension of the Asiatic High, which produces strong, persistent cold winds across the region from the east and southeast that often cause blizzard conditions and drift the snow, laying bare much of the territory and exposing it to deflation. This accounts for much of the loess covering the Ukraine. Occasionally dustfalls as far north as Scandinavia can be traced to this origin.

During summer the same region suffers frequent incursions of the so-called *sukhovey,* a desiccating episode of hot-dry weather that causes severe wilting of plants and may sharply curtail crop yields. Sukhovey conditions are generally the product of rapid surface heating of dry Arctic air that moves southward across the East European Plain and stagnates in a high-pressure cell around the lower Volga Region. The air initially has a low absolute humidity, and as surface heating becomes intense the relative humidity drops to very low values, and evaporation rates rise sharply.

In order to combat the effects of wind and sukhovey, the Soviets have planted many shelter belts in the eastern Ukraine and surrounding areas. These consist of broad strips of trees and shrubs of various varieties that produce ragged open belts of permanently vegetated surface several hundred meters wide. They are generally oriented north-south across the prevailing easterly winds, but they also may be planted in quadrangular patterns completely around peripheries of fields and farms. They are designed to break up the general flow of air into separate currents, some of which go over the barriers, some of which seep through the vegetation, and all of which rejoin on the lee side to form confused eddies that dissipate much of the forward motion. This serves to reduce the drifting of snow in winter and to hold a thin snow cover over the entire surface, thus reducing deflation during winter and providing spring melt water that significantly moistens the soil, rather than allowing the snow to accumulate in deep drifts in local areas that during spring will take a long time to melt. During summer the reduction of the wind significantly reduces evaporation and lessens the effects of sukhovey.

During the last two decades a tremendous number of apple orchards have been added to the shelter-belt system to serve the dual purpose of fruit production and wind control. The typical arrangement of vegetation along highways is a combination of scraggly shelter belts of trees and brush immediately along the highways stretching back from the road perhaps 200–300 meters, beyond which may be 20–30 rows of apple trees, and only

beyond that the open fields of annual crops. Thus, the tourist riding down a highway in a bus has a hard time determining what is planted in the fields away from the highway, and every time he attempts to take a picture out of the moving bus window a tree flashes into view just as he snaps his camera. This frustration has led many foreign tourists to contend that the Soviets have purposely planted all these trees and brush to obscure views of the fields. This probably is not the case; the real reason these belts of trees have been planted is to compensate the tourist for the lack of gasoline station rest stops on long bus rides.

Much of the Donets-Dnieper Region was originally grassland except for the higher parts of the Donets Ridge that stood out as an island of wooded steppe in the steppe around it. Even today the steeper slopes of ravines are occupied by so-called *buyerak* (ravine or gully) forests consisting mainly of oak and ash. But most of the rest of the area is under cultivation. The subhumid climate has been conducive to the formation of rich chernozem and chestnut soils, and the admixture of loess has increased the fertility.

AGRICULTURE

Much of the unurbanized area of the eastern Ukraine is cultivated, except for the steeper slopes of the valleys. Although the region is somewhat dry and therefore less productive than farther northwest in the Ukraine, the rich soils of the area make it one of the prime agricultural regions of the country. In the northern oblasts of the region, Kharkov, Poltava, and Sumy, where moisture is a little more abundant, sugar beets and winter wheat are the big crops with corn and sunflowers also very important. Significant amounts of hemp are grown and livestock grazing, particularly dairy cattle, is intensively developed. This is the eastern end of the sugar beet belt that becomes most intensive west of the Dnieper in central Ukraine. Much of the corn in this area is grown for silage because the growing season is a little too cool and short for corn to ripen many years.

Southward in the Donets Basin and the Dnieper Bend area corn and sunflowers become more important, and sugar beets drop out of the crop complex. Wheat remains very important. Vineyards are significant toward the Sea of Azov. Livestock raising remains important, and swine become a major part of the livestock effort.

The Donets Basin is in the heart of the sunflower belt, which extends in a crescent-shaped region from the southeastern Ukraine around the head of the Sea of Azov into the Kuban District of the North Caucasus. Sunflowers are ideally suited to this droughty area of sunny skies and fertile soils. They pro-

vide the basis for many vegetable oil and margarine-processing plants in the area. Both dairy cattle and swine utilize the refuse from sunflower processing as well as from the sugar beet processing farther north. The dairy cattle also make great use of the corn, much of which is chopped for either green fodder or silage. The swine make use of the grain corn, which is grown primarily in the same dryish crescent-shaped area as the sunflowers. Although southeastern Ukraine and the Kuban District are too dry for optimal corn growing, they are about the only extensive areas in the country with sufficiently warm and long growing seasons to ensure ripe corn most years. Therefore, drought is risked in these regions in order to gain heat. But even along

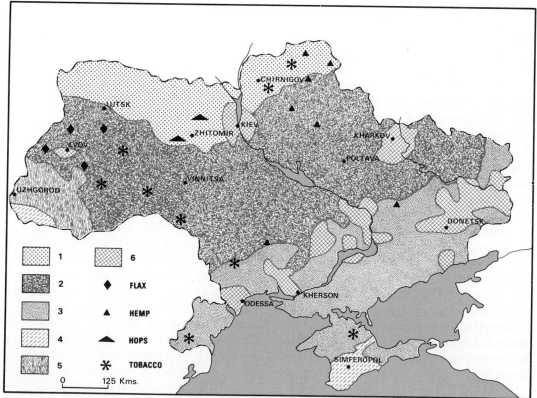

Figure 5-3 Agricultural regions. After Nikitin, p. 34.; 1-Flax, potatoes, milk-meat livestock, grain; 2-Sugar beets, wheat, milk-meat livestock, swine; 3-Wheat, corn, sunflowers, vineyards, vegetables, melons, apples, milk-meat livestock; 4-Vineyards, gardens, milk-meat-wool livestock; 5-Sheep and cattle grazing on mountain pastures, orchards in river valleys; 6-Urban oriented agriculture.

the shores of the Black and Azov Seas, significant amounts of the corn are chopped for fodder.

Around all the larger cities, urban-oriented agriculture has been developed to supply vegetables and fruits to the urban markets. This is particularly well developed in the Donbas, where many large cities lie in close juxtaposition to one another, as well as in the Dnieper Bend area where the same situation exists. It is also developed around the large city of Kharkov in the north.

MINERAL RESOURCES AND INDUSTRIES

No other region of comparable size in the U.S.S.R., and perhaps the world, is as well endowed with mineral resources as the Donets-Dnieper Region of the eastern Ukraine. Not only does the region contain the Donets coal basin and the Krivoy Rog iron basin in close juxtaposition to one another, but the world's largest manganese deposit is located in between, and the country's main rock salt deposit lies in the Donets Basin. Buried sand deposits in two areas are the Soviet Union's principal sources of titanium and zirconium. The largest gas-producing field in the country at present is situated southeast of Kharkov. There are also significant deposits of oil, mercury, uranium, graphite, phosphorite, kaolin, and limestone.

All of the major ingredients of the iron and steel industry lie within 250–300 kilometers of one another within the Donets-Dnieper Region, and the region is the major producer in the country of all of them. Since the Russian industrial revolution of the 1880s, the Donets Basin has been the primary producer of coal in the country, and the Krivoy Rog Basin has been the primary producer of iron ore. Around the turn of the century these two basins produced most of the coal and the iron ore in the Russian Empire. Although their relative shares have decreased during the Soviet period as other areas have opened up, they have retained their first-place standings, and

their absolute amounts of production have increased greatly.

The Donets coal basin is not the biggest or the richest coal deposit in the country by any means, and the great depth and complicated geology of the richer deposits make it very expensive to mine. Half the deposits lie at depths between 600 and 1200 meters, about one-third between 1200 and 1800 meters, and the remainder at even greater depths. Reserves down to a depth of 1800 meters have been estimated at 100 billion tons, which amounts to about 2.4 percent of the estimated reserves of the Soviet Union. Grades run all the way from anthracite to bituminous to lignite. It is estimated that 13.3 percent of all the coal reserves in the basin are suitable for coking. Shaft mines go down as deep as 2000 meters.

But the ideal location of the Donets Basin with regard to the other ingredients of the steel industry, as well as to the major markets of the country, has prompted its great development in spite of these drawbacks. In 1974 the entire Donets Basin produced 220 million tons of coal out of a U.S.S.R. total of 684 million. About 30–35 million tons of this production occurred in the eastern end of the basin that lies outside the Ukraine in Rostov Oblast of the R.S.F.S.R. Therefore, the Donets-Dnieper Region produced about 190 million tons. Of this, about 82 million tons was coking coal, which amounted to about half the coking coal production in the country. Most of the production comes from the central part of the basin in Donetsk and Voroshilovgrad Oblasts, but the coal seams extend northwestward, and production keeps expanding in that direction closer to the iron ore. The brown coal deposits actually extend across the Dnieper northwestward out of the region as far as Zhitomir west of Kiev. However, little of this is mined except for local heating and electric-generation purposes. The Donets coal is used not only locally but also throughout much of European U.S.S.R. west of the Volga River as far north as Moscow and Leningrad and as far south as the Transcaucasus.

The Krivoy Rog iron ore basin began to develop simultaneously with the Donets coal basin around 1880. It rapidly developed into the major iron-mining region of the country and for many years was credited with having the greatest reserves in the country. Now, with the opening of the Kursk Magnetic Anomaly in the Central Chernozem Region, the Krivoy Rog Basin has been relegated to second place in reserves, but it is still by far the largest producer in the country.

The ore exists primarily in a narrow strip of land 1–6 kilometers wide that stretches north-south for about 100 kilometers. High-grade ores averaging about 60 percent iron total about 2 billion tons, and iron quartzites averaging about 35 percent iron have reserves of 9–13 billion tons. Most of the rich ores lie at considerable depths and must be mined underground, while much of the quartzite lies near the surface and at the present time is all mined by open-pit methods. The Krivoy Rog ores constitute about one-fifth of all the known iron reserves of the Soviet Union.

In recent years two extensions of the basin have been discovered and opened for exploitation. The first is in the north about 15 kilometers east of Kremenchug on the left bank of the Dnieper River. A large concentrator has been constructed there to process low-grade ores, and there are long-range plans to construct an iron and steel plant in the area. The second region is south of Zaporozhye on the east side of the Dnieper near the town of Belozerka. The workers' settlement of Dneprorudnyy was established there in 1963 on the south shore of the Kakhovka Reservoir. The ore there is all rich at great depths. Many of the mineshafts go down about 600 meters.

Before World War II all of the iron mining in the Krivoy Rog Basin produced rich ores from shaft mines, but as the iron content of these ores slowly decreased to about 55 percent, it was found to be more economical to produce ore from the lower-grade quartzites by open-

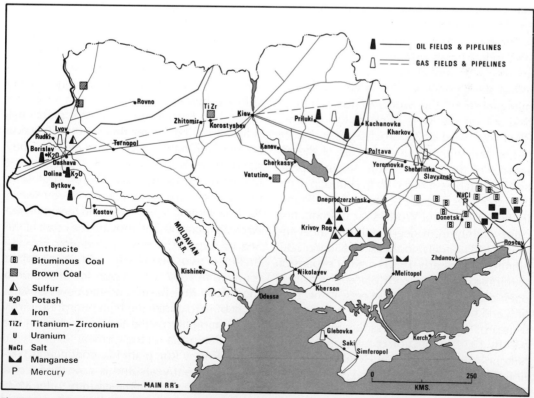

Figure 5-4   Minerals in the Ukraine.

pit methods and concentrate it to an iron content of about 65 percent. Beginning about 1955 large open-pit mines came into operation, and they are now producing more than half the usable ore.

In 1974 the Ukraine produced 122 million tons of usable ore out of a U.S.S.R. total of 225 million tons. Most of the Ukrainian ore came from the Krivoy Rog Basin. It has been estimated that about 5 million tons came from Kerch on the Crimean Peninsula, which will be discussed with the South Economic Region. Thus, it is estimated that about 117 million tons came from the Krivoy Rog expanded basin, of which about 50 million tons was direct-shipping ore and 67 million tons was concentrates from surface-mined low-grade quartzites.

Most of the Krivoy Rog ore is used locally in the many plants of the Donets-Dnieper Economic Region, but some moves northward to the Central Chernozem and Central Regions, and 40–45 million tons is exported annually to Czechoslovakia, Poland, Rumania, Hungary, East Germany, Bulgaria, Britain, Italy, and Japan.

The third major ingredient of the iron and steel industry is manganese, which is used at an average rate of about 10 pounds for every ton of steel produced. The largest deposit of manganese in the world is located near Nikopol on the west bank of the Dnieper River southwest of Zaporozhye. This deposit is credited with about four-fifths of the resources of the Soviet Union. Mining operations began here along with the buildup of the iron and steel industry of the eastern Ukraine in the 1880s. Until World War II production came mainly from deep, rich ores near the town of Marganets northeast of Nikopol. Beginning in the early 1950s a great expansion of mining operations took place, primarily of open pits with lower-grade ores. Concentration and beneficiating plants have been built in nearby towns to process this lower-grade ore. By 1974 production of manganese in the Nikopol area had increased to about 6.3 million tons out of a U.S.S.R. total production of 8.1 million tons. Most of this was used domes-

tically in the iron and steel plants of the U.S.S.R.

The happy juxtaposition of major deposits of coal, iron ore, and manganese, plus abundant limestone for fluxing, has prompted the construction of many large iron and steel plants in the Donets-Dnieper Region. Initially two major clusters of plants were built, one in the coal-mining area of the Donets Basin, and the other in the Dnieper Bend area between the iron and the coal. The Donets cluster consists of a great number of small to medium-sized plants in a number of different cities, none of which are of outstanding size. The largest plants are in Donetsk and the immediately adjacent cities of Makeyevka and Yenakiyevo. Other major plants are farther north in the cities of Konstantinovka, Kramatorsk, Kadiyevka, and Kommunarsk. In the Dnieper Bend area plants are concentrated in the three largest cities, Dnepropetrovsk, Zaporozhye, and Dneprodzerzhinsk. The Dneprodzerzhinsk plant, which dates from 1889, was the first to be built in the area, and until the major expansion of the new Krivoy Rog plant in the 1960s it was the biggest single producer of pig iron in the Ukraine. Coal moves westward from the Donets cluster and iron ore moves eastward from Krivoy Rog to serve all these plants at the two ends of the railroad shuttle.

The two largest iron and steel plants developed during Soviet times in the Ukraine are not within these two major clusters; they stand somewhat alone on either side. During the early 1930s two major iron and steel plants were constructed, one in Krivoy Rog in the iron-mining region itself and the other, the Azovstal plant, at Zhdanov on the coast of the Sea of Azov. The city of Zhdanov actually includes two plants, the old Ilyich plant founded in 1897, which gets its iron ore from the Krivoy Rog Basin, and the new Azovstal plant built to utilize the high phosphorus iron ore coming across the Sea of Azov from the Kerch Peninsula on the Crimea.

The Krivoy Rog plant has continued to expand in recent years and is now the second largest single plant in the country, after Mag-

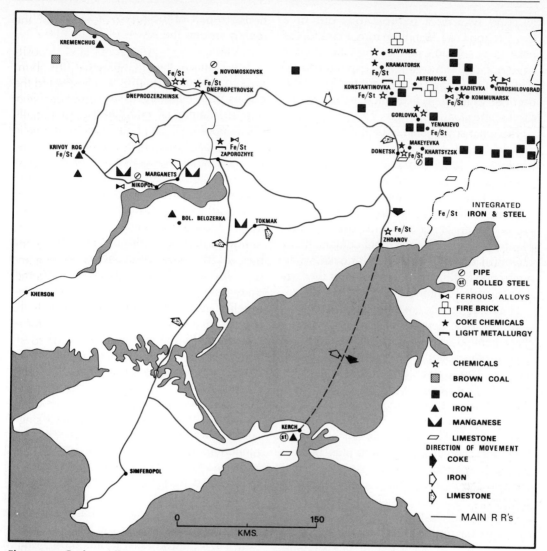

Figure 5-5 Coal, metallurgy, and chemicals in the Donets-Dnieper Region. After Nikitin, p. 29.

nitogorsk in the southern Urals. In 1974 it gained its number-9 blast furnace, which was described as the largest and most modern blast furnace in the world. It alone is capable of turning out 4.4 million tons of cast iron annually. The fully automated furnace has a new mold yard shaped like a circus building and serviced by two 22-ton ring cranes. Cast iron pours out of four taps into ladles that handle 154 tons each. It takes 26 railroad cars of fluxed sinter, iron ore, and coke per day to keep the furnace going. This is the Soviet Union's first 5000-cubic-meter blast furnace.

The total output of the Krivoy Rog complex in 1973 was about 10 million tons of pig iron and 13 million tons of steel. Plans for the late 1980s are to expand pig iron production to about 18 million tons and steel production to about 22 million tons. In 1974 the total pig iron production of the Ukraine was 44.6 million tons, which compared to a U.S.S.R. total of 99.9 million tons. The steel output of the

Ukraine was 52.4 million tons out of a U.S.S.R. total of 136 million tons. Plans for the next 15 years indicate that the Ukraine will have one of the most rapidly expanding iron and steel industries in the country. Thus, it is destined to retain its first place in the industry for the foreseeable future.

The great amount of coal coking in the iron and steel plants of the Donets-Dnieper Region produces a large quantity of coal tars and gases used as the basis for a highly developed chemical industry that turns out many intermediate products to serve the industries of the entire country. In addition to coke chemical plants at all the iron and steel centers, major chemical plants are found at Gorlovka, where a nitrogen fertilizer plant dates from the mid-1930s, and at a number of smaller cities.

In addition to the coke gases, local rock salt and limestone deposits are used in many of the chemical industries. The Artemovsk salt mines have been in operation since the 1870s. The Artemovsk deposit supplies around 40–45 percent of all the rock salt in the U.S.S.R. and is the major producing area in the country. This amounts to about 25 percent of the total salt production in the U.S.S.R. Nearby at Slavyansk an old soda plant processes salt and produces soda ash and caustic soda to supply chemical plants all over the country.

To the northeast another major chemical complex has built up in a number of cities surrounding the major center of Lisichansk. These use coking gases and hydrocarbons from natural gas brought in by pipeline from Shebelinka to the west. Farther south the city of Konstantinovka has a superphosphate plant associated with an older zinc smelter and refinery that processes long-haul zinc concentrates from other parts of the country. The superphosphate plant processes Kola Peninsula apatite and sulfuric acid as a by-product of the zinc smelter gases.

The Donets Basin has the Soviet Union's oldest mercury mine in a northern suburb of Gorlovka. It is still the leading producer in the country. During the 1960s it became apparent that one of the main uranium-producing areas in the U.S.S.R. was associated with the northern part of the Krivoy Rog iron-mining region around the towns of Terny and Zheltyye Vody.

The Donets-Dnieper Region is one of the principal natural gas producers. Most of this comes from the Shebelinka and Yefremovka deposits southeast of Kharkov. The Shebelinka deposit first went into operation in 1956 with the construction of a pipeline to Kharkov. Since then pipelines have been built west to Kiev, southwest to Odessa, north to Bryansk to join the Kiev-Moscow pipeline, and northeast to Ostrogozhsk to join the Kuban-Moscow pipeline. In 1965 the Yefremovka field was discovered and it was brought into production shortly thereafter. A new 40-inch pipeline was constructed from Yefremovka to Kiev parallel to the old 28-inch pipeline from Shebelinka to Kiev, and the pipeline system has been extended to Uzhgorod in the Transcarpathian Ukraine and on to the Czechoslovak border where natural gas is being transmitted to Czechoslovakia, Austria, Italy, West Germany, and France. Feeder lines have been built off the main gas lines to serve other cities of the area such as Krivoy Rog, Nikopol, Kishinev, Kremenchug, Cherkassy, Belaya Tserkov, and Vinnitsa. Most recently a pipeline has been constructed from Shebelinka southeastward to Slavyansk to join up with pipelines feeding various cities of the Donets Basin as well as Zhdanov on the coast of the Sea of Azov.

In 1974 the Ukraine produced 68.3 billion cubic meters of natural gas out of a total U.S.S.R. production of 261 billion cubic meters. It is estimated that at least 80 percent of the Ukrainian gas came from the Shebelinka-Yefremovka area. The rest came from the northern foothills of the Carpathians in the western Ukraine. In addition to Ukrainian gas, the Donets-Dnieper Region is served by pipelines leading northwestward across the very eastern part of the Ukraine from the North Caucasian gas fields through Rostov and Voroshilovgrad to Moscow.

The potential area for natural gas in the Donets-Dnieper Region extends over a long zone stretching from Voroshilovgrad in the southeast to Chernigov in the northwest north of Kiev. The western half of this zone also has oil possibilities. Wells are now producing in northern Poltava Oblast, southern Sumy Oblast, and western Kharkov Oblast. These are only minor producers, but they are important to the local area. In 1973 it was estimated that they produced 7–8 million tons of crude oil. Much of this was processed at the new Kremenchug refinery opened in 1966. The refinery at Kremenchug also processes some west Ukrainian crude oil, and since 1974 it has been served by a branch pipeline that comes in from Michurinsk in the Central Chernozem Region, where it taps off oil from the Friendship pipeline bringing Volga-Urals and Western Siberian oil across the region. A 28-inch pipeline connects the Kremenchug refinery with a smaller, older refinery at Kherson on the Black Sea coast. In 1975 it was reported that a new refinery was nearing completion at Lisichansk in the Donbas.

Water

The greatest lack in the Donets-Dnieper Region is water, not only for agriculture, but also for the heavy industries that require huge amounts for cooling and other purposes. By far the largest stream in the region is the Dnieper River, which gathers most of its water in the Pripyat Marshes and other humid regions in the headwater streams leading into the Dnieper. South of Kiev the Dnieper gains very little water, and by the time it reaches the Bend area it is losing water through evaporation and seepage. Thus, it has only a modest flow. The only other stream of any significance is the Northern Donets, which is a small stream indeed. It flows along the northern and eastern edges of the Donbas and supplies significant amounts of water to the heavy industries of that area. The Northern Donets-Donbas Canal has been constructed 125 kilometers into the Donbas to supply domestic and industrial water to many of the cities there. However, as cities and industries have grown, this source has become quite inadequate. Construction has started on a canal almost 600 kilometers long to bring in water from the Dneprodzerzhinsk Reservoir

on the Dnieper River to the Donbas via the Northern Donets-Donbas Canal. A branch canal will be constructed northward to Kharkov. Plans are to create a reservoir near Kharkov to store 10.5 billion gallons of water.

The Soviets have transformed the Dnieper River into a stairway of reservoirs, much as they have the Volga River. This system of dams and reservoirs was completed in 1972 and now consists of six major installations. Within the Donets-Dnieper Region there are three dams, the so-called Dnieper Dam at Zaporozhye, the Dneprodzerzhinsk Dam, and the Kremenchug Dam. In addition, much of the reservoir behind the Kakhovka Dam to the south lies within Zaporozhye and Dnepropetrovsk Oblasts.

The Dnieper dam and power plant (Dneproges) was the first installation to be constructed on the Dnieper and one of the first major undertakings in the industrialization of the Soviet Union. This was accomplished with a great deal of fanfare during the first five-year plan when the work was held up as a national symbol of new Soviet strength. It began operating in the autumn of 1932 and eventually developed a capacity of 558,000 kilowatts. Although its primary function was to generate electricity, the narrow reservoir behind the dam flooded the series of rapids in the constricted channel of the Dnieper Bend area where the river had cut into the old crystalline basement rock. This finally solved the problem of connecting the upper and lower portions of the river that had plagued this important trade route for more than 1000 years. The dam raised the water level more than 30 meters and drowned many of the rocky islands in the middle of the stream, although barren rocky crags still stick above the water in this region.

At the time Dneproges was constructed it was the largest hydroelectric plant in Europe. Early in World War II, in the face of the advancing Germans, the Russians dismantled the power plant and carried away all movable equipment. Later, as they retreated, the Germans blew up the dam. At the end of the war there was nothing left but a pile of concrete rubble and twisted steel in the riverbed. This was more than just a mortal blow to a power station; it was a blow to the young ego of the Soviet Union. After the war the dam was quickly reconstructed, and the power plant resumed operation in 1947 with a capacity of 650,000 kilowatts.

The Dnieper Dam was originally built with 48 spillways, 19 of which were to cope with floods. But with the building of other reservoirs on the river, spring floods have been greatly reduced, and these spillways no longer have any flood-control functions. Therefore, "Dneproges 2" is being built to convert these extra spillways into falls for power turbines. The first generating unit of this second stage went into operation in November 1974, and when the stage is completed the total plant will have a capacity of around 1.4 million kilowatts.

Meanwhile, the Kremenchug station was completed in 1960 with a capacity of 625,000 kilowatts, and the Dneprodzerzhinsk station was completed in 1964 with a capacity of 352,000 kilowatts. Earlier the Kakhovka Dam was completed in 1956 to the south of the Donets-Dnieper Region. This created a large reservoir in this flat area that is used primarily for irrigation. Major canals have been constructed southward to the Crimea and will be discussed in the South Economic Region, but also a small canal has been built northwestward to serve the Krivoy Rog iron mining and industrial area.

Although the primary reason for building the dams along the Dnieper was to produce hydroelectric power, the dams also enhance navigation and supply water for irrigation in certain regions. Some irrigation is now carried out in the vicinity of practically all the reservoirs, and there are plans to expand this in the future.

Other Industries

The great amount of industrial buildup in the Donets-Dnieper Region has required the construction of a tremendous number of thermal and hydroelectric plants to supply the great amounts of electricity required. Thermal plants have been built in most of the major

cities, and the six hydroelectric plants on the Dnieper have already been summarized. The great amount of electricity available has prompted the building of an alumina-aluminum plant in Zaporozhye. This began shortly after the Dnieper Dam was built in the 1930s. It originally used bauxite from a deposit east of Leningrad and in the Urals and eventually it shipped in alumina by rail from the Urals to be converted into aluminum. However, since 1955 the plant has operated primarily on Greek bauxite shipped in by sea. It annually processes enough bauxite to produce about 200,000 tons of alumina, which is enough to make 100,000 tons of aluminum. It also recovers vanadium from the bauxite. Zaporozhye also has a plant that produces magnesium and titanium.

The machine-construction industries are well developed throughout the eastern Ukraine, utilizing the great amounts of metal products being produced there. The products range all the way from agricultural machinery through milling and oil refinery equipment to transport equipment. Some of the main machine-building industries will be discussed with individual cities in the next section.

CITIES

As was mentioned in the beginning of this chapter, the Donets-Dnieper Region is a region of great cities. It has 25 cities with more than 100,000 population each, which is more than any other economic region.

Cities of the Donets Basin

One of the largest urban agglomerations in the country is in the Donets Basin. No one city stands out, but there are 13 cities with more than 100,000 population in Donetsk and Voroshilovgrad Oblasts. There are also many smaller cities. Most of these are coal-mining centers, and a number of them have iron and steel industries, which have already been mentioned. In addition, they have heavy chemical industries and many machine-building industries. Cement and glass industries are also included, as are many textile and food industries. In order of size the 13 largest cities are Donetsk (Yuzovka, Stalino) with a 1974 population of 934,000, Zhdanov on the Azov Sea coast with a population of 451,000, Voroshilovgrad (Lugansk) with a population of 423,000, Makeyevka with a population of 397,000, Gorlovka with a population of 341,000, Kramatorsk with a population of 162,000, Kadiyevka with a population of 140,000, Slavyansk with a population of 133,000, Kommunarsk (Alchevsk, Voroshilovsk) with a population of 127,000, Lisichansk with a population of 120,000, Konstantinovka with a population of 109,000, Krasnyy Luch with a population of 104,000, and Severodonetsk with a population of 104,000.

In addition to these larger cities, Khartsyzsk with a 1974 population of 55,000 has one of the largest pipe mills in the country. It turns out 1600-millimeter (64-inch) diameter pipe to be used on some of the longer pipelines in the country. In 1973 Khartsyzsk and other Ukrainian tube-manufacturing centers turned out 5.1 million tons of pipe out of a U.S.S.R. total of 14.4 million tons. Khartsyzsk also produces steel wire products and ductile iron.

Cities of the Dnieper Valley

The second largest agglomeration of cities in the Ukraine is situated in the Dnieper Bend area. Here are found six cities with more than 100,000 population if Krivoy Rog to the west of the Dnieper is included. In order of size they are Dnepropetrovsk with a 1974 population of 941,000, Zaporozhye (Alexandrovsk), "beyond the rapids," with a population of 729,000, Krivoy Rog with a population of 620,000, Dneprodzerzhinsk with a population of 242,000, Kremenchug with a population of 171,000, and Nikopol with a population of 137,000. The four largest cities have heavy industries based on the Krivoy Rog iron and the Donets coal, and Nikopol has metal-processing industries based on the local manganese ore. Kremenchug eventually is scheduled to get an iron and steel plant based on local iron ore deposits. In addition,

Zaporozhye, Dneprodzerzhinsk, and Kremenchug have large hydroelectric plants, and the other cities have large thermal electric plants. Other metal industries and machine-building industries are distributed throughout the cities. The aluminum industry has already been mentioned at Zaporozhye. Zaporozhye also contains a motor vehicle plant that builds the smallest and least expensive of Soviet passenger cars, the Zaporozhets, which went into production in 1960. It is a small four-passenger, four-cylinder car with an air-cooled engine located in the back with only 20–25 horsepower. Although the Zaporozhye plant is one of the least efficient and most neglected car producers in the country, by 1975 its production was 135,000 cars.

The smaller city of Kremenchug in the north seems to have been singled out for intensive industrialization. Not only is it the site of one of the large hydroelectric plants on the river and the economic center of the developing iron-ore mining region that may eventually get an iron and steel plant, but it is also the site of a heavy truck plant, a railroad car plant, and a carbon black plant. Its oil refinery has already been mentioned. The Kremenchug motor vehicle plant builds heavy cargo trucks of 12–14 tons capacity and a truck tractor that pulls a semitrailer with a payload of 30 tons. It currently turns out about 25,000 trucks a year. The trucks were designed after U.S. Army heavy prime movers supplied under lend lease during World War II. They are being used as military prime movers, for towing heavy industrial and construction equipment, and as dump trucks. A tire plant has been established in Dnepropetrovsk to serve the automobile plants in Zaporozhye and Kremenchug.

Kharkov

The largest city in the entire region, the second largest in the Ukraine and the sixth largest in the U.S.S.R., is Kharkov with a 1974 population of 1,330,000. It sits somewhat by itself in the northern part of the region on one of the main railroads running from the Donets and Dnieper industrial areas to the Central Region to the north. It owed its early preeminence to this function as a railroad junction — the second most important railroad node in the Ukraine, after Kiev. It also serves as the commercial center for a very rich agricultural region. At times the city has served important governmental functions. It was founded in 1650 by Ukrainian Cossacks, and from 1922 to 1934 it served as the capital of the Ukrainian S.S.R. During the Soviet period it has developed into one of the major machine-construction centers in the entire country. It specializes in agricultural machinery including tractors, but it also manufactures transport machinery. Many of the turbines for atomic power plants that are being built in the country are manufactured in Kharkov. It is the sixth city in the country to build a subway system. This began operating in 1975.

Other Cities

The other five cities of the region with populations of more than 100,000 are scattered. They are primarily trading centers for their respective regions. In order of size they are Poltava with a 1974 population of 254,000, Kirovograd with a population of 212,000, Sumy with a population of 189,000, Melitopol with a population of 149,000, and Berdyansk with a population of 113,000. Poltava in the northern part of the region is the oblast center for a very rich agricultural area. Historically it is primarily known as the site of Peter the Great's defeat of Charles XII of Sweden in 1709 in what the Russians consider to be a decisive battle of history. Kirovograd is an oblast center in a rich agricultural region west of the Dnieper Bend. It has some agricultural machine industries. Sumy in the far north of the region lies in another rich agricultural oblast and has developed a chemical complex concentrating primarily on the manufacture of superphosphates. Melitopol is on the main highway leading southward across the flat dryish plain toward the Crimea. Berdyansk is one of the lesser ports on the north coast of the Sea of Azov.

PROSPECTS FOR THE FUTURE

The Donets-Dnieper Region is a classic example of a closely knit network of interrelated heavy industries and their connecting railroads. In addition to its many mineral resources, the region derives benefit from gas pipelines running across it from the North Caucasus to the Central Region and an oil pipeline coming in from the northeast off the Friendship Line carrying Volga-Urals and Western Siberian oil. It is probably served by the best railroad transport system in the entire country, with several main lines running northward to the Central Region. Since its industrial complex is largely complementary to that of the Central Region, the two industrial areas together generate the heaviest traffic anywhere in the country. The eastern Ukraine, of course, is characterized primarily by heavy industry based on local resources, while the Central Region is characterized primarily by diversified finished goods based on capital accumulation, labor, and market. All indications are that the Donets-Dnieper Region will remain the primary region of heavy metallurgy in the country and one of the three leading industrial regions of the nation.

READING LIST

- Blazhko, N.I., "The System of Urban Places of the Donets Territorial-Production Complex," *Soviet Geography: Review & Translation,* February 1964, pp. 11–16.
- *Fiziko-geograficheskoye rayonirovaniye Ukrainskoy SSR* (The Physical Geographical Division of the Ukrainian S.S.R.), Kiev, 1968 (in Russian).
- Golikov, A.P., and V.M. Kravchenko, "Kharkov," *Geografiya v Shkole,* 1975, No. 2, pp. 6–11.
- Kryven, P., *Ukrainska RSR; ekonomiko-geografichna kharakterystyka* (Ukrainian S.S.R.; Economic-Geograpnic Characteristics), Kiev, 1961, 208 pp. (in Russian).

- Kubijovyč, Volodymyr, *Ukraine: A Concise Encyclopedia,* second edition, University of Toronto Press, 1971, 1397 pp.
- Kugukalo, I.A., et al., "Economic Regionalization of the Ukrainian SSR," *Soviet Geography: Review & Translation,* October 1960, pp. 23–32.
- Lanko, A.I., et al., "The Physical-Geographic Regionalization of the Ukrainian SSR for Agricultural Purposes," *Soviet Geography: Review & Translation,* December 1960, pp. 33–50.
- "Narodne gospodarstvo Ukraynskoy RSR u 1973 rotsi" (National Economy of the Ukrainian S.S.R. in 1973), *Statistical Yearbook,* Kyiv, 1974, 584 pp. (in Ukrainian).
- Pityurenko, E.I., "Tipy gorodskikh poseleniy Donetskoy oblasti i perspektivy ikh razvitiya" (Types of Urban Places in Donetsk Oblast and Prospects of Their Development), in Pavlovskiy, E.N., and O.A. Konstantinov, *Geografiya naseleniya v SSSR* (Geography of Population in the USSR), Akademiya Nauk SSSR, Moscow, 1964, pp. 168–182 (in Russian).
- *Ukrainskaya SSR* (Ukrainian S.S.R.), Akademiya Nauk Ukrainskoy SSR, Institut Ekonomiki, Part 1, Moscow, 1957, 556 pp., and Part 2, Moscow, 1958, 313 pp. (in Russian).
- Vernander, N.B., et al., "The Land Resources of the Ukraine; Their Evaluation and Inventory Methods," *Soviet Geography: Review & Translation,* January 1961, pp. 35–43.

Southwest Economic Region

	Area (km²)	Population	Persons/km²	Percent Urban
Kiev City	29,000	1,827,000	127.1	100
Kiev Oblast		1,858,000		39
Chernigov Oblast	32,000	1,529,000	47.9	38
Cherkassy Oblast	21,000	1,550,000	74.2	40
Zhitomir Oblast	30,000	1,598,000	53.4	39
Vinnitsa Oblast	27,000	2,110,000	79.6	30
Khmelnitsky Oblast	21,000	1,604,000	77.9	30
Ternopol Oblast	14,000	1,171,000	84.9	26
Chernovtsy Oblast	8,000	866,000	106.9	35
Lvov Oblast	22,000	2,488,000	114.1	50
Ivano-Frankovsk Oblast	14,000	1,286,000	92.5	33
Transcarpathia Oblast	13,000	1,100,000	85.9	34
Volyn Oblast	20,000	997,000	49.4	35
Rovno Oblast	20,000	1,076,000	53.6	30
Total	270,000	21,060,000	78.0	

chapter 6

the southwest economic region

The Southwest Economic Region includes 13 Ukrainian oblasts plus Kiev city, occupying the north central and western Ukraine, one of the most productive agricultural regions in the country and one of the most densely populated with rural people. It includes a territory of 270,000 square kilometers and a population of 21,060,000 people, which gives it an average population density of 78 persons per square kilometer. If the administrative unit of Kiev city is excluded, the entire region is predominantly rural. The 1970 census shows the region to have only 38 percent of the people classified as urban. This ties with the Central Asian Economic Region as the second lowest urbanized area in the country. Only adjacent Moldavia is less urbanized. During the intercensal period 1959–1970, the region showed a modest population growth, a little lower than the average for the entire Soviet Union. But one oblast, Vinnitsa, showed a modest population decline. This tendency for population decline spread to a couple of adjacent oblasts during the latter part of the 1960s. Practically all the region shows a negative migration balance.

The Ukraine west of the Dnieper has had a varied history as part of empires surrounding it. Very seldom has it enjoyed any independence of its own. Parts of its territory have been exchanged back and forth in loosely confederated structures of Russia, Lithuania, Poland, Austro-Hungary, and later Rumania.

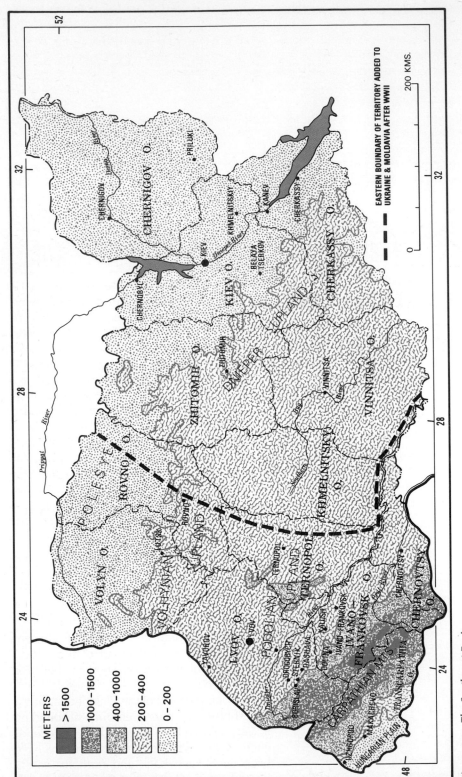

MAP LEGEND:
METERS
> 1500
1000–1500
400–1000
200–400
0–200

POLESYE

VOLYNIAN UPLAND

VOLYN O.

LVOV O.
LVOV

PODOLIAN UPLAND

TERNOPOL O.
TERNOPOL

DROGOBYCH
STERNIK
DASHAVA
BORISLAV
DOLINA
STRYI
KALUSH

IVANO-FRANKOVSK
IVANO-FRANKOVSK O.

CARPATHIAN MTS.

TRANSCARPATHIA

UZHGOROD
MUKACHEVO

HUNGARIAN PLAIN

CHERNOVTSY
CHERNOVTSY O.

Prut River

Dniester

RIVNO O.
RIVNO

Pripyat River

ZHITOMIR O.
ZHITOMIR

DNIEPER UPLAND

KIEV O.
KIEV
Dnieper River

CHERNOBYL

CHERNIGOV O.
CHERNIGOV
CHERNIGOV
KHMELNITSKY
Desna River

PRILUKI

BELAYA
TSERKOV

KANEV

CHERKASSY
CHERKASSY O.

KHMELNITSKY O.

VINNITSA
VINNITSA O.

Bug
Bug

Southern Bug

EASTERN BOUNDARY OF TERRITORY ADDED TO
UKRAINE & MOLDAVIA AFTER WWII

0   200 KMS.

52

32

28

24

32

28

24

48

Figure 6-1   The Southwest Region.

The most recent exchanges of territory took place immediately prior to and during World War II, when the two southeastern provinces of Poland, Volhynia and Galicia, were regained by the Soviet Union, provinces of Bessarabia and Bukovina were taken over from Rumania, and the so-called Ruthenian area in eastern Czechoslovakia was incorporated into the Soviet Union to become what is now known as the Carpathian Ukraine. This piece of territory from Czechoslovakia had never been in the Russian Empire and therefore is a totally new piece of territory for the Soviet Union. World War II thus resulted in a gain of territory for the Soviet Union within the Ukrainian Republic that amounts to about the western third of the Southwest Economic Region, west of the cities of Rovno and Ternopol.

PHYSICAL LANDSCAPE

Landform

The Southwest Economic Region consists of four geomorphic provinces, the Volhynian-Podolian Upland, the Pripyat-Dnieper Lowland (Polesye), the Carpathian Mountains, and the Hungarian Plain. Of these, the Volhynian-Podolian Upland and the Pripyat-Dnieper Lowland occupy by far the largest territories. Much of the region is taken up by the Volhynian, Podolian, and Dnieper Uplands that stretch in a west-northwest–east-southeast direction across the central Ukraine from the western border to the Dnieper River. This is the main body of the broad upwarp that runs across the Ukraine and continues east of the Dnieper as the Donets Ridge, discussed in the last chapter. The surface of the upland consists of a rolling plain that is greatly incised by river valleys and ravines. Elevations, generally between 200–400 meters above sea level, reach a maximum of 472 meters in the northwest in the so-called Kamula Mountains east of the city of Lvov. On the north and northeast, the upland adjoins the Polesye, a very flat lowland; the boundary is distinctly marked by a twisting scarp that in places is as high as 100 meters. This distinct boundary continues

southward along the east side of the upland as the high right bank of the Dnieper River. In the south the boundary is indistinct, and the upland gradually descends and merges with the Black Sea Steppes.

The Volhynian Upland covers only a small territory in the northwestern part of the region and is separated by a distinct break from the Podolian Upland to the south, an elongated lowland that was formed by glaciofluvial flows during the Quaternary. The Volhynian Upland overlooks the Polesye Lowland to the north across a scarp 60–70 meters in height. Small obsequent streams have dissected the cuesta edge and penetrated southward deep into the plateau, producing a ragged zone of cuesta-form hills. In places the river valleys are up to 100 meters deep.

The glaciofluvial lowland between the Volhynian and Podolian Uplands is a marshy region very similar to the Polesye to the north, frequently known as the "Little Polesye." The Podolian Upland to the south overlooks the Little Polesye along a scarp running 150–200 meters in height. The Podolian Upland is somewhat higher and more dissected than the Volhynian Upland in the north. A particularly dense network of river valleys, gorges, and ravines characterizes the slope facing the Dniester River on the south. The rivers here flow in deep, narrow gorges with vertical banks carved from limestone, marble, and various other rocks, and the watersheds are very narrow, in many places assuming the form of jagged ridges.

The foundation of the uplands consists of the Ukrainian Crystalline Shield that extends from northwest to southeast across the region. In the eastern part around the Dnieper, granites and other crystalline rocks come close to the surface and sometimes actually outcrop, usually in river valleys. Throughout much of the region the area underwent a prolonged continental period all the way from the Precambrian to the Tertiary, so that the Precambrian crystalline rocks are overlain directly by Tertiary deposits and a thin layer of Quaternary materials. But in the so-called Lvov depression west of the city of Khmelnitskiy, the crystalline rocks are downwarped greatly, and sedimentary layers of Paleozoic and Mesozoic age reach thicknesses of as much as 3000 meters. Limestones, sandstones, and chalk are widely distributed. In the northwest these crop out to form picturesque chalk mountains. These deep sediments along the northeastern foothills of the Carpathians are rather heavily mineralized.

East of a line through the cities of Terno-pol-Kamenets-Podolskiy there is a region of highly eroded limestones scarps known as the Toltry Mountains. They include fantastic erosion formations reminiscent of towers or ruins. The Toltry are formed from the erosion of the remains of a barrier reef formed in a Miocene sea by mollusks, calcareous algae, and even coral. The ridges composing the Toltry run in a northnorthwest-south-southeast direction for a distance of about 250 kilometers over a width of about 4–6 kilometers. Elevations above sea level reach more than 400 meters, but local relief runs only 50–60 meters.

East of the Southern Bug River the upland is known as the Dnieper Upland. Here the sedimentary overburden is shallow, and in many places river valleys cutting as deep as 130 meters intersect the crystalline basement rock.

Glacial deposits are found only along the northeast and northwest peripheries of the Podolian Upland, but much of the remaining area shows some effects of glaciation. The river valleys generally contain many outwash deposits, and the interfluves usually are covered by a thick mantle of loess, which was probably formed primarily during the melting of glacial advances when the river valleys were clogged with fine sediment that was reworked by strong winds blowing off the ice sheet. In places loess is as much as 3–6 meters thick and reflects two or three different stages of deposition.

The northern third of the Southwest Economic Region is occupied by the Pripyat-Dnieper Lowland, otherwise known as the Polesye, an ill-drained plain that extends northward into the southeastern half of Belorussia, and northeastward up the Desna River toward Bryansk and Kaluga in the Cen-tral Economic Region of the Russian Republic. The main body of the lowland forms a huge triangle between the cities of Brest in southwestern Belorussia, Mogilev in east central Belorussia, and Kiev in north central Ukraine.

The Polesye is the westernmost of the sandy lowlands forming a discontinous belt along the southern fringe of the Moscow glacial advance. Farther east, in the Central and Volga-Vyatka Regions, are similar lowlands known as the Meshchera in southeastern Moscow Oblast and the Volga-Vetluga Lowland father northeast. The Pripyat-Dnieper Lowland is by far the largest of these. It represents primarily a great proglacial lake bed with associated marshes and swamps that has been largely filled in by sedimentation and vegetative growth. Much of the sediment has been fine sand that was eroded out of crumbly sandstone farther north and washed into this shallow lake by the melt waters of the glacial sheet. Much of the sand has been reworked by the wind, which has blown the finer materials southward and deposited them as loess over a broad area of the Ukraine. A residue of sand, often in the form of dunes, remains in the area of the Polesye itself. Present streams are slowly carrying these materials southward, which accounts for the beautiful white sandy beaches and sandbars in such rivers as the Dnieper.

The Polesye was affected time and again during the Quaternary by glaciation. The Dnieper glacial stage was the thickest of all those covering the Russian plain, and it covered the Polesye with a thick mantle of ice that extended far to the south down the Dnieper Valley. But the present topography of the Polesye was formed during the last glacial stage, the Valday, that extended only to the northern edge of the Polesye. An enormous proglacial water basin was formed that eventually filled and overflowed eastward through the Tsna and Navlya Rivers into the valley of the Oka. Since the main body of the Polesye lies in Belorussia, further description will be delayed until that region is discussed.

With the acquisition of eastern Czechoslovakia after World War II, the Soviet Union came into possession of the central portion of the Carpathian Mountains. They consist of a system of separate ranges running northwest-southeast lying mostly at elevations from 500–1500 meters above sea level. Elevation generally increases southeastward, and the highest peak within the Soviet Union is reached at Mount Goverla in the headwaters of the Prut River at an elevation of 2061 meters above sea level. The mountains differ from one place to another because of the rock structure. The higher portions of the mountains are generally composed of crystalline rocks with rather sharp ridges, but in places where weaker sediments exist rounded summits are common. Frequent cuesta formations exist in sedimentary areas. These are generally capped by limestones or conglomerates and underlain by shales. On the southwestern side of the range is a region of extinct volcanic eruptions that have produced conical hills standing 700 meters or so above the lowland to the south.

The watershed range that forms the divide between northeasterly and southerly flowing streams is being eaten into from both sides by the Dniester and its tributaries on the north and the Tisza on the south, which is flowing down to the Danube. Since the Tisza has the lower base level, generally the watershed range is steeper on the southern side than on the north.

During the Dnieper glacial stage the continental ice moved southward into the foothills of the Carpathians and met mountain glaciers coming down the northern slopes of the mountains. In subsequent glacial stages the continental glaciation did not reach the foothills but the mountains accumulated glaciers on their slopes. Therefore, the present topography of the whole mountain range is strongly influenced by glacial features; corries, cirques, and tarn lakes abound. The mountains have more of an alpine aspect than one would expect just from their elevations.

The fourth geomorphic region covers only a very small area in the Soviet Union. This is the northeastern fringe of the Hungarian Plain that lies south of the Carpathian Mountains in the region known as Transcarpathian Ukraine. Within the Soviet Union this plain is only about 20 kilometers wide and has elevations of 100–120 meters above sea level. This is a piedmont depression with accumulated thick alluvium that has produced a monotonously flat floor broken here and there by low but conspicuous volcanic remnants.

Climate

The climate of the region is temperate continental. Temperatures during July average about 18°C (64°F) in the west and 22°C (72°F) in the eastern part of the region east of the Dnieper River. In the Transcarpathian area July averages around 20°C (68°F). During January temperatures average about −2°C in the southeast and −8°C in the northeast. Precipitation generally decreases from about 600–700 millimeters in the northwest to 450–500 millimeters in the southeast. In the Carpathian Mountains amounts may rise to 1200 millimeters. In the Transcarpathian Lowland annual precipitation is slightly over 700 millimeters. Thus, the climate of the southwestern region generally is a little cooler and a little more moist than it is in the Donets-Dnieper Region.

Characteristic of the climate in this region are the frequent winter thaws that may dissipate the snow entirely. These are usually associated with southern cyclones moving northeastward across the region.

The Southwest Region was originally an area of primarily mixed forests and wooded steppes. The Polesye in the north contained mixed and broadleafed forests of pine, oak, hornbeam, alder, ash, and aspen. Pine was the dominant tree. In the more ill-drained areas marsh grasses took over, and in some places occupied as much as 50 percent of the area. Although heavy lumbering operations have been carried on in the Polesye for many years and a significant amount of drainage and cultivation has been developed, forests still occupy a great deal of the area. They are best preserved in the southeast where they occupy 60 percent of the land.

In the upland to the south broadleaf forests predominated and were intermingled with steppe grasses. Oak, ash, Norway maple, linden, and hornbeam were the most common trees. Except for the steeper valley slopes, most of the forests and the grasses have been replaced by cultivation.

In the Carpathians up to elevations of about 600 meters the natural vegetation is mixed forests with a predominance of oak and mixtures of hornbeam, beech, maple, linden, and others. Between 600 and 1200 meters the forest changes to a beech-fir-spruce mixture. These forests are particularly dense. The beech often occur in pure stands. At higher elevations spruce begins to predominate. Between 1200 and 1500 meters the forests are almost pure spruce. Above 1500 meters few trees exist, and mountain meadows predominate. These are dotted with dwarf pine and mountain juniper.

Steppe grasses generally predominate in the Transcarpathian Lowland and also in the southeastern portion of the Dnieper Upland. Now almost all the grasses have been plowed under and the land put into cultivation.

Soils

Soils vary from northwest to southeast according to climatic characteristics and drainage conditions. In the Polesye in the north there are generally podsolized soils on the better-drained land and bog soils in the more poorly drained land. Throughout the Volhynian-Podolian-Dnieper Upland the soils are various grades of chernozems with very significant admixtures of loess. Thus, the rougher topography of the upland is counterbalanced by the very rich soil to make this region one of the most productive agricultural areas in the country. Chernozem soils also predominate in the Transcarpathian Lowland.

AGRICULTURE

The Southwest Economic Region is in first place among all economic regions in the Soviet Union in agricultural production. It annually averages about 10.2 percent of the total production of the U.S.S.R. It produces about 50 percent of all the granulated sugar of the country, 20 percent of all the potatoes, 16 percent of all the flax, 25 percent of all the potato and grain alcohol, 10 percent of all the starch, 10 percent of all the flour, 15 percent of all the tobacco, 12 percent of all the butter and milk products, and a wide variety of other crops.

Of course, the crops vary considerably from one place to another because of natural conditions. In the wooded steppe, which covers the bulk of the region, more than 40 percent of the sown area is in various grains, particularly winter wheat, barley, corn for grain, and buckwheat. Sugar beets are the specialty crop of the area. The oblasts of Vinnitsa, Cherkassy, Khmelnitskiy, Kiev, and Ternopol are the heart of the sugar beet belt of the entire country. Also, large acreages are occupied by legume crops and potatoes, and there is a significant amount of sunflowers, tobacco, southern hemp, corn for silage and green fodder, vegetables, and fruits. Hops is a specialty crop. (See Fig. 5-3)

In the Polesye, the main crops are rye, winter wheat, oats, flax, potatoes, and buckwheat. This is the main buckwheat-growing area in the Ukraine. Buckwheat is well adapted to the cool, moist conditions of the area and is used extensively for human food in various forms, particularly kasha, a gruel made of cooked whole grains of buckwheat.

On either side of the Carpathians and in some of the intermountain valleys there are many vineyards and orchards.

Livestock raising has been developed to a high degree throughout the Southwest Region. Most of it consists of dairy cattle and swine, particularly in the better farming areas. This region produces more butter, milk, and cheese than any other region in the country. In the Carpathians a significant number of sheep are grazed.

The rural population is very dense in the Southwest Region. The peasants live in large villages crammed helter-skelter in all the river valleys. Only in adjacent Moldavia is the rural population denser and the villages larger. Farther north population density diminishes and individual villages decrease in size.

RESOURCES AND INDUSTRIES

Agricultural resources are by far the greatest resources in the Southwest Region. Mineral resources are rather sparse, although in the northeastern foothills of the Carpathians there are significant deposits of coal, oil, gas, sulfur, and potassium and magnesium salts. There is some more oil and gas in Chernigov Oblast in the northeastern part of the region, brown coal and table salt in Transcarpathia, and large deposits of peat in the Polesye in the north. In most cases these are small deposits, important only to their localities. (See Fig. 5-4)

Probably of greatest national significance are the potassium and magnesium salt deposits, which, with those in the upper Kama River Valley of the western Urals and the more recently discovered deposits in southeastern Belorussia, constitute the only three significant producing areas in the country. The Carpathian deposits are credited with 7.5 percent of the U.S.S.R. potash reserves and about 14 percent of the potash production. Unlike the Urals and Belorussian deposits, which consist of chlorides only, the Carpathian deposits consist mainly of sulfates. Sulfates are used as fertilizers for crops that do not tolerate chlorine, such as potatoes, flax, alfalfa, tobacco, citrus fruits, and vineyards. An expansion program started during the 1960s involving both the production of commercial sulfate fertilizers and the development of a major chemical complex at Kalush, producing a wide range of products from magnesium metal to chlorine.

The centers of the potash mining are the towns of Kalush and Stebnik. Kalush has been developed into a highly complex chemical enterprise. It is now piping in ethylene from a Hungarian petrochemical plant and producing vinyl chloride. It is also now deriving hydrogen from natural gas for a large urea-resin unit, in addition to producing potassium sulfate and magnesium metal. Much of this development at Kalush took place during the late 1960s. The Stebnik-Kalush complex is one of the main potash-fertilizer-producing areas in the country.

Also of national significance is the sulfur mining area near Rozdol. This is the largest native sulfur operation in the Soviet Union. It annually accounts for about 80 percent of the Soviet Union's native sulfur output, although native sulfur itself accounts for only about 19 percent of total sulfur output in the country. A new deposit of sulfur at Yavorov near Rozdol in the Carpathian region is also being developed.

Probably the next most significant resource is the natural gas district around Dashava in the north Carpathians. This has been producing since before World War II when the region was acquired by the Soviet Union. Until the mid-1950s this was the only gas-producing region in the Ukraine and one of the major ones in the country, which at that time had very low overall production. Now it has been greatly overshadowed in the Ukraine by Shebelinka in the Donets-Dnieper Region and produced only about 20 percent of the Ukraine's total gas output in the early 1970s. The old west Ukrainian fields have thus been relegated to a minor role in the country's production as total production has expanded rapidly. (See Fig. 5-4)

The old pipelines radiating out from Dashava have been connected with those coming in from the southeast from Shebelinka and the North Caucasian fields, via Kiev, and from the northeast from the Western Siberian fields, and there has been reversal of gas flow on the pipelines leading northeast-southwest. The "Bratstvo" pipeline going to Czechoslovakia has been extended to Austria, Italy, West Germany, and France. Although the Dashava district supplies very little of this gas, the area is the focal point of the pipelines bringing in gas from the northeast, east, and southeast. An old gas-processing plant exists in the town of Borislav near Dashava, and a new one was built during the 1960s at the town of Dolina in the same general area. A gas plant is now being built in the Priluki fields of Chernigov Oblast east of the city of Kiev.

The oil fields of western Ukraine have been producing for quite a long time also, with the primary center at Drogobych. Oil refineries have been built in Drogobych and in the large city of Lvov to the north. But, as in the case of the gas fields, the old west Ukrainian oil fields have been superseded since 1960 by new discoveries on the left bank of the Dnieper, including the Chernigov area as well as the neighboring regions of Poltava, Sumy, and Kharkov Oblasts in the Donets-Dnieper Region, supplying the oil refinery at Kremenchug on the Dnieper. In 1970, the left-bank fields accounted for 80 percent of Ukrainian oil production (about 14 million tons).

In addition to local oil supplies, a branch of the Druzhba oil pipeline crosses the Southwest Region on its way to Czechoslovakia and Hungary. Oil can be tapped off the Druzhba line for use in the Southwest Region.

Both bituminous and lignite coal have been mined for a great number of years in the foothills of the Carpathians for local consumption, primarily for heating and electric power generation. The coal, gas, and oil of the region are all important in the generation of electricity, and the region has developed a number of large thermal electric plants. These are in addition to the two recently completed hydroelectric plants on the Dnieper at Kiev and Kanev. The Kanev Dam was the last of the construction projects on the Dnieper to be completed. It began power production in November 1972. It is to have an ultimate generating capacity of 420,000 kilowatts. Kiev began production in 1965. Its capacity is 352,400 kilowatts. (See Fig. 5-2)

The Sovets are now turning to nuclear power to solve the power needs of this region. Two large stations are under construction in the northern part of the region. The most advanced is at Chernobyl on the high right bank of the Pripyat River north of Kiev near the Belorussian border; it will have a capacity of 2 million kilowatts. A new urban settlement was established at the power site in 1972 and was named Pripyat. The other station is to be constructed near Rovno farther west.

The Southwest Region is crossed by the international electrical transmission line called "Mir." This branches in three directions from the Transcarpathian city of Mukachevo and goes to Rumania, Hungary, and Czechoslovakia. It is fed primarily by thermal plants in the Donets Basin, the Kharkov region, and the Kiev region.

A nickel mine and smelter went into operation at Pobugskoye on the Southern Bug River in 1972. The plant in Pobugskoye smelts the ore in electric furnaces with coke to produce a refined ferronickel that is suitable as an alloy in making special steels.

The processing of coal, oil, gas, salt, and sulfur has provided the basis for a rapidly expanding chemical industry in the region, particularly the production of gas-based mineral fertilizers, which are in great demand in this heavily producing agricultural area. Two large new nitrogen fertilizer plants were developed during the 1960s at Rovno and Cherkassy as nitrogen fertilizer production also shifted from coke-based gases in the Gorlovka and Dneprodzerzhinsk areas to the use of natural gas. The Ukraine now produces about one-fourth of all Soviet nitrogen fertilizer. Other chemical industries include plastics, synthetic fibers, and synthetic rubber. Recently an automobile tire factory was established in the city of Belaya Tserkov west of Kiev. This will supply such automotive factories as the truck plant in Kremenchug, the Zaporozhets automobile plant in Zaporozhye, the bus assembly plant at Lvov, and the new automobile plant that is being built in the city of Lutsk in the northwestern part of the Southwest Region.

The machine-building industries probably employ more people and have a greater value of manufacture than does any other group of industries in the entire Southwest Economic Region. These are scattered throughout many of the cities. In general, there are no outstanding individual plants or products, but a wide variety of small plants turn out electrical equipment, machine tools, durable consumer items, and transport equipment of various sorts. The two automotive plants in the region are the old bus assembly plant at Lvov, which produces about 10,000 city and intercity buses every year, and the new plant just mentioned at the city of Lutsk, which is to turn out a multipurpose vehicle called the "Volynyanka," primarily for rural use, which can carry six passengers or about half a ton of cargo. The two main centers of the machine-construction industry in the Southwest Region are Kiev and Lvov, the two largest cities in the region.

The food industries are highly developed in the Southwest Region, based on the rich agriculture and the high density of population. Such things as sugar refining, dairy processing, flour milling, and the manufacture of vegetable oils from sunflowers are outstanding, but there are a wide range of other food industries as well scattered throughout most of the cities.

In the intermontane valleys of the Carpathians the "Gutsuls" or "Verkhoviners" (mountain dwellers) are noted for their expertise in logging and wood carving.

CITIES

The Southwest Economic Region has not seen the tremendous urbanization that has gone on in such places as the Donets-Dnieper Region. Most of the cities are simply regional centers that serve their rich agricultural hinterlands and have industrialized to a certain extent in order to process local products and supply jobs for surplus laborers. The two large cities, Kiev and Lvov, owe their origins primarily to historical events. Both are very ancient cities and have been important regional centers for more than 1000 years. Most of the other larger cities are oblast centers that effectively control individual market areas, and a variety of smaller towns owe their existence to certain mining activities or certain industrial developments. Many of these have already been mentioned. A summary of the largest cities follows.

Kiev

The largest city in the region by far is Kiev with a 1974 population of 1,887,000. It is the third largest city in the Soviet Union after Moscow and Leningrad. It flourished during the ninth to thirteenth centuries as the capital of Kievan Rus and again from the fifteenth century onward as the cultural and religious focus of the Ukrainian Cossacks. In 1934 it was made the capital of the Ukrainian S.S.R. Damaged severely during World War II, Kiev has been rebuilt into perhaps the most beautiful city in the Soviet Union. The opportunity has been taken during the reconstruction to lay modern sewage, gas, and water lines and to build a subway system under the city.

The natural setting is magnificent. Situated on the high loess-covered western bluff of the Dnieper, at the confluence of its main left-bank tributary, the Desna, the city overlooks the blue water and white sandbars of the many-channeled river that flows in a large bend around the northern side of the city. Beautiful beaches abound along the banks of the river, for great quantities of white glacial sand have been carried down from the Polesye in the north. The wind has whipped some of this sand out of the immediate flood-plain of the river and has created extensive areas of sand dunes on the flat, low-lying meadowland to the east. A surprising number of boats ply the river, and considerable quantities of timber are floated down from the northern forests. With the completion of all the reservoirs, nagivation has been greatly improved, but many of the sandy beaches have been submerged.

Tree-lined double boulevards with broad sidewalks are modern innovations, but the gilded domes of St. Sophia's Cathedral, the oldest cathedral in the country (A.D. 1037), and the catacombs of the Pecherski Monastery in the loess bluffs are reminders of the old Kiev. A tall, graceful obelisk commemorating the heroes of World War II stands in a park along the rim of the high western bluff, overlooking the huge gray statue of St. Vladimir facing down the Dnieper. In addition to these monuments, Kiev is the center for the Ukrainian Academy of Sciences and has one of the main universities in the country; it dates from 1834. A great variety of institutes, museums, theaters, and other cultural institutions round out the amenities of this cultural center of the Ukrainians.

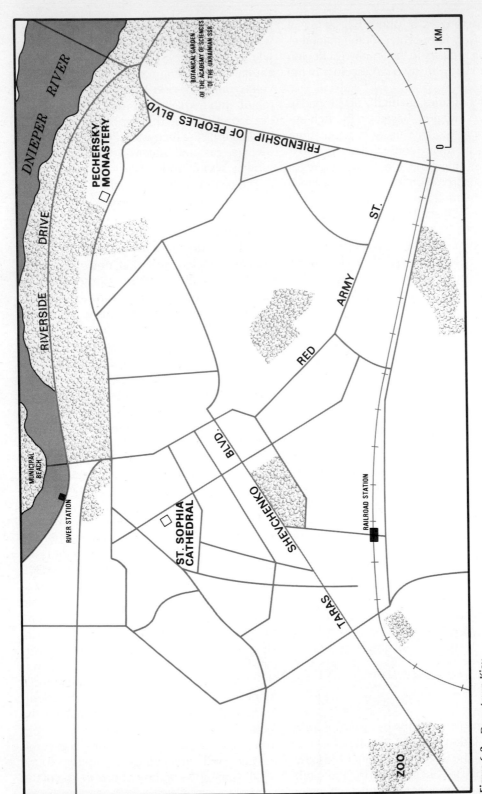

Figure 6-2 Downtown Kiev.

Modern Kiev has a wide variety of diversified industries. It manufactures riverboats and other marine craft, airplanes, streetcars, excavators, electrical equipment, machine tools and lathes, and telephone and cinema equipment. It is the main center for light industry in the Ukraine, turning out woolen, silk, and synthetic cloth, leather goods, and shoes. It is also a major center for the processing of food, including sugar, wine, butter, flour, baked goods, and so forth.

Lvov

Second largest city in the Southwest Region is Lvov, with a 1974 population of 605,000. It was founded in 1241 and has retained a medieval aspect with cobbled streets and high, narrow, steep-roofed houses. It was in the Austro-Hungarian Empire until 1920. With the breakup of the empire after World War I, it became part of Poland. In 1939 the Soviet Union annexed the territory and made it part of the Ukraine. As the cultural and religious center of western Ukraine, it is growing rapidly. Among the industries that have been established are a bus assembly plant, a fork-lift-truck plant, various industrial instruments, a large television factory, and other electronics industries, as well as glass works, chemicals, food industries, and light

industries. It is the third most important rail center in the Ukraine after Kiev and Kharkov. It also has a major university and one of the centers of the Academy of Sciences of the U.S.S.R.

Other Cities

The other cities of the Southwest Region are considerably smaller. Eleven more have populations between 100,000 and 300,000. Most of these are oblast centers or regional trading centers of one sort or another, and some of them are gaining important individual industries, which have already been mentioned. In order of size, these cities are Vinnitsa with a population of 264,000, Zhitomir with a population of 209,000, Chernigov with a population 205,000, Cherkassy with a population of 204,000, Chernovtsy with a population of 199,000, Rovno with a population of 147,000, Khmelnitskiy with a population of 144,000, Belaya-Tserkov with a population of 128,000, Ivano-Frankovsk with a population of 128,000, Lutsk with a population of 115,000, and Ternopol with a population of 112,000.

In addition, the smaller city of Uzhgorod, "the city on the Uzh River," is the governmental center of Transcarpathian Oblast. It is the cultural and economic center of the

Figure 6-3 Ukrainian village in dissected topography of Podolian Upland, central Ukraine.

Figure 6-4   Typical Ukrainian khata with whitewashed adobe walls and thatched roof, Kanev.

region that was acquired from Czecho-slovakia after World War II. The Soviets have established a university there that is one of the youngest schools for higher education in the country. In 1974 Uzhgorod had a population of 72,000.

PROSPECTS FOR THE FUTURE

The Southwest Economic Region, along with adjacent Moldavia, has perhaps the best combination of soils, moisture resources, and heat resources available in the Soviet Union for agriculture. It is somewhat more moist than the southeast Ukraine and somewhat warmer than much of the Central Chernozem Region. The Central Chernozem Region and the Kuban region of the North Caucasus would be its closest rivals. Therefore, it has always been a rich agricultural region and still is primarily agricultural. Although many di-

versified industries have been established in most of the larger cities of the region, there has been no major effort to increase the relative position of this economic region in the industrialization drive in the entire country. Therefore, it appears that the role of the Southwest Region will remain much as it is, one of the better agricultural regions of the country with a modest amount of urbanization and industrialization that supplements the agriculture. An existing pool of labor may be drawn increasingly into manufacturing industry as part of the Comecon integration program, as has been done at Kalush.

READING LIST

- Gerenchuk, K.I., *Priroda Ukrainskikh Karpat* (The Nature of Ukrainian Carpathia), Lvov, 1968 (in Russian).
- *Sovetskoe prikarpate* (Soviet Carpathia), Karpati, Uzhgorod, 1975, 219 pp. (in Russian).

South Economic Region

	Area (km²)	Population	Persons/km²	Percent Urban
Odessa Oblast	33,000	2,470,000	74.2	58
Nikolayev Oblast	25,000	1,181,000	47.8	57
Kherson Oblast	28,000	1,071,000	37.9	57
Crimea Oblast	27,000	1,943,000	71.9	65
Total	113,000	6,665,000	59.0	

chapter 7

the south economic region

The South Economic Region consists of the southwestern part of the Ukrainian S.S.R., primarily the so-called Black Sea Steppes and the Crimean Peninsula. Administratively this region is composed of Odessa, Nikolayev, Kherson, and Crimea Oblasts. These four oblasts total an area of 113,000 square kilometers and contain 6,665,000 people. Territorially this is the smallest economic region in the country, excluding Moldavia from the list of economic regions, as the Soviets do. It is second smallest in population, but does have more people than the huge Far East Region. Moldavia, next door to the South Economic Region, has less territory and fewer people than the South, and will be considered in the next chapter. The South Region has an average population density of 59 people per square kilometer, which varies from 38 in Kherson Oblast to more than 74 in Odessa Oblast. About 59 percent of the people in the South Region are considered to be urban dwellers, which is about average for the U.S.S.R. Crimea Oblast with its many resort areas is the most highly urbanized part of the region.

131

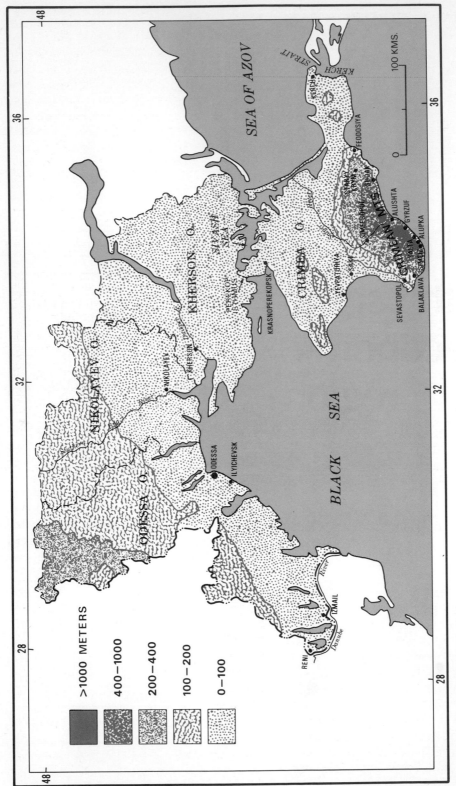

Figure 7-1 The South Economic Region.

TERRITORIAL ACQUISITION AND SETTLEMENT

The territory immediately to the north of the Black and Azov Seas was finally incorporated into the Russian Empire during the reign of Catherine the Great when the territory was taken over from the Turks during a series of campaigns in 1774–1791. Prior to its control by the Ottoman Empire the area had been subject to Greek settlement from the south and to a series of transgressions by nomadic tribes that crisscrossed the region even before the Christian era. Kerch is the site of the ancient city of Panticapaeum, the capital of the ancient Kingdom of the Bosporus. Archeological digs on Mithridates Hill in the city of Kerch have already unearthed a forum, galleries, and other structures. Burial mounds and other abundant archeological materials attest to the richness and variety of the early civilizations in this area. The greatest remains are those of the Scythians, whose burial mounds yield up great quantities of fine crafted utensils and other artifacts. But the Greeks probably left the greatest imprint on the present cities.

After the territory was secured for Russia in the eighteenth century, Catherine the Great, who was of German origin, encouraged rapid argicultural settlement of the land by large numbers of new German colonists, who became known as the Black Sea Germans. Thus, the area became a rich mixture of Greeks, Russians, Germans, Bulgarians, and a number of other nationalities in diminishing numbers. During World War II the Black Sea Germans were accused of collaborating with the German armies, and many were evacuated eastward. Many of those who remained in the region retreated westward later in the war with the retreating German armies back to Germany. Thus, at the present time there are few if any Germans in this region.

Also during World War II the Crimean Tatars were accused of collaborating with the enemy. The Tatars had occupied much of the north Crimean plain since the sixteenth century when the Golden Horde broke up into the three main groups centered in Kazan, As-trakhan, and the Crimea. In the Crimea most of them had become farmers. During the nineteenth and first part of the twentieth centuries Russians moved into many of the cities of the Crimea. As long as the Crimea was occupied primarily by Tatars and Russians, the territory remained under the jurisdiction of the Russian Republic. But after World War II Ukrainians occupied much of the land that had been vacated by the Crimean Tatars and the Black Sea Germans, and in 1954 the Crimea was made a part of the Ukraine; it eventually became a part of the South Economic Region. The Izmail district of southwestern Odessa Oblast was incorporated into the Russian Empire in 1812, but was then lost to the Austro-Hungarian Empire and eventually became part of Rumania. Then, as a consequence of World War II, it became part of the Soviet Union again. Most of the territory gained from eastern Rumania during World War II was incorporated into the Moldavian S.S.R., but the Izmail district was put into the Ukraine because its population was primarily Ukrainian. This has added considerable territory to Odessa Oblast and has caused it to take on a very elongated form in a crescent shape that wraps around the southern and eastern borders of the Moldavian S.S.R.

PHYSICAL LANDSCAPE

Landform

The South Economic Region contains two distinctly different geomorphic regions. The first is the very flat Black Sea Steppes occupying the northern fringes of the Black and Azov Seas on the mainland and extending across the narrow Perekop Isthmus onto the northern two-thirds of the Crimean Peninsula. The second is the Crimean Mountains along the southeastern fringe of the Crimean Peninsula. The southern fringe of the Podolian Upland is also in the northern parts of Odessa and Nikolayev Oblasts, but this type of topography was covered in the previous chapter and will not be repeated here.

The Black Sea Steppes are a flat alluvial

lowland that slopes gently southward toward the Black and Azov Seas. In places the feature-lessness of the landscape is broken slightly by low, indistinct abrasion scarps that mark former higher levels of the sea. A number of streams cross the steppes on their way south-ward to the sea; the major ones are the Dnieper, the Southern Bug, and Dniester. All of these are heavily silted and carry much sediment to the sea. The sediment is reworked by waves and long-shore currents in the shal-low northern part of the Black Sea and the Sea of Azov to produce sand spits and bars that extend for as much as 100 kilometers. In many cases these sand deposits have blocked the mouths of long estuaries that have been formed in the lower stream valleys by the postglacial rise in sea level to form stagnant lagoons. The most extensive such body of water is the Sivash Sea east of the Perekop Isthmus, cut off from the western end of the Sea of Azov by the very long Arabat sandbar. Everywhere along the northern coast, slopes are so gentle that the land merges into the sea, with many mud flats and deltaic peninsulas and islands. The wind has reworked much of the alluvial sediments in the Black Sea Steppes and formed broad, shallow deflation hol-lows that may contain temporary lakes during spring melt waters. In places dunes have been formed. In other places there are deposits of loess.

The flat dryish plain continues onto the northern two-thirds of the Crimean Peninsula, sloping gently upward toward the south, and then is suddenly terminated as the Crimean Mountains thrust up abruptly to heights of more than 1500 meters in the southeastern part of the peninsula. The highest peak is Roman-Kosh, which rises to 1545 meters.

The Crimean Mountains are a western ex-tension of the geosynclinal zone that con-tinues east-southeastward through the Caucasus into Central Asia. In the Black Sea area displacement along a major fault zone has separated the shallow northern shelf of the Black Sea from the deep-water basin to the south. Although folding and vulcanism have both entered the picture in the Crimean Mountains, the present mountain range was produced primarily by faulting along this major fault zone, so that the range exhibits the aspects of a massive fault block with its steep fault scarp on the south and its gentle dip slope on the north. Topographically there are three fairly distinct ranges, which owe their origins primarily to differential erosion on the tilted rock structure. The highest, or main, range lies on the south next to the sea and is made up primarily of a series of plateaulike

Figure 7-2   The southern slopes of the Crimean Mountains. Note the sheer limestone cliffs in the background. Vineyards are interspersed on the steep foothills that plunge abruptly to the sea.

uplands known locally by the Tatar word, *yayla,* which means upland pastures. These plateau segments have been formed by deep dissection by short, steep, intermittent streams flowing southward to the sea over massive limestone that in places rises unbroken in precipitous cliffs as much as 1000 meters. These cliffs form imposing backdrops to the coastal area of the Crimea. Their cloud-enshrouded tops look down on the sun-drenched avalanche and terrace topography of the foothills that plunge steeply down to the sea.

On the upland surfaces of the yayla there is a good deal of karst topography, especially in the west, due primarily to the trickling downward of melt waters from local snow fields through the jointed massive limestone. Much of this probably took place during the Pleistocene when the upper parts of the Crimean range were occupied by local mountain glaciers and snow fields, but the process is still going on. Much of the annual precipitation in the mountains falls as snow during winter, and winds drift the snow into the lower hollows where snow fields accumulate and persist through spring into early summer. Thus, there is a prolonged period each year of karstnival processes during the prolonged thawing period after winter.

Speleologists have explored more than 800 caves in the mountains and foothills of the Crimea. Some of these go 500 meters below the surface of the earth and contain caverns 90 meters deep. The Crimean Oblast Soviet has recommended that some of these be set aside as nature preserves. It is planned that the more spectacular ones will be opened to tourists.

The underground solution of limestone, combined with frequent earthquakes, provides the basis for many landslides, collapses, and avalanches. Much of southeastern coastal Crimea in the narrow strip between the limestone cliffs and the sea consists of a rumpled surface pitching steeply toward the sea that attests to the continuing landslide activity. It is particularly severe in areas where impervious clays underly friable layers and produce a water-slickened base. Occasionally roads, buildings, and conduits are destroyed. A special station for the study of landslides has been established in the Crimea. Where collapses of undermined limestone have occurred the piles of jumbled debris are referred to in Russian as *khaosy.*

The other two mountain ridges north of the yayla are two cuestas running parallel to the main range known as the second or "piedmont," and the third, or "outer," ranges. These are formed on fairly thick, resistant limestones underlain by shales. They are separated by inner lowlands dismembered by intermittent streams.

Figure 7-3   The beach at Yalta.

The streams of the Crimea are small and usually dry up completely during the dry summer. The largest is the Salgir, which heads in the main range and runs northward to the Sivash Sea. Its upper valley forms a low pass through the midsection of the mountains to provide a route for a highway that leads from the main Crimean transportation center of Simferopol southeastward across the mountains to Alushta and the other coastal cities.

The topography of the southern part of the Crimea is complicated by occasional volcanic features represented primarily by laccolithic remnants, but here and there also by eruptions of andesites. These are particularly prevalent in the hilly Kerch Peninsula, which is separated from mountain Crimea by the narrow Akmonay Isthmus. Here numerous mud volcanoes form low hills as much as 45 meters high that dot extensive fields of hardened mud. Their craters are full of ooze that sometimes emits bubbles of gas and gradually seeps onto the surrounding countryside. The gases contain petroleum hydrocarbons that are sometimes flammable.

Climate

The South Economic Region is the warmest region in the country outside of the Caucasus and the southern extremity of Central Asia.

This is undoubtedly why it is currently gaining population rather rapidly while regions around it are relatively static, and a few oblasts in the neighboring Southwest Region are actually losing population. Crimea Oblast is gaining population particularly rapidly. This is due primarily to heavy immigration. People seem to be moving southward for milder climatic conditions and more recreational amenities.

Highest average temperatures and mildest winters are found along the southeastern coast of the Crimean Mountains, which afford some protection from cold northerly air during the winter. Yalta averages 3.5°C during February, its coldest month, and the coldest temperature it has ever experienced is −15°C (5°F). Just to the north of the Crimean Mountains, Simferopol averages −0.6°C during February and has experienced temperatures as low as −29°C. The average temperature during summer also is significantly warmer in Yalta than in Simferopol, but the absolute maximum temperature is lower in Yalta. Yalta averages 23.9°C (75°F) in July, while Simferopol averages only 20.6°C. However, Simferopol has experienced a temperature as high as 40°C, while Yalta has experienced only 39°C. Farther west on the mainland, Odessa is warmer in summer and colder in winter than Simferopol. It averages 22.1°C

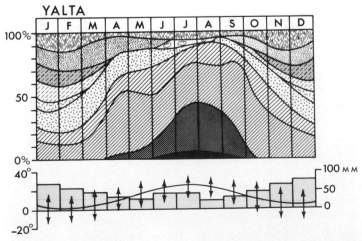

Figure 7-4   Weather types, temperature, and precipitation at Yalta. For legend, see page 6.

during July and −2.8°C during its coldest month, January. The growing season, as signified by the frost-free period, is relatively long at all three stations, 215 days at Odessa, 194 days at Simferopol, and 247 days at Yalta.

The South Region is known for its sunny summers. Yalta averages less than one day with overcast skies during July, Simferopol one, and Odessa only 2.1 during its clearest month, August. Winters are considerably cloudier. Yalta averages more than 16 days during December with overcast skies, Simferopol 14.5, and Odessa 19.7. The great difference in cloudiness between winter and summer is due to the regime of cyclonic storms, which are active during the winter and relatively absent during the summer. During winter the Mediterranean-Black Sea is a major route for cyclonic storms skirting the southern fringes of Eurasia.

On the mainland scattered thundershowers during summer bring more precipitation into the area than do the widespread cyclonic storms of winter. Odessa averages 116 millimeters of rainfall during June-August and only 85 millimeters during December-February. Simferopol shows a similar seasonal difference, with somewhat more precipitation in all seasons. Only at Yalta do the winter storms predominate, but not as much as is commonly assumed. Yalta averages 208 millimeters of precipitation during December-February and 113 millimeters during June-August. Therefore, even in Yalta there is considerable shower activity during summer.

Although the Crimean coast is often cited as the only area of Mediterranean climate in the Soviet Union, it is not a classic example. It is not very dry in summer and it is not very mild in winter. The famous resorts along the southeast Crimean coast do not enjoy the exalted climatic conditions of the typical Mediterranean region. And beaches are generally lacking. The mountains plunge off so steeply to the sea that the smaller intermittent streams flowing down their southeastern slopes carry jagged, coarse sediment onto the beaches and produce a rubble of subangular rocks several inches in diameter. Vigorous storm waves on the Black Sea wash away any finer materials that might be developed over time by wave action. Therefore, sunbathers find it necessary to rent slat platforms on which to lie to protect themselves from the sharp stones. There are broad sandy beaches in nonmountainous parts of Crimea, such as at Yevpatoriya on the west coast, which has become a popular children's resort, but here the winters are much more severe than along the southeastern coast.

All of the South Region suffers from drought. Of the three climatic stations cited, Yalta receives the greatest annual precipitation, 560 millimeters (22–23 inches). Simferopol receives 528 millimeters, and Odessa only 389. Therefore, without irrigation, agriculture is limited to drought-resistant crops. The region is known for its sukhovey conditions and dust storms, which are most noticeable in summer, but which may actually produce more severe soil erosion during winter when strong, persistent northeasterly winds blow across the snowless plains along the southern periphery of the western nose of the Asiatic High.

Although snow is fairly common during winter, and blizzard conditions can be experienced with strong northeasterly surface winds ahead of warm fronts in the northeasterly sectors of cyclonic storms moving across the region, the snow does not lie on the ground very long, and midwinter thaws are common. At Odessa on the average only 33 days per year have a consistent snow cover, and it accumulates to only about 5 centimeters (2 inches). Simferopol experiences 39 days with snow cover, with a maximum depth of about 12 centimeters. Yalta experiences only 11 days of snow cover with a maximum depth of about 6 centimeters. The uplands of the yayla, of course, receive considerably more winter snow, and it lies on the ground much longer. Snow collects in the karst depressions where it persists until the middle of summer, functioning as a sort of cistern supplying small reservoirs of water to feed springs near the southern coast.

Periods of thawing during winter are enhanced by foehn winds on either side of the mountains, depending on the wind direction.

Although they are not very strongly developed on either side, they are somewhat more significant on the northern slopes where they develop more intensely during the passage of southern cyclones.

Vegetation and Soil

Much of the Black Sea Steppes and plains of the Crimean Peninsula originally was vegetated by various grasses. These produced chernozem and dark chestnut soils with many areas of somewhat saline solonetzes. Practically all of these steppe areas are now under cultivation. Some stunted forests appear in river valleys and on islands in the Black Sea. These consist primarily of elm, black poplar, silver poplar, willow, oak, birch, and aspen. On the gently sloping northern sides of the two cuestas that form the northern ranges of the Crimean Mountains are widely scattered open oak forests. In the higher yayla, the aspect is drier in spite of the greater amounts of precipitation, because of the rapid seepage of water downward to a low water table in the karst features of the fissured limestone. Although some forest clumps exist, the typical vegetation in the yayla is upland pastureland. On the south slopes of the mountains a great variety of shrubs and low trees form a fairly dense cover of woody plants typical of Mediterranean climatic regions.

AGRICULTURE

The flatness of the land in the South Economic Region, except for the Crimean Mountains, and the fertile chernozem and chestnut soils have induced the plowing up of nearly all the

Figure 7-5 Cultivation of a young shelter belt in the Black Sea Steppes. Novosti.

Figure 7-6   Sunflowers and bee hives, Black Sea Steppes. Novosti.

area for the cultivation of crops that can withstand drought (Fig. 5-3). On the plains, winter wheat is ideally adapted to the climate since it matures before the onset of the summer heat and high evaporation rates. Sunflowers are also well adapted to the droughty conditions. Much corn is now grown in the region in spite of the fact that for optimal growth corn requires a considerable amount of moisture. Corn growing is not as important in this region as it is in other parts of the Ukraine where moisture is more abundant. Some sugar beets are grown, but they are not a major crop.

With the development of irrigation projects in large parts of the region, the crop complex has been expanded. Vineyards are widely distributed, particularly in Crimea and Odessa Oblasts. Except for the Moldavian S.S.R., the South Economic Region is the most important grape-growing area in the country. The town of Massandra in the Crimea is known throughout the country as the center of the wine industry. Rice has become a major crop, particularly in the irrigated areas south of the Kakhovka Reservoir. And there is a wide variety of fruits, berries, vegetables, and some aromatic herbs and tobacco.

Although some land has been irrigated for a number of years along the lower portions of the Dnieper, Southern Bug, Dniester, and Danube Rivers, the irrigated area has been greatly expanded since the mid-1960s with the construction of the Kakhovka irrigation project, which is based on a system of canals leading water southward and southeastward from the Kakhovka Reservoir on the lower Dnieper River. A major canal has been constructed across the plain southward to the Perekop Isthmus, on to the northern plain of the Crimea, and eastward all the way to the city of Kerch. This has now provided water to irrigate over 400,000 hectares (Fig. 5-2). Among other things, this irrigated area will provide another major rice-growing region in the country, a food grain the Soviets are eager to expand. The Soviets are also beginning to talk again about growing cotton in this region, although this time under irrigation rather than under dry-farmed conditions, as were the ill-fated attempts during the 1930s.

Figure 7-7 Tobacco and orchards on the northern slope of the Crimean Mountains south of Simferopol. Courtesy of Roy Meyer.

RESOURCES, INDUSTRIES, AND TRADE

Mineral Resources

The mineral resource base is weak in the Southern Economic Region. The primary development so far has been the Kerch iron ore, which is tied in with the economy of the Donets-Dnieper Region. The ore moves northward across the Sea of Azov primarily to the city of Zhdanov. Before World War II a small steel plant was constructed in the city of Kerch, and coal from the Donets Basin was transported southward across the Sea of Azov on returning ore boats. However, during the war the plant was destroyed, and it has never been reconstructed. The Kerch ore is all low grade and must be concentrated, and the deposit is a relatively minor one.

Recently the rich salt brines of the stagnant Sivash Sea have been put to use. A new chemical center, Krasnoperekopsk (Red Perekop), on the Perekop Isthmus has been developed to produce soda ash from the sodium carbonate in the brines. The first unit of the plant was opened in 1974 to produce disodium phosphate, a feed additive. Earlier, in 1972, an ammonium phosphate fertilizer unit was opened. A titanium pigment plant was opened in 1971. The raw materials for the titanium plant come from placer deposits west of Kiev and southwest of Dnepropetrovsk. The plant was located on the Perekop Isthmus so that sulfuric acid wastes could be discarded into the Sivash Sea. A natural gas pipeline is being constructed from Kherson to bring Shebelinka gas to this new chemical complex.

Recent maps of Ukrainian mineral resources that have appeared in Soviet geographical literature show an extensive area of potential oil and gas structures covering the entire northern two-thirds of the Crimean Peninsula, including the Kerch Peninsula, and the adjacent north shore of the Black and Azov Seas (Fig. 5-4). Although not enough drilling has been done yet to establish what does exist, there were reports in early 1975 of the opening of commercial gas wells in the Sea of Azov, and estimates of gas reserves under the sea indicate that this might be a major deposit.

Marine Resources

The northern Black and Azov Seas represent one of the largest marine resource areas of the Soviet Union, both in terms of port facilities and trade and in terms of the fishing industry. The Black Sea-Azov ports handle more than 20 percent of all the maritime freight in the Soviet Union. The Odessa-Ilyichevsk port facilities are the busiest in the U.S.S.R. The port of Odessa was established in 1794 shortly after the takeover of the Black Sea Steppes by the Russian Empire. It was built for both military and commercial purposes. During the nineteenth century it developed into the main grain-exporting port in the country. Since the early 1960s it has become one of the main grain-importing ports of the country. In 1952 the new port of Ilyichevsk was developed just to the southwest of Odessa to allow an expansion of port facilities in the area. Now a large new port is being built about 30 kilometers to the east of Odessa on Grigoryevka Lagoon to handle very large shipments of all sorts and to provide large areas of storage. The site is protected from storm winds and has excellent natural conditions for port structures. The port will be able to handle oil supertankers with displacements of as much as 180,000 tons. It will be a deeper water port than either Odessa or Ilyichevsk. Cargo handling will be mechanized and automated. A large chemical complex is to be built at the new port in connection with planned phosphoric acid shipments from the United States and exports of ammonia.

Other important port cities are Nikolayev at the mouth of the Southern Bug River and Kherson up the estuary of the Dnieper. In addition to port facilities, both cities contain shipbuilding yards. Nikolayev is particularly known for its construction of oceangoing vessels. To the southwest of Odessa the smaller ports of Izmail and Reni, up the mouth of the Danube, were acquired along with the Izmail district from Rumania during World War II. In the Crimea, the city of Sevastopol for many years has been one of the three main naval ports of the country, along with Kronshtadt near Leningrad and Vladivostok in the Far East. Sevastopol distinguished itself during both the Crimean War and World War II and has been designated as one of the hero cities of the Soviet Union because of its resistance

during World War II. Nearby Balaklava was the site of the Charge of the Light Brigade during the Crimean War, immortalized in Tennyson's poem. The South Economic Region contains three of the ten "hero cities" in the Soviet Union — Sevastopol, Odessa, and Kerch. Kerch is also an important port; its shipbuilding yards build supertankers.

The shallow northern part of the Black Sea and the shallow Sea of Azov are rich fishing grounds. During its prime production years, the Sea of Azov yielded about 5 kilograms of fish for each hectare of water. At that time the Sea of Azov was receiving about 25 cubic kilometers of water per year, primarily from its two main tributary rivers, the Don and the Kuban, and the salt content of the sea averaged slightly more than 1 percent. The Azov has an average depth of only 10 meters. But during the last 30 years water construction and irrigation projects on the Don and Kuban Rivers have reduced the inflow to the sea by about 6.25 cubic kilometers per year (25 percent). As a consequence the water balance of the Sea of Azov has become negative, and the currents through the Kerch Strait have reversed so that saltier Black Sea water has been entering the Sea of Azov. This has killed off a lot of fish and reduced the fish catch drastically.

Thirty Soviet research institutes have been assigned the task of considering various remedies, including bringing in water from the north. However, for the short run it has been considered to be much cheaper to control the salinity of the Sea of Azov within tolerable limits by constructing a 3-mile-long dam across the Kerch Strait to stop the inflow of Black Sea water. The dam is to consist of 34 spans with two rows of gates for migrating fish and two ship locks. A side benefit will be a considerable shortening of railroad and automobile routes between the Crimea and the Caucasus by providing for automobile and railroad traffic along the top of the dam. This will replace the ferry that presently carries this traffic across the Kerch Strait. Plans for the future of this area envision the bringing of additional water from the north via the

Volga-Don Canal system, but no details have been announced as to how they intend to lift the water over the Volga-Don Divide. Any such project would necessitate a considerable revision of the Volga-Don Canal itself.

Other Industries

The Soviets are becoming increasingly aware of the potential for seaboard industries in the Black Sea coastal cities to utilize foreign resources, as they expand their foreign trade and base it more on cost-benefit analyses. A good example is the alumina plant under construction near Nikolayev in the estuary of the Southern Bug River. This is to use bauxite imported from Greece, Yugoslavia, and Guinea. The Soviets are sponsoring a bauxite mine development in Guinea that will perhaps become the major supplier to this plant. The alumina from Nikolayev is expected to be hauled all the way to the aluminum plant under construction near the Sayan hydroelectric station in southern Siberia.

The city of Kherson has for many years had a small oil refinery that initially processed Baku crude oil brought in by tanker across the Black Sea from the port of Batumi in the Transcaucasus. Since the late 1950s the refinery shifted primarily to the processing of oil from the north central Ukrainian fields. The movement of this crude oil to Kherson has recently been enhanced by a 30-inch pipeline that carries the oil from Kremenchug to Kherson. This pipeline is also connected northward with the Friendship oil pipeline and can therefore tap off crude oil from the Volga-Urals and Western Siberian fields.

In addition to the industries already mentioned, a variety of light machine-building industries exist in various cities, and the food-processing industries are very important, based on local fruits and vegetables, as well as the fish of the neighboring seas.

CITIES

The South Economic Region is not known for its development of large cities. Only six have grown to more than 100,000 population. The largest by far is Odessa, which in 1974 had a population of 981,000. Its importance as a port city among other suburban ports has already been stressed. It handles more freight than any other port in the country. In addition, it is one of the country's primary resort and seaside health spas. The other two major port cities are Nikolayev with a 1974 population of 412,000 and Kherson with a population of 299,000. The fourth city is Simferopol, the commercial, transport, and governmental center for Crimean Oblast. It has the only major airport on the peninsula, and other cities must be served from it by bus or rail. Simferopol thus serves as the organizational center for the important resort industries in the cities along the southeast and western coasts of the peninsula. In 1974 it had a population of 275,000. The fifth city is the naval port of Sevastopol, which in 1974 had a population of 259,000. The sixth city is Kerch with a population of 145,000.

In addition to these larger cities, there are a number of famous resort cities of national significance. The best known of these to the outside world undoubtedly is Yalta, the site of the famous Yalta Conference during World War II between Stalin, Churchill, and Roosevelt. But a number of other cities are well known within the Soviet Union as health and vacation resorts to which people aspire to go. Some of the best-known resorts are at Miskhor, Alupka, Simeiz, Gurzuf, Alushta, Yevpatoriya, Saki, Feodosiya, Sudak, and Staryy Krym. None of these are very large cities. In 1974 Yalta had a population of 73,000. Feodosiya, with a population of 71,000, in addition to being a resort, functions as one of the main commercial ports for the Crimean Peninsula, along with Kerch.

PROSPECTS

At present the South Economic Region, particularly the Crimean Peninsula, is experiencing an influx of people moving in to enjoy the favorable climate and cultural amenities. The resort function is very important. Agriculture also makes up a major part of the economy, and with the expansion of irrigation networks, undoubtedly its role will continue to be very significant. The larger cities are gaining industries along with the rest of the country, but the industrial base is weak in the region, although this may be altered somewhat if major amounts of natural gas and oil are found. The port function is very important, but in the northern parts of the Black Sea and the Sea of Azov these are hampered by ice during winter. There is no indication that for the immediate future there will be any significant change in the trend of things in this region. The outlook is for development of coastal cities in connection with growing export-import functions and to make use of the growing labor pool stemming from increasing in-migration. The region will continue to be known for its resorts, its southern agriculture, and its maritime shipping.

READING LIST

- "Conference of the Southern and Donetsk Science Centers of the Ukrainian Academy of Sciences and of the North Caucasus Science Center on Ameliorating the Economic Uses of the Sea of Azov (Odessa, December 1973)," *Vodnyye Resursy,* 1975, No. 1, p. 201–202.
- Fisher, Alan W., *The Russian Annexation of the Crimea, 1772-1783,* Cambridge University Press, 1970, 180 pp.
- Fox, David J., "Odessa," *Scottish Geographical Magazine,* January 1963, pp. 5–22.
- Gnatyuk, L.V., "Some Aspects of the Economic-Geographic Situation of Odessa," *Soviet Geography: Review & Translation,* November 1963, pp. 43–51.
- Keller, P.C., *The German Colonies in South Russia,* 2 Volumes, Oriental Research Partners, Cambridge.
- Lynch, Donald Francis, "Approaches to the Physical Geography of New Russia: 1780–1837," *Professional Geographer,* October 1971, pp. 308–311.

Moldavian S.S.R.

	Area (km²)	Population	Persons/km²	Percent Urban
Kishinev City		415,000		100
Total	34,000	3,722,000	110.4	35

chapter 8

the moldavian s.s.r.

Moldavia is a nonregion. In their quaint way the Soviets say that their country is composed of 18 economic regions and Moldavia. Moldavia apparently is not considered important enough to warrant an economic region of its own, and yet it is not included in any other region.

The Moldavian S.S.R. is one of the 15 constituent republics of the U.S.S.R. It lies in the far southwestern corner of the Soviet Union next to Rumania and consists primarily of the territory called Bessarabia that was acquired from Rumania in 1940 early in World War II. The region had been passed back and forth several times before between neighboring empires. From the ninth to the thirteenth century the territory between the Dniester and Prut Rivers was considered part of Kievan Rus. During this time a Moldavian nationality became recognized. The people spoke a Rumanian dialect but used the Cyrillic alphabet. In the fifteenth century Moldavia was taken over by Turkey, but at the end of the eighteenth and beginning of the nineteenth centuries it again became part of the Russian Empire. After World War I and the Bolshevik Revolution the territory reverted to Rumania in 1920. In 1924 the Soviets constituted a Moldavian A.S.S.R., but this lay primarily east of the Dniester River in the western Ukraine and did not incorporate Moldavia proper. When the Moldavian S.S.R. was created in 1940 after the reacquisition of Bessarabia, the new republic did not

145

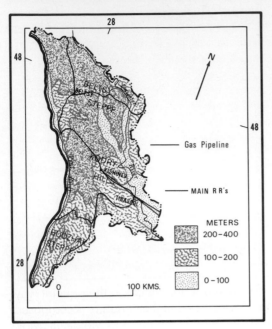

Figure 8-1   Moldavia.

include much of the territory that had been in the Moldavian A.S.S.R. This reverted back to the Ukraine. Therefore, it is quite obvious that the Moldavian A.S.S.R. was a political construct created with the hope of enticing the Moldavians across the border from Rumania. This technique of appealing to national minorities in foreign countries has been used a number of times along the borders of the Soviet Union.

The present Moldavian S.S.R. contains only 34,000 square kilometers (13,200 square miles), which is less than one-fourth the size of Wisconsin. This is by far the smallest of the economic regions, and the second smallest of the Soviet Socialist Republics, after Armenia. But in this relatively small territory the Republic contains 3,722,000 people, which is almost as much as the population of Wisconsin. Therefore, the population density in Moldavia is about four times that of Wisconsin. Within the Soviet Union, the Moldavian Republic has more people than Lithuania, Latvia, Estonia, Armenia, the Kirgiz Republic, or the Tadzhik Republic. With a population density of 110 people per square kilometer it is the most densely populated republic in the entire

country. Among the economic regions it is somewhat more densely populated than the Donets-Dnieper Region and almost twice as densely populated as the Central Region. Yet these two regions are highly urbanized while Moldavia is still 65 percent rural. Therefore, the rural population pressure on the agricultural land in Moldavia is quite great. Individual oblasts within the Central Region, the Donets-Dnieper Region, or some other region such as some of the irrigated districts of Central Asia, have greater population densities, but no entire republic or entire economic region is so densely populated, and only some of the intensively cultivated irrigated areas of Central Asia exceed the rural population density of Moldavia.

The present population of Moldavia is 65 percent Moldavian, 15 percent Ukrainian, 10 percent Russian, 3 percent Gagauz, 3 percent Jewish, 2 percent Bulgarian, and 1–2 percent Armenian, gypsy, Greek, and others. The Gagauz, who now number about 130,000 people, are a Turkic group who lived in the Balkans for as long as anyone can remember and then moved to the southern Moldavian steppes at the turn of the nineteenth century.

The population of Moldavia has a natural increase of about 1.25 percent per year, which is considerably above the 0.89 percent average for the U.S.S.R. The republic enjoys a small net in-migration, and therefore the total population growth rate is considerably above average for the country as a whole. The population growth density (population growth per unit area) ranks among the highest in the country.

PHYSICAL LANDSCAPE

Landform

Moldavia contains essentially four geomorphic regions, although they are not very distinct from one another. Much of the republic consists of rolling country, which in some places is quite hilly and in other places rather flat. The region rests on an arched structure that runs north-northwest–south-southeast through the entire republic. But intense erosion by the Dniester River and its tributaries have produced a contemporary topography that only locally conforms to rock structure. There are two uplands and two lowlands. The highest elevations lie in the south central portion of the republic, known as the Kodry ("forested") Hills. These contain the highest elevation in the entire republic (430 meters), Mount Megura, northwest of Kishinev.

In the very northern part of the republic is the Khotin Upland, which generally has elevations between 250–300 meters, although in places it rises to more than 340 meters. In places where Cretaceous rocks outcrop, this region becomes very picturesque because the marls composing many of the sediments have been shaped by transverse fissures that under erosion segment the bedrock into rectangular blocks that often comprise dazzlingly white chalky scarps 20 meters or more in height. Commonly these are covered with dense woods, and the green of the foliage and dazzling white of the background rocks present an unusually beautiful combination of colors. The Khotin Upland is also cut across by the Moldavian Toltry in a northwest-southeast direction. Like the Toltry farther northwest in the western Ukraine, the Moldavian Toltry appears as pinnacles and widely scattered cones capped with limestone with local relief up to 60 meters. The Toltry is made up of the raggedly eroded remnants of a barrier reef consisting of the remains of calcareous molluscs and corals.

Between the Khotin Upland and the Toltry lies the Beltsy Steppe, named for the major city in the northern part of the area. This flat-to-rolling lowland was formed by the Dniester River and its major right-bank tributaries, the Reum and Kubolta. The flattish landscape continues southeastward in the eastern part of Moldavia throughout the remaining length of the republic as the broad floodplain of the Dniester River.

The other lowland is the drier Budzhak Steppe in the southwestern part of Moldavia. Within the Moldavian Republic it is a rolling dryish plain, but it becomes much flatter southward as it stretches out of Moldavia into the Izmail district of southwestern Odessa Oblast in the Ukraine. Budzhak is a Gagauz term meaning "corner," which refers to this region as a remote corner of the world.

The present landform of Moldavia has been etched primarily by the Dniester and Prut Rivers, which head on the northern slopes of the Carpathians in the western Ukraine and flow southeastward in subparallel courses to the Black Sea. The Prut enters the Danube, which then flows into the sea. Much of the length of the Prut forms the international boundary between Moldavia and Rumania, and in its central portion the Dniester River for a short distance forms the republic boundary between Moldavia and the Ukraine. The lower third of the course of the Dniester lies entirely within Moldavia. These two streams have cut deeply into the landscape in northern Moldavia and follow tortuous courses between the steep slopes of convex hills. Their tributaries have extended toward each other in central Moldavia to dissect the upland into a narrow watershed. In its middle course, where the Dniester forms the republic boundary, the river has cut a steep-sided narrow gorge over rapids where it has intersected the underlying granite basement rock. This region is analogous to the rapids of the Dnieper Bend area.

Climate, Vegetation, and Soils

Moldavia enjoys some of the most favorable climatic conditions for agriculture of any region of the country, although the lowlands tend to be droughty. Summers are warm and sub-humid and winters are mild by Soviet standards. July average temperatures range from 23°C in the south to 21°C in the north. Maximum temperatures have reached as much as 40°C. January temperatures average about −2°C in the south and −4°C in the north. In the north temperatures have dropped as low as −30°C. Weather is extremely changeable during both winter and summer. From April through September the main airflow across the region comes from the northwest around the eastern side of the Carpathians, but occasionally warm, humid, sultry air penetrates from the southwest from the

Mediterranean and brings cloudbursts to the area. During winter such southwesterly flows bring frequent thaws. From September through March Moldavia is influenced primarily by the southwestern edge of the Asiatic High. Thus, the prevailing winds are from the northeast. Local topography may alter the surface winds to produce almost unidirectional flow. In Kishinev, for instance, the prevailing winds every month of the year are from the northwest, conforming to the trend of the individual ranges in the Kodry.

Moldavia is known as a sunny land. In the early morning from July to September, Kishinev usually has no more than four or five-tenths sky cover. As the day wears on and convective activity takes place, cumulus clouds build up to cover five or six-tenths of the sky. During November–February, seven or eight-tenths of the sky is usually covered, and the clouds then are generally of stratus form. Farther south there is considerably less cloudiness.

Precipitation decreases southward. In the Khotin Upland in the north, annual precipitation generally amounts to 500–600 millimeters. This drops to 400–450 millimeters in the Beltsy Steppe and then rises slightly again to around 500 millimeters in the Kodry. Southern Moldavia receives only 300–350 millimeters. In the central and southern portions of the republic, June generally has a pronounced maximum of precipitation and March a pronounced minimum. Father north the maximum lags into July. October frequently is dry, as the "old women's summer," (Indian summer) occurs with the establishment of a high-pressure ridge over the area.

Although snow occurs frequently during winter, the frequent thaws do not allow for a very consistent snow cover. In the north a consistent snow cover may last from eight to ten weeks during the year, but in the south it is generally less than two weeks. Southern Moldavia sometimes has snowless winters.

The higher elevations of Moldavia are generally forested, while the lower elevations are grasslands, which today are largely under cultivation. The Khotin Upland in the north lies in the wooded steppe zone.

The soils that have developed on the higher elevations under the forests are somewhat podzolic, but on the lower elevations they are chernozems and chestnuts. The best soils are in the Beltsy Steppe and along the floodplain of the lower Dniester, where they are developed on river alluvium. On the uplands they generally have a rich admixture of loess, which in some places reaches as much as 10 meters in depth.

AGRICULTURE

The physical landscape and agriculture of Moldavia are primarily western extensions of the Southwest and South Economic Regions of the adjacent Ukraine. However, with the higher population density, agriculture in Moldavia concentrates more on labor-intensive crops such as vineyards, truck gardens, orchards, tobacco, and so forth. Each year about 2 million hectares is sown. Of this about 100,000 hectares is under irrigation, primarily along the lower Dniester valley and in the Budzhak and Beltsy Steppes. Much of the cultivated land is taken up by grains, primarily corn and winter wheat. Corn is the largest grain crop in Moldavia, and here it has been grown for many years. Practically all parts of the plant are used. The grain is used both for animal and human food, and the stocks are used for thatching and fence making. Although corn and wheat are grown throughout the republic, they are concentrated most heavily in the Budzhak Steppe in the southwest. Sunflowers also occupy considerable acreage in this area. In the north sugar beets are combined with the wheat and corn and some sunflowers.

Although these four crops occupy most of the cultivated land, Moldavia is better known for its specialty crops, which yield more intensively on less area. It is particularly well known for its vineyards. Moldavia has often been called the "Champagne" of the Soviet Union. Moldavia occupies first place among all the economic regions for its vineyards. It annually produces about half of the country's grapes and about 30 percent of the country's

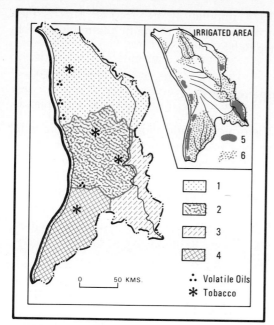

Figure 8-2 Agricultural regions and irrigation. After Nikitin, p. 78.; 1-Sugar beets, wheat, corn, sunflowers, milk and meat livestock; 2-Vineyards, orchards, sunflowers, tobacco, milk and meat livestock; 3-Orchards, vineyards, vegetables, milk and meat livestock; 4-Vineyards, wheat, corn, sunflowers, tobacco, milk and meat livestock; 5-Irrigated area; 6-Planned irrigated area.

abundant corn to feed to cattle and hogs. In the drier southern part of the republic the raising of sheep and karakul is important.

Most of the farming effort in Moldavia is organized in large collective farms. About 88 percent of the rural inhabitants live on collective farms, and only 12 percent live on state farms. They dwell in large rural villages that in many cases number more than 5000 persons each. These are strewn densely along the river valleys near sources of water. Almost 38 percent of the rural inhabitants of Moldavia live in villages with more than 3000 persons each, another 47 percent live in villages numbering between 1000–3000 persons, and only 15 percent live in villages of less than 1000 population. These are the largest rural villages in the country. Many of these large villages, particularly rayon seats, are constructing food-processing establishments, both to complement the agricultural economy and to provide work for excess labor on the farms. There is now great encouragement to form intercollective farm associations to operate large vineyards and orchards and to establish processing plants so that the farms can control their products all the way from the fields to the city markets. About 90 agroindustrial associations have already been established. One such superorganization involves 21 collective farms that have planted an orchard covering 5000 hectares and have equipped it with underground irrigation systems, plants for packing and processing the fruit, cold storage facilities, and a fleet of refrigerated trucks. This undertaking alone is expected to produce about 180,000 tons of fruit per year. In addition to these farm-related industrial activities, about 6 percent of the rural population in the central region of Moldavia is now journeying to work in urban places.

grape products. Large wineries have been built in the three largest cities, Kishinev, Tiraspol, and Beltsy. These turn out 17 percent of the country's high-quality wines. Vineyards occupy about 10 percent of the agricultural land in Moldavia. Although there is about an equal acreage under vineyards in the Ukraine, the average yield in Moldavia is 50 percent more than in the Ukraine. The heaviest concentration of vineyards in Moldavia is in the central region in the Kodry Hills around Kishinev.

Moldavia grows a great variety of other fruits, berries, and vegetables. Food canning and preserving of all sorts are major industries in all the larger cities. Moldavia annually provides about 10 percent of all the country's canned goods. It also produces about 15 percent of the country's tobacco.

The livestock industry is highly developed, partially to use refuse from canning factories, wineries, and sugar refineries. There is also

INDUSTRIES

Industries are poorly developed in Moldavia. There are no mineral resources of any note, although recently there have been tentative reports of the possibility of iron ore. Most of the industries are associated with the rich agriculture of the region. Machine-building industries in some of the larger cities turn out tractors for orchards and vineyards, refrigerators, and so forth. Food industries and textile industries are well developed.

Moldavia lacks its own resources for energy, but a natural gas pipeline has been built into Kishinev from the Shebelinka fields in the eastern Ukraine, and recently this pipeline has been extended to Bulgaria. One large thermal electric plant provides much of the electricity for the region, and some of this also is being exported to Bulgaria.

CITIES

There are only three cities in Moldavia with more than 100,000 population. This is the least of any economic region in the country. The capital city, Kishinev, is the largest. In 1974 it had a population of 432,000. It contains a diversified machine-construction industry, chemical industries, textiles, and food industries. It serves as the cultural center for Moldavia and has established a university and a branch of the Academy of Sciences of the U.S.S.R.

The second city in size is Tiraspol, located on the lower Dniester River in the southeastern part of Moldavia. In 1974 it had a population of 126,000. Its industries are concentrated on food preserving, certain types of machine construction, and cotton textiles.

In the north lies the city of Beltsy with a 1974 population of 115,000. This is the economic center of the rich farming area of the Beltsy Steppe.

PROSPECTS

There are no indications that Moldavia will change its role significantly. With its rich agricultural resources, it will probably remain primarily rural. Its almost total lack of mineral resources mitigates against industrial development, although many food and other light industries will be established in the cities and villages to utilize excess labor and serve local markets.

READING LIST

- Mirskiy, D.A., "Sovetskaya Moldaviya v novoy pyatiletke" (Soviet Moldavia in the New Five-Year Plan), *Geografiya v shkole,* No. 4, Moscow, 1972, pp. 13–15 (in Russian).
- Mytku, M.A., "Rural Settlement Trends in Moldavia," *Soviet Geography: Review & Translation,* November 1970, pp. 761–767.
- Odud, A.L., *Moldavskaya SSR* (Moldavian S.S.R.), Moscow, 1955, (in Russian).
- *Problemy geografii Moldavii* (Problems of the Geography of Moldavia), Kishinev, 1970 (in Russian).
- *Razvitie i razmeshchenie proizvoditelnykh sil Moldavskoi SSR* (Developments and Distributions of the Productive Forces of the Moldavian S.S.R.), Nauka, Moscow, 1972 (in Russian).

Belorussian Economic Region

	Area (km²)	Population	Persons/km²	Percent Urban
Brest Oblast	32,000	1,319,000	40.8	39
Vitebsk Oblast	40,000	1,388,000	34.6	50
Gomel Oblast	40,000	1,560,000	38.6	44
Grodno Oblast	25,000	1,126,000	45.1	36
Minsk City ⎱	41,000	1,038,000 ⎱	63.0	100
Minsk Oblast ⎰		1,533,000 ⎰		29
Mogilev Oblast	29,000	1,238,000	42.7	47
Total	208,000	9,202,000	44.3	48

chapter 9

the belorussia economic region

The Belorussian S.S.R. has been constituted as a separate economic region. However, it is considerably larger than the Moldavian S.S.R., and it has been divided into oblasts for administrative purposes, as shown on the preceding page. It includes a territory of 208,000 square kilometers and had a 1974 population of 9,202,000. Thus, it has a population density of over 44 persons per square kilometer, only 48 percent of which is considered to be urban. Like Moldavia, it is predominantly rural. However, it does not have nearly the agricultural base per unit area that Moldavia has. The climate is cooler and more moist, and the soils are less fertile and in many places ill drained. Therefore, its rural economy has been rather poor. Since World War II the Soviets have been pouring a great deal of industrial investment into the cities to remedy this. Thus, in the last 30 years, the Belorussian Republic has made much more progress toward industrialization and urbanization than Moldavia.

TERRITORIAL ACQUISITION AND POPULATION

Like Moldavia, the area that is now constituted as the Belorussian S.S.R. has been segmented and exchanged back and forth between neighboring powers throughout history. Never have the Belorussians had a state of their own, and at times most of the territory has been either in the Polish-Lithuanian Empire or the Russian Empire. But at times it was divided between them and thereby lost most of its identity.

From early times Belorussia occupied a midposition on the trade routes between the Varangians (Scandinavians) in the Baltic and the Greeks in the eastern Mediterranean. During the ninth century it became incorporated into the state of Kievan Rus. Already such cities existed as Polotsk, Turov, Brest, Vitebsk, Pinsk, Minsk, and Orsha. With the fall of Kiev to the Tatars in 1240, much of the Belorussian area came under the influence of the Lithuanian Empire, and with the union of Lublin in 1569 it became part of the Polish Empire. As a result of the three divisions of Poland in the late eighteenth century, all of the territory eventually became part of the Russian Em-

pire, where it remained until World War I. Between the two world wars, the territory of present Belorussia was divided. The eastern half was in the Soviet Union within the Belorussian S.S.R., which had been constituted on January 1, 1919, and the western half was in Poland, which had regained its independence after World War I. The Belorussian Republic became one of the four charter members, along with the Russian Republic, the Ukrainian Republic, and the Transcaucasian Republic, to constitute the newly formed Soviet Union on December 30, 1922.

The onset of World War II provided the opportunity once again to divide Poland, this time between the Soviet Union and Germany. Although this treaty was abrogated when Germany attacked the Soviet Union on June 22, 1941, the Soviets held onto the newly regained western portion of the Belorussian-

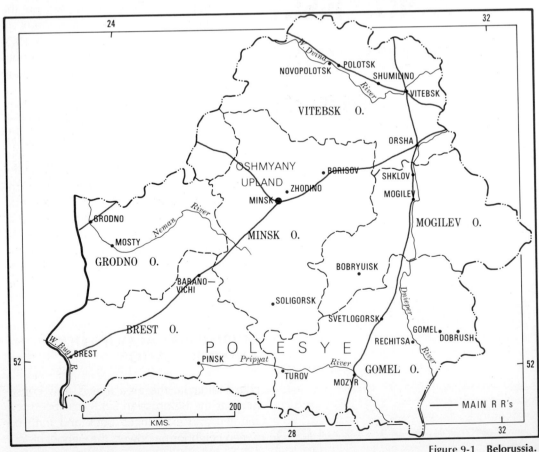

Figure 9-1 **Belorussia.**

occupied territory. At the end of the war when Poland was reconstituted in a more westerly position, the eastern territories of interwar Poland became the western half of the present territory of the Belorussian S.S.R.

This exchange of territories, whereby the western boundary of Poland was expanded well into what had been the eastern part of Germany and the western part of Belorussia was expanded into what had been the eastern part of Poland, necessitated the repatriation of many peoples into their respective newly created national areas. For a time this compounded the devasting effects of the war in this part of Eastern Europe, but it was eventually accomplished, and now the Belorussian S.S.R. probably occupies the best approximation of territory in which the Belorussians have dwelt through history.

However, it is hard to define this territory, as it is hard to define the Belorussians themselves, separately from the Russians and the Ukrainians, or even the Poles for that matter. The Belorussians, or "White Russians," are probably the least distinct among the eastern Slavs. However, they consider themselves to be of purer Slavic strain than the Russians, who have considerable mixtures of eastern peoples from the steppes of Central Asia as far east as Mongolia. The Belorussians express this attitude when the say, "scratch a Russian and you will find a Tatar."

Regardless of these identity problems, the 1970 census showed the population of the Belorussian Republic to consist of 81 percent Belorussians, 10.4 percent Russians, 4.3 percent Poles, 2.1 percent Ukrainians, 1.6 percent Jews, and 0.6 percent other nationality groups.

At present the Belorussian Republic has a birth rate that is a little lower than the national average, a death rate that is a little higher, and a natural increase that is about two-thirds that of the average for the entire country. However, the area is not out of line with its immediate surroundings, because the European part of the Soviet Union in general has considerably lower birth rates than do the Central Asian and Transcaucasian Republics. During the last 15 years or more, Belorussia has shown a more rapid rate of natural increase than has most of European Russia and the Ukraine, and it has experienced some in-migration, so its population has continued to grow at a modest rate.

Since World War II the Soviet government has poured much investment capital into Belorussia to rebuild the destroyed areas and rehabilitate the economy. As a result, the Belorussian Republic has shown a very rapid rate of industrialization and urbanization during the last 30 years. According to Soviet statistics, the industrial output of the republic increased more than 15 times between 1940 and 1972, which was somewhat greater than the national average. During this same time the urbanization increased from 21 percent to about 48 percent. Although this still leaves Belorussia about 11 percentage points below the national average for urbanization, the change within Belorussia during the past 30 years has been very striking.

PHYSICAL LANDSCAPE

Landform

The Belorussian Republic is divided into two geomorphic regions, the northwestern half and the southeastern half, that are distinguished by different glacial surface features, most of which relate to the latest glacial stage, the Valday. These two regions are separated from each other by the irregular terminal moraine that runs diagonally across the republic from the city of Brest in the southwest through Minsk in the center to Orsha in the northeast.

This morainic zone, which stands a little above the topography on either side, affords somewhat better drainage than either the southeast or the northwest and therefore has been traversed by the major highway and railroad running from Warsaw through Minsk to Moscow. It is along this route of travel that western invasions of Moscow have taken place, and hence such cities as Brest and Minsk, as well as the old center of Smolensk east of the border in the Russian Republic, have suffered much destruction time and time

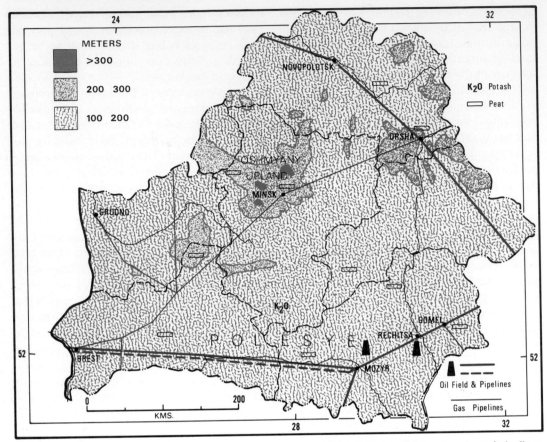

Figure 9-2 Landform, minerals, and pipelines.

again. The highest elevations in the entire Belorussian Republic are found within this morainal ridge just to the west and north of Minsk where maximum elevations rise to 340–345 meters above sea level. A spur of morainic material juts northwestward from this region toward Vilna in southeastern Lithuania in what is known as the Oshmyany Upland. Elevations here rise to about 320 meters.

Much of the rest of Belorussia is a flat-to-undulating lowland with elevations ranging about 175–225 meters above sea level. The northwestern half of the republic was covered by the Valday ice and therefore is a recently formed till sheet with various morainic and outwash materials superimposed on it. In the lower portions of the region drainage is poor, and there are many lakes. The southeastern half of the republic was not covered by the

Valday ice, but was greatly affected by it, as a vast proglacial lake or series of lakes formed and accumulated huge quantities of outwash sediments, particularly in the entire basin of the Pripyat River in the south and the upper portions of the Dnieper Basin in the eastern part of the Republic. With the recession of the ice, most of these lakes drained southward through the Dnieper, and today the old lake beds are occupied by extensive bogs, swamps, and marshes. Although many small lakes still exist in this region, they are not nearly so prevalent as they are in the northwestern part of the republic.

This southeastern part of Belorussia, of course, is the main body of the Polesye, which was discussed as the northwestern part of the Ukraine in Chapter 6. It is the largest and westernmost of the sandy plains that form a discontinuous belt through the central portions of the East European Plain along the southern margins of the Moscow glaciation. These surfaces are composed of reworked older glacial materials that were laid down primarily by the Dnieper stage, which extended farther southward.

The major streams of Belorussia are the headwaters of the Dnieper that flow southward through the eastern part of the republic, the Pripyat River that flows eastward through the entire southern width of Belorussia to join the Dnieper just outside the southeastern corner of the republic, the headwaters of the Western Dvina in the north that flow northwestward into the Gulf of Riga, and the headwaters of the Neman in the west that flow northwestward to the Kaliningrad area. In the far southwestern part of Belorussia begins the Western Bug, which flows westward to join the Vistula north of Warsaw. These streams and their tributaries are ill formed and pick their way slowly through the glacial debris, their valleys choked with drift, so that during flood stages they easily overflow their banks and join with interfluvial marshes to form continuous bodies of water extending for many kilometers in all directions. The watershed sections between the tributaries consist of undissected plains that are universally marshy.

Although the rivers are sluggish and filled with debris, they were the only routes of travel before the coming of railroads and highways. The Pripyat River is navigable throughout much of its length, and the upper Dnieper is navigable as far north as Smolensk. Old canals connect the headwaters of the Pripyat River with those of the Neman and Western Bug. There has been some talk of revamping these canals, but so far none of this has been accomplished.

Climate, Vegetation, and Soils

The climate of Belorussia is relatively cool and moist. In the center of the republic, Minsk has a July average temperature of only 17.6°C (64°F), and the maximum temperature ever attained was 35°C. In January the temperature averages −6.6°C and the absolute minimum temperature is −39°C (−38°F). Winter tem-

peratures decrease faster eastward than northward, thus signifying the influence of the Atlantic. Minsk receives 606 millimeters (24 inches) of precipitation per year, which is quite adequate in the cool temperatures that persist. Maximum amounts fall in July and August, frequently hampering the harvest. Flax must be cut with a binder and shocked for a prolonged period in order to cure, and often hay has to be hung on racks to dry. Relative humidities of the surface air are usually high, averaging 80 percent for the entire year. They average 90 percent in November. The air is also relatively cloudy, averaging over seven-tenths sky cover throughout the year. Summers are less cloudy than winters. November is the cloudiest month, with more than nine-tenths sky cover all the time.

The cool, humid climate has been conducive to the growth of mixed and broadleafed forests, which occupy up to 60 percent of the land in the south and southeast where the drainage is poorest. The pine is the predominant forest tree, particularly in the more sterile sandy soils and some of the boggier areas. Some pine forests have a well-developed second story of oak and hornbeam. Oak originally occupied some of the more fertile areas that are now being cultivated. There are also admixtures of ash and alder, as well as some aspen. Meadows occupy large areas of the Polesye, where drainage is too poor for tree growth.

Most of Belorussia is made up of weakly to moderately podsolized soils that are poor in humus and nutritive elements. In the poorly drained areas there are broad expanses of bog soils and peat beds consisting mainly of vegetable matter. Some of the bogs contain considerable amounts of bog iron ore. In places where limestone bedrock comes close to the surface, lime-rich rendzinas have been formed. These occur only sporadically but are the most productive soils of the entire area.

AGRICULTURE

In spite of the cool climate, the infertile soils, and the poor drainage, Belorussia has always

Figure 9-3　Flax harvesting near Minsk. Novosti.

been primarily an agricultural region, and a dense rural population has developed in the area. With less than 1 percent of the area of the U.S.S.R. and about 3.7 percent of its population, Belorussia produces about 5.1 percent of the agricultural output of the country. This output is concentrated on crops that can adjust to the cool, moist climate and acidic soils and on livestock. Much of the crop production, except for the major cash crop, flax, is oriented toward the high development of beef and dairy products, swine, and poultry.

In 1970 grain occupied 41 percent of the sown area of the republic. By far the most extensive grain was winter rye, and barley and some wheat were grown. Fodder crops, primarily hay, occupied another 37 percent of the sown territory, potatoes 16 percent, flax 4.7 percent, and vegetables 0.6 percent. In addition, buckwheat and millet are old traditional crops that have been used for food for centuries, although they do not occupy much area. Some hemp and sugar beets have been introduced recently. Apples and other fruits are also important. The Belorussian Republic produces about 22 percent of all the flax of the

U.S.S.R. and about 14 percent of the potatoes. Many of the potatoes are used as fodder for swine. Like Poland to the west, Belorussia for a long time has been known for its high-quality pork.

For several centuries desultory attempts have been made to drain the marshy areas of Belorussia and put them under cultivation. By the time of the Bolshevik Revolution about 500,000 hectares had been drained. By 1970 this had increased to about 1,578,000 hectares. Now there is a more concerted effort for land reclamation. During the ninth five-year plan, 1971–1975, additional irrigation was to have taken place on 1.1 million hectares of land, various other forms of amelioration were to have been performed on another 800,000 hectares, and meadows and pastures were to have been improved on yet another 900,000 hectares.

The most intensive drainage has taken place on the left bank of the lower Pripyat River between it and the Dnieper. North of the city of Mozyr, 30–40 percent of the sown area is in some drainage project (Fig. 9-5). Much of the southeast has at least 10 percent of its sown territory under drainage. The Pripyat drainage basin contains about two-thirds of all the drained land in the Belorussian S.S.R. Although drainage projects are scattered throughout the republic, there still remains much to do. Along with the drainage there

Figure 9-4 Digging drainage ditches in the marshes of the Polesye, Belorussia. Novosti.

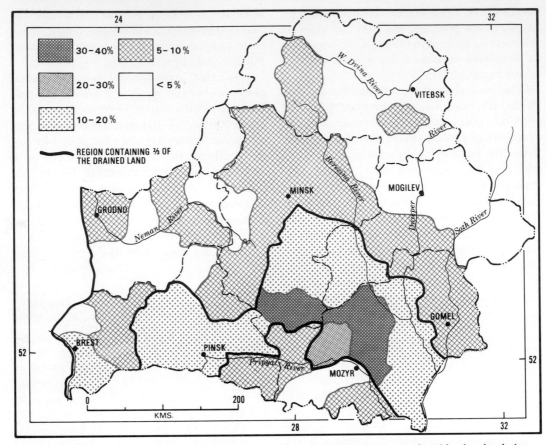

Figure 9-5   Percent of agricultural land under drainage.

must be a great deal of clearing of brush and small trees. Because of the drainage conditions, individual fields have remained rather small. With the more organized drainage and land-clearing projects, many of these fields can be consolidated and made more adaptable to mechanization.

INDUSTRIAL RESOURCES AND DEVELOPMENT

Mineral Resources

Until the early 1960s there was no significant mineral production in the Belorussian Republic other than peat. It is estimated that Belorussia contains about 50 percent of the Soviet Union's reserves of peat, presently used extensively for fuel and certain chemical products. But in 1963 the Soligorsk potash de-

posit was opened up, and a large mill was built to produce potassium fertilizers. This has been expanded in three stages and is now about equal to the Solikamsk-Berezniki area in the Urals in the production of potassium salts and fertilizers. Each produces around 45–50 percent of the country's production. The rest comes from the Kalush-Stebnik district of the northern foothills of the Carpathians, which was covered in Chapter 6. The Soligorsk potassium resources are now estimated at about 4 billion tons, which is more than one-fourth of all the proved reserves of potassium salts in the country. It is estimated that there are reserves of as much as 15–20 billion tons. This area also contains significant deposits of magnesium salts and about 20 percent of the Soviet Union's reserves of rock salt.

In 1964 oil production began in southeastern Belorussia, primarily around the town of

Rechitsa. By 1974 production had risen to 8 million tons. Although this is not a major deposit of oil, production here is very important to the western regions of the U.S.S.R. Actually the oil industry had already been established in the republic before oil was discovered there. The Friendship pipeline had been laid across southern Belorussia on its way from the Volga-Urals fields to the East European satellites. The pipeline forks at Mozyr, near Rechitsa, and one branch goes straight west through Brest to Poland and East Germany, while another branch goes southwestward to Czechoslovakia and Hungary. An oil and chemical complex was established at Polotsk in northern Belorussia when a branch oil line was run northwestward from the Friendship pipeline through Polotsk to the Latvian port of Ventspils for export. The Novopolotsk complex has become one of the biggest oil-refining and chemical-producing complexes in the country. Thus, Volga-Urals oil was being refined in the very area that local oil deposits were to be discovered a few years later. And now Western Siberian oil is also flowing through the Friendship pipeline. In 1975 a second Belorussian oil refinery was completed, at Mozyr, to use the local Rechitsa oil and oil from the pipeline. Mozyr grew in population from 25,700 in 1959 to 61,000 in early 1974. In conjunction with the oil refining, a gas-processing plant was to have opened in 1975 in the oil fields of Rechitsa.

Belorussia also contains significant deposits of oil shale and brown coal, but these have not yet been developed. Some of the coal lies at shallow depths no more than 100 meters below the surface and can be mined by cheap open-pit methods.

Forestry Resources

Lumbering and woodworking has always been an important part of the economy in Belorussia. Although the timber resource is not great, and lumbering has been decreasing in past years, the wood products industries are expanding all the time. The region specializes in certain prepared products that require a good deal of skilled labor. In 1970 the Repub-

lic produced about 3 million cubic meters of sawed lumber, 102,500 tons of paper, about 19 percent of all the plywood production, and 7.6 percent of the country's prefabricated housing. The main sawmilling centers are at river-rail junctions such as Bobruysk, Borisov, and Gomel. The main centers for the production of plywood, matches, and various construction materials are Rechitsa, Pinsk, Mozyr, and Mosty. The paper and cellulose industries are found primarily in the cities of Dobrush, Svetlogorsk, Shklov, and Borisov. A cellulose paperboard factory is under construction at Bobruysk.

Other Industries

The main industrial development since World War II has taken place in the machine-building and chemical industries. Many of the chemical industries are connected with either the petroleum refining at Mozyr and Polotsk or the potash mines of Soligorsk. These turn out various plastics and synthetics, as well as large quantities of mineral fertilizers. Some of the main synthetic fiber plants are at Novopolotsk, Grodno, and Mogilev. The first nitrogen fertilizer plant in Belorussia was established in Grodno in 1963 based on Carpathian gas. A second plant is to be built at Shumilino about halfway between Vitebsk and Polotsk in the northeastern part of the republic to utilize gas brought in by the Torzhok-Minsk gas transmission main. Belorussia now accounts for about 19 percent of the polyethylene produced in the Soviet Union and 10 percent of the chemical fibers.

Metal-processing and machine industries have been established throughout many of the cities of Belorussia, primarily since World War II. Belorussia now produces about 19 percent of all the tractors of the country, 13 percent of all the metal-cutting machines, and 17 percent of the motorcycles. One of the outstanding machine-building plants is the Minsk motor vehicle plant, which is the largest producer of heavy-duty cargo trucks in the U.S.S.R. Cargo capacities range from 4.5 tons on two-axle trucks to 14 tons on three-axle trucks. Since this plant cannot be expanded, the Soviets are considering the construction of a second plant in the Minsk area.

About 20 kilometers east of Minsk is the new Belorussian Motor Vehicle Plant at the small industrial settlement of Zhodino. This plant specializes in heavy off-highway dump trucks for mining and construction. It produces about 3000 trucks annually, primarily in two models with capacities of 27 and 40 metric tons, respectively. Trucks with as much as 180-ton capacities are planned.

The tractor plant in Minsk has become the biggest tractor producer in the country. It specializes in the "Belarus" light-wheeled tractor, which has become a major export item. The tractor-testing station at the University of Nebraska has approved it as a high-quality product. Some of these tractors are now being imported into the United States. A tire plant has been established in Bobruysk to supply large tires for the heavy trucks produced at Minsk and Zhodino and for the farm tractors produced in Minsk.

The production of glass from glacial sands, primarily in the Rechitsa and Bobruysk areas, is an old industry in the Belorussian area. At the time of the revolution more than 20 small glass factories existed in this region. Since

then eight large factories have been established in Borisov, Gomel, Grodno, Bobruysk, Novopolotsk, and other cities.

With the relatively high density of population and the concentration on agriculture, the Belorussian area has always had important food-processing industries and other light industries to utilize excess labor and serve local markets.

CITIES

Belorussia has nine cities with more than 100,000 population each. Except for Bobruysk, Baranovichi, and Orsha, these are all oblast centers that have grown primarily because of their governmental functions, which eventually has attracted a well-rounded manufacturing economy to each city.

Minsk

The largest city by far is the Belorussian capital of Minsk, which in 1974 had a population of 1,095,000. This placed it eleventh among

Figure 9-6 Dump trucks at the Zhodino plant east of Minsk.

the cities of the Soviet Union. It is one of the fastest growing of the large cities in the Soviet Union. It has more than doubled its population in the last 13 years. It is expected that by 1980 the population of Minsk will be about 1,500,000. Founded in 1067, Minsk has been the traditional cultural and economic center of the Belorussians for more than 900 years. However, it has never served as the capital of an independent country.

Located on the main route to the west along the terminal moraine, it has had much contact with the West and has suffered heavily during war. During World War II it was almost completely destroyed. Since then an impressive job of reconstruction has produced a major city with broad boulevards and squares and an abundance of parks. Initially most of the buildings were 5 stories high, but now 9–12 story buildings are preferred, and newer buildings are going as high as 16–18 stories. Grade-separated speedways are under construction, and a subway system is being built. A green belt has been set aside in the morainic landscape surrounding the city containing a "water necklace" — a system of connected lakes and man-made reservoirs — to provide recreational facilities for the city.

At present Minsk turns out about one-third of all the Belorussian Republic's industrial goods and contains a quarter of its labor force. Every sixth Soviet-made tractor and every sixth Soviet-made motorcycle is manufactured in Minsk. The motor vehicle plant has already been mentioned; it is the largest producer of heavy-duty cargo trucks in the country. At present a huge refrigerator factory is being constructed with French help that will be the biggest enterprise of its kind in Europe and will eventually have an annual output of more than half a million refrigerators.

Other Cities

The other eight larger cities in order of size are Gomel with a 1974 population of 324,000, Vitebsk with a population of 265,000,

Mogilev with a population of 244,000, Bobruysk with a population of 170,000, Grodno with a population of 161,000, Brest with a population of 150,000, Baranovichi with a population of 115,000, and Orsha with a population of 111,000. Most of these have been mentioned with regard to certain industries. Brest is the old city of Brest-Litovsk, which was the site of the separate treaty drawn up with Germany in 1918 after the Bolsheviks had taken over the Russian government.

PROSPECTS

Since World War II Belorussia has received a disproportionate share of capital investments from the Soviet Union for the improvement of industries and agriculture in the region. This has resulted in one of the most rapid industrializations and urbanizations in the country during the last three decades, and all indications are that these processes will continue. Although Belorussia is still considerably more rural than the national average, if it continues the same trends at the same rates, it will soon catch up with the rest of the country in industrialization and urbanization. At the same time its agriculture is being continually improved by land reclamation measures, particularly drainage. Like the western Ukraine, it may be called upon to develop more industry integrated with the East European members of Comecon.

READING LIST

- *Atlas Belorusskoy SSR* (Atlas of the Belorussian S.S.R.), Minsk, 1958, 140 pp. (in Russian).
- *Belorusskaya SSR* (Belorussian S.S.R.), Akademiya Nauk BSSR, Institut Ekonomiki, Moscow, 1957, 487 pp. (in Russian).
- Bogdanovich, A.V., *Goroda Belorussiy; Kratkiyekonomicheskiy ocherk* (The Cities of Belorussia; A Short Economical Essay), Nauka i tekhnika, Minsk, 1967, 183 pp. (in Russian).

- Borodina, V.P., et al., *Soviet Byelorussia,* Progress Publishers, Moscow, 1972, 169 pp.
- French, R.A., "Drainage and Economic Development of Polesye, U.S.S.R.," *Economic Geography,* April 1959, pp. 172–180.
- Kravchuk, A.N., et al., *Zanimatelnye voprosy po geografii BSSR* (Entertaining Questions on the Geography of the Belorussian S.S.R.), Minsk, 1968, 87 pp.
- Lubachko, Ivan S., *Belorussia Under Soviet Rule 1917–1957,* University Press of Kentucky, 1972, 219 pp.
- Motuz, V.M., "O proiskhozhdenii lyossovykh porod Belorusskogo polesya" (On the Origin of Loess in the Belorussian Polesye), *Vestnik Moskovskogo Universiteta, seriya geografiya,* No. 1, 1973, pp. 100–102 (in Russian).
- Rakov, A.A., *Naseleniye BSSR* (Population of Belorussia), Nauka i tekhnika, Minsk, 1969, 220 pp. (in Russian).
- Rogach, P.I., "Otsenka urovnya promyshlennogo razvitiya administrativnykh oblastey (na primere Belorusskoy SSR" (An Evaluation of the Level of Industrial Development of Oblasts — With Particular Reference to the Belorussian S.S.R.), *Vestnik Moskovskogo Universiteta, seriya geografiya,* No. 4, 1972, pp. 109–111 (in Russian).
- *Sovetskiy Soyuz: Belorussiya* (Soviet Union: Belorussia), Mysl, Moscow, 1967, 309 pp. (in Russian).
- Yurkevich, I., *Geograficheskaya tipologiya i rayonirovaniye lesnoy rastitelnosti Belorussii* (Geographic Typology and Regionalization of the Forest Vegetation of Belorussia), Minsk, 1965, 286 pp. (in Russian).

The Baltic Economic Region

	Area (km²)	Population	Persons/km²	Percent Urban
Lithuanian S.S.R.	65,000	3,233,000	49.6	54
Vilna City		409,000		100
Latvian S.S.R.	64,000	2,430,000	38.1	64
Riga City		765,000		100
Estonian S.S.R.	45,000	1,405,000	31.2	67
Tallinn City		386,000		100
Kaliningrad Oblast	15,000	761,000	50.4	75
Total	189,000	7,829,000	41.4	

chapter 10

the baltic economic region

The Baltic Economic Region contains three of the fifteen Union Republics of the Soviet Union: Lithuania, Latvia, and Estonia, and now Kaliningrad Oblast, which is under the political jurisdiction of the Russian Republic. These four political units constitute a territory of 189,000 square kilometers and a population of 7,829,000. The region has an average population density of 41.4 persons per square kilometer and is about 62 percent urbanized, which is about 3 percentage points above the national average.

TERRITORIAL ACQUISITION AND POPULATION

Like the territories of Moldavia, the western Ukraine, and western Belorussia, acquired as a result of World War II, the Baltic Region has had a varied history as parts of adjacent empires. But unlike the other three regions, the Baltic states between the two world wars tasted a brief moment of political independence that still fires their imaginations and unquestionably makes them among all the nationality groups the most rebellious against the Soviet system. Or, at least, they are most overt about it. Within the republics, individuals have gone so far as to set fire to themselves, and outside the region, the Lithuanian, Latvian, and Estonian governments in exile have maintained the rudiments of embassies in

167

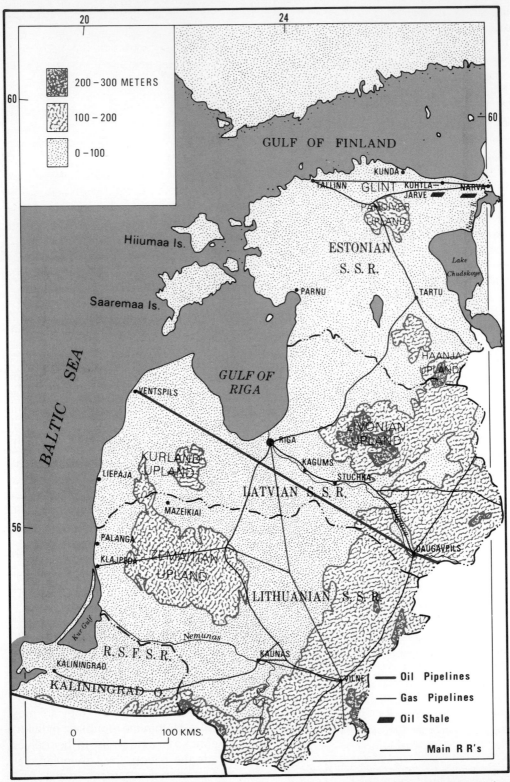

Figure 10-1   The Baltic Region.

other countries, although these are gradually disappearing as doddering 80-year-old staff members die off one by one.

The first acquisition of part of the Baltic territory was accomplished with the victory of Peter the Great over Charles XII of Sweden in the Northern Wars during the period 1700–1721. This resulted in the incorporation of what is now Estonia and the northeastern part of Latvia, along with the city of Riga, into the Russian Empire. The remaining part of Latvia and Lithuania came under the control of Russia in the latter part of the eighteenth century as a result of the partitions of Poland. With the large Russian market as a stimulant, the Baltic area underwent considerable industrialization, much of it with the help of foreign capital, during the second half of the nineteenth century. At this time ports were rebuilt, railroads were laid, and manufacturing plants were established to produce ships, railroad rolling stock, electrical equipment, textiles, and certain chemicals. The Baltic seaports became most essential in the trade between Russia and Western Europe.

The Baltic Region remained within the Russian Empire until World War I, and after the Bolshevik Revolution the Soviets established control in the area for a short time. But with the help of the Allies, the independent states of Lithuania, Latvia, and Estonia were established in 1918. With the onset of World War II, the Soviet Union annexed them in August 1940, and since the rest of the world was so preoccupied with the German threat no concerted protest was made from the outside. However, within the Baltic Republics, fierce fighting ensued for a number of years, even after the end of World War II, and a great deal of passive, and even some active, resistance still continues. It is obvious that the Baltic peoples swing a considerable amount of political clout, since they have been constituted as three of the fifteen Soviet Socialist Republics.

At the end of World War II the Soviet Union took over the northern half of what had been East Prussia, a part of Germany, before the war. But instead of attaching it to adjacent Lithuania, the Soviets expatriated the 1,500,000 Germans who were living in the area and moved in about 600,000 Russians. They then renamed the old city of Königsberg "Kaliningrad" and constituted the area as Kaliningrad Oblast within the R.S.F.S.R. Until recently Kaliningrad Oblast was considered part of the Northwest Economic Region, although it was detached from the main body of the region by the Baltic Republics in between. Only since the 1960s has Kaliningrad Oblast been considered a part of the Baltic Economic Region.

Apparently the Soviets were initially loath to trust this westernmost territory along the Baltic to the Lithuanians and other Baltic peoples who had only recently been acquired by the Soviet Union and who were fiercely resisting this acquisition. But the recent inclusion of Kaliningrad Oblast in the Baltic Economic Region signifies some lessening of these fears, and there has been some speculation that eventually Kaliningrad Oblast might be incorporated into the Lithuanian Republic. While this might enhance the overall position of Lithuania, the Lithuanians are somewhat leery of such an event, because the inclusion of Kaliningrad Oblast into their republic would instantly dilute their majority drastically within the population of such a newly constituted Lithuanian Republic. The Russians now make up about 9 percent of the population of Lithuania, and the addition of another 600,000 or more would increase their portion to about 30–35 percent. This would reduce the Lithuanian majority from around 80 percent to about 60 percent.

The present nationality structure of the Baltic Republics is shown in Table 10-1. The Russians have become very strong minorities in both Latvia and Estonia. They are not as strong yet in Lithuania because not as much industrialization has taken place there. Also, the Catholic Lithuanians maintain a higher birth rate than do the Protestant Latvians and Estonians. There has been an inevitable russification associated with industrialization, as is true throughout the country, because in many cases the local groups have not been able to staff adequately the new factories that have been built. In some parts of the country, particularly in Central Asia, this is because the native groups do not adjust well to factory life. But here in the Baltic Region, where the indigenous peoples are well organized and, if anything, more advanced than the Russians themselves, it has been due to low natural increases among the Baltic peoples, who are not providing enough new 16-year-olds to the labor force. Although the Estonians and Latvians often joke that the Russians are their hired help, they know that there is another side to the coin and that their cultural sovereignties are being badly eroded by a large influx of Russian laborers. Already the Latvians are in danger of losing their majority in their republic, which, according to the constitution, is one of the criteria for being a Union Republic, although certainly this would not be the first case of a titular group losing its majority without losing its Union Republic status.

The Baltic peoples have relatively low birth rates and relatively high death rates, because of their aging populations. Therefore, their natural increases are among the lowest in the country. This is particularly true of the Latvians and Estonians, whose natural increase rates are lower than the rest of the country,

except for the Central Region of the Russian Republic and perhaps some of the oblasts in the Northwest and Volga-Vyatka Regions. A modest net in-migration has compensated somewhat, so that during the last 15 years or so the region has shown a modest population growth.

PHYSICAL LANDSCAPE

Landform

The Baltic Region is a cuestaform plain covered with glacial drift. As such the surface is a series of alternating uplands and intervening lowlands complicated by irregular depths of glacial debris dumped on top. The outcropping bedrocks are Devonian and Silurian sedimentary strata that dip gently south-southeastward. Differential stream erosion on these slightly dipping rocks of varying resistances has produced a preglacial topography of two cuestas that run almost west-east throughout the western and central portions of the Baltic Region and then curve northeastward as they enter the Russian Republic to the east. The older of these two structures

Table 10-1 Nationality Composition of the Baltic Economic Region, 1970 (Percent of Total)

Lithuanian S.S.R.	100.0	Estonian S.S.R.	100.0
Lithuanians	80.1	Estonians	68.2
Russians	8.6	Russians	24.7
Poles	7.7	Ukrainians	2.1
Belorussians	1.5	Belorussians	1.4
Ukrainians	0.8	Finns	1.4
Jews	0.8	Jews	0.4
Other	0.5	Other	1.8
Latvian S.S.R.	100.0	Kaliningrad Oblast	100.0
Latvians	56.8	Russians	77.1
Russians	29.8	Belorussians	9.4
Belorussians	4.0	Ukrainians	6.6
Poles	2.7	Lithuanians	3.2
Ukrainians	2.3	Jews	0.6
Lithuanians	1.7	Poles	0.6
Jews	1.6	Mordvinians	0.4
Other	1.1	Tatars	0.4
		Chuvash	0.4
		Other	1.3

Source: *Itogi vsesoyuznoy perepisi naseleniya 1970 goda,* Volume 4, pp. 14, 15, 88.

forms an imposing cuesta escarpment along the south shore of the Gulf of Finland that extends the length of the north coast of Estonia and continues eastward into the Northwest Economic Region south of Leningrad and Lake Ladoga. This is capped by limestones primarily of Silurian age and is known as the "Glint" — the northern escarpment face of the Silurian Plateau that forms a gently rolling upland on the dip slopes of the rocks to the south.

On the eastern border of Estonia the Narva-Luga Depression, which drains the huge glacial Lake Chudskoye (Peipus) northward to the Baltic, forms a break in the Glint, and a low coastal plain extends inland as much as 30 kilometers. But westward the pre-Glint lowland between the escarpment and the sea narrows, in places to no more than 1 kilometer wide. West of Kunda along the central Estonian coast, the gentle coastline of eastern Estonia gives way to a hopeless labyrinth of capes, bays, inlets, and underwater reefs and shoals. Literally thousands of rocky limestone islands lie off the northern

coast of western Estonia. These represent fragments of the Silurian Plateau that have become detached from the main body of the rock structure but have not been completely eroded away and still remain above water level. The Gulf of Finland is an inundated section of the inner lowland between the Silurian escarpment to the south and the Baltic Shield to the north in Finland and the Karelian Isthmus. This lowland continues, partly under water, through the great lakes area, primarily Lakes Ladoga and Onega, in the Northwest Economic Region.

The Glint rises abruptly above the Gulf of Finland to elevations of as much as 150 meters, and the Silurian Plateau to the south is an undulating upland that reaches elevations as high as 166 meters in northern Estonia and 175 meters farther east in the Russian Republic. It is cut by a network of small streams that in places form gorgelike valleys with rapids and waterfalls; it is surrounded by hilly morainic and kame formations with a great number of eskers along its northern edge. In Estonia the eskers run in a northwesterly di-

Figure 10-2 Rock fragments on the coast of Estonia. Courtesy of Robert Jasiorkowski.

rection, and many of them are grouped on the border of the Pandivere Upland, the highest part of the Silurian Plateau in northern Estonia. The glacial deposits on top of the limestone plateau contain numerous kettles of water that slowly dissolve the limestone below to form typical karst features in many parts of the region.

The Silurian strata dip below Devonian structures in the south which form the second cuesta, the Devonian cuesta and upland in central Latvia. In between the Silurian and Devonian cuestas lies the broad Baltic Lowland, which extends eastward from the deep indentation of the Gulf of Riga through the large glacial Lakes Chudskoye and Pskov on the eastern border of Estonia and on to the Ilmen depression in the Russian Republic. Where this lowland intersects the Baltic Sea on the west, primarily around the Gulf of Riga, the shoreline is flat and sandy and rimmed by enormously extensive shoreline bars and dunes, particularly farther south where they grow completely across the mouths of river embayments to form bay bars and extensive lagoons such as Kur Gulf at the mouth of the Neman River in Kaliningrad Oblast.

The Devonian Plateau is represented by a number of disconnected remnants of a Devonian dolomite that forms such broad rolling uplands as the Kurland Upland in western Latvia, the Livonian Upland in northeastern Latvia, and the Haanja Upland in southeastern Estonia. Other segments of the upland continue east-northeastward in the Russian Republic. Elevations above sea level on these uplands average 200–250 meters but reach a maximum of as much as 318 meters in the Haanja upland. The surfaces of these uplands are dominated by hilly morainic topography with only small areas of intervening outwash. Around their edges, however, glaciofluvial deposits are very prominent.

Farther south a broad push moraine forms a belt as much as 100 kilometers wide that begins in northern Poland and extends east-northeastward through southeastern Lithuania, northern Belorussia, southeastern Estonia, and eastward into the Valday Hills area of the Northwest Economic Region. This broad morainic zone contains thousands of glacial lakes of small and intermediate size. The highest section of the moraine extends in a northwest-southeast orientation between the cities of Vilna in southeastern Lithuania and Minsk in central Belorussia. This is known as the Baltic Ridge, which reaches elevations as high as 309 meters. Other morainic material forms the Zemaitian Upland in western Lithuania, which reaches elevations of 228 meters. Although many streams wander aimlessly through the lakes and marshes of this glaciated region, only two form extensive river systems. The largest is the Western Dvina, which heads on the western slopes of the Valday Hills in Kalinin Oblast of the Central Region and flows westward through the northernmost part of Belorussia and then northwestward through the breadth of Latvia to the Gulf of Riga. In Latvia it is known as the Daugava. The other major stream is the Neman, which heads in western Belorussia and flows northwestward through southern Lithuania. In its lower portion it forms the boundary between the Lithuanian S.S.R. and Kaliningrad Oblast. In Lithuania it is known as the Nemunas. Both of these systems served as important trade routes before the coming of railroads, with canal connections from some of their headwater streams into the Dnieper system to the south.

One of the very short streams that might be mentioned is the Narva, which drains the large interconnected Lakes Chudskoye and Pskov northward to the Gulf of Finland and forms the republic boundary between Estonia and Russia. The city of Narva along its banks was the site of the first major battle between Peter the Great and Charles XII of Sweden during the early part of the eighteenth century.

Climate, Vegetation, and Soils

The climate of the Baltic Region is cool, humid, and cloudy. The presence of the Baltic, the Gulf of Finland, and the large glacial lakes serves to temper the climate and make it cooler in the summer and less severe in winter than one might expect for the latitude. The water basins also produce a skewness to the seasons, because they have great thermal capacities to heat slowly in spring and cool slowly in fall. Spring thawing of ice over these large water bodies delays the rise of temperature so that spring is late and very short. In autumn they delay the cooling of the surface air temperatures, so that falls are prolonged and relatively warm. However, the region is never very warm. Summers along the coast are definitely chilly, and occasional night frosts may occur in interior lowlands even during July. On the coast, Riga has experienced freezing temperatures during all months except July and August. The frost-free period in Riga averages only 133 days. July temperatures in Riga average 17°C (63°F) and temperatures have dropped in July to 3°C. In January temperatures at Riga average −5°C and have dropped as low as −35°C with incursions of arctic air from the northeast.

Frequent cyclonic passages along the Baltic route cause the weather to be very unstable, cloudy, and characterized by frequent prolonged light rain. There is a great deal of cloud cover throughout the year, but it is somewhat more prevalent in winter than in summer. During winter dull gray overcast skies, *pasmurnaya,* weather occurs more than two-thirds of the time. During summer this occurs only about one-third of the time, and many of the clouds at this time of year are cumulus. Sky cover averages about seven-tenths in July and more than nine-tenths in November, the cloudiest month. In Riga every other day of the year receives as much as 0.1 millimeter of precipitation, and many other days receive lesser amounts. Precipitation is more frequent in winter than in summer, but the summer months receive more than twice the amount of precipitation than the winter months do. July and August are the rainiest months of the year, which hampers the harvest in this area of short growing seasons. All the agricultural hazards of the cool, short growing season and the concentration of precipitation in late summer that were stressed in the chapter on the Belorussian Region are compounded in the Baltic Region. A significant amount of instability occurs in the warmer humid air of summer, so that cumuloform clouds are

common. On the average June receives five thunderstorms, July six, and August four.

Yearly precipitation totals 566 millimeters (23 inches) in Riga. This is quite adequate, since temperatures are generally cool and atmospheric humidity is high. The relative humidity of the surface air in Riga averages 80 percent year round. Yearly evaporation averages only 445 millimeters. Fog occurs 44 days of the year. Although snows are common in winter, frequent thaws limit the duration of snow cover. On the average only 93 days of the year have a snow cover, which reaches a maximum depth of only 11 centimeters.

The Baltic Region is transitional between taiga forests in the north and mixed forests in the south. In most places coniferous forests predominate, with the most prominent species being Norway spruce and Scotch pine with admixtures of white birch and aspen. But in sections of western Latvia broadleaf forests composed of ash, maple, oak, and linden are prominent. Large areas of marshy ground throughout the Baltic Region are occupied by meadows.

Soils in the Baltic Region tend to be podsolic with leaching of the basic minerals. The ill-drained areas are boggy. On some of the limestone uplands lime-rich rendzinas have developed, and these are the most fertile soils in the area.

AGRICULTURE

The cool climate, infertile soils, and poor drainage severely limit agriculture in the Baltic Region. Less than half the land can be used for agriculture. Forests and copse occupy more than 30 percent of the total territory; marshes, swamps, and lakes 10 percent; and roads, sand, and other infertile soils 20 percent. The cool, short, wet growing season limits crop choices to hay, primarily clover and alfalfa, a few small grains, and the cash crop, flax, which although scattered widely does not occupy a lot of area. Potatoes are very important as human food and as the main fodder base for swine. Some sugar beets have been introduced during the last couple of decades, and a variety of vegetables, fruits, and berries are grown that can adapt to the cool climate.

Because of the natural limitation on crop growth, heavy emphasis has been placed on livestock production. Per unit area of arable land, the Baltic Region produces twice as many milk cows and swine than the rest of the country as a whole. Much of the crop production, particularly the hay crops and potatoes, as well as some of the small grains, is grown to sustain the livestock industry. Almost 90 percent of all the marketable agricultural products in the Baltic Region are livestock products. One could characterize the agriculture of the Baltic Region by its marketable products, most of which would fall into three categories: milk, pork, and flax.

The agricultural settlements in the Baltic Region have always been very small. There is a gradual diminution in size in rural villages all the way from Moldavia northward through the Ukraine and Belorussia to the Baltic. In Lithuania original settlements were primarily in small villages, many with no more than three or four houses. In Latvia and Estonia most of the farmers lived in individual homesteads on their farms. Although the Soviets have nationalized and collectivized the land, most of the people still live in their small villages or in individual households. The collective farm is the primary unit of production in the three Baltic Republics, where strong attachment to the land existed long before the Soviets collectivized the area. But in Kaliningrad Oblast, where a mass exchange of farmers took place after World War II, state farms were set up over much of the region.

Although agriculture in the Baltic Region is severely hampered by the natural environment, and mechanization is hampered by the small sizes of fields between plots of woods and swamps, agriculture has been maintained at a respectably high level of yield through the use of some of the most scientific farming in the country. Much land reclamation, drainage, clearing of brush, application of mineral fertilizers, and reliance on livestock have produced a well-integrated agricultural economy that is adapted to the environment. The region now ranks first in the country in the application of mineral fertilizers and is one of the leading areas in the continuing process of drainage and consolidation of fields.

INDUSTRIAL RESOURCES AND DEVELOPMENT

Mineral Resources

Until recently the only mineral resource of any significance in the Baltic Region, other than widespread peat beds, was the Estonian oil shale, which has been under exploitation for quite a long time. Old underground mines located in the vicinity of the town of Kohtla-Jarve produced oil shale gases that were transmitted by pipeline eastward to Leningrad and westward to Tallinn. With the coming of natural gas into the Leningrad area from the east and southeast, the gas flow in the Baltic pipeline has been reversed, and natural gas is carried westward to Tallinn.

The old underground mines are being phased out as three open-pit mines and a large underground mine are being developed farther east in the Narva region. These are being constructed in conjunction with large mine-head thermal power plants that utilize about two-thirds of the shale production. In the same neighborhood the Baltic and Estonian thermal power stations, each with a capacity of 1.6 million kilowatts, have gone into operation.

In 1973 Estonia produced 25.4 million tons of oil shale out of a Soviet total of about 31 million tons. Most of the rest of the oil shale came from adjoining Leningrad Oblast in an extension of the Estonian oil shale basin. The two thermal stations have produced enough electrical power for Estonia to export some to Leningrad and the Latvian Republic. The third of the shale production that is not used for power generation is used for various chemicals and refined shale products.

Although within the context of the total U.S.S.R. fuel and power industry, this operation is a minor one, it is one of the biggest oil shale operations in the world, and it is very important to the fuel-poor Baltic and western regions of the country. It is not as significant for gas generation as it was before the coming of natural gas pipelines from other parts of the country. However, with its use switched primarily to electrical power generation, it can be used efficiently at the mine heads, and the power can be transmitted cheaply to other parts of the East European area.

In addition to the natural gas brought in through the old Leningrad-Tallinn pipeline, a major gas pipeline has been built westward from the Moscow-Leningrad transmission system at the town of Valday through Pskov to Riga. This brings in primarily gas from the Vuktyl field in the Komi A.S.S.R. in northeast European Russia. An older pipeline was built to Riga from the south to carry Dashava gas from the northern foothills of the Carpathians (now depleted) northward through Belorussia to Latvia. A branch line carries gas westward to the port of Liepaja on the coast of Latvia. The coming of all this gas to the region has allowed the Baltic Region to cut down on high-cost long-haul coal from the Donets Basin and establish nitrogenous fertilizer industries based on natural gas such as that in Kohtla-Jarve. Natural gas has also provided the basis for some thermal power plants and nitrogenous fertilizer plants in Latvia and Lithuania.

Latvia also relies heavily on long-haul fuel oil from refineries at Novopolotsk in Belorussia and in central Russia. A branch of the Friendship oil pipeline has been built from Polotsk to Ventspils to alleviate this hauling on the railroads, and recently a parallel pipeline has been built from Polotsk to Ventspils to facilitate export of oil from this west Latvian port. Tankers now sail from Ventspils to more than 20 countries in Europe, Asia, Africa, and South America. The deepwater harbor is being enlarged to cope with the increased demand for Soviet oil products. An oil refinery is now under construction at the small town of Mazeikiai in northern Lithuania near the Latvian border.

In the late 1960s the Soviets announced the possibilities of oil in Kaliningrad Oblast and the Lithuanian S.S.R. By 1974 nine producing wells had been drilled in Kaliningrad Oblast, and commercial crude began moving by railroad tank car to the Novopolotsk refinery. If production goes as predicted, a 300-kilo-

meter pipeline will be built from the Kaliningrad fields to the oil refinery that is now under construction at Mazeikiai. Although it is still too early to tell, this looks like a minor development. However, the Soviets are now hinting at the possibility of oil deposits beneath the Baltic.

All three of the Baltic republics have cement plants based on local limestone outcrops. Altogether there are four major plants that have made the Baltic Region self-sufficient in cement production. In addition, glacial gravels and other construction materials are readily available.

An unusual natural resource found in the Baltic Region is amber, a fossil resin from extinct coniferous trees. Two-thirds of the world's amber is produced in Kaliningrad Oblast and Lithuania S.S.R. Most is used for jewelry, but the amber not suitable for jewelry can be used for succinic acid, medicines, varnish, and reactive substances. It is also used for electrical insulation. There are impressive collections of amber at the amber-producing center in Kaliningrad and at the amber museum in Palanga, Lithuania. But the major collections have been gathered in the Hermitage Museum in Leningrad and the Armory in Moscow.

Water Resources and Fishing

The Baltic Region is heavily oriented toward the sea. Three of its major cities are ports that handle a significant amount of Soviet traffic moving westward through the Baltic. Riga has been an important commercial center since medieval times when it was a member of the Hanseatic League. Major ports exist at Riga, Tallinn, Kaliningrad, Ventspils, Liepaja, Klaipeda, Pärnu, and Narva. Many of these contain shipbuilding yards, and all of them are important fishing ports. The Baltic Economic Region accounts for about 25 percent of the fish catch of the U.S.S.R., and the Baltic seaports provide 90–95 percent of the fish catch of the region, mainly from the Baltic Sea and the North Atlantic Ocean. Major fish canneries have been established in many cities, particularly in Ventspils and Liepaja.

The lesser ports of Ventspils, Liepaja,

Klaipeda, and Kaliningrad, on the west coast of Latvia, Lithuania, and Kaliningrad Oblast, have the advantage of being essentially ice-free during winter, whereas the large port of Riga on the nearly enclosed Gulf of Riga is hampered by ice much of the time from December through May. Therefore, during winter these smaller ports carry a great deal of traffic. It appears that the port of Kaliningrad has never regained the eminence it had when it was Königsberg in East Prussia. Since this is the westernmost Soviet port on the Baltic, it would seem logical that it would become one of the main ports in the area. Apparently the Soviets are still wary of holding this far-westerly exposed territory.

Three hydroelectric plants have been built on the Daugava (Western Dvina) River in Latvia. In 1953 a small plant with a capacity of only 68,000 kilowatts was built at Kagums 50 kilometers southeast of Riga. In 1966 the much larger Plavinas station, with a capacity of 825,000 kilowatts, was completed at the town of Stucka 80 kilometers southeast of Riga. In 1975 the first stage of the Riga hydroelectric plant was in production at the suburb of Salaspils on the southeastern outskirts of Riga. This is to have an ultimate capacity of 384,000 kilowatts. These three hydroelectric plants supply less than 40 percent of Latvia's electrical consumption, and they serve primarily during peak-load periods. The bulk of Latvia's electricity is produced by thermal electric plants using local peat or natural gas piped in from other parts of the country. Although there have been several plans to build hydroelectric plants on the Neman River in Lithuania, one by one each of these has been abandoned, primarily because the proposed reservoirs would flood scarce farmland.

Manufacturing

The limitations imposed on the economy of the Baltic Region by the natural environment and the relative lack of nationally significant mineral resources have induced the people in the Baltic Region to be very innovative in augmenting their economy by developing a wide variety of light industries turning out consumer durables, all sorts of household gadgets, clothing, food, and so forth. Factories in this area often lead in the design of new appliances and conveniences for the home, in appearance often resembling those produced in Scandinavia across the Baltic. The region specializes in refrigerators, washing machines, motorcyles, and so forth. One-fifth of the radio sets and hi-fi systems used in the Soviet Union are manufactured in Riga. In addition, Riga is the leading producer in the country of electric and diesel trains and is one of the major producers of minibuses. The Baltic Region manufactures 27 percent of the country's railroad passenger cars and 22 percent of the streetcars.

The Baltic Region is also known for its woodworking, particularly the manufacture of plywood, paper products, and furniture. Although the forest resources of the region constitute only 0.8 percent of the country's total, the region produces 3 percent of the country's lumber, 10 percent of the paper, and 7 percent of the furniture.

All this manufacturing activity since World War II has shot the Baltic Region into first place in industrial growth rate in the country. According to Soviet statistics the Baltic Region increased its industrial output from 1940 to 1972 by more than 34 times, while the country as a whole increased by less than 14 times.

CITIES

Riga

The largest city in the Baltic Economic Region is Riga, with a 1974 population of 776,000. The city was founded in 1201 as a fortress and has long served as the focal city of the Latvian nationality group. Between the two world wars it served as the capital of the free Republic of Latvia. Sitting on the shore of the Gulf of Riga at the mouth of the Western Dvina River, it has been one of the major ports along the Baltic from early times, and during the Middle Ages it became one of the Hanseatic League cities. Its main function, therefore, has been one of commerce, with such industries as shipbuilding and fishing being of prime importance. However, since World War II many other industries have been introduced into the city, including such heavy industries as the construction of trains and streetcars, as already mentioned.

Vilna

Second in size is Vilna, the capital of the Lithuanian Republic, which in 1974 had a population of 420,000. Vilna apparently was founded in the twelfth century. After the downfall of the Livonian knights it became the cultural and religious center for Lithuanians and East European Jews. In 1323 Prince Gedimin made it the capital of the Duchy of Lithuania. By the sixteenth century it had lost some of its eminence due to the merging of Lithuania with Poland. In 1795 it was annexed by Russia along with much of Poland. The World War I peace treaty established Lithuania as an independent country, but in 1920 the Poles took over Vilna and the surrounding territory. In 1939 the Soviet Union restored Vilna to Lithuania as a political gesture to soften up Lithuania for annexation to the Soviet Union.

Vilna is not located on the coast and therefore does not serve as a port, as do Riga and Tallinn, the other republic capitals. However, in recent years it has grown faster than Tallinn, and it has now surpassed it in size. But it serves simply as the seat of government and a center of light industries and transport within the Lithuanian Republic.

Tallinn

The third city in size is Tallinn, the capital of the Estonian Republic, which in 1974 had a population of 392,000. It was founded as a Danish fortress in 1154, and later was known as Revel. Besides serving as the capital of Estonia, it is a fairly important port on the Baltic Sea, and it contains a variety of light industries.

Kaunas

Like Vilna, Kaunas is an important city on the Neman River in southern Lithuania. It is an old city that has grown with the traffic on the river. During the period between the two

Figure 10-3   The medieval city of Tallinn. Courtesy of Robert Jasiorkowski.

world wars when Lithuania was an independent country and Vilna was within Poland, Kaunas was the capital city of the independent country of Lithuania. During that time it underwent a great deal of growth. Since World War II it has lost its role as a capital city, but it has become a major railroad and industrial center. It turns out metalwork, lathes, electrical apparatus, and is a main center for silk, wool, and synthetic textiles, as well as food and furniture industries. It has a polytechnic institute, a medical center, and an agricultural academy. In 1974 its population was 337,000.

Kaliningrad

Fifth city in size is Kaliningrad, the seat of government of newly acquired Kaliningrad Oblast, which in 1974 had a population of 331,000. It is the old city of Königsberg, which was the main seaport in the section of East Prussia that was taken over by the Russians after World War II. The city was first established in 1255 as a fortress of the Livonian Knights. The present city has only about two-thirds the population of the former city, and so far it has not assumed the importance as a seaport that Königsberg had. However, its port facility is perhaps its main function along with fishing and shipbuilding. The Soviets have established some heavy transport equipment and other industries in the city.

Klaipeda

The sixth city in size is Klaipeda, on the west coast of Lithuania. This is the old town of Memel. It serves primarily as the port for the Lithuanian Republic. In 1974 it had a population of 160,000.

Daugavpils

The seventh and final city in the Baltic Economic Region above 100,000 population is Daugavpils on the Daugava River (Western Dnina) in southeastern Latvia. In 1974 it had a population of 109,000. It is simply a regional center for the area often called Latgale in southeastern Latvia.

One other old town that should be mentioned is Tartu, in southeastern Estonia, which in 1974 had a population of 96,000. This is the old university city of Dorpat.

Many of the port cities already mentioned have developed important resort functions along the Baltic, as have many smaller cities in between. Although the Baltic's waters never warm up much in summer, and although the skies are frequently overcast, the Baltic coast from Leningrad westward to Kaliningrad has become a major summer resort area for the Soviet Union.

PROSPECTS

The Baltic Economic Region has been the fastest industrializing region in the country since World War II. Industries turn out a great range of consumer goods including large appliances and are based on the highly skilled nature of the labor of the area. In many cases industries in this region serve as the leading stylists for finished goods throughout the country. Although the environment is very restrictive for agriculture, agriculture is improving constantly as land reclamation and better methods of farming are introduced.

The rapid rise in industrialization coupled with a low natural population increase has produced some severe labor shortages in certain sectors of the economy. This has induced a steady stream of Russian workers into the area, which has diluted the nationality groups in their own republics. It seems inevitable that this process will continue. Although there is still a great deal of antagonism toward the Russians by the native Baltic peoples, things have settled down very much since the annexation of the territories during World War II, and it now seems that the Baltic states are integral parts of the Soviet Union and will remain such for the foreseeable future. The economy of these republics has become very much integrated with the rest of the Soviet Union, and the large market of the Soviet

Union for Baltic products, as well as the large Russian hinterland for Baltic seaports, has been beneficial to the economic development of the region during the last 30 years.

READING LIST

• Danilevicius, E., *Lithuania in Questions and Answers,* Gintaras, Vilnius, 1970, 246 pp.

• Dunn, Stephen P., *Cultural Processes in the Baltic Area Under Soviet Rule,* University of California Press, Berkeley, 1966, 92 pp.

• *Estonskaya SSR* (Estonian S.S.R.), Akademiya Nauk Estonskoy SSR, Institut Ekonomiki, Moscow, 1957, 366 pp. (in Russian).

• Fedor, Thomas S., "Demographic Trends in Estonia," *Geographical Review,* July 1974, pp. 425–427.

• Gargasas, Peter, *Litovskaya SSR* (Lithuanian S.S.R.), Moscow, 1960, 126 pp. (in Russian).

• Idzelis, Augustine, *Industrialization of the Lithuanian SSR: A Case Study in Soviet Industrial Location Theory,* Master's thesis, Kent State University, 1971.

• Itsikzon, M.R., *Litovskaya SSR* (Lithuanian S.S.R.), Moscow, 1960, 63 pp. (in Russian).

• *Journal of Baltic Studies,* The Association for the Advancement of Baltic Studies, New York.

• Kolotiyevskiy, Anton M., *Latviyskaya SSR* (Latvian S.S.R.), Moscow, 1955, 117 pp. (in Russian).

• Krepp, Endel, *The Baltic States: A Survey of the International Relations of Estonia, Latvia, and Lithuania,* Stockholm, 1968, 20 pp.

• Lazdyn, V.K., and V.R. Purin, *Riga; ekonomiko-geograficheskiy ocherk* (Riga; Economic-Geographic Study) Moscow, 1957, 95 pp. (in Russian).

• *The Lithuanian Soviet Socialist Republic,* Novosti Press, Moscow, n.d., 64 pp.

• *Litovskaya SSR* (Lithuanian S.S.R.), Akademiya Nauk Litovskoy SSR, Institut Geografii, Moscow, 1955, 390 pp. (in Russian).

• "Narodnoe khozyaystvo Latviyskoy SSR v 1973 godu" (The National Economy of the Latvian S.S.R. in 1973), *Statistical Yearbook,* Liesma, Riga, 1974, 590 pp. (in Russian and Latvian).

• Parming, Marju Rink, *A Bibliography of English-Language Sources on Estonia: Periodicals, Bibliographies, Pamphlets, and Books,* Estonian Learned Society in America, New York, 1974, 72 pp.

• *Pribaltiyskiy ekonomicheskiy rayon* (The Baltic Economic Region), Nauka, Moscow, 1970, 308 pp. (in Russian).

• "Problemy prirodopolzovaniya v Sovetskoy pribaltike" (Conference on Resource Use in the Baltic Region — Riga, April 1972), *Izvestiya Akademii Nauk SSSR, seriya geograficheskaya,* No. 5, 1972, pp. 146–148 (in Russian).

• Purin, V.R., and M.I. Rostovtsev, "Sovetskaya Latviya v novoy pyatiletke" (Soviet Latvia in the New Five-Year Plan), *Geografiya v Shkole,* No. 3, 1973, pp. 11–17 (in Russian).

• Raman, K., *Priroda i landshafty Latvii* (The Natural Environment and Landscapes of Latvia), Riga, 1967 (in Russian).

• Rauch, Georg von, *The Baltic States: The Years of Independence: Estonia, Latvia, Lithuania, 1917–1940,* University of California Press, Berkeley, 1974, 265 pp.

• Rostovstev, M.I., and V. Yu. Tarmisto, *Estonskaya SSR* (Estonian S.S.R.), Moscow, 1957, 365 pp. (in Russian).

• Rostovtsev, M.I., "Zapadno-Dvinskiy Kaskad" (Western Dvina Cascade), *Geografiya v shkole,* No. 6, 1961, pp. 28–31 (in Russian).

• Sharkov, V.A., *Estonskaya SSR* (Estonian S.S.R.), Moscow, 1956, 118 pp. (in Russian).

• *Sovetskiy Soyuz: Estoniya* (Soviet Union: Estonia), Mysl, Moscow, 1967, 254 pp. (in Russian).

• *Sovetskiy Soyuz: Litva* (Soviet Union: Lithuania), Mysl, Moscow, 1967, 286 pp. (in Russian).

• Spekke, Arnolds, *History of Latvia,* Goppers, Stockholm, 1957, 436 pp.

• Tavydas, Stasys, *Litva* (Lithuania), Moscow, 1967, 285 pp. (in Russian).

• Tomingas, William, *The Soviet Colonization of Estonia,* Kultuur Pub. House, New York, 1973, 312 pp.

• Vardys, V. Stanley, "How the Baltic Republics Fare in the Soviet Union", *Foreign Affairs,* April 1966, pp. 512–517.

• Vardys, V. Stanley, *Lithuania Under the Soviets,* Praeger, New York, 1965, 299 pp.

• Varep, Endel, *Estoniya* (Estonia), Moscow, 1967, 253 pp. (in Russian).

• Weis, E.E., and V.R. Purin, *Latviyskaya SSR* (Latvian S.S.R.), Moscow, 1967, 439 pp. (in Russian).

The Northwest Economic Region

	Area (km²)	Population	Persons/km²	Percent Urban
Archangel Oblast	587,000	1,415,000	2.4	69
Nenets National Okrug	177,000	39,000	0.2	56
Vologda Oblast	146,000	1,288,000	8.8	52
Leningrad City	86,000	4,133,000 }	65.5	100
Leningrad Oblast		1,495,000 }		37
Murmansk Oblast	145,000	854,000	5.9	89
Novgorod Oblast	55,000	718,000	13.0	58
Pskov Oblast	55,000	864,000	15.6	47
Karelian A.S.S.R.	172,000	720,000	4.2	73
Komi A.S.S.R.	416,000	997,000	2.4	65
Total	1,663,000	12,484,000	7.5	76

chapter 11

the northwest economic region

The Northwest Economic Region encompasses the whole of northern European U.S.S.R. from Finland on the western border to the Ural Mountains on the eastern border. Most of the region lies north of the 60th parallel. It is the first of the far-northern regions in the U.S.S.R. to be discussed and the first of the very large, sparsely populated regions, which will occur so frequently in the remainder of the book. Its total area amounts to 1,663,000 square kilometers, which is almost four times as big as the Central Region to the south. However, its population is only 12,484,000, which is less than half that of the Central Region. The average population density is only 7.5 persons per square kilometer. Most of the region is sparsely populated, for much of it lies beyond the limits of agriculture. Only the large city of Leningrad alters this generalization significantly, and if the city of Leningrad is removed, Leningrad Oblast, which is the most populated part of the region, has a population density of only 17–18 persons per square kilometer. The density ranges downward through the rest of the region to a minimum of only 0.2 persons per square kilometer in the Nenets National Okrug.

Because of the poor prospects for agriculture, most of the people in the region are engaged in nonagricultural pursuits and are living in cities. The Northwest Region is 76 percent urbanized. The greatest urbanization appears in the far north, in Murmansk Oblast,

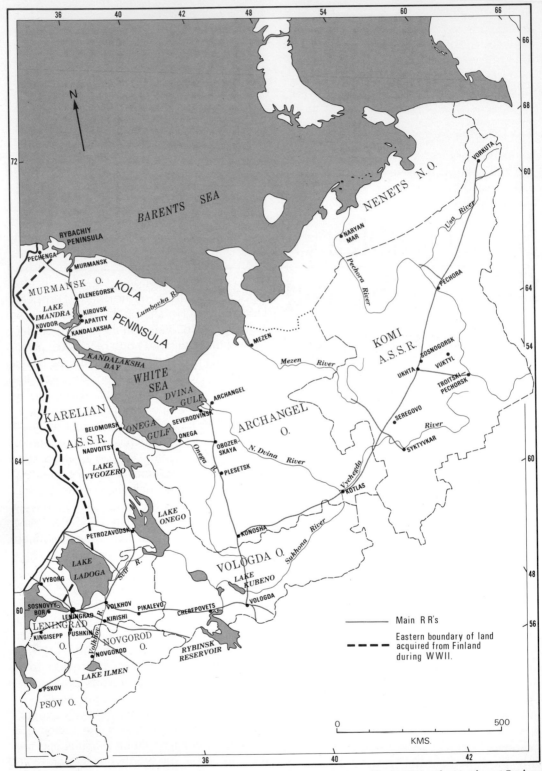

Figure 11-1 The Northwest Region.

where 89 percent of the population is classified as urban. Here there is very little opportunity for any other sort of economic activity. Along the southern fringe of the region, where agriculture is more possible, Leningrad Oblast, excluding the city of Leningrad, is only 37 percent urbanized, and Pskov Oblast is only 47 percent urbanized.

Although this extensive area is somewhat homogeneous in terms of climate, vegetation, and soils, it consists of two very different parts according to rock structure and mineralization. The western part has also been considerably more developed than the eastern part. Therefore, until 1963 this area was divided into two economic regions, the Northwest and the North. The striking differences between these two parts will become obvious as the discussion proceeds.

TERRITORIAL ACQUISITION AND POPULATION

The bulk of the territory encompassed by the Northwest Economic Region has been in the Russian Empire since the acquisition of the lands of Novgorod by Ivan III in 1478. The western part of the territory — which now comprises the Karelian A.S.S.R. and adjacent parts of Murmansk and Leningrad Oblasts — and Finland have been in contention for centuries, primarily between Russia and Sweden. The Leningrad area was acquired by Russia for good during the Northern Wars between Peter the Great and Charles XII during the first quarter of the eighteenth century.

From 1809 to 1918 all of Finland was in the Russian Empire. The peace treaty after World War I established Finland as an independent country, but the Soviets never fully accepted this arrangement, and they took the opportunity early in World War II to invade Finland. Two brief but bitter wars ensued between the two countries. Although the Soviet Union was unsuccessful in taking over Finland, several important boundary adjustments were forced upon the Finns. (Fig. 11-1). The largest areas transferred to the Russians lay in the extreme north and extreme south. The Pechenga area

in the north, or Petsamo as it was known to the Finns, is an area with important nickel and copper deposits. This area, along with the Rybachiy ("fishermen's") Peninsula, was taken over by the Russians in two different maneuvers in 1940 and 1944. In the south the entire Karelian Isthmus between Leningrad and Vyborg was ceded to the Soviet Union by the Finns, and this area was placed under the jurisdiction of Leningrad Oblast, probably for strategic and economic reasons. A number of small pieces of land were ceded to the Russians all along the Finnish border.

In 1923, shortly after the Soviet Union had been constituted, the Karelian area was made into the Karelian A.S.S.R. within the Russian Republic in order to give recognition to the Karelians, a Finnish-speaking Russian Orthodox group. Then, in 1940, with the onset of World War II, the area was reconstituted into the Karelo-Finnish S.S.R., apparently to entice the Finns to be more kindly disposed toward the Russians. It is quite obvious now that this was a purely political maneuver, because in 1956, without any forewarning or explanation, the union republic was downgraded once more to an autonomous republic and again was placed under the jurisdiction of the Russian Republic. The area never did warrant union republic status according to the constitution, which states that in order for an area to become a union republic it must have at least one million people with a majority of those people being of the titular nationality. According to the 1970 census, the Karelian A.S.S.R. still had only 713,451 people, of which only 11.8 percent were Karelians. The Russians made up 68.1 percent of the population, the Belorussians 9.3 percent, and the Ukrainians 3.8 percent. The Finns made up only 3.1 percent.

The Russians also greatly predominate in the Komi A.S.S.R. and in the Nenets National Okrug. In 1970 the Russians made up 53.1 percent of the population of the Komi A.S.S.R., while the Komi made up only 28.6 percent. In the Nenets National Okrug the Russians made up almost 65 percent of the population, and the Nentsy only 15 percent. Hence, none of these political units satisfy constitutional requirements. This situation is now true in most of the nationality-based political units below the republic level, and even the Kazakh and Kirgiz Republics do not satisfy constitutional requirements.

PHYSICAL LANDSCAPE

Landform

The northwestern portion of the Northwest Economic Region is composed of the eastern fringe of the Precambrian Baltic Crystalline Shield that underlies all of Scandinavia. Around this to the east and south lies a broad sedimentary plain whose more resistant strata have formed cuestas as erosion has stripped the sedimentary cover down the gentle dip slope toward the southeast. The contact zone between the sedimentary rocks to the south and crystalline rocks to the north is marked by a broad inner lowland at the northern foot of a prominent limestone escarpment, the western portion of which was referred to as the Glint in the last chapter. This lowland is marked by the large water bodies of the Gulf of Finland in the west, Lakes Ladoga and Onega in the center, and portions of the White Sea in the northeast. In between are many smaller lakes.

Superimposed on top of the rock-controlled topography throughout the entire region are more recent glacial materials, which in many places obscure the relationship between the rock structure and the surface topography. The older Dnieper glacial stage covered the entire region, the more recent Moscow stage covered most of the region, and the most recent Valday stage covered approximately the northwestern half, although glaciofluvial influences extended well beyond the edges of the ice. All of these glacial advances profoundly influenced the topography, but of course the older materials under the processes of subsequent erosion have become less distinctive than the younger. In the flat northern plains, particularly in the river basins of the Northern Dvina, the Mezen, and the Pechora, as well as parts of the Kola Peninsula and southern Karelia, postglacial transgressions of the sea im-

mediately after the ice was unloaded from the isostatically depressed land rewashed the glacial materials and obscured their surface forms.

The Baltic Shield within the Soviet Union is limited primarily to Murmansk Oblast and the Karelian A.S.S.R., although it does extend into the northern part of Leningrad Oblast and the western part of Archangel Oblast. The shield consists of Precambrian schists, gneisses, and granites that have been intruded by younger magmas. In places these are overlain by quartzites, sandstones, and shales. Everywhere the crystalline massif has been cut by tectonic fractures trending generally west-northwest–east-southeast parallel to the northeastern Murmansk coast. In places, particularly in the Kola Peninsula, there is also a set of tectonic fractures running south-southwest–east-northeast. Thus, the region consists of distinct blocks, some of which have been elevated and others depressed with respect to each other. The depressed zones are occupied by hundreds of interconnected lakes that are elongated in a northwest-southeast direction, as are the deep embayments of the White Sea, the Onega and Dvina Gulfs in the south, and Kandalaksha Bay in the north. Most of the tectonic movements date from Precambrian times and were accompanied by volcanic activity along the cross-fractures, which formed the massive laccoliths of the Khibiny Mountains and surrounding areas in the central part of the Kola Peninsula, containing rich deposits of apatite, copper, nickel, and iron. During the Tertiary, orogenic processes renovated many of the ancient cracks and fissures. At this time some of the sunken blocks were in part inundated by the White and Barents Seas.

The Kola Peninsula can be characterized as a rough, rolling peneplain with elevations of 400–500 meters above sea level. But in the central part of the peninsula the Khibiny, Lovozero, and Monche Tundras rise to a maximum elevation of 1191 meters above sea level in Mt. Chasnochor in the Khibiny. The term *tundra* here is used in its Laplander context meaning "bald mountaintop." The relief is much more uniform throughout much of

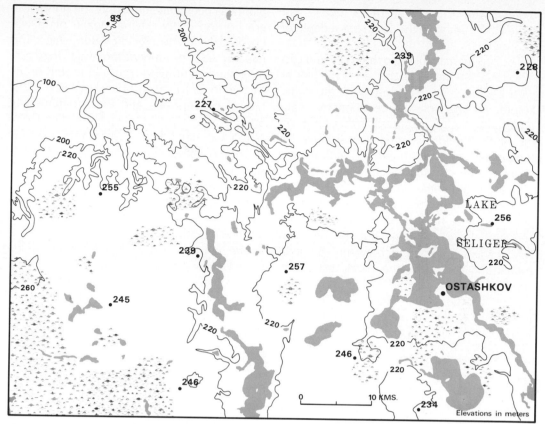

Figure 11-2 The morainal topography of the Valday Hills. From *Landscape Atlas of the USSR,* p. 38.

Karelia where elevations generally lie between 100–120 meters above sea level. However, in the southwestern portion of the region elevations above 250 meters are common, and the very highest point lies 658 meters above sea level.

Since the Baltic Shield was the center for the formation of continental glaciers in Europe, the chief ice action in the Kola-Karelia region has been one of ice scour, which has moved materials southward and southeastward out of the region to leave the higher summits polished clean of weathered debris. The hills tend to be rounded and smoothed off in the form of roches moutonnees. In between, the depressions have been partially filled with glacial till, on top of which in many cases are lakes, marshes, and swamps. The streams have not been able to re-form coherent valleys in the hard rock surface during the short period since glaciation, and they pick their way as best they can among the rocky hills from lake to lake, often forming sections with steep gradients and many rapids alternating with quiet lake impoundments. Most of the streams follow the ancient fissures in the bedrock from west-northwest to east-southeast. Although there are no large streams in the area, the steep gradients and light sediment load in the streams that do exist provide ideal conditions for water power development such as that along the Niva River flowing southward into Kandalaksha Bay. There are more than 11,000 small rivers throughout Karelia. Some of them contain waterfalls reaching heights of as much as 15–16 meters.

Karelia contains more than 50,000 lakes, which occupy 9 percent of the total territory. Most of them have depths of from 6 to 10 meters, with a maximum of 25 meters. But large Lake Ladoga in the south has a depth of 225 meters.

The sedimentary plain to the south and east of Karelia that makes up the rest of the Northwest Region contrasts greatly with the Baltic Shield. At one time the sedimentary strata underlying the plain lapped farther north on the Baltic Shield, but stream erosion over a long period of time stripped the sedimentary strata southeastward down their dip slopes and produced some prominent cuestas that run southwest-northeast across the plain. Some of these have been obscured by subsequent glacial deposits, but the one that marks the contact zone between the sediments and the crystalline rocks just to the south of the "great lakes" and the White Sea, known as the White Sea-Kuloy scarp, in places stands 60–70 meters above the lowland to the northwest. Above this to the south stands the relatively undissected Kuloy Plateau, 120–140 meters above sea level, which slopes gently southeastward.

The large triangular plain filling up the northeast corner of European U.S.S.R. north of the 60th parallel consists of two main parts divided from one another by the Timan Ridge running northwestward from the middle Urals to the Arctic coast and across the northern end of the Kanin Peninsula. This is a broad, low upwarp that separates the drainage basins of the Northern Dvina and Mezen Rivers in the west from the Pechora River in the east. Elevations in the Timan Ridge generally run 250–300 meters in height with a maximum elevation reaching 463 meters above sea level. The relief of the ridge in general is that of a plain with occasional elongated hilly sections. Outcrops of crystalline rocks, basalts, quartzites, and sandstones form ridges with steep slopes and conic hills. In the coastal belt they form capes that extend well out into the sea. Where limestones outcrop karst forms are in evidence. The streams flowing off the ridge to either side form narrow incised valleys with rapids and small waterfalls.

In contrast, the plain on either side is much flatter and lower, with average elevations running 100–200 meters. Although the entire plain has been glaciated, only the northwestern portion of the Dvina-Mezen plain was covered by the most recent Valday stage. This has formed a prominent morainic ridge running south-southwest from the mouth of the Mezen River to Lake Kubenskoye east of the city of Cherepovets and then southwest to Smolensk, Vilna in Lithuania, and then to the North German Plain. East of this morainic ridge the somewhat older glacial features have been subdued over a large area by postglacial transgressions of the sea that followed immediately on the heels of the glacial retreat before the isostatically depressed land had a chance to spring back.

The more prominent glacial features in the western part of the Dvina-Mezen Plain are augmented by karst features in outcropping limestones. Sinkholes 6–10 meters deep, many of them occupied by lakes, caverns, underground rivers, and abundant solution springs, are scattered in a broad area southwestward from the White Sea borderland to the southern shores of Lakes Onega and Ladoga.

Throughout this northern plain, particularly in the broad river basins, drainage is a severe problem. During spring when melting occurs, the headwaters of the northward-flowing streams thaw before the downstream portions do and produce broad-scale flooding behind ice jams on the lower rivers.

In the southwestern portion of the Northwest Economic Region a prominent feature runs south-southwestward from the southern shore of Lake Onega through what is known as the Tikhvin Ridge into the Valday Hills area. It forms part of a general upland formed by resistant Carboniferous limestones overlying Devonian friable sandy clays. This upland forms the prominent Valday scarp, 100–130 meters in height, overlooking the Ilmen Lowland to the west, in the center of which lies Lake Ilmen. The Valday Hills occupy the position on this scarp where the Valday terminal moraine crosses it at an acute angle to form a jumbled mass of hills and kettle lakes that occupy a region as much as 80 kilometers in width. The highest hills reach elevations of more than 300 meters, the single highest point of the upland being 346 meters near the northern shore of Lake Seliger. This is the largest and most complex of a series of more than 600 interconnecting lakes that occupy the broad swampy divide separating the drainage basins of the Volga to the east, the Dnieper to the south, the Western Dvina to the northwest, and the Lovat-Ilmen-Volkhov drainage northward to Lake Ladoga. (Fig. 11-2). The divide function of these hills lying among the headwaters of the major river systems on the East European Plain has accorded them their historical significance. Before the coming of railroads, the river trade routes focused on this portage area where boats had to be removed from one water system and lowered into another.

The helter-skelter nature of the morainic material, which in many places has buried the bedrock escarpment in glacial drift to depths of as much as 250 meters, has been made even more chaotic by sinkholes and other karst forms that have developed in the underlying limestone. Superimposed on top of the general morainic material are fields of kames, eskers, and drumlins, attesting to the fact that the topography of the area was formed near the edge of the ice cover. The abundance of lakes has caused the region often to be referred to as the *Poozerye,* "the lake region".

Climate, Vegetation, and Soils

The climate of the Northwest Economic Region everywhere is cool and humid. The western portion of the plain is tempered much more by the sea than the eastern portion, particularly during winter, when isotherms run more north-south than east-west across the plain. During winter little heat is received from insolation anywhere in the region, so land-sea effects are much more important than latitude. The northern part of the Kola Peninsula, as well as much of the Nenets National Okrug in the east, lies well north of the Arctic Circle and experiences a polar night for about one month during midwinter when the sun never rises above the horizon. Adding to the small effects of insolation during winter in this northern region is the high albedo of the snow, which reflects most of the small amount of sunlight that is received.

During January Leningrad averages −7.5°C (18°F), and the coldest temperature that has ever been experienced is −36°C. In the far north, at Murmansk, temperatures are about the same. January averages −9.9°C, and the absolute minimum is −38°C. In the eastern part of the region, Naryan-Mar near the coast averages −17.3°C in January and has experienced a minimum temperature of −51°C. Syktyvkar much farther south in the interior has experienced about the same temperatures, an average of −15.2°C during January and an absolute minimum of −51°C.

The city of Murmansk in the northern part of the Kola Peninsula sits near the head of the elongated, steep, narrow Kola Fjord and experiences a somewhat more severe climate than does the coast to the north. The seawater off the coast never freezes during winter because of the northerly extension of the North Atlantic Drift (an extension of the Gulf Stream), which brings warmer waters into the Barents Sea and produces an open-water area during winter that causes fog and low clouds along the Murman coast. In spite of its most northerly position, the port of Murmansk is one of the few open ports in the Soviet Union during the winter. It takes much of the traffic that would go to Leningrad during the ice-free season. At the narrow head of the Gulf of Finland, the port of Leningrad is hampered by ice from December through May. Also, the port of Archangel, much farther south than Murmansk on the nearly enclosed White Sea, is hampered by ice almost half the year.

During the long daylight periods of summer, latitude becomes the more important control of temperature, and isotherms tend to run west-east. In the southern part of the region July temperatures average 17.7°C at Leningrad in the west and 16.6°C at Syktyvkar in the east. Although Syktyvkar is a little farther north than Leningrad, its interior position allows warmer days occasionally during summer than in Leningrad. The absolute maximum temperature that has been observed at Syktyvkar is 35°C, while at Leningrad it is only 33°C. In the northern part of the

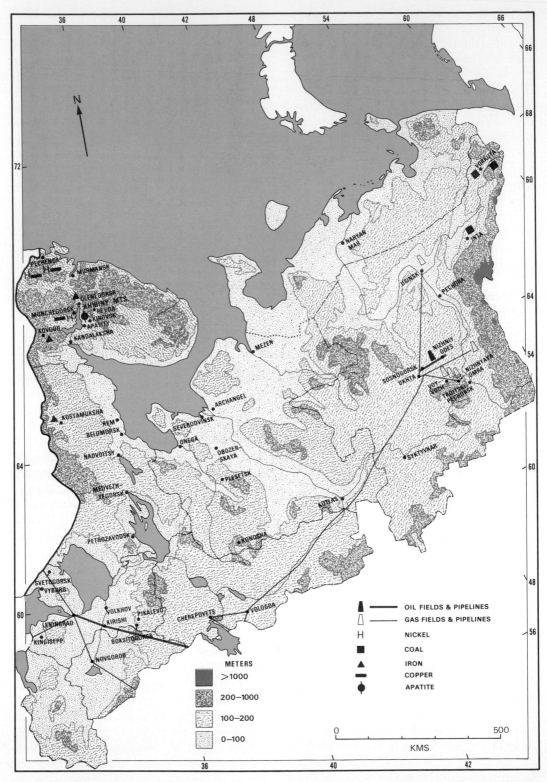

Figure 11-3 Landform, minerals, and pipelines.

region, July temperatures average 12.8°C at Murmansk in the west and 12.0°C at Naryan-Mar in the east. Both cities have observed temperatures as high as 33°C, which is exactly the same as the maximum temperature observed at Leningrad. Obviously the marine location is a major control on maximum temperatures.

The Northwest Region is extremely stormy. Favored storm tracks converge on the area along the Norwegian-Barents Sea route around the northern end of Scandinavia and along the Baltic route across the southern part of the region. Tight isobaric gradients in these storms frequently produce gale winds in the head of the Gulf of Finland that drive water into the lower parts of the city of Leningrad. They also produce large waves on Lakes Ladoga and Onega that may capsize boats. In the White and Barents Seas they may cause shipwrecks. During winter sharp temperature contrasts between land and sea along the Arctic Coast produce strong offshore winds much of the time.

The frequent cyclonic storms also cause much cloudiness and frequent precipitation. Almost all of this cloudiness is of the low stratus type, which produces the dull, dreary *pasmurnaya* days so characteristic of the north. Although precipitation falls frequently, it does not total very much, because no warm, unstable air masses are involved in these cyclonic storms. Air masses in this region are primarily of a maritime nature, coming in from both the Atlantic Ocean and the Barents Sea, and during winter continental arctic air may enter the region from the northeast. These air masses are all cool or cold, and although they generally have high relative humidities, their capacity to hold moisture is low. Hence, the precipitation amounts derived from them are meager. Leningrad receives measurable precipitation on 194 days of the year, but the annual total is only 559 millimeters (22 inches). Cloud cover averages eight to nine tenths from October through February and six to seven tenths from April through August; 172 days per year in Leningrad are overcast. Relative humidities of the surface air average almost 80 percent

throughout the year and reach a high of 88 percent during December. During December the sun is seldom seen; it never gets very high above the horizon, and it peeks above the horizon for only a short period of the day. During December 23 days are overcast. Typical winter weather in Leningrad is dark, dreary, overcast skies; raw, moisture-laden winds from the Gulf of Finland; and fine drizzle or light snow.

Summer skies are considerably clearer, with only 8.5 days being overcast in Leningrad in July. Precipitation falls on less than half the days, but it amounts to about twice as much as during winter. The maximum amount falls in August, which hampers the harvest in this poor farming area. During winter snow lies on the ground 132 days in Leningrad and reaches a maximum depth of 32 centimeters.

Farther north, Murmansk is even cloudier than Leningrad, and 191 days per year are overcast. Here the greatest amount of cloudiness occurs during autumn when arctic steam rises from the relatively warm Barents Sea into the cold air above to produce a great deal of fog and low stratus overcast along the Murman coast. Yearly precipitation reaches only 376 millimeters in Murmansk, but the cool temperatures, cloudy skies, and high atmospheric humidities make this region just as moist as the Leningrad area. Snow lies on the ground 195 days of the year in Murmansk and reaches a maximum depth of 64 centimeters. It reaches considerably greater depths on the northeastern slopes of the Khibiny in the central part of the Kola Peninsula, where northeastern winds in the advancing edges of cyclonic storms often drive moisture-laden air upslope along the low mountain ridges. Here snowpacks may accumulate to more than 100 centimeters in depth.

The great amounts of low cloudiness and frequent precipitation continue eastward throughout the region. Naryan-Mar has 200 days per year with overcast skies, and Syktyvkar in the interior has 201. Both cities have 201 days per year with measurable precipitation. Snow lies on the ground 221 days per year in Naryan-Mar and reaches a maximum depth of 64 centimeters. At Syktyvkar it stays on the ground 186 days and reaches a maximum depth of 56 centimeters.

The cool, humid climatic conditions have been conducive to the growth of a forest vegetation throughout most of the region, except for the northern fringe where summer temperatures are too cool even for tree growth. Tundra occupies all of the Nenets National Okrug in the northeast and a broad coastal strip westward almost to Archangel. It occupies most of the Kola Peninsula, except for the southern fringe and the foothills on the protected southern side of the Khibiny Mountains.

During the glacial period all vegetation in the Northwest Region perished, and then repopulated the lowland as the glaciers melted back. Vegetation encroached on the area both from the west and from the east. Therefore, today the western portions of the lowland in the Dvina-Mezen drainage basin are populated primarily by spruce, pine, and birch from Europe, while the Pechora Lowland in the east is populated primarily by Siberian forms, such as fir, cedar, and larch. The tree species in the Pechora Basin are much less valuable for lumber than are those in the Dvina-Mezen Basin.

Some of the best pine and spruce forests in the Soviet Union exist in the Onega, Northern Dvina, and Mezen River valleys. These stretch all the way from the western border of Karelia to the Urals in eastern Komi A.S.S.R. However, the western sections have been cut over rather heavily.

In the southern tier of oblasts, Vologda, Novgorod, and Pskov, as well as in adjacent parts of Leningrad Oblast, the forests have been cut over repeatedly, and a considerable portion of the land where drainage is not too poor has been cleared for agriculture. Minor areas of cultivation exist throughout the remainder of the forest zone, primarily on river floodplains, but it is a marginal effort at best. Although pine and spruce are the dominant forest species, there are significant admixtures of birch, aspen, and alder. And large sections of the land are too ill drained to support tree growth, so marshland is very extensive.

The soils throughout the Northwest Region are poor. The cool, humid climate, poor drainage, and coniferous forests and tundra vegetation have been conducive to extreme podsolization processes that have leached most of the plant minerals from the soil and created little humus content. In lowlands, bog soils predominate. Where agriculture is practiced, soils must be treated heavily with mineral fertilizers to keep them productive.

AGRICULTURE

This is a poor agricultural region at best. Most of the cultivation is limited to the three southwestern oblasts, Vologda, Novgorod, and Pskov. There is some cultivation in adjacent Leningrad Oblast, in southern Karelia in the west, and in the southern part of the Komi A.S.S.R. in the east, particularly around the capital city of Syktyvkar. In this southern part of the region the crops are primarily flax and potatoes. There is some growing of small grains, primarily oats and rye, and some hay. The agricultural economy is based heavily on livestock, particularly dairy cows. Vologda Oblast is known as the dairy belt of the Soviet Union, although it does not produce nearly as much dairy products as some of the better farming areas farther south. However, in this northern region dairying is the primary effort and therefore is characteristic. Urban-oriented agriculture has been developed during the last 20 years around most of the larger cities. This consists of the raising of a variety of vegetables and fruits that can be adapted to the cool, short growing season and to dairying, swine, and poultry raising. Cucumbers and tomatoes are grown in extensive greenhouses.

Throughout much of the rest of the forest zone, cultivation is very limited and is generally found in the natural meadowlands along the river valleys. In the northern tundra, agriculture is limited primarily to the herding of reindeer. This, along with fishing, is the main occupation of the Nentsy in the northeast, and also of the Laplanders of the Kola Peninsula, who continue to frustrate Soviet authorities by wandering back and forth at will across the international border into Norway.

This region is to benefit with the Central Region and the Volga-Vyatka Region in the 15-year plan to upgrade the agriculture of the nonchernozem part of European R.S.F.S.R. Drainage, land-clearing, and field-consolidation programs are to be carried out, as well as heavy mechanization, fertilization, and adaptation of new crops. The quality of rural life in the area is to be enhanced by reconstructing many villages, bringing electricity and natural gas to many of the villages, and building roads to provide access to the outside world. However, the shortness and coolness of the growing season will always limit this region to marginal agriculture.

INDUSTRIAL RESOURCES AND DEVELOPMENT

Mineral Resources

During the Soviet period, the northern part of European Russia has seen the development of quite a number of mineral resources that have provided the basis for the creation and growth of cities in certain parts of the area. In the west, in the crystalline Baltic Shield area, the metallic ores (iron, nephelite, bauxite, nickel, and copper) are of outstanding importance, as well as the nonmetallic ores (apatite and phosphorite.) In addition there are abundant supplies of limestone for various metallurgical and chemical industries and some of the rare metals. In the eastern part of the region in the broad sedimentary basin, particularly in the Pechora Basin, fairly extensive deposits of mineral fuels (coal, oil, and gas) have been found.

The first large development to be undertaken in this region by the Soviets was the utilization of the large apatite deposit in the Khibiny Mountains in the center of the Kola Peninsula. The town of Kirovsk was established in 1929 to act as the center of production in this empty mountain tundra region. Apatite production began in 1929 and by 1973 had reached a production of 13.4 million tons of concentrate, which accounted for

about 80 percent of all the phosphate materials in the country and served 26 superphosphate plants in European U.S.S.R. In 1963 a second and larger concentrater opened up at the new town of Apatity southwest of Kirovsk. About half of the present production is exported, primarily to East and West Germany, Czechoslovakia, Poland, Rumania, Hungary, Bulgaria, Finland, Norway, Belgium, and Sweden. Most of the concentrated ore for export moves northward by rail to Murmansk, where it is shipped to the other countries. The Kola apatite is by far the largest deposit of apatite in the world. Within the Soviet Union it is a resource of national significance.

As other areas begin to produce phosphatic ores, the share of total Soviet production represented by the Kola apatite will steadily decrease. It has already dropped from 87 percent of total production in 1965 to 80 percent in 1973. It was scheduled to drop to less than 70 percent by 1975. But the absolute production of apatite in the Kirovsk-Apatity area continues to rise.

A new source of phosphorus has been opened up in the Northwest Region at the phosphorite deposit near the town of Kingisepp in Leningrad Oblast, where a fertilizer-manufacturing center has been established to produce ammonium phosphate. Production began in 1963 and has been continually expanding since. It appears that some of the Kola Peninsula apatite is going to be mixed with the local phosphate rock. Kingisepp was scheduled to produce about 2.2 percent of the country's phosphate fertilizers in 1975.

The second major development that took place in this region was in the aluminum industry. Small scattered deposits of bauxite were exploited in the 1930s around the new town of Boksitogorsk east of Leningrad, and an alumina-aluminum plant was built at the town of Volkhov, the site of a newly constructed hydroelectric plant on the Volkhov River. Production began at Volkhov in 1932, and for a while this was the primary aluminum-producing center in the country. Later in the 1930s some of the alumina was shipped southward from Volkhov to a new aluminum plant at Zaporozhye on the Dnieper in the Ukraine. In 1938 production began in a new alumina plant in the town of Boksitogorsk itself. However, immediately after World War II, much larger bauxite mines were opened up in the Urals, and aluminum production shifted eastward to large new hydroelectric plants on the Volga and in Siberia.

As the bauxite ores around Boksitogorsk began to be depleted, a new source of aluminum ore was needed to serve the alumina plants at Volkhov and Boksitogorsk. The Soviets settled on the use of low-grade nephelite, which is associated with the apatite ores of the Kola Peninsula. The nephelite had been discarded on waste piles of the apatite mines for years and was available for reworking for its aluminum content. The nephelite contains between 20–30 percent alumina. It is now being converted to alumina at the Volkhov plant and at a newer plant at Pikalevo in the same general region.

The production of alumina requires at least two tons of limestone for every ton of nephelite, and therefore alumina plants tend to be situated near abundant limestone deposits. The final product from a mix of four tons of nephelite and eight tons of limestone is one ton of alumina, ten tons of cement, and one ton of soda potash. Thus, the alumina plants east of Leningrad have also become large cement producers. According to Soviet data published in 1974, the Kola nephelite now accounts for about 10 percent of the Soviet Union's aluminum production. The Kola Peninsula now ships about 1.5 million tons of nephelite concentrate each year. This produces 400,000 tons of alumina, about 300,000 tons of which are being produced at Pikalevo and 100,000 tons at Volkhov. It is planned eventually to ship Kola nephelite to alumina plants at Ulyanovsk and Mikhaylovka in the Volga Region.

Some of the alumina produced at Volkhov and Pikalevo is converted to aluminum at the Volkhov alumina-aluminum plant. However, this small plant is not very well supplied by electricity from the small Volkhov Dam. Therefore, new aluminum plants have been constructed farther north to utilize some of the water power of the Karelia-Kola area. Aluminum reduction plants have been established at Nadvoitsy in Karelia and at Kandalaksha in the Kola Peninsula. Thus, some of the nephelite ore moving southward from the Kola Peninsula to Volkhov and Pikalevo eventually finds its way northward again to aluminum plants in the Karelia-Kola area.

A new development in the aluminum industry is now taking place in the Northwest Region. Since 1949 the Soviets have known of a major bauxite deposit near the town of Plesetsk on the west bank of the lower Onega River. This is a compact, high-grade ore body that averages 53 percent alumina. The deposit originally was listed in the eighth five-year plan, 1966–1970, for development, but the remoteness of the site and the heavily waterlogged terrain resulted in a delay of several years. Now a 7-mile rail spur has been built to link the area with the main north-south railroad running from Konosha to Archangel, a power transmission line has been built into the area, and excavation is going on in a 60-meter-deep pit that when completed is to have a capacity of several million tons of bauxite per year. This will be one of the largest aluminum ore producers in the Soviet Union. Initially this Onega bauxite is to move to the alumina plant at Boksitogorsk, but there are plans eventually to construct a separate alumina plant somewhere nearby, and possibly a new aluminum project as well.

A third mineral ore industry that has been developed by the Soviets in the Baltic Shield area of the western part of the Northwest Region is based on the many small, low-grade deposits of iron ore that exist in the Karelian A.S.S.R. and the Kola Peninsula. Much of this ore contains 30–35 percent iron and must be concentrated for use. The first production began in 1954 at the town of Olenegorsk in Murmansk Oblast in conjunction with the building of the iron and steel plant at Cherepovets more than 1200 kilometers to the south in Vologda Oblast.

The plant at Cherepovets began to produce steel in 1955 and now employs more than 30,000 workers. It contains four blast furnaces, open-hearth furnaces, and electric furnaces, as well as eight coke-oven batteries, which produce 4.5 million tons of coke per year from coal brought in from the Vorkuta district in the far northeastern corner of the region. In 1974 the plant produced more than 5 million tons of pig iron, 6 million tons of ingot steel, and more than 5 million tons of rolled-steel products. Cherepovets provides practically all of the steel needs of the Northwest Region, including the large city of Leningrad, whose machine-building industries are heavy users of steel.

In 1962 a new iron-mining operation began at Kovdor, also in Murmansk Oblast, to supplement the Olenegorsk ores. By 1974 these two iron-mining districts were producing about 10 million tons of iron concentrates, which amounted to between 4 and 5 percent of the country's iron ore production. About 7 million tons of this iron concentrate was shipped southward to Cherepovets, and the other 3 million tons was exported through Murmansk. The Cherepovets iron and steel plant also uses iron ore from the Kursk Magnetic Anomaly about 1000 kilometers to the south. In 1974 it shipped in about 2 million tons of usable ore from Kursk.

The Cherepovets iron and steel plant has been expanded into one of the major plants in the country. Plans call for further expansion to an ultimate capacity of at least 9 million tons of pig iron, 12 million tons of ingot steel, and 10 million tons of rolled-steel products per year. It has been estimated that by 1980 the Olenegorsk and Kovdor mines will be able to supply Cherepovets with only about 50 percent of its ore needs. Therefore, another ore deposit is being developed at the town of Kostamuksha in the west-central Karelian A.S.S.R. near the Finnish border. The Kostamuksha ores consist of iron quartzites containing about 30 percent iron, which will have to be beneficiated to about 65 percent concentrate. Total reserves have been estimated at 1.2 billion tons, which is more than the combined reserves of Olenegorsk and Kovdor. At the planned rate of development the Kostamuksha ores will last about 70 years. These ores will be about 350 kilometers closer to

Cherepovets than the Murmansk ores, thus allowing for some reduction of costs of assemblage of materials for the Cherepovets plant, which has the longest hauls of iron ore and coal anywhere in the country. This will also allow for more export of the Murmansk ores. The Soviets have enlisted the help of the Finns to develop the Kostamuksha ores, and in turn will ship ore to the Finnish iron and steel works at Raahe. Production is scheduled to begin in 1978. It is planned to build a concentrator and a town with an ultimate population of 45,000 at the mining site, which is to have an ultimate production capacity of 24 million tons of crude ore that will be converted into about 8 million tons of usable concentrate. Development will require the construction of an 80-kilometer rail spur, motor roads, and power transmission lines.

Copper and nickel deposits are fairly abundant in the Kola Peninsula area. Production of nickel and some copper has been taking place for a long time in the far northwestern corner of the region, the so-called Pechenga area that was taken over from the Finns during World War II. Copper and some nickel mining have recently been developed in the Monche Tundra west of Lake Imandra across from the apatite mining region in the Khibiny Mountains of the central Kola Peninsula.

In the far northeastern corner of the Northwest Economic Region lies the Pechora coal basin, one of the main producing basins in the country. Development began in what has become the city of Vorkuta in 1940, and production expanded rapidly with the use of political prisoners and prisoners of war during and shortly after World War II. Initial development of the basin was greatly speeded by the fact that the Soviets had lost the Donets coal basin to the Germans and badly needed a replacement for the war effort. During the war years the Pechora railroad extending northeastward from Kotlas to Vorkuta was hurriedly completed to facilitate the exploitation of this coal. There was no time to build an organized city for the workers, and the initial coal miners lived underground in the shaft mines that they had dug. Thus, Vorkuta took on the form of an arc of a circle extending from west to north along the edge of the basin where the coal was not too far below the surface. Eventually, of course, aboveground houses were built, but the pattern of the present city still reflects this early beginning.

Because of the severity of the climate of the Vorkuta area and its remoteness from markets, development since World War II has proceeded only rapidly enough to serve the needs of the Northwest Economic Region. About half the production is consumed at the iron and steel mill at Cherepovets, and the other half is used primarily for electrical generation and domestic heating in the northern area. The cost of mining is high, comparable to that in the Donets Basin, and the extra length of haul rules out competition between Vorkuta coal and Donets coal in central European Russia. Thus, in spite of the fact that all Vorkuta coal is of coking grade, the region has not been highly developed. In 1974 the Pechora Basin, including the separate Inta coalfields 240 kilometers southwest of Vorkuta, produced 23.3 million tons of coal out of a country total of 684 million. It ranked behind not only the Donets Basin and the Kuznetsk Basin, but also the Karaganda and Ekibastuz Basins in Kazakhstan and even the Moscow Basin in the Central Region. The Vorkuta area produces about two-thirds of the Pechora coal, all of coking grade, and the Inta field produces about one-third, all lower-grade steam coal.

The Soviets desire to make greater use of the rich Pechora coal reserves, and from time to time they have carried on lengthy discussions regarding how this can be done economically. Most of the discussions center around the use of these coals in the heavy metallurgy of the central and southern Urals. A number of rail routes have been proposed utilizing sections of existing routes to bring this coal southward into the Urals. However, the inevitable conclusion to all these discussions seems to be that in spite of the fact that Vorkuta is next to the northern end of the Urals, it is just as far from the industrial part of the Urals as the coalfields of Western Siberia and northern Kazakhstan. And the far north-

ern location of Pechora makes the coal more costly to mine. Therefore, under present conditions, it seems that the Pechora coal cannot compete in the central and southern Urals. If railroads are extended northward in the Urals to utilize mineral deposits farther north in the mountains themselves, then eventually the extension of a line into Vorkuta might be justified. Or, if an all-water route might be provided by the joining of the headwaters of the Pechora and Kama Rivers, the economic use of Vorkuta coal in the metallurgy of the Urals might be achieved. However, at present there are no definite plans for any of these schemes.

The western edge of the Pechora Basin along the eastern slope of the Timan Ridge has proved to be a fairly rich oil and gas region. Oil production began around the city of Ukhta during World War II and after 1960 increased as new fields were discovered in the area. By 1974 the Ukhta oil fields were producing about 7 million tons. Since 1970 a new field has opened up on the Usa River about 400 kilometers north of Ukhta. The new oil town of Usinsk was founded in 1971 and is expected ultimately to reach a population of 70,000. Oil production in this region began in 1973. A pipeline has been built from this new field southward to Ukhta, to a refinery at Yaroslavl on the Volga River, and on to a refinery in Moscow. A new rail line also is being built from the Kotlas-Vorkuta line northwestward to Usinsk. It is planned eventually to extend the line all the way to Naryan-Mar to serve the development planned for several oil and gas deposits that have been discovered along the way in the Nenets National Okrug. Also, it has been hinted that bauxite deposits have been discovered in this far northern region that might rival those of the Urals in magnitude.

It is suspected that large oil and gas reserves might exist under the continental shelf of the Barents Sea north of the Nenets National Okrug. A geological team, using Naryan-Mar as a base, is drilling exploratory wells in the shelf around Kolguyev Island.

An oil refinery went into production in 1966 in the new city of Kirishi 100 kilometers southeast of Leningrad. It uses crude oil from the Volga-Urals fields that originally was brought in by tank cars on the railroads. In 1969 a crude-oil pipeline was completed from the Volga-Urals fields to Kirishi, and in 1971 a pipeline for refined products was built between Kirishi and the Leningrad metropolitan area.

Natural gas production began in the Komi A.S.S.R. during World War II in the area about 50 kilometers southeast of Ukhta. This remained only a small production until the mid-1960s, when a larger field was opened up near Vuktyl about 175 kilometers east of Ukhta. This field began producing in 1968 with the completion of a 48-inch transmission line to Ukhta that was extended in 1969 to Rybinsk and Torzhok, the main gas distribution center on the Moscow-Leningrad pipeline. It reached Minsk in 1975 and is being extended to the Czechoslovak border to feed the gas transmission system to Western Europe. A parallel second pipeline from Vuktyl to Torzhok, with a diameter of 56 inches, is under construction. It is envisioned that eventually these pipelines will be utilized to transmit Western Siberian gas to the Central Region when pipelines are built from the Western Siberian gas fields to Ukhta.

The Vuktyl gas field now produces at a rate of about 17 million cubic meters per year. It also yields about 4 million tons of gas condensates, which is about half of the Soviet total. The condensates move over a 182-kilometer pipeline west to a gas processing plant that has been built at Sosnogorsk just to the northeast of Ukhta.

In early 1975 it was reported that the first truck convoy had left Naryan-Mar near the Barents Sea over winter roads through the tundra to begin development of the Laya-Vozh gas field 100 kilometers to the east of Naryan-Mar. This is the beginning of development of a number of gas fields that have been discovered in the Nenets National Okrug. Altogether, reserves in this area have been tentatively set at 5 trillion cubic meters. It is thought that eventually the operation here might rival that being developed east of the Ob Estuary in Western Siberia. Thus far, the production of oil and gas in the Komi A.S.S.R.

occupies only a minor position in the total production of the entire country, but it appears that perhaps at least the natural gas production might eventually become a major component in that industry. The fact that the Komi fields lie on a direct line between the Western Siberian fields and the Central Region will enhance their development, because the same pipelines can serve both fields.

The Ukhta area may also become a source for titanium. This has been found just below a depleted oil deposit and can be extracted using three drill holes that were used to extract the petroleum from above it. It is planned to convert this titanium into pigment using chlorine to be supplied by a caustic-chlorine plant to be built on a salt deposit at Seregovo north of Syktyvkar. The titanium pigment plant would be located nearby.

Forest Resources

The Northwest Economic Region is by far the largest wood producer in the country. In 1973 it produced a total of 96.9 million cubic meters of wood out of a country total of 387 million, or exactly 25 percent of the total. By contrast the second largest producer, the huge Eastern Siberian Region, produced 66 million cubic meters, and the third largest producer, the Urals, produced 57 million cubic meters. In 1973 the Northwest Region produced 16.3 percent of the country's saw timber, which was slightly higher than that of the Eastern Siberian Region. But the region is even more outstanding in paper production than in total wood production. In 1973 it produced 35.2 percent of the country's paper of all sorts. It was 70 percent above the second paper producer, the adjacent Urals Region. It was also the largest paperboard producer of all types. In fact, Archangel Oblast alone produced more paperboard than the second place Central Region just to the south.

Although the timber reserves of the Northwest Region total only 10.5 percent of the country's total and are greatly exceeded by those of the much larger areas in Western Siberia, Eastern Siberia, and the Far East, the timber stands in the Northwest Region are much more compact and generally of higher quality than those of the eastern regions. And, of course, the Northwest Region is much nearer to domestic markets than the eastern regions. Therefore, the Northwest Economic Region has been much more highly developed than the eastern regions, but even here development is still far from complete. Lumbering railroads constantly are being built into new areas to open up hitherto unused forest resources. In many cases these efforts are combined with efforts to reach important mineral resources, or to link up with other developed areas. A good example is the 160-kilometer railroad that has been built from Sosnogorsk east of Ukhta to Troitsko-Pechorsk. This has been built to open up rich timber resources in the Troitsko-Pechorsk area, but it is the beginning of a rail line that is planned to be completed to the important chemical center of Solikamsk on the Kama River, now the northern rail head of the western Urals. This would then provide a link between northeast European U.S.S.R. and the Urals. A similar situation is the Archangel-Karpogory lumber railroad, which eventually is to be extended southeastward to link up with lumber railroads in the Komi A.S.S.R.

Within the Northwest Region, Archangel Oblast is the biggest wood producer, followed by the Komi A.S.S.R., Vologda Oblast, and the Karelian A.S.S.R. Archangel Oblast also ranks first in the production of saw timber, but in this case the Karelian A.S.S.R. is second, Komi A.S.S.R. is third, and Leningrad Oblast is fourth. The Karelian A.S.S.R. is by far the largest paper producer, producing almost half that of the Northwest Region. Second rank Archangel Oblast produces only about one-third as much. The Karelian A.S.S.R. forests have been cut over much more than those in the more remote Archangel and Komi areas. Therefore, much of the timber is of lower quality and is utilized primarily for paper production.

Among individual political units, Archangel Oblast is exceeded only Irkutsk Oblast in the Eastern Siberian Region in the production of total wood and saw timber. Because

Irkutsk Oblast is somewhat larger than Archangel Oblast, wood production per unit area is about the same in the two oblasts.

The Northwest Economic Region has been holding its own through the last decade in total wood production. Expansion has been at about the same rate as across the rest of the country. There has been some relative decrease in the Northwest's share of saw timber, because the absolute amount of saw timber produced in the Northwest Region has remained essentially the same, while the rest of the country has been increasing slowly. Paper production has been increasing rapidly in the Northwest Region, as it has in the rest of the country, so that the Northwest's share of total production has remained at about the 35-percent level.

The Northwest Economic Region is by far the largest exporter of wood from the Soviet Union, primarily through the port of Archangel, but also through lesser ports along the Arctic coast, such as Mezen, Onega, and Naryan-Mar, as well as the port of Leningrad, which handles much of the exports from the Karelian A.S.S.R. Timber is floated down the northward-flowing streams to the Arctic ports during the open summer season and is piled along the many distributary channels in the delta areas. By autumn the city of Archangel, for instance, appears to be nothing but watery corridors between huge piles of logs. During winter freezeup much of the wood is sawed into lumber, and then with the breakup of ice during the following spring it is exported to other countries while new logs are floated down the streams. Heavy log floating on the Northern Dvina River has made this stream the second most important freight carrier in the entire U.S.S.R., after the Volga.

Most of the woodworking centers of the interior have developed along the two main rail lines, the Northern Railroad running from Vologda to Archangel, and the Pechora Railroad extending northeastward from Konosha through Kotlas to Vorkuta. The two outstanding inland centers are Kotlas at the juncture of the Pechora Railroad with the Northern Dvina River, and Syktyvkar, the capital of the Komi A.S.S.R. on the Vychegda River and a spur rail

Figure 11-4   Timber floating in one of the channels of the Northern Dvina
at Archangel. Novosti.

line southeast of the Pechora Railroad. Large pulp and paper complexes have been built recently in the suburbs of both Kotlas and Syktyvkar. In addition to the production of various types of paper, these complexes produce plywood and other pressed-board products and viscose for rayon, paper bags, boxes, and so forth.

Although the rivers of the Northwest Economic Region serve the Arctic ports fairly well, they do not serve the domestic markets, most of which lie to the south, because they flow in the wrong direction. Therefore, most of the timber sawed in the Northwest Region for deomestic use must travel on railroads southward to the central and southern parts of European U.S.S.R.

Fishing

The Northwest Region ranks third in the country in fish catch. The Barents Sea, with its meeting of the cold arctic waters and the warmer Gulf Stream around the northern end of Scandinavia, is a very rich fishing ground, and ships from the port of Murmansk range the entire Atlantic. Many other ports along the Barents and White Sea coasts add to the fishing industry, as does Leningrad on the Baltic. Also, the thousands of inland lakes and rivers on the glaciated plains of the Northwest Region contribute large amounts of freshwater fish. Fishing is one of the two main occupations of the Laplanders and Nentsy in the tundra lands of the north, where the only other occupation of any note is reindeer herding.

Electric Power Industry

The rapid expansion of mining and industries in the Northwest Region has prompted the need for a great amount of electrical power. In hilly Murmansk Oblast many small hydroelectric plants built on the small, steep rivers provide about 80 percent of the present electrical power.

To a lesser extent this is true in Karelia. But in the rest of the region there is little opportunity for hydroelectric development, other than a few plants, such as the Volkhov plant, which has already been mentioned in conjunction with aluminum production. And even in the Kola Peninsula, much of the hydroelectric potential has already been realized, so that expansion of electrical production must be done by other means. Large thermal electric plants have been built throughout the region, utilizing local oil, gas, and coal. Outstanding among these is the Kirishi electric station near Leningrad, which is associated with the oil

Figure 11-5 Part of the fishing fleet in Murmansk harbor. Note the barren, rocky cliffs of the ice-scoured tundra shore. Novosti.

refinery. In 1974 it had a capacity of 1.6 million kilowatts, and there were plans to expand this to perhaps 2.5 million kilowatts.

But it appears that the Soviets intend to solve many of their new electric power needs in the north by constructing nuclear power plants. In December 1973 the first 1-million-kilowatt reactor of the Leningrad nuclear electric station began generating in the new town of Sosnovyy Bor in the pines and sand dunes along the south shore of the Gulf of Finland 80 kilometers west of the city of Leningrad. This is the sixth major nuclear power station to become active in the Soviet Union. It is planned to add another 1-million-kilowatt reactor to expand the station to a total capacity of 2 million kilowatts. Farther north the first 440,000-kilowatt reactor of the Kola nuclear power station began operation in June 1973, and the second began in December 1974. The station is situated at the new town of Polyarnyye Zori ("Polar Dawns") situated on a small peninsula on the south shore of Lake Imandra in the central part of the Kola Peninsula. This station may be expanded by another 880,000 kilowatts during the five-year plan 1976–1980. A 500-kilovolt transmission line is being constructed southward to Leningrad.

An interesting development is the experimentation with tidal power in the far north. In 1968 the first experimental station with a capacity of 400 kilowatts went into operation at Kislaya Bay, a narrow fjordlike inlet of the Barents Sea about 50 kilometers north of Murmansk. The power-generating unit was manufactured in France. A second unit is to raise the total capacity to 800 kilowatts. It is intended to build much more ambitious tidal power projects at the mouth of the Lumbovka River on the northeast coast of the Kola Peninsula and at the mouth of the Mezen River at the entrance to the White Sea. The planned capacity of the Lumbovka station is 320,000 kilowatts, and that at the Mezen station is 14 million kilowatts. High tides in these deep narrow inlets can be controlled both coming in and going out by building proper dam structures, and truly astronomical amounts of electricity can be realized from this double use of tidal water.

The Soviets are continually struggling for a solution to the need for quick power supplies at new and temporary settlements in the far north that are associated with oil and gas drilling and pipeline laying. A Tyumen shipyard in Western Siberia is building small floating power plants to serve these needs. One is being installed at the town of Pechora in the Komi A.S.S.R. to provide temporary power to the construction site of the Pechora central electric station, and another is under construction for use at Naryan-Mar.

TRANSPORT

In this vast, sparsely settled area, transportation is the lifeline to the economy. Until the coming of railroads during the latter half of the nineteenth century, transportation in this northern area was wholly dependent on waterways. A number of old canal systems were built, three of which led from the Central Region around Moscow northward and northwestward to the Baltic area. Some of these have been revamped by the Soviets and others have been added to them.

The first major water construction project undertaken by the Soviets was the White Sea-Baltic Canal, which opened in 1933. It leads southwestward from the White Sea at Belomorsk utilizing many lakes, such as Lake Vygozero, or Crescent Lake, in its course to Lake Onega about 225 kilometers away. From Lake Onega westward this system links up with the canal system that leads down the Svir River to Lake Ladoga, around the southern end of Lake Ladoga, and then down the Neva to Leningrad and the Baltic. The part from Lake Onega westward to the Gulf of Finland follows the lakes and intervening short rivers that occupy the lowland between the limestone escarpment to the south and the Baltic Shield to the north. Canals skirt the larger lakes, which frequently have storm waves too dangerous for barge trains and other water craft that ply the canal system. The stretch of the canal from Belomorsk to Lake Onega utilizes 19 locks. During World War II the Finns destroyed some of the system, but it was quickly reconstructed after the war.

Of course, the canal is closed by ice at least half of the year, so that the region still is primarily dependent on the Kirov Railroad constructed from Leningrad northward to Murmansk.

During the early 1960s the 150-year-old Mariinsk Canal system was revamped to handle Volga-size steamers. A dam was built across the Sheksna River where the Northern Railroad crosses the stream near Cherepovets. The dam backed up water 225 kilometers to form the Cherepovets Sea, which completely inundated the valley of the Sheksna as well as Beloe Lake to the north and raised the water level up the Kovzha River all the way to the divide. Six large modern locks now lower the boats down the north slope of the divide into the Vytegra River and to Lake Onega, where connections are made to the west down the Svir River, Lake Lodoga, and the Neva River to the Gulf of Finland, and to the north through the Baltic-White Sea Canal to the White Sea. This modern Volga-Baltic waterway provides a canal 4 meters deep that connects the Central Region, the Northwest, the Urals, and the South. Large Volga barges are able to navigate all the way to Leningrad. Transport costs have been cut to one-third that of the railroad, and travel time from Cherepovets to Leningrad has been reduced several times. It is hoped that these improvements will induce increased movement to the Leningrad area via water of grain, wood, petroleum, salt, cotton fibers, potash, and building materials. Also, iron ore from the Kola Peninsula and coal from Vorkuta can be brought to Cherepovets mainly by water to reduce production costs of steel there and make it an economical enterprise. Steel products can be shipped from Cherepovets to Leningrad, Gorkiy, Yaroslavl, and Moscow entirely by water. Wood can be shipped in barges all the way from sawmills in northern European Russia to the Central, Volga, and South Regions. Grain from Western Siberia, the Volga, and the Kama area is expected to move westward along the water routes, and apatite from the Kola Peninsula can be shipped through the Baltic-White Sea and Volga-Baltic waterways to nearly all the superphosphate plants of European Russia.

A bonus benefit realized from this system is additional water brought into the upper Volga from Lake Kubeno and the Sukhona River, the major left-bank tributary of the Northern Dvina. Water from these sources can be dumped into the Cherepovets Sea at the rate of about 3.5 cubic kilometers per year, thereby increasing the flow of the Volga. This increase enhances navigation and electric production in the power stations on the upper Volga. The Cherepovets Sea on the Sheksna has filled the old Northern Dvina Canal and provides for a better connection between the old Mariinsk and the Northern Dvina Canal systems. Additional improvements are planned along the Northern Dvina waterway.

A grand scheme that has been talked about for many years is the Vychegda-Pechora diversion project. This proposal would reverse the flow of some of the water in the Pechora and Vychegda Rivers from uselessly flowing out to the Arctic Ocean to run southward into the headwaters of the Kama River and eventually into the Volga and the Caspian Sea. At times in the past it looked as though this project was going to be accomplished in the very near future, but counterarguments always appeared and shelved it temporarily. At present things look optimistic again, but environmentalists are raising their voices once more, and nothing definite has been done.

The plan would entail the building of one or two large dams in the midsection of the Pechora River, a large dam on the Vychegda, the main right-bank tributary of the Northern Dvina, a dam on the upper Kama River, and many smaller dams on many of the tributary streams in the region. These dams would impound a huge reservoir, almost equal in size to Lake Ladoga, that would connect the headwaters of these major river systems. Water could be pumped up into the reservoir from the Pechora and Vychegda Rivers and be allowed to flow by gravity southward into the Kama (Fig. 11-6). The many dams would be necessary to keep the water from backing up all the small streams in the area and thereby flooding a tremendous area with only a small depth of water.

The advantage of this project would be the

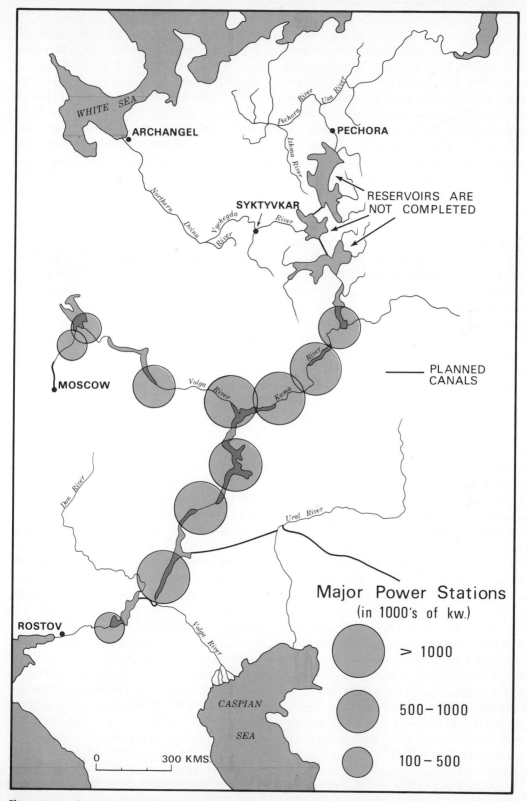

Figure 11-6 The Vychegda-Pechora diversion project. From Micklin, p. 201.

addition of water to the Volga, which reaches a very low stage in middle and late summer just when the Pechora River is reaching its greatest flow. This would enhance navigation along the Volga, would help to regulate the level of the Caspian Sea, would provide additional water for the power plants along the Volga south of Kazan, thus allowing them to be run closer to capacity, and would provide considerable amounts of water for irrigation in the east Volga lowlands south of Kuybyshev, including the proposed Volga-Ural River canal system that would provide irrigation water for large areas in the North Caspian Lowland. It might also eventually provide more water to the lower Don, via the Volga-Don Canal, in order to stabilize the level and salinity of the Sea of Azov. This latter project would require considerable additional construction along the Volga-Don Canal, since the Volga River is much lower than the Don at this point. It has been pointed out by enthusiastic economists that the additional power that could be generated by the existing hydroelectric plants on the lower Volga would amount to the present output of the Kuybyshev Dam, and that this alone would pay for the entire project in a short period of time.

However, local authorities in the Komi A.S.S.R. have pointed out that all the benefits accrue to the south while all the detriments occur in their region. The reservoir would flood much of their better farmland along the floodplains of the Pechora and Vychegda Rivers; it would flood a large section of prime forest land; it would alter the ground water table and might kill forests over another area equal to that occupied by the reservoir itself; most important, from an economic standpoint, it would flood parts of the potential oil and gas fields, making them more expensive to exploit. On the ecological side, it would alter the microclimate of the immediate surroundings, delay the coming of spring by the long period of ice melting in the reservoir, and so forth.

Yulian Saushkin, professor of geography at Moscow State University and one of the leading authorities on the economic geography of the Soviet Union, says that if the Vychegda-Pechora-Kama diversion project ever is built it should be used only for transport purposes in the Northwest Region and should not involve the unrealistic idea of seeking to maintain the level of the Caspian or the uneconomical objective of providing additional hydroelectric output on the Kama and Volga Rivers. Interestingly, his statement harks back to the primary purpose that was initially attached to the project when it was first discussed in 1933–1934 by the Institute of Water Design, which at that time viewed the transfer of water southward to the Volga as of only incidental importance. Saushkin points out that such a waterway in the Komi A.S.S.R. would provide a largely all-water route from the Vorkuta coal fields to the Urals metallurgical area and westward to the center and south of European U.S.S.R. He says that when this water connection is completed there then should be defined a new "West Urals Economic Region," which would have a production complex based on Komi and Western Siberian natural gas, Pechora coal, Solikamsk salt, Kama, Pechora, and Vychegda timber, iron and steel based on ores from the Kursk Magnetic Anomaly and coals from Pechora, and heavy machine building. The city of Perm on the upper Kama River would be the region-forming center of such a West Urals Economic Region.

Some concrete indication that the Soviets are thinking very seriously of going ahead with this project was revealed at an international meeting on atomic energy in Vienna in February 1975 when a group of Soviet scientists described an experimental underground atomic explosion in 1971 that created a 2300-foot-long, 1100-foot-wide, 35–50-foot-deep channel in the divide area between the Pechora and Kama Rivers. They reported that 250 such nuclear charges could excavate the entire canal system, costing only about one-third as much as the building of the system by conventional methods.

The Northwest Economic Region also contains the western portion of the Northern Sea

Route that skirts along the Arctic coast of the Soviet Union all the way from its western terminus at Murmansk eastward to the Bering Sea and southward into the Pacific. The Barents Sea portion of the route is the least hampered by ice and carries the most traffic. Murmansk is the primary home port for the ships plying the route. The world's largest diesel-electric ice breaker, the *Yermak,* has recently been added to the nuclear icebreakers, the *Lenin* and the *Arktika,* to convoy ships eastward along the Northern Sea Route. Sections of this route will be discussed in more detail in the Siberian and Far East chapters.

In spite of the impressive construction of waterways in the Northwest Region, railroads handle most of the freight, just as they do in all regions of the country. Four main lines set the general pattern for the region and are augmented by interlacing and feeder lines. The oldest of these by far is the first major line built in Tsarist Russia during the middle of the nineteenth centruy, running from Leningrad to Moscow. In 1916 during World War I the Kirov Railroad was constructed from Leningrad to Murmansk in the far north. The Northern Railroad was built northward from Moscow through Vologda to Archangel. During World War II the Pechora Railroad, leading northeastward from the Northern Railroad, was hurriedly constructed through Kotlas and Ukhta to Vorkuta. During the early part of World War II, the "Obozerskaya Bypass" was completed between Belomorsk on the Kirov Railroad eastward to Obozerskaya on the Northern Railroad. This provided a detour route for the heavy flow of lend-lease goods that was coming into Murmansk to be moved south to the Moscow area without going through the German-occupied Leningrad region.

Highways are not of much significance in this northern region, except in the southern fringes where they connect the farm settlements with the towns. But the "Great North-South Highway" is under construction from Leningrad through Petrozavodsk to Murmansk. This will augment the role of the Kirov Railroad, which it will parallel. The most re-

cent additions to the transportation system are the oil and gas pipelines, which have already been mentioned in conjunction with the oil and gas industries of the area.

CITIES

Leningrad

By far the largest city in this area, and second largest in the Soviet Union, is Leningrad, which in 1974 had a population of 4,243,000. Although the city suffered terribly during World War II when for more than 900 consecutive days it was under continuous siege by the German army, the population has steadily regained its prewar size, and now Leningrad has more people than ever before.

The city was founded in 1703 by Peter the Great in the watery swamps of the Neva River delta at the head of the Gulf of Finland, which had been newly secured from Sweden. In spite of its inauspicious location, it became Peter's "window on the west" and was made the capital of the Russian Empire from 1713 until the Bolshevik Revolution. So in spite of its poor hinterland, it prospered and became the largest city in the Russian Empire. From 1713 to 1914 it was known as St. Petersburg, but in 1914, after the beginning of World War I, it was renamed Petrograd, to eliminate the German terminology. In 1924, after Lenin's death, it was named Leningrad to commemorate the foremost leader of the revolution.

Leningrad has the most vivid history of any of the cities of the Soviet Union, having acted as the capital during the momentous years of the growth of the Russian Empire that culminated in the revolution and the formation of the Soviet Union. Tsarist society reached its zenith here and left its mark in the form of many monumental buildings and spacious grounds. Revolutionary resistance groups formed and grew up in St. Petersburg under the very eyes of the so-called third section, the secret police arm of the tsars. Because of this historical background, it is still perhaps the most interesting city of the country from the standpoint of tourism, although it has lost out to Moscow in most economic and cultural aspects.

Leningrad is built on the many low, muddy islands that separate the distributaries in the delta of the Neva River. With its more than 500 bridges, it has been likened to Venice in Italy. Although it is only 125 kilometers long, the Neva is about 1.5 kilometers wide, and it has a consistent flow because it drains the large glacial Lake Ladoga into the Gulf of Finland. The river does not flood, but the delta on which Leningrad sits is so flat and so low above the sea that a strong west wind can raise the water level in the Gulf of Finland enough to inundate the lower sections of the city. During some years gales on the Baltic drive water into parts of the city seven or eight times during the year. Particularly high water

levels were reached exactly 100 years apart in 1824 and 1924. Marks on the outside walls of downtown buildings show these two levels — 4.5 meters and 4 meters above normal. Now the Soviets are planning a 25-kilometer-long dam across the eastern end of the Gulf of Finland to protect the city from these storm waves. The rock and earth dam will be built across the 35-meter-deep eastern end of the gulf, utilizing Kotlin Island on which the naval base of Kronstadt is located. A breakwater atop the dam will rise 8 meters above the sea. This will protect Leningrad against floods up to 6 meters above normal. The dam will have ship gates and spillways that ordinarily will be open, but that can be closed by 130-meter-long concrete walls on rollers. A motor road is to be built along the top of the dam.

Nevsky Prospect, the main street of Lenin-

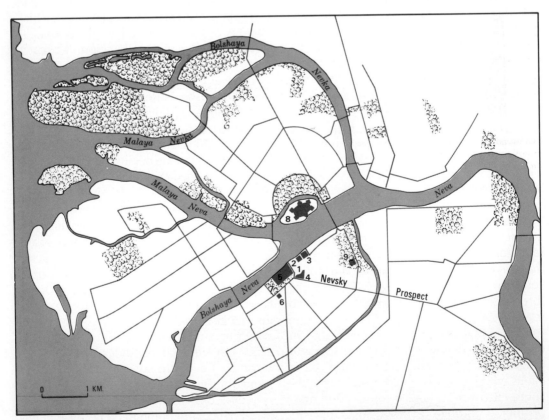

Figure 11-7   Downtown Leningrad.; 1-Palace Square; 2-Winter Palace; 3-Hermitage Museum; 4-General Staff Building; 5-Admiralty Building; 6-St. Isaac's Cathedral; 7-Decembrist's Square; 8-Saints Peter and Paul Fortress; 9-Russian Museum.

grad, is lined by rows of five-story buildings that culminate on the southeast bank of the Bolshaya Neva, the main distributory of the Neva River, in a series of large squares surrounded by palaces, government buildings, and monuments reminiscent of empire days. The largest of these squares is Palace Square, hemmed in by the Winter Palace and the Hermitage Museum along the river, the semicircular arch of the General Staff Building, and the Admiralty Building with its gilded spire. In the center of the square a slender red granite monolith 50 meters high, with the figure of an angel at the top, commemorates the victory over Napoleon. The angel has the face of Alexander I. Another square is dominated by the massive St. Isaac's Cathedral, whose dome reaches a height of 100 meters, the highest point in the city. In front of it is Decembrists' Square, a broad formal garden fronted on the river by a 4000-ton, rough-hewn granite monolith surmounted by the

Figure 11-8   The Winter Palace across Palace Square, Leningrad. The granite spire commemorates the 1812 victory over Napoleon. It is surmounted by the figure of an angel with the face of Alexander I.

Figure 11-9   "The Bronze Horseman," Peter the Great, Decembrist's Square, Leningrad.

figure of Peter the Great on a rearing horse.

Most of these monumental buildings are painted pale yellow and trimmed in pale green in classic style, although many of them look as if they have had very little paint added to them since the revolution. The Winter Palace is perhaps the most imposing structure; a five-story green building facing on the Neva River, it served as the home of the royal family during the long winters in Petersburg. During the reign of Catherine the Great a large addition was added to the building to provide for a private art gallery for Catherine. This addition became the Hermitage Museum, which now also occupies much of the Winter Palace and houses one of the most superb art collections in the world. Outside, the palace appears as a dull, dirty green building, but inside all is polished mahogany and gold leaf with crystal chandeliers dominating the rooms.

On an island across the broad channel of the Neva sits the red brick-walled fortress of

Figure 11-10   In the Hermitage Museum. Courtesy of Clara Dundas Taylor.

Sts. Peter and Paul, which in the beginning served as the kremlin for the initial town in the area. At that time the fort was composed of crude buildings enclosed by a log and earthen wall. The wall was later replaced by granite and brick, and more imposing cathedrals and governmental buildings were built inside. The cathedrals eventually became the burying places for the tsars, and the casement walls became one of the most infamous prisons in the Russian Empire. During the second half of the nineteenth century, many of the leading thinkers in Russia were imprisoned sooner or later in Sts. Peter and Paul Fortress.

Fringing Leningrad on the south and west are a number of old tsarist estates that in most cases served as summer homes for the royal families. The best preserved of these is Petrodvorets, about 30 kilometers west of Leningrad, along the southern shore of the Gulf of Finland. Again, there are pale yellow buildings with gold-leaf trim, but they are in much better repair and are much shinier in appearance than the buildings in Leningrad. The huge grounds surrounding the palace are landscaped with hundreds of fountains in various arrays, fed by a natural head of water from the limestone escarpment to the south. Farther east are other tsarist grounds, the most elaborate of which is Tsarskoye Selo, the "Tsar's Village," which since the revolution has been renamed Pushkin, because Alexander Pushkin attended a lycee nearby. The Soviets have restored this area since World War II and have made it into a combination museum and weekend recreational park.

It was in St. Petersburg that the Industrial Revolution made its greatest inroads during the 1890s. Here all sorts of prototypes of industrial products were manufactured, and here a semiskilled labor pool, or proletariat, was developed. Leningrad produced the first Soviet tractors in 1924 and the first synthetic rubber in the 1930s. Under the Soviets, Moscow largely has preempted these functions of industrial innovation, but Leningrad still has a monopoly on certain industries that require special skills, such as the manufacture of very fine machine tools and giant hydroelectric turbines. The chief industries of Leningrad at

Figure 11-11 "Meteor Ship," hydrofoil boat on the Neva River in front of Saints Peter and Paul Fortress.

Figure 11-12   Peterhof (Petrodvorets). Peter the Great's summer palace is noted for its beautiful displays of fountains.

present are the machine-building, chemical, textile, food, and printing industries. All raw materials for the industries of Leningrad must be provided from other parts of the Soviet Union, and many of the finished products of the region must find markets in the rest of the country.

Leningrad utilizes about 10 percent of the steel output of the U.S.S.R. The main steel center to serve the machine industires of Leningrad has been established in Chere-povets, at the north end of the Rybinsk Reservoir, utilizing coal from Vorkuta and iron ore from the Kola Peninsula. Shipbuilding is an important industry, as might be expected in one of the biggest ports in the country, and the

naval base of Kronshtadt sits on Kotlin Island just offshore. In 1955 Leningrad got its first subway, which has since been expanded into a comprehensive system. Construction workers ran into a lot of water in the swampy delta region, but solved the problem by freezing the earth with liquid nitrogen before tunneling through it.

Archangel

The second city in size is the lumber port of Archangel at the mouth of the Northern Dvina River on the White Sea. In 1974 it had a population of 369,000. Archangel was founded in 1584 by Ivan the Terrible as the first port of the Russian Empire to establish trade with England and later with other countries. The first Russian shipbuilding yards were set up here in 1693. The Solombola sawmill in Archangel is the largest in Europe, as is the wood chemical complex that turns out cellulose paper, cardboard, plywood, fodder yeast, and so forth. The Archangel "Pomor" fishermen have been fishing the adjacent water for centuries. The annual catch is now over 330,000 tons.

Murmansk

Murmansk, with a 1974 population of 347,000, is the largest polar city in the world.

It was founded in 1915 at the northern terminus of the Kirov Railroad. The city sits near the head of Kola Fjord about 65 kilometers from the sea. Although the climate here is cold and raw much of the year, the sea remains ice-free in the winter because of the Gulf Stream. Murmansk replaces Leningrad as the northern port of the Soviet Union from December through May. As the home base for the fishing fleets in the Barents Sea and the western terminus of the Northern Sea Route, it has developed important shipbuilding and ship-repair yards. It also has a naval base equipped with submarine pens. Much of the apatite of the Kirovsk area moves through the port of Murmansk. During World War II it served as the port of entry for most of the lend-lease goods shipped from the United States to the U.S.S.R.

Cherepovets

The fourth city is Cherepovets, the steel center for northern European U.S.S.R. In addition to its steel plant, which began operating in 1955, Cherepovets contains a major chemical complex that produces superphosphate using Kola apatite and Urals pyrites and a nitrogen fertilizer plant that uses ammonium sulfate, which is a by-product of the coke oven gases. With this great amount of industrialization, Cherepovets has increased its population from only 35,000 in 1947 to 223,000 in 1974. Its trading function has also been enhanced by the rebuilding of the Volga-Baltic waterway, of which it is the southern terminus.

Vologda

Vologda was founded in 1147 at the boat portage between the headwaters of the Sukhona and the Sheksna Rivers. It provided an all-water route from the Northern Dvina Basin to the Volga Basin and thus controlled the trade route from Archangel to Moscow. During the sixteenth century it prospered, along with Archangel, with the growing trade between Muscovy and England. In 1974 it had a population of 205,000.

Petrozavodsk

Petrozavodsk, with a 1974 population of 203,000, is the capital of the Karelian A.S.S.R. It owes its name, "Peter's plant," to the fact that Peter the Great established a rudimentary ironworks on the west shore of Lake Onega during his reign. Among its industries are the Onega tractor plant and the largest mica plant in the country.

Severodvinsk

Severodvinsk, on the western edge of the Northern Dvina delta, is a satellite city of Archangel. Its main industry is submarine construction. In 1974 it had a population of 166,000.

Novgorod

The famous old city of Novgorod occupied the northern position on the early river trade routes between the Baltic and Black Seas. It was here that Rurik in A.D. 862 established the first Slavic state. With the removal of the seat of government to Kiev after Rurik's death, Novgorod remained the second most important city in Kievan Rus and became an important commercial center peopled by international merchants who had connections with the Hanseatic League cities westward along the Baltic. After its fall to Muscovy in the fifteenth century, it declined in importance and practically dropped from view during the early Soviet period. During World War II heavy German fighting leveled it to the ground, but since the war the Soviets have restored the kremlin and monumental churches and have rebuilt the town into a pleasant city that is now one of the main tourist attractions of the country. A round trip by bus, made in a day from Leningrad, provides time for a leisurely tour of the Novgorod kremlin and various anti religious museums as well as a boat excursion up the Volkhov River and around Lake Ilmen. Since 1964 Novgorod has been revitalized by the construction of a large chemical complex that uses natural gas from the main lines running between Moscow and Leningrad. This has caused a spurt in growth from 61,000 in 1959 to 180,000 in 1974.

Syktyvkar

Syktyvkar is a major pulp and paper processing center on the Vychegda River and the capital of the Komi A.S.S.R. For many years it was a sleepy backwoods town with no modern transport connection to the outside world. But during the 1960s a branch rail line was extended southeastward from the Pechora Railroad into the city to provide it with an all-weather outlet. In 1974 Syktyvkar had a population of 148,000.

Pskov

The ancient city of Pskov in western Russia was one of the major cities of Kievan Rus along with Kiev, Novgorod, and Smolensk. Since that time it has become a sleepy regional center in a relatively poor agricultural area. Although it has received some industrialization during the Soviet period, it seems to have remained a backwater place. In 1974 its population was 146,000.

PROSPECTS

The Northwest Economic Region is an area of severe climate, poor soils, and bad drainage. Only the southern fringes have significant agriculture, and even under the 15-year program to upgrade the nonchernozem zone, one cannot expect too much change, because of natural limitations. The minerals, the forests, the fisheries, and the port facilities of the area have stimulated growth during the Soviet period. The apatite of the Kola Peninsula is of national significance. The other minerals are only of local importance, although eventually aluminum may also be nationally significant. The coming of natural gas and oil to the region has stimulated various industries that heretofore were unknown. Therefore, the major cities are getting more rounded economies. Leningrad, of course, has a great drawing power as a city and continues to grow in population in spite of governmental policies against the growth of big cities. The region

Figure 11-13   The walled city of Novgorod on the bank of the Volkhov River north of Lake Ilmen. Novosti.

undoubtedly will remain the primary lumber region in the country for many years, because it is much closer to markets than the more expansive regions east of the Urals.

READING LIST

- Altman, L.P., and M.L. Dolkart, "Leningrad kak promyshlennyy tsentr i osnovnyye problemy ego razvitiya" (Leningrad as an Industrial Center and Its Main Problems of Development), *Vestnik Leningradskogo Universiteta, seriya geologiya-geografiya,* No. 3, 1969, pp. 91–100 (in Russian).
- Altman, L.P., and M.L. Dolkart, "Problems of Economic Development in the Northwest Economic Region During the New Five-Year Plan (1966–70), *Soviet Geography: Review & Translation,* January 1968, pp. 11–23.
- *Atlas Pskovskoi oblasti* (An Atlas of Pskov Oblast), Moscow, 1969 (in Russian).
- Dmitrevskiy, Yu. D., *Geografiya Vologodskoy oblasti* (Geography of Vologda Oblast), Vologda, 1961 (in Russian).
- Golovanov, S.S., ed., *Leningradskaya Oblast: priroda i khozyaystvo* (Leningrad Oblast: Nature and Economy), Leningrad, 1958, 344 pp. (in Russian).
- Gorovoy, V.L., "The Timber Industry of Northern European Russia," *Soviet Geography: Review & Translation,* April 1961, pp. 53–59.
- Granik, G.I., "Location of Productive Factors in the European Part of the Soviet North," *Problems of the North,* No. 9, 1965, pp. 11–20.
- Greer, Deon Carr, *The Russo-Finnish Border Change of 1940–1944 and its Effect Upon Finland,* Dissertation, University of Indiana, 1969, 230 pp.
- Helin, R.A., "Soviet Fishing in the Barents Sea and the North Atlantic," *Geographical Review,* July 1964, pp. 386–408.
- Inber, Vera, *Leningrad Diary,* St. Martins Press, New York, 1971, 207 pp.
- Isachenko, A.S., *Fiziko-geograficheskoye raionirovaniye Severo-Zapada* (The Physical Geographical Regionalization of the Northwest), Leningrad, 1965 (in Russian).
- Kanev, G., *Ekonomicheskaya effektivnost selskogo khozyaystva evropeyskogo severa* (The Economical Effectiveness of Agriculture of the European North), Nauka, Moscow, 1974, 224 pp. (in Russian).
- *Karelskaya ASSR* (Karelian A.S.S.R.), Karelskiy filial akademii nauk SSSR, institut geografii, Moscow, 1956, 335 pp. (in Russian).
- Kirillova, V.A., *Ozera Leningradskoi oblasti* (The Lakes of Leningrad Oblast), Leningrad, 1971 (in Russian).
- *Leningrad za 50 let, statisticheskiy sbornik* (Leningrad after 50 Years, a Statistical Collection), Lenizdat, Leningrad, 1967, 174 pp. (in Russian).
- Micklin, Philip P., "Soviet Plans to Reverse the Flow of Rivers: The Kama-Vychegda-Pechora Project," *The Canadian Geographer,* XIII, No. 3, 1969, pp. 199–215.
- Mikhaylov, Yu. P. "Vliyaniye perebroski rechnogo stoka severnykh rek na prirodu taezhnykh geosistem" (A Conference on the Impact of Northern River Diversion on the Natural Environment of Taiga Geosystems), *Izvestiya Vsesoyuznogo Geograficheskogo Obshchestva,* No. 1, 1975, pp. 80–84.
- Miller, Wright, *Leningrad,* Barnes and Noble, New York, 1970, 82 pp.
- Moskvin, B.V., "Severo-Zapad RSFSR v novoy pyatiletke" (The Northwest of the R.S.F.S.R. in the New Five-Year Plan), *Geografiya v Shkole,* No. 4, 1972, pp. 8–13 (in Russian).
- Pokshishevskiy, V.V., et al., ed., *Severo-Zapad RSFSR* (The Northwest of the R.S.F.S.R.), Mysl, Moscow, 1964, (in Russian).
- "Problems of Developing Productive Factors in the Northern European Part of the USSR," *Problems of the North,* July 1969, pp. 1–149.
- Rom, V. Ya., "Historical Geography of Industry in the Cherepovets Country," *Soviet Geography: Review & Translation,* May 1974, pp. 299–310.
- Rom, V. Ya., "The Volga-Baltic Waterway," *Soviet Geography: Review & Translation,* November 1961, pp. 32–43.
- Ryabkov, N.V., "Drevnyaya gidrograficheskaya set na mezhdurechye Kamy, Pechory i Vychegdy" (An Ancient Drainage Net in the Interfluve of the Kama, Pechora and Vychegda Rivers), *Izvestiya Akademii Nauk SSSR, seriya geograficheskaya,* No. 1, 1971, pp. 100–107 (in Russian).
- Ryabkov, N.V., "Zandrovye polya severo-vostoka russkoy ravniny" (The Glacial Outwash Plains in the Northeast Part of the Russian Plain),

Izvestiya vsesoyuznogo geograficheskogo ob-shchestva, No. 4, 1972, pp. 263–268 (in Russian).

- *Severo-Zapad evropayskoy chasti SSSR* (The Northwest European Part of the U.S.S.R.), Leningrad, V., 1963 (in Russian).
- Shishkin, N.I., "On the Diversion of the Vychegda and Pechora Rivers to the Basin of the Volga," *Soviet Geography: Review & Translation,* May 1962, pp. 46–56.
- Taskin, George A., "The Soviet Northwest: Economic Regionalization," *The Geographical Review,* April 1961, pp. 213–235.
- Vendrov, S.L., "Geographical Aspects of the Problems of Diverting Part of the Flow of the Pechora and Vychegda Rivers to the Volga Basin," *Soviet Geography: Review & Translation,* June 1963, pp. 29–41.

The Urals Economic Region

	Area (km²)	Population	Persons/km²	Percent Urban
Kurgan Oblast	71,000	1,068,000	15.0	47
Orenburg Oblast	124,000	2,052,000	16.6	57
Perm Oblast	161,000	2,972,000	18.5	70
Komi-Permyak National Okrug	33,000	193,000	5.9	20
Sverdlovsk Oblast	195,000	4,336,000	22.3	83
Chelyabinsk Oblast	88,000	3,323,000	37.8	80
Udmurt A.S.S.R.	42,000	1,430,000	34.0	61
Total	680,000	15,181,000	22.3	72

chapter 12

the urals economic region

The Ural Mountains stretch in a nearly north-south direction from the Pay-Khoy Upland on the shore of the Kara Sea at latitude 69°30'N to the Mugodzhar Upland in northern Kazakhstan at a latitude of about 50°N. The northern third of the range, southward to about 62° latitude, consists of a single narrow ridge no more than 50 kilometers wide that forms the boundary between the Pechora Basin of the Komi A.S.S.R. on the European side and the Ob Basin of Tyumen Oblast on the Asiatic side. The Urals Economic Region does not include this northern portion, which is not considered an integral part of any economic region, but simply the boundary between the Northwest Economic Region and the Western Siberian Economic Region. Neither does the Urals Economic Region cover the Mugodzhar extension in Kazakhstan. Thus, the Urals Economic Region is not really coextensive with the physical feature, the Ural Mountain chain, but is a region established to incorporate much of the industrialized portion of the Urals metallurgical area. This includes the south-central portion of the range from about 62°N to 51°N and considerable territory on the west and east sides of this portion of the range.

Politically the Urals Economic Region consists of Sverdlovsk and Chelyabinsk Oblasts on the eastern slopes of the Urals, Perm Oblast on the western slope, and Orenburg Oblast elongated east-west across the south-

213

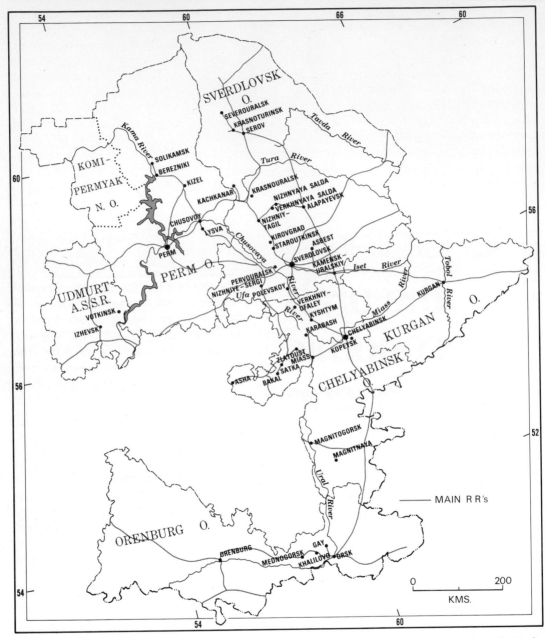

Figure 12-1   The Urals.

ern end next to the Kazakh border. The Bashkir A.S.S.R., which occupies the western slope between Perm and Orenburg Oblasts, made up a considerable portion of the Urals Region for a number of years, but in the early 1970s it was transferred to the Volga Region, because its oil-dominated industry is more integrated with the Volga oil fields than it is with the metallurgy of the Urals. In addition, more removed from the Urals Range, is the Udmurt A.S.S.R. west of Perm Oblast, and Kurgan Oblast east of Chelyabinsk Oblast, which was recently transferred from the Western Siberian Region. The Udmurts are another Finno-Ugrian group, as are the Komi-Permyaks, who form a national okrug within Perm Oblast.

In 1973 these political units totaled 680,000 square kilometers of territory and contained 15,181,000 people. The average population density was 22.3 persons per square kilometer, but this varied from 5.9 persons per square kilometer in undeveloped Komi-Permyak National Okrug to 37.8 persons per square kilometer in highly industrialized Chelyabinsk Oblast. As a whole, the region is very urbanized; 72 percent of the entire population of the region is considered to be urban. The urban portion is as high as 83 percent in Sverdlovsk Oblast and 80 percent in Chelyabinsk Oblast. All of the political units are well above the national average for urbanization, except Kurgan and Orenburg Oblasts, which have much higher agricultural potentials than the rest of the region, and the Komi-Permyak National Okrug, which is the least developed part of the entire region and has only 20 percent of its people living in urban places. The Urals Region contains 15 cities of more than 100,000 population, which ties for fourth place with the North Caucasus and Kazakhstan. It has three cities with more than 900,000 population, which ties for first place with the other region of heavy industry, the Donets-Dnieper Region.

The Urals came under the influence of the eastward-advancing Russians as early as the thirteenth century and was definitely incorporated into the empire in the later part of the sixteenth century after the fall of Kazan and the expansion into Siberia. Considerable settlement had taken place in the area between the thirteenth and sixteenth centuries as a result of the salt industry on the upper Kama River. In the seventeenth and eighteenth centuries the area became the primary metallurgical region of Russia, using charcoal as fuel. Although it lost this preeminence to the eastern Ukraine during the later part of the nineteenth century when coke superseded charcoal, it became once again one of the main heavy industry areas of the country under the Soviet regime.

During the Soviet period the region has had its ups and downs. During the 1920s and 1930s it lay somewhat dormant as primary efforts were poured into the rehabilitation of European Russia and the opening up of new mining and industrial areas in Siberia and the Far East. But World War II forced an eastward movement of people and industries out of European U.S.S.R., giving the Urals a new growth impetus that lasted for about a decade after the war. But during the latest intercensal period, 1959–1970, it appears that once again the Urals Region has somewhat stagnated with respect to some of the other industrial areas of the country. During this period the population of the area increased by only 7 percent, while the country as a whole increased 16 percent and the heavy industrial area of the Donets-Dnieper Region increased 13 percent. Most of the region experienced net out-migration, and practically every city in the region experienced a diminishing growth rate. The present population in the Urals has a birth rate somewhat below the national average, a death rate the same as the national average, and a natural increase significantly below the national average.

THE PHYSICAL LANDSCAPE

Landform

The Ural Mountains, or "Stone Belt," as the Russians often called it in the past, rise abruptly from the flat Arctic coastal plain about 40 kilometers inland from the Kara Sea to a height of 1363 meters in Konstantinov Kamen. From there southward to a latitude of about 62°N the Urals extend as one continuously high and narrow ridge. A truly wild and rocky region, this section is well above the treeline and has been heavily glaciated. Local mountain glaciers still exist in some of the protected upper valleys. On either side the ridge drops off abruptly to an extremely flat plain that has recently been washed by the waters of the Arctic Ocean. This northern section of the mountains, at approximately 65°N latitude, contains the highest elevation in the

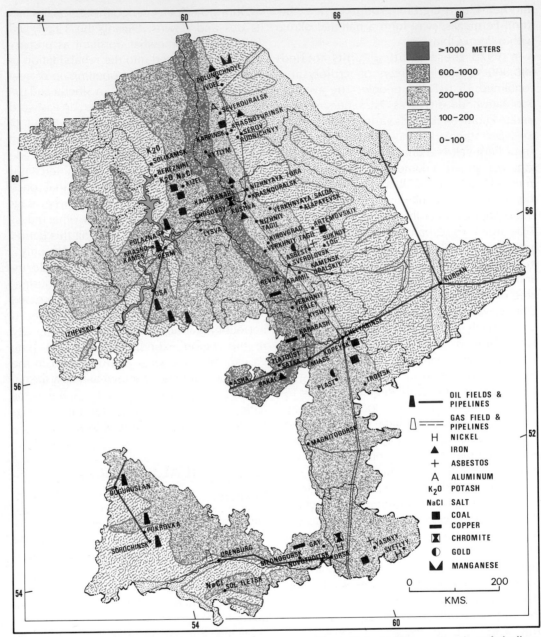

Figure 12-2   Landform, minerals, and pipelines.

Urals, Narodnaya Gora, or "People's Mountain," which reaches an elevation of 1894 meters.

To the south the Urals split into two or more ranges and become softer in outline as pine, fir, and larch forests begin to cover the slopes. From 61° latitude southward to approximately 55°, in the region usually known as the middle Urals, the mountains are comprised of from two to ten ranges, all ill defined, broken, and low in elevation with only occasional peaks rising to 1000 meters or more. In many places this midsection is not mountainous at all; branches of the Trans Siberian Railroad cross the range without difficulty. The pass on the Sverdlovsk railroad is only 410 meters high. The mountains in this section do not drop off abruptly on either side, particularly on the west where the land slopes gradually westward toward the Volga River in a broad mountain foreland. Much of the foreland has been deeply dissected by streams, which in some places have eroded the upland into a series of rounded hills and in others have cut canyon-like valleys below plateau- and mesa-like divides. The northern part of this foreland in the Kama River area is known as the Uvaly, or "hummocks." The central section is the Ufa Plateau, a tableland deeply dissected by the Ufa River and its tributaries. This lies primarily in the Bashkir A.S.S.R., which recently has been shifted to the Volga Region. Farther south the upland is known as the Obshchiy Syrt, which means "upland erosion surface."

The southern Urals, south of 55° latitude, continue to fan out in a series of indistinct ranges that here and there rise to mountainous proportions, among which the highest peak, Yamantau, reaches an elevation of 1640 meters. South of the Russian-Kazakh border the mountains trail out in a broad, eroded, semiarid upland known as the Mugodzhar Mountains, whose highest elevations are little more than 400 meters.

The Ural Mountains are an old mountain range that have undergone three main stages of development and a number of substages that have worn down the mountains to their bare stumps and exposed many varieties of rocks at the surface. The first stage occurred during the Paleozoic era and was predominantly a period of uplift after a long period of subsidence and accumulation of sediments. The uplift intricately folded and faulted the mountains, causing thrust faults and great pressures that metamorphosed many of the rocks and caused widescale intrusions of igneous magma. This stage was followed by the second stage in the prolonged Mesozoic-Paleogene, when the high mountains were destroyed by erosion and peneplains were formed. At the end of the Paleogene, the site of the present Ural Mountains was nothing more than a rolling peneplain. The third stage, the Neogene, was a period of disjunc-

tive uplifts that produced primarily block faulting that lifted different sections of the Urals to different elevations and resulted in a series of elevated sections of old peneplains surmounted by monadnock remnants. Many of the higher blocks consist of resistant quartzites whose steep slopes are buried in accumulations of talus composed of unweathered quartzite blocks that have fallen off the upper cliffs and worked their way downhill under the force of gravity. Rock streams are common in both the higher northern and southern portions of the range.

The Neogene block faulting produced some lateral movements that caused conspicuous elbow turns in streams along the eastern slopes of the main ranges. It also produced an abundant series of sagponds with a chain of good-sized lakes at the eastern foot of the ranges just to the west of the city of Chelyabinsk. The lakes extend northward in a discontinuous zone west of Sverdlovsk as far north as Nizhniy Tagil.

During the Quaternary the Urals were covered by the Dnieper stage of glaciation as far southward as the 60th parallel. It may be that the highest peaks in the northern Urals were not inundated by the ice, but remained exposed as nunataks. South of the glacial sheet, individual glaciers formed on mountain summits. Later, the Valday glaciation caused individual mountain glaciers to form on some of the same summits in the northern Urals that had previously been ridden over by the Dnieper stage. Mountain glacial forms such as cirques and horns are common in the higher portions of the northern Urals where many small snow fields and glaciers now are present.

The sedimentary cover has been stripped off broad sections of the eastern slopes of the mountains to expose the underlying igneous and metamorphic rocks that are rich in many types of metallic ores and gemstones. But on the western slope the broad foreland area is covered with thousands of meters of sediments that have accumulated in a long-subsiding mountain foredeep that has since been warped upward in a broad arch. These sedimentary strata contain the rich Volga-

Urals oil deposits, natural gas, coal, and various salts. In places they exhibit considerable karst features.

The Ural Mountain system is drained by tributaries of major river systems that flow on either side of the range. In the far northwest they are tributary to the Pechora River, which flows northward into the Arctic. In the central western slopes they are tributary to the Volga system. On the eastern slopes they are tributary to the great Ob River system, and in the south to the minor Ural River, which drains southward, then westward, and then southward again to the north Caspian.

Within the confines of the Urals Economic Region itself is the Kama River in the west. Its main left-bank tributary is the Chusovaya, which actually heads on the eastern side of the mountains southwest of the city of Sverdlovsk and flows completely across the range to the northwest to join the Kama just north of the city of Perm. Two large construction projects have been completed on the Kama within the Urals Economic Region, the Kama plant above Perm that was completed in 1956 with a generating capacity of 504,000 kilowatts, and the Votkinsk plant farther south that was completed in 1964 with a capacity of 1 million kilowatts. A third plant is under construction farther downstream at Naberezhnyye Chelny in the Tatar A.S.S.R., discussed in the chapter on the Volga Region.

The possibility of bringing water into the upper Kama from the Pechora and Vychedga Rivers was discussed in the preceding chapter on the Northwest Region. If this project ever materializes, all-water routes for Pechora coal and other commodities from the Northwest could penetrate into the heart of the industrial Urals via improved waterways on the Chusovaya and Belaya River systems. The Belaya River begins near the town of Beloretsk not far west of Magnitogorsk, and the Ufa River begins just west of Chelyabinsk. They follow roundabout routes through the Bashkir A.S.S.R. and finally join near the capital city of Ufa, after which they flow northwestward to join the Kama River in the northeastern part of the Tatar A.S.S.R. It would not be too difficult to join the headwaters of the Ufa River with the Miass, which flows eastward through the city of Chelyabinsk to join the Iset, or even to join the headwater of the Iset River, which flows eastward through the city of Sverdlovsk, with the headwater of the Chusovaya River, which starts just to the west of Sverdlovsk. Thus, with some effort the three major industrial centers on the east side of the Urals — Sverdlovsk, Chelyabinsk, and Magnitogorsk — could be served by all-water routes from the west.

Magnitogorsk, of course, sits on the upper portion of the Ural River, which drains the southern Urals southward to the Caspian. This flows primarily through steppe and desert territory and therefore does not have a very great flow of water. If the Volga-Ural Canal ever materializes, the flow in the lower portion of the Ural River in western Kazakhstan will be significantly increased by additional water from the Volga.

The eastern slopes of the Urals within the Urals Economic Region are drained eastward by the Tobol River system with its main left-bank tributaries the Iset, the Tura, and Tavda Rivers. The Tobol is tributary to the Irtysh River, which in turn is tributary to the Ob River in Western Siberia.

Climate, Vegetation, and Soils

Since the Urals Economic Region stretches north-south about 11° of latitude, climate varies considerably from one end to the other. Since the entire region experiences very short days during midwinter and high surface albedos due to deep snow cover, radiation effects are minimized, and temperatures do not vary much from south to north during the winter. Orenburg in the south averages −15°C during January and has experienced a minimum temperature of −44°C. Serov in the north averages −16.9°C in January and has experienced a minimum temperature of −51°C. The temperatures vary more during summer when radiational effects are more influential and isotherms run more latitudinally. During July Orenburg averages 22°C, while Serov averages only 16.7°C. However, on individual days during summer all lowland areas in the Urals can become quite warm. Orenburg has experienced temperatures as high as 41°C, while Serov has experienced temperatures as high as 36°C.

There are also significant climatic differences between the western and eastern slopes of the mountains, but these differences relate more to the cloud and precipitation regimes than to temperatures. The Urals Region is crossed by many cyclonic storms, most of them moving from southwest to northeast. During winter, when they are best developed, they most frequently follow a route around the southern end of the Urals northeastward into the Western Siberian area or a northerly route eastward along the Arctic coast. The southerly storms generally bring widespread cloudiness in their northeastern quadrants ahead of slowly moving warm fronts that is added to by orographic uplift as the storms approach the western slopes of the mountains. This produces considerable cloudiness throughout the mountain range, but more on the windward western slope than on the leeward eastern slope. Perm in the west has 176 days per year with overcast skies. October, the cloudiest month, averages more than 22 days with overcast. June averages only 8.4. On the eastern side of the mountains,

Sverdlovsk averages 156 days per year with overcast. It has an annual regime similiar to that of Perm, but the differences between winter and summer are not so great. The cloudiest month, November, has 19.3 days with overcast skies, while the clearest month, June, has 9.2 days.

Perm averages 570 millimeters of precipitation a year, while Sverdlovsk averages only 462. Farther north, Serov averages 446, and in the south Orenburg averages 358. All stations have a fairly pronounced summer maximum of precipitation. Generally the maximum falls in July, although in some localities it is August. Throughout most of the region the annual precipitation is quite adequate, but in Orenburg Oblast potential evaporation is about double precipitation. Also, Kurgan Oblast in the east experiences some deficit of moisture.

The rising air ahead of northeastward-moving cyclones during winter produces much fogginess and drizzle in the Urals that often freezes on trees, transmission lines, and other objects in the form of either glaze or rime ice. In some particularly exposed localities this may accumulate to as much as 10 centimeters in diameter and cause great destruction because of its weight.

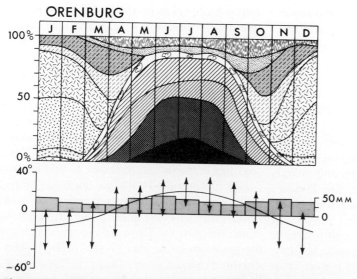

Figure 12-3 Weather types, temperature, and precipitation, Orenburg. For legend, see page 6.

Precipitation occurs frequently throughout the middle Urals. Perm records at least 1 millimeter of precipitation on 198 days of the year. During the winter there is frequent snowfall, which locally can be quite heavy. The western slopes of the middle Urals accumulate some of the greatest snow depths in the county. At Perm the annual average maximum snow depth is 76 centimeters, and snow remains on the ground an average of 176 days of the year. Farther east at Sverdlovsk, the snow accumulates to only 44 centimeters and remains on the ground 166 days of the year. The western slopes of the mountains experience some winter thaws, while on the eastern slopes these are very rare. During summer there is considerable convective activity. Perm experiences 21 thunderstorms from May through August, and Sverdlovsk experiences 25.

The intermontane basins generally experience strong temperature inversions during winter, so there is an inversion in vegetative cover. Thus, on western slopes of the southern Urals, it is common to find pine-birch forests growing on valley floors, while above them exist oak, and still higher linden with admixtures of maple and elm. It is not uncommon to find a 20°C increase in temperature with an elevation increase of 400–500 meters.

The low central Urals, which cover most of the Urals Economic Region, nowhere reach above the treeline, and forests are still the predominant vegetation, even though much of the middle Urals has been cut over a number of times, and the better soil areas have been put under cultivation. The best forests exist in the northwest and the northeast, in Perm and Sverdlovsk Oblasts, respectively. There spruce forests generally occupy the slopes between 800–1000 meters, fir forests between 600–800 meters, and mixed forests consisting of pine, birch, oak, linden, maple, and other broadleaf species below 600 meters.

In the southern part of the region where mountains are higher, tundra occupies the upper slopes above 1000–1200 meters, and larch forests are immediately below. In the south the dryish lower slopes and inter-montane basins originally were occupied by grasslands, which now have been largely plowed up and put under cultivation. The low southern extension of the Urals in Orenburg Oblast everywhere is steppe country, and this is almost entirely under cultivation.

The soils of the Urals vary from podsolic types in the northern part of the region and on the higher slopes of the mountains to steppe and chernozem soils in the south. The southern soils are the most fertile, but agriculture there is hampered by drought. Nevertheless, because of the fertile soils, the south has the greatest crop agriculture. Farther north agriculture depends heavily on livestock. Kurgan Oblast in the east has the greatest potential for agriculture. It has fertile chernozem soils in combination with subhumid moisture conditions and relatively warm summers.

AGRICULTURE

Within the Urals Economic Region as a whole, grains occupy about 70 percent of the cultivated land. They are by far the most prevalent in the steppe zone of the south where spring wheat is overwhelmingly dominant. In the forest zone farther north rye becomes very important. Fodder crops, primarily clover and alfalfa, occupy another 25 percent. Industrial crops occupy 1.5 percent of the cultivated area. In the south this is primarily sunflowers and in the north flax. Flax growing is most important in the Udmurt A.S.S.R. and Perm Oblast. Some sugar beets have been introduced into the area, but these are primarily in the Bashkir A.S.S.R., which has been transfered to the Volga Region. Potatoes and vegetables occupy 3 percent of the cultivated land. They are scattered throughout the region, but are most important in the cool, humid north.

During the mid-1950s the southern Urals saw a significant expansion of cultivated land under the Virgin Lands program, which stretched from the Trans Volga region across the southern Urals into Western Siberia and northern Kazakhstan. Initially these new lands were occupied almost entirely by spring wheat, but gradually a more rounded live-

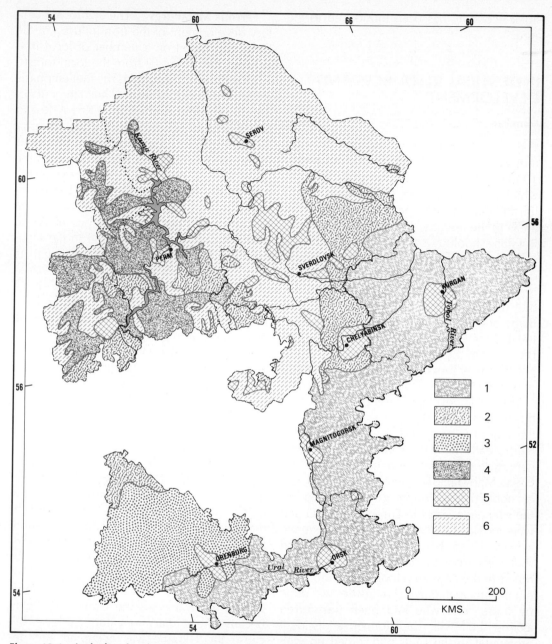

Figure 12-4   Agricultural regions. After Saushkin, p. 148,; 1-Wheat,
meat-milk livestock, fine-wooled sheep; 2-Grain, milk-meat livestock, swine;
3-Wheat, rye, oats, millet, sunflowers, meat-milk livestock, fine-wooled
sheep; 4-Flax, dairying, grain, livestock; 5-Urban oriented vegetable and
potato growing with dairying and other livestock products; 6-Forestry,
hunting, and gathering, with some vegetable growing and livestock raising.

stock economy has been introduced to the area.

INDUSTRIAL RESOURCES AND DEVELOPMENT

Minerals

The Ural Mountain range is one of the most mineralized on earth. It contains more than 1000 different exploitable minerals, many of which carry special Ural names, such as uralite and ilmenite. It is one of the oldest mining areas in the country. The story goes that if a Russian schoolboy is asked where the country gets a certain mineral, if he says the Urals he is correct. Although the Urals are not quite as important relative to the country as a whole as they used to be, because of the opening up of many new mining areas, they remain one of the major mining areas of the country, probably equal to the Donets-Dnieper in total output, and they turn out a much greater variety of minerals than the Donets-Dnieper Region.

The Urals developed iron and copper industries in the early eighteenth century during the reign of Peter the Great and expanded them greatly in the latter half of the eighteenth century during the reign of Catherine the Great. Many factories were set up in the Urals by noblemen who were going bankrupt on their landed estates in European Russia and were looking for alternate forms of economic activity where they could invest capital and shift serfs from the land to their factories. Much of the early development of the Urals mining and metallurgical industries was done by these serfs who had been transferred against their will. They formed a dissident proletariat in the Urals and joined up with Pugachev in a revolt during the reign of Catherine that nearly toppled the empire. Nevertheless, by 1800 the region yielded about 80 percent of Russia's iron and virtually all of its copper, as well as precious stones, gold, and salt. By this time the Urals had become the largest iron producer in the world, and actually shipped pig iron to Britain.

Ferrous Metallurgy. The eighteenth century development of the iron industry in the Urals was based on a number of local iron deposits and charcoal from the local forests. During the next century, as the fuel emphasis shifted from charcoal to coal and larger richer iron mines were opened up at Krivoy Rog in the eastern Ukraine, the Urals iron industry rapidly became eclipsed by the new industries in the eastern Ukraine. The eastern Ukraine underwent a particularly rapid expansion after 1880. The share of Russian pig iron produced in the Urals dropped from 70 percent in 1860 to 20 percent on the eve of World War I. Industrial growth lapsed in the Urals until the 1930s when the Soviets began to construct the Urals-Kuznetsk Combine based on the newly opened rich iron deposits at Magnitnaya in the southern Urals and the large coking coal reserves of the Kuznetsk Basin in Western Siberia. Iron and steel plants were constructed at Magnitogorsk in the west and at Stalinsk (now Novokuznetsk) in the east to utilize railroad cars moving both directions along the Trans Siberian Railroad. Iron ore moved east and coal moved west. Actually, this shuttle didn't last very long, because local iron ore deposits were found around the southern end of the Kuznetsk Basin, but coking coal continued to move westward in great quantities subsidized by artificially low freight rates set by the central government to make possible the continued development of the Magnitogorsk steel plant. But the real revitalization of industry in the Urals came with World War II when whole plants were relocated in the area from the western regions. During the war years the Urals once again became the primary metallurgical base, because the Ukraine was occupied and destroyed by the Germans.

By the end of the war it was evident that the higher-grade ores were running out at Magnitnaya, which fed the giant blast furnaces of Magnitogorsk, and at Blagodat and Vysokaya on either side of the other large iron smelting center of Nizhniy Tagil farther north. The old iron mines at Bakal, which for years had supplied highest-grade ore to the fine steel center of Zlatoust west of Chelyabinsk, had always been a relatively small operation and could not be expected to take up the slack. For a few years Soviet planners contemplated the gradual diminishing of the iron industry in the Urals and the building of new plants in other regions of the country. Then, in the mid-1950s, reports came in from geological survey teams that seemingly inexhaustible supplies of low-grade iron ore lay in widespread deposits in northern Kazakhstan and Western Siberia immediately adjacent to the Urals and within the Urals themselves. Overnight this transformed the picture of the future, and plans were changed to develop rapidly large open-pit mines equipped with huge concentrators to process the ore, much of which had no more than 16 percent iron content, into a pelletized aggregate of iron, manganese, limestone flux, and coke, to feed efficiently into the furnaces of the Urals that were to undergo major expansion. It appears that most of these plans are successfully being carried out on schedule, and the iron industry of the Urals is assured of a major role for the foreseeable future.

Within the Urals, the most outstanding new iron deposit is at Kachkanar northwest of Nizhniy Tagil. The Kachkanar deposit is now credited with half the reserves in the Urals. Several large deposits are strung in a north-south line through Tyumen Oblast in Western Siberia, Kurgan Oblast in the Urals Region, and Kustanay Oblast in northern Kazakhstan. All of these low-grade deposits lie near the surface and can be exploited by inexpensive open-pit mining.

In 1974 the Urals Economic Region produced 26 million tons of usable iron ore out of a U.S.S.R. total of 225 million tons. Adjacent regions in northern Kazakhstan produced another 16 million tons. This is contrasted to 122 million tons in the Ukraine and 30 million tons in the Kursk Magnetic Anomaly. The great amount of expansion in iron and steel capacity of the plants of the Urals that has taken place during the last 20 years since the

discovery of the large low-grade deposits of iron ore has kept the need for iron ore in the Urals ahead of the supply, and in 1974 the Urals found it necessary to import about 10–12 million tons of iron ore from the Kursk Magnetic Anomaly.

Ferrous alloys such as manganese, nickel, tungsten, and chrome are found in some quantities in the Urals, with nickel and chrome being especially abundant in the Orsk-Khalilovo area in the south. The Russians claim that they have found the largest deposit of chrome in the world across the Kazakh border at Khrom-Tau. A new steel industry has been established in this southern extension of the Urals to utilize the iron ore, nickel and chrome deposits for the production of high-grade nickel-chrome steels.

The last 20 years have witnessed major expansions of iron and steel facilities throughout the Urals. The Kachkanar concentrator began in 1963 to process 16 percent iron ore containing vanadium and very low percentages of sulfur and phosphorus. The Kachkanar ore has become the principal source of vanadium for the iron and steel industry throughout the entire Soviet Union. Much of this is made usable for the steel industry at the nearby Chusovoy plant. By 1975 the capacity of the Kachkanar iron ore concentrator complex had expanded to about 45 million tons of crude ore per year, which produced about 8 million tons of concentrate. The principal consumer of the Kachkanar concentrate is the Nizhniy Tagil iron and steel plant, inaugurated in 1940. The plant has been expanded into one of the principal iron and steel producers of the Urals. Its pig iron capacity now apparently exceeds 5 million tons.

The largest iron and steel plant in the Urals, and in the entire country, is at Magnitogorsk. This plant has undergone continual expansion since 1955 to increase its pig iron capacity from about 6 million tons per year to about 15 million tons in 1975. Although it is rapidly being overtaken by the newer Krivoy Rog plant in the Ukraine, it appears that the Magnitogorsk plant will continue to be expanded somewhat during the foreseeable future. Construction began on Magnitogorsk in 1929 next to the magnetite deposit of Magnitnaya Mountain near the Ural River. The first blast furnace went into production in 1932, and the first steel was made in 1933. Now that the Magnitnaya ores are running out, at least half of the ore used at Magnitogorsk comes from the new mining center of Rudnyy in the low-grade surface deposit in Kustanay Oblast in northern Kazakhstan. A significant portion of the ore is now coming from the Kursk Magnetic Anomaly in the Central Chernozem Region.

A second large integrated iron and steel plant exists in Chelyabinsk Oblast, in Chelyabinsk city. This was established during World War II when it was based on Bakal ore, 300 rail kilometers to the west. Now that the Bakal ore is running out after 200 years of mining, the expanded plant at Chelyabinsk is using primarily ore from Rudnyy and some from the

Figure 12-5   Steel smelting at Magnitogorsk. Novosti.

Kursk Magnetic Anomaly. It was reported that in 1975 Chelyabinsk produced 7 million tons of 550 kinds of steel. It also had one of the main steel pipe plants in the country. Both Magnitogorsk and Chelyabinsk are expected to utilize greater amounts of Kursk ore in the future in order to make use of empty freight cars returning from the west.

In the very southern part of the Urals Region, the new center of Novotroitsk was established in the early 1950s to contain the site of the new iron-nickel-chrome steel plant that began operation in 1955. This is officially known as the Orsk-Khalilovo iron and steel plant. It was designed to use the local naturally alloyed ore containing chrome and nickel, but technical problems have sidetracked this effort, and the plant gets most of its ore supply from Rudnyy. It has been reported that in 1973 the pig iron capacity of the plant was about 3.5 million tons.

In 1974 the Urals produced 26 million tons of pig iron out of a U.S.S.R. total of 100 tons and 42 million tons of crude steel out of a U.S.S.R. total of 136 million tons. This was second to the Ukraine, which produced 44.6 million tons of pig iron and 52.4 million tons of steel. About 80 percent of the Urals pig iron and 70 percent of the steel comes from the four big integrated plants at Magnitogorsk, Chelyabinsk, Nizhniy Tagil, and Orsk-Khalilovo. Smaller integrated plants that turn out both pig iron and steel exist at Alapayevsk, Beloretsk, Serov, Chusovaya, Asha, and Verkhniy Ufaley. Pig iron only is produced in Satka, Nizhnyaya Salda, and Staroutkinsk. Steel and rolled-steel products only are produced at Lysva, Izhevsk, Zlatoust, Revda, Nizhniye Sergi, Verkh-Iset (part of Sverdlovsk City), Verkhnyaya Salda, and Minyar. Steel pipe is produced in Chelyabinsk, Pervouralsk, Kamensk-Uralskiy, and Polevskoy.

Nonferrous Metallurgy. The Urals have been known for their nonferrous metallurgy for a great many years. Copper, zinc, lead, silver, gold, and platinum have been mined for a long time and until recently were mined almost exclusively in the Urals. During the last 25 years the production of bauxite has become very important. At present the Urals produce most of the aluminum ore in the country. As other areas open up, the Urals are becoming less significant relative to the country's total production of nonferrous metals, but are still the leading producer of most of them.

Copper ores are scattered up and down the length of the Urals, and these have provided the basis for a number of smelters and refineries in Krasnouralsk, Kirovgrad, Revda, Karabash, Kyshtym, and Mednogorsk. As local ores ran out, the Urals were overextended in copper smelting, and copper ore had to be hauled in from Kazakhstan to supply the Ural smelters. Some of that long-distance hauling has been alleviated recently with the opening of a very large copper mining district at Gay Near Orsk in the south in Orenburg Oblast as well as at Uchaly in the Bashkir A.S.S.R. The first underground mine went into operation at Gay in 1961, followed by the first open-pit mine in 1963 and the first stage of a concentrator in 1966. This has rapidly beome one of the principal copper ore producers in the Urals. It is said to have one of the largest reserves of copper in the country. A zinc refinery has been in operation in Chelyabinsk since 1935.

In 1934 bauxite mining began in the Krasnaya Shapochka ("Red Riding Hood") mines at Severouralsk in the northern part of the Urals Region near Serov. In spite of a flooding problem in the karst limestone surrounding the region, these mines rapidly became the major suppliers of aluminum ore in the country. The bauxite is shipped to alumina plants at Krasnoturinsk nearby and Kamensk-Uralskiy farther south, originally founded in 1939 on a small local bauxite deposit, which soon became depleted. Some of the alumina at Krasnoturinsk and Kamensk-Uralskiy is reduced to aluminum locally, but much of it is now shipped to large new aluminum plants at major hydroelectric stations in Siberia because large amounts of electricity are needed to reduce alumina to aluminum. Some of the alumina used to be shipped to the Transcaucasus, particularly Yerevan, but it appears now that this practice has ceased.

For a long time the Urals were the major

producer of gold and silver in Russia, but during the Soviet period the region has been far surpassed by the Far East, Central Asia, and the Transcaucasus. However, gold is still mined in many small scattered centers in the Urals. The Urals also used to be the world's largest producer of platinum, but this has been eclipsed by a new operation in conjunction with nickel production at Norilsk in Eastern Siberia.

Fuels and Power. Unfortunately the Urals are poor in fuels. The region contains 0.5 percent of the country's energy resources and consumes 15 percent of the country's energy production. It is particularly short in coal, which is so necessary for the many metallurgical industries. The best deposits of coal are in the northwest at Kizel, but even these cannot be used in blast furnaces. Other than the Kizel coals, the Urals are limited to scattered deposits of lignite, generally along the eastern flanks of the mountains, particularly in Chelyabinsk Oblast. Coal must be shipped in for the steel and other metallurgical mills from the Kuznetsk Basin more than 1600 kilometers to the east and from Karaganda more than 950 kilometers to the southeast in Kazakhstan. Because the Karaganda coal is high in ash, it cannot be used alone in blast furnaces. Generally the mix contains one-third Karaganda coal and two-thirds Kuznetsk coal. The Urals are also now shipping in large quantities of Ekibastuz coal from northeastern Kazakhstan for power generation and heating purposes.

Except for the heavy metallurgical industries, the fuel problems in the Urals may largely be solved by oil and gas, which lie in abundance on either side of the Urals and which can be piped in from the gas fields of Central Asia and Western Siberia. The largest producing oil fields in the country lie between the Volga River and the Ural Mountains on the western flanks of the fold. The major producing area in the Urals was the Bashkir Republic, which has recently been transferred to the Volga Region, but Perm Oblast has increased its oil production to more than 20 million tons per year, and there are reports

that the Udmurt A.S.S.R. has a number of significant deposits. The Udmurt Republic produced about 3 million tons in 1974. An oil refinery was established in the city of Perm in 1958 and has been expanded into a major refinery complex. A much older refinery exists in Orsk in the south at the northern terminus of a pipeline that for many years has been carrying crude oil northward from the Emba oil fields along the northern Caspian coast. Crude oil from Baku in the Transcaucasus is brought by steamer to Guryev on the North Caspian coast, where it is then transferred to the pipeline. In 1969 a gas processing plant was established at Perm to process oil well gases in the region.

In 1963 the first gas line to the Urals from Bukhara in Central Asia was inaugurated. Now two pipelines from the Bukhara district supply about 20 billion cubic meters of gas per year to the Urals. In 1966 the first pipeline from the Punga field along the lower Ob in Western Siberia was completed to Serov and Nizhniy Tagil. The line now carries about 10 billion cubic meters a year to the Urals. A second line is now under construction, and the first line has been extended to Perm and Berezniki. Recently three pipelines have been completed from the huge Medvezhye gas field along the Arctic coast east of the Ob Estuary to the Urals.

In 1967 a large natural gas deposit was discovered in Orenburg Oblast. It is now evident that this is one of the largest fields in the country. Reserves are estimated to be about 1.7 trillion cubic meters, which rival those of Central Asia. The gas has a high sulfur content and is rich in liquid petroleum fractions and helium. It is treated before transmission by a complex of processing plants that have been built in the area. A gas transmission main carries the dry-processed gas to fuel the Zainsk thermal power station in the Tatar A.S.S.R., another pipeline carries liquid petroleum fractions to the Bashkir petrochemical center at Salavat, and a third short pipeline carries gas to the Kuybyshev area on the Volga. The Soviet Union and its East European satellites are building a 3000-kilometer pipeline southwestward from Orenburg to

Uzhgorod on the Czechoslovak border where it will link up with existing gas distribution systems serving eastern Europe.

Thus, the Urals seem now to be well supplied with the necessary fuels to power a great number of large thermal electric-generating stations that have been built in the region. In addition, one of the major atomic power stations in the country exists at Beloyarskiy east of Sverdlovsk. The first unit was built in 1964. A third stage under construction in the mid-1970s will raise its total capacity to 900,000 kilowatts.

Other Minerals. Many nonmetallic ores are mined in the Urals Region. Chief among these are the salts and potash deposits of the Berezniki-Solikamsk twin cities on the upper Kama River. The salt works were established as early as the fifteenth century when the Russians first settled the western slopes of the Urals. In the 1870s the first ammonia-soda plant, using natural brines, began production at Berezniki. During the Soviet period a modern chemical industry has been established on the basis of the potassium chloride and associated carnalite, hydrous potassium-magnesium chloride. The first potash plant was opened in Solikamsk in 1934, and a magnesium plant was opened in 1936. A second potash plant was opened in Berezniki in 1954. Both plants have been expanded, and in the mid-1970s the region had a capacity to turn out about 10.8 million tons of potash fertilizer per year. This was about half the total Soviet production, exceeding the Soligorsk region in Belorussia by about 2 million tons. Berezniki has a nitrogenous fertilizer plant that, in addition to fertilizers, turns out about one-third of the Soviet Union's aniline dyes. A second magnesium plant established in Berezniki during World War II has also added to the production of titanium.

Pyrites from the Urals continue to be the principal sulfur-bearing raw material in the Soviet Union. Sulfuric acid is derived from by-product smelter gases at all of the copper smelters in the region. Three of the Urals copper smelting centers — Revda, Krasnouralsk, and Kirovgrad — have established super-

phosphate industries to utilize sulfuric acid derived from their copper smelters to process Kola apatite into superphosphate fertilizers.

The Soviet Union produces about half the world's asbestos. About 90 percent of this is produced at the town of Asbest in the Urals. A new asbestos mill is being constructed with the help of Comecon countries at the town of Yasnyy in Orenburg Oblast.

The Urals have long been known for their gems and semiprecious stones. Chief among these are emeralds, jasper, agate, and malachite, a mottled green stone that has been used for centuries to decorate tabletops and other articles of furniture as well as for sculpture of various forms. The malachite room in the Hermitage Museum in Leningrad displays some of the most notable specimens of this stonework.

Chemical and Machine-Building Industries

The great amount of coal coking, oil and gas processing, and ore smelting in the Urals Region has provided the basis for a wide complex of chemical industries. Some of the main ones have already been mentioned at the Berezniki-Solikamsk area and in the major copper-smelting cities. The metallurgical industries have also provided the basis for a wide range of machine-building industries, ranging all the way from precision tools to heavy mining equipment.

The very large "Uralmash" machine-building plant in Sverdlovsk is known throughout the country for its construction of heavy mining equipment. Also, the automotive industry is well represented here. A new plant at Izhevsk, the capital of the Udmurt Republic, went into operation in 1970. It is to turn out about 200,000 Moskvich model passenger cars annually. This will be equal in production to the Moscow plant and larger than either the Zaporozhye or Gorkiy plants. It will be equal to about one-third the output of Togliatti on the Volga. In addition, the Urals Motor Vehicle Plant built in the city of Miass during World War II now specializes in the building of three-axle heavy cargo trucks of 5–7.5-ton capacity. Many of these are used for military transport operations over rough terrain. The city of Kurgan on the plain east of the Urals is one of the main schoolbus-producing cities in the country. A tire plant has been established in Sverdlovsk to serve these automotive industries.

Nizhniy Tagil is known for its railroad car construction. In total machine construction the two most important cities are the two largest cities of the Urals, Sverdlovsk and Chelyabinsk.

Forestry

The Urals Economic Region is the third most important wood-producing region in the country, after the Northwest Region and the Eastern Siberian Region. In 1973 it produced 57 million cubic meters out of a U.S.S.R. total of 387.6 million cubic meters. Over 90 per-cent of the Urals production came from Sverdlovsk and Perm Oblasts, which ranked fourth and fifth in wood production among all the political units of the country. The Urals Region also ranked third in saw timber pro-duction in the country, and Sverdlovsk Oblast ranked fourth among the political units. In paper production the Urals Region ranked second after the Northwest Economic Region, and Perm Oblast ranked first among all the political units in the country, including the Karelian A.S.S.R., which was the first-ranking political unit within the Northwest Economic Region. The Kama River region of Perm Oblast on the western slopes of the Urals is the most important paper-producing area in the whole country.

A great deal of the timber logged in the Kama River region is floated southward down the Kama and into the Volga to the southern regions of the country. But most of the Urals timber is loaded onto trains and carried by rail to domestic markets, primarily in European U.S.S.R. Unlike the Northwest Economic Re-gion, which produces large amounts of wood for export, most of the Ural production is used within the U.S.S.R. Most of this moves by rail, as does 80 percent of all freight traffic in the Urals.

CITIES

As mentioned at the beginning of this chapter, the Urals Economic Region is almost three-fourths urbanized. It has 15 cities with more than 100,000 population, and three cities with more than 900,000 which ties it for first place with the Donets-Dnieper Region.

Sverdlovsk

The largest city in the Urals is Sverdlovsk, which in 1974 had a population of 1,122,000. This has been the largest city in the Urals for centuries and has often been called the capital of the Urals, although, of course, the Urals never have been a political unit. The city was founded in 1721 under a governmental decree by Peter the Great to establish mining industries in the area. The city was called Yekaterinburg. In 1924 it was renamed Sverdlovsk after the famous rev-olutionary. Sverdlovsk is known primarily for its machine construction industries. The large "Uralmash" plant has already been mentioned. It also has some heavy and light metallurgy, chemical industries, and wood-working industries. Seven railroad lines make it the most important rail junction in the Urals.

Chelyabinsk

Second largest city is Chelyabinsk, with a 1974 population of 947,000. It was founded in 1736 as a fortress. During the Russian Em-pire it had an infamous reputation as the trans-fer point for exiled peasants awaiting ship-ment into Siberia. It was largely a barracks town for transients laying over and awaiting assignment to new regions. Most of them were in a confused, depressed state of mind, and they left with very bad impressions of the town. But with the coming of the Trans Sibe-rian Railroad in 1890 Chelyabinsk got a great boost in importance and soon replaced Tyumen as the gateway to Siberia.

Early in the 1900s, Chelyabinsk went through a growth period in which flour mill-ing, based on local wheat growing, was the most significant industry. But today Chelyabinsk has evolved into another important machine-building town like Sverdlovsk. Its machine industries range from fine machine tools to aircraft industries, but it is probably still best known for its tractor works. It is the main center for the production of heavy caterpillar tractors in the Soviet Union. Much other agricultural machinery is built there to service southwestern Siberia and northern Kazakhstan. It also has heavy and light metallurgy. Its recently expanded iron and steel plant is now second in size in the Urals, after Magnitogorsk. The town has one of the largest zinc smelters in the country. Chemical industries are based on low-grade coal mined locally and natural gas brought in by pipeline from Central Asia in the south and Western

Figure 12-6   The Chelyabinsk tractor plant. Novosti.

Siberia in the northeast. A large-diameter pipe mill has been built to produce pipe for the oil and gas mains that are being laid in many regions of the country.

Perm

Third in size is Perm, the metropolitan center on the Kama River in the northwestern part of the Urals Region. In 1974 it had a population of 920,000. The city was founded in 1780, and from the mid-1930s to 1957 it was named Molotov. When it was finally renamed Perm, geologists around the world were relieved because this was the region from which the Permian geologic period had derived its name. The city's primary function is to serve as the urban center for the Kama River region, which is important in chemical industries, machine building, oil refining, and wood-working.

Izhevsk

Izhevsk, the capital of the Udmurt A.S.S.R., has been the most rapidly growing city in the Urals since the late 1950s. In 1974 it had a population of 489,000. Its new car assembly plant has already been mentioned. In addition, it manufactures many other kinds of machines, including motorcycles and paper-making equipment. It also produces a great deal of ordnance, including sporting rifles. One of its major plants is a steel plant.

Orenburg

The fifth largest city in the Urals is Orenburg, with a 1974 population of 400,000. It was established in the steppes in the south along the Ural River as one of a series of Russian fortifications against the steppe peoples to the southeast. It eventually became the center of an important agricultural region specializing in growing spring wheat and raising sheep and horses. After the successful polar flight from Moscow to Vancouver, Washington, by its native son, Valery Chkalov, and his companions in 1938, Orenburg was renamed Chkalov. But in 1957, when several towns

reverted to their prerevolutionary names, Chkalov again became known as Orenburg. For many years Orenburg remained rather stagnated compared to many of the other cities of the Urals that were undergoing much more industrialization. Recently, with the development of the huge gas deposit in the area, as well as a general metallurgical site in the Orsk-Khalilovo area nearby, Orenburg has taken a spurt in growth and has surpassed Nizhniy Tagil and Magnitogorsk.

Nizhniy Tagil

The sixth city is Nizhniy Tagil with a 1974 population of 390,000. It is primarily known as an old iron and steel center in the north-central Urals. During Soviet times it has expanded into one of the largest steel centers in the Urals. For a number of years it was second only to Magnitogorsk in iron and steel production. Now it has been surpassed by Chelyabinsk. It is also known for its freight car manufacturing, as mentioned earlier.

Magnitogorsk

Seventh in size is the heavy metallurgical center of Magnitogorsk, with a 1974 population of 384,000. The city was established in 1931 next to Magnitnaya Gora, the important iron deposit in the hills just outside of town, as part of the widely publicized Ural-Kuznetsk Combine, to utilize the iron ore in the Magnitogorsk area and the coal in the Kuznetsk Basin. Iron and steel mills were built at both ends of the shuttle in order to utilize railroad cars in both directions. As usual, the most important steel mills were built closest to the markets, in this case Magnitogorsk. By 1939 Magnitogorsk had developed into one of the major metallurgical centers of the U.S.S.R., and it has continued to expand and has remained the biggest single plant in the country. In mid-1970s it had an estimated steel capacity of 15 million tons.

During the early development of the steel plant, the town grew like Topsy with no planning whatsoever. Iron and steel mills were erected and laborers were shipped into the area with no living accommodations. People were living in caves and lean-tos strung without pattern. The citizens of Magnitogorsk are still trying to eliminate the chaos of the past and rebuild the city in a rectangular pattern. The old city is situated on the east side of the Ural River. A new workers' settlement has been established on the west side of the river, and most of the people have moved across the river into apartment houses there.

Southeast of the old city a hill of iron ore rises 160 meters above the river to an elevation of about 650 meters. The steel plant stretches about 5 kilometers between "Magnetic Mountain" and the river. Ten coke ovens all in a row belch black smoke across the barren landscape as they convert coal to coke for the blast furnaces and open-hearth furnaces. A complete chemical complex makes use of the by-product gases and tars. The pig iron from the furnace goes directly as hot metal to the open-hearth shops, where it is joined by scrap metal to make steel ingots. Rolling mills turn out sheet steel for such large metal-fabricating centers as Chelyabinsk 250 kilometers to the northeast. Magnitogorsk steel is shipped all over the country and even abroad, since little metal fabrication is done in the city itself.

Until recently practically all of the iron ore for the plant came from the neighboring "Magnetic Mountain." This mining activity has left two enormous pits, one on either side of the hill. The west pit is about 2500 meters long, 2000 meters wide, and 350 meters deep. The east pit is somewhat smaller and is cut into the side of the hill so that it is level with the terrain on the east and rises to a 150-meter cliff against the hill on the west.

The metallurgical plant uses more water than the cities of Moscow and Leningrad combined. This is a problem of the first magnitude in this dryish region. A dam across the small Ural River forms a reservoir just outside town, providing barely enough water for industrial and domestic use. Little is left over for maintenance of lawns and gardens. Magnitogorsk is not as pleasant a place to live as most of the cities farther north in the more humid parts of the Urals.

Kurgan

Kurgan, with a 1974 population of 278,000, is the regional center of Kurgan Oblast, recently transferred from the Western Siberian Economic Region to the Urals. It is the commercial center of a rich farming area, and its primary industries are agricultural machine building. Its bus assembly plant has already been mentioned.

Orsk

In the south along the Ural River lies the city of Orsk, with a 1974 population of 237,000. It is very similar in aspect and function to Orenburg just to the west. For a number of years it has been the northern terminus of an oil pipeline from the Emba oil fields in the North Caspian Lowland, and it has a small refinery. With the development of the Orsk-Khalilovo metallurgical area, the city of Orsk is growing rapidly. The new city of Novotroitsk has been built nearby to serve as the iron and steel center for the region.

Zlatoust

Zlatoust, with a 1974 population of 188,000, is the old metallurgical center in the mountains west of Chelyabinsk. It has a small steel plant based on the very high-grade Bakal iron ores in the vicinity. It is known for its production of high-grade steel.

Kamensk-Uralskiy

Kamensk-Uralskiy (rocks of the Urals), with a 1974 population of 178,000, is the important alumina-producing center southeast of Sverdlovsk.

Berezniki

Berezniki, with a 1974 population of 161,000, is one of the twin cities on the upper Kama River known for its salt and chemical industries.

Kopeysk

Kopeysk, with a 1974 population of 156,000, is one of the main coal-mining centers in the Urals. It is located just east of Chelyabinsk on the Chelyabinsk brown coal basin.

Miass

Miass, with a 1974 population of 141,000, is the truck assembly city on the eastern edge of the Urals about 75 kilometers west-southwest of Chelyabinsk.

Pervouralsk

Pervouralsk, with a 1974 population of 122,000, is an iron-mining center in the mountains about 50 kilometers west of Sverdlovsk.

Serov

Serov is an old metallurgical center in the northern part of the Urals Economic Region. From 1970 to 1973 its population decreased from 101,000 to 99,000 and then increased to 100,000 in 1974.

PROSPECTS

The Urals Economic Region for a long time has been one of the three main industrial regions of the country, after the Central Region of European Russia and the Donets-Dnieper Region of the eastern Ukraine. Like the eastern Ukraine, its industries are based on the mining activities of the area. But unlike the eastern Ukraine its eastward position places it in a precarious economic situation. It prospers during times of crisis and tends to stagnate during times of relative quiet. At present its population is growing much less rapidly than the country as a whole, and its urbanization process has particularly slowed down. Most of the cities in the Urals showed decreased growth rates during the last intercensal period. Its position as the third most important industrial region in the country is being challenged by the Volga Region to the west,

particularly now that the oil-rich Bashkir Republic has been transferred from the Urals to the Volga Region. However, its metallurgical plants keep expanding, and with an apparently firm basis for mining the abundant low-grade surface iron ores just to the east of the mountains, the metallurgical industries seem to be assured for the foreseeable future. The economy would be put on a more firm basis if more machine-building industries were established in the area to utilize the products of the many metallurgical industries, much of which are now being shipped out of the region to other parts of the country. One of the key problems in the Urals is the need for modernizing industry, which dates largely from the 1940s and has yet to benefit from the latest technology. It is hoped that modernization will raise labor productivity and thus compensate to some extent for the increasing labor shortage.

READING LIST

- *Atlas orenburgskoy oblasti* (An Atlas of Orenburg Oblast), Moscow, 1969 (in Russian).
- Clark, M. Gardner, "Magnitogorsk: A Soviet Iron and Steel Plant in the Southern Urals," in Thoman, Richard S., and Donald J. Patton, *Focus on Geographic Activity*, McGraw-Hill, New York, 1964, pp. 128–134.
- Komar, I.V., *Ural; ekonomiko-geograficheskaya kharakteristika*, Moscow, 1959, 366 pp. (in Russian).
- Olenev, A.M., *Ural i Novaya Zemlya: Ocherk prirody* (The Urals and Novaya Zemlya: An Essay on Their Natural Environment), Izdatelstvo mysl, Moscow, 1965, 216 pp. (in Russian).
- Scott, John, *Behind the Urals: An American Worker in Russia's City of Steel,* Indiana University Press, Bloomington, 1973, 279 pp.
- Stepanov, P.N., *Ural*, Moscow, 1957, 163 pp. (in Russian).
- *Ural i Priuralye* (The Urals and the Ural Foreland), Nauka, Moscow, 1968 (in Russian).
- Varlamov, V.S., "The Economic-Geographic Situation of Orenburg," *Soviet Geography: Review & Translation,* June 1961, pp. 14–20.
- Varlamov, V.S., "On the Economic Links of the Industry of Orenburg," *Soviet Geography: Review & Translation,* March 1961, pp. 54–60.

The North Caucasus Economic Region

	Area (km²)	Population	Persons/km²	Percent Urban
Krasnodar Kray	84,000	4,639,000	55.5	49
Adyge Autonomous Oblast	8,000	399,000	52.4	42
Stavropol Kray	81,000	2,378,000	29.5	46
Karachay-Cherkess Autonomous Oblast	14,000	353,000	25.0	34
Rostov Oblast	101,000	3,936,000	39.0	66
Dagestan A.S.S.R.	50,000	1,503,000	29.9	37
Kabardino-Balkar A.S.S.R.	13,000	625,000	50.0	55
North Osetian A.S.S.R.	8,000	579,000	72.4	66
Chechen-Ingush A.S.S.R.	19,000	1,119,000	58.0	42
Total	355,000	14,779,000	41.6	52

chapter 13

the north caucasus economic region

The North Caucasus occupies the southern part of the European plain that stretches from the Sea of Azov and the Black Sea on the west to the Caspian on the east and from the lower Don region in the north to the main range of the Caucasus in the south. This encompasses a territory of 355,000 square kilometers and a total population of 14,779,000, which gives the region an average population density of 41.6 persons per square kilometer. The population density varies from 72.4 per square kilometer in the North Osetian A.S.S.R., which contains a fairly dense rural settlement coupled with 66 percent urbanization, to a low of 25 people per square kilometer in the Karachay-Cherkess Autonomous Oblast, which is only 34 percent urbanized. Certain parts of expansive political units, such as eastern Stavropol Kray and the northern part of Dagestan A.S.S.R., as well as the high mountain regions of the south, have very few people.

The entire region is within the Russian Republic, but a number of important non-Russian nationality groups form political subdivisions. The Caucasus in general has long been a very complex area of nationalities, many of which have been able to maintain their identities in isolated mountain basins and valleys. There are many smaller groups who are too few to be constituted as separate political units. Most of these peoples are known simply as Caucasian peoples, al-

235

Figure 13-1 The North Caucasus Region.

though the Osetians are Iranian (Indo-European), and the Azerbaydzhanis, Nogay, Karachay, and Balkar are Turkic. Those who have their own political units are listed in the table at the beginning of the chapter. As can be seen, some of them have been grouped. The Dagestan group is made up of 10 small groups that are listed by name in the 1970 census plus others who individually are too few to list.

The Russians came into the area during the eighteenth century as one after another outpost was established farther and farther to-

ward the southeast. Rostov was established at the mouth of the Don River in 1761, Vladi-kavkaz ("ruler of the Caucasus"), the modern Ordzhonikidze, was established in 1784 at the northern entrance to the main pass over the midsection of the Great Caucasus, and Yekaterinodar (modern Krasnodar) was established in the Kuban River basin in 1794. After the turn of the century the Russians crossed the Caucasus into Transcaucasia.

World War II complicated the nationality picture in the North Caucasus as many of the non-Russian groups were looked upon as potential collaborators with the enemy and were moved bodily eastward into Central Asia, Kazakhstan, and Western Siberia, and their political units in the North Caucasus were abrogated. Then, in 1957, Premier Khrushchev issued an amnesty decree to these peoples and allowed them to return to their homelands where their political units were reestablished much as they had been before the war. Most of these peoples did return to their homelands, although not exactly where they had been before the war. Also, many other people, particularly from Western Siberia, accompanied them to the North Caucasus and one way or another settled on collective farms and in the cities of the region. The North Caucasus Region is one of the southern areas that have experienced considerable in-migration during the last couple of decades. This has produced some problems; because there is not work for everybody, many people simply squat in a semilegal manner on small plots of ground where they

eke out a living. The government considers such people to be lost to the socialist labor force.

As can be seen in Table 13-1, the Russians are strongly represented even in the non-Russian political areas. They form a large majority in the Adyge Autonomous Oblast and a large plurality in the Karachay-Cherkess Autonomous Oblast. Although the titular groups in the four A.S.S.R.s are still more numerous than any other groups, it is only in Dagestan ("mountain country") that the various Dagestani groups as a whole form a very strong majority.

PHYSICAL LANDSCAPE

Landform

The North Caucasus Economic Region contains two very contrasting topographic units, the broad plain in the north and the Great Caucasus in the south. A third element, the

Table 13-1 Nationality Composition of Nationality-Based Political Units (Percents of Total)

Dagestan A.S.S.R.	100.0	Chechen Ingush A.S.S.R.	100.0
Dagestanis	74.3	Chechens	47.8
Russians	14.7	Ingush	10.7
Azerbaydzhanis	3.8	Russians	34.5
Chechens	2.8	Dagestanis	1.8
Jews	1.6	Armenians	1.4
Other	2.8	Ukrainians	1.2
Kabardino-Balkar A.S.S.R.	100.0	Other	2.6
Kabardiny	45.7	Adyge Autonomous Oblast	100.0
Balkars	8.7	Adyge	21.1
Russians	37.2	Russians	71.9
Ukrainians	1.8	Other	7.0
Osetians	1.6	Karachay-Cherkess Autonomous Oblast	100.0
Other	5.7	Karachays	28.2
North Osetian A.S.S.R.	100.0	Cherkess	9.0
Osetians	48.7	Russians	47.1
Russians	36.6	Other	15.7
Ingush	3.3		
Armenians	2.4		
Georgians	1.9		
Ukrainians	1.7		
Dagestanis	1.2		
Other	4.0		

Source: Itogi vsesoyuznoy perepisi naseleniya 1970 goda, Volume 4.

Stavropol Upland in the south-central portion of the plain, divides the lowland into two parts, the Kuban-Azov Lowland in the west and the Kum-Ter Lowland bordering on the Caspian in the east. Both of these lowlands are quite flat and are drained in their southern portions by major stream systems that head in the mountains to the south.

The western plain in its southern portion is drained by the Kuban River, which has many headwater streams flowing northward out of the high west-central Caucasus.

The river traverses the breadth of the plain westward through Krasnodar to form a large delta in the southeastern portion of the Sea of Azov. This region is often referred to simply as the Kuban and is known throughout the U.S.S.R. as one of the better farming regions of the country. Many small streams north of the Kuban River flow northwestward down the gentle dip of the plain to the east coast of the Sea of Azov where they form a very complex coastline of mud flats, islands, sandbars, stagnant lagoons, and marshes.

The Taman Peninsula juts out into the Sea of Azov from the delta of the Kuban River. It consists of a small archipelago of low islands made up of shales, marls, and shell limestones

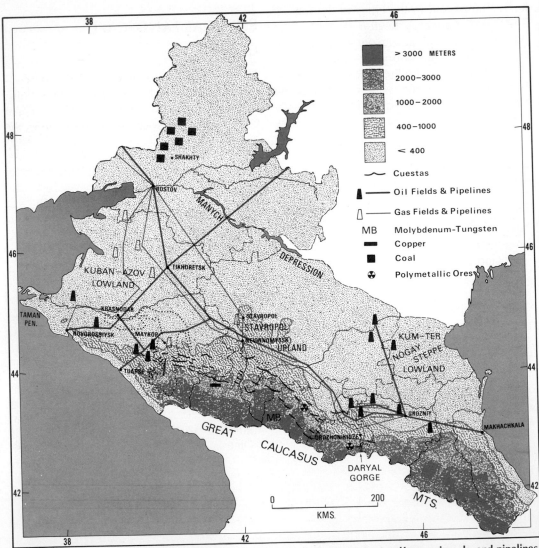

Figure 13-2   Landform, minerals, and pipelines.

that have been cemented together by the alluvial deposits of the Kuban River. Low folds are lined up with the Caucasus to the southeast and the Crimean Mountains to the northwest. The highest point of these folded ridges reaches 164 meters above sea level. There are about 25 large mud volcanoes on the peninsula that are reminiscent of those across the Kerch Strait on the Kerch Peninsula. Hydrogen disulfide emitted from the mud volcanoes undergoes spontaneous combustion and results in smoke and flames. Farther north along the eastern Azov coast is the city of Yeysk, which is a resort town with therapeutic mud and sulfur springs.

If anything, the eastern plain is even flatter than the west. The eastern half of the Kum-Ter plain (named for the Kuma and Terek Rivers) lies below sea level and is part of the North Caspian Lowland that during glacial times was part of the Caspian seabed. Few streams interrupt this plain, because the climate is quite dry. The Terek River is the counterpart of the Kuban River, flowing eastward out of the central high Caucasus to form a large marshy delta on the northwestern coast of the Caspian Sea. The Kuma River heads in the same general district on the northern slopes of the central Caucasus and flows northeastward to the Caspian where its lower portion forms the northern boundary of Dagestan A.S.S.R. and the North Caucasus Economic Region. Much of the time the Kuma dries up before it reaches the Caspian.

The eastern and western plains are connected north of the Stavropol Plateau by a structural sag through which glacial Lake Caspian spilled over to the northwest to the Sea of Azov during the Pleistocene when the water level of the Caspian was above sea level. This structural trough is known as the Manych Depression, at present occupied by the sluggish Manych River and various salt pools that at times of high water flow northwestward to the Don but during dry periods separate into salty pools of water. The Manych depression forms the northern boundary of the North Caucasus Economic Region in its eastern section, but in the west the region extends northward into the valleys of the Don

and its major left-bank tributary, the Sal River.

North of the Don lies the eastern extension of the Donets Ridge containing the eastern end of the Donets coal basin. Rostov Oblast, which is included in the North Caucasus Region, includes the lower Don Valley and this eastern extension of the Donets Ridge. The northern part of Rostov Oblast is a rolling plain dissected by the lower portion of the Northern Donets River and its tributaries.

The Stavropol Upland is a broad, dome-shaped uplift that in the southwestern and central portions includes high plateau surfaces armored with relatively resistant limestones and sandstones. The highest elevation is in the southwest where the surface rises to 832 meters. These rock-defended uplands are cut through by deep, asymmetrical valleys that characteristically are terraced, thus indicating successive uplifts. The upland slopes gradually down toward the northwest, north, and east, but terminates in an abrupt scarp in the southwest where the Kuban River has etched out a cuesta along the strike of northeasterly dipping strata.

Between the southeastern edge of the Stavropol Plateau and the main mass of the Caucasus Mountains to the south lies the Mineralnyye Vody ("mineral waters") region, which geologically is a synclinal ravine between the two uplifts on either side. Fractures have formed within this ravine along which acid magmas have risen to form some 80 laccolithic mountains whose jaggedly eroded spires stand up with fantastic silhouettes several hundred meters above the open plains surrounding them. The best known are the five peaks that form the backdrop for the city of Pyatigorsk ("five mountains"). A great number of mineral springs associated with the intrusive volcanism have formed the bases for the health resorts of Mineralnyye Vody, Pyatigorsk, Kislovodsk, and some other smaller cities in the area. These mineral health spas are of national significance.

The North Caucasian Plain is separated from the Transcaucasus by the Great Caucasus Range, which is actually a system of several ranges. Its width varies from about 32 kilometers around the western end, to 180

Figure 13-3   The approach to Pyatigorsk.

kilometers in the west-central portion, to 160 kilometers in the east. The overall structure of the system is one of a great asymmetrical fold that slopes gently on the north but almost overhangs on the south. Thrust faults have occurred in places on the southern side. The drainage divide follows the Main Caucasus Range in the southern part of the Great Caucasus system. This is paralleled on the north by the Front or Peredovyy Range, which is less continuous but contains the highest peaks in the entire system: Mt. Elbrus at an elevation of 5642 meters, Mt. Kazbek at 5033 meters, and about a dozen other such peaks above the 5000-meter level.

North of the Front Range lie three other subparallel ranges that are really giant cuestas eroded in massive limestone and sandstone rocks dipping northward underneath the plain. The southernmost and highest of these cuestas is the Skalistyy ("rocky") Range, which reaches elevations of as much as 3300 meters. The central cuesta is the Pastbishchnyy ("pasture") Range, which reaches elevations as high as 1500 meters. And the northernmost, lowest cuesta is the Lesistyy ("forest") or Chernyy ("black," from the forest cover) Range, which reaches elevations around 600 meters. This belt of cuestas extends for about 540 kilometers along the northern slope of the western half of the Great Caucasus (Fig. 13-2). The width of the belt

varies from about 12 kilometers south of Krasnodar to as much as 64 kilometers near the Cherek River to the east. Everywhere these cuestas exhibit steep escarpments on the southern sides that lie at angles of up to 30° and gentle dip slopes on the northern sides that slope at not more than 5°. In places the dip slopes take on the character of plateaus. Rivers flowing down the north slope of the Main Range have cut these cuestas into separate segments divided by gorgelike stream valleys. All of the cuestas exhibit prominent karst phenomena on their gentle northern slopes. Most of these northern slopes support broadleaf forests and fertile mountain meadows, while the longitudinal valleys lying in the rain shadows between the ranges are predominantly of steppe character.

North of the Main Range erosion has produced features essentially in parallel alignment from northwest to southeast, but south of the Main Range it has proceeded in a radial pattern to form many short ranges jutting southward from the Main Range at high angles.

The high central section of the Main Range is composed mainly of crystalline rocks, primarily metamorphic gneisses, schists, and slates. Magmatic intrusions are common, and some sedimentary cover exists in places. The higher peaks such as Elbrus and Kazbek are dead volcanic cones sitting on top of the rest of the structure. They are now being attacked vigorously by glacial and stream action. Toward either end of the Main Range the elevation becomes lower, and the rocks turn to primarily sedimentary flysch, easily eroded shaly limestones and marls, in which the headwaters of streams have eroded very narrow canyons with precipitous cliffs that are full of solution features, particularly in the low Black Sea Caucasus in the west. Hundreds of caves honeycomb the hills. Along the coast waves have hollowed out some of these caves at sea level and provided shelters where for centuries prior to the Soviet period pirates hid out to prey on maritime shipping along the coast. East of the Daryal Gorge of the Terek River the mountains are composed more of easily eroded shales that in a semiarid climate have been transformed into almost a badlands topography of enormous magnitude. The Sulak River canyon in this region is cut to a depth of 1500 meters. Mud torrents are common in this region during summer downpours.

The higher parts of the Caucasus exhibit extreme glaciation. Even the higher crests of the first cuesta north of the Front Range exhibit glacial features. During the Ice Age the boundary of perpetual snow in the humid western Caucasus lay at 2000 meters, about 800 meters lower than it is at present. In the drier, eastern part glacial features are not so prominent. The high central portion of the Main Range and the higher parts of the Front Range are cut by U-shaped valleys with hanging tributaries along which landslides and avalanches are very common. The drainage divide along the crest of the Main Range has been eaten into from both sides by cirque formations that have sharpened the ridge into a sawtoothed line of individual mountain horns with jagged peaks and precipitous slopes. The higher peaks are all snow-capped, and glacial tongues extend down some of the valleys to elevations as low as 2000 meters.

The southern boundary of the North Caucasus Economic Region follows the republic boundary between the R.S.F.S.R. on the north and the Georgian and Azerbaydzhan Republics on the south. This political boundary in most cases follows the highest crest of the Main Range, but it does jump back and forth between the Main Range and the Front Range and deviates from both ranges completely at either end. In the west the Russian Republic extends across the low Black Sea Caucasus to include the entire mountain range and the Black Sea coast southward beyond the city of Sochi. In the east the republic boundary suddenly cuts northeastward to the Caspian leaving the last 100 kilometers of the mountains, which still have heights of more than 4000 meters, in the Azerbaydzhan Republic to the south.

Climate, Vegetation, and Soils

The climate varies drastically across the region because of great differences in elevation, in exposure to the Black and Caspian Seas, and in contact with preferred cyclonic routes. During summer most of the plain is dominated by a slow northerly drift of air around the eastern end of the Azores High. This brings to the region a continental type of air that is relatively hot and subject to convective activity. Some influx of moisture from the west produces considerable thundershower activity. During winter the plain is dominated by an easterly flow of surface air around the southern periphery of the western nose of the Asiatic High. This brings relatively cold stable air to the region that often exhibits strong surface temperature inversions. In the western part of the plain this is frequently broken up by cyclonic passages moving along a route from the Black Sea northeastward across the western section of the plain. The Black Sea coastal area south of the western Caucasus is usually sheltered from the colder air to the north except on occasions when cold bora winds blow from northeast to southwest through the passes and interrupt the mild winter climate in the coastal cities. The Novorossiysk bora are famous around the world for their frequency and strength. They often whip up waves along the coast and blow spray off the breaking whitecaps that freezes over all the moorings and piers along the harbor.

During summer temperatures in the plain

average around 23°C in July at Krasnodar in the middle of the Kuban district, only 33 meters above sea level. Higher up at Pyatigorsk at 573 meters, the temperature in July averages 21.6°C. Both cities have experienced temperatures as high as 41°C. Farther east in northern Dagestan temperatures get even higher. Along the Black Sea coast maximum summer temperatures lag into August. Sochi averages 23°C and Novorossiysk farther north 23.7°C. But maximum temperatures are cooler than they are on the northern plain because of marine influences. At Sochi the maximum temperature ever recorded was 38°C. During winter temperatures on the northern plain average well below freezing. Krasnodar averages −2.1°C and Pyatigorsk −4.3°C. Farther north, Rostov averages −6.3°C in January. Minimum temperatures have reached −36°C in Krasnodar. On the Black Sea coast Sochi averages 5.7°C in January and has experienced a minimum temperature of −14°C. Farther north Novorossiysk averages 2.5°C and has experienced temperatures as low as −24°C with the cold northeastern bora winds.

The winter cyclones coming in off the Black Sea move northeastward across the western portion of the plain and do not perceptibly affect the area east of the Stavropol Plateau. Therefore, there is a great change in the annual regime of precipitation from west to east. The coastal area and adjacent mountains along the Black Sea exhibit a decided winter maximum of precipitation, which comes with prolonged periods of overcast skies associated with these cyclonic storms. Sochi receives maximum precipitation in December when it averages 107 millimeters. The minimum in May averages only 71 millimeters. Total for the year is 1356 millimeters. Not far inland, the precipitation regime reverses. Krasnodar receives its maximum precipitation, 64 millimeters, in June and its minimum, 50 millimeters, in March and April. The precipitation is much more evenly distributed throughout the year than at Sochi and totals only 640 millimeters, which is generally adequate but not abundant for the long warm summers in this agricultural region. Farther east on the northern plain the annual precipitation drops steadily, and the summer maximum becomes much more pronounced as the winter precipitation diminishes. At Pyatigorsk in the south-central portion of the plain the annual precipitation totals only 482 millimeters. A maximum of 77 millimeters

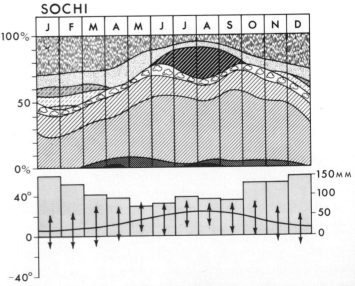

Figure 13-4   Weather types, temperature, and precipitation, Sochi. For legend, see page 6.

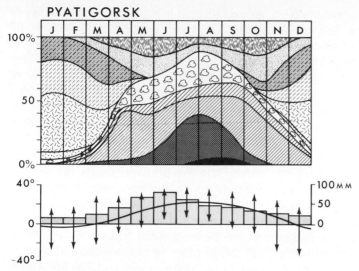

Figure 13-5 Weather types, temperature, and precipitation, Pyatigorsk. For legend, see page 6.

falls in June and a minimum of 13 millimeters in January. Summer thunderstorms caused by convection due to surface heating are the most significant form of precipitation in the central and eastern portions of the plain. But as the humidity of the air decreases eastward, the amount of precipitation derived from summer thunderstorms also decreases. As the Caspian coast is approached annual precipitation falls to about 300 millimeters in northern Dagestan.

The Kuban district in the southwestern part of the plain is the only part of the northern plain that receives enough precipitation to carry on a wide range of crop cultivation without irrigation. The precipitation diminishes eastward, northeastward, and northward. Rostov at the mouth of the Don in the north receives only 483 millimeters per year. Of course, the mountains generally receive much more precipitation than the plain. The Black Sea section of the Great Caucasus Mountains receives the heaviest precipitation in the Soviet Union. In places on the southwestern slopes of these mountains exposed to the cyclonic incursions from the Black Sea, precipitation during the year totals more than 3000 millimeters. Much of this falls during winter in the form of snow as a consequence of the combination of cyclonic and orog-

raphic uplift. Exceedingly heavy snow pack exists in the southwestern part of the Great Caucasus. On northeastern slopes, precipitation probably amounts to no more than 1000 millimeters. Precipitation in the mountains diminishes rapidly eastward and supports little forest growth east of the Terek Valley. Also, the precipitation regime shifts to a strong summer maximum eastward as convective activity along the mountain slopes becomes the major mechanism producing precipitation. The Caucasus are known for their summer thunderstorms that cause considerable hail damage to high cost crops such as vineyards and citrus in the Transcaucasus.

Throughout the plains, snow cover is not very consistent during the winter. Frequent thaws occur, and strong winds from the east drift the snow very unevenly across the surface. In the eastern part of the plain, where little snow falls, much of the area is blown bare during the winter, and severe duststorms may occur. In the dry Nogay Steppe between the Kuma and Terek Rivers in northern Dagestan, aeolian forms such as deflation hollows and barchan dunes are common. Farther west where there is more moisture wind erosion is not so damaging. But the sukhovey still occurs frequently during summer. In Krasnodar snow covers the ground 42 days on the average and reaches a maximum depth of 18 centimeters. Little snow falls on the Black Sea coast. Novorossiysk has snow on the ground only 14 days of the year, and Sochi farther south only 8 days.

There is much winter cloudiness in the North Caucasus Region, particularly in the west where cyclonic storms cause low-lying stratus overcast. During January and February Krasnodar averages more than eight-tenths sky cover and has 15–17 days per month with overcast. Summers are much sunnier. July averages only three days of overcast and August less than three days. Clouds at that time of year are more cumuloform. In the higher mountains the cloud maximum occurs during summer when convective activity is strongest. During winter the upper slopes lie well above the low-lying stratus decks.

The eastern parts of the Stavropol Plateau exhibit unusually high frequencies of low cloudiness, fog, and glaze ice during winter. This is due to the gradual upslope motion of the cold, easterly air moving up the eastern slope of the Stavropol Plateau underneath a strong surface inversion. The inversion often intersects the surface of the land near the crest of the plateau and hence traps all the condensed moisture underneath the inversion at ground level at that point. Pyatigorsk experiences 100 days per year with fog, which occurs every other day from the beginning of December through the end of March. Glaze ice is a constant hazard during this time of year. On the western side of the Stravopol Plateau, the air descends and the moisture evaporates. Krasnodar experiences less than half as much fog as Pyatigorsk.

The original vegetation of the North Caucasus Plain was primarily steppe grasses. On the river floodplains there were forests, composed primarily of willow, poplar, ash, alder, maple, pear, and apple, with some oak forests on the better-drained natural levees. These are still in place in the more humid western part of the plain, particularly in the Kuban drainage basin, but they have been largely cut down in the Stavropol Plateau, and they were never well developed in the drier eastern plain. The Nogay Steppe between the Kuma and Terek Rivers was vegetated primarily by sagebrush and feather grass, now badly overgrazed and the sandy soils subject to wind erosion. In spring in this region there is a great deal of ephemeral vegetation that provides valuable grazing, but this is short-lived and disappears before the heat of summer arrives. Near the Caspian shore the vegetation gets

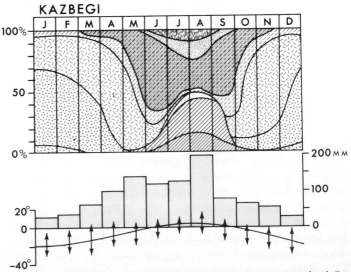

Figure 13-6   Weather types, temperature, and precipitation, Kazbegi. For legend see page 6.

very poor; thistles predominate. The marshy deltas of the Terek and Sulak Rivers on the western shore of the Caspian, as well as much of the marshy land along the Azov coast in the west, are vegetated by reeds.

The soils on the North Caucasus Plain grade from chernozems throughout much of the Kuban and western part of the Stavropol Plateau, through chestnut soils throughout eastern Stavropol Plateau and the northern part of the plain in Rostov Oblast, to lighter chestnut and brown saline soils with some solonchaks in the dry steppe and semidesert parts of the Kum-Ter Plain. Thus, except for certain saline areas, the soils are quite good and can be made very productive if supplied with enough moisture.

In the mountains, of course, altitudinal zones of vegetation and soils exist. Also, there is a gradual change from humid conditions in the west to dry conditions in the east. The western half of the mountains is forested on lower slopes. Due to the much heavier snowfall on the southwestern slopes, the snowline and alpine meadows extend to lower elevations on the southwest side of the mountains than on the northeast. On the southwestern slopes beech forests occupy the area up to about 1000–1200 meters, and conifer forests take over between 1200–2000 meters. In the western part of the region firs are predominant among the conifer forests, but farther east spruce plays a greater role. On the north slopes the conifer forests extend upward to about 2300 meters. The deciduous forests below them consist of beech, hornbeam, ash, maple, elm, linden, apple, pear, and plum.

Above the conifer forests extend the alpine meadows, grasses with many mixtures of beautiful flowering plants. These extend upward to 2900–3000 meters, above which are the perpetual snowfields and glaciers.

Eastward to the Georgian Military Highway between Tbilisi and Ordzhonikidze along the valley of the Terek, most of the forests have disappeared because of the drying climate. The forests are pinched out of the middle slopes by the rising limits of drought below and the continuing limit of cold above. The mountains of southern Dagestan have very few trees, generally only on certain sheltered northern slopes where some pines may grow. Many of the slopes are almost completely barren. But a sparse growth of mountain xerophytes, shrubs with limited leaf structures and spiny needles, covers much of the area.

Mountain soils vary from brown forest types in the west to mountain chernozems in the east at lower and intermediate elevations. On the higher elevations they are mountain tundras and undeveloped rocky rubble produced by strong pereglacial action.

AGRICULTURE

Much of the North Caucasus Region is used one way or another for agriculture. The economic region contains 16 million hectares of arable land and more than 8 million hectares of permanent pastures. Three million hectares are under irrigation, and continual expansion is taking place. Irrigation projects are involved primarily with the Terek and Sulak Rivers in the southeast, the Kuban in the southwest, and the lower Don in the north. (Fig. 13-7).

The Kuban district is by far the best farming area in the region, and one of the very best in the entire country. Its soil and moisture resources are similar to those in the better parts of the Ukraine and the Central Chernozem Region, and its heat resources are greater than either of those regions. Soviet regional comparative studies of agriculture often use Krasnodar Kray, which includes much of Kuban district, as the standard against which other political units in the country are judged with regard to such things as crop yields and farm profits. Recently the area has been chosen as the site of a unique genetic bank that will be a repository for a world seed collection holding about 400,000 samples of seeds of the most diverse cultivated plants all over the world. A storehouse will be constructed consisting of 24 reinforced concrete underground chambers, each holding as much as a railroad car. The latest automatic equipment, refrigeration installations, and a signaling system will pro-

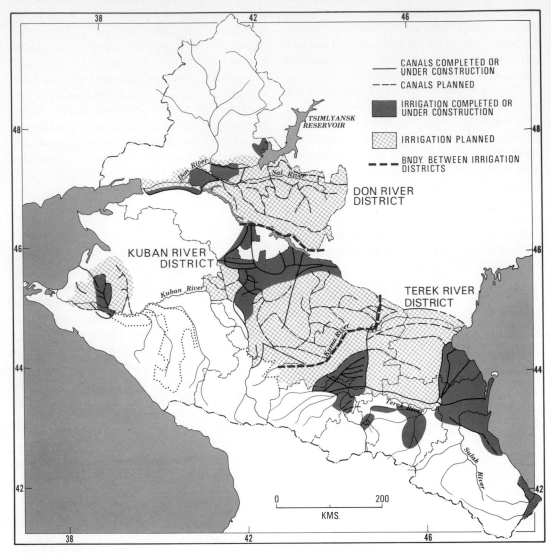

Figure 13-7   Irrigation. From Saushkin, p. 128.

vide the required microclimate for each set of seeds.

The Kuban district generally has enough moisture to grow a wide variety of crops without irrigation. It has traditionally grown primarily winter wheat and sunflowers. But in the middle 1950s it became the primary region for the introduction of corn. Sugar beets were simultaneously introduced to the point where this region has become the second most important sugar-beet-producing area in the country after the old traditional belt in the north central Ukraine and adjacent southern part of the Central Chernozem Region. Rice has been introduced into the lower Kuban region, as well as in the delta of the Terek in the east, and the North Caucasus is now the third most important region of rice production in the country. The rice is grown under irrigation, as are some areas of fiber crops, southern hemp, and kenaf. Such specialty crops as tobacco and aromatic herbs (roses, sage, and lavender) are also grown in the area.

North and east of the Kuban River the climate becomes drier, and such wide choices are not feasible without irrigation. The lower

Don region is the midsection of the main sunflower belt of the country, stretching both westward into the Ukraine and southward into the Kuban. Although the belt stretches continually across the lower Don, the fields thin in the vicinity of the Don, and the culture is not as concentrated as it is either to the west or to the south. Winter wheat occupies more cultivated land in the Don area than any other single crop, and that is true also in the central and eastern portions of the Stavropol Plateau. East of the Stavropol Plateau little cultivation is possible without irrigation. The driest part of the region, the Nogay Steppe in northern Dagestan between the Kuma and Terek Rivers, is primarily grazing country.

In the irrigated areas are grown a great variety of grapes, vegetables, melons, and so forth. Vineyards are particularly concentrated in the lower Don region as well as southward along the shores of the Azov and Black Seas in the west and the Kuma Valley, Terek Delta, and Caspian coastal area in the east. The Black Sea coastal area of Krasnodar Kray southwest of the western extension of the Caucasus grows a great variety of fruit, including some citrus as the Georgian border is approached in the south. There are plans to expand tea plantations northward along this section of the coast.

The rich crop agriculture of the North Caucasus Region has prompted the development of a great many food-processing industries. For instance, the Kuban and lower Don districts grow about half of all the sunflowers and produce about half of all the sunflower margarine in the Russian Republic. The area has become the second most important sugar refining area in the country. Flour milling and rice processing are important in many towns. The area has also become one of the main regions of the country for the canning of fruits and vegetables, making preserves of various sorts, and making wine.

Livestock raising is very important in the region. In the better farming areas of Krasnodar and Stavropol Krays and Rostov Oblast are found dairy cattle, swine, and poultry. These have provided the basis for meatpacking and dairy industries and for the large

leather-working and shoemaking industries in Rostov and Krasnodar. In the dry steppes of Dagestan and in the high mountains sheep grazing is the primary economy. Seasonal transhumance of the flocks is practiced on a grand scale. The sheep are pastured in the alpine meadows above the forest belt during summer and on the lowland steppes in winter. During spring and fall the mountain roads are clogged with flocks of sheep moving to their new pastures. Nevinnomyssk in the southern part of the Stravopol Plateau has become one of the main wool washing centers of the country. Krasnodar is the main center for the production of worsted cloth. Altogether the North Caucasus Region turns out about 16 percent of the country's wool.

The agriculture of the North Caucasus Region is currently being enhanced by several water projects, which among other things will provide more irrigation water. Until now much of the irrigation on the lower Don Val-

Figure 13-8   Transhumance of sheep in the Caucasus. Novosti.

ley has used water from the Tsymlyansk Reservoir, built as part of the Volga-Don Canal system in the early 1950s. Now a smaller dam has been built farther downstream on the Don at the village of Nikolayevskaya. In addition to improving navigation on the lower Don, it will provide water to irrigate about 125,000 hectares of additional land. At the present time more than one-fifth of the flow of the Don River is being used for irrigation. Even greater use of the Don water for irrigation will upset the balance of the Sea of Azov even more than it already has been. Therefore, a dam has been planned to shut off the Kerch Strait. This was discussed in the South Economic Region.

In 1972 a third large irrigation reservoir, known as the Krasnodar Reservoir, was completed on the Kuban River just above the city of Krasnodar. It is situated between the Tshchik Reservoir farther upstream and the Shapsug Reservoir downstream. It is much larger than either of the other two. It is supposed to irrigate an additional 200,000 hectares of rice in the lower reaches of the Kuban River. Some of the water will also be used for the irrigation of corn.

In the eastern part of the plain additional projects are being completed on the Terek River and its tributaries. A canal has been built to carry some of the Terek water to the Kuma River.

INDUSTRIAL RESOURCES AND DEVELOPMENT

Energy Resources

Other than the rich agricultural ones, the main resources of the North Caucasus Region are related to energy. This includes all the mineral fuels plus water power. First to be developed was the eastern end of the Donets coal basin in Rostov Oblast. Exploitation began here in the 1860s and has continued to expand slowly ever since along with the rest of the Donets Basin across the border in eastern Ukraine. At present Rostov Oblast is credited with about 70 billion tons of reserves, mostly anthracite, with some bituminous coal

of coking quality in the northeastern part of the basin. The region annually produces about 35 million tons, which compares to about 185 million tons produced annually in the western part of the basin in eastern Ukraine. The primary producing centers are Shakhty ("mine"), Novoshakhtinsk ("new mine"), and Krasnyy Sulin. Most of the coal is used for power generation, and about 70 percent of it is shipped out of the region for that purpose. Some of the bituminous coal mined in the northeast is used for coking purposes in metallurgical industries in Krasnyy Sulin and Taganrog, the main Rostov Oblast port on the north coast of the Sea of Azov. These cities produce steel, rolled steel, and steel pipe. Novoshakhtinsk contains a coke-chemical combine, and Kamensk-Shakhtinskiy has a combine for the production of synthetic fibers.

The next mineral fuel to be exploited was petroleum, initially around the city of Groznyy in the Chechen-Ingush area. Oil has been produced there since 1893. An oil refinery was built in Groznyy and development progressed simultaneously with the larger development at Baku in the Transcaucasus. The largest producing fields in the area have grown up around the town of Malgobek. In 1928 a crude-oil pipeline was built from the Groznyy fields 600 kilometers westward to the port of Tuapse on the Black Sea to export Groznyy crude to other parts of the country. The Groznyy region was then producing about 4 million tons, which was about one-third of the Soviet production. An oil refinery begun at Tuapse in 1929 was dismantled in 1942 because of the German threat and was reasssembled at Krasnovodsk on the eastern coast of the Caspian. A new refinery was built in Tuapse in the late 1940s, and it has been expanded into a major operation since then.

The Groznyy fields reached a peak production of about 8 million tons of crude oil in 1931 and then declined to about 2 million tons in the mid-1950s. However, deeper drilling in the late 1950s discovered new oil deposits in older rocks, and production soared again to over 20 million tons in the early 1970s. This was as much as the famous old oil development around Baku had ever been able to produce. During the last few years, however, it seems that oil production here has peaked again and is now on a gradual decline.

During the years of lean production in Groznyy, a pipeline was built in 1936 from the Caspian Sea terminal of Makhachkala to move Baku crude oil to the Groznyy refinery to make use of the refining capacity there. In the early 1950s crude oil was hauled all the way from the Volga-Urals oil fields to Groznyy for refining. However, with the major expansion during the 1960s, all importation of crude oil into the Groznyy refinery ceased, and crude oil was shipped out of the Groznyy region through the old pipeline to Tuapse. It was also shipped through a new pipeline opened in 1969 to connect the Malgobek fields with an existing pipeline system at Tikhoretsk in northeastern Krasnodar Kray. The oil then moved southwestward through an older pipeline to an oil refinery at Krasnodar and on to the sea port of Novorossiysk for export. A pipeline also runs northwestward from Tikhoretsk through Rostov to the Donets Basin where it is assumed that eventually some of the Groznyy crude will be refined in a new refinery being constructed in Lisichansk.

A large petrochemical complex opened in the Groznyy area in 1954 and has since expanded several times. Gas-processing plants to extract natural gas liquids from the petroleum produced in the Groznyy area have been built in a number of surrounding towns. A smaller gas plant was opened in the early 1960s in the Krasnodar oil fields.

Another old oil-producing area of the North Caucasus around Maykop south of Krasnodar has reached a peak production of around 3 million tons per year. In recent years significant new deposits of oil have been opened up in a number of places along the foothills of the mountains in southwestern Krasnodar Kray and also in the western portion of the Nogay Steppe in northwestern Dagestan A.S.S.R. and adjacent northeastern Stavropol Kray. A crude-oil pipeline has been constructed from these Nogay Steppe fields to the Groznyy re-

finery. Total oil production in the North Caucasus Region has now reached a level of about 30 million tons per year.

It appears now that there are small deposits of oil scattered in many localities throughout the North Caucasus Region. Most of the oil has a paraffin base that will allow light fractions to be refined that will be of national significance. High-grade lubricating oils are shipped to all parts of the country, even to the Volga-Urals where the petroleum is all asphalt based. However, the Caucasus oil lies at great depths, generally between 3000–4000 meters, and is costly to exploit.

The Black Sea ports of Novorossiysk and Tuapse have developed into major oil-exporting ports. The Tuapse oil-loading pier, which dates from the 1920s, has recently been expanded and modernized to handle oceangoing tankers with drafts of up to 12 meters. Tuapse is now being connected directly by rail to Krasnodar by a new 140-kilometer railroad that has been under construction since the late 1960s. It takes a tortuous route through the western end of the Great Caucasus where more than 30 bridges and a long tunnel underneath the crest of the mountains are being built. The oil-exporting facilities of the port of Novorossiysk have been greatly enhanced by the construction of a 1500-kilometer pipeline from the Volga oil center of Kuybyshev completed in late 1974. The Novorossiysk port now loads about 30 million tons of oil per year, which amounts to about 30 percent of all Soviet oil exports.

During the mid-1950s the exploitation of the third mineral fuel, natural gas, began in recently discovered deposits, primarily in Stavropol and Krasnodar Krays. This gas was dry gas unassociated with oil fields. Two pipelines were completed from the Stavropol fields to Moscow in 1956 and 1957, and a third pipeline was completed in 1959 from the northern Krasnodar fields to Serpukhov south of Moscow where it hooked up with a gas pipeline system to the Soviet capital that continues on to Leningrad. Since then other gas fields have been opened in Krasnodar Kray, the largest being about 15 kilometers north of Maykop in the southern part of the region. Two pipelines have been built from Stavropol through Ordzhonikidze southward over Krestovyy Pass in the Great Caucasus to Tbilisi in eastern Georgia where they hook up with the Transcaucasian pipeline system.

The North Caucasian gas fields were the largest producing fields in the country for a very short period of time, but almost simultaneously with the development of these fields came the development of the Shebelinka field in the eastern Ukraine. This field soon surpassed the production of Stavropol and Krasnodar, as did the gas fields of Central Asia a little later. Now all of these fields are to be eclipsed by the huge deposits being opened up along the Arctic coast in Western Siberia. In 1975 the North Caucasian fields were producing about 6 percent of the Soviet Union's gas.

The North Caucasian gas has provided the basis for many new chemical industries. The largest chemical complex based on gas in the region has been developed at the town of Nevinnomyssk south of Stavropol. The chemical plant was inaugurated in 1962 with an ammonia unit, and it has been expanded several times since and diversified into many other products. Some of the expansion has taken place with the technical help of Japanese and American engineering companies. The plant is one of the largest nitrogen fertilizer producers in the Soviet Union.

Because of the steep slopes and heavy precipitation in the western half of the high Caucasus, the North Caucasian Region has great hydroelectric potential. It has been estimated that the region has a total potential of 127 million kilowatts. However, little of this has been realized, and even the installations that have been constructed on many of the streams for the purposes of irrigation do not include hydroelectric generating facilities. A number of small generating plants built on several of the mountain streams apparently have a total generating capacity of about 10–11 million kilowatts. The largest hydroelectric station to be constructed so far is the recently completed Chirkey hydroelectric plant in the canyon of the Sulak River. It has a 230-meter-high arched dam and a total generating capacity of 1 million kilowatts. A much smaller station already existed downstream on the Sulak, and construction is scheduled in the near future on another smaller station in between the two existing ones. The ninth five-year plan projected construction of a hydroelectric plant on the Terek River in the Daryal Gorge and on a couple of other smaller rivers. On the northern plain, the Tsymlyansk hydroelectric plant went into operation on the lower Don in 1952 in conjunction with the Volga-Don Canal. It has a generating capacity of 164,000 kilowatts.

Other Minerals

The North Caucasus Region is not rich in metallic ores. However, some polymetallic deposits of nonferrous minerals exist in the southern part of the North Osetian A.S.S.R. These ores contain lead, zinc, copper, silver, gold, cadmium, germanium, thallium, indium, selenium, and mercury. The lead-zinc industry began in this area as early as 1853 when a mill was opened to smelt ores for silver and lead. This old smelter was replaced in 1904 by a zinc refinery at Vladikavkaz (the present Ordzhonikidze), the oldest in the country. In 1933 it was converted to the electrolytic method of zinc recovery when the small Gizeldon hydroelectric station went into operation with a capacity of only 23,000 kilowatts. Another small hydro plant was built on the Terek River above Ordzhonikidze in 1954.

Since the 1930s, the zinc refinery has been supplemented by a smelter that recovers the lead and many of the other metals from the ore. It also derives sulfuric acid from copper pyrites for chemical industries. The Ordzhonikidze refinery outgrew the local mines, and ores had to be shipped in from as far away as the Urals, the Altay Mountains of Western Siberia, and even the lead mines of Tetyukhe in the Soviet Far East. Since the early 1960s other mines have been developed to make this smelter and refinery complex more self-sustaining.

Another significant region of metallic ore development is in the Kabardino-Balkar

A.S.S.R., where complex ores of molybdenum and tungsten are found. A smelter was opened in 1961 at Nalchik, the capital of the Kabardino-Balkar A.S.S.R. The process also yields valuable by-products such as bismuth. During the 1960s a large copper deposit was developed at the town of Urup in the Karachay-Cherkess Autonomous Oblast. This is turning out copper concentrate.

In addition to the metallic ores just mentioned, there are enormous deposits of marls that provide the basis for one of the most important cement industries in the country, glass sands, a variety of construction materials, and rock salt. The Novorossiysk cement complex on the Black Sea coast has been one of the major producers of cement in the country for many years. It now produces about 4.5 million tons per year out of a national output of around 110 million tons. In 1974 a new plant was opened near Groznyy in the eastern part of the region. There is also a plant in Ust-Dzheguta, Cherkess Autonomous Oblast.

Other Industries

The North Caucasus Economic Region has developed a significant number of machine construction industries, concentrating primarily on agricultural machinery and transport machinery. These will be discussed with individual cities in the next section, as will some of the light industries and service trades.

CITIES

Rostov

The largest city by far in the North Caucasus Region is Rostov, at the mouth of the Don River, with a 1974 population of 867,000. This large city relates more to the Donets-Dnieper economy than it does to the rest of the North Caucasus. It is a major transport node and commercial trading center for the southeastern part of European R.S.F.S.R. The railroads and pipelines from the Caucasus Region focus on Rostov and then continue

northwestward to the Central and Northwest Regions. Rostov is the major port on the Sea of Azov. This role was enhanced by the completion of the Volga-Don Canal in 1952. Over the years the city has developed huge agricultural machine construction combines. The main ones are "Rostselmash" ("Rostov agricultural machinery") and "Krasnyy Aksay" ("Red Aksay," named after the old Don Cossack center of Aksay upstream from Rostov).

Krasnodar

The next city in size is Krasnodar, the capital of Krasnodar Kray with a 1974 population of 519,000. It sits in the center of the rich Kuban farming area and serves as the commercial center for the oil and gas industries of Krasnodar Kray. It has an oil refinery and has developed food and light industries as well as machine construction industries. It has a major cotton textile factory. The city was founded in 1792 by Zaporozhian Cossacks as the fortress of Yekaterinodar. There are still many Cossack farmers in the surrounding countryside.

Groznyy

The third city in size is Groznyy, the capital of the Chechen-Ingush A.S.S.R., with a 1974 population of 369,000. It serves as the commercial and oil refining center for the Groz-

Figure 13-9   River station at aksay, the old Don Cossack stronghold on the high west bluff near the mouth of the Don River just upstream from the present large city of Rostov.

nyy oil fields and has developed a major petrochemical complex.

Taganrog

The fourth city is Taganrog, the seaport on the north coast of the Sea of Azov, with a 1974 population of 272,000. In addition to its port function, Taganrog has a steel plant. Like Rostov, its industries are oriented toward the Donets Basin.

Ordzhonikidze

Ordzhonikidze, the capital of the North Osetian A.S.S.R., had a 1974 population of 265,000. It was established in 1784 as the fortress of Vladikavkaz at the northern entrance to Krestovyy Pass in the central portion of the Great Caucasus through which the Georgian Military Highway has been built. Therefore, it occupies a very strategic point on the major mid-Caucasian transport route. Its name was changed to Ordzhonikidze in 1931 after one of the Bolshevik revolutionaries. The name was changed again to Dzaudzhikau in 1944, and then back to Ordzhonikidze in 1954. Its industries are heavily based on the polymetallic ores of the region.

Sochi

Sochi is the largest of the resort cities along the eastern Black Sea coast. In 1974 it had a population of 244,000. The city sits on a hilly section of land where the mountains plunge abruptly to the Black Sea, and though it is all very picturesque, the beaches are narrow and filled with cobbles. Level land in Sochi is so lacking that the city cannot be served directly by air; planes must land at Adler about 30 kilometers to the south on a small river delta, and passengers must be conveyed to Sochi by open-air buses over a bumpy, winding mountain road. In 1961 the city limits of Sochi were extended southward to include Adler. In Sochi are all the facilities considered by the Russians to be significant to the self-indulgence of the idle vacationer: glistening white resort hotels perched on the hills high

above the Black Sea, funicular railways, and large expanses of parks with circuses, opera houses, and cinemas. Besides these strictly resort amenities, there are many health sanitoriums and a botanical garden that contains many subtropical plants collected from all over the world.

Stavropol

Stavropol, with a 1974 population of 226,000, is almost a replica of Krasnodar, only on a smaller scale. The city sits at the crest of the arch of the Stavropol Plateau in the midst of a relatively good farming region, and it serves as the seat of government for large Stavropol Kray. Like Krasnodar, since 1955 large gas fields have been developed in the area, adding to the industries of Stavropol, but they are now approaching depletion.

Shakhty

Shakhty ("coal mines") is the main coal-mining center of the Russian part of the Donets Basin. In 1974 it had a population of 217,000. Until 1920 it was known as Aleksandrovsk-Grushevskiy.

Makhachkala

Makhachkala, the capital of the Dagestan A.S.S.R., had a 1974 population of 214,000. It is a major seaport on the west coast of the Caspian and serves as a fish center and a transfer center for Baku oil coming by boat to Makhachkala and continuing by pipe to Groznyy, Rostov, and the Ukraine.

Nalchik

Nalchik, the capital of the Kabardino-Balkar A.S.S.R., had a 1974 population of 182,000. It has a smelting complex to treat molybdenum and tungsten ores.

Novocherkassk

Novocherkassk, northeast of Rostov on the small Aksay River just upstream from its junc-

Figure 13-10 Metallurg Sanatorium in Sochi.

tion with the Don, had a 1974 population of 178,000. It is the major coke-chemical and coal-electrical generating center in the Russian part of the Donets Basin.

Armavir

Armavir, with a 1974 population of 155,000, is a regional center for a rich farming area along the Kuban River upstream from Krasnodar. It occupies an important rail junction on the line running from Rostov along the northern foot of the Caucasus to Baku. A branch line runs southwestward from Armavir across the western Caucasus to the Black Sea coast at Tuapse.

Novorossiysk

Novorossiysk is one of the most important seaports along the eastern Black Sea coast. It recently has been connected by pipeline to the Western Siberian oil fields, and therefore serves as an export point for that rich oil-producing area. It also is one of the major cement-producing cities of the country. In 1974 it had a population of 143,000. It has been proclaimed one of the hero cities of World War II. It recently has become the site of the first Pepsi Cola plant in the U.S.S.R.

Maykop

Maykop, the capital of the Adyge Autonomous Oblast, had a 1974 population of 124,000. It is primarily a regional center for a relatively rich farming and oil-producing area.

Novoshakhtinsk

Novoshakhtinsk ("New Shakhty"), with a 1974 population of 101,000, is one of the major coal-mining towns of the eastern part of the Donets Basin. It has a small coke-chemical combine.

PROSPECTS

The North Caucasus Region undoubtedly will remain one of the main farming regions of the country and one of the gas- and oil-producing areas. People are continuing to shift southward into the region to add to the complexity of the population pressure and nationality mix already existing. The continuing heavy in-migration may induce the Soviet planners to expand labor-intensive industries in the region. Another factor likely to stimulate its development is its coastal location on the Black

Sea, in view of growing trade ties with the outside world.

READING LIST

- Geiger, Bernhard, *Peoples and Languages of the Caucasus,* Mouton, The Hague, 1959, 77 pp.
- Kazanbiyev, M.K., "Karst uzvestnyakovogo Dagestana," *Izvestiya Vsesoyuznogo Geograficheskogo Obshchestva,* No. 1, 1975, pp. 54–58.
- Kvezereli-Kopadze, N.I., "The Problem of Year-Round Traffic Through the Pass of the Cross on the Georgian Military Highway," *Soviet Geography: Review & Translation,* March 1974, pp. 163–174.
- Nove, Alec, and J.A. Newth, *The Soviet Middle East,* Praeger, New York, 1967, 160 pp.
- Pyshnova, Yu. T., "Historical-Geographic Aspects of the Development and Settlement of the Black Sea Coast of the Caucasus," *Soviet Geography: Review & Translation,* March 1974, pp. 156–163.
- *Severnyy Kavkaz* (Northern Caucasus), Akademiya Nauk S.S.S.R., Institut Geografiya, Moscow, 1957, 508 pp. (in Russian).
- Vodovozov, S.A., "Severnyy Kavkaz ekonomicheskiy rayon" (The North Caucasus Economic Region), *Nauchnye Trudy, Tsentralnyy Nauchno-Issledovatelskiy Ekon. Institut,* 1, 1969, pp. 295–310 (in Russian).
- Vodovozov, S.A., and O.D. Chuvilkin, "Osnovnye zvenya khozyaystva Severnogo Kavkaza v devyatoy pyatiletke" (Basic Economic Indices of the North Caucasus During the Ninth Five-Year Plan), *Geografiya v Shkole,* No. 5, 1972, pp. 12–16 (in Russian).

The Transcaucasus Economic Region

	Area (km²)	Population	Persons/km²	Percent Urban
Georgian S.S.R.	70,000	4,835,000	69.4	49
Tbilisi City		946,000		100
Abkhaz A.S.S.R.	9,000	494,000	57.5	45
Adzhar A.S.S.R.	3,000	328,000	109.3	44
South Osetian Autonomous Oblast	4,000	102,000	26.3	38
Azerbaydzhan S.S.R.	87,000	5,421,000	62.6	51
Baku City		1,337,000		100
Nakhichevan A.S.S.R.	6,000	215,000	39.0	25
Nagorno-Karabakh Autonomous Oblast	4,000	153,000	34.7	40
Armenian S.S.R.	30,000	2,667,000	89.5	62
Yerevan City		842,000		100
Total	186,000	12,923,000	69.4	

chapter 14

the transcaucasus economic region

At the beginning of the nineteenth century the Russians moved into Transcaucasia primarily by invitation and default. In 1801 Alexander I, who was becoming looked upon as the "savior of Europe" because of his resistance against Napoleon, was invited by the Christian Georgian prince to protect the area from the Moslem Persian shah. Thus, the Russian armies crossed the Great Caucasus and gained a foothold in Tbilisi, the capital city of Georgia, whence they moved to the Azerbaydzhanian center of Baku in 1806 and to the Armenian center of Yerevan in 1828. Here Russia met the growing influence of the British in Persia, and a stalemate resulted; with minor boundary changes, it remains to this day.

Thus, by 1828 the Russian Empire had acquired an extensive chunk of land peopled largely by non-Russian groups who had national traditions in the area of more than 2000 years duration. The Georgians and Armenians seldom have enjoyed the status of independent countries, but they are both proud old nationality groups who consider themselves culturally ahead of the Russians, the Turks, and the Persians, the three great powers that have surrounded them from time immemorial. Since the revolution the Transcaucasians have voiced their desires strongly and have played significant roles in national political maneuvering. During the chaotic period of the civil war following the revolution, each of the

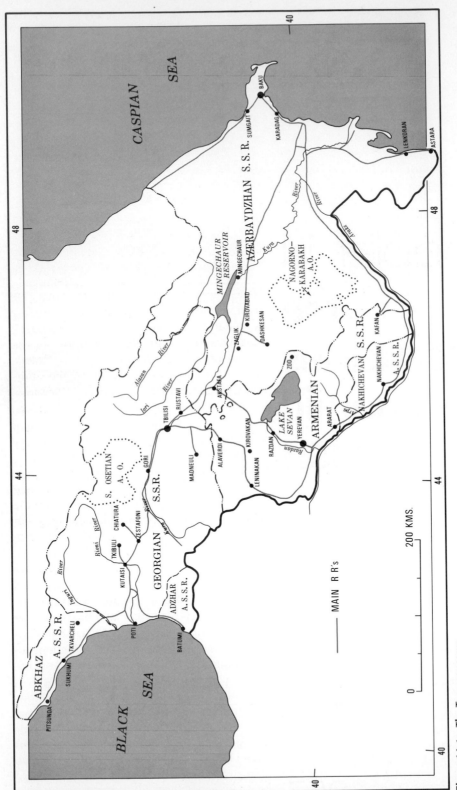

Figure 14-1 The Transcaucasus.

major nationality groups set up independent governments. These governments ultimately were crushed by the Bolsheviks, and the entire Transcaucasian area was included in the newly constituted Soviet Union on December 30, 1922, as the Transcaucasian Soviet Federated Socialist Republic, one of the four republics making up the Soviet Union at that time. Agitation for national recognition continued, however, and when the Soviet Union was reconstituted in 1936 each of the three major nationality groups was accorded Union Republic political status. Thus, a region containing less than 1 percent of the area of the Soviet Union and about 5 percent of its population contains three of the fifteen Union Republics of the country.

POPULATION

The present political breakdown of the Transcaucasus is shown in the table at the beginning of this chapter. The three largest nationality groups, the Georgians, the Azerbaydzhanians and the Armenians, each have been accorded the status of Union Republic. Lesser nationality groups form A.S.S.R.s and autonomous oblasts within these republics. The Georgian Republic contains the Abkhaz A.S.S.R. in the northwest, the Adzhar A.S.S.R. in the southwest, and the South Osetian Autonomous Oblast in the high mountain country in the north. The Azerbaydzhan Republic includes a detached piece of land called the Nakhichevan A.S.S.R., which is separated from the main body of Azerbaydzhan by Armenia. This region is peopled primarily by Azerbaydzhanians, and because it has adequate transport and communication connections with the Azerbaydzhan Republic, it has been constituted as part of that republic. However, the Nagorno-Karabakh region in western Azerbaydzhan, which is peopled by Armenians, has been constituted as an autonomous oblast within the Azerbaydzhan Republic because it has no adequate connections with the Armenian Republic. It sits on the highest part of the Armenian Plateau, which has been deeply dissected by stream canyons, and transportation routes out of the area are tortuous. The three capital cities of the three Union Republics have been accorded political status separate from their immediate surroundings and jurisdictionally are responsible directly to their respective Union Republics. Therefore, they constitute separate political entities, as do many of the large cities in the Soviet Union.

All together these political units total a territory of 186,000 square kilometers, slightly smaller than that occupied by the Baltic Region, which also contains three Union Republics, and the Transcaucasus Region contains 12,923,000 people, which is 65 percent more population than the Baltic Region contains. The average population density of the Transcaucasus is 70 persons per square kilometer, but this varies drastically from place to place; it is very sparse in high mountains and some low desert areas and very heavy in intensively cultivated wet lowlands and foothills. The Adzhar A.S.S.R. in southwestern Georgia, the climatically mildest part of the entire region, averages 109 people per square kilometer, while the South Osetian Autonomous Oblast in the high mountains in the north-central part of the region averages only 26. Within both of these subregions, population densities vary greatly over short distances, because of the great differences in topography. In portions of the wet foothill areas of western Georgia there probably are as many as 200 people per square kilometer, and in some of the more rugged mountain areas of the South Osetian Autonomous Oblast there are probably no permanent dwellers at all.

Urbanization throughout the region is similar to that throughout the rest of the country. Armenia is a little more urbanized than average, while Georgia and Azerbaydzhan are a little less urbanized than average. Georgia particularly is retaining its rural nature, because in many places it has a climatic environment that is conducive to the intensive development of crops that are exotic to the rest of the country.

In addition to the nationality groups represented by the nationality-based political units, there are a number of smaller groups that have not been accorded political status. Like the North Caucasus, the Transcaucasus Region contains a wide variety of nationalities, many of whom have retained their distinctive identitites. During the last 150 years, the Russians and other Slavic groups have formed significant minorities in the region (Table 14-1).

The Abkhaz and Adzhar A.S.S.R.s have no constitutional bases for existence. The Georgians are overwhelmingly in the majority in both areas; even the Russians outnumber the Abkhaz, and the Armenians are almost as numerous. The Adzhars are not a nationality, but Moslem Georgians who were converted under Turkish rule.

The Transcaucasus is the beginning of a belt of high birth rates and high natural population increases that extends eastward through Central Asia. The region as a whole has a natural population increase about twice that of the average for the entire country. However, there are wide differences among the Transcaucasian Republics. Georgia has reduced its birth rate and natural growth much more than Armenia and Azerbaydzhan. Azerbaydzhan particularly has much higher birth rates than the other two, but it also is undergoing a decline. In 1973 Azerbaydzhan had a birth rate of 25.4 people per 1000 population, a death rate of 6.4, and a natural increase of 19.0. Georgia had a birth rate of 18.2 per thousand, a death rate of 9.3 per thousand, and 8.9 per thousand natural increase. Not only are the birth rates higher than the average in the Transcaucasus, but the

Table 14-1 Nationality Composition of Political Units (Percents of Total)

Georgian S.S.R.	100.0	Jews	0.5
Georgians	66.8	Abkhaz	0.4
Osetians	3.2	Others	1.6
Abkhaz	1.7	Nakhichevan A.S.S.R.	100.0
Armenians	9.7	Azerbaydzhanis	93.8
Russians	8.5	Armenians	2.9
Azerbaydzhanis	4.6	Russians	1.9
Greeks	1.9	Kurds	0.5
Jews	1.2	Others	0.9
Ukrainians	1.1	South Osetian Autonomous Oblast	100.0
Kurds	0.4	Osetians	66.5
Others	0.9	Georgians	28.4
Azerbaydzhan S.S.R.	100.0	Russians	1.5
Azerbaydzhanis	73.8	Jews	1.4
Russians	10.0	Armenians	1.2
Armenians	9.4	Others	1.0
Lezgins	2.7	Abkhaz A.S.S.R.	100.0
Others	4.1	Abkhazi	15.9
Armenian S.S.R.	100.0	Georgians	41.0
Armenians	88.6	Russians	19.1
Azerbaydzhanis	5.9	Armenians	15.4
Russians	2.7	Greeks	2.7
Kurds	1.5	Ukrainians	2.5
Others	1.3	Jews	0.9
Adzhar A.S.S.R.	100.0	Others	2.5
Georgians	76.5	Nagorno-Karabakh Autonomous Oblast	100.0
Russians	11.5	Azerbaydzhanis	18.1
Armenians	5.0	Armenians	80.6
Ukrainians	2.3	Russians	0.8
Greeks	2.2	Others	0.5

Source: Itogi vsesoyuznoy perepisi naseleniya 1970 goda, Volume 4.

death rates are also lower than average, because of the youthful structure of the population as compared to much of European U.S.S.R. However, the birth rates in Transcaucasia are dropping significantly. In 1965 Azerbaydzhan had a birth rate of 36.6 per thousand and a natural increase of 30.2 per thousand. The Transcaucasus Region is also experiencing a modest in-migration, so that absolute growth rates are moderate to heavy as compared to the rest of the country.

PHYSICAL LANDSCAPE

Landform

The Caucasus Mountains consist of two systems of ranges, the Great Caucasus, which has largely been discussed with the North Caucasus Economic Region, and the Lesser Caucasus farther south. In between the two a synclinal lowland runs the entire length of the isthmus between the Black and Caspian Seas, but this has been divided into two parts by the transverse Surami Range, which runs south-southwest–north-northeast between the Lesser and Greater Caucasus in east-central Georgia. Although the Surami Range lies at an elevation of only about 1000 meters, it forms a very distinct topographic and climatic break between the flat swampy Colchis Lowland to the west and the more extensive dry Kura Lowland to the east. The lower portions of both of these lowlands are exceedingly flat, because both of them in the recent past have been parts of seabeds.

At the start of the Quaternary the Colchis Lowland was the Colchis Gulf of the Black Sea. It has been filled in with alluvium by such streams as the Rioni, Kodori, Inguri, and Tskhenis Tskhali. None of these streams are very long, but they have great flow, since they drain a very wet region. The Rioni River alone carries an average annual load of 10 million cubic meters of alluvium. The shore at the city of Poti advances into the sea at an annual rate of about 12 meters. The aggraded lowland is very marshy and is filled by numerous abandoned channels, oxbow lakes, natural levees, and meander scars.

The large, flat lower section of the Kura Valley lies below sea level and represents an old arm of the Caspian Sea that has been filled in with alluvium from the Kura and Araks Rivers and their tributaries. The Kura River is by far the longest stream in the Transcaucasus. It heads in northeastern Turkey and flows much of the length of Georgia, cutting through the Surami Range, and then eventually runs the full length of the Kura Lowland to the Caspian. Throughout eastern Georgia and western Azerbaydzhan the lowland is a rolling plain interspersed by low mountains with elevations as high as 1300 meters. Only in its lower portion, downstream from the Mingechaur Reservoir, does the lowland become an utterly flat plain. Before the Kura River empties into the Caspian, it is joined by its major right-bank tributary, the Araks, which also heads in northeastern Turkey and for about 500 kilometers forms the international boundary between the Soviet Union on the left bank and Turkey and Iran on the right bank.

The Kura Lowland continues southward along the coast of the Caspian to the Iranian border in a narrow strip of land 5–30 kilometers wide between the Caspian shoreline on the east and the Talysh Mountains on the west. This narrow coastal plain is known as the Lenkoran Lowland, which is a miniature replica of the Colchis Lowland in the west. Here the climate is very wet and warm, and the vegetative growth is lush. Along the immediate shore of the Caspian is a strip of low, sandy dunes 4–6 meters-high, interspersed with marshy areas where many small streams flowing down from the Talysh Range cut through the lowland to the sea.

The Kura Lowland is terminated on the north by the eastern extension of the Great Caucasus that lies entirely within the Azerbaydzhan S.S.R. The mountains decrease gradually in elevation from about 4200 meters along the border of Dagestan to sea level and below on the Apsheron Peninsula, which juts out into the Caspian for 80 kilometers or more. The upwarped structure of the Great Caucasus continues across the Caspian in an underwater ridge that divides the southern

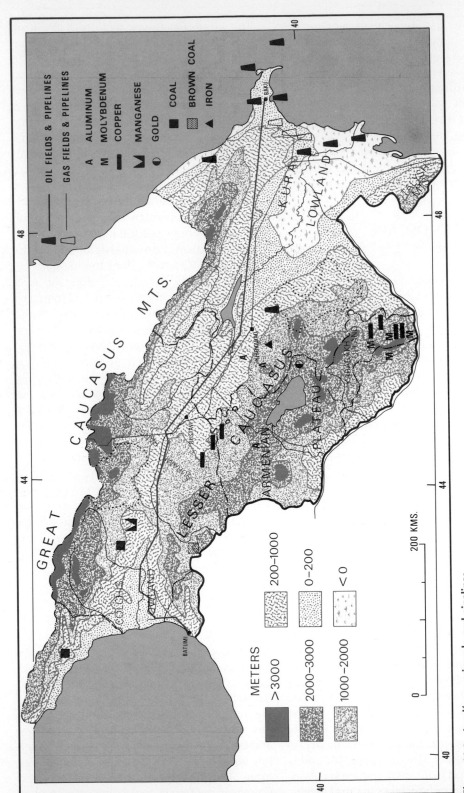

Figure 14-2 Landform, minerals, and pipelines.

Figure 14-3   The Kura River cuts through the surami Range at Tbilisi.

Caspian into two separate deep basins and then comes up on the eastern side as discontinuous small mountains in western Turkmenia. The underwater ridge lies no more than 200 meters below the surface, but the basin on the north reaches a depth of 800 meters and the basin on the south 1025 meters.

To the south of the synclinal lowland lies the Lesser Caucasus — eight discontinuous ranges subparallel to the Great Caucasus in the north. Elevations generally range from 1500–2500 meters, but maximum elevations reach as high as 3373 meters just north of Lake Sevan. The ranges of the Lesser Caucasus consist of strongly dislocated Tertiary, Jurassic, and Cretaceous rocks that have been folded and faulted and interbedded with a great number of volcanic facies. The folds generally are overturned toward the north. Hence, the synclinal lowland is faced by overturned folds on either side with very steep slopes leading up to both the Lesser Caucasus in the south and the Greater Caucasus in the north.

The folded nature and individual alignments of the ranges of the Lesser Caucasus are in many places obscured by a merging of enormous quantities of volcanic material that have poured out along fissures in the folded structure and filled up all the intervening valleys and in fact have covered many of the ranges themselves. These lavas consist primarily of andesites, basalts, and dacites interbedded with many tuffs. These eruptions occurred during the Neogene and Quaternary. Repeated eruptions of lava along various fissures were concluded with the formation of convex, shieldlike massifs that, as a result of subsequent movements, were raised high above the surrounding surfaces of the volcanic plateaus. On these shieldlike massifs are superimposed volcanic piles that represent the highest elevations in the area.

This volcanic region, which extends into northeastern Turkey and northern Iran, is known as the Armenian Plateau and has been peopled by Armenians for at least 2000 years. The plateau surface generally lies between 2500–3500 meters. The highest part of the upland is the Karabakh Upland in southwestern Azerbaydzhan, where elevations run 3500–3600 meters. Here is located the Nagorno-Karabakh Autonomous Oblast. But the absolutely highest points are the volcanic cones rising above the rest of the plateau. Within the Soviet Union the highest peak is Mt. Aragats, northwest of Yerevan, the capital city of Armenia, with an elevation of 4090 meters. The highest peak on the entire Armenian Plateau is across the border in Turkey, about 65 kilometers south of Yerevan; Mt. Ararat reaches a maximum elevation of 5156 meters. On clear days these snow-capped peaks form a magnificent backdrop to the city of Yerevan.

Streams are few and often intermittent on

the Armenian Plateau, not only because of the dryness of the climate, but also because of the high permeability of much of the basalt and tuff that allows rapid penetration of precipitation to a low groundwater table. The major stream in the Armenian Plateau is the Araks River, which flows eastward through the length of the plateau to join the Kura before flowing into the Caspian. A number of small tributary streams flow into the Araks on either side; the most significant is the Razdan, which drains the large Lake Sevan southward through the Yerevan Basin to the Araks.

Lake Sevan is the largest of a number of lakes on the Armenian Plateau that occupy downdropped blocks lying between fault lines. Numerous severe earthquakes along these fault lines have caused much destruction to cities and other man-made structures throughout the history of human occupancy of this region. Lake Sevan sits at an elevation of 1900 meters above sea level and has a surface area of about 1400 square kilometers. It is one of the largest high lakes of the world. Its maximum depth is about 35 meters. This large body of water provides a steady flow to the Razdan River, which during its short course of less than 100 kilometers descends about 1000 meters to the Araks River south of Yerevan and provides considerable water-power potential.

Climate, Vegetation, and Soils

The Transcaucasus is looked upon by the Soviets as the mildest climatic region in the country. It is generally considered to be subtropical. However, the climate varies drastically from one place to another within the Transcaucasus because of the great differences in elevation, exposure to sunshine, general flows of air, and local wind regimes. Temperatures on the uplands of the Armenian Plateau during winter are just as severe as they are on the North Caucasian Plain, although day-to-day weather on the Armenian Plateau is much different from that on the North Caucasian Plain. Mean January temperatures vary from −6 to −12°C, and the absolute minimum is −30°C. A thin, irregular snow cover persists in some places for 4–5 months per year. Even in Yerevan at an elevation of 907 meters, January temperatures average −4°C and a minimum of −31°C has been observed. Snow lies on the ground in Yerevan for 49 days of the year and reaches a maximum depth of 10 centimeters. Thus, only the lowlands in Transcaucasia can be considered subtropical. The Black Sea port of Batumi in southwestern Georgia averages 6.4°C in January and has experienced a minimum temperature of only −8°C. Here snow lies on the ground only 13 days during the winter. At Baku on the Caspian, temperatures average a little colder than at Batumi, but because of the meager amount of winter precipitation, snow lies on the ground only 7 days of the year and the maximum depth is only 2 centimeters. Even in the foothills around Batumi, hard frosts occur every winter and are very hazardous to citrus and other subtropical agriculture. The lower Colchis Lowland, because of cold air drainage during the coldest winter nights, experiences even lower temperatures that generally rule out citrus growing on the basin floor.

Summers are definitely hot in much of Transcaucasia and, except for the western Georgian area, are relatively dry. July–August temperatures along the Black Sea coast average 23–24°C and reach a maximum of 40–41°C. July temperatures in Yerevan average more than 25°C and reach a maximum of 41°C. Along the Caspian coast July–August temperatures average more than 25°C. At inland stations in the Kura Lowland, July temperatures may average as much as 28°C.

Too often the Transcaucasus Region is thought of as having a simple winter rainfall maximum associated with cyclonic storms that affect the whole of the Middle Eastern region at this time of year. Actually, this is true only along the Black Sea coast, and even there the regime varies considerably from north to south. Two rainfall mechanisms affect the Transcaucasus: winter cyclonic storms and summer thunderstorms. The winter cyclonic storms tend to take northeasterly courses across the region and affect primarily the western part. In summer the thunderstorms bring much more rainfall to the western part than to the eastern part, because of the general west-east flow of moisture across the region. Thus, annual amounts of rainfall decrease from around 3000 millimeters (120 inches) on the southwestern slopes of the Great Caucasus in northwestern Georgia and 2504 millimeters (100 inches) at Batumi in southwestern Georgia to only 238 millimeters (9 inches) at Baku on the southern shore of the Apsheron Peninsula jutting into the Caspian Sea. The Armenian Plateau generally receives about 300 millimeters per year, although higher elevations may receive as much as 500–600 millimeters. Tbilisi, on the eastern slope of the Surami Range, receives 513 millimeters. East of the Borzhomi Gorge of the Kura River, potential evaporation considerably exceeds precipitation. Thus, only the western fourth of the Transcaucasus can be considered humid.

Along the Black Sea coast, the two precipitation controls generally produce two maximums during the year, with the winter cyclonic controls being predominant. Far up the coast at Novorossiysk, the primary maximum falls in January, a secondary maximum occurs in July, and minimums occur in August and May. Thus, there is a midwinter maximum of cyclonic activity and a midsummer maximum of thunderstorm activity. The winter cyclonic storms cause much more cloudiness and more frequent precipitation than the summer thunderstorms. Down the coast toward the southeast, the winter rainfall maximum backs up to December at Sochi and Sukhumi. South of Sukhumi the summer maximum advances to August, and then to September, as the winter maximum diminishes and finally disappears. Total annual rainfall increases steadily southward along the coast. At Batumi, there is almost four times as much annual precipitation as there is at Novorossiysk, and a single maximum occurs in September and a single minimum in May. The May minimum persists all along the Black Sea coast, no doubt due to the maximum atmospheric stability reached at this time of the year when the sea reaches its coldest stage with respect to the air above it. There is almost an opposite seasonality along

the Black Sea coast between the number of rainy days and the amounts of rain received. March, April, and May generally have the greatest number of days with more than 1 millimeter of precipitation, but May generally has the minimum amount of rainfall during the year. During spring there are many prolonged, foggy, low-stratus, drizzly spells of weather along the Black Sea coast.

Not too far inland the rainfall regime changes drastically. At the eastern apex of the triangular-shaped Colchis Lowland, Kutaisi has a primary maximum of rainfall in June and a primary minimum in February, with a secondary maximum in December and a secondary minimum in August. Hence, the two rainfall mechanisms are still apparent there. But farther east, the Armenian Plateau generally shows a single maximum and a single minimum. The maximum rainfall throughout most of the rest of the Caucasus, both in the highlands and the lowlands, occurs in May, which seems to be the period of most frequent thunderstorms throughout most of the region. However, toward the Caspian Sea, the maximum jumps abruptly to October–November. Astara, which has the highest precipitation in the Talysh region of southeastern Azerbaydzhan, has a primary precipitation maximum in October and a secondary maximum in March. October is the month of most frequent cold fronts in the area, and March appears to be the beginning of the thunderstorm activity. The Lenkoran Lowland in this region receives about 1500 millimeters (60 inches) of precipitation, which causes this region to be a hot, humid area similar to the Colchis Lowland in the west.

Among other things, the Transcaucasian climate is known for its sunnyness. This is especially true in the Armenian Plateau during summer, when generally less than three-tenths of the sky is covered by clouds. Winter is considerably more cloudy, with six to seven-tenths covered. The Black Sea coast and the intermediate slopes of the mountains are cloudy but still exhibit a good deal of sunshine, because many of the clouds during the rainiest period are cumuloform in nature and do not cover the entire sky. It is interesting to note that at Batumi the rainiest month, September, has the clearest skies of any month of the year. The middle slopes of the mountains generally have summer maximums of cloudiness because of increased convective activity during that time of year. The lower slopes are usually below the clouds, and the upper slopes are frequently above the clouds.

The Transcaucasus Region has the highest incidence of thunderstorms and hail in the country. A hail-supression experimental station has been established in the Transcaucasus to attempt to find a way to trigger thunderstorms before they reach the hail stage, thus lessening the damage to such valuable, fragile crops as grapes, citrus, tobacco, and a wide variety of other fruits and vegetables.

Temperature inversions are well formed in many areas. During summer a local high-pressure situation generally sits over the Armenian Plateau and produces a subsidence inversion that traps much of the moisture, dust, and other pollutants near the surface to produce a very hazy surface atmosphere. This is particularly noticeable in the Yerevan Basin during summer, when the snow-capped volcanic peaks in the surrounding region are usually obscured from view.

Local wind regimes abound in the Caucasus where the relief is so great. Foehns are very noticeable in many regions, particularly in the eastern Colchis Lowland around Kutaisi during winter when the airflow is often from the east around the southern periphery of the Asiatic High. During these times, the air descends the western slopes of the Surami Range and blows with great velocity into the city of Kutaisi to produce relatively high temperatures and extremely low relative humidities that may cause fruit trees to drop their fruit, and even their leaves, and cause great damage to agriculture in general. Kutaisi experiences more than 100 days per year with foehns. During the height of their occurrence in midwinter they may be present as much as 50 percent of the time. Maximum wind speeds of 36 meters per second (75 miles per hour) can be expected every year, and 55

meters per second (120 miles per hour) once in 20 years. During one extreme case in December the temperature in Kutaisi rose to 17.5°C and the relative humidity fell to 8 percent. This same flow continued southwest to Batumi and caused a temperature of 38°C. During winter foehns may cause rapid evaporation of the thin snow cover. During summer they appear as hot, desiccating winds that after several hours may cause forms of vegetation to drop their leaves. Foehn occurrences usually last no more than 2–10 hours, but occasionally they may last up to a week, and after such duration much vegetation withers and dies. In the high mountains, on either side of the Great Caucasus, and in the higher elevations of the Lesser Caucasus as well, foehns during winter cause rapid melting of snow and disastrous avalanches.

As the climate varies in the Transcaucasus, so do the natural vegetation and soils. The low, swampy floor of the Colchis Lowland, as well as the wet foothills surrounding it, generally have lush growths of vegetation — a combination of trees such as alder, willow, oak, chestnut, and hornbean, under which is a rich mixture of plants and vines. Farther up the well-watered slopes of the Black Sea Caucasus are thick stands of conifer forests. Eastward, as the climate becomes drier, the vegetation turns to a brushy chaparral type, and east of the Surami Range steppe grasses originally covered much of the lowlands and gradually graded into desert thorny shrubs near the Caspian Sea. On the Armenian Plateau grasses and shrubs are the typical natural vegetation. There are very few trees anywhere in Armenia.

The soils of the Colchis Lowland and the surrounding hills are typical subtropical red and yellow podsols. In the subhumid-semiarid part of the Kura Lowland they are chernozem and chestnut soils, which grade into gray desert soils eastward toward the Caspian. On the Armenian Plateau there are many areas of chernozemlike volcanic soils. Throughout the Transcaucasus in the river valleys, of course, alluvial floodplains often contain the best soils of the region.

AGRICULTURE

The subtropical climate allows the Trans-caucasus to specialize in crops that are exotic to the rest of the Soviet Union. Tea and citrus are probably the most characteristic. They are grown in the humid western portion of the Transcaucasus, although not right on the valley floor of the Colchis Lowland. Here winter frosts are too frequent and too severe for such sensitive crops. Tea, citrus, and tung nuts compete for the same foothill areas sur-rounding the wet Colchis Lowland, where they can benefit from both air and soil drain-age. In some places these three crops occupy as much as 90 percent of the agriculturally usable acreage. This is particularly true in the Adzhar A.S.S.R. in the southwest where the climate is the mildest of all. This foothill region surrounding the Colchis Lowland and extending northward along the Black Sea coast almost as far as Sochi grows about 98 percent of all the tea and citrus in the country. The other 2 percent is grown on the wet eastern foothills of the Talysh Moun-tains bordering the Lenkoran Lowland in southeastern Azerbaydzhan.

Tea is the national drink of the Soviet Un-ion. In old Russia, afternoon tea pouring was as much of a ceremony as it is in England. Also, the non-Russian nationality groups of Soviet Central Asia and parts of the Transcau-casus are traditional tea drinkers. The Uzbeks have a saying: "with tea you have strength; without it you do not." Therefore, the Soviets have wanted to expand tea production as much as possible in spite of a rather limited area that is suitable for tea growing. For com-mercially worthwhile production, tea re-quires a minimum of about 1250 millimeters (50 inches) of rain per year, well distributed throughout the year, with no month getting less than about 50 millimeters (2 inches). Dur-ing the bearing season, temperatures less than 13°C (55°F) may damage the leaves and halt the growth of new leaves; during the dormant season temperatures below −14°C (7°F) may kill the bush. The well-drained red and yellow podsolic soils on the foothills immediately to

the north and south of the swampy floor of the Colchis Lowland best satisfy these growing requirements and contain more than 50 per-cent of all the tea planting in the Soviet Union. The Zugdidi foothills on the northern side of the lowland contain more than 30 percent of the tea planting and the southern foothills more than 20 percent. The next most impor-tant region is the Abkhaz A.S.S.R., which is a northern continuation of the Zugdidi foothills, and plantings here continue northward along the steep coast of Krasnodar Kray in the Rus-sian Republic. The farther north one pro-ceeds, however, the greater the frost hazard and the more severe the erosion problems, because the Caucasus Mountains crowd the shoreline in this area, and the slopes plunge very steeply down to the sea. In the vicinity of Sochi the slopes are so steep that tea planta-tions must be terraced. In this area, frosts limit planting to below 300 meters elevation.

South of the Colchis Lowland, as winter temperatures become progressively milder, tea is often crowded out by citrus, which gen-erally has less tolerance to frost than tea does. Thus, in Adzharia, which has the highest yields of tea in the Soviet Union, tea occupies only about 9 percent of the cultivated area, whereas citrus occupies almost 40 percent.

The Soviets have done an admirable job in attempting to become self-sufficient in tea. Before the revolution, tea growing was lim-ited largely to the foothills around Batumi in the warmest, wettest part of Georgia, which produced less than 1 percent of the country's consumption. During the years 1928–1940 the Soviets planted about 4500 hectares of tea per year and increased the total tea area from only 3500 hectares in 1928 to 55,300 hec-tares in 1940. World War II interrupted the tea-planting program, but after the war there was another rapid expansion, and by 1955 the Soviet Union was 87 percent self-supporting. In 1955, however, the per capita consumption of tea was only one-third what it had been in 1913. Obviously, the amount of tea being made available to the average citi-zens did not reflect their desires. After the death of Stalin, relaxations on imports of con-

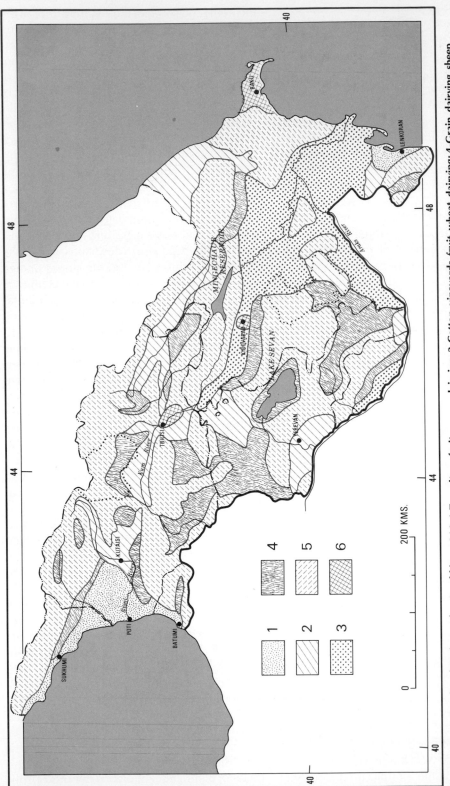

Figure 14-4 Agricultural Regions. After Saushkin, p.314. 1-Tea, citrus, fruit, silkworms, dairying, corn, tobacco; 2-Fruit, vineyards, vegetables, silkworms, dairying; 3-Cotton, vineyards, fruit, wheat, dairying; 4-Grain, dairying, sheep raising; 5-Livestock on seasonal pastures; 6-Urban oriented agriculture.

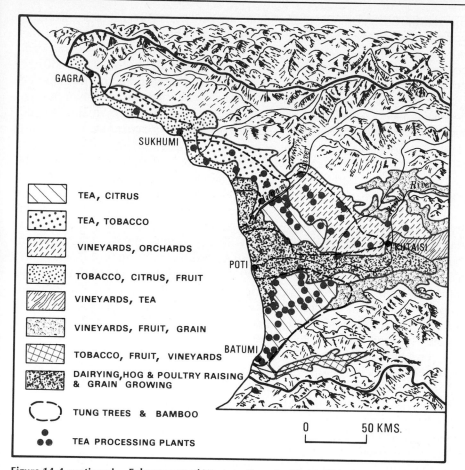

Figure 14-4 continued.   Enlargement of Western Georgia. After Nikitin, p. 170.

sumer goods allowed the consumption of tea to spurt ahead while the domestic production was growing at only a normal pace, and therefore the percentage of consumption supplied domestically has declined. It appears that the Soviets are more likely to import more tea in the future than to continue to try to expand tea production into marginal regions. Contrary to many Soviet statements to the effect that there are abundant opportunities for further expansion of tea production, it appears that all the prime land for tea growing has already been occupied. In fact, some reduction of tea acreage might be expected in the near future as marginal lands are taken out of production and put to better use.

Citrus growing in Georgia is limited to special Georgian varieties of tangerines, oranges, and lemons. Winter temperatures are too severe for other types, as well as for grapefruit. Of the three fruits grown, lemons are the least frost-resistant. A temperature of $-5°C$ damages the leaves and new sprouts, and $-9°C$ kills the trees. Therefore, lemons are limited primarily to Adzharia in the far southwestern part of Georgia, whereas other citrus are grown in Abkhazia in northwest Georgia and in the foothills surrounding the Colchis Lowland. Conditions deteriorate rapidly inland from the Black Sea coast, so that the interior part of Georgia raises very little citrus.

Citrus fruit is another food product that is in

very much demand in the Soviet Union. So far the quantity grown has been very limited and the quality has been very poor. Although the Soviets have been desirous of becoming self-sufficient in citrus, it appears that they have no possibility of coming anywhere near that goal. The Soviets have never produced more than about 20 percent of the annual consumption of citrus, and the amount of citrus made available to the public, primarily through imports, probably has never scratched the surface of potential demand. If the demand for citrus fruit in the Soviet Union were to be developed fully and satisfied, domestic production would undoubtedly prove to be only a drop in the bucket.

At the outset of the enthusiasm for the growing of citrus in the late 1930s, the acreage in Georgia was rapidly increased from about 3300 hectares to 25,000 hectares in 1940. Production was alwasy poor, however, and complaints were constantly made regarding the sloppy way in which the citrus crop was being tended. Then in the winter of 1949–1950 a disastrous freeze killed about 19,000 hectares of citrus trees, which reduced the remaining acreage in Georgia to less than one-third of what it had been one decade earlier. Although the acreage has been expanded since then, it has fluctuated up and down drastically, and the latest report seems to indicate that the present acreage (about 10,000 hectares) is not significantly more than that surviving the 1949–1950 freeze. Therefore, it would appear there is not much chance of further expansion of citrus acreage, although production might be increased somewhat by better attention to the groves that already exist. Also, better marketing methods would reduce much of the spoilage that now occurs before the fruit reaches markets. Therefore, the Soviet Union seems destined to remain a large citrus importer, particularly if it tries to satisfy ultimate consumer demands.

During recent years tung trees have occupied more acreage than have citrus trees. Tung is grown for the production of oil in the use of paints, lacquers, and so forth. Other intensive crops traditionally grown in humid Transcaucasia are grapes, tobacco, and a great variety of fruits and vegetables. Tobacco is heavily concentrated on the steep seaward slopes of Abkhazia where it has been a traditional crop for centuries. More than 8000 hectares of tobacco in this region make up over 98 percent of all the tobacco grown in western Georgia. Grapes are more widely scattered, but are somewhat concentrated on the eastern margins of the subtropics between the Colchis Lowland and the Surami Range, in the Surami Range itself, particularly around the Georgian capital of Tbilisi, and in many irrigation districts farther east. Viticulture is an ancient part of the agriculture in Transcaucasia, but with the development in the southern Ukraine, Moldavia, North Caucasus, and Central Asia, the Transcaucasus relatively has reduced its role in this part of the economy. It now produces about 20 percent of all the grape products of the country and less than 10 percent of the wine.

Although frosts severe enough to damage tea and citrus do not occur every year in the Colchis Lowland, since it takes at least five years for a tea plant or a lemon tree to regenerate itself after a killing freeze, seven killing frosts which occurred during 1910–1960 were enough to wipe out two-thirds of the potentially bearing years over the 50-year period. Therefore, more hardy annual crops are raised in this wet lowland wherever the land has been drained enough for cultivation. Since the middle 1920s about 67,000 hectares has been drained out of the 220,000 hectares of marshlands that exist in the Colchis Basin. Of this drained land, 37,000 hectares is in crops and orchards, and the rest is in forest, shrub, pasture, and nonfarm use. Considerable areas have been planted with eucalyptus trees in an effort to get rid of some of the groundwater through rapid transpiration into the air. The crops grown on the drained land are primarily grains, fodder crops, root crops, and vegetables. The main grain is maize, which has been a basic food crop in this region for centuries. Rice also is a traditional basic food here and is being grown more and more extensively on some of the wetter lowlands. Mulberry trees line the banks of many of the streams and provide the basis for a long-established silk industry.

Figure 14-5   Spring in a rural village near Tbilisi. Novosti.

In the dry Kura Lowland east of the Surami Range, farm practices and crop complexes are quite different. The primary need here is irrigation. The main crop grown under irrigation is cotton, and its rotation crop is alfalfa, which gets rid of some of the secondary salinization and fixes nitrogen in the soil. It also serves as a green manure crop when it is plowed under. Many fruits and vegetables, as well as grapes, are grown in the irrigated districts. Rice is grown in the swampy delta area of the Kura River, as well as in some of the swampier parts of the middle valley.

Mulberry trees grown along most of the

Figure 14-6   Cotton picking in the Kura Lowland, Azerbaydzhan. Novosti.

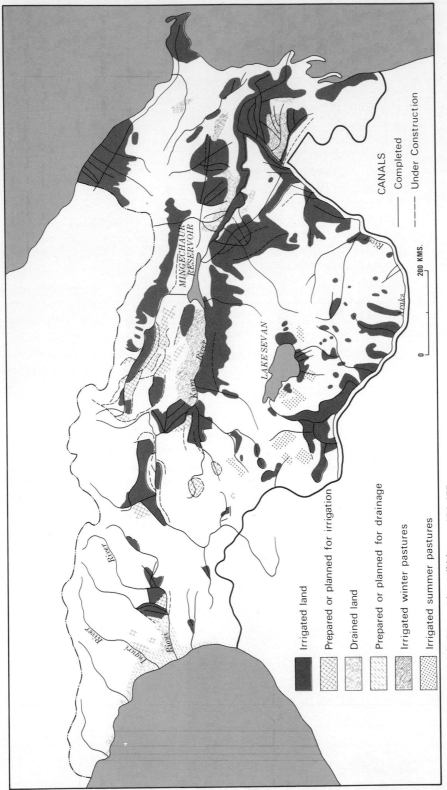

CANALS

—— Completed

---- Under Construction

200 KMS.

MINGECHAUR RESERVOIR

LAKE SEVAN

Araks River

Kura River

Kura River

Inguri River

River

River

Irrigated land

Prepared or planned for irrigation

Drained land

Prepared or planned for drainage

Irrigated winter pastures

Irrigated summer pastures

Figure 14-7   Irrigation and drainage. After Nikitin, pp. 154-155.

irrigation canals in the Kura Lowland and other irrigated areas provide the basis for a silk industry, just as they do along the drainage canals of the Colchis Lowland. The Transcaucasus Region produces more than 30 percent of all the country's raw silk, most of which is shipped out of the region for processing. Wheat and some other small grains are grown without irrigation in some of the moister foothills surrounding the lowland.

The agriculture of the Kura Lowland extends up the narrow floodplain of the Araks Valley as far as the Yerevan Basin and beyond. Here the crop complex is identical to that in the Kura Lowland.

In the highlands agriculture is limited primarily to grazing. Transhumance is practiced on a grand scale. Flocks of sheep and herds of cattle are moved in spring from the *kishlag* ("winter pastures") in the lowlands to the *eilag* ("summer pastures") on the mountain meadows, and back again in the fall where the flocks are shorn. They are then sorted, some for slaughter and some for retention as breeding stock, to be fed on the alfalfa hay and pastures of the lowlands in the winter.

Some irrigation agriculture is carried out in the Armenian Plateau, utilizing water primarily from two systems: the Sevan-Razdan drainage basin in central Armenia and the Alazan River basin in southeastern Georgia. There are also numerous small irrigation proj-

ects scattered about the area (Fig. 14-7). The irrigated crops of the Armenian Plateau are primarily wheat, tobacco, sugar beets, grapes, and other fruits. Some grain is dry farmed in the moister areas.

Climate or land amelioration is necessary in most of the cultivated areas of the Transcaucasus. The drainage projects of the Colchis Lowland have already been mentioned. In addition, many shelter belts, composed primarily of Lombardy poplar and eucalyptus trees, have been planted throughout the cultivated areas of the Colchis Lowland and the surrounding hills to combat the influences of the desiccating foehns that blow down the western slopes of the Surami Range and, on occasion, some of the other surrounding mountain slopes. Irrigated land now amounts to about 1.2 million hectares in Azerbaydzhan, 300,000 hectares in Armenia, and 200,000 hectares in Georgia. Most of the irrigation projects are tied in with multipurpose water construction projects, and they will be discussed in conjunction with those projects in the next section.

WATER AND POWER

Although most of the streams of the Transcaucasus are not very large in size, their steep gradients and consistent flows give them great

Figure 14-8 Irrigation canal near Lake Sevan, Armenian Plateau. Volcanic cone in background. Courtesy of J. H. Glen Burke.

Figure 14-9   The irrigated basin of Arpa-Chaya, Nakhichevan, A.S.S.R.,
Azerbaydzhan. Novosti.

hydroelectric potential. These flows are enhanced by the fact that most of the streams do not freeze during winter, and many of them are fed by snowfields and high-level lakes. Many small and medium-sized hydroelectric plants have been operating for quite a long while on a great number of these short, swift streams. A few major multipurpose water construction projects are worthy of mention.

The first was the Mingechaur multipurpose water management project on the middle Kura River, completed during 1950–1955. The project was to control floods, provide irrigation water, generate electricity, eradicate malaria swamps, and provide a navigable channel about 2 meters deep. Before the dam was built, the Kura River in its lower portion flowed between natural levees above the general level of the floodplain, and broad flooding occurred annually. Sweeping through the dry sedimentary plain, the river carried 14 million cubic meters of sediment per year, which generally was strewn across the floodplain. Now all the sediment is collected in the reservoir behind the dam. The hydroelectric plant has a generating capacity of 371,000 kilowatts. On completion of the

project, 135,000 hectares of new land was immediately put under irrigation, and this has since been increased to about 450,000 hectares. Twenty-five percent of this irrigated land is planted in cotton, 25 percent in perennial grasses, 15 percent in corn, 5 percent in vineyards, 4 percent in orchards, and the rest in small grains. Rice is grown extensively in areas with controlled flooding. The project is equipped with fish hatcheries and stocking basins to enable an integrated effort to raise fish on a commercial basis. About 200,000 hectares of agricultural land that has become saline through prolonged irrigation is now being flushed out by water from Mingechaur.

The Sevan-Razdan Cascade is a project involving a series of dams and reservoirs on the small Razdan River that drains Lake Sevan southward through Yerevan to the Araks River. The Razdan River is only about 100 kilometers long, but in that distance it drops more than 1000 meters from Lake Sevan to its junction with the Araks. Its flow is very consistent because it drains the large lake, so the natural conditions are ideal for the development of water power. Originally it was planned over a 50-year period to

Figure 14-10   Lake Sevan. Note exposed shorelines of previously higher lake levels.

drain Lake Sevan down to a level about 50 meters below its natural surface and thereby reduce its area to about one-seventh of its original size. At this point it was calculated that a balance would be reached between run-in, evaporation, and water necessary for power development on the cascade. By 1960 six stations with an aggregate capacity of 620,000 kilowatts had been constructed on the Razdan. The largest of these was constructed underground in a tunnel that had been dug through a small mountain range to increase the outflow of water from the lake. The building of more projected dams was stopped when it was discovered that the lake bed being exposed along the edges was not as immediately usable for agriculture as had first been anticipated, and the lowering lake level had drastically increased erosion along the slopes of the mountains surrounding the lake. Also, the need for hydroelectrical power in the Yerevan area diminished as natural gas became available. Therefore, the project was stopped during the mid-1960s, and there is now an effort to raise the level of Lake Sevan partway back up to its normal level. This is being done by building a dam on the Arpa River about 60 kilometers south of the lake. Water from this reservoir will be piped through a 48-kilometer-long tunnel being driven through the Vardenis Range and dumped

into a short canal that will carry the water into the southern end of Lake Sevan. Much of this water will be used for additional irrigation around Lake Sevan, and only partial use will be made of the installed hydroelectric capacity along the Razdan River.

The Sevan-Razdan Cascade has supplied water to irrigate more than 100,000 hectares of new land along the Razdan Valley and in the Yerevan Basin. In addition, the Sevan-Razdan Cascade has generated an urban development along the Razdan River between Yerevan and Lake Sevan. The first of a series of new towns was founded in 1959 and was named Razdan. Since than an alumina plant has been under construction in the town to utilize nearby nephelite-syenite deposits to produce alumina for the aluminum plant in Yerevan, making use of some of the electrical power of the valley. With the cutback of the Sevan-Razdan project, new thermal electric stations have had to be built, of much larger size than the hydroelectric stations, to supply power to the industries established in the area.

Another major irrigation district lies in arid southeastern Georgia between the Alazan and Iori Rivers. The first irrigation canal to be built there was the lower Alazan Canal, 91 kilometers long and opened in 1930. This irrigated about 34,000 hectares of land. The upper Alazan project is now under construc-

Figure 14-11   The town of Razdan on the Armenian Plateau.

tion. This is to be completed in two stages with an ultimate irrigation expansion of about 108,000 hectares.

The largest hydroelectric development in the Transcaucasus is now nearing completion on the Inguri River in northwestern Georgia. This drains the southwestern slopes of the western end of the Caucasus that receive the greatest amount of precipitation in the Soviet Union. Therefore, although the Inguri is a fairly short stream, it has a large flow. Plans for the project called for a 300-meter-high arched dam on the Inguri River and a 17-kilometer-long diversion tunnel taking water to a main underground plant with a capacity of 1.3 million kilowatts. The water would then go into the Gali Reservoir on the Eris-Tskali River, which was to have four smaller power stations with a combined capacity of 300,000 kilowatts on a 24-kilometer-long canal linking the Gali Reservoir with the Black Sea. The four smaller stations were completed in 1971–1972, but there have been unwarranted delays in the construction of the tunnel and the main underground plant. As a temporary measure, the flow of the Inguri River is now being diverted on the surface to the Eris-Tskali River to make fuller use of the four small stations already completed.

A smaller hydroelectric project under development is the construction of three dams on the short, steep Vorotan ("thunderous") River in southern Armenia east of the Razdan.

This stream, which is less than 200 kilometers long, plummets 3000 meters down the steep southern slope of the Vardenis Mountains to the Araks River. Together these three hydroelectric plants will have a generating capacity of over 400,000 kilowatts.

Although small hydroelectric plants are still being constructed on many of the Caucasian streams, the expansion of industries in Transcaucasia during the Soviet period has far outrun the availability of hydroelectric power, and thermal electric plants have been constructed in many cities, dwarfing the plants on the rivers. About 75 percent of the present electricity of the Transcaucasus is being generated by thermal plants. Most of these burn natural gas or fuel oil. In addition, a nuclear power plant is being constructed about 50 kilometers west of Yerevan. It is identical to the one being constructed on the Kola Peninsula south of Murmansk. The plant is to have a capacity of 880,000 kilowatts, with the possibility of future expansion.

INDUSTRIAL RESOURCES AND DEVELOPMENT

The Caucasus Mountains are a young system with much sedimentary and volcanic overburden. Therefore they are not highly mineralized near the surface. But there are some minerals of national significance, and others are important to the local economy. By far the largest development has been Baku oil. Commercial production dates back to the 1870s, and for a short time around the turn of the century Baku was the world's principal petroleum producer. It retained a prominent position within the Soviet oil industry until World War II, when output dropped sharply because of the war and never fully recovered. In 1940 the Azerbaydzhan Republic was producing 22.2 million tons of crude oil, which was 71 percent of the Soviet Union's total. With the German threat during the war, Baku oil production dropped to around 11.5 million tons, and then after the war it slowly recovered and eventually approached the 1940 level around 1968. But in the meantime the Volga-Urals oil fields had come into production, as well as some other oil fields, and the Baku production had slipped to only about 7 percent of the Soviet Union's total.

The postwar recovery of oil production around Baku was made possible by drilling deeper wells to reach deposits in older rocks and by drilling wells in the sea floor among the many small islands east, south, and southwest of the Apsheron Peninsula. A causeway connects the small islands and provides a base for drilling rigs and an oil workers' town over the surface of the Caspian Sea. The various branches of this causeway total about 240 kilometers in length. A submarine pipeline is now being laid to connect the oil field of Neftyanyye Kamni ("oil rocks") with Baku. The pipe will lie about 30 meters below the surface of the sea and will pump both oil and gas. It is being assembled on the shore and floated by pontoons into place. This recent development produced about 11 million tons of oil in 1974 out of a total Azerbaydzhan production of 18 million tons. The present Azerbaydzhan production includes some fields farther south along the Caspian near the mouth of the Kura River, northward along the Caspian coast north of the Apsheron Peninsula, and in west-central Azerbaydzhan. But the Baku area with its offshore satellite fields is still the major producer in Azerbaydzhan.

The Baku area also early became the major oil-refining center of the country (until the early 1950s it was about the only one). A pipeline was laid as early as 1907 westward through the entire length of the synclinal valley to the Black Sea coast at Batumi in southwestern Georgia to facilitate exports through the Black Sea, and a refinery was built at Batumi. Since then two more pipelines have been laid to Batumi.

Although Caucasian oil now makes up only a very small portion of total Soviet oil production, it is still of national significance because of its low sulfur content, which allows it to be refined into high-octane gasolines and high-grade lubricating oils that cannot be produced from many of the other sources of petroleum in the country. Therefore, Baku oil products are still distributed throughout much of the country. The thermal power plants in Transcaucasia, which are still burning fuel oil, ship it in from other areas of the country rather than use the valuable Baku oil.

The Soviets have experimented with wells as deep as 15 kilometers with facilities to extract oil simultaneously from several different layers one on top of another. But even with these efforts, the oil production on the mainland in the Baku area has been steadily declining in recent years, and only the expansion of offshore drilling has maintained the Azerbaydzhan production at a fairly constant level. Although the Soviets state that they eventually intend to exploit the submerged anticyclinal ridge that crosses the Caspian from the Apsheron Peninsula to Cheleken Peninsula on the east side of the Caspian in the Turkmen Republic, it is questionable how far they can go into deeper water. Therefore, it appears that the Baku area is destined to continue to decline both absolutely and relatively in the oil industry of the U.S.S.R. Some of this decline might be compensated for by significant oil deposits recently struck in Georgia. This area is now under development.

Before World War II, Baku also produced all the gas in the country. This was casinghead gas recovered as a by-product from the oil wells. In 1940 this production totaled about 2.5 billion cubic meters. At that time the Soviet Union made very little use of gas as a fuel. In the mid-1950s, large gas deposits were discovered around Stavropol and Krasnodar in the North Caucasus, in Central Asia, and in the eastern Ukraine. Natural gas production expanded rapidly during the next decade and the casinghead gas became only a small part of the total production. A natural gas deposit was discovered southwest of Baku near the town of Karadag ("black mountain"). At first this was thought to be a major deposit, and a pipeline was laid westward through the synclinal valley to Tbilisi, and a branch line extended southwestward from Akstafa to Yerevan. However, it was soon found that this was not such a large deposit and that reserves would run out after a few years. Therefore, a pipeline was laid southward from Stavropol through Ordzhonikidze across the Great Caucasus through Krestovyy Pass along the Georgian Military Highway to Tbilisi where it linked up with the Transcaucasian pipeline. Gas moved southward through this line from the Stavropol fields to supply most of the needs of the Transcaucasus.

In recent years a pipeline has been built northward from Iran through southeastern Azerbaydzhan to join the Transcaucasian pipeline west of Baku. Iranian gas is now being fed into the Transcaucasian system, and as gas consumption goes up all over the country it is envisioned that the gas flow along the Stavropol pipeline will be reversed, and Iranian gas will flow northward across the Caucasus. The depleted gas structures beneath the ground at Karadag are being utilized as a storage basin for Iranian gas until it can be piped westward. Eventually it is assumed that this 40-inch pipeline from Iran will transmit about 10 billion cubic meters of gas per year to the Soviet Union. It is also speculated that eventually a second pipeline might be built from central Iranian fields directly to Yerevan in southern Armenia. A second 40-inch pipeline has been built up the synclinal valley parallel to the old 28-inch pipeline built in 1959–1960 to carry the enlarged volume of Iranian gas flow.

In the late 1960s and early 1970s the Bakhar gas field about 25 miles southeast of Baku was developed along with some offshore oil fields. This gas field is now producing about 6 billion cubic meters of gas per year, which is twice as much as the Karadag field produced at its peak in 1960.

The production of natural and casinghead gas has prompted the development of several gas-processing plants and provided the basis for a large chemical industry in Transcaucasia. The first gas-processing plant was built in Baku in the 1920s to process oil well gases. Since then a much larger plant has been built in Baku, and a second smaller plant has been opened in the new chemical center of Sumgait on the northern coast of the Apsheron Peninsula.

The third mineral fuel, coal, occurs in the Transcaucasus only in small amounts, primarily at Tkibuli and Tkvarcheli, in the foothills on the northeastern side of the Colchis Lowland. The Tkibuli mines produce more coal than Tkvarcheli, but it is of lower grade and cannot be used in metallurgical industries for coking. The Tkvarcheli coals are not very high-grade coking coals either, and have to be mixed with Donets coal for metallurgical purposes. In 1974 Georgia produced about 2.15 million tons of coal, of which about 1.7 million tons was coking coal. Compared to the U.S.S.R. total production of 684 million tons, the Georgian production was almost negligible. However, it provided the basis for many of the early thermal electric plants in the area, most of which have since been shifted to natural gas, and it also provided the fuel for a small ferromanganese plant at the nearby town of Zestafoni. This coal is also feeding the iron and steel plant constructed in the new town of Rustavi in eastern Georgia, based on the small Dashkesan iron ore deposit in nearby western Azerbaydzhan. However, about 1.5 million tons of Donets coal has to be shipped in yearly to mix with the Georgian coal in this plant.

In the same general area as the coal in Georgia lies the Chiatura manganese deposit. This is second only to Nikopol in the eastern Ukraine in size of reserves and production. For many years the Chiatura ore, which is richer than the Nikopol ore, was the primary producer in the Soviet Union and in the world. Production started in 1879. Much of it was exported to other countries, as it still is. Until World War I Chiatura accounted for about half of the world's manganese trade. However, as the grade of ore declined in Chiatura, larger open-pit mines were developed in the eastern Ukraine, and Georgia's production declined. In 1974 Georgia produced 1.8 million tons of manganese ore, which compared to 6.3 in the Ukraine and 8.1 for the U.S.S.R. as a whole. However, the Chiatura manganese is still of national significance, and Chiatura is the primary exporter of manganese from the Soviet Union. Part of the ore moves directly to the port of Poti for export or for shipment to the Ukraine through the port of Zhdanov. Since 1933 part of the ore has been smelted at the Zestafoni ferroalloys plant for use in the steel industries throughout the country.

In the early 1950s a small iron and steel plant came into being in eastern Georgia in the new town of Rustavi to utilize the nearby iron deposit at Dashkesan and the coal and manganese in western Georgia and to serve all the steel needs of the Transcaucasus. However, as mentioned, the Georgian coals are not rich enough, and about 1.5 million tons of coal has to be shipped in annually from the Donets Basin. Also, for a while in the late 1960s and early 1970s the ore-processing plant at Dashkesan was modernized before the steel plant at Rustavi was altered to handle the new form of ore, and iron ore actually had to be shipped in from Krivoy Rog in the Ukraine, while the Dashkesan ore was shipped to the Ukraine. The Rustavi iron and steel operation has been costly, but it serves most of the steel needs of the Transcaucasus — mainly steel pipe for the oil and gas industries. Rustavi turns out about 60 percent of the pipe requirements of the Transcaucasus and Sumgait the other 40 percent. In 1974 the Rustavi plant turned out about 780,000 tons of pig iron, which was less than 1 percent of the country's total, and 1,430,000 tons of crude steel, which also was less than 1 percent of the country's total. In addition to the iron and steel production at Rustavi, a large chemical complex has been established, based at first on coke chemicals and now also based on

natural gas brought in by pipeline from the Baku area.

Some of the largest and oldest mining industries of Transcaucasia involve various nonferrous metal complexes. Copper mining is one of the oldest industries in the region, and it is constantly being expanded. Silver and copper were mined as early as the ninth century around Alaverdi in northern Armenia where a copper smelter was built sometime before the Bolshevik Revolution. Copper, lead, zinc, and some other metals have been mined since the Middle Ages in the southeastern panhandle of Armenia around the little town of Kafan. Attention at present is concentrated on copper and molybdenum complexes. This ore moves to Alaverdi for smelting, and the molybdenum is moved to other parts of the country for processing. A molybdenum-processing plant is supposed to be built in Kirovakan. The most recent development in the copper industry is taking place near the town of Madneuli in Georgia southwest of Tbilisi. This ore also contains lead, zinc, and barite. Madneuli already has become one of the main barite-producing regions of the country. The copper ore from this region also will move to the Alaverdi smelter. A new goldfield is opening up just east of the eastern end of Lake Sevan at the town of Zod. This gold lode is expected to make Armenia one of the Soviet Union's principal producers. A flotation mill is under construction southeast of Yerevan near the town of Ararat near the Araks River to avoid pollution of Lake Sevan.

The aluminum industry was attracted to the cheap hydroelectric and thermal electric power in the Transcaucasus when a plant went into operation at the new city of Sumgait on the northern shore of the Apsheron Peninsula in 1955. At first this plant used long-haul alumina from the Urals. For a few years it even hauled alumina from the Leningrad area and from Hungary. The development of local raw materials lagged until the early 1960s when a plant finally went into operation at Kirovabad in the middle Kura Valley based on alunite ores at nearby Zaglik. The Kirovabad plant now produces alumina, sulfuric acid, and potassium sulfate. Its alumina is being shipped to aluminum plants at Sumgait and Yerevan. Another alumina plant has been under construction since 1960 at the new town of Razdan along the Razdan River in Armenia. This is to be based on local nephelite. It will use limestone from the vicinity of Ararat, and the plant will turn out about 300,000–400,000 tons of alumina per year and four to five times as much cement. The alumina section of the plant still had not opened by 1975, but the cement plant opened in 1970. There is an earlier cement plant at the town of Ararat. With the development of alumina plants at Kirovabad and Razdan and the aluminum plants at Sumgait and Yerevan, the Transcaucasus may become a major aluminum-producing region. However, it is not on the magnitude of the new plants in Siberia, and its resource base is limited and difficult to utilize.

In addition to metallic ores, the Transcaucasus contain important nonmetallic minerals such as bentonite, mercury, and a wide range of building materials. Bentonite is a clay used as drilling mud in oil and gas wells where it acts as a lubricant, keeps drill cuttings in suspension, and helps prevent the loss of drilling fluids by forming impervious coatings on drill hole walls. It is also now being used in great quantities in the iron pelletizing industry to bind the pulverized iron ore into pellets. Bentonite has been mined for some time in Georgia, and during the early 1970s a much larger complex was developed in northern Armenia. It appears that the Armenian development may turn out at least one-third of the Soviet Union's bentonite.

A new mercury-mining complex has been built in west-central Azerbaydzhan. It appears that this might become one of the major four or five mercury-mining areas in the country, putting the Soviet Union in third place in the world in mercury production. There is no lack of building stones in the Transcaucasus. Perhaps the most developed industry is in the Armenian Platau, where volcanic tuffs constitute an easily worked pinkish stone used for major buildings in most of the cities of the area. The multistory downtown buildings in Yerevan, for instance, are all composed of

neatly cut blocks of this stone that are fit together so perfectly that little mortar has to be used. Varying hues of pink, tan, and brown have been used to produce artistic patterns in the stonework. The volcanic Armenian Plateau is often referred to as "the land of stone."

The mineral fuels and metallurgical industries of the Transcaucasus have prompted the development of many chemical industries. Sumgait is perhaps the most outstanding example, because the new city was developed specifically for the development of chemical complexes. Its construction began in 1944 around a small chlorine-caustic chemical plant, which was based on a salt deposit near Nakhichevan, and since then the city has gained a small steel plant and pipe-rolling mill, a synthetic rubber plant, a superphosphate plant, and petrochemical and gas-processing plants. The small Sumgait steel plant utilizes scrap metal and pig iron from the Ukraine. At Rustavi in eastern Georgia, the metallurgical coke gases have provided the basis for a nitrogen fertilizer plant and a synthetic fiber complex, which have been augmented by the coming of natural gas to the area. Rustavi produces nitrogenous fertilizers for Georgian tea, citrus, and wine growers.

At Kirovakan in northern Armenia, a chemical complex opened in 1932 to produce calcium carbide from local limestone. This eventually was used as the basis for a synthetic rubber plant in Yerevan, and later a nitrogen-based chemical complex was added to the Kirovakan chemical industries. Now an artificial corundum plant has been established at Kirovakan that will produce synthetic rubies and sapphires for industrial uses such as jewels in watches, lasers, and precision instruments. Chemical complexes also exist in the large cities of Baku and Yerevan, which among other things produce synthetic rubber tires.

Several machine-building industries have been established in the Transcaucasus to satisfy the markets there. Many of these have to do with the oil, gas, and mining industries. Truck assembly plants have been established in Kutaisi, the commercial center of the Colchis Lowland, and in Yerevan, the capital of the Armenian Republic. The Kutaisi plant builds cab-over-engine truck tractors with trailers designed for hauling general cargo weighing up to 15 tons. Yerevan produces off-highway trucks for mining and construction work.

Textile industries have been in the Transcaucasus for a long time, using local raw materials for silk, cotton, and wool. However, the industries have not been developed much beyond local market needs. Much of the raw materials are moved to the Central Region for processing. Although the Transcaucasus Region produces more than 30 percent of the raw silk of the country, it produces only about 5.5 percent of the silk cloth. Most of this is produced in Tbilisi and Yerevan. Most of the cotton raised in Azerbaydzhan and Armenia moves to the Central Region for processing. Only about 15 percent of the cotton raised in the Transcaucasus is used there to produce cotton cloth. Major mills exist in Baku, Kirovabad, Mingechaur, and Gori (a small city northwest of Tbilisi, which is the birthplace of Stalin). The Transcaucasus Region is one of the major wool-producing areas of the country, and much of the wool moves to the Central Region also.

TRANSPORT

One of the problems of the Transcaucasus is its relative isolation from the rest of the country because of the Great Caucasus Range, which has no low breaks. Only two railroads connect the Transcaucasus with the rest of the country, one going along the shore of the Black Sea around the western end of the Great Caucasus and one along the shore of the Caspian around the eastern end of the Caucasus. Both of these are slow, heavily overloaded routes. Of course, there is steamer service on both the Black and Caspian Seas, and these link up with the Volga-Don waterway. But they are slow and very circuitous. The main Black Sea ports within the Transcaucasus are Batumi, with its important oil terminal, and

Poti at the mouth of the Rioni River, the exporting port for Chiatura manganese. Baku dominates the sea trade on the Caspian, and most of the movement out of there is oil, but Baku also handles cotton, wood, grain, and machinery.

Three roads, all in close proximity to one another, were built across the mountains in the Georgian area shortly after the acquisition of the Transcaucasian region. These are known as the Georgian, Sukhumi, and Osetian Military Highways, so called because initially they had to be guarded by military personnel to protect travelers from bands of wild tribesmen who lived in the mountains and pillaged the traffic. Today these military roads are unguarded. The Georgian Highway has been converted into a two-lane blacktop motor road. It follows a tortuous route, in many places hanging on sheer cliffs, and traffic over it is very light. Avalanches of snow in winter frequently block the roads for long periods of time and have induced the construction of long snow sheds over the highways at particularly vulnerable spots. In the summer of 1967 mud flows destroyed parts of the Georgian Military Highway and the parallel Stavropol-Tbilisi gas pipeline passing through Daryal Gorge on the upper Terek River.

The Georgian Military Highway, built over Krestovyy Pereval ("the pass of the cross") in 1861, is the most usable of the three highways. It rises 2384 meters over Krestovyy Pass. It has been paralleled by two gas pipelines running from Stravopol to Tbilisi, and now it is tentatively planned to build a railroad along the same route. This would be the highest railway in Europe with the longest tunnel, needing many shorter tunnels, bridges, and viaducts. The new electrified line is planned to carry fast heavy trains that would reduce the transport time between the Transcaucasus and the Central Region by as much as 3½ days.

The Transcaucasian Mainline Railroad runs from Baku westward through the synclinal valley to Poti and Batumi on the Black Sea coast. Branch lines connect various cities on either side, and a major branch line runs up the Araks Valley to connect with a north-south line in western Armenia that runs northward to the Transcaucasian Mainline east of Tbilisi. Another major north-south line is under construction from Yerevan northward directly to the Transcaucasian Mainline at Akstafa. An oil pipeline runs the full length of the synclinal valley from Baku to Batumi, and a gas pipeline runs from Baku to Tbilisi with a branch southward to Yerevan. At Tbilisi the line connects northward through Krestovyy Pass to Stavropol. Roads are poorly developed in the Transcaucasus and must take very circuitous routes because of the topography.

CITIES

The only three very large cities in the Transcaucasus are the three capital cities, Baku, Tbilisi, and Yerevan.

Baku

Metropolitan Baku is the largest city, with a 1974 population of 1,359,000. It is the fifth largest city in the Soviet Union. The city was probably founded in the ninth century as a stopover point along a constricted segment of the trade route between the Orient and Europe around the southern end of the Caspian Sea. It grew rapidly in the later part of the nineteenth century under the impetus of oil production and has been maintaining this growth ever since. Although oil production has declined, Baku is still one of the leading oil-refining and commercial oil cities in the country.

Had it not been for oil, Baku undoubtedly would not have gained the eminence that it has today, for it sits on the barren, windswept southern shore of the Apsheron Peninsula where the rainfall is less than 8 inches per year. Water supply is a serious problem in the large city. Before 1917 drinking water had to be brought in from the Kura River by tankers. Then a pipeline 200 kilometers long was constructed to bring in good mountain water for drinking, but it did not supply anything for irrigation. There are very few lawns in the city. Therefore, the city is a rather unpleasant place in which to live. It is very hot and dry in summer and subject to strong winds throughout many months of the year. During summer hot, dry winds funnel around the eastern end of the Great Caucasus and blow dust across the city from the steppes to the north. The name Baku means "blow of the wind." Since 1936 it has served as the capital city of the Azerbaydzhan Republic; this has enhanced its standing. During the Soviet period chemical industries and machine-building industries of many types have been established. Recently a subway system has been built.

Tbilisi

Tbilisi, with a 1974 population of 984,000, is the capital of the Georgian Republic. It has served as the center of the Georgian culture since its founding in A.D. 458. Unlike Baku it is a lovely city sitting in the rolling hills and low mountains where the Kura River cuts through the Surami Range. It has no major heavy industries, but it has many diversified industries. The most important are the textiles, concentrating on silk, and machine and food industries. It is famous for its wines, cognac, and champagne. *Tbilisi* comes from the Georgian word "warm." The city sits atop several hot mineral springs. Occasionally one of these breaks through the asphalt of the streets and explodes like a geyser. Therapeutic waters are piped to baths in health resorts within the city limits. The city stretches for about 55 kilometers in the gorge along the Kura River and in places is jammed between mountains in a strip of land no more than a kilometer wide. Urban transportation is therefore somewhat difficult. In 1966 the first subway line opened, which has now been expanded to a total length of about 7 kilometers with 11 stations. Construction on the subway system is still continuing. Funicular railways and cable cars carry tourists to the top of Mt. Mtatsminda, about 300 meters above the downtown portion of the city, where they can get a bird's-eye view of the urban area. New

Figure 14-12   Cable car in Tbilisi.

apartment buildings are being built on hill-sides so steep that residents have to move up and down by elevators.

Yerevan

Third in size is Yerevan, the capital of the Armenian Republic, with a 1974 population of 870,000. It was founded in 783 B.C. Like Tbilisi, it has been the cultural center of an important nationality group that has occupied the area for over 2000 years. Under the Soviets it has flourished because of its function as the capital of the Armenian Republic and because of rapid industrialization. It is a lovely old city, sitting at an elevation of about 1000 meters in a basin surrounded by higher land on three sides that opens on the south onto the Araks River Valley. Dotted across the Armenian Plateau within sight of the city are several snow-capped volcanic peaks, the highest of which is Mt. Ararat across the border in Turkey. Unfortunately, the stable air in the basin produces a dust haze that generally obscures these magnificent cones from view. Irrigated crops of fruits and vegetables surround Yerevan and serve the urban market. The Soviets seem to have singled out Yerevan

Figure 14-13   Yerevan. Snow capped volcanic cones in background.

to become one of the main industrial cities of the Transcaucasus. Aluminum, chemical, and machine-building industries have been established there. The Sevan-Razdan Cascade supplies much electricity to the city, and the natural gas pipeline coming in from the northeast brings in the needed fuel.

Kirovabad

A large population gap occurs between the three largest cities and the fourth city, Kirovabad, which had a 1974 population of 203,000. Kirovabad is the economic center of the Kura Lowland. It is well served by a railroad and a gas pipeline running along the synclinal valley, and it has been provided with an alumina plant to process alunite ores from nearby Zaglik.

Leninakan

Leninakan, an old city on the western edge of Armenia, was formerly known as Alexsandropol. It is an important rail junction and manufactures carpets, textiles, light machinery, and has a meat-canning industry. Mining of tuff stone for building materials takes place in the vicinity. In 1974 Leninakan had a population of 180,000.

Kutaisi

Kutaisi is the economic and rail center of the Colchis Lowland. In 1974 it had a population of 169,000. It has diversified light industries, and during the last 15 years a truck assembly plant has been established in the city.

Sumgait

Sumgait is the chemical center established in 1944 on the north coast of the Apsheron Peninsula. Its chemical, steel, aluminum, and synthetic rubber plants have already been discussed. In 1974 it had a population of 152,000.

Kirovakan

Kirovakan is the chemical center in north central Armenia. In 1974 it had a population of 123,000.

Rustavi

Rustavi, the iron and steel center established in eastern Georgia during the 1940s, had grown to a population of 117,000 by 1974, more than twice the size originally intended for it. It also has an important chemical complex, which has already been discussed.

Sukhumi

Sukhumi is a seaport on the Black Sea coast of Georgia. It is primarily known as a resort town and as the site of a subtropical botanical garden. In 1974 it had a population of 112,000.

Batumi

Batumi is the oil port on the Black Sea coast in southwestern Georgia. It has an oil refinery and some light industries. It is one of the main oil export ports from the Transcaucasus to the Ukraine and other parts of the Soviet Union, as well as abroad. In 1974 it had a population of 111,000.

PROSPECTS

Transcaucasia, because of its subtropical climate, holds a unique position in the agriculture of the Soviet Union. Undoubtedly it will continue to serve as the sole domestic producer of such products as tea, citrus, and tung. But the population pressure will force a continued urbanization, and as the Soviets establish basic industries in the area the urbanization process will be speeded even more. The Caucasian peoples still have rather high birth rates, but these are diminishing rapidly as the area is being drawn more and more into Soviet ways of life. The Caucasus area has lost its monopoly on the Soviet oil industry and is now dependent to a certain extent on oil and gas from the outside. Connections with the rest of the country are being enhanced slowly as new transportation lines are developed. However, Transcaucasia remains one of the most identifiably separate regions of the Soviet Union. It cannot be expected that its role within the Soviet economy and culture will change significantly in the foreseeable future.

READING LIST

- Altounyan, Taqui, "Land of Great Ararat: Armenia's Modern Capital," *The Geographical Magazine,* No. 3, December 1969, pp. 194–199.
- *Armyanskoy SSR* (Armenian S.S.R.), Akademiya Nauk SSSR, Institut Geografiya, 1955, 282 pp. (in Russian).
- *Atlas Armianskoy Sovietskoy Sotsialisticheskoy respubliki* (An Atlas of the Armenian S.S.R.), Yerevan, 1961, 111 pp. (in Russian).
- *Atlas Azerbaydzhanskoy SSR* (Atlas Azerbaydzhan S.S.R.), Akademiya Nauk Azerbaydzhanskoy SSR, Baku, 1963, 213 pp. (in Russian).
- *Atlas Gruzinskoy SSR* (Atlas of the Georgian Republic), Tbilisi, 1964, 269 pp. (in Russian).
- *Azerbaydzhanskaya SSR* (Azerbaydzhan S.S.R.), Akademiya Nauk Azerbaydzhanskoy SSR, Moscow, 1957, 445 pp. (in Russian).
- Bone, Robert M., "Soviet Tea Cultivation," *Annals of the Association of American Geographers,* June 1963, pp. 161–173.
- *Gruzinskaya SSR* (Georgian S.S.R.), Akademiya Nauk Gruzinskoy SSR, Moscow, 1958, 400 pp. (in Russian).
- *Gruzinskaya SSR; ekonomiko-geograficheskaya kharakteristika* (Georgian S.S.R.; Economic-Geographic Characteristics), Akademiya Nauk SSSR, Moscow, 1956, 348 pp. (in Russian).
- Hovannisian, Richard G., *The Republic of Armenia,* "The First Year, 1918-1919," Vol. 1, University of California Press, Berkeley, 1971, 547 pp.
- Jensen, Robert G., "Soviet Subtropical Agriculture: A Microcosm," *Geographical Review,* April 1964, pp. 185–202.
- Kozlov, I.V., *Sovetskiye subtropiki* (The Soviet Subtropics), Moscow, 1959, 125 pp. (in Russian).
- Lang, David Marshall, *The Georgians,* Praeger, New York, 1966, 244 pp.
- Lang, David Marshall, *A Modern History of Soviet Georgia,* Grove Press, New York, 1962, 298 pp.
- Magakyan, G.L., "The Mingechaur Multi-Purpose Water Management Project," *Soviet Geography: Review & Translation,* December 1961, pp. 43–50.
- Shaginyan, Marietta, *Journey through Soviet Armenia,* Foreign Languages Publishing House, Moscow, 1954, 215 pp.
- *Sovetskiy soyuz: Armeniya* (Soviet Union: Armenia), Mysl, Moscow, 1966, 342 pp. (in Russian).
- *Sovetskiy Soyuz: Gruziya* (Soviet Union: Georgia), Mysl, Moscow, 1967, 318 pp. (in Russian).
- *Soviet Georgia: Its Geography, History, and Economy,* Academy of Sciences of the Georgian SSR, Vakhushti Institute of Geography, Progress Publishers, Moscow, 1967, 182 pp.
- Valesyan, L.A., *Proizvodstvenno - territorialny komplex armyanskoy SSR* (The Territorial-Production Complex of the Armenian S.S.R.), Yerevan, 1970 (in Russian).
- Valesyan, L.A., "Sovetskaya Armeniya v novoy pyatiletke" (Soviet Armenia in the New Five-Year Plan), *Geografiya v shkole,* No. 1, 1973, pp. 7–12 (in Russian).

The Central Asia Economic Region

	Area (km²)	Population	Persons/km²	Percent Urban
Uzbek S.S.R.	447,000	12,896,000	28.8	37
Andizhan Oblast	4,000	1,156,000	268.9	26
Bukhara Oblast	143,000	1,032,000	7.2	32
Dzhizak Oblast*	21,000	396,000	18.9	19
Kashka Darya Oblast	28,000	881,000	31.0	18
Namangan Oblast	8,000	932,000	119.4	31
Samarkand Oblast*	25,000	1,527,000	62.1	30
Surkhan Darya Oblast	21,000	731,000	35.1	16
Syr Darya Oblast*	5,000	394,000	85.7	30
Tashkent City		1,504,000		100
Tashkent Oblast	16,000	1,584,000	197.9	40
Fergana Oblast	7,000	1,466,000	206.5	33
Khorezm Oblast	5,000	606,000	134.6	19
Kara Kalpak A.S.S.R.	166,000	762,000	4.6	36
Kirgiz S.S.R.	199,000	3,145,000	15.8	38
Frunze City		463,000		100
Issyk Kul Oblast	44,000	330,000	7.6	30
Naryn Oblast	50,000	203,000	4.0	16
Osh Oblast	74,000	1,341,000	18.2	31
Tadzhik S.S.R.	143,000	3,188,000	22.3	38
Dushanbe City		411,000		100
Kulyab Oblast*	13,000	418,000	32.2	27
Leninabad Oblast	26,000	1,031,000	39.5	38
Gorno-Badakhshan Autonomous Oblast	64,000	107,000	1.7	1.3
Turkmen S.S.R.	488,000	2,360,000	4.8	48
Ashkhabad City		272,000		100
Ashkhabad Oblast*	95,000	334,000	3.5	32
Krasnovodsk Oblast*	138,000	283,000	2.0	82
Mary Oblast*	87,000	549,000	6.3	33
Tashauz Oblast	74,000	447,000	6.1	30
Chardzhou Oblast	94,000	506,000	5.4	45
Total	1,277,000	21,589,000		

*January 1, 1974. Created or altered, December 1973.

chapter 15

the central asia economic region

Stretching all the way from the Caspian Sea to China is the inland desert empire now known as Soviet Central Asia. Politically, this region is composed of four union republics that are further subdivided into oblasts, autonomous republics, and autonomous oblasts. Together these constitute an area of 1,277,000 square kilometers containing a population of 21,589,000 people. The average population density is less than 17 persons per square kilometer, but this varies drastically from less than 2 persons per square kilometer in the Gorno-Badakhshan Autonomous Oblast in the high mountains of the Tadzhik Republic and in Krasnovodsk Oblast in the desert of the Turkmen Republic to more than 206 persons per square kilometer in the irrigated agricultural area of Fergana Oblast of the Uzbek Republic. In fact, it probably varies more widely than that, since there are large areas of desert and mountains within political units that probably have no people at all, and there are sections of political units in the Fergana Basin that probably have as many as 300–400 persons per square kilometer in intensively irrigated agricultural districts. The region is still heavily rural. Most of the native groups have not yet become very integrated into the Soviet social and economic system and have not moved into cities. The entire region has less than 40 percent of its people classified as urban. Separate political units in some of the

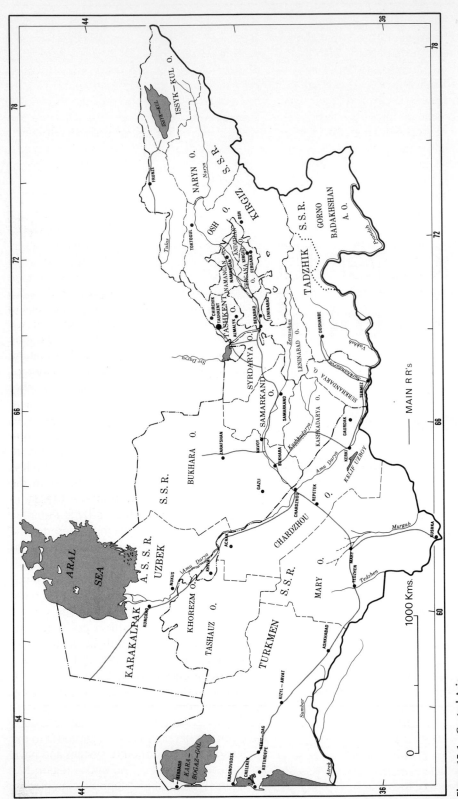

Figure 15-1 Central Asia.

more intensively irrigated agricultural districts have no more than 16 percent of their people classified as urban. In the high mountains of Gorno-Badakhshan Autonomous Oblast only 13 percent of the population is classified as urban.

The Central Asian peoples have the highest birth rates and highest natural growth rates in the country. Individually all four republics rank considerably above any other republic in the country. The highest birth rate and highest natural growth rate of any individual republic is the Tadzhik Republic, which in 1973 had a birth rate of 35.6 per thousand, a death rate of 7.2 per thousand, and a natural increase of 28.4 per thousand. The Uzbek and Turkmen Republics were close behind, and the Kirgiz Republic somewhat behind those. But even the Kirgiz Republic had a natural growth rate 4 percent higher than the Azerbaydzhan Republic, which was fifth after the four Central Asian republics.

These high natural growth rates of more than 20 per thousand in Central Asia are keeping the average for the country at the modest level of 8.9 per thousand. And the Central Asian republics have retained such high growth rates only because they have not been integrated into the Soviet system as much as other parts of the country. As these areas are pulled more and more into the socio-economic stream of things in the Soviet Union, undoubtedly their birth rates and natural growth rates will decrease also, and then the average population growth in the entire country will drop significantly. There is already an indication of this trend. In the Tadzhik Republic since 1965 birth rates have declined by 1.2 points, death rates have increased by 0.6 points, and the natural growth has declined by 1.8 points.

It is obvious that the Central Asian republics are just emerging from the second stage of population development when improved health care and reduced infant mortality greatly diminish the death rate in a population that is heavily balanced toward the young while the birth rate remains at a high level. Therefore, the natural increase is at its highest stage, higher than previously when under-developed conditions resulted in high death rates, and higher than it will be in subsequent periods when urbanization and industrialization reduce birth rates. The Central Asian republics during the first half-century of the Soviet period have gone through this second stage of population development and are now entering the third stage when birth rates begin to drop drastically as death rates remain constant or even rise a little as the population becomes older.

In addition to the high natural increase, the Uzbek Republic is experiencing a moderate net in-migration, and the Tadzhik and Kirgiz Republics are experiencing a modest net in-migration. The Turkmen Republic, on the other hand, is experiencing a small net out-migration. In general, the Central Asian people have not been very mobile. Most of the in-migrants are Russians and other Slavic groups from European U.S.S.R. and Western Siberia. The small out-migration from the Turkmen Republic is probably going into the neighboring republics. As a result of combined natural increase and migration, during the intercensal period 1959–1970, much of Central Asia registered some of the highest population growths in the country.

HISTORY, ETHNOGRAPHY, AND POLITICAL ORGANIZATION

This vast inland region is peopled by a variety of nationalities whose colorful pasts long antedate the Russian incursion into the area and reflect several millennia of nomadic conquests and assimilations in this crossroad between Europe, the Orient, and the Middle East. Archeological evidence in the thick layers of silt deposited on the densely populated floodplains of the annually flooding rivers attests to the existence of various riverine civilizations that date back to at least 3000 B.C. The juxtaposition of loess-covered steppe and desert plains, with long warm summers, and high fringing mountains along the southern border, whose peaks catch considerable amounts of winter precipitation in the form of snow, provides an ideal combination for primitive civilizations based on irriga-tion agriculture. The mountain snows and glaciers assure reliable flows of summer meltwater in the streams that cascade down the northern slopes and partially traverse the desert floors before ending in the sands or depositing their waters in some interior drain-age basin, such as the Aral Sea.

Greek and Persian reports of early expedi-tions into the region of the Oxus (Amu Darya) and Jaxartes (Syr Darya) speak of thriving civilizations that were contemporary with Byzantium, Babylon, and the Nile. Farther north, the nomadic herdsmen roamed the steppes all the way from the Volga to China, and although they left little evidence in the form of permanent settlements, their influ-ence on the present stock of peoples was probably no less than that of their more seden-tary neighbors, since they often marauded the towns to the south and became assimilated into those populations.

Thus, for thousands of years the area has had identifiable settlements in the river val-leys of the south and has been overrun throughout by nomadic herdsmen belonging to many clans. In addition, from time to time it has been overwhelmed by outside invaders from the east and the south, primarily the Mongols and the Arabs. Under Tamerlane the region was organized into an effective power base. But none of the indigenous peoples in the area had much sense of definite territorial occupance or patriotism beyond that of clan or tribal organization. Therefore, the area was a sort of no-man's-land or political vacuum between more powerfully organized neigh-bors until the nineteenth century when the Russians intervened. Throughout much of this long history, China was more or less an or-ganized state in the east, although its western territories were not very directly attached to China proper, and in the south the Persian and Ottoman Empires exerted some influence, as did India and later the British in India. Thus, the region was often a stage for a three-way struggle between the encroaching Russians from the north, anarchic and rebellious indig-enous peoples, and other powers on the east and south.

There was little recorded history in the re-gion before the Arab invasions of the seventh and eighth centuries. Therefore, it is very dif-ficult to unravel the origins of the many peoples who now bear nationality designa-tions. Such distinctions were not generally made before the Soviet period. Most of the people in the area identified themselves only with small clans or tribes through blood rela-tions and did not think of themselves as mem-bers of larger national groups. The identifica-tion of broad national groups as they exist today is largely a product of Sovietization, which, although it made use of traditional group names, nevertheless codified the na-tional classification scheme as it had never been codified before. In fact, the Soviet codification brought to light a great deal of confusion. The Russians themselves were not very well acquainted with local ethnic his-tories. This was particularly true in the deline-ation between the Kazakhs and the Kirgiz. The expansive steppes of what is now north-ern Kazakhstan originally were known by the Russians as the Kirgiz Steppes, and after the Revolution when the Central Asian area was first constituted into political subdivisions, this region became known as the Kirgiz A.S.S.R. It was only in 1925 that this confu-sion was cleared up.

Sogd is the only part of the entire region about which any coherent information is available from before the seventh century. Sogd lay between the Oxus and Jaxartes Riv-ers in the region that was later to become known as Transoxania. The people of Sogd were of Iranian origin, and they formed a small part of a vast nomadic Turkic empire that stretched from the Urals to Mongolia and southward into the mountains bordering China and India. During the seventh century the Persian Empire was overrun by Arab forces centered in Damascus, and these Arabs moved northeastward into Transoxania and occupied what they regarded as Chinese Tur-kestan. In spite of the fact that the Arab power was soon replaced by the Persians once more, the Arab imprint was lasting, in the form of religion and rudimentary administration such as law, taxation, and land tenure. Originally, the Islamic culture was confined pretty much to the Iranian settlements of the south, but by the fifteenth century it had spread to the Turkic nomads in the northern steppes.

From about A.D. 1000–1200, the region was under the influence of various Turkic rulers and dynasties who quickly embraced Islam. The Mongol invasion under Genghis Khan early in the thirteenth century quickly overran all of Turkestan and part of the steppe region to the north, but the Mongol forces consisted largely of locally recruited Turks, so that the number of Mongols who settled in the region was negligible, and the lasting cultural effects of the conquest were minor. By the middle of the fourteenth century all the Mongol rulers had become Turkicized and had embraced Islam. The Mongol period reached its zenith under Timur (Tamerlane) and his successors during the fifteenth and early sixteenth centuries when the Timurid Dynasty was finally overthrown by a part of the nomad Kazakhs, who had embraced Islam and become known as Uzbeks. They moved southward from the region northwest of the Aral Sea and overwhelmed the southern settlements.

Because the Arab invasion had not penetrated northward as far as the Kazakh Steppes, the early history of the Kazakhs has never been recorded. In the first half of the seventeenth century the people in that area were referred to as Uzbeks. But by the second half of the seventeenth century a so-called Kazakh Union had been formed to establish contact with the Russians, who by this time had conquered the Mongol Khanate of Astrakhan at the mouth of the Volga. During the seventeenth and early part of the eighteenth centuries the various Kazakh hordes found it necessary to become more or less united against the Kalmyk or Oyrot invasions directed against their region from what is now Sinkiang in western China. It was partly in order to gain help against these invasions that some of the Kazakhs submitted to Russian rule around 1730. Thus, the stage was set for Russian occupance. The Russians were already in possession of Western Siberia and had established a line of Cossack settlements along the Ural River in the west. Five years later they established the city of Orenburg as an outpost to act as a fortress against the steppe peoples who periodically moved northward toward the Urals. The Cossack settlements and Orenburg were the beginning of what was to become a line of fortified settlements, such as Omsk, Akmolinsk, Semipalatinsk, Pavlodar, and Barnaul, in an effort to form a cordon around the north and eastern borders of the Kazakh area.

Toward the end of the eighteenth century three khanates came into being in Bukhara, Khorezm (Khiva), and Kokand. At that time, these three khanates occupied most of the territory that now constitutes the four Central Asian republics, but there were no clearly defined boundaries and there was constant war among the khanates. For a time the Russians believed that they could negotiate with these khanates, which appeared to them to be properly constituted nation states, but by the first part of the nineteenth century the Russians realized that this was far from actuality and that they would have to neutralize the khanates by force if they were to advance until they reached the frontiers of organized states. By this time, Central Asia had become a very isolated region of the world. The caravan routes, which from the second century B.C. had intimately connected Central Asia with the Middle and Far East, had long since given way to sea routes between southern Chinese ports and the Persian Gulf. Also, events in other parts of the Middle East had cut off the Central Asian area from the rest of the Moslem world. Therfore, on the eve of the Russian march southward, the Central Asian khanates, and still more the steppe region to the north, were the most backward parts of the whole Moslem world, and nation-forming processes could hardly be said to have been underway there. In surrounding areas, the Mogul Empire in Persia was beginning to disintegrate, British power in India had not yet been firmly established, and the Chinese government had liquidated the Oyrots in Dzungaria but had failed to establish Sinkiang formally as a province of the Chinese Empire. Thus, the Russian expansion southward began at an auspicious time when other powers adjoining the region had either abandoned their designs on it or were too weak to pursue them.

The Russians had no difficulty moving across the Kazakh Steppes where there were no cities or permanently settled areas or any organized military force other than small followings at the disposal of individual tribal leaders. In the settled khanates, however, things were quite different. Here despotic khans and emirs ruled with iron hands and maintained strict social organization and military might. It was against these hotbeds of resistance that Russian efforts were directed beginning in 1855 in an all-out effort to nullify the relatively impotent, but nevertheless harassing, military forces of the native groups who were in the habit of swooping northward to new Russian settlements and carrying off hostages to be sold as slaves in Khiva or Bukhara. Consequently, without too much difficulty, the Russians captured Yangi (now Dzhambul) in 1864, Tashkent in 1865, Khodzhent (now Leninabad) in 1866, Bukhara and Samarkand in 1868, and the last remaining khanates of Khiva in 1873 and Kokand in 1876. Finally, in the early 1880s, the Russians succeeded in overrunning Transcaspia and the Merv Oasis after several fierce battles with the Turkmen, who were the most warlike of all the natives of Central Asia.

Suddenly the Russians found themselves in semicontrol of this entire inland empire. Once again they had come into contact with British influence, in India, and in 1888 boundaries were agreed upon that established Afghanistan as a buffer country between Russia and India. Some of the Moslem colonies, such as Bukhara and Khiva, remained nominally independent under the Russian regime until 1920, when finally the Bolsheviks won the civil wars in the area and established Soviet rule.

As in Transcaucasia, the Russian Revolution brought complete chaos to Central Asia. Actually, what was to follow the 1917 revolution was portended in 1916 when a great native revolt broke out in Central Asia in response to a Russian imperial decree to call up 500,000 men from among the Central Asian natives to serve as support laborers in the rear of Russian forces engaged on the German front. This was the first time that the Central Asians had been called upon to perform any sort of military duty for the Tsar, and to add insult to injury they were not being asked to fight but to dig trenches and do other menial tasks to support the Russian forces. Native wrath was turned largely against the Russian settlers in the area, and full-scale massacres took place on both sides. In addition, it has been estimated that about 300,000 people fled eastward into Chinese territory to escape punitive operations following the revolt.

The Russian Revolution that followed quickly thereafter was received in Central Asia initially by indifference, except for those 3 percent of the people who were literate and had some idea of what was going on. However, the activities of the Tashkent Soviet, which was set up to administer the general region, and opposition forces in the area, made up largely of Russian settlers and dissident loyalist groups from among the higher echelons of previous Tsarist elements, eventually embroiled most of the native groups in disastrous fighting that caused widespread destruction and famine across the entire area. Native resistance finally culminated in a massive guerrilla movement known as the Basmachi Revolt. It lasted for over five years, in spite of the fact that by the end of 1920 the whole of the area was pretty well controlled by the Bolsheviks. The Basmachi movement finally collapsed in 1923, and the Central Asian natives resigned themselves to the fact that no material assistance was forthcoming from the outside and no dream of self-determination was going to be realized. Obviously, the Soviets had no more intention of relinquishing the territory gained by the Tsars in the nineteenth century than the Tsars themselves had had.

As early as 1920 the Soviets constituted the Kirgiz A.S.S.R., in what is now much of the Kazakhstan Republic (they were still confusing the Kirgiz and the Kazakhs), and the Turkestan A.S.S.R., which included the rest of Central Asia. Both these A.S.S.R.s were put under the jurisdiction of the R.S.F.S.R., since that was the only general political entity that existed at the time; the U.S.S.R. was not formed until December 30, 1922. In 1923 and early 1924 the areas controlled by Khiva and Bukhara were constituted as the People's Soviet Republic of Khorezm, and the People's Soviet Republic of Bukhara, respectively. In October 1924 the Turkestan, Khorezm, and Bukhara political units were abolished and in their place were established the Uzbek and Turkmen S.S.R.s, the Tadzhik A.S.S.R., and the Kirgiz and Kara-Kalpak Autonomous Oblasts. When the Stalin constitution was written in 1936, the Kazakh (Kirgiz) and Tadzhik A.S.S.R.s and the Kirgiz Autonomous Oblast were upgraded to the status of S.S.R.s,

and the Kara-Kalpak Autonomous Oblast was upgraded to an A.S.S.R. Hence, by 1936 the five most populous nationality groups in Soviet Central Asia had been accorded the highest political status possible within the structure of the Soviet Union, and the sixth group had been given the second highest status. Five of the groups eventually became parts of the Central Asian Economic Region.

In 1973 it was estimated that Central Asia contained 21,589,000 people, a mixture of native groups and others who have moved in, particularly Russians and Ukrainians (Table 15-1). The four most populous groups give their names to the four union republics.

The Uzbeks are the largest Turkic group in the Soviet Union and the second largest in the

Table 15-1   Numbers of People by Nationality by Union Republic, 1970

	Number of People (thousands)	Percent of Total		Number of People (thousands)	Percent of Total
Uzbek S.S.R.	11,799	100.0	Tatars	71	2.4
Uzbeks	7,725	65.5	Germans	38	1.3
Russians	1,473	12.5	Kirgiz	35	1.2
Tatars	574	4.9	Ukrainians	32	1.1
Kazakhs	476	4.0	Jews	15	0.5
Tadzhiks	449	3.8	Turkmen	11	0.4
Karakalpaks	230	2.0	Kazakhs	8	0.3
Koreans	148	1.3	Others	50	1.7
Ukrainians	112	0.9	Turkmen S.S.R.	2,159	100.0
Kirgiz	111	0.9	Turkmen	1,417	65.6
Jews	103	0.9	Russians	313	14.5
Turkmen	71	0.6	Uzbeks	179	8.3
Other	329	2.7	Kazakhs	69	3.2
Kirgiz S.S.R.	2,933	100.0	Tatars	36	1.7
Kirgiz	1,284	43.8	Ukrainians	35	1.6
Russians	856	29.2	Armenians	23	1.1
Uzbeks	333	11.3	Others	86	4.0
Ukrainians	120	4.1	Total, Central Asia	19,791	100.0
Germans	90	3.1	Slavic groups	3,285	16.6
Tatars	69	2.4	Russians	2,986	15.1
Uigurs	25	0.8	Ukrainians	299	1.5
Kazakhs	22	0.8	Titular native groups	13,933	70.4
Tadzhiks	22	0.7	Uzbeks	8,903	45.0
Others	111	3.8	Tadzhiks	2,101	10.6
Tadzhik S.S.R.	2,900	100.0	Turkmen	1,499	7.6
Tadzhiks	1,630	56.2	Kirgiz	1,430	7.2
Uzbeks	666	23.0	Others	2,573	13.0
Russians	344	11.9			

Source: Itogi vsesoyuznoy perepisi naseleniya 1970 goda, Volume 4.

Figure 15-2 Uzbek men drinking their afternoon tea on a carpet-covered raised platform beside a shady irrigation ditch north of Tashkent.

world after the Turks of Turkey. With a total of more than 9 million, they are the third most numerous nationality in the Soviet Union. Their name was probably derived from Uzbek, one of the khans of the Golden Horde. Originally they occupied the area between the lower Volga and the Aral Sea, but in the sixteenth century they migrated southward and conquered the settled regions of Bukhara, Samarkand, Urgench, and Tashkent. Here they became mixed with earlier settlers, including the ancient Iranian population of Khorezm and Sogd. At present more than 80 percent of the Uzbeks lives in the Uzbek Republic, and most of the remainder lives in the four neighboring republics. There are over 1 million Uzbeks outside of the Soviet Union, primarily in Afghanistan, and a few thousand in the Sinkiang-Uighur Autonomous Region in China.

The Turkic Kazakhs are the sixth most numerous nationality in the Soviet Union, with a total of more than 5 million people. About 80 percent lives in Kazakhstan and the remainder in bordering republics.The origin of the Kazakhs is obscure. The word itself does not appear until about the eleventh century, when a general term meaning "riders of the steppe" was used to describe the peoples of the area. During the Soviet period there has been a great effort to collectivize and settle the Kazakh nomads, which has resulted in large fluctuations in the population. They showed a decrease of about one-fourth be-

tween the 1926 and 1939 censuses. Since that time they have been on the increase again. About 500,000 Kazakhs live on the Chinese side of the border in the Ili-Kazakh Autonomous District of Sinkiang. The Kazakhs differ somewhat in appearance from the Uzbeks in that they have fuller, rounder faces, broader noses, and yellower skins. The Uzbeks tend more toward a dusky complexion, which belies their relation to the Iranians on the south.

The Turkmen are probably the most distinctive Turkic group in Central Asia. They remained quite aloof from the khanates in the settled river valleys to the east, and today they are characterized by long heads with sharp, bony features. Their origin is very obscure, but their language indicates origins from the west rather than from the east. Of the 1,525,000 Turkmen in the U.S.S.R., about 1,417,000 live in the Turkmen S.S.R. and the remainder in the Uzbek S.S.R. There are about 330,000 in Iran and 270,000 in Afghanistan.

The Tadzhiks are undoubtedly the oldest ethnic element in Central Asia. They are closely related to the Iranians and Afghans to the south. Of the 2,136,000 living in the U.S.S.R. in 1970, 1,630,000 were living in the Tadzhik S.S.R. and the rest in the Uzbek and Kirgiz S.S.R.s. The bulk of the Tadzhiks live outside of the Soviet Union, however. There are about 2,100,000 in Afghanistan. There are also Tadzhiks in northern Iran and in the Sinkiang Uighur Autonomous Region of China.

The Kirgiz appear to be closely related to the Kazakhs, but their origin is obscure. It appears that before the ninth century they were living in the upper reaches of the Yenisey River and migrated from there to their present position in the eastern Tien Shans. The 1970 census showed 1,452,000 Kirgiz in the Soviet Union, of whom 1,284,000 lived in the Kirgiz S.S.R. The remainder lived in the Uzbek and Tadzhik S.S.R.s. In addition, there are about 70,000 Kirgiz living in the Sinkiang Uighur Autonomous Region of China. Like the Kazakhs, the Kirgiz have yellow complexions and round facial features.

The Karakalpaks numbered 236,000 in 1970, almost all in the Karakalpak A.S.S.R. in

Figure 15-3   The interior of the home of a Kazakh collective farmer. The
samovar in the foreground provides hot water for making tea that is drunk
out of bowls. Novosti.

Figure 15-4   Turkmen women rug weavers listening to newspaper reading
during lunch. Novosti.

Figure 15-5   Tadzhik men playing chess in a tea garden near Dushanbe.
Novosti.

the Uzbek Republic south of the Aral Sea. They appear to be closely related to both the Kazakhs and the Uzbeks, probably more closely to the former.

In addition to these six main Asian nationalities, there are Russians, Ukrainians, Jews, Germans, Poles, Belorussians, Tatars, Koreans, Uighurs, and Dungans living in the area. Russians, Ukrainians, and Belorussians have been rapidly migrating into the cities of the area, and consequently the cities are very Russian in aspect. In the capital city of Alma Ata, one sees scarcely anyone but Russians. In the oases of Central Asia where the native populations are more dominant there is little connection between the native life in the rural villages and the Russian life in the larger cities. The natives live and work the land much as they did before the revolution, whereas in the cities the factories are being run as they are in Moscow. Most of the natives still live in adobe huts with thatched roofs. The donkey is the universal beast of burden and the donkey cart the chief means of transport of produce.

The population of Central Asia is distributed very unevenly. In general it is concentrated in areas that afford high potentials for agriculture. Such areas are determined primarily by factors of soil and climate, which in turn are closely related to topography. A few major centers of population and a considerable number of scattered minor settlements owe their existence to the mining of mineral resources, and this is closely related to the geology of the region.

Figure 15-6   The felt covered *yurt* is the summer home of Kirgiz shepherds in the mountain pastures of the Tien Shans. Novosti.

PHYSICAL LANDSCAPE

Landform

The Central Asian Region encompasses a wide variety of landforms, from flat desert plains to rocky eroded uplands to the highest mountains in the Soviet Union. The plains part of the region is occupied by two broad structural basins running roughly north-south with intervening higher land between. On the west is the Caspian Basin, and down the center of the region runs the Turanian Lowland, which contains the Kara Kum desert in the south, the Aral Sea in the center, and the Turgay Lowland farther north, which will be discussed in the next chapter on Kazakhstan.

The southern half of the eastern side of the Caspian Basin falls within the Turkmen Re-

public. This includes the large Kara-Bogaz-Gol ("black mouth bay"). The gulf is bordered on the south, east, and north by steep cliffs of surrounding plateau surfaces that rise 100 meters or more above the water level of the gulf. The water level itself lies at 31 meters below sea level. On the west the gulf has been almost completely cut off from the main body of the Caspian by sandbars that have grown from either side to within about 200 meters of each other so that the strait between the Caspian and the gulf is now only about 200 meters wide and 3 meters deep. The gulf averages about 10 meters in depth, and according to the Soviets it has a surface level that often falls as much as 4 meters below the level of the Caspian. Thus, a considerable current flows from the Caspian into the gulf, and the gulf

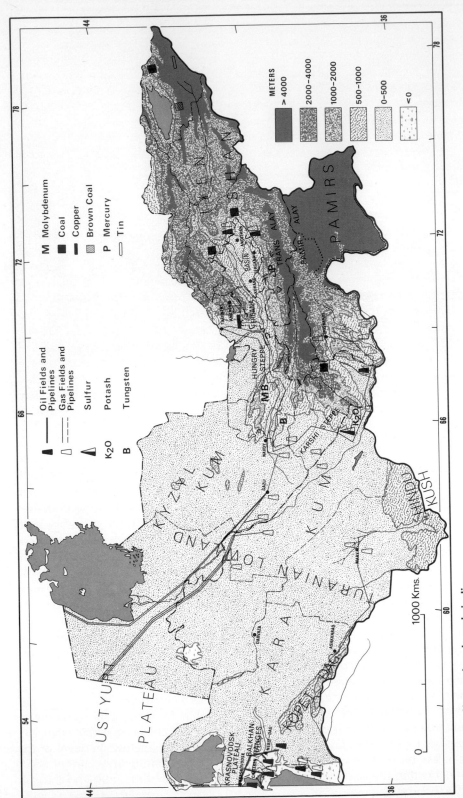

Figure 15-7 Landform, minerals, and pipelines.

acts as a final evaporation pan for the Caspian. It has been calculated that between 10–20 cubic kilometers of water is evaporated from Kara-Bogaz-Gol annually. The salt content there is understandably very high.

South of Kara-Bogaz-Gol is a peninsula formed by the Krasnovodsk Plateau that rises 100 meters or more above the Caspian and again plunges off to the sea in steep cliffs. The city of Krasnovodsk ("red water") clings to the base of the cliff on a narrow coastal plain bordering the Caspian. Southeast of the Krasnovodsk Plateau lie several anticlines of thick limestone known as the Balkhan Ranges, which reach a maximum elevation of 1880 meters. The ranges are surrounded by a broad *takyr* (clay pan) that represents an old lake bed. The shallow basin was undoubtedly filled with water at one time during the glacial period when a connection existed between the Aral Sea and the Caspian. There are terraces along the slopes of the Balkhans as high as 70 meters above the present surface of the plain. A series of dry stream channels known as the "Uzboy System" leads through the plain, which only a few hundred years ago served as the spillway from the Aral Sea to the Caspian. Nebit-Dag and other low hills rising 50 meters or more above this vast *solonchak* are topographic expressions of dislocated tertiary sediments that yield considerable quantities of petroleum.

West of Nebit-Dag ("oil mountain") lies Cheleken Island, or, since the drop in water level in the Caspian, actually Cheleken Peninsula, another fault block that rises abruptly from the Caspian to elevations of about 100 meters. It has been described as a broken plate, a tertiary, oil-bearing, highly faulted section of sandstone and other sediments underlain by young volcanic magma. Mud volcanoes and petroleum seeps abound and have turned the sand into an asphalt-cemented rock that has split into basaltic-like prisms to form spectacular mesas and buttes. Gases are emitted from some of the mud volcanoes, and gas bubbles constantly rise through the water from the bottom of the Caspian. This sort of activity continues southward along the below-sea-level coastal plain to the mouth of the small Atrek River, which forms the international boundary with Iran.

Stretching northeastward from Kara-Bogaz-Gol to the Aral Sea is the Ustyurt Plateau, the southern and eastern portions of which lie in the Turkmen and Uzbek Republics. This is a dry, flat, barren upland of nearly horizontal sedimentary strata. At its greatest elevation in southern Kazakhstan it lies about 340 meters above sea level. In most places around its periphery it drops off in steep cliffs. In fact, in the southeast, south, and southwest it drops off to enclosed depressions that lie below sea level. On its eastern edge it plunges in a fault scarp about 150 meters down to the Aral Sea. No streams of any significance head in this area, and no water is available for irrigation. Hence, it seems to be destined to remain an almost unused area.

East of the Ustyurt Plateau, in the midsection of the Turanian Lowland, lies the Aral Sea, the fourth largest lake in the world, with a surface area of about 64,000 square kilometers. It is a shallow sea, with depths of only 10–20 meters throughout much of its extent, and it contains thousands of islands. The name *Aral Sea* means "island sea." The greatest depth, about 70 meters, is found along the western edge at the base of the fault scarp of the Ustyurt Plateau. Hence, the lake basin ends abruptly at a fault scarp on the west, but rises gradually eastward into the sands of the Kyzyl Kum and southward into the sands of the Kara Kum. The Syr Darya is building a large delta into the lake in the northeast, and the Amu Darya is building a large delta from the southern side. Apparently, until only a few hundred years ago, the Aral Sea drained southwestward through the Uzboy System into the Caspian. Hence, the Aral Sea has less than 1 percent salt. By comparison the southeastern part of the Caspian has about 14 percent salt.

Precipitation in the Aral Sea area totals less than 100 millimeters (4 inches) per year. If it were not for the surface inflow of the two large rivers fed by the melting snows of the high mountains to the southeast and subsurface seepage of artesian water from fissured aquifers below, the sea would immediately dry up.

As it is, the sea seems to be gradually diminishing, so much so in fact that the problem of the falling water level of the Aral Sea has gained nationwide attention similar to that of the Caspian, except on a smaller scale. As more water is taken out of the two large streams for irrigation purposes, the falling level of the Aral Sea will be accelerated. Some planners advocate that the sea be dried up completely. However, this would interrupt a rich fishing industry and might have serious effects on the ground water of the surrounding area.

Southwest of the Amu Darya lies the Kara Kum, the most extensive sand desert in Central Asia. Although the name means "black sands," the name comes not from the color of the sand, which is standard yellow-gray desert sand, but from the uninhabited, unknown nature of the area. About 90 percent of the area is covered by elongated ridges of relatively fixed sand topped by smaller, shifting barchan dunes of loose sand. Most of it is quite unfit for agriculture. Only the southernmost margins bordering on the mountains along the south and the northern section near the mouth of the Amu Darya have rich alluvial soils that are supplied with irrigation water to support a thriving agriculture.

Across the Amu Darya to the northeast is the Kyzyl Kum ("red sand") desert, which occupies much of the area lying between the Amu Darya and the Syr Darya. The Kyzyl Kum is higher, rockier, and more devoid of sand than the Kara Kum and shows more variety in its relief. Stubby, worn-down outcrops of old Paleozoic formations reach elevations of 700–900 meters in the central portions of the region. Like the Kara Kum, the Kyzyl Kum is a very dry desert that is little utilized except along its margins where some irrigation water can be derived from either the Syr Darya or the Amu Darya. In its southern portion, southwest of Tashkent, lies an extensive ancient lake floor that is exceedingly flat and filled with alluvium. This is the so-called Golodnaya ("hungry") Steppe, which has been almost completely irrigated and sown with cotton.

Everywhere on the south and east Central Asia is bounded by high, rugged mountains. In the west, bordering on Iran, are the Kopet Dag ("dry mountains"), a fault block range cut sharply on its northeastern side by a major fault system that runs in a straight line from southeast to northwest along the Transcaspian Railroad through the cities of Ashkhabad and Kizyl Arvat and continues on northwestward through Nebit Dag and the Balkhan Mountains to the Caspian. The Kopet Dag reaches an elevation of 2246 meters in the Soviet Union, but the area is so dry that even in their highest elevations the mountains are practically devoid of vegetation. Erosion, in the process of stripping the sedimentary layers down their dipslopes toward the southwest, has produced a series of jagged, overhanging cuesta escarpments facing northeastward overlooking the sandy desert of the Kara Kum. The spectacular scenery standing out in bold relief in this dry climate has induced the Soviets to establish the city of Ashkhabad as one of the film making centers of the Soviet Union. Western-type movies are produced here, utilizing the magnificent backdrop of the Kopet Dag. No streams of any proportions originate in the Kopet Dag, but several small streams provide water for local domestic use and restricted irrigation in areas such as Ashkhabad. Also, wells and underground canal systems, constructed centuries ago by the Persians, are still utilized to provide water supplies.

Eastward from the Kopet Dag rise the ranges of the Hindu Kush. Although they lie entirely in Afghanistan, they provide the watershed for small streams flowing northward into Soviet Central Asia. The two largest of these streams, the Murgab and Tedzhen Rivers, end in the sand of Turkmenistan and form the two oasis around the cities of Mary (the old Merv) and Tedzhen.

The Hindu Kush ranges rise in eastern Afghanistan to join the Pamir Knot, which straddles the boundaries of Afghanistan, Pakistan, China, and the Soviet Union. On the Soviet side, the Pamirs fan out to the west in a series of east-west oriented ranges known as the Pamir Alay. These contain the first and

Figure 15-8   A relic on the barren high Pamirs, Tadzhik SSR. Novosti.

third highest peaks in the Soviet Union, Mt. Communism (formerly Mt. Stalin) in the Academy of Sciences Range at an elevation of 7495 meters, and Mt. Lenin in the Trans Alay Range at an elevation of 7134 meters, both in the Tadzhik Republic. The Pamir Alay ranges also contain Fedchenko Glacier, one of the most extensive mountain glaciers on earth, which emanates from Communism Peak and surrounding peaks.

In the east, near the Chinese border, where the Pamir Alay ranges merge into the Pamir Knot, the region is simply a barren high upland without any distinctive individual ranges. Summit areas lie way above the cloud systems and hence receive practically no precipitation. They are also very cold, and therefore nothing grows. But in their western extremities, the Pamir Alay ranges are deeply dissected by the headwaters of the Amu Darya, especially by the two main headwater streams, the Vakhsh and the Pyandzh. Throughout much of its course the Pyandzh forms the international boundary between the

Soviet Union and Afghanistan. The Vakhsh and several smaller streams flow southwestward across a gently rolling upland in southwestern Tadzhikistan, providing irrigation water to transform the steppe into the primary agricultural area of the Tadzhik Republic. North of this rolling upland lie three subparallel mountain ranges oriented essentially east-west. These are, from south to north, the Gissar Range, the Zeravshan Range, and the Turkestan Range. Between the Zeravshan and Turkestan Ranges, the Zeravshan River flows westward in a deep, narrow valley fed by mountain glaciers in the higher portions of the western Alay Range on the Tadzhik-Kirgiz border. The river emerges from the mountains near the western border of Tadzhikistan and continues to flow westward through the foothills and desert for another 250 kilometers past the famous old cities of Samarkand and Bukhara. After leaving the mountains, it takes on a braided course and loses water to the desert sands until eventually, shortly beyond Bukhara, it ends in a stagnant pool known as

Figure 15-9 **The Gissar Range, Tadzhik SSR. Novosti.**

Karakul ("black lake") just short of joining the Amu Darya.

The Trans Alay Range forms the northern-most range of the Pamir Alay Mountains, and northward across the Alay Valley the Alay Range forms the southernmost range of an extensive mountain system known as the Tien Shan, a Chinese term meaning "heavenly mountains." The Tien Shan system stretches all the way from northern Tadzhikistan, through the Uzbek and Kirgiz Republics, to eastern Kazakhstan east of Lake Balkhash into China. The individual ranges in this system are oriented primarily west-east, and gener-ally they are rather widely spaced with broad steppe basins in between. The broadest of these mountain basins is the Fergana Basin just north of the Alay Range. This flat-floored alluvial basin, extending approximately 160 kilometers east-west and 15–35 kilometers north-south, is a major agricultural area of Central Asia. It is a steppe area and requires irrigation.

North of the Fergana Basin the main ranges of the Tien Shan form a bold escarpment on the north overlooking a string of important irrigated oases and cities built on the alluvial fans at their base. Many small streams flowing northwestward out of the mountains bring the all-important water to these settlements. Issyk Kul, as well as several smaller lakes, lies within these ranges. The headwaters of the Syr Darya, particularly the Naryn, head along the southern slope of the ranges and flow the entire length of the Fergana Basin before en-tering the desert to the northwest. These lakes and streams are fed by melting glaciers during the summer and reach their greatest flow at that time, a fact that is very significant to ag-riculture in the area. Most of the precipitation in these mountains comes during the winter in the form of snow when cyclonic storms from the Mediterranean, Black, and Caspian Seas, and from the Middle East, penetrate the Cen-tral Asia Region. The precipitation is stored in the form of snow until it is needed for irriga-

Figure 15-10   The Great Uzbek Road through the Gate of Tamerlane on the Zeravshan River near Samarkand. Novosti.

tion in the summer. Were it not for this natural storage, agriculture in this area would be extremely limited.

The Tien Shan in general are folded mountain ranges, but faulting has occurred, and some volcanism has broken out along various fault lines. Issyk Kul ("hot lake") gets its name from the fact that volcanic activity in the immediate vicinity produces warm water in certain portions of the lake. Many different names are given to individual ranges in this broad mountain system. In the north, overlooking the desert, the main ranges are the Kirgiz, the Kungey-Alatau, and the Trans-Ili

Alatau. The word *alatau* means "mottled mountains," which comes from the fact that during summer patches of snow and glaciers remain on their higher slopes, giving them a mottled appearance from a distance. Several fault block ranges branch out in a general northwesterly direction from the northern side of these main ranges into southern Kazakhstan. The two major ranges of this type are the Karatau and Chu-Ili Range, which will be discussed in the next chapter, as will the remainder of the Tien Shan ranges along the Chinese border northward from the Kirgiz Republic.

Climate, Vegetation, and Soils

The outstanding characteristic of Soviet Central Asia, and the characteristic that most unifies it, is aridity. Most of the lowland area receives less than 200 millimeters (8 inches) of precipitation per year, and large sections in the central part of the region, along the eastern Caspian and along western Lake Balkhash, receive less than 100 millimeters (4 inches) per year. The extensive foothill areas and intermontane basins generally receive 200–400 millimeters per year. Intermediate mountain slopes receive 400–1600 millimeters, and some of the more exposed slopes may receive more than 1600 millimeters (64 inches). These wetter slopes generally face southwestward and catch heavy winter snows from advancing warm fronts in cyclonic storms that frequent the area at that time of the year. Above 5000 meters elevation, mountain peaks generally receive very little precipitation, since they are above most of the cloud formations. It has been estimated that the eastern Pamirs receive as little as 75 millimeters (3 inches) per year.

The dryness of the area is due to the extreme interior continental location. The high mountains rimming the entire southern edge of the region largely rule out any importation of moisture from the Indian Ocean and its surrounding seas. In addition, the surface airflow is generally from the north, around the eastern end of the Azores High during summer and along the southern periphery of the western extension of the Asiatic High during winter. Therefore, most of the air that is imported into the region comes from the dry plains of Kazakhstan and surrounding areas to the north. These northerly winds are so constant that the orientation of elongated sand dunes in the southern part of Central Asia reveals very clearly their prevailing direction. Also, the thick loess deposits along the foothills fringing the southern mountains attest to the great amount of wind deflation and sifting

Figure 15-11 Prevailing surface winds as revealed by dune orientation.
After Lydolph, *World Survey of Climatology*, Vol. 7.

action in the desert sands to the north that have blown the fine dust southward and lodged it against the mountain foothills.

During winter the region is generally filled up with cold Siberian air from the north and northeast along the southern periphery of the Asiatic High. Therefore, winters on the average are not as mild as might be expected, and absolute minimum temperatures are severely cold. Tashkent averages −1°C (30°F) in January and has experienced a temperature as low as −30°C. Even at Kushka on the Afghan border, the most southerly station in the entire

Soviet Union at latitude 35° 17′N, January temperatures average only 2°C (35°F), and a minimum temperature of −33°C has been experienced. Farther west, Krasnovodsk on the Caspian Sea coast experiences about the same temperatures on the average, but does not experience the extreme minimums. There the absolute minimum temperature is −17°C. The growing season at Tashkent is 204 days, and at Kushka 207 days. In the high mountains, the station of Tien Shan at an elevation of 3614 meters averages −21.9°C in January and has experienced temperatures as low as

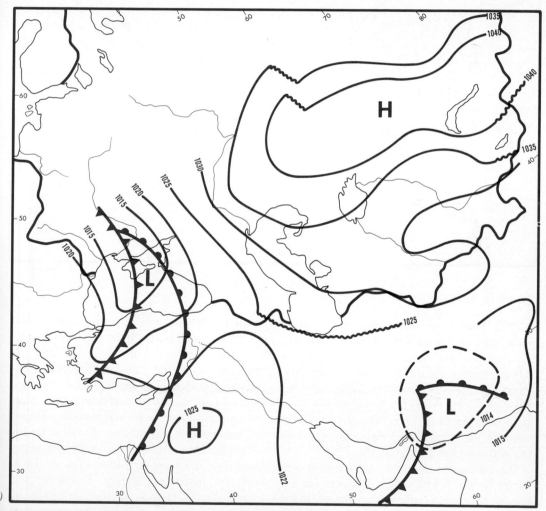

Figure 15-12   The procession of winter cyclones across Central Asia. Weather maps for (A) 1500 hours, 12/14/49, (B) 0300 hours, 12/15/49, (C) 1500 hours, 12/15/49, (D) 0300 hours, 12/16/49. After Lydolph, *World Survey of Climatology*, Vol. 7.

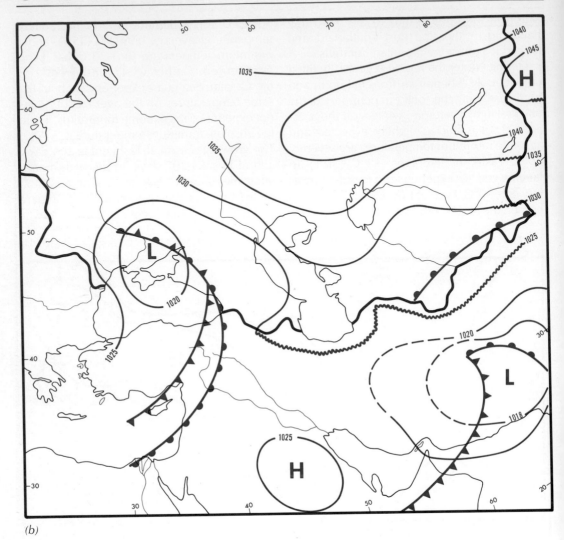

(b)

−48°C. Frosts may occur any time of year. Snow lies on the ground at Tien Shan 212 days per year and reaches a greatest depth of 30 centimeters. On the plain there is very little snow; Tashkent experiences snow cover 43 days per year which accumulates to a maximum depth of 11 centimeters. At Krasnovodsk there are only 5 days per year with any snow on the ground at all.

The constancy of the winter weather produced by the Asiatic High is broken up frequently by cyclonic storms that move into the region during this time of year. These generally follow three favored tracks, the south

Caspian, the Murgab, and the upper Amu Darya. As they approach the high mountains, they slow up, and fronts wrap around the mountain spurs and cause many topographically induced occlusions that may stagnate for long periods of time and dump considerable amounts of snow on southwestern slopes at intermediate elevations. On the plains winter weather is relatively cloudy, and every third day experiences a little rain. At Tashkent, for instance, January, February, and March all average more than seven-tenths sky cover with almost half the days experiencing overcast. Rain amounting to 0.1 millimeters

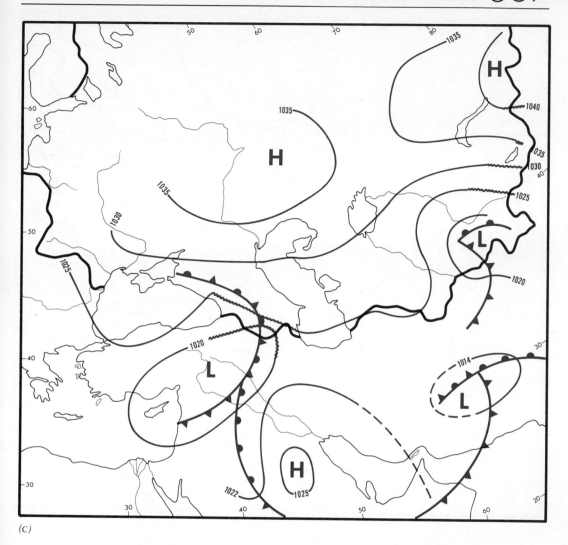

(C)

or more falls 9–11 days per month. Tashkent receives 417 millimeters (16 inches) of precipitation per year, with the maximum amount falling in March. July, August, and September are almost rainless. Most of the Central Asia Region has a March maximum of precipitation. This grades into April toward the north, and in the central Aral Sea area begins to jump toward June as summer thundershower precipitation becomes dominant in Kazakhstan to the north. Few of the Central Asian winter cyclones penetrate very far northward. Most of them die in the high mountains to the south.

Most of the lower-lying intermontane basins have yearly regimes similar to that of the plains, but being more sheltered they are generally drier than the more exposed foothill areas. The city of Fergana in southeastern Fergana Basin receives only 169 millimeters (6.5 inches) of precipitation per year. Of course, the central Kara Kum is even drier.

During summer the Central Asia Region is filled with hot, dry surface air that generally produces a shallow low-pressure system in the southeastern part of the region. Airflows focus toward this region from the north and northwest around the eastern end of the

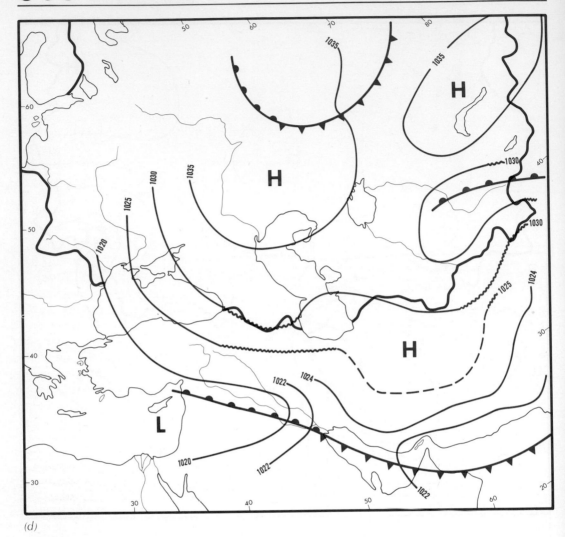

(d)

Azores High. Surface heating raises surface air temperatures to high levels. At Kushka, July temperatures average 27.6°C (81.5°F) and the temperature has risen to 46°C (115°F). Ashkhabad, the capital of the Turkmen Republic, is even hotter. It averages 31.2°C in July and has experienced a temperature as high as 47°C. These are by far the highest summer temperatures in the Soviet Union and are characteristic of much of the plains and lower foothill areas of Central Asia. In the mountains, of course, temperatures drop rapidly. At Tien Shan, July averages only 4.5°C, and the maximum temperature ever reached is 19°C.

There is little cloudiness and precipitation throughout much of Central Asia during summer. At Kushka, sky cover averages only 0.05 during July–September. Precipitation is nil during July and August. Evaporation rates are exceedingly high. The potential evaporation during the year in Kushka totals 1084 millimeters, almost seven times the actual evaporation, which is limited by the lack of water. Relative humidities of the surface air average about 30 percent during June–September. Tashkent has a little more summer cloudiness and precipitation, but not much. Higher mountain slopes may exhibit a seasonality opposite to that of the plains below.

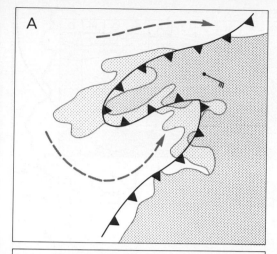

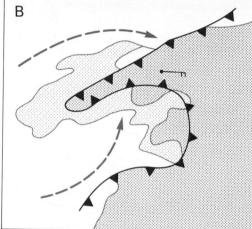

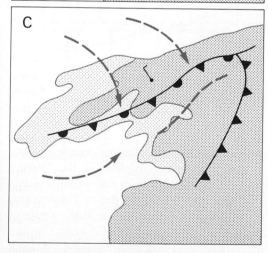

Figure 15-13 Topographically induced occlusion. (A) 1300 hours, 12/4/37, (B) 1900 hours, 12/4/37, (C) 0100 hours, 12/5/37. After Lydolph, *World Survey of Climatology,* **Vol. 7.**

Much of the cloudiness in the higher mountains is due to cumulus buildup during summer. During winter these slopes may be above most of the stratus clouds associated with cyclonic storms.

Local winds abound in Central Asia, as they do in most mountain, desert, and coastal areas. Some of these are well developed and have been given local names. Outstanding are some foehn winds, which are often accentuated by constriction of airflow between approaching storms and mountain slopes. Such winds, coupled with strong thermal activity, keep the surface air and dust stirred up so that there is always a hazy, whitish hue to the lower atmosphere in Central Asia. Repetek averages 69 days with dust storms per year.

Foehn winds generally occur along the advancing edges of cyclonic storms, and therefore are much more developed in winter than during summer. They bring much thawing of snow and even sublimation directly from solid to vapor, keeping cattle pastures open year-round on many of the mountain foothills. There is a saying in the Tien Shan that "two days of foehn are worth two weeks of sunshine." This signifies the favorable effects that foehns have on life in general during winter. Since they usually occur with southerly flow along leading edges of cyclones, the strongest foehns are generally experienced descending northern slopes of mountains. The northern slopes of the Kirgiz Range are so frequented by foehns during the winter that at a height of about 3 kilometers the snow cover is very thin and in some years lies only in patches, while at the same time on the southern slopes of the same range snow cover may be 2 meters or more thick.

An outstanding foehn condition, known as the *garmsil,* occurs primarily during summer in southwestern Tadzhikistan where the air is sometimes constricted between advancing cyclonic storms and the high mountains to the east. These southeasterly winds produce high velocities, low relative humidities, high temperatures, and great amounts of dust. The garmsil in Tadzhikistan has raised temperatures to as high as 47.8°C and dropped rela-

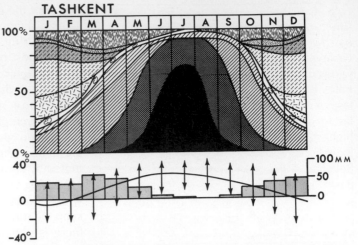

Figure 15-14 Weather types, temperature, and precipitation at Tashkent. For legend, see page 6.

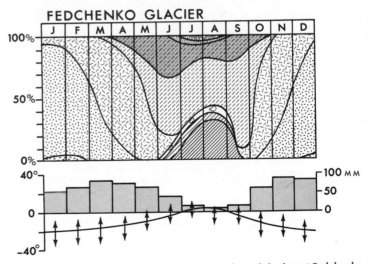

Figure 15-15 Weather types, temperature, and precipitation at Fedchenko Glacier in the Pamirs at an elevation of 5240 meters. For legend see page 6.

tive humidities to 8 percent with wind speeds of 6 meters per second. Under such conditions trees drop their leaves and fruit. Such winds may lower yields of cotton by 20–50 percent after blowing for only a few hours.

Another outstanding foehn wind is the so-called *ursatyevskiy*. This is an east-to-southeast wind that blows with great force through the narrow western throat of the Fergana Basin onto the flat plains of the Hungry Steppe to the west. It takes its name from the railroad junction of Ursatyevskaya, which lies in the southeastern portion of the Hungry Steppe usually directly in line with the winds issuing from the Fergana Basin. These winds occur almost always along the leading edge of the northeastern quadrant of a south Caspian or Murgab cyclone approaching the area from the southwest, and along the southwestern periphery of the Asiatic High, which lies to the northeast during the winter. This general pressure pattern sets up the easterly flow of air that collects in the Fergana Basin, builds up pressure, and then funnels westward through the narrow neck at the western end of the basin. Ursatyevskaya averages 69 days per year with winds of more than 12 meters per second (25 miles per hour). Generally such winds may last for one or two days, but on occasion they last for as long as seven consecutive days. The highest wind speeds associated with these foehns occur above ground over the city of Bekabad in the western throat of the Fergana Basin. Wind speeds as high as 60 meters per second (125 miles per hour) have been observed over this region at a height of 1360 meters above the ground.

Foehn winds of a less spectacular nature flow southwestward down the Chirchik River into the large metropolitan area of Tashkent. All the trees along the river valley lean toward the southwest. Such winds may blow from one to four days on end and cause serious sand storms. These foehns have raised January temperatures to as much as 24°C and dropped the relative humidity to 19 percent.

A characteristic postcold frontal wind is the *Afghanets*. This is a strong, dry wind that generally blows from a westerly direction after the passage of a winter cold front and produces huge dust storms, particularly in the upper reaches of the Amu Darya after crossing the Kara Kum. Dust is sometimes carried to heights of more than 3000 meters and takes 10 days to settle after the winds die down. In extreme cases the winds may last for five days. Electrical phenomena may develop in the air due to static electricity that has built up by friction on dust particles.

Vegetation varies primarily with elevation in Central Asia. On the low-lying desert floors sparse stands of sagebrush and other xerophytic shrubs dot the area with much bare earth in between clumps. In very sandy areas where the surface materials are frequently on the move, little vegetation takes hold. This includes large sections of the Kara Kum and smaller portions of the Kyzyl Kum. One woody plant that is unique to this area is the so-called saxaul tree, which grows to a height of as much as 7 meters in sandy areas where nothing else will grow. This has been very useful in stabilizing sands, but it has also been the chief source of firewood for nomadic herdsmen for thousands of years, and therefore it has been largely destroyed. The wood is very hard, heavier than water, and burns like charcoal. An effort has been made in recent years to reestablish growths of saxaul and protect them from extinction. In spring after the late winter and early spring rains and the thawing of winter snow, an abundance of ephemeral vegetation springs up and causes the desert to bloom for a period of two to three months before it subsides to the summer heat. Many bulbous grasses provide good desert pastures at this time of year.

The desert vegetation extends upward into the foothills to elevations of 1200–1500 meters. However, at these higher elevations, particularly on loess soil, steppe grasses are more prevalent. In the rockier heads of alluvial fans sagebrush may take over. From about 1200 meters to about 2300 meters, depending on the exposure of the slope, mountain broadleaf forests are the dominant vegetation; in places they grow in separate groves among meadow steppes. Persian walnut, maple, apple, cherry, plum, and buckthorn are common. Above 2300 meters coniferous forests, consisting primarily of spruce, fir, and juniper, occupy the slopes up to 2800–3000 meters, above which subalpine meadow steppes prevail. Above 5000 meters little vegetation exists. Many of the higher summits are covered with perpetual snow and glaciers.

The desert soils are typical sierozems that in many low-lying places are salty or alkaline. Broad takyrs, clay pans in playa lake beds, occupy the lowest-lying interior basins between higher sand-dune or rocky upland areas. At the mouths of major streams, particularly the Amu Darya, broad delta and floodplain alluvial deposits provide rich soils for irrigation agriculture. In the southern foothills loess deposits in places reach thicknesses of more than 100 meters. This is one of the great loess belts of the world. The loess has provided the basis not only for a rich agriculture, but also for building materials for adobe houses, clay walls around fields, and all sorts of pottery, tile, and brick work. Thus, the

Figure 15-16   Saxaul trees in the Kyzyl Kum. Novosti.

juxtaposition of rich loess deposits, rivers, and winter snows in the mountains provides the ideal combination necessary for the early riverine civilizations of the area.

In the moister foothills chestnut and even some chernozem soils have developed under steppe grasses on the loess deposits. At higher elevations brown forest soils prevail, and they become more podsolized at higher elevations where the trees grade into conifers and eventually into tundra. Many intermontane basins lying at intermediate elevations contain fertile chernozem and chestnut soils.

WATER, AGRICULTURE, AND CONSTRUCTION PROJECTS

Water is the key commodity in Soviet Central Asia, as it is in most dry regions of the earth. With water the native population can carry on extensive irrigation agriculture; without it they must struggle as best they can with dry farming in the moister areas and with exten-

sive grazing in the drier areas. As has been pointed out, the entire plains area of Soviet Central Asia is dry. Certain areas are moister than others, but none classify as humid. Streams that originate on the plains flow primarily only as spring freshets when the thin snow cover melts. Many of them dry up completely before the summer is over. All end

Figure 15-17   The "fences" around the fields and barnlots near Tashkent are loess walls.

either in one of the three great interior drainage basins, the Caspian Sea, the Aral Sea, or Lake Balkhash, or in some salt-encrusted playa lake bed. None of the runoff in this area reaches the sea; evaporation eventually accounts for all the precipitation that falls.

Perennial streams are limited primarily to those whose headwaters lie in the high mountains and are fed throughout the summer by melting snows and glaciers. The two outstanding streams of this nature are the Amu Darya and the Syr Darya, the two great rivers of Soviet Central Asia that flow northwestward into the Aral Sea. But many smaller streams flow out of the southern mountains, some of which already have been named. These smaller streams, such as the Zeravshan between the Syr Darya and the Amu Darya, and the Sokh in the southwestern part of the Fergana Basin, were utilized most extensively by early civilizations. They did not have the technology to harness the larger streams. The Soviets, on the other hand, have concentrated on the larger streams and have greatly expanded irrigation systems, which now constitute a discontinuous belt along the northern slopes of the Tien Shan all the way from Taldy Kurgan in southeastern Kazakhstan westward through Alma Ata, Frunze, Dzhambul, and Tashkent, and then eastward into the Fergana Basin and southwestward to Samarkand and Bûkhara. Separate districts lie in southwestern Tadzhikistan, along the lower Amu Darya south of the Aral Sea, and in scattered smaller oases along the southern Turkmen Republic from Mary westward through Tedzhen to Ashkhabad and beyond. Northwesterly extensions of this irrigation belt continue down streams such as the Syr Darya, the Chu, and the Ili into south central Kazakhstan (Fig. 15-18).

Central Asia contains about half the irrigated land of the Soviet Union. The specialty crop for which these irrigated lands of Central Asia are best known is cotton. But many other crops are raised that also utilize the long, hot summers and good loess soils. Although the Soviets have forced a continual expansion of cotton acreage in the irrigated areas at the expense of wheat, a considerable amount of irrigated land is still occupied by grain crops,

particularly wheat and rice, the staple foods of Central Asia, and by a great variety of fruits and vegetables. Certain regions are known for their vineyards and winemaking. And recently sugar beets have been introduced into the area rather heavily. Other specialty crops are raised, such as tobacco and kenaf, a fiber crop used in the making of ropes and burlap bags. Not all these crops are scattered throughout the entire region; the physical environment varies from place to place, and individual regions are best suited to certain complexes of crops. Cotton growing is limited to the regions with the longest and hottest growing seasons, which eliminates it from the northeastern slopes of the Tien Shan east of the Talas River Valley around Dzhambul in southern Kazakhstan.

Beginning in the east, the first major irrigation district in Central Asia is associated with the headwaters of the Chu River near the city of Frunze, the capital of the Kirgiz Republic. The Chu flows northwestward into southern Kazakhstan and eventually dries up in the sands. Much of its irrigated agriculture lies within the Kazakh Republic, but the southern portion of the district lies within the Kirgiz Republic. About 90 percent of the irrigated acreage in the Chu Valley is planted with grain crops, particularly winter wheat and barley, but the valley is probably best known for its sugar beets, introduced by Russian and Ukrainian settlers. The Chu Valley has been dubbed "sugar beet valley."

The cotton belt begins farther southwest with the Syr Darya and its many complex irrigation districts. The Syr Darya heads in the high mountains of the southeastern Kirgiz Republic in its major headwater stream, the Naryn. The Naryn flows westward the entire length of the Kirgiz Republic and enters the northeastern edges of the Fergana Basin where it is joined by some other streams to form the Syr Darya. The Syr Darya continues westward through the entire length of the Fergana Basin and cuts through the narrow western throat of the basin to debauch out onto the Golodnaya (Hungry) Steppe, an exceedingly flat alluvial plain southwest of Tashkent. After traversing this flat desert plain it turns north-

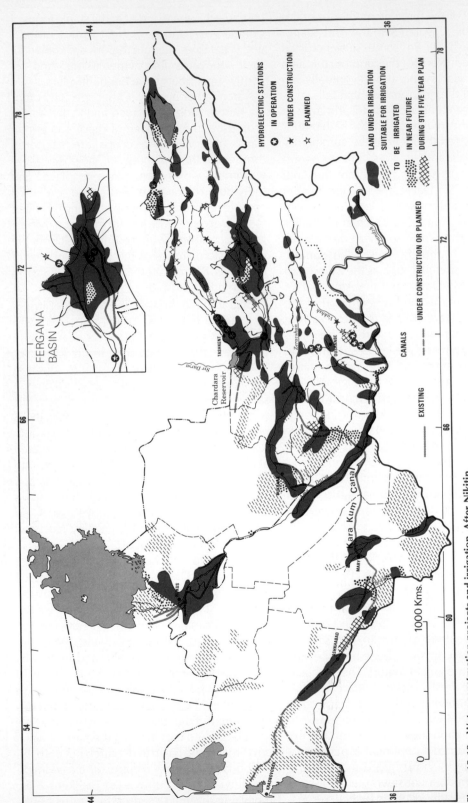

Figure 15-18   Water construction projects and irrigation. After Nikitin,
pp. 250-251.

ward and then northwestward to continue through the southern Kazakh Republic to the northeastern corner of the Aral Sea.

The biggest irrigation district connected with the Syr Darya is the Fergana Basin. Until Soviet times the Syr Darya lay unutilized in the basin. Only small tributary streams, particularly those descending the northern slopes of the southern mountains, were utilized before they entered the Syr Darya. These streams formed large alluvial fans on the valley floor sloping northward, which produced an asymmetrical floor in the Fergana Basin with its lower portions near the northern side. Small dams impounded small reservoirs of water on each of these streams, and irrigation water was allowed to flow northward by gravity across entire surfaces of fans. A classic example of this arrangement is the alluvial fan

of the Sokh River, at the base of which sits the old Moslem center of Kokand (Fig. 15-19).

The Soviets initiated the first major water construction project in Central Asia in the 1930s when they undertook to build the Great Fergana Canal. This became one of the three big construction projects during the early five-year plans, along with the Dnieper Dam in the Ukraine and Magnitogorsk in the southern Urals, held up as symbols of new national strength to capture the imagination of young volunteers to work on the projects during their spare time and on weekends without pay. The Great Fergana Canal was completed in 1939 and ran the full length of the southern side of the basin, consolidating many of the smaller canal systems on individual alluvial fans along the way. The North Fergana Canal was opened in 1940, the Cen-

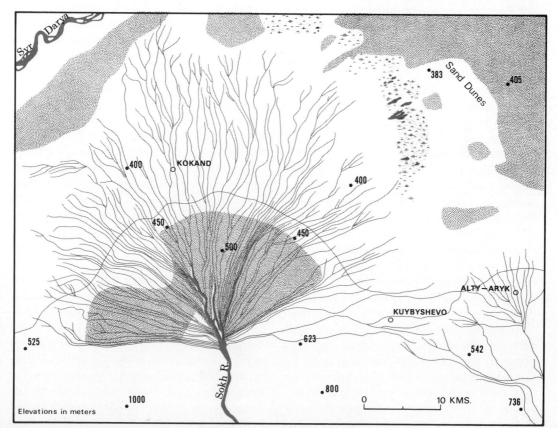

Figure 15-19   The alluvial fan of the Sokh River on the Southern side of the Fergana Basin. The Syr Darya flows westward along the northern edge of the basin. From *Landscape Atlas of the USSR*, p. 125. (Numbers represent elevations in meters.)

tral Fergana Canal, later called the Andizhan Canal, was completed later, and now the Great Namangan Canal is being completed just north of and parallel to the North Fergana Canal. These four major canal systems, with their feeder canals, have provided irrigation water to almost the entire floor of the Fergana Basin. To supply water to these canal systems, a number of dams have been built on the Naryn River and tributary streams. The largest of these installations, completed in the mid-1970s, is the Toktogul Station, which has a power-generating capacity of 1.2 million kilowatts. It is planned eventually to build 22 dams on the Naryn River, with a total annual electrical output of more than 30 billion kilowatt hours. The largest structure planned, the Kambaraty project, with a designed capacity of 2.2 million kilowatts, is supposed to be built sometime during the 1980s. This project involves the unique building of an earthen dam by a direct explosion using 2.5 million tons of TNT.

The main crop in the Fergana Basin is cotton, as it is in most of the irrigated districts of Central Asia, and the second most important crop is alfalfa, which is used in rotation with cotton to add nitrogen to the soil and absorb some of the salts that accumulate through prolonged irrigation. In addition, a wide variety of grains, fruits, and vegetables are grown. Irrigated wheat and barley cover considerable acreages, as does rice, the basic food crop of the region. Around the larger cities vegetables and fruits of all types are grown for the urban markets. Grapes for wine are grown throughout the area. Such specialty crops as kenaf are being introduced. Mulberry trees have been grown for centuries along the irrigation ditches to provide the basis for a silk industry.

At the western end of the Fergana Basin where the noisy Syr Darya rushes through a gorge in the Mogol Tau on its way to the Hungry Steppe to the west, the Farkhad Dam was constructed primarily to provide hydroelectricity to the many industries that were being located in Central Asia, particularly to a variety of chemical and synthetic industries. But it also provided water to expand irrigation in the Hungry Steppe just west of the Fergana

Basin. This was augmented in 1957 by the Kayrak Kum project, with its Druzhba Narodov ("friendship of nations") hydroelectric station that formed a reservoir known as the Tadzhik Sea just upstream from the Farkhad Reservoir. Water for the Hungry Steppe was further increased in 1964 when the Chardara Dam and hydroelectric station (100,000 kilowatts) came into being on the Syr Darya at the downstream side of the Hungry Steppe. In addition to allowing the expansion of cotton land, this provided water for the addition of 200,000 hectares of new rice lands during the early 1970s.

With only a short break, the irrigated lands of the Hungry Steppe continue northward around the large city of Tashkent. Here complex works on the Chirchik and Angren Rivers, tributaries of the Syr Darya, provide water for irrigation and domestic use. Since 1932 sixteen small power stations with an aggregate capacity of 330,000 kilowatts have been built on the Chirchik River alone. A much larger project was completed in 1972 on the Chirchik at Charvak Gorge 70 kilometers northeast of Tashkent. The generating capacity is 600,000 kilowatts, and the Charvak Reservoir expands irrigation and serves recreational needs for the large city of Tashkent. An access railroad and a highway have been built to facilitate its use. More construction projects are still planned for the Chirchik. The irrigated lands around Tashkent extend northward down the Syr Darya into nearby Kazakh S.S.R.

The next large irrigation district lies along the Zeravshan River, which extends southwestward from the Hungry Steppe. This district includes the ancient cities of Samarkand and Bukhara and is the oldest riverine civilization in Central Asia. But the Soviets have added much water and irrigated land to the district. Most recently water has been added to the lower reaches of the Zeravshan Valley by building a major canal system from the Amu Darya just above Chardzhou to the Zeravshan near Bukhara. This allows for the transfer of water from the large Amu Darya to the smaller Zeravshan. This system is still being expanded.

Also, during the last decade another major

Figure 15-20 Orchards, fields, and rice paddies in the Fergana Valley. Novosti.

canal system has been built to alter the use of Zeravshan water. In this case it is a matter of diverting part of the Zeravshan River southward to add water to the new cotton-growing district of the Karshi Steppe southeast of Bukhara. The Kashka Darya runs westward, then northwestward through the Karshi Steppe, and ends shortly south of the Zeravshan, but its limited water resources have been adequate to irrigate only about 10 percent of the irrigable area of the Karshi Steppe. The Kashka Darya water has now been augmented by the Zeravshan water. In addition, in 1973 the first section of an irrigation system was put into operation to divert water from the Amu Darya to the Karshi Steppe. The main canal diverts water from the Amu Darya just upstream from the town of Kerki across the

river from the entrance to the Kara Kum Canal, which leads Amu Darya water westward through the Turkmen Republic. It is said that the cotton potential of the Karshi Steppe is equivalent to one-third of the entire output of the Uzbek S.S.R., the major cotton producer in the Soviet Union. The importance of this new cotton-growing district was signified in 1964 when work was begun on the Amu Darya-Karshi Canal by the reestablishment of Kashka Darya Oblast in southeastern Uzbekistan as a separate political unit to administer the irrigation project.

Southeast of the Karshi Steppe, across the Kugitang Tau mountains, lies the extensive Yavan-Obi-Kiik Upland in southwestern Tadzhikistan. It is dissected by a number of tributaries of the Amu Darya flowing southwestward across the region. The main rivers in this district used for irrigation are the Surkhan Darya and the Vakhsh. The Surkhan Darya provides an old irrigation district that has been added to since 1960 by the building of an earthen dam across the river. This has provided irrigation water for an additional 180,000 hectares in the lower part of the valley just upstream from where the river enters the Amu Darya at Termez. This is one of the warmest spots in the Soviet Union and thus affords the possibility of high cotton yields and second cropping after the cotton harvest. The project was deemed worthwhile in spite of the necessity to flush the generally saline soils.

The Vakhsh River has the greatest water potential of any of the streams crossing southwestern Tadzhikistan. It heads in the high mountains and carries melt water from glaciers and snow fields. In its course down to the Pyandzh it cuts deep canyons with steep gradients. In the Tadzhik language, the word *Vakhsh* means "mad." During the mid-1970s a major construction project was completed on the Vakhsh just southeast of the Tadzhik capital of Dushanbe. This is the Nurek Dam, which is the highest dam in the Soviet Union and has the largest hydroelectric plant in Central Asia. Situated in a deep gorge, the dam is about 315 meters high and 1 kilometer long. The ultimate capacity of the electric plant will be 2.7 million kilowatts. The electrical generation has provided the basis for new aluminum and chemical industries to be established in the area as well as for irrigation of a number of districts in the vicinity. Since level land is limited along the Vakhsh River itself, some of the water is diverted through tunnels under low mountain ranges to adjacent valleys. One of these tunnels, about 8 kilometers long, runs westward through the Kara Tau Mountain Range to irrigate part of the originally arid Yavan Valley, and another tunnel runs southward to the Dangara Valley.

Far to the northwest in the lower reaches of the Amu Darya lies the ancient irrigation district of Khiva, which at present is divided between Khorezm Oblast and the Kara Kalpak A.S.S.R. within the Uzbek Republic and Tashauz Oblast in the Turkmen Republic. This area is hot and dry and contains excellent soils that have been deposited by repeated floodings of the river through the ages. This is one of the main cotton-, alfalfa-, and rice-growing regions in Central Asia and has been for many centuries. The Soviets have added a number of canals to the system to bring additional Amu Darya water to the region and expand the irrigated acreage. One of the most ambitious flood-control and irrigation-construction projects in all of Central Asia was announced in the late 1960s to be added to this area. This is the Tyuyamuyun project on the lower Amu Darya where the river is constricted in a narrow gorge about 600 meters wide. Construction was to have gotten under way during the 1970–1975 period on a series of reservoirs and a spillway dam that would have an associated hydroelectric station with a capacity of 100,000 kilowatts. The dam and reservoirs were to regulate the very irregular flow of the Amu Darya, which does not provide enough water in spring for application before planting or in fall for leaching of salts out of the ground after the harvest. During flood stage in July and August, on the other hand, heavy sediment silts up irrigation headworks. How this project is faring is unknown at present.

The largest canal project so far undertaken in Central Asia is the Kara Kum Canal, which takes water from the Amu Darya upstream at Kelif and carries it westward through the oases at Mary and Tedzhen to Ashkhabad, adding water to ancient irrigation districts along minor streams, such as the Murgab and Tedzhen Rivers, along the way. This was a major undertaking involving the building of a canal through 650 kilometers of shifting sands, which during any windstorm could destroy the work already completed. The Amu Darya carries 250 million cubic meters of silt and sand every year, and 8 million cubic meters enter the canal. Therefore, the canal starts in the form of three wide branches. A quarter of the sediment remains in these branches, and 17 excavating pumps continually remove it. The rest settles in the Kelif Lakes, a series of eight stagnant lakes connected by shallow channels that occupy the old Kelif Uzboy, the bed of an old tributary of the Amu Darya, that has been all but swallowed up by the shifting sands of the Kara Kum. Now that the Amu Darya water has returned to the Kelif Uzboy, life has reappeared on the lakes, which are overgrown with reeds and water plants and swarm with birds. The water plants are a serious problem to the canal. Tractors pull special floating cutting machines through the canal to pull weeds from the bed. This is a very expensive operation.

The canal was completed to Ashkhabad in 1962, and there are long-range plans eventually to extend it all the way to Krasnovodsk on the Caspian. Whether or not there is enough water to warrant this is questionable. Only a third of the Amu Darya water that enters the canal reaches as far westward as the Murgab Oasis at Mary. The rest is lost in evaporation and filtration or is used for irrigation. The canal is also used for navigation by shallow-draft boats, and the Soviets envision its completion to Krasnovodsk as a necessary link in a water system that will run all the way from the Baltic through the Volga system and the Caspian into the heart of Central Asia.

To augment the waters of the canal, new construction projects have been completed on such small streams as the Murgab and Tedzhen Rivers along the way. The Tedzhen River carries 90 percent of its annual flow during spring when the rains come and the snow begins to melt in the mountains. To remedy the shortage of irrigation water in summer, the large Khauz-Khan Reservoir was built on the Kara Kum Canal between the Murgab and Tedzhen Rivers to store water flow from the canal during winter as well as the spring meltwater from the Tedzhen River until it is needed for irrigation along the canal during the summer.

Figure 15-21   The Kara Kum Canal cuts through the sand dunes near Mary.
Novosti.

If the canal is ever completed westward to Krasnovodsk, it is planned to build a spur canal southwestward around the low western end of the Kopet Dag Mountains into the small valleys of the Sumbar and Atrek Rivers in southwestern Turkmenistan, where winters are the mildest anywhere in Central Asia. Then perhaps irrigated citrus and other crops can be grown in this limited area.

Another use of the Amu Darya water has often been talked about, but so far it has seemed to be unrealistic. This is the so-called Great Turkmen Canal, which would lead off water from the Amu Darya near its mouth at the city of Nukus, run southwestward through the old Uzboy System around the southern perimeter of the Ustyurt and Krasnovodsk Plateaus, and go all the way to the Caspian at Krasnovodsk. This was one of Stalin's pet projects, but after his death in 1953 all plans for the project were dropped. Now, with the long-range vision of bringing northern water into the Aral Sea area from the swamps of Western Siberia, talk has been renewed about the Great Turkmen Project. If water is ever brought in from Western Siberia, it might provide the necessary volume to justify the construction of the Great Turkmen Canal. But this is speculative and at best far in the future.

Most of the many water construction projects in Central Asia are primarily or exclusively to serve the purpose of irrigation. There are a few exceptions, such as the high Nurek and Toktogul Dams, which also have the major objectives of producing large amounts of hydroelectricity and controlling flooding. But generally the needs of irrigation are incompatible with those for flood control and electrical generation. Irrigation would require that reservoirs be kept as full as possible for peak use during the growing season, while flood control would require that they be kept as empty as possible for emergency use during sudden high-water stages. Electrical production would require a steady flow through the turbines, while irrigation and flood control would require highly irregular flows.

Although there is some navigation by small boats on the waterways of Central Asia, this is minimal, and navigation can be considered to be insignificant in determining construction projects. The streams and canals all carry very heavy sediment loads that make navigation difficult and necessitate constant dredging even for irrigation and other purposes. In the newer reservoirs in mountain areas, diversion dams usually are constructed upstream from major empoundment dams to trap much of the sediment before it enters the irrigation and flood control reservoirs. Such complicated dam structures render navigation impossible.

In addition to the irrigation agriculture of Central Asia, there are two other forms of agriculture — dry farming and extensive grazing. Dry farming of grain has been carried on for a long time in the moister loessial foothills where annual precipitation averages 250–400 millimeters. During the Virgin Lands Program of the middle 1950s, Russian and Ukrainian farmers were established in extensive state farm villages composed of new single-family dwellings with unpainted clapboard walls and corrugated sheet-metal roofs. These new villages contrast greatly with the native villages of adobe walls and thatched roofs in the older established irrigated districts. Although these new state farms are in hazardous climatic areas where wheat yields are never very high, the farming of thousands and thousands of hectares of new land has provided some of the grain to the Central Asian area that was displaced by cotton during the early part of the Soviet development. Most of these new wheat lands lie in the adjacent Kazakh Republic just to the north.

Some grazing of livestock is carried on nearly everywhere, but it becomes the dominant economy in the drier desert lowlands and in the high mountains where cultivation is impossible. Grazing is poor throughout the drier areas; in many localities it is limited to spring and early summer after the melting snows have produced an abundance of ephemeral vegetation. Thawing and refreezing of the winter snows, as well as ice storms, may form hard crusts of ice over the surface of the plains during winter, making it impossible during prolonged periods for the livestock to reach the grass underneath. On the other hand, in the immediate forelands of many of

Figure 15-22 Women coming with their buckets and yokes to obtain water at the village pump on a state farm north of Alma-Ata. The new rural dwellings of unpainted boards and sheet metal roofs are typical of new single-family dwellings throughout the Soviet Union.

the mountains, foehn winds during the winter frequently produce balmy spells of weather that dispel the snow and provide open grazing throughout the year.

Sheep and camels predominate in the lowland deserts. Camels have been used extensively as beasts of burden in the deserts of Central Asia, particularly along the medieval caravan routes from China to Europe. Such cities as Tashkent and Samarkand were long important as stopover points along the "silk road" between China and Europe, and the camel very early became established as the best means of transport across the Central Asian deserts. Today camels seem to be decreasing in importance; they are no longer seen in the vicinity of the larger cities. Cattle and sheep are becoming the dominant animals, for their meat, and the donkey is the most common beast of burden in the native villages of Central Asia.

The karakul sheep are admirably suited to desert conditions, having originated in the Kara Kul ("black lake") oasis at the end of the Zeravshan River. Karakul are black, curly-haired sheep that are raised for the skins of their newborn lambs, which bring very high prices on the world market. They are raised in various places scattered about the desert, and in the mountains to some extent, but they are concentrated in the Zeravshan area. The Kara

Kalpak A.S.S.R. south of the Aral Sea owes its name to these sheep. The term *Karakal-pak* refers to the large karakul hat worn by the natives in this area. Today factories in Tashkent and in some of the other cities of Central Asia are turning out synthetic karakul cloth.

Sheep, goats, and cattle utilize the desert pastures in winter and spring, but they must be driven to the mountains during the summer. Transhumance is practiced on a grand scale. Yak are grazed in some of the high mountains of the Tadzik and Kirgiz Republics. With the Soviet expansion of cotton growing in Central Asia and its rotation with alfalfa, the grazing industry has been revolutionized by the abundance of large amounts of alfalfa hay. Thus, the livestock industry has been greatly enhanced during the Soviet period. This is particularly true of dairying and beef production.

INDUSTRIAL RESOURCES AND DEVELOPMENT

The mountains of Central Asia are relatively young geologically and are not highly metalliferous. However, some minerals are being mined for local uses. But the big development in the last decade has been the mineral fuels, primarily natural gas and oil, in the desert plains of the Kara Kum. The natural gas is of national significance.

Gas was first discovered in the early 1960s in western Uzbekistan around Bukhara, and by 1963 a pipeline was carrying gas from the major field, Gazli, over 2000 kilometers to Chelyabinsk in the Urals. In 1965 a second line was laid from Gazli to Sverdlovsk in the Urals. A pipeline also was laid eastward to serve the larger cities along the northern base of the Tien Shan and in the Fergana Valley. The pipeline along the northern foot of the Tien Shan has been extended all the way to Alma Ata. By 1966 the Gazli field was producing about 22 billion cubic meters of gas, which rivaled the production in the Ukraine and the North Caucasus. The new city of Navoi was established in the Gazli area and has since been expanded into a major chemical center and thermal electric generating

Figure 15-23   Drying karakul skins. Novosti.

center. The Navoi complex now includes a nitrogen fertilizer plant, a cellulose acetate plant, an acrylic fiber plant, and a cement plant.

In 1966 gas was discovered in the Turkmen Republic across the Amu Darya from the Uzbek fields. The first field to be opened in the Turkmen Republic was Achak, and since then other fields have been opened up in the same area of northeastern Turkmenistan, as well as along the southern border near Mary. Most recently gas finds have been reported near the town of Chardzhou along the middle Amu Darya.

The development of the gas fields along the middle Amu Darya has prompted the development of a gas pipeline system from Central Asia to Central Russia. The first 40-inch line was laid in 1967 from Achak to Moscow. A second parallel line, 48 inches in diameter, was completed in 1972–1973. A third line, also 48 inches in diameter, was being built during the middle 1970s. Also, a fourth stage, a 56-inch-diameter gas pipeline, has been built over a distance of about 450 kilometers from a huge new gas field in southern Turkemia to Khiva in the north where it hooks up with the Central Asia-Central Russia pipeline system. This new gas field, Shatlyk ("happiness") west of Mary, is now credited with having reserves of 1.5 trillion cubic meters, by far the largest field in Central Asia. It began production in 1973 utilizing a Turkmenian pipeline running from the older Mayskoye field, also near Mary, to markets in Ashkhabad and nearby Bezmein where it serves a thermal electric station and a cement plant. In 1974 the Turkmen fields altogether produced 39.3 billion cubic meters of gas, and the Uzbek fields produced 37.0 billion cubic meters. A small amount of the Turkmen gas was produced in conjunction with the oil wells in western Turkmenia, and some of the Uzbek gas was produced in conjunction with oil wells in the Fergana Valley, but most of the gas was produced in the large gas fields already mentioned. In addition, some gas was produced in the Tadzhik Republic south of the capital city of Dushanbe, but amounts there are almost negligible.

In 1974 Central Asia produced almost 80 billion cubic meters of natural gas out of a U.S.S.R. total of 261 billion. The Central Asian production was larger than that in any other economic region in the country. It is planned that the Turkmen fields will increase production rapidly while the Uzbek fields will decline a little. The plan for 1975 was 53 billion cubic meters in Turkmenia and 36.8 billion in Uzbekistan. Although eventually it is envisioned that the Western Siberian fields will outproduce all other fields in the country, it appears that for the immediate future Central Asia will be the primary producer of the country.

In addition to domestic gas production in Central Asia, gas is now being imported from northern Afghanistan through a 250-kilometer pipeline to Kelif on the Uzbek-Afghan border and then to the Tadzhik capital of Dushanbe. The Soviet Union has been importing Afghan gas through this 32-inch pipeline since 1967. It supplies much of the needs of the Tadzhik Republic, along with the local gas production of the area, which in 1973 amounted to about 520 million cubic meters.

Oil has been produced in Central Asia longer than natural gas, but it has never reached the eminence of the recent development of natural gas. The oldest fields lie on Cheleken Peninsula, which until the recent drop in sea level was an island off the east coast of the Caspian. Dug wells date back to the thirteenth century, and drilled wells began in the 1870s. "The Nobel brothers from Sweden were the first foreign capitalists to reach their rapacious paws toward Cheleken." Simultaneously drilling began in the Nebit Dag ("oil mountain") 125 kilometers east of Cheleken. These oil deposits are trapped in

disturbed sedimentary structures associated with the major fault zone that runs northwestward along the edge of the Kopet Dag and continues in an underwater anticline across the Caspian to the Great Caucasus Mountains farther northwest.

The Cheleken and Nebit Dag fields have never been large producers. Until World War II they annually produced 1–2 million tons of oil, which at that time was about 1–2 percent of the country's production. During World War II a small refinery was relocated from Tuapse on the Black Sea coast to Krasnovodsk on the east coast of the Caspian just north of Cheleken, and drilling began in earnest to find deeper and richer deposits in the Cheleken-Nebit Dag area. Consequently, production has expanded there considerably during the last 30 years, and during the late 1950s a newer, richer field was brought into production at the town of Koturdepe halfway between Cheleken and Nebit Dag. Also, production has been developed on Zhdanov Bank under the water of the Caspian about 17 kilometers west of Cheleken, and some small new fields have been opened up southward along the Caspian coast three-fourths of the way toward the Iranian border.

As a result of all this renewed activity, the Turkmen Republic has increased its crude oil production to 16 million tons. Although this is still only about 3.4 percent of the U.S.S.R. production, the expanded production here has been very important to Central Asia, and has necessitated the export of Turkmen oil to other regions of the country. The Krasnovodsk refinery has been expanded several times, crude oil is being shipped to Groznyy in the North Caucasus and to Volgograd in the lower Volga Region, and a second oil refinery is planned to be built at the town of Neftezavodsk (Shagal) about 50 kilometers northwest of Chardzhou across the Turkmen Republic on the Amu Darya. A new refining and petrochemical city is to be built there to produce synthetic rubber, fibers, and plastics out of petroleum products. A pipeline is to be built across the Turkmen Republic from Nebit Dag to Neftezavodsk ("oil refinery"), and eventually it will be extended eastward to the oil refineries in the Fergana Valley. Eventually a pipeline might also bring Western Siberian crude to Neftezavodsk.

Some gas is produced in the Cheleken-Nebit Dag fields in conjunction with oil. A carbon-black plant has been established in Cheleken to utilize oil well gases from Kotur-depe and the Zhdanov Bank to produce about half of the Soviet Union's carbon black.

A little petroleum has been produced for a long time in the southeastern part of the Fergana Valley. A small refinery was built in 1908 in the small town of Alty Aryk near Fergana. This has now been expanded into a major refinery complex, and the town has been renamed Khamza. In addition, a refinery has been built in Kirgili, a northeastern suburb of Fergana. This began operation in 1959. Since then the Kirgili refinery has been expanded, and a nitrogenous fertilizer plant has been added to it. Most of the crude oil being refined by these two refineries near Fergana now comes from the west Turkmen deposits, hauled in by rail tank cars. Their operation will be greatly facilitated by the pipeline when it is finally built from western Turkmenia. Some Western Siberian oil may eventually be refined here. There is also a small amount of crude oil brought in from a few oil wells in the Surkhan Darya valley in the southwestern part of Uzbekistan; they have been producing a little oil since the 1930s.

A few small coal deposits have been found in Central Asia and are now being exploited to a certain extent. These lie primarily in the mountains surrounding the Fergana Basin, in the eastern Tien Shan in the eastern part of the Kirgiz Republic, and in the Surkhan Darya Valley in the southern part of the Uzbek Republic. The best fields by far, and the ones that are producing the most coal, are around Angren near the head of the Angren River valley east of Tashkent. The first commercial coal was produced there in 1942, and since then production has expanded to about 5 million tons per year, which is less than 1 percent of the U.S.S.R. production. It is of subbituminous quality and is rather hard to transport since it crumbles easily. It is utilized only for electric power production and heating pur-

poses. Its further development will hinge on the utilization of the kaolin overburden as a source for alumina. If the technology is successful, the Angren area can become the primary source of alumina for the Regar aluminum plant in the Tadzhik Republic near the Nurek Dam. At present, Regar uses alumina from the Urals.

Central Asia is not self-sufficient in coal by any means. Considerable quantities must be imported from the Karaganda and Ekibastuz coal mines of Kazakhstan and the Kuznetsk Basin of Western Siberia. Among other things these imported coking coals are used in the small steel plant that has been established at Bekabad to serve some of the steel needs of Central Asia. There is no iron ore source for this plant, and the steel is produced from scrap metal and pig iron shipped in from Karaganda and Novokuznetsk. The Bekabad plant produces only about 400,000 tons of steel annually, which meets only 15–20 percent of the steel needs of the Central Asian republics.

About 100 kilometers southeast of Tashkent lie the ore-rich Kurama Mountains facing on the northwestern side of the Fergana Basin. Here copper is found in conjunction with molybdenum, lead, and zinc. The city of Almalyk has become the industrial center of this mining region. A copper-processing complex, established during the years 1961-1970, carries the copper ore all the way from the smelting stage through final copper-rod milling. A concentrator also treats lead and zinc ores. The lead concentrate moves to a smelter at Chimkent in nearby Kazakhstan, but since 1970 the zinc concentrate has been refined in a new plant opened in Almalyk. In 1967 the copper smelter was equipped to extract sulfuric acid from the copper smelting process, and this is now used in an ammonium phosphate plant that treats phosphate rock from the Karatau Mountains nearby in Kazakhstan and ammonia from the Chirchik gas-based nitrogen chemical center. Although the Almalyk operation is far surpassed in copper production by plants in the Urals and Kazakhstan, and the lead-zinc operation is surpassed by plants in eastern

Kazakhstan and other parts of the country, the Almalyk complex has become the major non-ferrous metallurgical center in Central Asia.

Molybdenum is produced in association with copper at Almalyk, and it is also mined together with tungsten north of the Zeravshan Valley in Samarkand Oblast. The tungsten and molybdenum concentrates are refined and manufactured into high-temperature alloys, wire, rods, and other end products at the Chirchik alloys plant northeast of Tashkent, opened in 1956. The Uzbek S.S.R. is now one of the Soviet Union's leading producers of tungsten and molybdenum. The Kurama Range is also a major producer of uranium ore. A major antimony and mercury complex has been under construction since the late 1950s in the Gissar Range in the northwestern Tadzhik Republic.

Most recently several gold lode deposits have been developed in the Kurama Mountains and across the Fergana Valley on the slopes of the southern mountains about 100 kilometers north of Kokand. Gold lodes have also been located in the central area of the Kyzyl Kum desert about 250 kilometers northwest of the chemical city of Navoi. A railroad was built during the early 1960s from Novoi to these gold lodes to exploit a huge open-cut mine under construction there. A miners' city called Zarafshan ("gold bearing") has been erected at the site. Apartment buildings 9–14 stories high, air-conditioned against the desert heat, are planned for the new town, and a 48-inch aqueduct has been completed from the Amu Darya 200 kilometers away to bring water to the gold operation.

The nonmetallic minerals play an important role in Central Asia. Sodium sulfate and other types of salts are being derived from Kara-Bogaz-Gol and processed at the town of Bekdash on the narrow sandy spit on the north side of the entrance to the gulf. Salts are also derived from various other surface lake deposits. In the very southeastern corner of the Turkmen Republic native sulfur has been produced for a number of years at Gaurdak. This, together with the Rozdol deposits of the northwestern Ukraine, produce most of the native sulfur in the country. Of course, native

sulfur does not account for most of the sulfur production in the country, because much of it comes from the processing of pyrites and natural gas. A large sulfur recovery plant based on natural gas went into operation in 1973 in Central Asia at Mubarek in the gas fields of southwestern Uzbek S.S.R. about 100 kilometers south of the chemical center of Navoi.

In addition to industries based directly on mining, Central Asia has been establishing some machine-building industries and light industries, particularly cotton textiles based on locally grown cotton. Such industries will be mentioned in conjunction with individual cities. However, most of the raw cotton still moves to the Central Region of European Russia for processing, as well as to many other cities in other parts of the country. The Soviets have found it difficult to establish factories in Central Asia, because the native groups do not seem to want to work in them. In most cases the establishment of factories in Central Asian cities has meant a large influx of Russians, Ukrainians, and others to staff the factories. This has caused major cities of the area to take on a definitely nonnative look.

CITIES

Tashkent

The metropolis of Central Asia is Tashkent. With a 1974 population of 1,552,000, it is fourth in size in the Soviet Union. Tashkent has served an important historical role since the seventh century as the main stopover point in Central Asia for the caravan routes between China and Europe. It has shared with Samarkand and Bukhara the function of the seat of governmental control over Moslem Middle Asia. In 1865 the Russians took over the area and established a new town outside the old Moslem center. Since that time, and particularly during the Soviet regime, the new city of Tashkent has grown and engulfed the old city, and in the process of transformation many of the old adobe huts have been torn down and replaced by brick and concrete

apartment buildings. But many new individual homes are being economically built by
Uzbeks of adobe bricks made from extensive
loess deposits.

Today Tashkent is a thriving, bustling city of
streetcars and taxis peopled by Russians and
Ukrainians as well as by Uzbeks. It sits in the
heart of a rich cotton-growing area at a
strategic position on the northwest corner of
the Tien Shan around which all transportation
routes must funnel. It has been selected by the
Soviets as the primary manufacturing city of
Central Asia, and machine-building industries and textile industries have been developed to the highest degree. Thus, it serves
more than the function of political capital of
the Uzbek Republic; it is the commercial capital of the entire Central Asia area.

Tashkent sits at a rather low altitude, 500
meters, and has long, hot, dry summers. Its
annual rainfall is only 14.6 inches, and practically all of it comes during the winter. Because the growing season is hot and dry, irrigation is necessary for all agriculture, as well
as for growing trees and lawns in Tashkent.
Small *ariqs,* or water-distributing ditches,
gurgle along both sides of every street in the
city. Often the ditch is a cemented trench
from 1 to 2 feet wide and of about equal depth
running between the sidewalk and the street,
but sometimes it is simply a shallow channel
in the earth that is allowed to wander at will
alongside footpaths.

Although factories and apartment buildings
have been built in Tashkent, many of the
Uzbek residents have maintained much of
their old way of life. The native bazaar is still a
main feature of the commercial life of the city,
as it is in most Central Asian cities. Farmers
bring their produce to the market early in the
morning and spend the day selling their own
vegetables and fruits. As long as the farmer
does not hire someone else to sell his produce
for him, private retailing is not considered to
be capitalistic. The labor forces in the larger
factories are made up largely of Russians and
Ukrainians who have moved into the area.
Thus, there is a considerable racial and social
split between the society staffing the larger

Figure 15-24 An Uzbek woman and boy resting beside
an ariq in Tashkent.

factories and the society carrying on agriculture and much of the retail trade.

An earthquake-proof subway, 15 kilometers in length and containing nine stations,
is now being built in the city. Disastrous
earthquakes in 1966 caused heavy losses in
Tashkent, and reminded the citizens of their
precarious position along the base of the tectonically unstable Tien Shan.

Frunze

Second in size is Frunze, the capital of the
Kirgiz Republic, with a 1974 population of
474,000. Frunze sits on the northern slopes of
the Tien Shan among the headwaters of the
Chu River. It thus lies within a rich agricultural
area specializing in grains and sugar beets. Its
industries are concentrated on machine
building, textiles, and food processing.
Among other things it produces off-highway
dump trucks for construction work. It was
founded in 1878 as the Russian fortress of
Pishpek, and was renamed Frunze in 1926
after a Bolshevik military leader who was
born there. At present, Frunze is one of the
fastest-growing cities in the Soviet Union.

Dushanbe

Third in size in Central Asia is Dushanbe, the
capital of the Tadzhik Republic, with a 1974

population of 422,000. Dushanbe exemplifies the rapid growth of a native village after it becomes the seat of government for a newly established republic. From 1927 until 1961 it was known as Stalinabad, but with the further downgrading of Stalin in 1961 it reverted to its old Tadzhik name. The city sits on the southern side of the Gissar Range of the Tien Shan on the upper portions of the plateau in southwestern Tadzhikistan. It serves as the governmental and commercial center for a relatively rich cotton-growing region, and cotton textiles are its primary industry. Machine-building and food industries also are important. It is destined to benefit industrially from the nearby Nurek hydroelectric project and from natural gas that is being piped in from Afghanistan.

Samarkand

Fourth in size is Samarkand, with a 1974 population of 293,000. Samarkand is situated on the Zeravshan River, the ancient cradle of civilization in Central Asia. The modern city sits on hills of thick loess deposits that cover the remains of many former cities dating back as far as 3000 B.C. During the fourteenth and fifteenth centuries Samarkand served as the center of Tamerlane's far-flung empire, which at times encompassed all the territory from eastern China to the Volga. During this time, many magnificent mosques were built to commemorate important individuals. Ruins of these beautiful mosques still dominate the urban scene, their blue tiles sparkling in the desert sun. Some of the mosques are now being reconstructed out of bricks made from the loess clay in the same manner as the originals. Archeologic excavations are unearthing predecessor cities.

In 1868 the Russians established a new town next to Samarkand; it has grown and gradually engulfed the old city. It might be said that Samarkand at present is a small-sized Tashkent that lags behind Tashkent in transformation by a period of 10 or 15 years. Samarkand still has the native aspects to a much greater degree than does Tashkent, but

Figure 15-25   The tomb of Tamerlane in Samarkand.

as fast as it can be accomplished the native quarters are being torn down and apartment buildings constructed. Some light industries have come to Samarkand, particularly the textile industries.

In 1964 the fabled city was threatened with extinction by flood from a rapidly rising lake that formed behind a huge landslide that had blocked the upper Zeravshan. Only frantic efforts that succeeded in cutting a diversion channel saved the city from certain destruction.

Ashkhabad

Fifth in size is Ashkhabad, the capital of the Turkmen Republic, with a 1974 population of 280,000. It was founded in 1881 as a Russian fortress and was known as Poltoratsk from 1919 to 1927. Ashkhabad sits on the major fault zone at the northern base of the Kopet Dag on the southern edge of the Kara Kum. In 1948 it was virtually destroyed by earthquake. It is in a remote and barren desert area with only a limited amount of irrigation agriculture developed around it. If it were not for its function as the capital city of the Turkmen Republic, Ashkhabad would not have prospered significantly, because it is away from the main activity in Central Asia. It is connected with the port of Krasnovodsk on the Caspian and with the major cities of Central Asia to the east by the Transcaspian Railroad. If it were not for this single lifeline, it would be isolated indeed. Its function as one of the main filmmaking centers in the Soviet Union already has been mentioned. Also, it has some textile and machine-building industries.

As was the case in Transcaucasia and in the Baltic and Belorussian Republics of the northwest, it can be seen clearly here in Central Asia that the function as a governmental seat is of prime importance to the development of a town. Among the five largest cities in Central Asia, four are the capitals of the four republics. Only Samarkand does not serve that function at present. Samarkand, of course, got its start as the center of early civilization and later benefited greatly as the governmental seat of a loosely constructed empire, so in a sense it too might be considered to have grown because of its governmental function.

Other Cities

Eight more cities in Central Asia have populations of more than 100,000, and a number of other lesser cities that have special significance have already been mentioned in conjunction with specific industries. The first four of the next eight cities in size lie in the Fergana Basin. These are Andizhan with a population of 210,000, Namangan with a population of 202,000, Kokand with a population of 147,000, and Osh with a population of 143,000. These old cities have served as cultural and commercial centers of rich agricultural areas for centuries, and in part that is their function today. Their industries are based largely on the processing of local cotton, silk, and a variety of foods.

The next city in size is the famous old Moslem center of Bukhara near the end of the Zeravshan River, which had a 1974 population of 133,000 This is followed by the old oil-refining center of Fergana in the southeastern part of the Fergana Basin, with a 1974 population of 124,000. Next is the city of Chirchik up the Chirchik Valley northeast of Tashkent. It has been made into one of the main chemical and ferro-alloy centers in Central Asia. In 1974 it had a population of 121,000. The last city above the 100,000 mark is Leninabad, the Tadzhik urban center

in the southwestern part of the Fergana Basin. In 1974 it had a population of 116,000. The Fergana Basin is divided politically among the Uzbek, Kirgiz, and Tadzhik Republics on the basis of ethnic groups. An endeavor to keep nationality groups on the correct sides of boundaries, coupled with an endeavor to include mountain watershed areas with corresponding plains at their bases to which they supply water, has made for intricate boundary delineations in the area. The Tadzhik Republic has a narrow, irregular neck of land that extends northeastward into the southwestern part of the basin. Leninabad is situated here in a semiisolated part of the Tadzhik Republic that is cut off from the productive southern part by high mountain ranges. Like the other cities of the Fergana Basin, Leninabad and Fergana are important textile centers.

TRANSPORTATION AND TRADE

In this far-flung area of isolated settlements transportation lines become of utmost importance, and in this arid region the burden falls even more heavily on the railroads than it does in the rest of the Soviet Union.

The streams by and large are unsuitable for navigation. The major streams head in high mountains where rapids and gorges prevent traffic, and when they issue forth on the dry, sandy plains they spread out, become shallow, and divide into many separate, shifting channels with extremely fluctuating levels of flow during different times of the year. There is local navigation on the Amu Darya, but this stream leads nowhere at either end.

Soviet policy since the beginning of the five-year plans has brought about both a great increase in the production and consumption of Central Asia and a strict specialization of crops raised in the area. Both factors have thrown an increasingly heavy burden on the railroads. The fact that these heavily populated irrigated areas are separated from other populous areas of the Soviet Union by wide expanses of steppe and desert, together with the increasing specialization of the agriculture, has brought about some of the longest rail hauls in the Soviet Union. Although the Central Asian republics now produce more than 90 percent of the country's raw cotton, the Central Industrial Region around Moscow still produces more than 70 percent of the country's cotton textiles. Hence, much of the raw cotton of the country must be shipped more than 3000 kilometers to be processed. Also, with the intense specialization in cotton in Central Asia, grain must be shipped into the area all the way from northern Kazakhstan and Western Siberia and from even more removed areas such as the Trans Volga and the Caucasus.

An increasing demand for lumber products associated with the great buildup of industries and cities in Central Asia has greatly increased long hauls of lumber from Western and Eastern Siberia as well as from the Volga and Urals areas. The industrialization of Central Asia has brought about greater movement of coal and petroleum products between different regions within the Central Asian republics. A large volume of trade with regions outside the area has been generated by the total absence of pig-iron production in the Central Asian republics and the inadequate assortment of locally produced, rolled-steel products.

Before the turn of the century, when the interregional trade of the area was largely undeveloped and the bulk of the irrigated acreage was occupied by wheat and other food crops for local consumption, the camel caravan served as the main means of transportation of the small quantities of high-cost goods that were exchanged over long distances. Since that time, interregional trade has increased a hundredfold, and railroad lines have been constructed. The railroads now carry more than 90 percent of the total freight. Until 1906 the Transcaspian Railroad, connecting the towns along the foothills of the southern mountains between Krasnovodsk and Tashkent, was the only railroad in the area, and its only connection with the rest of the country was by ferry across the Caspian from Krasnovodsk to Baku. This railroad served primarily to bring in oil from Baku to fuel-deficient Central Asia and to export raw

cotton from Central Asia westward across the Caspian to European Russia. At that time the Turkmen oil fields around Nebit Dag were producing very little so that the small need for oil products in Central Asia had to be provided for primarily from the Caucasus oil fields. Also, at that time, the cotton export trade in Central Asia was not very flourishing, and much of the cotton textiles that were produced in the Central Industrial Region were produced from raw cotton imported from Egypt, India, and the United States.

Then in 1906 a line leading directly northwestward from Tashkent to Orenburg was completed. This linked up with railroads leading to the west and provided a direct route for increasing shipments of cotton northwestward and grain and lumber southeastward. By the end of the 1920s this Kazalinsk Line, as it came to be known, was so overburdened that new efforts were made to complete the Turk-Sib Railroad to relieve the congestion and at the same time to make possible an increase of shipments of cotton, grain, and lumber to provide for an even more intense specialization of cotton growing in Central Asia.

The Turk-Sib Railroad, running from Semipalatinsk to Arys, had been started in 1912, but it was abandoned during World War I and the ensuing chaos of the civil war and was begun again only in 1927. Finally completed in 1931, the Turk-Sib Railroad provided a link around the eastern end of Lake Balkhash between the cities of Central Asia and the Trans Siberian Railroad in southwestern Siberia. It was built specifically to induce a movement of raw cotton northeastward into newly developing industrial centers in Siberia and to bring about a shift in the supply areas of lumber and grain for Central Asia. Until this time much of the grain consumed in Central Asia was raised in the Trans Volga region, the North Caucasus and Transcaucasia, the Urals, and Ukraine, with only about one-tenth of the grain consumption of Central Asia being supplied by Western Siberia. Also, most of the lumber consumed in Central Asia came from either the Volga area or the Urals. It was hoped that the Turk-Sib Railroad would induce a change in these supply areas so that

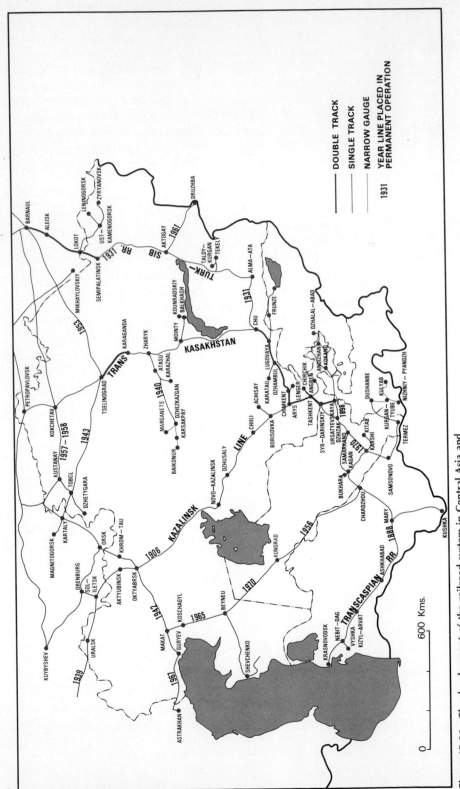

Figure 15-26 The development of the railroad system in Central Asia and Kazakhstan. Updated from Taaffe.

Western Siberia, particularly the Kulunda Steppe, would supply much of the grain needs of Central Asia, and the slopes of the Altay Mountains and the plains of Western Siberia would supply much of the lumber needs. By developing textile industries in the growing cities of Siberia, raw cotton shipment north-westward on the Kazalinsk Line could be reduced, and the shipment of cotton textiles from the Central Region to Siberia over the heavily burdened Trans Siberian line could be halted.

These shifts in interregional trade came about agonizingly slowly, and it appeared for a time that the Turk-Sib Railroad was going to be an economic failure. The production of lumber did gradually pick up in Siberia, however, and the lumber demands of Central Asia grew rapidly as industrialization and urbanization took place. The opening of the virgin lands in southwestern Siberia and northern Kazakhstan since 1954 has greatly increased grain production in that area, so that now the aims of the Turk-Sib Railroad have largely been accomplished, and a new line to the west of it has been built to supplement its function. In 1953 the last link of the so-called Trans Kazakhstan Trunk Line was completed between Mointy and Chu around the western end of Lake Balkhash. This provides a direct route from the new grain-growing areas of northern Kazakhstan and Western Siberia through the area of heavy industry around Karaganda to the major cities of Central Asia. Northern Kazakhstan now fills most of the wheat needs of Central Asia.

Since the early 1930s a number of paralleling and branch rail lines have been constructed either to link major cities more directly or to provide access into new mining and industrial areas. In 1956 a rail line paralleling the Amu Darya was completed from its junction with the Transcaspian line at Chardzhou to Kungrad near the mouth of the river. This provided the first big leg of a second direct all-rail link between Central Asia and European Russia. In the mid-1960s the completion of a rail line from Guryev through Beyneu to the new oil port of Shevchenko on the Mangyshlak Peninsula provided another leg, and the completion of the Guryev-Astrakhan line in 1967 provided still a third. The last, rather difficult, leg across the Ustyurt Plateau between Beyneu and Kungrad was finally completed in 1970.

PROSPECTS

The old civilizations of Central Asia that have fallen within the Soviet sphere seem finally to have submitted to a state of passive acquiescence as the Russians and other Slavic groups steadily flood the area to establish industries and build cities and transportation lines. Although the older elements of the native populations still remain quite aloof from the economic and social revolution that is taking place in the cities within their midst, the young people are being educated in Soviet schools, and the brighter of these students are being assimilated into the inevitable stream of events. No one can dispute the fact that material life is now much better than it was, and it is generally better on the Soviet side of the border than it is among related groups across the international boundaries in the Middle Eastern countries. Little wonder, then, that present generations have lost sight of former fierce struggles against the Tsar and against the Bolsheviks, civil war, and collectivization. It appears that the Moslem cultures under the Soviets are doomed to extinction. What roles the Central Asian peoples ultimately will play within the Soviet framework is still uncertain. High birth rates generally are increasing their proportions within the total population, but in their own republics they are being diluted by heavy in-migrations of Russians and other Slavs.

Economically, Soviet Central Asia will continue to become more integrated with the total Soviet economy, and should play a larger role as its natural gas, oil, and other mineral deposits are fully exploited. It will continue to have a virtual monopoly on raw cotton production, and absolutely all agricultural production will continue to expand as more and larger river construction projects provide for the irrigation of more land.

Some Soviet geographers suggest that a far larger portion of investment should be allocated to Central Asia in the future to provide employment for the large and growing labor resources. Such investment priorities are considered more urgent than the investment in Siberian manufacturing.

READING LIST

- Abdushkurov, T., *Nekotorye problemy povysheniya proizvoditelnosti truda v promyshlennosti Uzbekistana* (Some Problems in Raising the Productivity of Labor in Industry of Uzbekistan), Tashkent, 1970 (in Russian).
- Albitskaya, Kaleriya A., *Kirgizskaya SSR* (Kirgiz S.S.R.), Moscow, 1958, 59 pp. (in Russian).
- Asanov, G.R., "Uzbekistan v devyatoy pyatiletke" (Uzbekistan in the Ninth Five-Year Plan), *Geografiya v Shkole*, 1973, No. 3, pp. 5–11 (in Russian).
- *Atlas tadzhikskoy SSR* (An Atlas of the Tadzhik S.S.R.), Gugk, Moscow, 1968, 200 pp. (in Russian).
- *Atlas uzbekskoy SSR* (An Atlas of the Uzbek S.S.R.), Tashkent, 1963, 53 pp. (in Russian).
- Bacon, Elizabeth E., *Central Asians Under Russian Rule*, Cornell University Press, Ithaca, New York, 1966, 273 pp.
- Batyrov, A., *Selskoye resseleniye v zone karakumskogo kanala imeni V.I. Lenina* (Rural Settlement in the Kara Kum Canal Zone), Ylym, Ashkhabad, 1972 (in Russian).
- Becker, S., *Russias Protectorates in Central Asia; Bukhara and Khiva, 1865–1924,* Harvard University Press, 1968, 416 pp.
- Bubnow, B., *An Assessment of the Mineral Resource Base in Soviet Middle Asia and Kazakhstan: Coal, Iron Ore, Manganese, Oil and Natural Gas,* Master's thesis, Kent State University, 1969.
- *Canadian Slavonic Papers,* Carleton University, Ottawa, Vol. XVII, Nos. 2 & 3, 1975. (Special double issue on Russian and Soviet Central Asia).
- Caroe, Olaf, *Soviet Empire: The Turks of Central Asia and Stalinism,* St. Martin's Press, New York, 1967, 2nd ed., 308 pp.
- *Central Asian Review,* Central Asian Research Center, 66 Kings Road, London SW 3; various issues.
- Coates, W.P., and K. Zelda, *Soviets in Central Asia,* Greenwood Press, New York, 1969, 288 pp.
- Dyker, D.A., "Industrial Location in the Tadzhik Republic," *Soviet Studies,* No. 4, April 1970, pp. 485–506.
- Esenov, Rakhim, *The Turkmen Soviet Socialist Republic,* Novosti, Moscow, 1974, 134 pp.
- Field, Neil C., "Amu-Darya: A Study in Resource Geography," *Geographical Review,* 1954, pp. 528–542.
- *Fizicheskaya geografiya Priissykkulya* (Physical Geography of the Issyk Kul Basin), Ilim, Frunze, 1970 (in Russian).
- Freikin, Z.G., *Turkmenskaya SSR* (Turkmen S.S.R.), Moscow, 1957, 450 pp. (in Russian).
- Frumkin, Gregoire, "Archaeology in Soviet Central Asia. VII. Turkmenistan," *Central Asian Review,* Vol. XIV, No. 1, 1966, pp. 71–90.
- Grousset, R., *The Empire of the Steppes: A History of Central Asia,* Rutgers University Press, New Brunswick, 1970, 687 pp.
- Hostler, Charles Warren, *Turkism and the Soviets,* Praeger, New York, 1957, 244 pp.
- Isayev, A., and M.M. Kartavov, "Kirgizskaya SSR v devyatoy pyatiletke" (The Kirgiz S.S.R. in the Ninth Five-Year Plan), *Geografiya v Shkole,* No. 5, 1972, pp. 8–11 (in Russian).
- Jankunis, Frank J., *Samarkand: An Urban Study,* Dissertation, University of California, Los Angeles, 1969, 231 pp.
- Kolbin, L., *Kirgizskaya SSR* (Kirgiz S.S.R.), Moscow, 1960, 46 pp. (in Russian).
- Leontyev, O.K., and A.N. Kosarev, "Problemy Kara-Bogaz-Gola" (The Problems of Kara-Bogaz-Gol), *Geografiya v Shkole,* No. 6, 1969, pp. 20–24 (in Russian).
- Leontyev, O.K., V.A. Lyubanskiy, and L.G. Nikiforov, "Izmeneniya dinamiki beregovoy zony p-ova cheleken v rezultate vozvedeniya gidrotekhnicheskikh cooruzheniy," (Changes in the Coastline Dynamics of the Cheleken Peninsula Following the Introduction of Engineering Structures), *Vestnik Moskovskogo Universiteta, geografiya,* No. 1, 1975, pp. 92–94.
- Lewis, Robert A., "Early Irrigation in West Turkestan," *Annals of the Association of American Geographers,* September 1966, pp. 467–491.

- Lewis, Robert A., "The Irrigation Potential of Soviet Central Asia," *Annals of the Association of American Geographers,* March 1962, pp. 99–114.
- Lopatin, G.V., *Delta Amu Dari* (The Delta of the Amu Darya), Nauka, Moscow, 1958 (in Russian).
- Luknitsky, Pavel, *Soviet Tadjikistan,* Foreign Languages Publishing House, Moscow, 1954, 254 pp.
- Maltsev, A. Ye., *Zemelno-vodnyye resursy Sredney Azii i ikh selsko khozyaystvennoye ispolzovaniye* (Land and Water Resources of Central Asia and Their Agricultural Utilization), Ilim, Frunze, 1969 (in Russian).
- Matley, I.A., "The Golodnaya Steppe: A Russian Irrigation Venture in Central Asia," *Geographical Review,* No. 3, July 1970, pp. 328–346.
- Mints, A.A., *Srednyaya Aziya* (Central Asia), Mysl, Moscow, 1969, 502 pp. (in Russian).
- Mizan, Central Asian Research Center, London, quarterly. Preceded by *Central Asian Review,* 1953–1968.
- Morris, A.E.J., and Basil Booth, "Tashkent — City of Seven Earthquakes," *Geographical Magazine,* Vol. 46, No. 8, 1974, pp. 409–416.
- Murzaev, E., *Srednyaya Aziya: fiziko- geograficheskaya kharakteristika* (Middle Asia: Physical-Geographical Characteristics), Akademiya Nauk SSSR, Institut Geografiya, Moscow, 1958, 647 pp. (in Russian).
- Nikolayeva, G.M., and G.M. Chernogayeva, "Karty elementov vodnogo balansa Azii" (Maps of the Water-Balance Elements of Asia), *Izvestiya Akademii Nauk SSSR, seriya geograficheskaya,* No. 2, 1974, pp. 88–97 (in Russian).
- Nove, Alec, and J.A. Newth, *The Soviet Middle East,* Praeger, New York, 1967, 160 pp.
- Nove, Alec, and J.A. Newth, *The Soviet Middle East: A Communist Model for Development,* Praeger, New York, 1966, 160 pp.
- *Ocherki prirody Kara-Kumov* (Studies of the Natural Habitat of the Kara Kum Desert), Akademiya Nauk, Institut Geografiya; 1955, 405 pp. (in Russian).
- O'Donovan, Edmund, *The Merv Oasis,* Arno, New York, 1970, 500 pp.
- Pavlenko, V.F., "The Transport-Geography Situation and Interregional Links of Central Asia," *Soviet Geography: Review & Translation,* November 1963, pp. 27–33.
- Rakowska-Harmstone, Teresa, *Russia and Nationalism in Central Asia; The Case of Tadzhikistan,* Johns Hopkins Press, Baltimore, 1970, 325 pp.
- Riazantsev, Sergei N., *Kirgizskaya SSR; ekonomiko- geograficheskaya kharakteristika* (Kirgiz S.S.R.; Economic-Geographic Character), Moscow, 1960, 483 pp. (in Russian).
- Schuyler, Eugene, *Turkestan: Notes of a Journey in Russian Turkestan, Kokand, Bukhara and Kuldja,* Praeger, New York, 1966, 340 pp.
- Schuyler, Eugene, *Turkistan* (edited by Geoffrey Wheeler), Praeger, New York, 1966, 303 pp.
- Semenov-Tian-Shanskii, P.P., *Putishestviye v Tian-Shan* (Expedition to the Tien Shan), Moscow, 1958, 277 pp. (in Russian).
- Sheehy, Ann, "Population Trends in Central Asia and Kazakhstan," *Mizan,* London, No. 3, May–June 1969, pp. 152–259.
- Sheehy, Ann, "Some Aspects of Regional Development in Soviet Central Asia," *Slavic Review,* September 1972, pp. 555–563.
- Sheehy, Ann, "The Tashkent Earthquakes," *Central Asian Review,* Vol. XIV, No. 3, 1966, pp. 261–269.
- Sinitsyn, V.M., *Tsentralnaya Aziya* (Central Asia), Moscow, 1959, 455 pp. (in Russian).
- Skosyrev, Petr G., *Soviet Turkmenistan,* Foreign Languages Publishing House, Moscow, 1956, 231 pp.
- Skosyrev, Petr G., *Turkmenistan,* Moscow, 1955, 293 pp. (in Russian).
- *Soviet Geography: Review & Translation,* June 1968. (Almost the entire issue is devoted to Soviet Central Asia.)
- *Srednyaya Aziya* (Central Asia), Mysl, Moscow, 1969 (in Russian).
- *Strany i narody Vostoka* (Countries and Peoples of the East), Nauka, Moscow, 1971 (in Russian).
- Taaffe, Robert, *Rail Transportation and the Economic Development of Soviet Central Asia,* Department of Geography Research Paper No. 64, University of Chicago, 1960, 186 pp.
- Taaffe, Robert, "Transportation and Regional Specialization: The Example of Soviet Central Asia," *Annals of the Association of American Geographers,* March 1962, pp. 80–98.
- *Tadjikskaya SSR* (Tadzhik S.S.R.), Akademiya Nauk Tadjikskoi SSR, Moscow, 1956, 227 pp. (in Russian).

- *Tadzhikistan,* Mysl, Moscow, 1968, 239 pp. (in Russian).
- *Turkmenistan,* Mysl, Moscow, 1969, 276 pp. (in Russian).
- Ukrainski, F. Ya., "Vozmozhnyye puti razvitiya oroshaemogo zemledeliya Sredney Azii i budushcheye Aralskogo morya" (Possible Ways of Developing Irrigated Agriculture in Central Asia and the Future of the Aral Sea), *Izvestiya Akademii Nauk SSSR, seriya geograficheskaya,* No. 1, 1972, pp. 60–71 (in Russian).
- *Uzbekskaya SSR* (Uzbek S.S.R.), Tashkent Universitet geograficheskii facultet, Moscow, 1956, 470 pp. (in Russian).
- *Uzbekskaya SSR: ekonomiko-geograficheskie ocherki* (Uzbek S.S.R.: Economic-Geographic Studies), Akademiya Nauk Uzbekskoi SSR, Tashkent, 1963, 483 pp. (in Russian).
- Vambery, Arminius, *History of Bokhara,* Arno Press, New York, reprint of 1873 edition.
- Vitkovich, Victor, *A Tour of Soviet Uzbekistan,* Foreign Languages Publishing House, Moscow, 1954, 246 pp.
- Wheeler, Geoffrey, *The Modern History of Soviet Central Asia,* Praeger, New York, 1964, 272 pp.
- Wheeler, Geoffrey, *The Peoples of Soviet Central Asia,* The Bodley Head, London, 1966, 126 pp.
- Wheeler, Geoffrey, *Racial Problems in Soviet Moslem Asia,* Oxford University Press, London, 1962, 67 pp.

The Kazakhstan Economic Region

	Area (km²)	Population	Persons/km²	Percent Urban
Aktyubinsk Oblast	300,000	580,000	1.9	46
Alma Ata City ⎱ Alma Ata Oblast ⎰	105,000	794,000 ⎱ 771,000 ⎰	15.0	100 19
East Kazakhstan Oblast	97,000	862,000	8.9	58
Guryev Oblast	112,000	354,000	3.2	58
Dzhambul Oblast	145,000	843,000	5.8	43
Dzhezkazgan Oblast	313,000	432,000	1.4	77
Karaganda Oblast	86,000	1,211,000	14.1	84
Kzyl Orda Oblast	227,000	524,000	2.3	56
Kokchetav Oblast	78,000	597,000	7.6	32
Kustanay Oblast	115,000	919,000	8.0	44
Mangyshlak Oblast	167,000	199,000	1.2	89
Pavlodar Oblast	128,000	738,000	5.8	53
North Kazakhstan Oblast	44,000	553,000	12.5	40
Semipalatinsk Oblast	180,000	736,000	4.1	47
Taldy Kurgan Oblast	119,000	641,000	5.4	40
Turgay Oblast	112,000	243,000	2.2	28
Uralsk Oblast	151,000	538,000	3.6	35
Tselinograd Oblast	125,000	787,000	6.3	55
Chimkent Oblast	116,000	1,373,000	11.8	39
Total	2,717,000	13,695,000	5.0	52

chapter 16

the kazakhstan economic region

The Kazakh S.S.R. has been established as a separate economic region. It is a poorly defined region because different parts of its vast territory have very disparate types of land, people, and economy. The southeastern part of the republic is part of the irrigated strip along the northern foothills of the Tien Shan, and the economy is much like that of the rest of Central Asia. The northern tier of oblasts is a southern continuation of the chernozem steppe zone that runs through the southern part of Western Siberia, whose economy is based on dry farming of wheat and related crops. In between these two very different types of farming regions lies a broad expanse of desert that, except for mining activities and related urban development, is largely devoid of population and has little in the way of a farming economy other than extensive grazing. In the west the Kazakh Republic includes the eastern half of the North Caspian Lowland with its generally flat, below-sea-level terrain, while in the east are the first ranges of the Altay Mountain system that continues into Western Siberia and China. Thus, peripheral parts of the Kazakh Republic are much more similar to adjacent territories across the Kazakhstan border than they are to each other, and they are separated goegraphically from one another by a large, sparsely occupied desert region.

The republic is not held together by homogeneity of people either. In fact, the Kazakh

Republic does not satisfy constitutional nationality requirements. The Kazakhs are a minority in their own republic. The 1970 Soviet census showed that the Kazakhs made up only 32.6 percent of the total population of the Kazakh Republic, while Russians alone made up 42.4 percent. There is an unusually broad spectrum of other nationality types in this wide, empty land, which never has had well-defined borders and which has always attracted a mobile type of population from the outside.

Although the nomadic Turkic "riders of the steppe" were generally known as Kazakhs at least as early as the beginning of the eighteenth century, they occupied no specific territory, but roamed at will with their herds across the endless steppes east of the Volga all the way to China and did not effectively occupy any territory. Their allegiance was to tribal groups, and they did not recognize any broader nationality relationships. Therefore, the Kazakh area is not a traditional old political region, such as the Ukraine, but is a Soviet construct with little real meaning. As pointed out in the last chapter, for a while during the 1920s there was some confusion as to whether this was to be called Kazakh or Kirgiz. However, since its inception with the so-called Stalin Constitution on 5 December 1936, the Kazakhstan S.S.R. has remained surprisingly inviolate. Only a few minor exchanges of territory have taken place with

neighboring Central Asian republics in the south, particularly the Uzbek Republic, as irrigation districts have been added to or altered.

It appeared in 1960 that the central government might be preparing to split off the northern tier of oblasts to combine them with adjacent Western Siberia. After the opening of the Virgin Lands in the two adjacent territories brought great influxes of Russians, Germans, Ukrainians, Belorussians, and others into the new farming lands on both sides of the republic boundary, a new type of political unit, Tselinnyy Kray, was established to encompass much of the new lands in northern Kazakhstan, which included several oblasts within the kray and did not include any nationality-based territorial unit. However, in short order several other krays were formed in other parts of the republic that also incorporated oblasts, and then in 1965 the kray structure was dismantled and the republic returned to a breakdown directly into oblasts. Thus, at present, the Kazakh Republic consists of 19 oblasts plus the capital city of Alma Ata, which is responsible directly to the republic.

In 1973 the Kazakh Republic covered a territory of 2,717,000 square kilometers and contained 13,695,000 people, for an average population density of 5 persons per square kilometer. Fifty-two percent of the people were classified as urban, which was 7 percentage points below the U.S.S.R. average. The population density of all the oblasts is rather low, but most oblasts cover considerable territory and contain many internal variations. This is particularly true of those oblasts containing large desert areas that are essentially devoid of population and irrigated oases that may have population densities rivaling those of the irrigation districts of Central Asia. The percent of urbanization also varies greatly from one part of the republic to another. Karaganda Oblast, which contains the large city of Karaganda but is too dry for much farming, is 84 percent urbanized, while the farming oblasts in the north generally range from 28–35 percent urban.

The nationality mix also varies greatly from one part of the republic to another. In general,

Table 16-1 Nationality Composition of the Kazakh S.S.R. (Percents of Total)

Kazakh S.S.R.	100.0
Kazakhs	32.6
Russians	42.4
Ukrainians	7.2
Germans	6.6
Tatars	2.2
Uzbeks	1.7
Belorussians	1.5
Uigurs	0.9
Koreans	0.6
Dungans	0.1
Others	4.2

Source: Itogi vsesoyuznoy perepisi naseleniya 1970 goda, Volume 4.

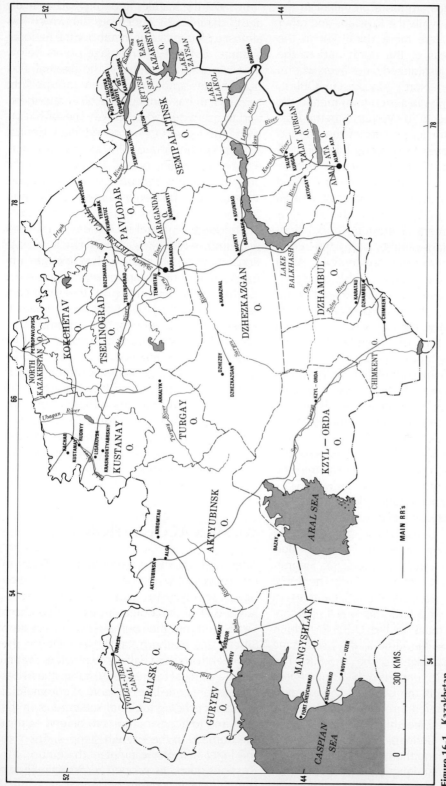

Figure 16-1 Kazakhstan.

the native groups are more prevalent in the southern oases, while the Russians and other Indo-Europeans are more dominant in the dry-farming areas of the north and in the larger, more industrialized cities everywhere. For instance, in North Kazakhstan Oblast, which is primarily an agricultural area in the new lands adjacent to Western Siberia, Russians account for 63 percent of the population, Kazakhs only 15 percent, Ukrainians 8 percent, Germans 7 percent, Tatars 3 percent, and Belorussians about 1.5 percent. In Kzyl Orda Oblast, in an irrigated agricultural area along the lower Syr Darya, the Kazakhs number 70 percent of the total population, while the Russians number only 19 percent. In the southeastern part of the republic, Alma Ata Oblast shows Kazakhs and Russians almost equally balanced, each accounting for about 35 percent of the total population of the region. But in Alma Ata City Russians account for 70 percent of the population, while Kazakhs account for only 12 percent. In the central part of the republic, heavily industrialized Karaganda Oblast shows 51 percent of the population to be Russians, 19 percent Kazakh, 10 percent Ukrainians, and 9 percent Germans.

The Germans are heavily represented throughout much of Kazakhstan and to some extent in parts of Central Asia as well. They are particularly numerous in the new lands of northern Kazakhstan and in some of the more industrialized cities. These are primarily Germans who were evacuated eastward during World War II from the Black Sea Steppes and the Volga German A.S.S.R. The 1970 census showed a total of 858,077 Germans in the entire Kazakh S.S.R. This was 53 percent of all the Germans in the U.S.S.R., which incidentally was the same as the percentage of the total Kazakhs in the U.S.S.R. The Kazakh Republic contains only 53 percent of all the Kazakhs in the U.S.S.R. The Kazakhs are widely scattered throughout the country, particularly in the neighboring Central Asian Republics. The Germans are concentrated in certain places in northern Kazakhstan enough to publish German-language newspapers and operate German-language radio stations.

In 1973 the Kazakh Republic had an average birth rate of 23.2 per thousand, which was almost 6 percentage points above the national average, but 7–12 percentage points below the Central Asian republics. The greater influx of Russians and other alien groups into Kazakhstan has reduced the birth rate there, and the seminomadic Kazakhs never had as high birth rates as the more sedentary Central Asians. The death rate in Kazakhstan was only 6.5 per thousand, one of the lowest in the country, mainly because of the young age structure, due primarily to in-migrants, most of whom are youths in their early twenties. Therefore, the natural increase was 16.7 per thousand, which was almost twice the national average, but again well below the Central Asian republics and somewhat below the Azerbaydzhan Republic in the Transcaucasus. The Kazakh Republic everywhere is experiencing a modest net in-migration. Coupled with the above-average natural increase, this has resulted in a moderate-to-heavy population growth rate during the last 15 years or more. The oil-bearing districts in Mangyshlak and Guryev Oblasts along the northeastern part of the Caspian Sea Lowland experienced some of the highest percentage growth rates of population in the country during the last intercensal period.

RUSSIAN ACQUISITION

After the Russians had subdued the Tatars in the Volga Valley and opened up Siberia, they began seriously to settle the fertile steppelands east of the Volga, across the southern Urals, and into the southern part of Western Siberia and northern Kazakhstan. During the eighteenth and first half of the nineteenth centuries a string of towns were established in this chernozem zone both to serve as commercial centers for the agricultural settlements in the area and to act as outposts to defend against the nomads in the Kazakh steppes. Then, in the latter half of the nineteenth century, the Russians quickly swooped across Kazakhstan into the Moslem towns of Central Asia.

Russian-Chinese Conflict

The Russian drive through Kazakhstan brought the Russians once more into contact with the Chinese, their long-standing rivals in Eastern Siberia and the Far East. The Chinese periodically had exercised nominal control over much of the desert region of Central Asia, in spite of the fact that local uprisings largely prevented continuously effective control from the central Chinese government. The Chinese formed only a small minority of the population in the region. Practically all of the population in the area, including the Ili and Dzungarian districts east of Lake Balkhash in the Tarim Basin, was of Turkic origin. About three-quarters of the population was made up of so-called Uighurs, Turkic Moslems who apparently had migrated into the area from the Mongolian Plateau sometime during the eighth or ninth century. Kazakhs, Kirgiz, and Uzbeks made up much of the rest. Only about 5 percent of the population in this district was Chinese, and that was largely made up of the so-called Dungans, Chinese Moslems who felt little if any common bond for the Chinese proper. The small minority of Chinese officials who were located in the area were greatly hated by the national groups. The Chinese had never attempted to settle the area but tried to maintain control in order to exact tribute through local chieftains.

The high point of Chinese influence in this area was reached under the Ching Dynasty in the latter half of the eighteenth century when Dzungaria and Kashgaria were united into the New Dominion, translated as Sinkiang. During this period the khanates of Kokand and Bukhara, as well as many of the Kazakh hordes, submitted to Chinese influence. However, as the Russian drive got under way during the following century it became evident that the corridors of the Ili Valley and the Dzungarian Gate, through which Genghis Khan and his hordes swept westward in the thirteenth century, were less than one-third as far away by camel ride from the outposts of Russian civilization in southwestern Siberia as they were from China proper. Through a series of treaties drawn up between Russia and China between 1860 and 1881, a division of ancient Turkestan was effected between these two great powers. The resulting international boundary divided people of common ethnic, cultural, and religious characteristics. The Kazakh nomads who had wandered across the region freely with their flocks and herds in the past suddenly found themselves confronted with an international boundary. The half million Kazakhs in the Ili Kazakh Autonomous District of the Sinkiang Uighur Autonomous Region undoubtedly have been the most dynamically rebellious element of the population ever since.

Although the Russian-Chinese boundary set in the late 1800s has not changed significantly since, the Russians have not abandoned designs upon adjacent parts of Chinese territories. Throughout the first half of the twentieth century the Chinese were experiencing internal difficulties, and the Russians were on the offensive in the area. This offensive was largely an economic one, although the Russians did not shy away from political advantages when the opportunities presented themselves. Shortly after the establishment of the international boundary in the 1880s, the Russian government, eager to secure its position against the nomads as well as the Chinese, settled 15,000 crop-cultivating Cossacks in Dzungaria and Ili districts. The Kazakh nomads were very resentful that their best grasslands had been occupied and that their nomad routes of transhumance from summer to winter pastures had been cut. Bloody uprisings were staged against the Russians, and when the Russian Revolution occurred many of the Kazakhs joined the Bolsheviks hoping that their own cause would be benefited. It soon became evident to the Kazakhs that this was not the case, and 100,000 Kazakhs sought asylum in Sinkiang.

It was quite evident that on the eve of World War I Russia had been seriously intending to annex Dzungaria, but the chaos of war, and internal difficulties within China, allowed Sinkiang to live for several years as a semi-independent state under a local Chinese governor. The relative calm ended in 1931 when China sent in a mass migration of thousands of

Chinese, and the native Dungans revolted against the local Chinese administration. Turkic-speaking Moslems in the area, indirectly supported by the British, proclaimed a Republic of East Turkestan. The local Chinese governor, who had been very pro-Soviet throughout the 1920s, called on the Soviet Union for assistance to put down the revolt, and it was jointly crushed in 1934. Shortly thereafter the Soviets backed a local coup, and from then on they became the dominant political and economic force in the region. They followed up their advantage very quickly with the establishment of theaters, libraries, and other institutions that became centers for the dissemination of communist propaganda. An intense Sovietization drive was underway. At the same time Stalin was pursuing an all-out drive for collectivization that was generally playing havoc with the Kazakh population on the Soviet side of the boundary. It appears that between 1926 and 1939 the Soviet Kazakhs declined from about 4 million to around 3 million people. It appears that at least 250,000 Kazakhs moved south and east with their herds and flocks, some going over the mountains into India while others attempted to settle in Chinese territory.

The pro-Soviet Chinese governor in Sinkiang allowed the Soviets to establish military bases in Sinkiang and to monopolize the exports of Sinkiang's raw materials. However, in 1942, when it looked as though the Soviet Union was going to lose World War II to the Germans, the Chinese governor in Sinkiang did an about-face and began a massive purge of the communists in the area. The Soviets began a retaliation after World War II, but in 1949 the Chinese communists came into power, and a major Chinese force marched into Sinkiang to occupy the territory. In deference to their "communist brothers," the Soviets pulled out of the region, and the Chinese communists have proved their ability to exercise tight control over the area ever since. Since the Chinese communists have taken over the area, population movements largely have been in the opposite direction; Kazakhs, Uighurs, and Dungans have been

fleeing westward into the Soviet Union to escape the bloody reprisals of the new Chinese regime.

PHYSICAL LANDSCAPE

Landform

The two structural troughs of Central Asia continue northward through Kazakhstan and continue northward into European U.S.S.R. and Western Siberia on either side of the Urals. These are the Caspian Basin on the west and the Turanian Lowland in the center. In Kazakhstan they are separated by a southerly extension of the Urals, the Mugodzhar Upland, in the north and the northwestern part of Ustyurt Plateau in the south. East of the Turanian Lowland lies the Kazakh Hillocky Upland, which merges eastward into the Altay.

In the west, the Kazakh Republic includes the eastern half of the North Caspian Lowland, a flat part of the Pleistocene lake bed that wraps itself around the northeastern end of the Caspian Sea. This flat, dry plain slopes gently toward the Caspian and for the last 100–150 kilometers lies below sea level. It is crossed from north to south by the small, sluggish Ural River, which heads in the dry southern Urals, and from northeast to southwest by the Emba River, which has its meager headwaters in the Mugodzhar Upland and generally does not have enough flow to reach the Caspian Sea. Other small streams head to the north and northeast and flow partway into the lowland before they dry up completely. Most of these flow only as spring freshets during the thawing period. The only topographic features of any note on the plain are a number of broad, shallow dome structures produced by salt plugs beneath the surface that have not compacted as much as the sediments around them. These have provided traps for petroleum to form the Emba oil fields around the mouths of the Emba and Ural Rivers. A number of autoprecipitating salt lakes occupy portions of the plain.

The Caspian Lowland ends on the south against the faulted structure of the Mangyshlak Peninsula, which consists of two or

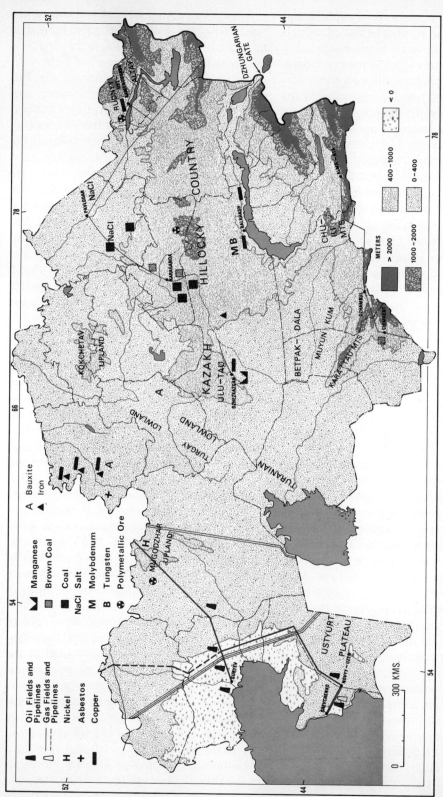

Figure 16-2 Landform, minerals, and pipelines.

three steep-sided horsts and intervening grabens. The central portion of this plateau is known as the Kara Tau ("black mountain"). Highest elevations reach 556 meters. Down-dropped blocks on the southwest and southeast lie 132 meters and 70 meters below sea level, respectively. The below-sea-level depression on the southeast then rises southeastward across a cliff 340 meters above sea level onto the Ustyurt Plateau.

The Ustyurt Plateau is a broad, flattish upland composed of nearly horizontally lying strata and fringed by fault zones on all sides. The western part lies in the Kazakh Republic, the eastern part in the Uzbek Republic, and the southern fringe in the Turkmen Republic. The bounding cliffs are generally known as "chinks." In a number of places these chinks descend into below-sea-level depressions. On the east they overlook the Aral Sea in a scarp that is about 200 meters high in the south but descends to a height of about 25 meters in the north. North of the Ustyurt Plateau lies a lowland about 250 kilometers wide, north of which rises the Mugodzhar Upland, a peneplain surface surmounted by monadnock ridges that reach a maximum elevation of 657 meters.

East of the Ustyurt and the Mugodzhar Upland lie the central and northern portions of the Turanian Lowland. The central portion is occupied by the Aral Sea and a broad, flat plain surrounding it. As mentioned before, the Aral ("island") Sea is a shallow body of water interspersed with thousands of small mud islands, from which the sea gets its name. Along the northeastern shore of the sea is the extensive delta of the Syr Darya. Along the northwestern coast extending northward for about 100 kilometers are the Bolshiye ("big") and Malyye ("little") Barsuki, elongated sand ridges oriented south-north.

About 200 kilometers north of the Aral Sea, the Aral basin narrows into a structural trough that continues northward between the foreland of the Urals in the west and the westerly extensions of the Kazakh Hillocky Country in the east. This trough is known as the Turgay Lowland after the Turgay River that heads along its middle slopes and flows southward to end in a brackish pool of water in the desert northeast of the Aral Sea. It is also known as the Turgay Tableland, because the trough is occupied by flat-topped mesa and butte remnants of a formerly higher surface that has been stripped by much larger volumes of water that probably poured southward through the lowland during the Pleistocene. In between the mesa and butte uplands the valley floor is occupied by elongated sand dunes and stagnant pools of water. The divide in the Turgay Lowland, between the southward-flowing Turgay River and the northward-flowing Ubagan, lies about 150 meters above the Aral and West Siberian basins to the south and to the north. Thus, any plans to utilize the Turgay Lowland as a spillway for diverting some of the northward-flowing waters from the West Siberian Lowland southward into the desert will have to take into account that the water will have to be pumped up 150 meters over the divide.

The northeastern quadrant of Kazakhstan is occupied primarily by the Kazakh Hillocky Country. This old, worn-down area is part of the Urals-Tien Shan geosynclinal belt that has reached relative stability in its northwestern and central portions, but is still quite active in the southeast. It is a rough, eroded upland with dome- and conical-shaped summits that here and there are aligned in ill-defined ridges running essentially west-east. Its highest portions lie south and east of Karaganda where a maximum elevation of 1565 meters is reached. The Nura River rises on the northeastern edge of this upland and flows westward through Karaganda to its terminus in Lake Tengiz, which lies in a structural depression in the west-central portion of the upland. The Ishim River rises in this upland basin and flows westward and then northward to the Irtysh and eventually to the Ob. This basin is fringed on the southwest and the north by higher outliers of the Hillocky Upland. In the southwest the Ulutau Mountains rise to a maximum elevation of 1133 meters, and in the north the Kokchetav Upland rises to a maximum elevation of 947 meters. Northeast of the Hillocky Upland lies a broad, flat plain through which the Irtysh River flows northwestward. The plain continues eastward across the Kazakhstan boundary into Altay Kray of Western Siberia.

South of the Kazakh Hillocky Country stretches a broad desert plain before the land rises again into the high mountains in the south. The western part of this plain is occupied by the Betpak Dala ("evil, perilous plain"), so named because of its many mirages during the heat of the summer days. This is an expansive, flat, utterly dry plain devoid of any streams; it can be utilized only for extensive grazing. It is bordered on the south by a conspicuous scarp overlooking the Chu River, which flows northward out of the Kirgiz Mountains and then turns westward along the base of the southern scarp of the Betpak Dala to end in a stagnant pool within a sandy depression. On the west the Betpak Dala is bounded by the valley of the Sary Su River, which flows southward out of the Ulutau to end in the same structural depression as the Chu River. South of the Chu River lies a broad, sandy desert reminiscent of the Kyzyl Kum and Kara Kum deserts farther southwest in Central Asia, except on a smaller scale. This is known as the Muyun Kum. The Talas River flows northward from the Kirgiz Mountains through the city of Dzhambul to end eventually in the sands of the Muyun Kum.

In the east the desert plain is occupied by a structural basin, along the northern borders of which lies the large Lake Balkhash and its eastern extensions, Lakes Sasykkol and Alakol within the Soviet Union and Lake Ebi-Nur in China. The surface level of Lake Balkhash at 342 meters above sea level lies considerably higher than that of the Aral Sea, which lies only 53 meters above sea level, or the water level of the Caspian, which lies 28 meters below sea level. The lake basin is being pinched along its southern side by the continual growth of large alluvial fans that are being built by the rivers flowing out of the high mountains along the U.S.S.R.-Chinese border northwestward into the lake. The largest of these rivers by far is the Ili, which heads in a major range of the Tien Shan in the Sinkiang Uighur Autonomous Region of China and flows westward through a deep graben between high mountains in southeastern Kazakhstan in the vicinity of Alma Ata on the south and the Dzungarian Alatau Mountains on the north. Several smaller streams flow into the lake farther east, particularly the Karatal, the Aksu, and the Lepsy.

During Pleistocene times Lake Balkhash was considerably more extensive and included the smaller lakes to the east in one water body that extended all the way into China. As the water level dropped and the streams built alluvial fans farther and farther toward the north, the eastern part of the lake was segmented into separate pools of water. One of the distributary channels of the Ili River delta has built a sand spit about three-quarters of the way across Lake Balkhash in the central portion of the present lake. The great amount of fresh water poured into the western end of the lake by the Ili River keeps the western half of the lake fairly fresh, fresh enough for drinking and irrigation, but the eastern half of the lake has a negative water balance that is replenished from the western half through the narrow strait in the central portion of the lake. Therefore, the eastern half of the lake acts as the final evaporation pan for much of the water of the entire lake and is quite salty.

The southeastern boundary of the Kazakh Republic generally follows the crests of some of the major mountain ranges forming the bold northern escarpment of the Tien Shan, and therefore many of the northern slopes of the high mountains lie within the republic, as do certain ranges branching out from the main mass of the mountains toward the northwest. The most westerly mountain range in the Kazakh Republic is the Kara Tau, which branches northwestward between the Syr Darya on the west and the Talas River on the east. This is a fault block range with its higher scarp facing northeastward. Its highest elevation lies in the center of the range 2176 meters above sea level. The range is composed of gray somber shales, limestones, and sandstones that are barren of vegetation and form prominent cliffs on the eastern side. East of the Kara Tau, the Kazakhstan boundary follows the crest of the Kirgiz range, which reaches elevations of more than 4000 meters. The border then turns northward to cross the lower portions of the alluvial fans formed by the Chu River in the vicinity of the Kirgiz capital of Frunze, and then continues eastward along the crest of the Kungey Alatau, north of Issyk Kul. Another branch range trends northwestward from this area between the Chu River on the west and the Ili River on the east. This is the Chu-Ili Range, which reaches a maximum elevation of 1294 meters and then lowers northward to merge with the Betpak Dala west of Lake Balkhash.

The Kazakh border continues eastward south of Alma Ata into the high glacier-covered mountain knot on the border of the Kirgiz and Kazakhstan Republics with China where the second highest peak in the Soviet Union, Pobeda Peak, reaches an elevation of 7439 meters on the Kirgiz side. Here the border turns northward to cross the upper Ili Valley and rises again into the Dzungarian Alatau where a maximum elevation of 4464 meters is reached, and then northeastward across the Dzungarian Gate, a fault graben that has formed a narrow low-level pass through the high mountains that presents the only complete break in the mountain chains between the U.S.S.R. and China. The Dzungarian Gate has been the main outlet from western China to the Middle East and Europe ever since the early caravan days. Northeast of the Dzungarian Gate the border rises again into the Tarbagatay Mountains where a maximum elevation of 2992 meters is reached, and then descends into the broad graben that is the site of Lake Zaysan on the upper Irtysh River. Northeast of that begin the Altay Mountain ranges. Within the Kazakh Republic, the Altay reaches elevations as high as 3373 meters.

Climate, Vegetation, and Soils

The climate throughout Kazakhstan is very continental: relatively hot in the summer, relatively cold in the winter, and relatively dry. Of course, the summers are hottest in the south and the winters are coldest in the north. In the south, Kzyl Orda along the lower Syr Darya has July temperatures that average

24.6°C and has experienced a temperature of 46°C (115°F). January temperatures average −9.6°C, and a minimum temperature of −38°C (−37°F) has been experienced. In the north, Kustanay has July temperatures that average 20.4°C with a maximum temperature of 42°C. January temperatures average −17.8°C, and an absolute minimum of −51°C (−60°F) has been experienced.

There is a general decrease in precipitation southward, although precipitation varies somewhat with topography. In the north Kustanay averages 268 millimeters (11 inches) per year, while in the south Kzyl Orda averages 114 millimeters. Karaganda at an elevation of 537 meters in the Kazakh Hillocky Country gets a little more precipitation, 273 millimeters per year, and Alma Ata at an elevation of 848 meters in the mountain foothills of the southeast receives 581 millimeters per year. However, the entire republic, except perhaps a few spots in the Altay and the Tien Shan, has an arid climate. It is steppe to semi-desert in the northern tier of oblasts south to about the 48th parallel, and south of that is desert.

Perhaps the most striking change in the climate throughout the republic is the shift in season of maximum rainfall from late winter to spring in the south, associated with the winter cyclonic storms of Central Asia, to midsummer in the north, associated with the convective activity of the East European and Western Siberian plains. The shift takes place rather abruptly between Kzyl Orda and Balkhash, between the 45th and 47th parallels, where both seasonal influences can be seen and the season of maximum precipitation bounces back and forth over a narrow zone before changing to one regime or the other. Kzyl Orda shows a definite winter maximum. From December through April each month averages 13–15 millimeters of precipitation, while June through September average 3–5 millimeters. Balkhash is in the transitional zone where monthly averages do not display any coherent pattern. From January to December the monthly averages are as follows: 10, 8, 10, 11, 9, 19, 11, 9, 4, 8, 9, 12. Although June is decidedly the wettest month of the year, or more accurately, the least dry month of the year, other months are not arranged around it symmetrically. Figures 16-3 and 16-4 illustrate this changeover very nicely. Much of the northern half of Kazakhstan experiences a July maximum of precipitation. The precipitation often diminishes through August and September and then increases a little again in late autumn and early winter.

Winters in Kazakhstan are definitely rigor-

ous. The north-central portion of the republic is often occupied by the western nose of the Asiatic High with its cold, relatively calm conditions. However, storms sweep across the entire width of Kazakhstan frequently during the winter and bring blizzards to the barren, windswept plains. In the north snow lies on the ground about 150 days of the year and reaches a maximum depth of 24–30 centimeters (1 foot). It drifts very unevenly on the ground. In the south snow lies on the ground

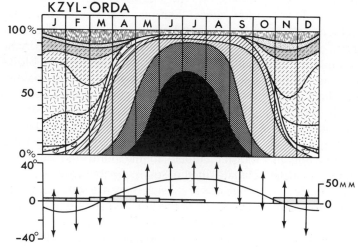

Figure 16-3   Weather types, temperature, and precipitation at Kzyl Orda. For legend see page 6.

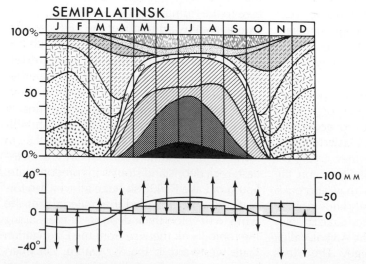

Figure 16-4   Weather types, temperature, and precipitation at Semipalatinsk. For legend see page 6.

about 60 days per year and reaches a depth of only 6 centimeters. In the southern foothills, Alma Ata has snow on the ground 111 days per year with a maximum depth of 31 centimeters. Along the east Caspian coast, Fort Shevchenko has snow on the ground only 18 days per year with a maximum depth of only 4 centimeters. Throughout much of the southern half of Kazakhstan brief midwinter thaws, associated with northward-moving cyclones, followed by renewed outbreaks of cold air from the north cause ice encrustations on the surface that may severely hamper winter grazing and cause hazardous road conditions. Glaze ice has always been a problem for the nomadic herdsmen of Kazakhstan.

In the high mountains of the south and east local wind regimes become important. Foehn winds are most prevalent, and they have great significance to winter grazing in the foothills and avalanche occurrences in the mountains. By far the best known foehns throughout the entire Soviet Union are those blowing in either direction through the Dzungarian Gate east of Lake Balkhash between the Soviet Union and China. The Dzungarian Gate, oriented in a north-northwest–south-southeast direction, is a narrow, flat-floored, steep-sided, downdropped, graben between high mountains on either side. At its narrowest point near Lake Zhalanashkol it is only 10 kilometers wide. The town of Zhalanashkol has strong winds 100 days per year with maximum velocities reaching 70 meters per second (about 150 miles per hour). January and December are the windiest months, with strong winds about 18 days during each month. Often after temperatures have been hovering around −20 or −30°C, the foehn winds cause thaws to occur and clouds to dissipate. The southeasterly winds are the best known because they create intense, broad-scale foehn conditions on the Soviet side of the border as they approach Lake Alakol. These are generally known as the *ibe* because they blow out of the Lake Ebi-Nur region. Local inhabitants in the Alakol Valley call these storm winds the *evgey*. The winds that blow from the northwest across Lake Alakol into the Dzungarian Gate are known as the *saykan*.

Winds blow through the Dzungarian Gate as if they were blowing through a wind tunnel. During the late 1950s and early 1960s when a railroad was being laid through the pass to the Chinese border weather records showed that wind gusts reached peak speeds of 80 meters per second (about 175 miles per hour). The meteorological station had to be built especially to withstand such winds, and the observation tower had to be tied down to the station with cables so that it would not blow away. During such winds, not only snow and sand are lifted into the air, but also light gravel. Visibility is reduced to zero. Miserable as the winds are while they are blowing, after they subside they produce balmy, sunny winter days over broad areas of pastureland east of Lake Balkhash.

The vegetation and soils of Kazakhstan lie primarily in east-west zones that reflect the moister climate in the north and the drier climate in the south. In the very northern fringe of Kazakhstan there are some southerly extensions of the wooded steppe that lies to the north in Western Siberia. But much of the southern half of Kazakhstan is made up of open-steppe and semidesert country, with chernozem soils reaching southward to about the 50th parallel, beyond which the drier climate and sparser grasses have been conducive to the formation of chestnut soils, which extend southward to about the 48th parallel. The southern part of Kazakhstan is much like Central Asia. The vegetation and soils are desert types. Ephemeral grasses and herbaceous plants cover the desert floors for short times after the late winter and spring rains. In some of the hillier parts of the Kazakh Hillocky and Mugodzhar Uplands, as well as in some of the mountain foothills in the southeast, rock debris and stony soils predominate. South of Lake Balkhash huge alluvial fan formations have provided the materials for the wind to develop thick deposits of loess along the foothills all the way from the Dzungarian Gate westward to the Syr Darya. On intermediate slopes of the alluvial fans wind work has created sand-dune areas. These are most extensive in the Muyun Kum between the Chu and Talas Rivers.

AGRICULTURE

As of 1970, only 15.4 percent of the territory of the Kazakh Republic was considered arable. Desert and mountain pastures occupied 80.6 percent, and the rest consisted of desert and mountain areas that were not even suitable for pasturing. For the republic as a whole, grain occupied 73.2 percent of the arable land, and wheat alone occupied 56.4 percent. Fodder crops, particularly alfalfa, occupied 24.8 percent, and the remaining 2 percent was occupied by technical crops such as cotton, sugar beets, sunflowers, flax for seed, grapes, melons, potatoes, and a variety of vegetables.

There is much areal variation of crops. In the south lie extensive areas of irrigated agriculture adjacent to those of Central Asia. Most of the irrigated land in the Kazakh Republic has too short a growing season for cotton, which is limited to the Talas Valley around Dzhambul and Chimkent and to pockets of cultivated land southwestward toward Tashkent. Much of the irrigated land along the northern foothills of the Tien Shan, ranging from Dzhambul through the capital city of Alma Ata and northeastward to Taldy Kurgan, is in grain and sugar beets plus a variety of fruits and vegetables. Many apple orchards have been established around Alma Ata, which, according to the Soviets, is the area of origin of the apple. Tobacco is also a specialty crop in many of the oases. Along the lower Syr Darya vast rice plantations have been established. Agricultural aviation is used to plant, fertilize, and dust the crops over the flooded ricefields that stretch for hundreds of kilometers along the river. The Soviets say that the total length of all the canals in this irrigated rice district would equal the length of the equator.

In between the irrigated oases in the south, the fertile soils of the loess belt are occupied by dry-farmed grain wherever the precipitation is sufficient. Some of this land was included in the Virgin Lands Program of the middle 1950s, and large state farms were established at that time. Wheat occupies by far the greatest portion of these lands, although some barley is grown.

The other crop area lies in northern Kazakhstan where precipitation becomes sufficient for the dry farming of wheat, barley, and a smattering of other crops, such as sunflowers and flax grown for linseed oil. Cultivation in this area extends southward to the city of Karaganda in the Kazakh Hillocky Country, but generally it does not extend quite that far south in the lowlands on either side. Selected portions of this steppe region had been cropped since the Russian settlement of the region in the eighteenth and nineteenth centuries, particularly in the more humid northern fringe bordering on Western Siberia. But the bulk of the territory came under cultivation during the execution of the Virgin Lands Program during the middle 1950s. Northern Kazakhstan became the core area of the project, which extended into the adjacent Western Siberia, southern Urals, and Trans Volga regions. The entire Virgin Lands area that stretches all the way from the middle Volga to the Altay Mountains saw the opening up of about 42 million hectares (104 million acres) of new land during the seven years 1954–1960. This is more than the total wheat acreage of the United States, Canada, and Australia combined. These lands are now producing about 27 percent of all the grain harvested in the Soviet Union and 50–60 percent of all the wheat. Much of this grain is grown in hazardous climatic conditions with annual precipitation averaging no more than 8–16 inches.

The Soviets recognize that agriculture in this region is a gamble with the weather, that average yields per acre are going to be low, and that inevitably crop failures will be experienced perhaps half the time. But over the long run they believe that the endeavor is worth the effort. Also, they view the Virgin Lands Project as only one part of an integrated

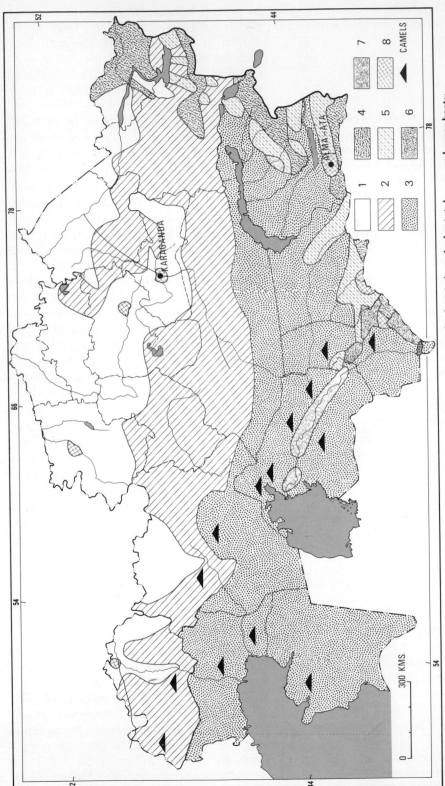

Figure 16-5   Agriculture. From Nikitin, p. 217.; 1-Spring wheat, millet, dairying, and fine-wooled sheep; 2-Cattle for meat, tallow, and milk; semifine-wooled sheep, horse breeding on steppe and semidesert pastures; 3-Sheep and karakul on desert and semidesert pastures; 4-Mountain grazing of cattle, sheep, and yak; 5-Irrigated wheat, tobacco, and sugar beets; 6-Irrigated cotton; 7-Irrigated rice; 8-Irrigated urban oriented truck gardening and dairying.

program for agriculture for the entire country that was initiated by Khrushchev in 1953. The stimulus for this program was the great expansion and improvement of animal products. In order to achieve this, a sufficient fodder base had to be established, primarily in the better farming areas of southern European Russia and the Ukraine. A new crop, corn, was introduced into this rich farming region, which was best suited for it, and something had to give. The crop that was removed was wheat, and new lands had to be found for it, because the Soviets did not want to sacrifice their total wheat production. Bread is still the staff of life in the Russian diet, and the Soviet Union consumes more wheat than any other country. Therefore, the steppes of Kazakhstan and adjacent regions were chosen for the new home of much of this wheat, because soils were fertile, the topography was flat, and the vegetation was grass, which could easily be plowed up and put into crops the very first year after the decision was made. No other area in the Soviet Union could have been reclaimed for cultivation so quickly.

Also, some agroclimatologists have pointed out that climatically the new wheat areas in the Virgin Lands complement the old wheat areas in the Ukraine. Rarely does drought occur in both places the same year; in fact, when one area is dry, the other most likely will have above-normal precipitation. This is not pure happenstance. Ukraine and Kazakhstan are separated by a distance approximately equal to one half of a wavelength of the circulation of the upper troposphere. Therefore, it is to be expected that they would experience opposite types of weather. Thus, the Virgin Lands Program has been justified on the assumption that insurance is being provided that somewhere in the Soviet Union there will be a good wheat crop every year.

On the other hand, some agricultural specialists fear that a huge dust bowl is being created. During the growing season southwest and west winds commonly sweep this area with velocities up to 30 meters per second. Tselinograd, in the midst of the new lands, experiences dust storms 53 days per year. During the 1960s wheat yields in the

Figure 16-6   Wheat field in northern Kazakhstan. Novosti.

area dropped consistently, apparently due primarily to constant monoculture and lack of fallowing. But during the great drought year of 1972, when much of European U.S.S.R. had disastrous crop failures, the Virgin Lands proved their worth by producing the largest crop ever. Now large state farms that have been carved out of the open steppe have an air of permanency about them.

At first, young single people were recruited to work on the Virgin Lands, and they lived in tents and in other temporary dwellings. Most of these Komsomols, Young Communist League members, have in one way or another found their way back to more civilized areas, however, and the Virgin Lands today are being built up with permanent dwellings in big rural villages peopled by families. There is a constant striving to make the economy of these areas more well-rounded, so there is a great drive to recruit people to develop animal husbandry, dairying, poultry raising, vegetable and fruit growing, and so forth.

The huge semidesert and desert midsection of Kazakhstan is utilized primarily only for extensive grazing. The main livestock are cattle and sheep, but Karakul sheep also occupy some of the drier desert areas. Camels are still raised as a beast of burden in the region along the banks of the Syr Darya and extending northwestward beyond the northern end of the Aral Sea to the Ural River in the northwest, and southward along the eastern coast of the Caspian.

WATER RESOURCES AND CONSTRUCTION PROJECTS

Lack of sufficient water is the primary limitation on agriculture in Kazakhstan, just as it is in Central Asia. A number of small water-construction projects have been built on the streams that flow northward out of the Tien Shan to provide irrigation water to the adjacent plains and to provide some hydroelectricity to some of the cities, such as the capital city of Alma Ata. The largest of these constructions so far is the recently completed

Kapchagay hydroelectric station on the Ili River north of Alma Ata. The old city of Ili was flooded by the reservoir and a new town was established at the site of the dam, originally called Novoiliysk, then shortened to Iliysk, and finally renamed Kapchagay. A dam 50 meters high has formed a reservoir on the Ili River about 200 kilometers long. The reservoir began to fill in September 1969, and the electrical plant went into operation late in 1970. The ultimate capacity of the plant is to be 434,000 kilowatts. A great deal of controversy revolved about this construction project, because many conservationists were fearful that the construction of the dam and reservoir would reduce the flow into Lake Balkhash and hence lower its water level.

The only stream in the north of any significance is the Irtysh, the main left-bank tributary of the Ob, fed by mountain headwaters in China and the large Lake Zaysan to maintain a steady flow throughout the summer. Other streams, such as the two main Irtysh tributaries, the Ishim and the Tobol, as well as many small streams radiating out of the Kazakh Hillocky Country, are only spring freshets fed by thawing snow and ground, and they have very little water in late summer. The main river in the Kazakh Hillocky Country, is the Nura, only 160 kilometers long, which flows westward through the heavily industrialized area of Karaganda. A reservoir has been constructed on the Nura to supply domestic, mining, and industrial needs of Karaganda, but it has proved to be woefully inadequate.

Several construction works have been planned for the Irtysh River to utilize its water better. The Ust-Kamenogorsk Dam was completed in 1953 to create the so-called Small Irtysh Sea. Upstream, near the mouth of the Bukhtarma River, the Bukhtarma Dam was completed in 1960. This dam raised the water level 67 meters and backed water up the Irtysh 600 kilometers to create the Large Irtysh Sea, which engulfed Lake Zaysan and raised its water level 6 meters. The power plant has a capacity of 675,000 kilowatts. Construction of a third dam is planned downstream from

Ust-Kamenogorsk. These dams are primarily to improve navigation along the middle Irtysh and to provide hydroelectricity.

Recently a dam was constructed at Yermak about 30 kilometers south of Pavlodar to provide water for the newly constructed Irtysh-Karaganda Canal to supply water to the growing industries in central Kazakhstan. It will also allow the irrigation of about 37,000 hectares of land along the way, to be cultivated to supply vegetables, potatoes, and fruit to the developing urban markets in the area. The canal runs westward through the coal-mining center of Ekibastuz and near the future copper mines of Bozshakul, then turns southwestward to follow up the Shiderty River to Karaganda. The total length of the canal is 480 kilometers. Twenty-three pumping stations raise the water to an elevation of 520 meters at the divide between the headwaters of the Shiderty and the Karaganda area. The canal was formally dedicated on January 1, 1972. Part of the canal construction was done by blasting. The excavating of the canal turned up a long chain of burial mounds along the route that apparently date back to the

Figure 16-7 **Blasting the Irtysh-Karaganda Canal. Novosti.**

seventh–sixth centuries B.C. Archeologists have found thousands of bronze, iron, and bone articles. A unique find is a molded belt buckle depicting a hunting scene: a tiger attacking a wild camel. The clasp has been estimated to be about 25 centuries old. Work has already begun on a 480-kilometer extension of the canal westward to the copper-mining complex of Dzhezkazgan.

In northwestern Kazakhstan the Volga-Ural River project has been revived. It was first proposed in 1950 to connect the Ural River with the Volga and utilize some of the Volga water to irrigate large sections of the North Caspian Lowland. However, it was abandoned for lack of sufficient water, but in 1973 the Soviet government gave its final approval, and construction was to have started in 1974. It is estimated that the project will require 15 years to construct. The canal will lead off from the northern end of the Volgograd Reservoir northeastward for a distance of 464 kilometers to the Ural River just south of the city of Uralsk. Three pumping stations will raise the water to an elevation of 44 meters above sea level, after which the water will descend by gravity to the Ural River. Feeder canals will flow southward under the force of gravity down the gentle slope of the North Caspian Lowland to irrigate about 300,000 hectares of land. It will also benefit millions of acres of pasturelands and revive some of the stagnant pools of water in old channels of the Ural River and thus encourage waterfowl and fishing. It would appear that unless northern waters are brought into the Volga, the Volga-Ural Canal system will suffer from a deficit of water. Therefore, the initiation of the Volga-Ural Canal would seem to be yet another clue as to Soviet intentions regarding the Pechora-Vychegda diversion project in northeast European Russia.

Another colossal project, which incidentally might also solve the Volga-Ural water problem, has been mentioned off and on since as early as 1868, but has not been taken very seriously until recently. This is a plan to take water from the Ob-Irtysh River system, and eventually perhaps even from the Yenisey, in Siberia southward into Kazakhstan and Central Asia. The initial stages of this project seem definitely to be under consideration at present. Several variants of this scheme have been considered, and some of them may eventually be combined. These range all the way from the construction of a huge dam in the lower Ob Basin, which would back up a tremendous reservoir all the way to the junction of the Irtysh with the Ob and provide water that could be pumped over the Turgay Divide to flow southward into the Aral Sea area, to the diversion of water from the upper reaches of the Ob, the Katun, the Irtysh, and perhaps even the upper Yenisey to lead water into the existing Bukhtarma Reservoir and then westward, perhaps by an extended Irtysh-Karaganda Canal, into central Kazakhstan. Whatever scheme is chosen, it will require a great deal of pumping, because the Turgay Divide lies about 150 meters above the West Siberian Lowland to the north and the Aral Sea basin to the south, and much of the irrigable land in the northern steppe region lies 100–300 meters above the Turgay Divide.

It has been estimated that about 80 million hectares (over 200 million acres) of irrigable land in Kazakhstan and Central Asia remains unirrigated because of lack of water. Much of this lies in the northern steppe zone, which is already being dry farmed but whose production could be greatly increased by irrigation agriculture. The rest lies in the vicinity of the Aral Sea, the lower Syr Darya and the Amu Darya regions, and in western Kazakhstan in the northern part of the Caspian Lowland.

The scheme that appears to be the most feasible for the immediate future is a plan to divert water from a reservoir to be constructed on the Irtysh River near the town of Tobolsk. Water would be pumped up the course of the Tobol River and its tributary the Ubagan to the Turgay Divide and then southward through the Turgay Valley to the Aral Sea region. This envisions a Volga-size stream flowing southward through the Turgay Lowland. One extension of this canal could skirt the eastern side of the Aral Sea across the lower Syr Darya and Amu Darya to irrigate about 4 million hectares of fertile land, which used to be irrigated in ancient times, and another 2 million hectares of desert land in southwestern Turkmenia along the Uzboy System between the Aral and Caspian Seas. Another extension of this canal could be constructed westward north of the Aral Sea into the North Caspian Lowland to supplement Volga River water in the Ural River irrigation system that is now being constructed. An ultimate extension of the system is a plan to dump water into the Volga upstream from the entrance to the Volga-Don Canal to be pumped through the canal into the lower Don to replenish the freshwater inflow of the Sea of Azov. Also, some water may be dumped into the Aral Sea to maintain the level of that body of water, if it is deemed the best thing to do.

The Aral Sea presents a problem similar to that of the Caspian, only on a much smaller scale. The sea level has been dropping rapidly since the increased utilization of the Syr Darya and the Amu Darya for irrigation purposes upstream. The lake level dropped 176 centimeters between 1960 and 1967. It was expected to drop another 3 meters by 1975 and 9 meters by 1985. Because the prevailing depth of the Aral Sea is only 10–20 meters, such a drop would cause a drastic reduction in area. During the early 1960s the average annual inflow into the Aral Sea was about 50 cubic kilometers. This had declined to about 23 cubic kilometers in 1975 and is expected to cease entirely by 1990. The advancing shoreline has hampered access to harbor facilities at the few small ports along the banks and has caused a drastic decline in the annual fish catch, from about 40,000 tons in 1962 to around 6,000 tons in 1970. Some planners look on the desiccation of the lake as inevitable and point out that the expanded irrigation in Central Asia more than compensates for the loss of the Aral Sea shipping and fisheries. In addition, the salt flats being exposed provide raw materials for chemical industries. On the other hand, there are fears that the complete drying up of the lake might cause a drastic drop in the water table in the surrounding area, a significant climatic change, and widespread wind erosion of the exposed salt flats that would produce salinization of a huge territory surrounding the basin.

Another potential source of water for mining, industrial, and agricultural purposes in central Kazakhstan are huge reserves of groundwater that collects in the basin structures of sedimentary aquifers dipping into the Aral Sea area both from the high mountains in the south and from the West Siberian Lowland in the north. It has been estimated that there is more water under the Kazakhstan desert than there is in Lake Baykal in Eastern Siberia, the largest freshwater lake in the world. In many areas this water is trapped between impervious layers and would flow without pumping through artesian wells to be utilized on the surface for irrigation of crops and supplemental water to expansive pasturelands. If this underground water is tapped extensively sometime in the future, its replenishment may depend on bringing in more northern water through the Turgay Canal system.

In the meantime experiments are under way to desalt saline water from the Caspian, the Aral Sea, and smaller salt lakes dotted throughout the central part of Kazakhstan. The largest of these projects so far is at the new oil town of Shevchenko on the arid Mangyshlak Peninsula. This is in conjunction with the production of electricity through an atomic breeder plant opened there in 1972. The plant has a generating capacity of 350,000 kilowatts, and it uses 200,000 of these kilowatts to desalt 120,000 tons (26.5 million gallons) of fresh water daily for use in the city of Shevchenko and the mining area surrounding it. In addition to the Shevchenko atomic experiment, several electrodialysis units have been designed at railroad towns in central Kazakhstan to desalt brackish water from local surface lakes. Such units are now operational in Mointy and Aktogay in Kazakhstan and at Gyaurs in Turkmenia.

MINERAL RESOURCES AND INDUSTRIALIZATION

Kazakhstan has proved to be one of the most highly mineralized regions in the Soviet Union. Resources range from mineral fuels, through iron ore and nonferrous metals, to nonmetallic ores, many of which are of national significance. Perhaps the greatest industrial development thus far has been based on the mineral fuels, primarily coal. The large city of Karaganda, now the center of the largest industrialized region in the republic, sits atop the Karaganda coal basin in the Kazakh Hillocky Country, credited with reserves of about 8 billion tons. Production began in earnest here in the early 1930s in conjunction with the development of the Magnitogorsk steel mill in the southern Urals. It was envisioned that because this mining area was only about half as far from Magnitogorsk as the Kuznetsk Basin in Western Siberia, Karaganda would quickly become the major supplier of coal to the Urals. However, high ash content has limited the use of Karaganda coal for coking, and it must be mixed with higher-grade Kuznetsk coal on a ratio of about one to two. Nevertheless, large quantities of Karaganda coal move to the metallurgical plants of the Urals, and large quantities of lower-grade coal are used for steam electric production in the Urals and throughout Kazakhstan and Central Asia.

Production in the Karaganda area has steadily increased to 45.2 million tons in 1974, which was about 6.6 percent of the U.S.S.R. production. Of this, 17.7 million tons was coking coal. The Karaganda Basin ranked third in the country in both total coal production and coking-coal production, after the Donets Basin in eastern Ukraine and the Kuznetsk Basin in Western Siberia. It has held third place in coking-coal production since its beginning in the 1930s, but it has only recently surpassed other producing areas such as the Moscow Basin and scattered fields in the Urals in total coal production. Thus, its mining operation has been expanding more rapidly in recent years than in those other areas. The marketing of Karaganda coal has been enhanced by the electrification of the railroad from Karaganda to Magnitogorsk. The Karaganda coal basin has prompted the construction of a large iron and steel plant in the Karaganda area. It opened during the middle 1960s and now utilizes large quantities of Karaganda coal. Although the Karaganda coal is primarily used in the Urals and locally, it moves as far away as the Central Chernozem Region and the Volga-Vyatka Region in the west and supplies most of the coal used throughout Central Asia in the south.

More recently the Ekibastuz coal basin has been brought into production in northeastern Kazakhstan; it is credited with about the same reserves as Karaganda. However, the Ekibastuz coal is not of coking quality. It also has a high ash content, but it is a good steam coal and has a higher heat potential than the Moscow coal. Modern production began during the early 1950s when the area was traversed by the South Siberian Railroad that was constructed between Pavlodar and Tselinograd. The Ekibastuz coal lies near the surface in thick seams and is all mined by inexpensive open-pit methods. This is one of the cheapest coal-mining regions in the country. Its production has been expanding more rapidly than any other coal basin, and in 1974 its production totaled 42 million tons, almost equal to that of Karaganda. This made it the fourth-largest coal-producing area in the country. Most of the Ekibastuz coal moves to the Urals for electric power generation, but more and more of it is being used locally as large thermal electric stations are being constructed in the mining area. The first large thermal electric station to be built in the area was in the new ferro-alloys center of Yermak on the Irtysh River south of Pavlodar, where a 2.4-million-kilowatt station went into operation in 1968. Immediate plans call for the construction of four 4-million-kilowatt stations at the mines themselves. Huge amounts of electric power generated by these stations will be transmitted over a 1.5-million-kilovolt dc line to be built to a proposed power terminal near Tambov in the Central Chernozem Region for distribution throughout central European U.S.S.R. Also, it is envisioned that large amounts of electricity will be used at Pavlodar where an alumina plant is operating and an oil refinery and petrochemical industries are being developed. In addition, power will be sent to the Leninogorsk-Ust Kamenogorsk metallurgical district in the Altay.

In addition to the two large coal-producing areas, Kazakhstan contains more than 100 separate deposits of coal that have been discovered in such areas as the Turgay Lowland.

Most of these are low-grade brown coals that will probably never be exploited for anything other than small local uses. However, because many of the coal beds are very thick and lie very near the surface, increased power needs might bring them into production for the thermal generation of large amounts of electricity. The Soviets estimate that by the year 2000 Kazakhstan will be producing about 250 million tons of coal annually, much of which will be consumed locally in large thermal power stations that will transmit cheap electricity by high-voltage lines to the Urals and the central parts of European U.S.S.R.

Oil has been produced in northwestern Kazakhstan since the first wells were drilled at Dossor in 1911 and at Makat in 1915 in the Emba oil fields formed by the salt domes in the North Caspian Lowland. Although oil production here never expanded significantly, the area continued to produce about 1–2 million tons of oil per year despite high production costs because it yielded high-paraffin lubricating oils with low freezing points, especially useful oils in the northern part of the country during winter. The crude was shipped to an old oil refinery near Yaroslavl specializing in the manufacture of lubricants, and after 1935 by pipeline to a newer refinery at Orsk in the southern Urals. The port of Guryev shipped much of the oil by tanker along the north Caspian and up the Volga to the central part of the country. In 1945 a refinery constructed with United States wartime aid opened in Guryev. It was designed to produce gasoline and diesel fuel from crude oil from the Volga Region, Turkmenia, and Baku. After 1958 the Guryev refinery also began to use some Emba crude oil.

In the late 1950s oil development began on the Mangyshlak Peninsula. The first commercial crude oil was shipped in 1965 over a new railroad that had been completed from Makat to the new industrial center of Shevchenko on the Caspian coast. This oil moved to both the Guryev and Orsk refineries. Shallow-draft tankers carried crude from Shevchenko to the Volgograd refinery. The first long-distance pipeline from Mangyshlak was completed in

1970 to the Kuybyshev refining complex over a distance of 1800 kilometers, with a branch along the way to the Guryev refinery.

Pipeline transmission of Mangyshlak crude presents special problems because the crude is about 30 percent paraffin, which solidifies at a temperature of 32°C (90°F). Fourteen heating stations had to be installed on the Mangyshlak-Kuybyshev pipeline to keep the crude oil at a temperature of 60°C (140°F). To facilitate extraction of the high-paraffin crude, water is brought 150 kilometers from the Caspian Sea, is desalted, and is brought to the boiling point and injected at high pressure into the oil-bearing horizons. The necessity of such complicated procedures has slowed development of the Mangyshlak fields.

The 1975 plan for Mangyshlak production recently has been revised to 23.8 million tons instead of the original five-year-plan goal of 30 million tons. Production at Mangyshlak now far outstrips the Emba production of about 3 million tons annually and accounts for most of the Kazakhstan production. To handle the increased flow of oil, the Guryev refinery has been expanded, and an associated petrochemical plant has been built. In March 1973 a new political unit, Mangyshlak Oblast, was created to incorporate this oil- and gas-producing region. It was carved out of the southern portion of Guryev Oblast. The administrative seat is the new city of Shevchenko, which in 1974 had a population of 89,000. Other cities of note are the oil center of Novyy Uzen with a 1974 population of 29,000 and the old fishing port of Fort Shevchenko, with a population of 10,000.

In eastern Kazakhstan a pipeline is being laid from Omsk in Western Siberia to Pavlodar and on to Chimkent in southern Kazakhstan. Oil refineries are under construction at Pavlodar and Chimkent. These will both be fed primarily by West Siberian crude.

Although little gas is being produced in Kazakhstan, except small quantities in conjunction with the oil in the west, major pipelines cross the area from the Central Asian fields to the Urals and the central European area. Two pipelines run from the Bukhara area along the west coast of the Aral Sea to the

Urals, and three pipelines run northwestward across the Ustyurt Plateau and through the Emba oil fields to the middle Volga Valley and on to the Central Region. Also a pipeline carries gas from the Bukhara area along the northern foothills of the Tien Shan as far as Alma Ata. Therefore, gas can be served to the intervening areas.

A gas-processing plant has been established at Novyy Uzen to separate natural gas liquids from gas in preparation for pipeline transmission. Mangyshlak gas is fed into the main pipeline system running from Central Asia to Central Russia. The Mangyshlak fields are now turning out about 5 billion cubic meters of gas per year, which is about 2 percent of the country's total. A 150-kilometer, 20-inch gas pipeline has been constructed from the gas and oil fields at Mangyshlak to the city of Shevchenko to supply an ammonia synthesis plant, and the natural gas liquids will be used as feedstocks at a big polystyrene plant at Shevchenko.

The Bazay gas deposit on the northwest shore of the Aral Sea began production in 1969. Gas is being fed into the Bukhara-Urals pipeline at the rate of about 1.5 billion cubic meters per year. No projections have yet been made regarding the ultimate scale of this operation. Soviet geologists expect to find large reserves of oil and gas in the Ural River district in northwestern Kazakhstan. Test wells are now being drilled over a zone several hundred kilometers long.

Probably the second most important mineral resource after coal in Kazakhstan is iron ore, which together with the Karaganda coal has prompted the establishment of a major iron- and steel-producing center at Karaganda. Actually, the Karaganda iron and steel plant was under construction before the discovery of large deposits of low-grade iron ores in Kustanay Oblast in northern Kazakhstan. The city of Karaganda came into being in the early 1930s when the large development of coal mining was initiated, and a small steel plant, the Kazakh Metallurgical Plant, which used long-haul pig iron, was completed during World War II in the northern satellite city of Karaganda named Temirtau ("iron moun-

tain") on the west shore of an artificial reservoir on the Nura River. This steel plant reached a production of 400,000 tons by 1960. However, in the 1950s the Karaganda area was selected as the site of one of the Soviet Union's new integrated iron and steel complexes. Although it was called the Karaganda Metallurgical Plant, it also became administratively part of the city of Temirtau. The first blast furnace was opened in 1960. Since then continual expansion has taken place, and in 1974 this plant produced about 3.4 million tons of pig iron and 4.4 million tons of steel. With these two plants, the Kazakh Republic produced 4.8 million tons of steel in 1974. The 1975 plan is for Kazakhstan to produce 4.5 million tons of pig iron and nearly 6 million tons of steel. This, then, has become one of the major iron and steel plants in the country, considerably smaller than Magnitogorsk in the southern Urals or Krivoy Rog in the eastern Ukraine, but in the same first-order class with them, joining such other plants as Cherevopets in the Northwest, Lipetsk in the Central Chernozem Region, Chelyabinsk in the Urals and Novokuznetsk in the Kuznetsk Basin of Western Siberia.

The iron ore source for the Karaganda iron and steel complex originally was intended to be the Atasu deposit at the town of Karazhal about 250 kilometers southwest of Karaganda. However, in the early 1970s it was supplying only 20 percent of Karaganda's needs. Rudnyy ("ore-town") and Lisakovsk in Kustanay Oblast supplied the other 80 percent. The Atasu open-pit mine has been shipping 55 percent direct-shipping ore to plants in the Urals since 1956. For some reason, about half of this ore production at Karazhal still is being shipped to the Urals, mainly to Nizhniy Tagil. The better ores are beginning to run out at Karazhal, and costs are becoming higher as mining takes place in deeper shaft mines. It is intended that in the future Lisakovsk in Kustanay Oblast will become the primary provider of iron ore to Karaganda. Atasu will continue to supply some manganese to Karaganda.

The opening of seemingly inexhaustible low-grade ore deposits in Kustanay Oblast during the late 1950s and early 1960s seems to have solved the bulk of the iron-ore needs of Karaganda and the Urals for many years to come. The main exploration so far has been in the Sokolovka and Sarbay deposits near the new town of Rudnyy. These two deposits consist of magnetite with about 45 percent iron content and have reserves of 800 million tons at Sarbay and 600 million tons at Sokolovka. Both deposits lie near the surface at depths of about 65 meters and are exploited in open-pit mines. Operation of the Sokolovka mine began in 1957 and in the Sarbay mine in 1960. Initially the total output was shipped westward about 350 kilometers to Magnitogorsk, Novotroitsk, Chelyabinsk, and Nizhniy Tagil in the Urals. Now some of the ore is being shipped eastward to Karaganda.

Two more large deposits are being opened up in Kustanay Oblast at Kachar and Lisakovsk. Greater priority has been given to the development of the huge Lisakovsk deposit, which consists of phosphoritic limonite with an iron content of about 36 percent and high phosphorous and alumina contents. The ore is accessible by strip mining, but its use presents many technological problems. However, an intermediate product can yield phosphatic fertilizer, which helps to make the use of the ore economically feasible. Ultimately the Lisakovsk deposit is expected to support two very large mining and concentrating complexes, each with a capacity of about 36 million tons of crude ore per year.

In 1974 Kazakhstan produced 20.2 million tons of usable ore out of a U.S.S.R. total of 225 million tons. Of the Kazakhstan ore, Rudnyy produced 15 million tons, Livakovsk 1 million tons, and Karazhal 3 million tons. More than half of the Rudnyy ore was processed into pellets, which is the most advanced stage of ore preparation for blast furnaces.

A manganese mine was developed at Dzhezdy during World War II when Ukrainian and Transcaucasian manganese sources were cut off. It declined after the war but has been revived since the mid-1960s as a source of manganese for the new ferro-alloys plant at Yermak.

The Soviet Union's first chrome-ore con-
centrator went into operation in 1974 at Khrom Tau, the U.S.S.R.'s principal chrome-mining center in the Mugodzhar Upland of northern Kazakhstan. The Soviet Union is the leading chromite producer in the world, and the Khrom Tau deposit produces about 85 percent of the Soviet Union's chromite, which in 1970 amounted to 3 million tons. The Soviet Union exports about 40 percent of its production to the United States, Japan, West Germany, France, and Sweden. Development began at Khrom Tau in 1943, along with a ferro-alloys plant at nearby Aktyubinsk, to which most of the ore is shipped. Nickel-cobalt ores also are mined in the Aktyubinsk area and are transported north to a refinery at Orsk.

The mining and smelting of copper has been an industry in Kazakhstan for quite a number of years, during which it has dispersed into new parts of the republic. The oldest operation, begun in 1938, is at the city of Balkhash on the north shore of Lake Balkhash. This plant makes use of the ore deposit at Kounrad just to the north and now processes the ore through the entire manufacturing cycle. In addition, the Balkhash plant extracts molybdenum and other rarer metals.

The second major center for copper production in the Kazakh Republic, the largest copper ore producer in the entire country, is at Dzhezkazgan in the western portion of the Kazakh Hillocky Country. This is reported to be the biggest copper reserve in the Soviet Union. A small operation began as early as 1928, but modern commercial production was initiated around 1940. At first the copper ore was shipped to the Urals, but in 1954 a concentrator was opened at Dzhezkazgan and the concentrate moved to the Balkhash smelter. Finally, the Dzhezkazgan complex has become fully integrated with the completion of an electrolytic refinery in 1971 and a blister copper plant in 1973. A rail line has been built southwestward from Karaganda to Dzhezkazgan, and in 1973 Dzhezkazgan Oblast was created out of the large southern portion of what had been Karaganda Oblast. The city of Dzhezkazgan, which in 1974 had a population of 74,000, is the administrative

Figure 16-8   Open pit copper mine at Kounrad near Balkhash. Novosti.

seat. With satellite mining towns, the Dzhez-kazgan area has a population of over 150,000. The new oblast also includes the city of Balkhash with a population of 80,000 and the iron-ore-mining center of Karazhal with a population of 20,000.

Copper is also being produced in several other spots in Kazakhstan, often in conjunction with other metals such as lead, zinc, and barite. In 1974 a new polymetallic ore deposit was opened northwest of Karazhal. It contains lead, zinc, copper, barite, and some rare precious metals. There are prospects of a large new copper development at Bozshakul near the Irtysh-Karaganda Canal southwest of Pavlodar.

Lead and zinc have been produced in Kazakhstan for quite a number of years. The major development has been in the Altay Mountains in eastern Kazakhstan. The deposits extend in two parallel belts along the eastern side of the Irtysh River. Nearest the river the zinc deposits are associated with copper. About 60 kilometers east zinc deposits are associated with lead. These ores also contain gold, silver, cadmium, arsenic, antimony, bismuth, and a variety of rare metals. All these ores have been exploited since the early nineteenth century. Much of the ore in the zinc-copper zone near the Irtysh River has been smelted at the town of Glubokoye, but future development of the zinc-copper zone is expected to focus on the large Niko-layevka copper deposit when the large East Kazakhstan copper chemical plant is completed at Ust-Talovka. This ore deposit in the northwestern part of the zone yielded lead, silver, and copper during the eighteenth and

nineteenth centuries, but these high-grade ores have been depleted, and a surface deposit of copper is now being exploited.

The city of Leninogorsk ("Lenin mountain") has become the urban center for the eastern lead-zinc zone. The town, which was originally called Ridder after the discoverer of the mineral-rich ores, has been a mining center since the late eighteenth century. During the Soviet period a lead smelter was opened at Leninogorsk in 1927, and a zinc refinery was opened in 1966. This refining activity has been enhanced by a new hydroelectric plant on the Irtysh River, built during the late 1950s and early 1960s to augment some very small stations that had been built earlier on some tributary streams.

The city of Ust-Kamenogorsk has become the regional metallurgical center and rail hub for all this mining activity in the Altay. The city's industrial development began largely during World War II and has been expanded since, along with the provision of cheap electric power from hydroelectric stations on the Irtysh River. In 1947 a zinc refinery was opened, and in 1952 a lead refinery was completed. In 1952 the first section of the Ust-Kamenogorsk hydroelectric station came into production; at the time it was the third largest producer in the Soviet Union. Later when the Bukhtarma station opened, the additional power supply prompted the construction of a second and larger zinc refinery in Ust-Kamenogorsk, opened in 1955. In 1965 a titanium-magnesium plant was opened.

In additon to the lead-zinc production in the Altay, Kazakhstan also has important lead production in the south. The largest lead smelter in the Soviet Union was founded in 1934 in Chimkent to smelt the lead-zinc ores of the local region. Chimkent also handles lead concentrates from scattered mines throughout Central Asia and has developed a large chemical industry based on by-product gases as well as natural gas brought in by pipe from the Bukhara region.

In the early 1970s a concentrator was put into operation at the lead-barite deposit of Karagayly east of Karaganda. In addition to lead and barite, the deposit yields zinc and copper as well as a wide range of other products. Lead concentrate will probably move to the Chimkent refinery. The barite component will add to Kazakhstan's leading position in the Soviet Union as the main barite supplier of a weighting agent in oil-well drilling muds.

One of the most significant developments in nonferrous metals during the last 20 years has been the exploitation of a bauxite deposit near the town of Arkalyk in the Turgay Lowland in southeastern Kustanay Oblast. The town of Arkalyk was founded as a workers' settlement in 1956. The first bauxite ore moved to a new alumina plant at Pavlodar in 1963. Since then a second alumina plant has been built in Pavlodar, and it is to be supplied with bauxite from a new deposit discovered at Krasnooktyabrskiy ("red October"), whose reserves are said to exceed those of Arkalyk. An aluminum plant is to be built at Pavlodar when the local power base expands, but in the meantime alumina is being shipped from Pavlodar to the large new aluminum plants in Siberia at Novokuznetsk, Krasnoyarsk, Bratsk, and Shelekhov near Irkutsk. In 1970 Arkalyk was made the capital of a new political unit, Turgay Oblast, which was carved out of parts of Kustanay and Tselinograd Oblasts. At that time its population was around 16,000. Now that it is the seat of an oblast, the town is expected to grow rapidly. It had a population of 30,000 in 1974.

Many other nonferrous metals are mined at scattered locations in Kazakhstan, primarily in the Kazakh Hillocky Country or in the Altay. Among these are gold and silver. During the last 15 years, eastern Kazakhstan has become one of the main gold-lode mining centers of the Soviet Union. The town of Auezov ("gold") was founded in 1962 to act as the commercial center for this mining activity.

Kazakhstan has significant deposits of several of the nonmetallic minerals. Outstanding among these is the phosphorite of the Kara Tau Mountains in the southern part of the republic between the cities of Dzhambul and Chimkent. The Kara Tau phoshorite deposit has become the Soviet Union's second most important supplier of phosphate raw materials after the Kola apatite. Although the Kara Tau operation is much smaller than the Kola one, it has become the primary supplier to all of Central Asia and Kazakhstan. It is now apparently contributing about one-quarter of the Soviet Union's phosphate raw material.

The first mining operation in the 100-kilometer-long Kara Tau phoshate zone began in 1946 at the town of Chulak Tau, which since has been renamed Kara Tau. Since then other mines have been opened up over a wide area. The ground phosphate moves to superphosphate plants at Dzhambul in the Kazakh Republic and at Kokand, Samarkand, and Chardzhou in Central Asia. Also, in 1966 a plant to produce elemental phosphorus was established in Chimkent. It provides a base for detergents, animal-feed additives, and a wide range of other chemicals. A similar phosphorus plant was established in Dzhambul in 1973, in addition to the superphosphate plant opened in 1950. The Chimkent and Dzhambul elemental phosphorus plants, which treat the phosphate rock by thermal reduction method, are two of only three such plants in the country, the third being at Togliatti in the Volga Region. This elemental phosphorus is very cheap and easy to transport and is now being shipped as far as the superphosphate plants in the Ukraine and North Caucasus for conversion into fertilizer.

The Soviet Union's largest borax deposit is located in the Ural River valley 130 kilometers north of Guryev. The borax is processed at the town of Alga near Aktyubinsk, where there is also a double superphosphate plant that processes Kola apatite. The borax plant produces boric acid and boron compounds including additives for the fertilizer industry.

New applications for boron compounds have been found in atomic reactors and in space exploration as a coating material for solar batteries. This has stimulated the industry in Alga, which has been producing since the late 1930s.

Other nonmetallic ores include a wide variety of salts, such as natural sodium sulfate in the Aralsulfat area near the northeast tip of the Aral Sea, as well as the asbestos complex of Dzhetygara in the Aktyubinsk region of northwestern Kazakhstan. The Dzhetygara complex is the second largest asbestos producer in the Soviet Union after the town of Asbest in the Urals. The Dzhetygara complex was initiated in 1965, and by the middle 1970s was producing about 600,000 tons, or one-fourth of the country's asbestos.

CITIES

Alma Ata

The largest city in Kazakhstan is the capital, Alma Ata. This is a relatively new, non-Kazakh city that sits in the very southern extremity of the republic. In 1974 it had a population of 813,000. It was founded in 1854 as the Russian fort of Zailiysk (Trans-Ili) and was renamed Vernyy in 1885 and Alma Ata in 1921. It definitely is a Russian city; few native Kazakhs are to be found. Its rapid growth has taken place largely since it became the capital of the Kazakh Republic. Its present form reflects the chaotic growth that has taken place. The town does not have the look of a major metropolitan center, as does, for instance, Tashkent to the southwest, but it has certain site advantages. It sits at a somewhat higher elevation and is nestled directly within the foothills of the Tien Shan. Thus, Alma Ata is cooler than Tashkent, has a magnificent backdrop of mountain scenery, and is better watered by many little rushing streams that crisscross the alluvial fan surfaces on their way from the snow-capped mountains in the south to the deserts surrounding Lake Balkhash in the north. Alma Ata has a widely diversified industrial base, composed primarily of various types of machine-building and light industries.

Alma Ata has become one of the major cities on the tourist circuit in Central Asia. Two new hotels are under construction, and outside of town, located at an elevation of about 1650 meters above sea level in the Trans-Ili Alatau, is the world-famous Olympic Medeo skating rink. The clear glacial waters of the Alma Atinka River provide the ideal water situation for the rink, and a system of pipes 135 kilometers long keeps the ice at a constant temperature below freezing. Many world speed records have been set there. The old skating rink was destroyed in the mid-1960s by a major earthquake and flood caused by a broken dam at a small lake upstream from the rink. An earthquake-recording station has been established in the area, and an unusual slow-running tape recorder has been developed in Alma Ata to record the "pulsebeat" of the earth.

Karaganda

The second largest city in Kazakhstan is the new city of Karaganda, with a 1974 population of 559,000. It was founded in 1926, and since then has been the most rapidly growing city in Kazakhstan. Its founding and growth have been stimulated by coal mining in the local area and the establishment of the large iron and steel plant in the suburban city of Temirtau. The city sits in somewhat barren landscape in the Kazakh Hillocky Country at about the southern limits of the dry-farming region of northern Kazakhstan. The small Nura River flows through the city and provides water, which recently has been supplemented by the Irtysh-Karaganda Canal. Like Alma Ata, Karaganda is definitely a Russian City.

Chimkent

Chimkent is the metallurgical-chemical center in southern Kazakhstan west of the Kara Tau Mountain range. It has phosphorus industries based on the Kara Tau phosphate rock, other chemical industries based on natural gas from the Bukhara region, and is getting an oil refinery that will be supplied by pipe from the West Siberian fields. It also has the largest lead smelter in all Eurasia. In 1974 Chimkent had a population of 287,000.

Semipalatinsk

Semipalatinsk, on the Irtysh River in eastern Kazakhstan, was one of the fortified outposts established by the Russians during the eighteenth and nineteenth centuries to contain the nomads to the south. Since then it has developed into a regional center for grain growing and food processing and is a main station on the Turk-Sib Railroad. It is also the governmental seat of Semipalatinsk Oblast. In 1974 its population was 265,000.

Ust-Kamenogorsk

Ust-Kamenogorsk is the main urban center of the Altay nonferrous metallurgical district. In 1974 it had a population of 252,000. Its industries have already been mentioned with respect to lead and zinc smelting. It is also the site of a major dam and reservoir on the upper Irtysh River.

Pavlodar

Pavlodar, with a 1974 population of 228,000, is another major industrial center on the Irtysh River in eastern Kazakhstan. It seems to have been singled out for industrialization in spite of the fact that it is not in very close juxtaposition to any mineral resource. An alumina plant has been established there to use the Arkalyk bauxite halfway across the Kazakh Republic, and an oil refinery is being established to utilize West Siberian petroleum. In addition, a tractor plant in Pavlodar has been producing the "Kazakhstan" tractor since 1968. In the near future it is planned that the alumina plant will be expanded to include aluminum production utilizing cheap elec-

tricity from large thermal electric stations to be established in the Ekibastuz coalfield.

Dzhambul

Dzhambul is the phosphate and chemical center in southern Kazakhstan on the other side of the Karatau Mountains from Chimkent. The two cities have developed rather similarly, although Dzhambul does not have the nonferrous metallurgy that Chimkent has. In 1974 it had a population of 228,000. Until 1936 the city was known as Aulie Ata.

Tselinograd

Tselinograd, with a 1974 population of 209,000, is one of the main centers in the Virgin Lands district of northern Kazakhstan. Until 1961 it was known as Akmolinsk, but it was renamed when it became the administrative seat of the now-defunct Tselinnyy Kray, so named from the word *tselina,* which means "virgin soil."

Temirtau

The iron and steel city of Temirtau on the northern side of Karaganda has grown to a 1974 population of 192,000.

Other Cities

The next four cities in size are also oblast centers in the northern tier of oblasts in the wheat-growing region of Kazakhstan. In order of size these are Petropavlovsk, with a 1974 population of 188,000, Aktyubinsk with a population of 170,000, Uralsk with a population of 149,000, and Kustanay with a population of 143,000. The next city is Kzyl Orda on the lower Syr Darya, which had a 1974 population of 135,000. This sits in the center of an irrigated rice-growing area and from 1924 to 1929 served as the capital of the Kazakh (Kirgiz) A.S.S.R. The last city above the 100,000 size is the port city of Guryev near the mouth of the Ural River on the north Caspian coast. Its function as an oil-refining and oil-shipping center has already been mentioned. In 1974 it had a population of 125,000.

PROSPECTS

The Kazakh Republic has proved to be a treasure house of mineral resources that have prompted development of many metallurgical and chemical industries. The Virgin Lands Project of the 1950s gave a large spurt to its agricultural economy, and the irrigated districts to the south have been under continual slow expansion. After an initial shock when the Soviet system radically changed the ways of life and drastically reduced the numbers of the Kazakh natives, the population has recovered, and the republic now exhibits one of the higher birth rates, growth rates, and immigration rates in the country. Although the population has become heavily Russian, the Kazakh population during the last few decades has also experienced rapid growth. What before the Soviet period was a desert wasteland of roaming nomad herdsmen has now become a settled agricultural and industrial region integrated with the economy of the rest of the country. If additional large amounts of water can be supplied from some source, such as the Ob River system, then another spurt in the economy may lift the region to still another higher plateau of development.

READING LIST

* Alampiev, P., *Soviet Kazakhstan*, Foreign Languages Publishing House, Moscow, 1958 186 pp.
* Ashimbayev, T.A., *Nadeleniye i trudovyye resursy gorodov severnogo Kazakhstana* (Population and Labor Resources in the Cities of Northern Kazakhstan), Nauka Kazahkstanskoy SSR, Alma Ata, 1970, 273 pp. (in Russian).
* *Atlas Kustanayskoy oblasti* (An Atlas of Kustanay Oblast), Gugk, Moscow, 1963 (in Russian).
* *Atlas Tselinnogo Kraya* (Atlas of Tselinny Kray), Moscow, 1964, 49 pp. (in Russian).
* Berkalov, I.A., "O gryazevykh vulkanchikakh Tsentralnogo Kazakhstana" (About the Little Mud Volcanoes of Central Kazakhstan), *Izvestiya Vsesoyuznogo geograficheskogo obshchestva*, No. 1, 1972, pp. 40–44 (in Russian).
* Buyanovsky, M.S., "Balkhash-Ili, A Potential Major Industrial Complex," *Soviet Geography: Review & Translation*, October 1965, pp. 3–15.
* Dando, W.A., *Grain or Dust: A Study of the Soviet New Lands Program 1954–1963*, Ph.D. Dissertation, University of Minnesota, 1970, 187 pp.
* Davitaya, F.F., ed., *Agroklimaticheskiye i vodnyye resursy rayonov osvoyeniya tselinnykh i zalezhnykh zemel* (Agro-Climatic and Water Resources in the Regions of the Reclamation of the Virgin and Idle Lands), Leningrad, 1955, 464 pp. (in Russian).
* Demko, G.J., *The Russian Colonization of Kazakhstan, 1896–1916*, Indiana University Press, Bloomington, 1969, 271 pp.
* Durgin, Frank A., Jr., 'The Virgin Lands Programme 1954–1960,' *Soviet Studies*, 1962, pp. 255–280.
* Jackson, W.A. Douglas, *Russo-Chinese Borderlands*, Van Nostrand, Princeton, 1968, 2nd ed., 156 pp.
* Jackson, W.A. Douglas, and Richard Towber, "The Continuing Perplexities of Soviet Agriculture: The Performance of Northern Kazakhstan," in B.W. Eissenstat, Ed., *The Soviet Union: The Seventies and Beyond*, Lexington Books, Lexington, Mass., 1975, pp. 169–180.
* Karsten, A.A., "The Virgin Lands Kray and Its Prospects of Development," *Soviet Geography: Review & Translation*, May 1963, pp. 37–46.
* Kasimov, N.S., and N.A. Shmelkovo, "Landshaftno-geokhimicheski osobennosti zon razlomov kazakhstana (na primere Mugodzhar, Severnogo i Tsentralnogo Kazakhstana)' [Landscape-Geochemical Characteristics of Fracture Zones in Kazakhstan (with Particular Reference to the Mugodzhar Hills, Northern and Central Kazakhstan)], *Vestnik Moskovskogo Universiteta, geografiya*, No. 1, 1975, pp. 84–91.
* Kleyner, Yu. M., 'O karstye Ustyurta i Mangyshlaka' (On the Karst of the Ustyurt and the Mangyshlak), *Izvestiya Akademii Nauk SSSR, seriya geograficheskaya*, No. 5, 1970, pp. 53–55 (in Russian).
* Mayeva, S.A., A.N. Kosarev, and Ye. G. Mayev, "On the Connection between Level Fluctuations in the Caspian Sea and the Aral Sea," *Soviet*

Geography: Review and Translation, April 1975, pp. 231–239.

- Nikolayev, V.A., "O proiskhozhdenii Kazakhskogo melkosopochnika" (On the Origins of the Kazakh Hill Country), *Vestnik Moskovskogo Universiteta, seriya geografiya,* No. 3, 1972, pp. 39–43 (in Russian).

- Ovchinnikov, G.D., "O stroenii griv v severo-kazakhstanskoy oblasti" (On the Structure of Ridges in North Kazakhstan Oblast), *Izvestiya vsesoyuznoye geograficheskoye obshchestvo,* No. 3, 1970, pp. 293–294 (in Russian).

- *Razvitie narodnogo khozyaystva Kazakhstana za 50 let soveticheskoy vlasti* (Development of the National Economy of Kazakhstan after 50 Years of Soviet Power), Nauka, Alma Ata, 1967 (in Russian).

- Scott, G.A.K., *The Formation of the Turkestan Frontier Between Russia and China in the Eighteenth Century,* Ph.D. Dissertation, Oxford University, 1972.

- Shnitnikov, A.V., "Rekonstruktsiya vodnogo balansa ozero Balkhash" (The Reconstruction of the Water Balance of Lake Balkhash), *Izvestiya Vsesoyuznogo geograficheskogo obshchestva,* No. 3, 1973, pp. 223–229 (in Russian).

- *Tselinyy Kray; kratkie ocherki o prirode, naselenii i khosyaystve* (Tselinyy Kray; Short Study of Nature, Population, and Economy), Akademiya Nauk Kazakhskoy SSR, Alma Ata, 1962, 188 pp.

- Viktorov, S.V., *Pustynya Ustyurt i voprosy yeye osvoyeniya* (The Ustyurt Desert and Problems of Development), Nauka, Moscow, 1971 (in Russian).

The Western Siberia Economic Region

	Area (km²)	Population	Persons/km²	Percent Urban
• Altay Kray	262,000	2,631,000	10.1	50
Gorno Altay Autonomous Oblast	93,000	163,000	1.8	27
• Kemerovo Oblast	96,000	2,908,000	30.4	84
• Novosibirsk Oblast	178,000	2,522,000	14.1	68
• Omsk Oblast	140,000	1,845,000	13.2	59
Tomsk Oblast	317,000	813,000	2.6	63
Tyumen Oblast	1,435,000	1,489,000	1.0	54
Khanty-Mansi National Okrug	523,000	332,000	0.6	67
Yamal-Nenets National Okrug	750,000	103,000	0.1	51
Total	2,427,000	12,208,000	5.0	65

chapter 17

the western siberia economic region

The huge expanse of land generally known as Siberia that lies east of the Urals and north of the Kazakhstan boundary constitutes well over half the territory of the Soviet Union. The name comes from the small Tatar town of Sibir on the eastern side of the Urals. It was captured at the outset of the conquest of the territory in 1583 by a small band of Cossacks under the leadership of Yermak who was commissioned by the Stroganov family to open up the area for fur trading. After the fall of Sibir, the Russians met with very little resistance in their eastward sweep to the Pacific, which took place in the short span of approximately 50 years. The area was essentially unoccupied except for a few thousand widely scattered Finnic tribes who busied themselves with reindeer herding, hunting, and fishing. The harsh land did not immediately entice the Russian adventurers to attempt to homestead, and so their forward advance was not slowed by individual settlement. Rather, they attempted to exercise control over the area through the establishment of forts and trading posts to facilitate the collection of furs from native hunters.

During the seventeenth and eighteenth centuries many of the fur-trading centers of Western Siberia gave way to agricultural settlements, farther south, and many new villages were established to accommodate the influx of Russian farmers. By the end of the nineteenth century the southern wooded-steppe and steppe strip of Western Siberia presented the aspect of a continuously settled area with a population that was predominantly rural. The coming of the Trans Siberian Railroad in the 1890s connected the elongated string of settlements with the more populous west and initiated urbanization. Wherever the railroad crossed a major river, a new town was established to handle the commerce. The river-rail towns grew and soon surpassed the old regional centers that lay to the north of the main rail line. Flour milling, textiles, and lumbering industries soon developed in the new towns. Later metallurgical industries became predominant as mining developed in the Kuznetsk Basin. Rail lines, hooking up with the Trans Siberian Railroad, spread out both north and south to tap all parts of the steppe zone.

Although the name Siberia ("sleeping land") has become known throughout the world, generally connoting a cold, frozen wasteland, most people outside the Soviet Union are not exactly sure what territory it includes. It is not a political entity, but the Soviets have its boundaries well in mind. It lies wholly within the Russian Republic, and therefore is bounded on the south by the Kazakhstan border. Under the currently used economic regionalization, it does not extend to the Pacific. In fact, it falls far short of that, hardly reaching more than halfway to the Pacific. The eastern half of the Asiatic part of the country is known as the Far East. The rest of the territory is generally divided into two parts, Western Siberia and Eastern Siberia, although this is a rather arbitrary division. Climatic, vegetation, and soil zones generally tend to run east-west across the two regions, and both regions contain a fairly well-settled southern fringe and broad expanses of empty land in their northern territories. Nevertheless, the tripartite division of the territory east of the Urals into Western Siberia, Eastern Siberia, and the Soviet Far East has become fairly well established in Soviet minds.

Western Siberia is the westernmost fifth of the territory east of the Urals. Politically it consists of the huge Tyumen Oblast, which stretches all the way from the Kazakhstan border to the Arctic coast and contains two national okrugs; Altay Kray in the southeast, which contains the Gorno Altay Autonomous Oblast in the high mountain region; and Omsk, Tomsk, Novosibirsk, and Kemerovo Oblasts along the Trans Siberian Railroad and its branches in the south. The total territory is 2,427,000 square kilometers, and the total population is 12,208,000. This gives the region an average population density of 5 persons per square kilometer. But this varies drastically from one part of the region to another. Highly industrialized Kemerovo Oblast has 30.4 people per square kilometer, while Tyumen Oblast has only 1 person per square kilometer, and the Yamal-Nenets National Okrug in the northern part of Tyumen Oblast has only 0.1 person per square kilometer. Huge tracts of forests and swamps, as well as some of the Altay Mountains in the southeast, have practically no people at all. Because much of the area has little potential for agriculture, the region is fairly highly urbanized — an average of 65 percent of the population lives in cities. This varies from 84 percent in Kemerovo Oblast to only 27 percent in the Gorno Altay Autonomous Oblast.

Most of the people in the region are Russian. There are also significant numbers of Ukrainians, Germans, Belorussians, and neighboring people such as Kazakhs, as well as some of the Volga Bend people such as the Chuvash and Mordvinians who are relatively mobile. The native groups are quite small. The 1970 census showed only 46,750 Altay in the Gorno Altay Autonomous Oblast; 21,000 Khanty and 8,000 Mansi, primarily in the Khanty-Mansi National Okrug; and 29,000 Nenets, primarily in the Yamal-Nenets National Okrug. The present population, then, is little different from that in European Russia. Birth rates are relatively low, death rates average, and national growth rates only modest. During the 1930s and 1940s there was rapid in-migration into the region, partially instigated by the movement of forced labor into new mines and industries in the region and the relocation of industries and personnel due to World War II. But after the 1957 amnesty decree many people began

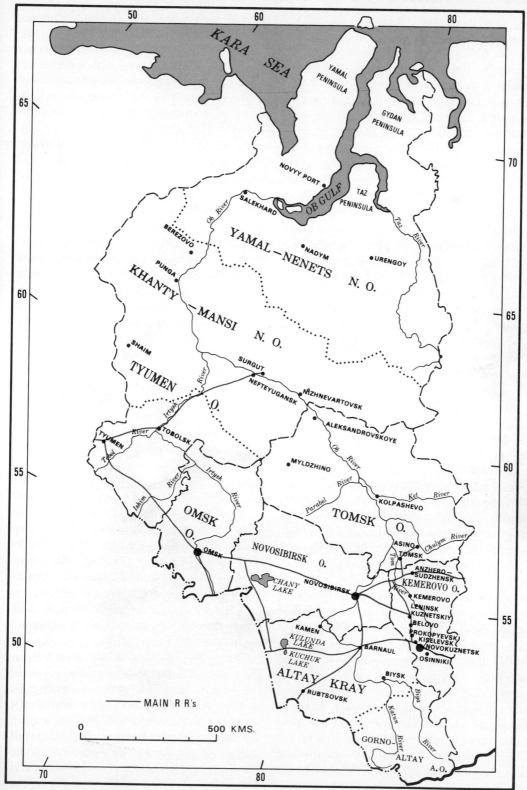

Figure 17-1   Western Siberia.

moving westward back to European U.S.S.R., and since that time much of the region, except Tyumen Oblast, has experienced a net out-migration. Therefore, the total population growth from the 1959 census to the 1970 census was only modest throughout most of the region. Tyumen Oblast was an exception because of the influx of oil and gas workers beginning in the mid-1960s, adding a significant portion to the small population that already existed there. The midsection of Tyumen Oblast showed one of the highest percentage growth rates anywhere in the country. But this did not mean a great influx of people. It simply meant that the original population had been sparse and that a significant number of people had been moved into the area to open up the rich oil and gas fields. In terms of population growth density (population growth per unit area), this region merges with the rest of Siberia and the Far East as being in the lowest category of growth density in the entire country.

PHYSICAL LANDSCAPE

Landform

The Western Siberia Economic Region contains two distinctively different geomorphic regions: the West Siberian Lowland and the northwestern extension of the Altay Mountain system. The region is not quite coextensive with the West Siberian Lowland, but ends with the western boundary of Krasnoyarsk Kray west of the Yenisey River before the lowland ends and the Central Siberian Upland begins. Also, in the south the lowland extends into northern Kazakhstan. Much of the lowland is drained by the great Ob River system, which also drains much of the Altay Mountains through the headwater streams, the Biya and the Katun, the major left-bank tributary, the Irtysh and its tributaries, and the main right-bank tributaries, the Tom and the Chulym. Much of the West Siberian Lowland is a very flat plain that has been washed by the sea a number of times in recent geologic periods. The most extensive transgression of the sea took place during the Eocene, at which time almost the entire plain was inundated and the West Siberian sea basin was connected with the Aral-Caspian depression through the Turgay Strait. Marine sediments up to as much as 10,000 meters in thickness cover an underlying basement of complex folded and intruded structures.

The lowland is generally concave toward the central part, which causes poor drainage. But through the center in an east-west direction runs a series of loosely connected slightly higher rises that are known collectively as the Siberian Ridges. They divide the basin into two concavities, to the south and to the north. In the south lies the vast Vasyugan Swamp, which occupies the broad central zone in which the Irtysh has its juncture with the Ob. To the north is a broad swampy lowland that includes the lower portions of the Ob River on the west and the entire length of the short Taz River on the east, both of which flow into an extensive estuary system that has recently been inundated by the sea. The Ob and Taz Gulfs penetrate the coastline more than 500 kilometers inland and divide the coastal area into huge peninsulas, the Yamal ("end of the earth") Peninsula on the west, the Taz in the center, and the Gydan on the east. The coastal zones of these peninsulas, inland as far as 100 kilometers in places, are occupied primarily by series of sea terraces on which the prevailingly strong winds have formed barchan dunes as high as 7–8 meters. The dunes migrate actively enough to keep the meager tundra vegetation from taking hold. The central parts of the peninsulas are occupied by low, hilly, morainic materials that have been dumped irregularly to form many kettle-lake basins.

During the Pleistocene, the West Siberian Plain was affected by three glacial advances: the Samara, the Taz, and the Zyryan. The Samara stage corresponds to the Dnieper stage in European U.S.S.R., the Taz stage to the Moscow stage, and the Zyryan stage to the Valday stage. The earlier glaciations constituted continental ice sheets that descended onto the plain from two sources, the Novaya Zemlya Mountains and polar Urals in the

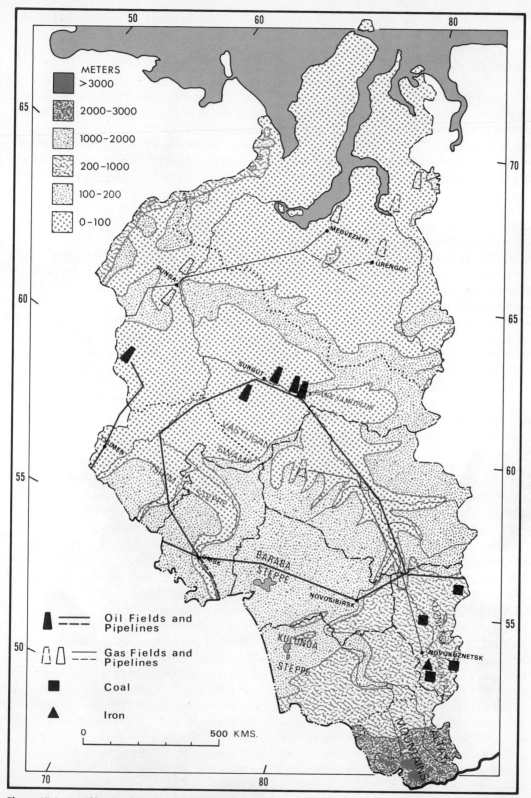

Figure 17-2 Landform, minerals, and pipelines.

northwest, and the Byrranga and Putorana Mountains on the northern portion of the East Siberian Upland to the northeast. These two sources are clearly marked on the plain by differentiations in the boulder beds in glacial deposits. In the western part of the plain along the lower reaches of the Irtysh and Ob Rivers, these boulder beds consist primarily of granites and granodiorites from the Urals, while in the eastern part of the plain, trap (volcanic) fragments have been brought from the Taymyr Peninsula.

During the oldest stage, the Samara, the continental ice sheet moved over the flat plain south to about the 58th parallel. It thus covered much of the two saucer-shaped depressions on either side of the Central Siberian Ridges as far south as the southern edge of the present taiga zone. Only the southern steppes were not covered by this ice sheet. But the steppe region also was greatly affected; the ice blocked northward-flowing streams and formed exceedingly extensive lakes that filled up the steppe lowlands, such as the Ishim, Baraba, and Kulunda steppes, and produced a great overflow of water toward the southwest into the Turgay Strait and southward toward the Aral Sea.

The Baraba and Kulunda Steppe regions, as well as the Ob Plateau just to the east, show the influences of this meltwater action most spectacularly. The whole region between the Irtysh and Ob Rivers south of the 56th parallel is streaked by these Pleistocene spillways that run northeast-southwest and today contain many small rivulets that flow either southwestward toward the Irtysh or northeastward toward the Ob, as well as a great number of elongated brackish lakes and chains of lakes that are all oriented in a northeast-southwest direction. These are huge features of low relief, usually detectable only by airplane or by mapping. On the ground their scale is too expansive to be grasped by the untrained eye. The ancient rills or valleys generally measure 5–15 kilometers in width, while the broad, flat ridges between them measure 15–50 kilometers wide. Elevation differences between rill bottoms and ridge tops amount to only 5–10 meters. The rills may extend for

250–300 kilometers in a northeast-southwest direction. Many of the small streams do not run their full lengths but end in small lake basins within the rills.

Today the extensive glacial lake beds are represented by the very flat, fertile steppe lowlands in the southern part of Western Siberia known by three regional names: the Ishim Steppe in the west between the Tobol and Irtysh Rivers through the center of which the Ishim River flows; the Baraba Steppe, which extends along the 56th parallel between the Irtysh and Ob Rivers; and the Kulunda Steppe, which also extends between the Irtysh and Ob River systems southeast of the Baraba Steppe. Loess-like loams occupy the surfaces of much of these steppe regions. These were probably laid down as delta formations in the glacial lake beds and were reworked to some extent by eolian processes. Perhaps significant thicknesses of loess were blown over the region from the north as the ice sheet melted and thereby exposed huge expanses of fine melt-water sediments that were drying out and being subjected to deflation. These lacustrine plains, which today are flat, fertile, subhumid steppes, are the best farmlands in Western Siberia.

During the early stages of interglacial periods the northern part of the West Siberian Lowland was inundated by transgressions of arctic water from the Kara Sea to the north. The farthest penetration of this seawater was to approximately the 63rd parallel along the slight rises of the Siberian Ridges running through the center of the basin. These transgressions of the sea rewashed glacial materials and erased much of the evidence regarding their extent.

The last glacial advance did not form an ice sheet over the plain. Individual mountain glaciers descended from the Urals in the west and the Taymyr-Putorana regions in the east and did not extend very far from their sources. Their extents are well marked by arrangements of terminal moraines around these highlands and the absence of morainic deposits in the northern part of the West Siberian Lowland.

The Ob and Irtysh Rivers have cut huge

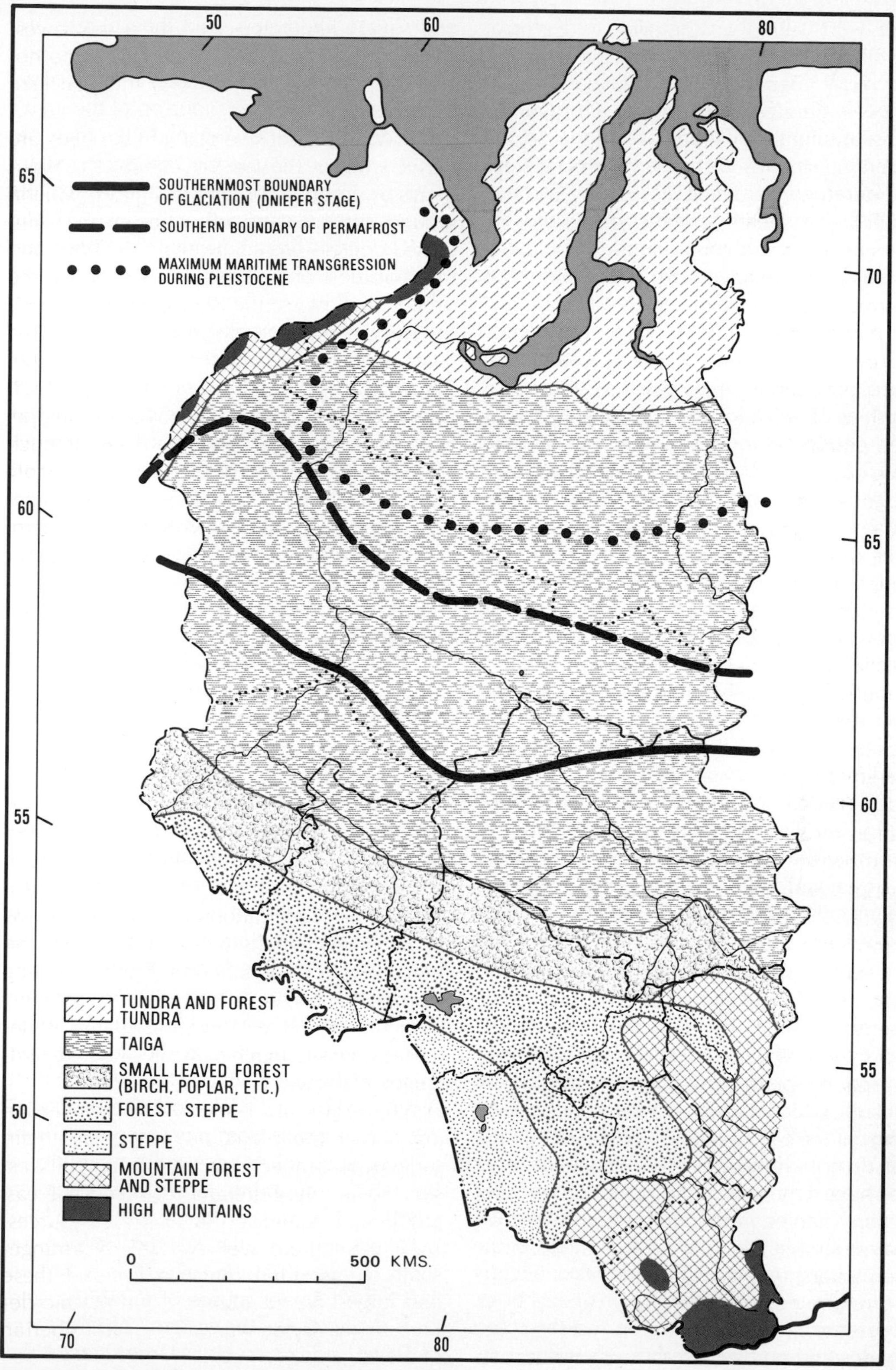
50
60
80
65
60
55
50
70
65
60
55
70
80
SOUTHERNMOST BOUNDARY OF GLACIATION (DNIEPER STAGE)
SOUTHERN BOUNDARY OF PERMAFROST
MAXIMUM MARITIME TRANSGRESSION DURING PLEISTOCENE
TUNDRA AND FOREST TUNDRA
TAIGA
SMALL LEAVED FOREST (BIRCH, POPLAR, ETC.)
FOREST STEPPE
STEPPE
MOUNTAIN FOREST AND STEPPE
HIGH MOUNTAINS
0
500 KMS.

Figure 17-3 Vegetation, soils, permafrost, and glaciation.

valleys 80–120 kilometers wide to depths of 60–80 meters that run through the length of the West Siberian Lowland. Generally, the valleys include a number of low, broad terraces at slightly different elevations. In between the streams are broad upland sections of undrained land that have not yet been reached by stream systems. Thousands of lakes of various origins abound on the plain. In the river floodplains are many enormous oxbow lakes and meander scars marking old cutoff meanders of the various streams. These features, along with their low, flat, natural levee formations, may cover widths of as much as 20–40 kilometers. During the spring melt period, when the southern headwaters thaw out before the northern lower portions of the streams do, ice jams on the lower streams cause widespread floods that fill up these old river channels to produce "sor" lakes that stretch over hundreds of square kilometers in territory and are generally 1–3 meters in depth. Many of the river channels themselves reach depths of 5–10 meters. During summer the water gradually recedes into the main riverbeds, and by the end of summer the subsiding lakes leave flat silt covered areas behind them. These "sor" lakes are favorite fish stocking areas, because they warm up rapidly during early summer and are rich in food.

In interfluve areas, the lakes may occupy basins of various formations. Some extensive, very shallow lakes occupy original shallow depressions on the otherwise flat marine and lacustrine plains. Others may occupy smaller, somewhat deeper depressions, in some cases resembling sinkholes, formed by thermokarst processes — the heaving and unequal sinking caused by permafrost (permanently frozen subsoil), which underlies much of the territory north of the 64th parallel. These lakes generally do not exceed 2–3 kilometers in diameter and have depths of 10–15 meters. Other lakes occupy kettles in morainic deposits, which may resemble the hummocky surfaces of the thermokarst regions. Still other lakes occupy basins formed by the destruction of peat bogs. These are generally found on marshy forest divides and on river terraces. Their size may range from only several square meters to several square kilometers, and their depths are usually only 1.5–2 meters.

In the southern steppes lakes may occupy depressions formed by suffusion of the lacustrine deposits. Fine dust particles may be washed out of the loosely compacted sediments by groundwater action, after which the ground surface gradually subsides and enclosed depressions are formed. The development of most of the basins of the numerous broad, shallow, saline and alkaline lakes of the steppes is apparently due to this process. Also, even in this southern region, thermokarst processes may have been active in the past when the earlier ice sheets lay just to the north. Undoubtedly, contemporary wind deflation processes have also added to these basin formations.

The generally high water table in the lowland, which is essentially a huge artesian basin, intersects many of the deeper hollows and maintains lakes in their lower portions throughout the year. But in the shallower basins the surface runoff collected during the thawing period in spring may evaporate completely by late summer, and nothing is left but salt encrustations on the surface. Attempts have been made to reduce evaporation and retain sufficient amounts of water in many of the lakes to keep them fresh enough to water livestock throughout the summer. Such measures include erecting embankments around the lake basins, planting trees, constructing snow-retention devices around the catch basins, and connecting several lakes into integrated catch basins so that water from broader areas can be concentrated into smaller lakes.

The water in the lakes of the steppe region ranges all the way from fresh through saline to alkaline. Many of the lakes are autoprecipitating, deriving salts from plugs underneath the surface. Such lakes have large quantities of salt, soda, mirabilite, and other chemical products. The most productive of these lakes is Lake Kuchuk in the Kulunda steppe just south of large Kulunda Lake. This is the second largest Soviet source of mirabilite, after Kara-Bogaz-Gol of the eastern Caspian. Many of the larger lakes, such as large Chany Lake, with a surface area of 2600 square kilometers, are of commercial fishing value. Also, large numbers of waterfowl find havens in the reed fields and sedges around the edges of the lakes during their migrating seasons in spring and autumn. Large numbers of geese and ducks are bred annually on the lakes of the Baraba Steppe. In this region muskrats were introduced from America in 1935; they readily acclimatized and spread over the entire region.

The rivers of the West Siberian Plain carry large volumes. The Ob River annually discharges 394 billion cubic meters of water into the Kara Sea. This is equal to the amount of water carried by 14 rivers the size of the Don. Many of the rivers are navigable, and in the region north of the Trans Siberian Railroad they are about the only menas of transportation. The Ob and its larger tributaries—the Irtysh, the Tobol, the Vasyugan, the Parabel, the Ket, the Chulym, the Tom, the Charysh, and a number of others — are regularly used for navigation purposes. The total length of navigable routes within the West Siberian Plain is more than 20,000 kilometers.

Unfortunately, many of the streams do not flow in the direction of the main flow of traffic. Much of the traffic crosses the area from west to east, and most of the streams run from south to north. The east-west sections of streams, such as the latitudinally flowing midsection of the Ob River in the central part of the basin, are most useful to navigation. In the early days of conquest before the coming of the Trans Siberian Railroad, the east-west portion of streams, connected by portages, were most useful to the Russian advance to the east. The Russians have long dreamed of connecting some of these east-west flowing portions to form a single east-west route across the territory.

This desire was part of the motive behind a proposed lower Ob dam near the mouth of the Ob at Salekhard. The dam would create a huge reservoir backed upstream past the juncture of the Irtysh with the Ob and flood the east-west portion of the Ob and some of its tributary streams eastward toward the Yenisey Divide. This might allow an easy connection between some of the small tributaries joining the Ob with the Yenisey. Of course, this connection would be only a side benefit from the diversion of the water southward, for which the reservoir would be primarily built. This scheme was discussed to some extent in the last chapter. However, the creation of such a huge reservoir in the West Siberian Lowland might have detrimental environmental effects, and it certainly would increase the difficulty of exploiting the rich oil deposits in the middle Ob Basin that are now under development. Since the discovery and exploitation of this oil, little has been said about the construction of this huge reservoir. It appears that the consideration of the oil basin has tipped the balance against the construction of the lower Ob dam. Any diversion projects that might be attempted in the future will probably be on smaller scales, perhaps involving only the Irtysh River and sections of the upper Ob.

The streams of Western Siberia also represent a very large hydroelectric potential. However, there are not very good dam sites on much of the West Siberian Plain. The narrow rocky valley of the Irtysh River between the confluence of the Bukhtarma and the city of Ust-Kamenogorsk is the most suitable for dam sites. Consequently, the Ust-Kamenogorsk and Bukhtarma electric plants have already been built on the Irtysh within eastern Kazakhstan. Also, a major reservoir has been created on the upper Ob by a dam at Novosibirsk, where the Ob River has cut a fairly narrow channel through the Ob Plateau. The hydroelectric plant at Novosibirsk has a capacity of 400,000 kilowatts. The dam has backed the water up one of the northeast-southwest-oriented ancient valleys occupied by the Ob for a distance of about 240 kilometers in an elongated reservoir that is as much as 20 kilometers wide in places. The reservoir extends to Kamen-na-Obi ('rock on the Ob') where it is planned to build a second dam. The Kamen dam is to back water upstream beyond the city of Barnaul and provide water to irrigate more than 2 million hectares of land in the Kulunda Steppe. The power plant is to have a capacity of 630,000 kilowatts.

In the southeastern corner of the Western Siberia Region lie the northwestern extensions of the Altay Mountains, whose main mass is in Mongolia and China. Much of the Soviet portion of the mountain mass lies in the Gorno-Altay Autonomous Oblast within Altay Kray. All of this oblast is occupied by high, rugged mountains rising to as much as 4506 meters in Mt. Belukha on the Kazakhstan border. The highest peaks in this region are covered with glaciers and snowfields that feed the headwaters of the Ob, the Biya and the Katun. Higher elevations throughout this district generally run about 2500 meters. The higher ridges are composed of cirques and horns separated by gorgelike U-shaped glacial valleys.

Two lower prongs of the Altay extend north-northwestward on either side of the Tom River between the Ob and the Yenisey to form the Kuznetsk Basin. On the west is the low Salair Ridge, whose maximum elevation rises to only 590 meters, and on the east is the Kuznetsk Alatau, which reaches a maximum elevation of 2178 meters. The two prongs join in the south in what is known as the Gornaya-Shoriya area, where elevations lie around 1500–1800 meters before merging southward with the Gorno-Altay area and the Western Sayans.

Climate, Vegetation, and Soils

The climate of Western Siberia is severe. Winters are colder than in any region discussed thus far. Because of the great continentality, midsummers are still relatively warm, so that seasonal changes are very great. As is true in all high-latitude areas, the transitional seasons are very short, temperatures falling rapidly between summer and winter and rising rapidly between winter and summer. Winter is by far the longest season. Spring is almost nonexistent. The deep snow cover during winter takes much of the spring heating for melting purposes, so that the temperature of the surface air does not rise significantly above freezing until all the snow is gone, the top soil has thawed, and much of the meltwater has evaporated. By this time, the season has progressed far along toward the summer solstice so that the high amounts of radiation

during almost 24-hour daylight periods cause the surface temperatures to rise almost instantaneously once the heat of fusion and evaporation is no longer needed. During fall no such change of state of water comes into play, temperatures descend somewhat more slowly, and a definite period can be identified as autumn. The weather graph for Omsk (Fig. 17-4), illustrates this fairly well. The long winter is also evident. Omsk, of course, lies along the southern fringe of Western Siberia. In the northern part of the territory the winter is still longer and the asymmetry of spring and fall even more pronounced.

July temperatures at Omsk average 19.5°C. and have reached a maximum of 40°C (104°F). Thus, midsummer is rather warm for the latitude of 55°N. However, summer is short. The growing season is only 115 days on the average. Killing frosts may occur any month except July. During January temperatures average −18.9°C and have reached as low as −49°C (−56°F).

Farther north at Surgut in the middle of the lowland, winter temperatures are colder, reaching a minimum as low as −55°C. Summers, of course, are cooler, and killing frosts can occur all months of the year. In the far north, at Salekhard near the mouth of the Ob River, summer temperatures are somewhat cooler, but winter temperatures are not perceptibly colder than they are at Surgut. January temperatures average about 2°C colder at Salekhard than at Surgut, but the absolute minimum temperature at Salekhard is 1°C warmer than at Surgut.

The minimum temperatures are held up a little bit by the influence of the Arctic Ocean during winter where the surface air gains some heat through the ice from the unfrozen water underneath. This keeps surface air temperatures significantly warmer over the Arctic ice cap than over the adjacent land to the south and causes constant offshore winds to blow from south to north along the coast during the winter. During summer the situation is reversed. While the land is warming up rapidly, the melting ice in the Arctic keeps the surface water temperatures about at the freezing point, which keeps surface air tempera-

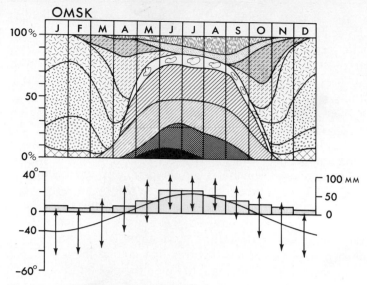

Figure 17-4 Weather types, temperature, and precipitation at Omsk. For legend see page 6.

tures at about the same level. Thus, the air over the water is much cooler than it is over the adjacent land, and there is a constant sea breeze during summer blowing from the cold sea to the warm land. This seasonal reversal of wind direction along the Arctic coast is monsoonal in nature and is so called by the Russians.

Although minimum temperatures during winter are generally colder in the interior than they are along the Arctic coast, the wind chill factor along the coast is much higher than it is in the interior. Farther east along the Arctic in the Eastern Siberia and Far East Regions, wind chill factors along the coast reach temperature equivalents of −125 to −135°C, probably the coldest wind chill factors on earth. On exposed headlands and islands along the coast, winter is truly unbearable. On Dikson Island along the northeastern coast of the Yenisey estuary, wind speeds average 7–8 meters per second (15–17 miles per hour) every month of the year and reach speeds of 15 meters per second (30 miles per hour) or more on 84 days of the year. The average wind speeds are a little greater in winter than in summer, and high wind speeds occur much more frequently during the winter. At Surgut, on the other hand, wind speeds of more than

15 meters per second are experienced only 18 days per year. Farther south in the steppes, wind speeds pick up somewhat. At Barnaul in the Kulunda Steppe in the far southeastern part of Western Siberia, wind speeds of more than 15 meters per second are experienced 45 days per year. However, there are many days with very light winds at Barnaul, so that the average wind speed is considerably less than it is at Surgut. Most of the high winds at Barnaul are associated with cyclonic storms during winter that may produce strong blizzards, the so-called buran or purga.

Western Siberia has about the greatest cyclone frequency anywhere in the U.S.S.R. This is particularly true in the north along the Ob Gulf. Two favorite routes of cyclones converge on this area, one from the west that crosses Scandinavia, the Baltic, and the Barents Sea and skirts along the Arctic coast, and the other from the southwest that sweeps in from the Black and Caspian Sea areas around the southern end of the Urals and northward through the Ob Basin. The storms are a little more frequent and more intense during winter than during summer, but there are significant numbers in summer as well. During summer they carry greater moisture and are enhanced by local thundershowers, so that the whole

Western Siberia Region exhibits a pronounced summer maximum of precipitation. For instance, Omsk, in the south, receives a yearly average of 325 millimeters of precipitation, 72 millimeters of which comes during July, and only 6 millimeters during February (Fig. 17-4). In the center of the plain, Surgut receives 492 millimeters of precipitation per year, which is a little more evenly distributed throughout the year. However, the summer is still much wetter than winter. July averages 68 millimeters, while February averages only 19. In the far north absolute atmospheric humidities decrease because of the decreasing capacity to hold moisture due to decreasing temperatures, so that the annual precipitation diminishes a little. Salekhard averages 464 millimeters of precipitation per year, with a maximum of 57 during both July and August and a minimum of 20 millimeters during February. At Salekhard and Surgut there is ample precipitation to take care of all evaporation during the year and leave a surplus, while at Omsk potential annual evaporation is almost twice as much as annual precipitation. The bulk of the West Siberian Lowland, then, would classify as a humid area southward to

about the 56th parallel, but south of there it becomes semiarid.

Throughout the entire plain the second half of summer generally has significantly more precipitation than the first half. And the precipitation maximum lags from July in the south to August in the north. This is not the best distribution through the summer for agriculture. Late summer and fall rains often make the harvest very uncertain during a season that is very short anyway and that may be brought abruptly to a halt by an early snowstorm. Excessive moisture at this time of year has induced the Soviets to practice time-consuming two-stage wheat harvesting, which involves first cutting the wheat and allowing it to lie on the ground to cure, and then later picking it up with combines and threshing it (Fig. 17-5).

During winter when much of Eastern Siberia and the Far East is dominated by the Asiatic High, which sends an elongated nose westward across the northern part of Kazakhstan as well, much of the Western Siberia Region, except for the southeastern fringe, lies in a concavity along the northwestern edge of the high in the eastern extension of the Ice-

Figure 17-5   Two-stage wheat harvesting in Western Siberia. Novosti.

landic Low. Thus, the winter weather of much of Western Siberia is very different from that in most of Eastern Siberia and the Far East. It is much stormier, much cloudier, and not as cold as farther east. Cloud cover at Surgut averages seven to nine tenths of the sky throughout the year. It is clearest during early summer and midwinter when it averages about six to seven tenths and cloudiest in fall when during October it averages almost nine-tenths. Overcast skies occur 154 days per year at Surgut. The situation is very similar in the far north at Salekhard. Farther south at Omsk cloudiness is reduced somewhat but is still surprisingly high, averaging six to eight tenths every month of the year.

Snow accumulates to considerable depths during winter. Some shadow effect is produced by the Urals in the western part of the basin, but snowfall and snow accumulation pick up again farther east. Snow depth reaches 75–90 centimeters along the eastern fringe of the basin in the middle Yenisey Valley. This is some of the heaviest snow accumulation in the country, rivaling the western slopes of the middle Urals and parts of the Khibiny Mountains on the Kola Peninsula. In the middle of the basin at Surgut snow lies on the ground 205 days of the year and reaches a maximum depth of 75 centimeters. In the south at Omsk it lies on the ground 157 days per year and reaches a maximum depth of 31 centimeters. In the far north at Salekhard it lies on the ground 233 days per year and reaches a maximum depth of 59 centimeters.

During summer consistent southward flows of air onto the landmass from the Arctic Ocean carry maritime arctic air deep into the basin. Although this air does not hold a great deal of moisture, it is nearly saturated, and under strong surface heating undergoes considerable convective activity that produces many short, showery bursts of precipitation during the summer, occasionally reaching thunderstorm proportions. For instance, Surgut receives 14 days with thunderstorms per year, with 5 during July. Even in the far north Salekhard receives 6 thunderstorm days per year. In the south Omsk experiences thunderstorms 20 days per year, with 7 occurring during July.

Natural vegetation on the West Siberian Plain is organized in essentially zonal belts that reflect the increasing coolness and shortness of summer toward the north and the moisture deficit along the southern fringe. Drainage conditions, particularly along the Siberian Ridges in the central part of the basin, induce irregularities in the zonal pattern. Along the Arctic coast tundra vegetation extends southward to about the Arctic Circle, covering all the large peninsulas and extending in a narrow strip along the main continental landmass. This grades into a narrow zone of forest tundra and eventually into the taiga, which covers the bulk of the basin southward to about the 56th parallel (Fig. 17-3).

Near the forest-tundra fringe, the forest is primarily a sparse larch stand. This is interspersed with numerous flat, hummocky sphagnum marshes. Toward the south larch becomes mixed with spruce, birch, and cedar. The central part of the taiga zone is what is known as the dark coniferous forest, very dense and forbidding. Fir and cedar with admixtures of larch, birch, and aspen are the predominant trees. Pine groves with sphagnum marshes dominate the area west of the Ob-Irtysh River system. In the south the taiga consists primarily of fir with mixtures of birch, aspen, and linden. There is very little in the way of a mixed forest east of the Urals. The coniferous forests of the north give way to a thin zone of deciduous forests made up primarily of fluffy birch, white birch, and aspen, with some mixtures of spruce and fir. Pine forests grow in the sandier areas. In the south this zone gives way to the forest steppe and eventually to the open steppe. Here drought and sukhovey (dry winds) are common, being most frequent during the first half of summer.

Soil zones correspond to these vegetation zones, with intrazonal irregularities produced by drainage differences. The tundra and forest soils are relatively poor, badly leached and podsolized, and are not of much use for agriculture. The forest-steppe and steppe zones of the south are a continuation of the chernozem belt that starts in the western Ukraine and runs through the south-central portion of European U.S.S.R. The belt crosses the southern Urals in intermontane basins and continues to cross the southern part of the West Siberian Plain in a zone approximately 300 kilometers wide. It ends rather abruptly at the Altay Mountains but is continued eastward in a discontinuous string of mountain basins all the way to the Pacific. The Kuznetsk Basin between the prongs of the Altay has wooded-steppe and steppe vegetation with rich chernozem soils. Much of the Baraba and Kulunda Steppes have rich chernozems, grading into chestnuts and solonchalks (saline) and solonets (alkali) soils in the drier portions toward the southwest.

In the Altay, the climate, vegetation, and soils are arranged very much in vertical zones, with some influence from direction of exposure to prevailing winds, storms, precipitation, and sunlight. In the high Altay the steppe and forest-steppe zones generally extend upward to about 250–500 meters, above which a zone of mixed forests of pines, spruce, birch, and some broadleaf trees extends upward to about 500–600 meters. Above this the dark coniferous forests rise to about 1400–1600 meters, above which is a cedar forest rising to 2000–2200 meters. Subalpine meadows and brush continue up to about 2500 meters, above which lie alpine meadows that form a discontinuous zone, absent in some of the mountains. Forest tundra occupies the higher peaks up to 3000 meters or more, above which the highest peaks extend above the snow line.

These vertical zones vary considerably from one part of the Altay to another, generally being lower in the southwest and rising higher in the northeast. The low Salair Ridge rises only into the lower parts of the dark coniferous forest, and the Kuznetsk Alatau rises into the alpine meadows. It is only the higher peaks of the Gorno-Altay region that rise above this into the perpetual snows. Throughout the Altay, there are many basins and river valleys that contain steppe climate and good chernozem and chestnut soils. These are the areas of limited cultivation, above which rise the mountains that are used only for grazing and lumbering.

AGRICULTURE

Agricultural land in Western Siberia amounts to about 35 million hectares, which is only about 14 percent of the total territory of the region. Of this about 20 million hectares is arable, 7 million in permanent fodder, and 8 million in pasture. Much of the arable land is in the chernozem forest-steppe and steppe zones in the south. There is little cultivation north of 56°N latitude. During the 1950s southwestern Siberia shared in the Virgin Lands Program, and the crop land increased from 12 million hectares in 1953 to 18 million hectares in 1967. Land is now being used that receives no more than 200 millimeters (8 inches) of precipitation per year. Fortunately, more than two-thirds of this precipitation falls during the growing season, but, as pointed out previously, in many cases more of it falls during the second half of the season than during the first half. This causes moisture deficits during the early stages of rapid growth and poor drying conditions when the crops are ready to be harvested.

The steppe zone of the southern part of the region northward to about the Trans Siberian Railroad is occupied primarily by spring wheat, with some mixtures of corn for silage, sunflowers, and a few other drought-resistant crops. Cattle are raised for meat and milk, and fine-wooled sheep are raised. North of the Trans Siberian in a strip of land about 150 kilometers wide the agriculture is a mixture of spring wheat, flax, and dairying. The high mountains of the Gorno-Altay region, as well as the southern part of the Kuznetsk Alatau, are utilized for grazing of sheep and cattle. In the Kuznetsk basin and around some of the other major cities urban-oriented agriculture of vegetables and fruit has developed. North of the 57th or 58th parallel the rural economy is based primarily on reindeer herding, hunting, fishing, and lumbering.

Agriculture in the steppe lands of the Western Siberian Plain may be enhanced in the near future by irrigation networks that would convert the agriculture from dry farming to irrigation farming. This would allow much more intensive cultivation and higher yields. Work has already begun on the so-called West Siberian Irrigation Canal, which will run 180 kilometers from Kamen on the Ob River into the Kulunda Steppe where it is to irrigate 20,000 hectares of land by 1980. It is ultimately to be extended to Pavlodar on the Irtysh River to increase the flow of the Irtysh in preparation for diverting water from the Irtysh southward through the Turgay Lowland into Kazakhstan and Central Asia.

It is now envisioned that in the not-too-distant future a dam will be constructed on the Irtysh near Tobolsk. This dam will back water up both the Irtysh and the Tobol Rivers and provide a large reservoir out of which can be pumped water up the Tobol Valley and across the Turgay Divide into the Aral Sea basin. Once this is done, additional Ob water might be made available by building a canal from the Ob at Kolpashevo through the Vasyugan Swamp to the Irtysh River. It is hoped that at the same time this northern water is made useful in the southern deserts, its extraction from the swamps in the West Siberian Plain will improve their water balance. In addition, it is planned that some parts of the West Siberian Plain may be drained by creating gigantic water-collecting basins with a series of nuclear explosions that would, in addition to producing surface basins, crack up the subsurface rocks to provide for better percolation, and make more readily available certain mineral deposits, such as oil.

FORESTRY

About one-third of the Western Siberia Region is covered by forests. The usable resources total about 8.6 billion cubic meters, out of which 4.5 billion cubic meters is found in Tyumen Oblast and 2.5 billion cubic meters in Tomsk Oblast. About two-thirds of the trees are conifers. Most of the rest are birch and alder. The densest stands of forests are actually in Altay Kray on the mountain slopes. Much of the forest cover in the Ob Basin is relatively sparse and spindly. Toward the north larch is the predominant tree, but it is not the best for lumbering. In addition to its poor quality, larch wood is very heavy, and logs tend to get water-logged and sink in streams, which makes log floating very difficult.

According to 1973 figures, Western Siberia contains 12.6 percent of the timber reserves of the U.S.S.R. This puts it in third place among the economic regions after Eastern Siberia and the Far East. But none of these huge eastern regions have the density and quality of stands of some parts of the Northwest and Urals Regions. Permanently frozen subsoil and poor surface drainage conditions drastically limit the species that can grow and the quality of the trees that do grow. Larch is admirably suited to growth over permafrost because it has a shallow-spreading root system that can feed off the thin cover of thawed topsoil during summer.

In 1973, Western Siberia produced 31.4 million cubic meters of wood of all types, which was about 8.1 percent of the country's total. This put it in fifth place after the Northwest, Eastern Siberia, the Urals, and the Far East. It was only slightly ahead of such small areas as the Central Region and the Volga-Vyatka Region. Distance from market, of course, is the determining factor in that comparison. Western Siberia produced even less saw timber than the Central Region, but it outproduced the Far East in this regard, so it retained its fifth-place standing in the country. Within the Western Siberia Region, two-thirds of the wood is produced in Tyumen and Tomsk Oblasts. More remote areas of good stands of timber are being made available in these regions by the building of special railroads branching off either the Trans Siberian Railroad in the south or railroads running along the eastern slopes of the Urals. One such special railroad is the Ivdel-Ob Railroad, which was completed in 1967 specifically to open up new timberlands.

Some railroads are serving the dual functions of making accessible new mineral deposits and opening up new lumbering areas along the way. The Tyumen-Surgut Railroad is one such example. The railroad has been built from Tyumen through Tobolsk to Surgut primarily to facilitate the tremendous development in the oil industry taking place around Surgut. But, incidentally, the railroad has opened up a stretch of land about 650 kilometers long for new lumbering activity. Another railroad of similar note is being extended northward from Tomsk to Asino to Belyy Yar and beyond, eventually perhaps to the oil fields on the Tomsk-Tyumen Oblast border.

Asino was established in 1946 at the end of a Trans Siberian rail spur near the Chulym River, a major logging stream. It has developed into the biggest lumber-products center in Western Siberia. By 1970 Asino's population had grown to 29,000. The railroad to Belyy Yar on the Ket River was designed to open up rich new timberlands to feed the Asino complex. The Ket River timberlands are some of the highest-quality timberlands in Western Siberia. One-half to three-fourths of their trees consist of valuable commercial species such as pine and spruce.

MINERALS AND INDUSTRIES

The minerals in Western Siberia consist overwhelmingly of the mineral fuels. Coal, oil, and natural gas occur in great abundance. It is now thought that Western Siberia contains the largest oil and gas fields in the country. And the Kuznetsk coal basin has long been the second most important coal producer in the country after the Donets Basin in eastern Ukraine.

The exploitation of the Kuznetsk coal has been going on since the 1890s when mines were opened up at Anzhero-Sudzhensk to supply steam coal to the newly completed Trans Siberian Railroad. Since then, the coal mining has provided the basis for development of many heavy industries in the Kuznetsk Basin, as well as in neighboring cities such as Novosibirsk just to the west. During the early period of Soviet industrialization in the 1930s, coal-mining centers developed at Leninsk-Kuznetskiy, Kiselevsk, Prokopyevsk,

and Osinniki, as well as in some minor centers in the Kuznetsk Basin. At the same time an iron and steel plant was developed at the town of Stalinsk, now Novokuznetsk ("new Kuznetsk") at the eastern end of the rail shuttle of the so-called Urals-Kuznetsk Combine, which moved Magnitogorsk ore eastward and Kuzentsk coal westward.

A zinc refinery was constructed in Belovo in 1930 to process lead-zinc ores from the Salair Ridge just to the west. However, these small ore deposits soon became depleted, and Belovo began shipping in concentrates from other mines as far east as Tetyukhe near the Pacific coast. The Salair Ridge now yields mainly gold, silver, and barite.

Coke ovens first went into operation in the city of Kemerovo in 1934, and this laid the basis for a complex of coke-chemical industries that now turn out analine dyes, nitrogen fertilizers, and kapron. Kemerovo is now the Soviet Union's largest producer of kapron. During World War II the small aluminum plant at Volkhov, near Leningrad, was evacuated and reassembled at Novokuznetsk, and since then it has been expanded into one of the largest aluminum producers in the Soviet Union. It originally used alumina from the Urals, but now most of the alumina comes from Pavlodar in Kazakhstan.

The Urals-Kuznetsk Combine did not operate very long as a coordinated unit because Novokuznetsk began using local iron ores in the Gornaya-Shoriya mines in the hills along the southern periphery of the Kuznetsk Basin. Additional ores were later brought into production to the east in the Kuznetsk Alatau within the Khakass Autonomous Oblast and finally much farther east at Zheleznogorsk ("iron mountain") east of Bratsk in Irkutsk Oblast of Eastern Siberia. A railroad was built from Abakan through Tayshet to Zheleznogorsk, and since then some new iron deposits have been opened up in southern Krasnoyarsk Kray along this railroad, particularly in the Irba district.

During World War II, Novokuznetsk gained a ferro-alloys plant, and during the mid-1960s a new integrated iron and steel plant was built about 16 kilometers northeast of Novokuznetsk. This new plant, called the West Siberian Plant, has expanded beyond the size of the old Kuznetsk plant. In 1974 the West Siberian Plant produced about 6 million tons of steel as compared to about 4.5 million tons at the Kuznetsk Plant. Small plants in some other cities brought the total West Siberian steel production in 1974 to 12 million tons. This was 9 percent of the country's total. Pig iron production in Western Siberia in 1974 totaled 9 million tons, which also was about 9 percent of the country's total. Plans call for the expansion of the West Siberian Plant to a capacity of 20 million tons of steel by 1985. This is to be achieved by the construction of new basic oxygen converters and electric furnaces. Together with the older Kuznetsk Plant, the West Siberian Plant is to supply all the steel-sheet needs of Siberia by 1985.

In 1972 the Soviets announced the beginning of the construction of a coke-chemical plant in the town of Zarinskaya east of Barnaul in Altay Kray. A coke-chemical plant is ordinarily the beginning of an iron and steel complex. There have been some hints in published materials that the Soviets are seriously considering another large iron and steel complex at this location. The site lies on the recently completed South Siberian Railroad between Barnaul and the Kuznetsk Basin where the railroad crosses the Chumysh River, a log-floating stream from the Altay Mountains. No recent information has been received regarding this project.

The Kuznetsk coal basin rapidly became the second most important coal producer in the country after the Donets Basin in the eastern Ukraine. The reserves at Kuznetsk are much greater and of higher quality generally than those in the Donets Basin, but because of its more remote location with respect to the nation's markets the Kuznetsk Basin has not developed as highly as the Donets Basin. Its reserves are surpassed only by those of the Tunguskan and Lena coalfields in Eastern Siberia, neither of which has significant production. The Kemerovo part of the Kuznetsk Basin has 40 working seams ranging 2–50 meters in thickness, with an aggregate thick-

ness of 70 meters. The seams are thicker and not quite so broken up by tectonic activity, nor as deep below the surface, as those of the Donets Basin, so mining operations are considerably cheaper in Kuznetsk. About 75 percent of the present production is by shaft mines in steeply pitching seams in the southern part of the basin, and 25 percent is by open-pit mining in the more nearly horizontal beds that are closer to the surface toward the northern part of the basin. In 1974 the Kuznetsk Basin produced 128 million tons of coal out of a U.S.S.R. total of 684 million. This compared to 220 million tons in the Donets Basin, which was first in production, and 45 million tons in the Karaganda Basin, which was third in production. Thus, the Donets and Kuznetsk Basins stand well above any other basins in production. About 40 percent of the Kuznetsk coal is of coking quality, and this accounts for about 30 percent of the coking-coal production in the U.S.S.R.

Shipments of coal from the Kuznetsk Basin travel farther than they do from any other coal basin in the country. This is because of the high quality and relatively low cost of production of the coal. Kuznetsk coal serves part of the needs of about half the territory of the U.S.S.R., from central European Russia to Eastern Siberia. About 40 percent of the coal produced in the Kuznetsk Basin is used in Western Siberia, and the rest is shipped to such places as the Urals, the Central Region, the Volga Region, Kazakhstan, and Central Asia. The greatest share goes to the Urals where the many metallurgical industries use large quantities that are not locally available. In spite of the fact that the Karaganda coal is closer, its high ash content has limited its use in metallurgical industries, and Kuznetsk coal still supplies about two-thirds of the needs of the Urals metallurgy. If an all-water route is ever provided from the Pechora coal basin to the middle Urals, the Pechora coal may replace some of the Kuznetsk coal in the Urals metallurgical centers. But this is a very indefinite prospect.

Since the late 1950s the silence of the swamps of Western Siberia has been broken by the clanking steel of oil derricks and the rumble of heavy construction equipment. The once-empty land has witnessed a tremendous oil boom that has brought not only workers from the oil districts of Azerbaydzhan, Tataria, and Bashkiria, but also construction workers and their families to build towns, highways, railroads, pipelines, and electrical transmission lines. Much of this activity has taken place around the old town of Surgut near the confluence of the Irtysh and Ob Rivers in the seemingly inaccessible central portion of the Vasyugan Swamp.

Commercial oil was first struck farther west near the small center of Shaim on the Konda River in 1959 whence the first crude oil moved by barge during the summer of 1964 down the Konda and then up the Irtysh to a refinery at Omsk. The following year a 400-kilometer pipeline carried the crude oil to Tyumen, where it was transferred to rail tank cars and carried to Omsk. However, the Soviets were eager to move their oil completely by pipe, and in 1967 a pipeline was completed from the Ust-Balyk field about 45 kilometers southwest of Surgut to Omsk. The 1000-kilometer, 40-inch pipeline picked up oil from several other fields along the way. In 1969 a 30-inch pipeline was connected into this line from Samotlor, which has proved to be the biggest oil producer in Western Siberia. Also in 1969 the pipeline system was extended to fields in Tomsk Oblast.

In 1972 a second major pipeline 800 kilometers long and 48 inches in diameter was completed from the Tomsk fields around Aleksandrovskoye to Anzhero-Sudzhensk in the Kuznetsk Basin where it hooked up with the Trans Siberian oil pipeline that had been built earlier to carry Volga-Urals oil eastward to Irkutsk. Some of the oil flowing southward to Omsk was also being transmitted eastward through this same transmission system to the refinery at Angarsk near Irkutsk. In 1970 the oil flow in the western section of the Trans Siberian pipeline system was reversed so that West Siberian oil started moving westward from Omsk to Ufa in the Bashkir Republic, rather than eastward from Bashkiria to Siberia as it had been doing up to that time.

A third major pipeline was completed in 1973 from Nizhnevartovsk near the Samotlor field through Nefteyugansk, Tobolsk, Tyumen, and Kurgan, to Almetyevsk in the Tatar Republic where it hooked up with the Friendship oil pipeline going across European U.S.S.R. to the East European satellites. This pipeline, 1844 kilometers long and 48 inches in diameter, is known as the Asia-Europe oil pipeline. A second pipeline was completed to Anzhero-Sudzhensk that same year and has since been extended eastward to Krasnoyarsk. Initially it was planned to extend this pipeline all the way to the Pacific, perhaps with the help of Japan, but Japanese companies seem to be reluctant to become involved this deeply in the extraction of Siberian oil for export to them. It now appears that the pipeline will be built only to Tayshet parallel to the pipeline that already exists there, and then the oil will be transferred to railroad tank cars and carried to the Pacific over the new Baykal-Amur Mainline.

In 1974 a 1500-kilometer pipeline was completed from Kuybyshev on the Volga to Novorossiysk on the eastern Black Sea coast to facilitate export of West Siberian oil, now being brought to Kuybyshev by pipe. Pipelines already run northwestward from Kuybyshev to the Baltic at Ventspils, so that Western Siberian oil now has outlets for export through both the Baltic and the Black Seas.

In addition to the many pipelines built from the Surgut area, the important access railroad from Tyumen was completed to the left bank of the Ob River in 1973. In 1975 a long bridge was completed across the broad floodplain of the Ob into the city of Surgut on the right bank of the river.

The West Siberian oil development has proceeded at an unprecedented rate, in spite of the fantastic hazards presented by the natural environment. In the short period of one decade, production in Western Siberia has increased from zero in 1963 to 116 million tons in 1974. This is twice the developmental rate of the Volga-Urals fields that took place earlier. The 1975 production plan was for 146 million tons. The Soviets envision an ultimate annual production from Western Siberia of at least 500 million tons, which is more than the total production in the entire U.S.S.R. in 1975.

The Soviets claim to have found more than 100 separate deposits of oil in Western Siberia, and they are looking for more below the gas fields along the Arctic coast. Also, there has been a recent report that oil has been found in older rocks in Novosibirsk Oblast farther south. The continued development of oil production in Western Siberia has been listed as one of the big projects planned during the years 1975–1990, along with the construction of the BAM railroad in Eastern Siberia and the Far East and the improvement of agriculture in the non-chernozem zone of European Russia.

The biggest oil pool located so far in Western Siberia lies beneath Lake Samotlor ("trap lake") in the middle of the Vasyugan Swamp, which is really a floating bog about 250 square kilometers in size, covered by 1–2 meters of water under which lies a 15–20-meter layer of quaking decomposed peat. This may well be the largest single oil field in the world. In 1974 the Samotlor area produced 61.2 million tons of petroleum, and the goal for 1975 was 86 million tons. It is estimated that the area is capable of producing 160 million tons per year.

The exploitation of the oil at Samotlor has required all the ingenuity that the Soviets could muster. The first corduroy (log) roads that were built into the bog were irrevocably sucked into the quagmire in about a month, and $-58°C$ temperatures during the following winter caused steel rigging to become brittle and break and lubricating oils to freeze. But eventually a hard-surface road was constructed across the bog on a floating foundation of frozen peat covered by dry earth to protect it from thawing during the summer. Small islets were filled in to provide platforms for drilling rigs, from which as many as 20 sloping shafts could be sunk from a single platform to exploit oil in a wide surrounding area by the procedure known as "bunch drilling."

The most recent chapter in the economic development of Western Siberia has been written by natural gas. Exploitation started a little earlier than that of oil, but has not proceeded as rapidly, because much of the natural gas has been found in even more remote areas. The first development took place in 1953 in what turned out to be relatively small deposits on the left bank of the lower Ob around the town of Berezovo. Eventually the largest field in this particular region turned out to be at Punga, and in 1966 a 40-inch pipeline was laid from there to Serov and Nizhniy Tagil in the Urals. But this development has been overshadowed by the opening of the huge Medvezhye gas field along the Arctic coast east of the Ob Estuary, to be followed by the even larger Urengoy field. These, together with the Zapolyarnoye ("transpolar") fields on the lower Taz River and the Novyy ("new") Port fields on the west bank of the Ob Estuary on the Yamal Peninsula, represent the largest known gas deposits on earth. They are now credited with about three-fourths of total Soviet gas resources. The reserves at Urengoy are estimated to be 6 trillion cubic meters and those at Medvezhye to be 1.5 trillion cubic meters. The Soviets are continuing to explore the area and are also investigating the shelf of the Kara Sea offshore. In addition to gas, some oil has been found in deeper horizons below the gas, and it is now thought that major oil fields exist in this area also.

The new town of Nadym near the Medvezhye field has become the collection center for much of the gas in this area. A pipeline was completed in 1972 from Nadym to Punga, and it was extended at the other end of the existing line from Nizhniy Tagil to Perm on the western slopes of the Urals. A second line parallel to this one was completed in 1972. A third string was under construction in 1975. In late 1974 the pipeline was extended westward from Perm through Izhevsk, Kazan, Cheboksary, and Gorkiy to Moscow. A branch line from Izhevsk carries the gas to the Tatar town of Naberezhnyye Chelny where the Kama River truck plant is under construction.

The entire pipeline from Nadym to Moscow is more than 3000 kilometers long and is mostly 48 inches in diameter. It had to be laid across the Ural Mountains, 23 rivers, including the Ob and Volga, and 253 swamps. This is undoubtedly the greatest pipeline-laying feat yet accomplished in the world. An earlier plan to lay the so-called Northern Lights Pipeline across the northern Urals through the Komi gas fields to the west was postponed in favor of laying pipelines farther south where they could serve more populous areas. A pipeline from Nadym through Punga across the Urals to Vuktyl is now under construction.

A whole new technique has been worked out for laying pipelines of such magnitude through such harsh environments. Construction workers have been housed in series of caravans mounted on sledges. The caravans contain not only living quarters but also dining rooms, shower-baths, and power plants. The mobile settlements move across the taiga cutting trenches ahead and leaving lines of welded pipes behind. Water supply for these shifting settlements has become a major problem during winter when temperatures as low as −50°C freeze the shallow rivers and lakes to the bottom. This has necessitated bringing in water, usually by airplane, from far away.

The gas fields are so far away from civilization that it has been deemed inexpedient to establish permanent settlements in many of the construction sites. High wages have to be paid to get men to work in these areas, and shipping materials over such long distances causes construction costs to be exceedingly high. To supply all the amenities of life to construction workers and their families, as well as to great numbers of support personnel, would be excessively costly. Therefore, a shuttle has been proposed to fly construction workers into the gas fields from central settlements for a week or a month at a time and then fly them back to their families while other workers alternate on the jobs. It has been found that during the long, dark winters, when the sun never rises above the horizon, workers cannot remain in the far north for too long without getting what has become known as "arctic hysteria."

The huge Urengoy gas field is now scheduled to go into production in 1977. Experimental wells have already been drilled, but no significant commercial production has yet occurred. The supply problem to this remote field has been a major one. It was finally partially solved in 1974 by a 130-kilometer railroad that was completed from Nadym to the Medvezhye field. It is assumed that this line will be extended to the Urengoy field, and then supplies brought to Nadym by water can be forwarded to Urengoy by rail. The Taz Gulf and Pur River are also to be used as an access route to Urengoy. The Soviets have carried on much negotiation with American gas companies to see if something can be worked out to cooperate on the development of this huge gas resource. It has been proposed that the so-called North Star pipeline be constructed from the Urengoy field westward along the Arctic coast to Murmansk where liquified gas can be shipped by sea to the east coast of the United States. However, it appears now that the United States companies are not going to become involved in the construction of such a pipeline for the time being. Nevertheless, United States companies are eager to purchase some of the liquified gas from Urengoy if the Soviets can arrange a way for it to be done. One possibility is to liquefy the gas on the site and move it out of the region entirely by sea during the summer when the Northern Sea Route is open.

While all this development of gas has been taking place in the far north, some development has taken place in Tomsk Oblast in conjunction with the adjacent Samotlor oil field across the oblast boundary in Tyumen Oblast. In addition, there is also a good-sized gas field at Myldzhino in the middle of the Vasugan Swamp in Tomsk Oblast that is not associated with oil.

By 1974 gas production in Western Siberia had risen to about 28 billion cubic meters, of which Tyumen Oblast produced about 25 billion, about two-thirds from the far northern fields and one-third from the Punga area along the lower Ob. The Western Siberian gas production represented about 9 percent of the country's production in 1974, still lagging significantly behind that of Central Asia, the Ukraine, and the North Caucasus. The difficulty of developing this far-northern region and of building pipelines through very hostile environment has slowed the development somewhat behind plans. Nevertheless, it is envisioned that in the near future the Western Siberia area will supply by far the largest portion of the gas of the country. Thus, Western Siberia is destined soon to become the largest gas producer, as well as the largest oil producer, in the country.

The rapid development of the oil in Western Siberia has been achieved with some discontinuity in production processes. For instance, gas-processing plants have not been able to keep up with the expansion of new oil wells, so that billions of cubic meters of gas are being flared off uselessly in the oil fields. The Soviets have been trying to remedy this, and several large gas plants are under construction. A gas plant has apparently been completed at Nizhnevartovsk near the Samotlor oil fields to process the oil-associated gas and provide liquid concentrates as feedstocks for petrochemical complexes being built in Tobolsk and Tomsk. Another gas-processing plant is nearing completion in the Pravdinsk oil field southwest of Surgut, and still another gas plant is being completed in the Balyk oil field south of Surgut. Some of the gas is being used as fuel in the Surgut power station. Tobolsk and Tomsk have been singled out as sites for large petrochemical complexes; construction on both of these was to have begun in 1974. These will be added to the already existing large petrochemical center of Omsk, which was developed during the 1950s after pipelines were built eastward from the Volga-Urals oil fields. Tire plants exist at Omsk and at Barnaul, farther southeast in the Kulunda Steppe, where synthetic fibers are also being produced.

TRANSPORT

The Trans Siberian Railroad is the lifeline of Siberia. The section between the Kuznetsk Basin and the Urals is the most heavily trafficked railroad in the world. Most of the largest cities of Siberia have grown up either along the line or along its branches. Older cities, originally the largest in Siberia, found themselves stagnated when they were by-passed by the new line in the 1890s.

Most of the goods destined for settlements off the railroad system are shipped along the rail line and then transferred to riverboats to be floated down the streams toward the north during summer. The only other alternative is to move materials by ship along the Arctic coast and then upstream to the interiors. But the much-touted Northern Sea Route along the Arctic coast is open at best only three months of the year, and it is navigated during that short period with great difficulty and high cost. Complex support facilities, such as weather stations, icebreakers, planes, and helicopters, are needed to help convoys of boats pick their way through the broken ice during the summer. Thus, except for certain bulky commodities (ores and timber), which are moved in quantity along the coast itself, the Northern Sea Route has proved to be of little commercial value. Few supplies moved by it penetrate very far up the river systems into the continent.

The role of the Trans Siberian Railroad will be enhanced by a motor road being built along its route from Chelyabinsk in the Urals to Chita east of Lake Baykal. Work on the road began in 1962, and by mid-1975 about 2300 kilometers had been completed and asphalted. Eventually it is hoped to extend this line in both directions so that a transcontinental motor highway will stretch all the way from Brest on the western border of Belorussia to the port of Vladivostok in the Far East. The sections of the highway already completed have proved to be a great relief to the rail line by siphoning off much short-haul local freight traffic.

Since much of Siberia and the Far East is unserved by rail lines or highways, the region has come to depend very heavily on the airplane. Even bulky construction materials and equipment are flown into new mining regions where no other transport facilities exist. Because of the great difficulty of building roads

and railroads across the swamps and permafrost of Siberia, the region will probably remain heavily dependent on the airplane.

CITIES

Novosibirsk

Chief among the new rail towns, and now the
largest in all of Siberia, is Novosibirsk, at the
important rail crossing of the Ob River.
Founded in 1903 as Novonikolayevsk, it was
renamed Novosibirsk ("new Siberia") in
1926. By 1974 it had grown to a population of
1,243,000. The industries of Novosibirsk are
varied, and their importance is shared by
commerce. The city acts as the metropolis for
the whole of Western Siberia, and it is the
regional center for the heavily industrialized
Kuznetsk Basin, although the city itself is not
located within the basin. Consequently, it has
often been called the "Chicago of Siberia."
Diversified machine construction and metalworking are the primary industries in Novosibirsk, but there are also heavy metallurgical,
chemical, and food industries. A specialized
satellite town, Akademgorodok ("academic
town"), situated in a pine- and birch-covered
hilly area, recently has become famous as an
experiment in isolated, concentrated living
for top-level research personnel and their
families.

Omsk

The second largest city in Siberia is Omsk,
with a 1974 population of 935,000. Like
Novosibirsk, it occupies a river crossing of the
Trans Siberian Railroad. In this case the river
is the Irtysh. However, Omsk existed long
before the railroad. Founded in 1716 as a
fortress, it is one of the older cities in Siberia.
When the Trans Siberian Railroad reached it
in 1894, the town became a storage depot for
goods brought to Siberia from European Russia. It grew rapidly and developed many types
of small manufacturing plants. During the
Soviet period it has been singled out for development as the primary oil-refining and

petrochemical center of Western Siberia.
These plants were built originally to process
Volga-Urals oil brought in by four pipelines
from the west. But with the great development
of West Siberian oil, pipelines have been constructed southward from the Siberian fields to
Omsk, and oil is now piped westward from
Omsk to the Volga-Urals. The petrochemical
industries in Omsk turn out many products,
including synthetic rubber and plastics. In
addition to these types of industries, Omsk
has many machine-construction and metalworking industris, as well as textile and food
industries.

Novokuznetsk

The main iron and steel center of the Kuznetsk
Basin is Novokuznetsk, which grew from essentially nothing in 1930 to 519,000 in 1974.
Its population has recently surpassed that of
Kemerovo, the oblast center of the Kuznetsk
Basin. The iron and steel industries and
coke-chemical industries of Novokuznetsk
have already been mentioned, as has the large
aluminum plant.

Barnaul

Barnaul, with a 1974 population of 488,000,
is the urban center of the rich agricultural
region of the Kulunda Steppe. Founded in
1771, its name was possibly adopted from a
Kazakh term meaning "good pastures." Like
Novosibirsk, Omsk, and Novokuznetsk, Barnaul has outgrown its function as a regional
center and is rapidly becoming an industrial
city. It sits at the junction of the South Siberian
Railroad coming in from the southwest from
Pavlodar and Tselinograd, the northern extension of the Turk-Sib Railroad coming in
from the south from Semipalatinsk, and the
new Omsk-Barnaul line coming in from the
northwest. These railroads join at Barnaul on
the left bank of the Ob River, and a single line
crosses the river and continues eastward to
the Kuznetsk Basin. Barnaul long has been an
important center for cotton textiles, utilizing
raw cotton shipped in from Central Asia over

the Turk-Sib Railroad to supply cheap cotton goods to markets of southwestern Siberia. It now has major synthetic fiber factories, a tire plant, and machine-building, woodworking, and food industries. The possibility of the construction of a large new iron and steel center to the east of Barnaul has already been mentioned.

Kemerovo

Kemerovo, with a 1974 population of 425,000, is the governmental seat of Kemerovo Oblast, which is essentially co-existent with the Kuznetsk Basin. Kemerovo used to be the largest city in the basin, but it has recently been surpassed by Novokuznetsk. Kemerovo is primarily a coal-mining town, and its industries are primarily chemical ones based on the coking industry. It also has some machine construction and metalworking.

Tomsk

Tomsk is one of the older cities in Siberia. It was founded in 1604, and together with Tobolsk and Tyumen farther west it dominated urban life in Siberia for a couple of centuries. But when the Trans Siberian Railroad was laid south of all these cities, they stagnated with respect to new, faster-growing towns. Eventually Tomsk was connected to the Trans Siberian Railroad by a 100-kilometer rail spur, and now with the great development of oil to the north it is beginning to prosper economically. It has been singled out as one of the three main petrochemical centers of Western Siberia, along with Tobolsk and Omsk. By 1974 it had grown to a population of 386,000. Tomsk is the site of the first university in Siberia, and long has been regarded as the cultural center of southwestern Siberia.

Tyumen

Tyumen, the oldest Russian city in Siberia, was founded in 1585 near the mouth of the Tura River where it joins the Tobol at the western head of navigation on the Ob-Irtysh River system. Although the major rivers of Siberia flow northward, it was their west-east-flowing segments that were important during the early days of eastward penetration into Siberia, so the fact that Tyumen occupied the westernmost point of navigation made it a very strategically located city. Later it was the eastern terminus of the old Perm-to-Tyumen railroad, and as such it served as the main entrepôt into Siberia until it was replaced by Chelyabinsk when the Trans Siberian Railroad became established to the south. With the building of the northern branch of the Trans Siberian Railroad from Sverdlovsk to Omsk, Tyumen gained a position on a major rail line. However, its main function remained only as an important river-rail transfer point for lumber and grain, and it did not regain its former importance until recently, when it became the supply base for the vast northern oil region.

Tyumen is now situated on the railroad and oil pipelines connecting the oil fields of Western Siberia with the rest of the country. New industries are being located in Tyumen in connection with the oil activity. One such unique industry is the construction of so-called Northern Lights floating thermal electric power stations, which are being used in the far north where permanent sources of power have not yet been established. Each station has a capacity of 20,000 kilowatts and has a crew of 40 people. These vessels, as tall as five-story buildings, are floated down the rivers to their new locations. Tyumen's industries are concentrated primarily on machine building, woodworking, and chemicals. By 1974 Tyumen had grown to a population of 312,000, which indicated a recent growth that was faster than some of the other cities of its size in Western Siberia.

Prokopyevsk

Prokopyevsk is a satellite city on the northwest side of Novokuznetsk. Concentrated on metalworking and chemicals, it has grown rapidly during the Soviet period to a 1974 population of 269,000.

Biysk and Rubtsovsk

Biysk, with a 1974 population of 203,000, and Rubtsovsk, with a 1974 population of 163,000, are two more important regional centers in the Kulunda Steppe. They are primarily trading centers for rich farming districts. Rubtsovsk has grown into a manufacturing center for agricultural machinery. Biysk takes its name from the Biya River, which joins the Katun at this location to form the Ob.

Other Cities of the Kuznetsk Basin

Four other cities in the Kuznetsk Basin are in the 100,000 category: Leninsk-Kuznetskiy, with a 1974 population of 130,000; Kiselevsk, with a 1974 population of 125,000; Belovo, with a 1974 population of 110,000; and Andzhero-Sudzhensk, with a 1974 population of 103,000. These are all coal-mining centers, and Belovo has a zinc-smelting plant. The population of Andzhero-Sudzhensk has decreased steadily from 1959 when it had a population of 116,000.

PROSPECTS

The opening of the huge oil and gas fields in Western Siberia has presented a whole new order of magnitude to the economy of the region. However, the exploitation of these mineral fuels does not portend a great population growth in the region. The fuels are being moved by pipe out of the area as fast as possible into the old settled areas of the Urals and European Russia. Some new industries, such as the petrochemicals at Tobolsk and Tomsk, of course, are developing along with the oil and gas production, but these too will not require many working personnel. Since the late 1950s it appears that Western Siberia has been experiencing a net out-migration. With the continually declining birth rate, even in the new areas, the population growth of the region has slowed, particularly in the more heavily populated southern portions of the region. Some of the more heavily populated, more urbanized parts of the southern oblasts

are actually losing population. It appears that the initial spurt of population and urban growth that took place in Western Siberia during the 1930s and 1940s is largely over, and that in the future the region will remain one whose function is primarily to supply natural resources to the west. Plans are to continue some expansion of the iron and steel industry in the Kuznetsk Basin, as well as perhaps in some other areas of Western Siberia, but these expansions will be made only as needed in the eastern regions and will not be prompted by continued economic development in the west.

READING LIST

- Armstrong, T., "Oil and Natural Gas in Northwest Siberia," *The Polar Record,* No. 92, May 1969, pp. 613–617.
- *Atlas novosibirskoi oblasti* (An Atlas of Novosibirsk Oblast), Gugk, Moscow, 1970 (in Russian).
- Budkov, S.T., "The Forest Products Industry, A Specialized Activity of the Sosva Valley Section of the Ob Basin," *Soviet Geography: Review & Translation,* November 1970, pp. 767–774.
- Chernetsov, V.N., and W.I. Moszynska, *The Prehistory of Western Siberia,* McGill-Queens University Press, Quebec, 1974.
- Dibb, Paul, *Siberia and the Pacific: A Study of Economic Development and Trade Prospects,* Praeger, New York, 1972, 288 pp.
- Hajdu, Peter, *The Samoyed Peoples and Languages,* Indiana University Publications, Uralic and Altaic Series, Bloomington, Vol. 14, 1963, 114 pp.
- Holzman, Franklyn D., "Soviet Ural-Kuznetsk Combine: A Study in Investment Criteria and Industrialization Policies," *The Quarterly Journal of Economics,* August 1957, pp. 368–405.
- Hooson, D.J.M., *A New Soviet Heartland?* Van Nostrand, Princeton, 1964, 132 pp.
- Hooson, David, "Plan for the Ob River," *Geographical Magazine,* April 1967, pp. 977–979.
- Izyumskiy, O.A., "Transport Development of the Middle Ob Oil District," *Soviet Geography: Review & Translation,* October 1970, pp. 655–660.
- Levin, M.G., and L.P. Potapov, eds., *The Peoples of Siberia,* University of Chicago Press, 1964, 948 pp. (translated from the Russian edition pub-

lished by U.S.S.R. Academy of Sciences in 1956).

- Malik, L.K., "Ob izmenenii nekotorykh elementov rezhima rek nizhney obi pri regulirovanii stoka (V Svyazi s problemoy pereraspredeleniya vodnykh resursov v Sredinnom regione)" 'On Changes in Some Elements of the River Regime of the Lower Ob in the Regulation of Runoff (in Connection with the Redistribution of Water Resources in the Midland Region)", *Vestnik Moskovskogo Universiteta, geografiya,* No. 1, 1975, pp. 70–76.

- Misevich, K.N., and V.I. Chudnova, *Naseleniye rayonov sovremennogo promyshlennogo osvoyeniya severa Zapadnoy Sibiri* (The Population of the Regions of Contemporary Industrial Development in the Northern Part of West Siberia), Novosibirsk, 1973.

- Morozova, T.G., *Ekonomicheskaya geografiya Sibiri* (Economic Geography of Siberia), Vysshaya shkola, Moscow, 1975, 263 pp. (in Russian).

- Morozova, T., et al., *Novaya geografiya Sibiri* (New Geography of Siberia), Prosveshcheniye, Moscow, 1972, 223 pp.

- Mosalova, L.M., "Regonal Peculiarities in the Formation of Industrial Nodes in the Middle Ob Region," *Soviet Geography: Review & Translation,* October 1973, pp. 519–525.

- Moskalenko, N.G., "Osobennosti protsessa vosstanovleniya rastitelnogo pokrova na trassakh lineynykh cooruzheniy Severa Zapadnoy Sibiri" (The Rehabilitation of Plant Cover along Linear Engineering Structures in the Northern Portion of Western Siberia), *Izvestiya Vsesoyuznogo Geograficheskogo Obshchestva,* No. 1, 1975, pp. 62–66.

- North, Robert N., "Soviet Northern Development: The Case of Northwest Siberia," *Soviet Studies,* No. 2, October 1972, pp. 171–199.

- North, Robert, N., *Transport and Economic Development in Western Siberia,* Ph.D. Dissertation, University of British Columbia, 1968, 704 pp.

- O'Brien, Kathy, *The Petroleum Resource of West Siberia,* Master's thesis, University of Washington, 1973.

- Ojala, Carl F., "A Study of Population Increases in the Greater Kuznetsk Region, USSR, 1897–1966: As Shown by Growth of Cities Greater than 50,000 in 1966," *Professional Geographer,* 1968, pp. 303–312.

- Orlov, B.P. "Objectives of Long-range Development of the Siberian Economy," *Problems of Economics,* August 1974, pp. 41–65.

- Orlov, B.P., *Sibir segodnya: problemy i resheniya* (Siberia Today: Problems and Remedies), Mysl, Moscow, 1974, 207 pp. (in Russian).

- Pomus, M.I., *Zapadnaya Sibir* (Western Siberia), Moscow, 1956 (in Russian).

- Preobrazhensky, A.A., *Ural i Zapadnaya Sibir v kontse XVI – nachale XVIII veka* (The Urals and Western Siberia from the End of the XVI to the Beginning of the XVIII Centuries), Nauka, Moscow, 1972, 392 pp. (in Russian).

- Revyakin, V.S., "Predelnoye oledeneniye Altaya" (The Glaciation Line in the Altay Mountains), *Izvestiya vsesoyuznogo geograficheskogo obshchestva,* No. 2, 1974, pp. 97–103 (in Russian).

- Shpolyanskaya, N.A., "Prognozno-geotermicheskoya rayonirovanie Zapadnoy Sibiri" (A Predictive Geothermal Regionalization of Western Siberia), *Vestnik Moskovskogo Universiteta, seriya geografiya,* No. 2, 1974, pp. 49–54 (in Russian).

- Slyadnev, A.P., *Geografiya Zapadnoy Sibiri* (Geography of Western Siberia), Novosibirsk, 1969 (in Russian).

- St. George, George, *Siberia: The New Frontier,* David McKay, New York, 1969, 374 pp.

- Sukhanov, Ya. B., *From the Urals to the Pacific,* Progress Pub., Moscow, n.d., 291 pp.

- Vendrov, S.L., "A Forecast of Changes in Natural Conditions in the Northern Ob Basin in Case of Construction of the Lower Ob Hydro Project," *Soviet Geography: Review & Translation,* December 1965, pp. 3–18.

- Zvyagintseva, K.M., "On the Three Fuel and Energy Supply Zones of Siberia," *Soviet Geography: Review & Translation,* October 1974, pp. 491–498.

The Eastern Siberia Economic Region

	Area (km²)	Population	Persons/km²	Percent Urban
Krasnoyarsk Kray	2,402,000	3,012,000	1.3	65
Khakass Autonomous Oblast	62,000	462,000	7.5	63
Taymyr National Okrug	862,000	41,000	0.05	62
Evenki National Okrug	768,000	13,000	0.02	30
Irkutsk Oblast	768,000	2,381,000	3.1	75
Ust-Orda Buryat National Okrug	22,000	143,000	6.4	18
Chita Oblast	432,000	1,180,000	2.7	60
Aga Buryat National Okrug	19,000	68,000	3.6	26
Buryat A.S.S.R.	351,000	834,000	2.4	47
Tuva A.S.S.R.	171,000	245,000	1.4	39
Total	4,123,000	7,652,000	1.9	65

chapter 18

the eastern siberia economic region

The Eastern Siberia Economic Region encompasses a huge territory including much of the Central Siberian Upland and the high mountains along the south on either side of Lake Baykal. Its total area amounts to 4,123,000 square kilometers, which is by far the largest region yet discussed. It is almost twice as large as either the Western Siberia Region or the Kazakhstan Region. Its area is surpassed only by the Far East, which will be studied in the next chapter. A few years ago it was the largest region in the country, but recently the Yakut A.S.S.R., which alone has a territory of 3,103,000 square kilometers, was transferred from the Eastern Siberia Region to the Far East Region.

The Eastern Siberia Region includes huge Krasnoyarsk Kray, which stretches north-south almost the entire width of the Soviet Union. Only the small Tuva A.S.S.R. separates its southern boundary from Mongolia, and in the north it continues to the Arctic coast. Krasnoyarsk Kray alone contains 2,402,000 square kilometers. It includes the Khakass Autonomous Oblast, which lies on the eastern slopes of the Kuznetsk Alatau in the south, and the Evenki and Taymyr National Okrugs in the central and northern portions. Eastern Siberia also includes Irkutsk and Chita Oblasts, west and east of Lake Baykal, each of which contains minor Buryat National Okrugs, and the Buryat and Tuva A.S.S.R.s. The Tuva region was quietly incor-

393

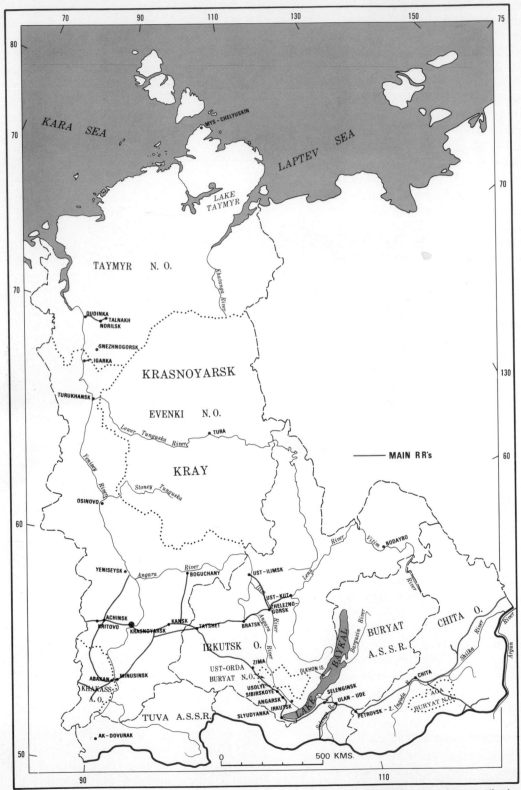

Figure 18-1 Eastern Siberia.

porated into the Soviet Union in 1944 during World War II after it had earlier been split off from Mongolia as a defacto protectorate of the Soviet Union. In 1944 it was constituted as the Tuva Autonomous Oblast directly under the jurisdiction of the R.S.F.S.R., and later it was raised to the status of A.S.S.R.

In spite of the huge territory, Eastern Siberia contains only 7,652,000 people, one of the smallest populations of any of the economic regions. The population density, then, is very low, exceeding only that of the Far East Region. The average population density in Eastern Siberia is 1.9 persons per square kilometer, but this varies considerably throughout the region. Most of the region has very little if any population, while individual settled basins along the Trans Siberian Railroad with major cities have much higher population densities. Such local settlements are generally submerged in population figures, because almost all political units incorporate both well-settled parcels of land and large empty spaces. The Evenki and Taymyr National Okrugs have very few people anywhere. Their average population densities are 0.02 and 0.05 persons per square kilometer, respectively. The Eastern Siberia Region tends to be fairly highly urbanized; 65 percent of its people are considered to be urban, which is significantly above the national average. However, most of the native areas are still very rural.

Although Eastern Siberia includes quite a number of nationality-based political units, the Russians are in the huge majority throughout all of the region except the Tuva A.S.S.R., where the Tuvinians still make up 58.6 percent of the population. However, even here the Russians make up 38.3 percent. In the Buryat A.S.S.R. the Russians make up 73.5 percent of the population, while the Buryats make up only 22 percent. The Russians make up 78.3 percent of the population of the Khakass Autonomous Oblast, 67.1 percent of the Taymyr National Okrug, and 61.1 percent of the Evenki National Okrug.

The native groups of Eastern Siberia are a mixture of Mongol, Turkic, Samodian (Uralian), and Tungus-Manchu peoples. The Mon-gol Buryats occupy the territory of the Buryat A.S.S.R. as well as two small national okrugs in Irkutsk and Chita Oblasts. The Tuvinians are Turkic, as are the Khakass. The Evenki are a Tungus-Manchu strain. In the Taymyr National Okrug, named after the Taymyr Peninsula in which it is located, two very different native groups are combined — the Turkic Dolgans and the Samodian Nenets.

During the 1959–1970 intercensal period, the Eastern Siberia Region experienced a moderate natural population increase, heaviest in the Tuva A.S.S.R. However, this was counterbalanced somewhat by out-migration from most of the region, except for much of Irkutsk Oblast, the Tuva A.S.S.R., and the very southeastern portion of Krasnoyarsk Kray. There was particularly heavy out-migration from Chita Oblast and modest out-migration from much of Krasnoyarsk Kray and the Buryat A.S.S.R. It appears that Eastern Siberia was losing population to both the Far East and to the new oil and gas regions in Tyumen Oblast in the west. The net result was that much of the Eastern Siberia Region experienced only a modest population increase. Largest population increases took place in the native areas, particularly in the Tuva and Buryat A.S.S.R.s.

PHYSICAL LANDSCAPE

Landform

Much of the Eastern Siberia Economic Region is occupied by the Central Siberian Upland, which stretches essentially from the Yenisey River in the west to the Lena River in the east and therefore extends eastward out of the region into the Far East. This is one of the old stable blocks of the earth's crust that has resisted recent geologic movement and has acted as an anchor against which weaker and more mobile zones around it have been crushed upward into higher, younger mountain ranges. This is particularly true along the southern and eastern sides and to some extent in the north. The general elevation of the upland ranges from 500–700 meters, but local sections rise above that, and deep river val-

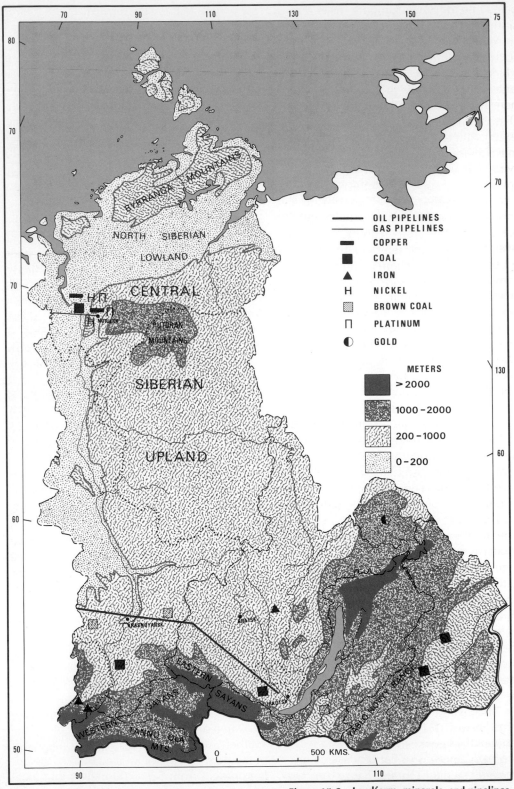

Figure 18-2   Landform, minerals, and pipelines.

leys are incised well below it. The highest portion of the upland is the Putorana Mountains in the northwest where an elevation of 1701 meters is reached. Other promontories include the Yenisey Ridge in the southwest along the right bank of the Yenisey River where an elevation of 1104 meters is reached.

The upland generally is underlain by complex crystalline rocks that over much of the surface are buried in deep layers of sedimentary rocks intermingled with colossal flows of trap (volcanic) rock and intrusive sills and laccoliths. Right-bank tributaries of the Yenisey, such as the Angara that drains large Lake Baykal, the Stony Tunguska, and the Lower Tunguska, and left-bank tributaries of the Lena, as well as shorter streams flowing northward out of the region to the Arctic, such as the Khatanga, Anabar, and Olenek, have dissected the upland into separate watersheds that look like isolated flat-top mountains or elongated ridges. Some of the volcanics rise above the monotonously flat surfaces to form low-domed promontories.

The Putorana area consists of a combination of volcanic and sedimentary layers that have not subsided as much as the area around them in relatively recent geologic movements. In most cases the upland drops off abruptly around its peripheries, particularly in the west along the Yenisey where it forms an escarpment almost the entire length of the river. This is also true in the north, particularly in the northwest where the slopes of the Putorana Mountains in their lower portions plunge abruptly to the North Siberian Lowland that runs east-west across the region and connects the West Siberian Lowland with the Lena Delta and separates the Central Upland from the Byrranga Range in the northern part of the Taymyr Peninsula.

The Byrranga Range is primarily a horst, an uplifted fault block, higher on its southern edge and sloping downward toward the north. The highest point reaches an elevation of 1146 meters. The upfaulted block is split into several portions, so that the mountains take on the appearance of a series of low, flat-topped ranges. On their northern and eastern sides they are generally bordered by a narrow coastal plain.

Most of the rivers of the upland have incised their valleys very deeply, and where they cut through volcanic trap rock or crystalline intrusives they cut gorgelike valleys with narrow rocky cliffs and many rapids and low waterfalls.

There are many traces of Pleistocene glaciation in the higher parts of the upland. These are particularly distinctive in the Putorana Mountains where the higher peaks stand out above the general dome structure of the region as sharp horns eaten into by cirques, separated by narrow, elongated valleys that have been gouged into U-shapes now containing a well-developed system of finger lakes that radiate outward toward the west and south from the central portion of the dome. There are also U-shaped glacial valleys in the Byrranga Mountains, where contemporary glaciers still exist in the higher eastern portions of the ranges where the snow line lies at elevations above 1100 meters.

Valley glaciers in both the Putorana and Byrranga Mountains left high moraines that retained glacial meltwaters and produced elongated lakes in the U-shaped valleys. Huge Lake Taymyr occupies a graben that has been strongly affected by glacial activity. The lake is about 200 kilometers long, up to 80 kilometers wide, and up to 26 meters deep. It is surrounded by morainic materials and roch moutonnées — ice-scoured rock hills. There are also many small, shallow thermokarst lakes in the northern part of the region. In the central part of the upland between the upper reaches of the Lower Tunguska and Vilyuy Rivers is a considerable area of karst that contains many small lakes.

Continental glaciation at its greatest extent covered the area southward to a line extending from about the mouth of the Stony Tunguska River along the middle Yenisey northeastward to the middle reaches of the Olenek River near the delta of the Lena.

The extensive areas of thick sedimentary cover contain massive coal seams that spread over more than a million square kilometers.

The largest coal basin in the U.S.S.R. is the so-called Tunguskan Basin concentrated around the Lower Tunguska River. Reserves in this basin — plus the Lena Basin farther east, which is now in the Far East Economic Region — are estimated to account for as much as 80–90 percent of the total reserves of the U.S.S.R. Coal is also scattered in wide areas outside of these two huge basins, in the Khatanga depression of the North Siberian Lowland and in various intermontane basins along the southern fringe of Siberia near the Trans Siberian Railroad. It is thought that large quantities of oil and gas may also exist in these broad, deep sedimentary formations, and many other minerals, especially iron ore and diamonds, have been found in some of the other types of rocks. Kimberlite diamond pipes intrude limestones and dolomites at a number of places in the central part of the upland.

In the southern part of the Eastern Siberia Region elevations become much higher, and the topography becomes much more rugged as folded and fault block mountains interspersed by deep, broad intermontane basins become the dominant forms. In the west the Sayan Ranges combine with the Kuznetsk Alatau on the east side of the Kuznetsk Basin to form a complex of intersecting mountain ranges that encircle a number of significant steppe basins. The Sayan Mountains are divided into two separate systems. One is the so-called Western Sayans, which run southwest-northeast across the upper Yenisey Valley between the Tuva Basin to the south and the Minusinsk Basin to the north. At their eastern extremity, the Western Sayans intersect the midsection of the Eastern Sayans, which are oriented northwest-southeast along the divide between the tributaries flowing westward to the upper Yenisey and those flowing northward and eastward into the Angara River. Along the Yenisey River, the Batenev Ridge of the Eastern Sayan system separates the Yenisey-Chulym Basin from the Minusinsk Basin to the south.

The Minusinsk Basin is a triangular-shaped lowland on the upper Yenisey River centered on the two cities of Minusinsk and Abakan and completely surrounded by mountains. On the west is the Kuznetsk Alatau, which reaches elevations as high as 1820 meters. On the southwest are the Western Sayans, which in their highest portions rise to 2930 meters, and in the northeast are the Eastern Sayans, which rise to 3492 meters. South of the Western Sayans in the very upper reaches of the Yenisey River lies the central Tuva Basin, which, together with the eastern and western Tuva Basins, is also completely surrounded by high mountains. In the south lie the Tannu-Ola Mountains, which reach elevations of 2972 meters. These mountains separate the Tuva Basin from the Ubsu-Nur Basin containing the large Lake Ubsu-Nur in northern Mongolia. The northern fringes of this basin lie within the Tuva A.S.S.R. In the western end of the Tuva A.S.S.R. the eastern ranges of the Altay system reach elevations of 3579 meters.

Between the upper Yenisey and Angara Rivers lies a southern extension of the Central Siberian Upland that has been eroded by subparallel streams flowing north or northwestward to join the Angara. These streams have divided the area into a system of north-south parallel ridges that generally lie only a few hundred meters above sea level. The highest portion lies along the Angara in the Bratsk Reservoir area, where maximum elevations over 800 meters are achieved. This region is separated by a deep tectonic trough from the eastern extension of the Sayan Mountains along the international boundary toward the southwest. This trough extends northwestward from the outlet of the Angara at the southwestern end of Lake Baykal and provides a broad, low break in the upland for the route of the Trans Siberian Railroad from Kranoyarsk to Irkutsk.

As Lake Baykal is approached, the land again becomes higher, and the topography takes on a definite fault-block, horst-graben nature that is oriented parallel to the shores of Lake Baykal in a south-southwest–north-northeast direction. The alternating horst-and-graben nature of the topography is most distinctive in the immediate vicinity of Lake Baykal, particularly around its northern end where high, flat-topped mountains alternate with low, broad, elongated basins. Lake Baykal itself occupies the major graben, which is really three downdropped blocks that over a long period of time have all become submerged below the water of the lake. Much of the basin form took shape during the Tertiary about 25 million years ago, which, according to the Soviets, makes this the oldest lake in the world.

The lake has many other unique features. It has the greatest depth and greatest volume of any freshwater lake in the world. Its greatest depth, which occurs in the middle depression, is 1620 meters (more than 1 mile). In the southern basin a maximum depth of 1443 meters is reached, and in the northern basin a maximum of 989 meters. These depths compare to about 400 meters for Lake Superior and only about 300 meters for Lake Michigan in North America. Thus, although Lake Michigan has nearly twice the surface area of Lake Baykal, it does not have nearly the water volume. The water volume of Lake Baykal is exceeded in the world only by the Caspian Sea (which is really a lake), but the Caspian, of course, is salty, and therefore Lake Baykal has the greatest volume of fresh water in the world. It is credited with having about one-sixth of all the fresh water on the surface of the earth. It has nearly as much water as all five of the North American Great Lakes combined. Its total volume amounts to about 23,000 cubic kilometers. This is equal to 23 Aral Seas or 92 Azov Seas. The lake is 636 kilometers long, 25–79.5 kilometers wide, and has a surface area of 31,500 square kilometers. Its shoreline stretches for about 2000 kilometers.

The lake generally freezes over in early January and remains frozen until mid-May. Ice reaches a maximum thickness of about 2 meters. The water is so clear that skaters during the winter can watch schools of omul, a salmon found only in the lake, swimming beneath the ice. Because of its great depth, the lake warms up very slowly in spring and cools off very slowly in autumn. Water temperatures never get very warm during summer. In the open lake, surface water temperatures during summer hover around 40–50°F, while some semienclosed bays have temperatures that rise to 60°F.

The surface of Lake Baykal lies 455 meters above sea level. The lake is surrounded almost entirely by steep, precipitous mountains that along the northern half of the lake, and in the southern end as well, reach elevations well over 2000 meters. The highest elevations of the surrounding mountains are generally in very close proximity to the lake shore. The overall structure of the Baykal region is a broad arch that has cracked under lateral pressures into parallel fault lines running south-southwest–north-northeast, and various segments of the cracked arch have fallen in. Continued lateral pressure from the west and from the east has caused overthrusts along the faults that have produced upturned edges along the graben sides. Therefore, Lake Baykal finds highest elevations in its immediate surroundings and does not receive water from a very broad drainage basin. Many of the rivers that head near the lake flow away from the lake. This is particularly true of the headwaters of the Lena River that begin only a few kilometers to the west of the central portion of the west shore of Lake Baykal and flow northward to the Arctic without affecting the lake at all.

The catchment basin for the lake covers an area of about 55,700 square kilometers, which is less than twice the area of the lake itself. Most of the streams flowing into the lake — there are 336 streams — are only short rivulets that plunge down the steep cliffs during rains or during the spring thaw. The major stream flowing into the lake is the Selenga, which flows northward from Mongolia through the basin surrounding Ulan-Ude, the capital of the Buryat A.S.S.R., and then westward to form a large delta in the southeastern portion of the lake. This provides 51 percent of the inflow to the lake. Other streams of some size are the Barguzin along the middle portions of the eastern side of the lake and the Upper Angara at the northern end of the lake. These two streams occupy two broad, downdropped grabens that lie between high, steep mountain ranges on either side. They flow through broad, flat, marshy basin floors, which suggests that some time in the past they might have been arms of the lake itself.

Only the Angara River flows out of the lake. It carries the water northward and westward to the Yenisey and eventually to the Arctic. Its course is so steep and its current so swift near the outlet in the southwestern corner of the lake that the Yenisey does not freeze during winter in its upper portions in the vicinity of Irkutsk. The large volume and constancy of flow provided by the lake imparts tremendous hydroelectric potential to the Angara and the Yenisey farther downstream.

This deeply faulted area still is very tectonically active. In 1806 a severe earthquake transformed 100 kilometers of the lake's shoreline into a large bay. Twenty-two mountainous islands exist in the lake; the largest is Olkhon along the midsection of the western shore. Many jagged, rocky crags jut above the water along the shorelines. Hot mineral springs abound, and there are plans to build a number of health resorts. Lake Baykal has recently become part of the first national park in the Soviet Union.

The lake is also unique for its plant and animal life. A limnological institute along its shore has identified about 600 plant species and 1200 animal species, about three-fourths of which are found nowhere else in the world. Some of the most interesting species are the omul, a large salmonlike fish; the golomyanka, a viviparous, transparent fish; and the nerpa, the world's only freshwater seal.

East of Lake Baykal, the southwest-northeast trend of the mountains continues in one after another range separated by river valleys. Maximum elevations generally are around 1500–2000 meters. One of the more prominent ranges is the Yablonovyy Range, which separates the basin around Ulan-Ude in the Buryat A.S.S.R. on the west from the basin around Chita in Chita Oblast on the east. The city of Chita sits on the Ingoda River, flowing eastward into the Shilka, which eventually joins with the Argun to form the Amur just before leaving Chita Oblast. The Argun forms the international boundary with China for a distance of about 600 kilometers, after

which the Amur forms the boundary much of the rest of the way to the Pacific. In the northern part of the Trans Baykal region the Vitim River flows northward through the Vitim and Patom Plateaus northeast of Lake Baykal eventually to join the Lena River. Thus, the Arctic-Pacific drainage divide lies in the far south between the headwaters of the Vitim and the Ingoda Rivers in Chita Oblast.

All the high mountains of the south, from the Sayans eastward to the Yablonovyy, have been heavily glaciated by mountain glaciers on their higher crests. Therefore, they exhibit strong glacial features throughout. Around Lake Baykal mountain glaciers descended down the valleys into the lake during the Pleistocene and left boulder trains and morainic deposits in many places along the shore. Some of the higher mountain slopes, particularly in the west where precipitation is greater, still contain perpetual snowfields and small glacial tongues of ice. This is particularly true on the southwestern slopes of the Sayan Ranges, which are exposed to the main moisture-bearing winds from the southwest.

Climate, Vegetation, Soils, and Agriculture

The climate of Eastern Siberia is one of the most continental on earth. This is particularly true of the southern part, which is dominated almost all the time during the winter by the core area of the Asiatic Maximum (Siberian High). During the winter the cold, dense air over the landmass forms a consistently located sea-level atmospheric high-pressure cell that is generally centered in the intermontane basins of northwestern Mongolia and adjacent Tuva A.S.S.R. about halfway between Lake Baykal and Lake Balkhash. From this core area, two high-pressure ridges extend — one toward the northeast into the upper reaches of the Yana, Indigirka, and Kolyma River valleys east of the Lena-Vilyuy-Aldan Lowland, and the other westward across Kazakhstan into southern European U.S.S.R.

This high-pressure system, which is revealed by sea-level equivalent atmospheric pressures, is what has become known

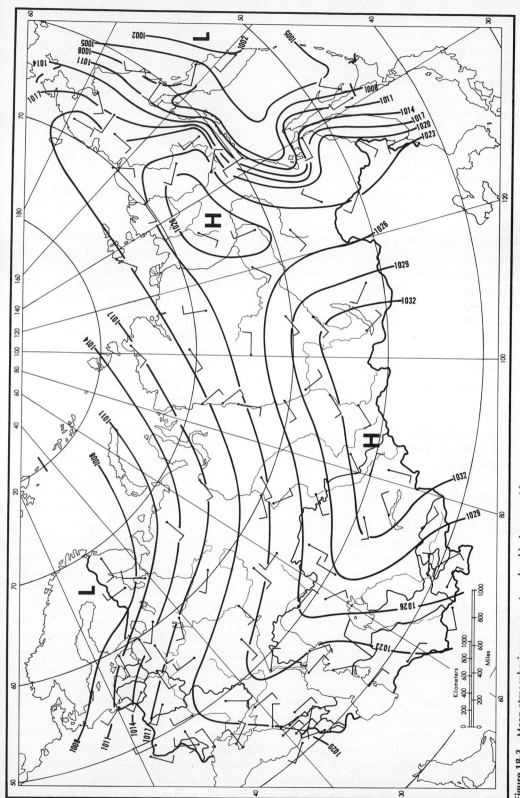

Figure 18-3 Mean atmospheric pressure at sea level in January. After Lydolph, *World Survey of Climatology,* Vol. 7.

throughout the world as the Siberian High. However, it is usually not centered in Siberia, and it does not cover all of Siberia. It also extends westward well out of Siberia. Soviet climatologists usually refer to it as the Asiatic Maximum. It is not a circular-shaped pressure system, nor even an oval one; it is eaten into on its northwestern side by a huge concavity that represents the eastern extremity of the Aleutian Low during winter. This low-pressure system during winter occupies much of the East Siberian Uplands and accompanying coastal lowlands north of the Putorana Mountains. Its boundary extends in a southwest-northeast direction from about the mouth of the Stony Tunguska River in the middle reaches of the Yenisey northeastward to beyond the delta of the Lena.

Therefore, during the winter Eastern Siberia is divided climatically into two distinct parts. The northwest, including the Putorana Mountains and adjacent northern fringes of the Central Siberian Upland, the North Siberian Lowland in the Khatanga Depression, and the Byrranga Mountain region on the Taymyr Peninsula, is dominated by dull, dreary, overcast skies, frequent storms, high winds, and significant snowfalls associated with the eastern end of the Aleutian Low. It is the eastern portion of the confluence area of cyclone tracks coming in from the west along the Arctic coast and from the southwest from the Black Sea region northeastward across the southern and central Urals through the West Siberian Lowland. In contrast, the remainder of Eastern Siberia is dominated much of the time by high pressure with associated clear, calm, extremely cold weather, with intensive formations of surface temperature inversions that cause temperatures on the floors of intermontane basins to be 15–30°C colder than they are a few hundred meters up the mountain slopes.

These cold pockets of air in intermontane basins give the illusion of an integrated atmospheric high-pressure cell. Since much of the region is relatively high in elevation, reduction of station pressures to sea level inherently induces considerable bias. The extrapolation downward of conditions in the cold,

dense air beneath inversions in intermontane basins by standard formulas produces extremely high sea-level pressure equivalents that reach as much as 1075 millibars southwest of Lake Baykal. But upper-air data reveal that even as low as the 850-millibar level (about 1300–1500 meters above sea level), the isobaric pattern turns into a pronounced low-pressure trough that extends northwest-southeast across Siberia from the vicinity of Novaya Zemlya in the northwest to the northwest coast of the Sea of Okhotsk in the southeast. This low-pressure trough intensifies upward until it forms a large, closed, low-pressure system at the 500-millibar level (about 5000–6000 meters above sea level).

Since many mountain ranges in the Sayan and Baykal areas poke well above the 850-millibar level, it is unrealistic to attempt to define a sea-level pressure system. Hence, the Asiatic Maximum is more a hypothetical construct — derived from extrapolations downward of atmospheric conditions in separated intermontane basins — than it is a real entity that spreads continuously across a major portion of the region. The surface atmosphere, particularly in the southern parts of Eastern Siberia, consists of isolated, cold, dense pools of air trapped beneath strong temperature inversions in intermontane basins, which have little connection with air masses and fronts that may go skimming across their tops (Fig. 18-5).

During summer much of the region becomes part of a shallow, expansive, diffuse, low-pressure system that forms over the surface as land temperatures warm up rapidly and the heated surface air becomes less dense than that over surrounding seas. The local effects of topography and interior location that produce the intensely cold pools of surface air during winter now act to produce anomalously high surface temperatures for such high latitudes in surface air that is stagnated in intermontane basins.

During both winter and summer much of the Eastern Siberia Region experiences light surface winds and little exchange of air with outside areas. Only along the Arctic coast in the north, where great surface temperature

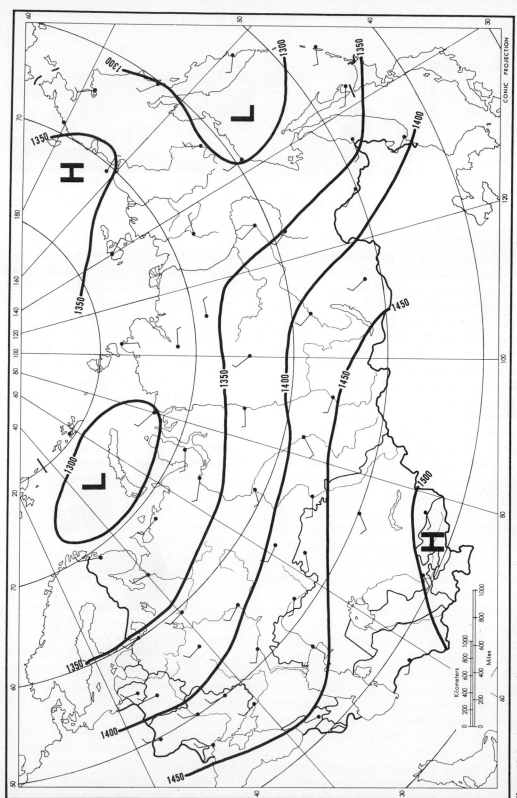

Figure 18-4 Contours at the 850 mb. level in January. After Lydolph, *World Survey of Climatology*, Vol. 7.

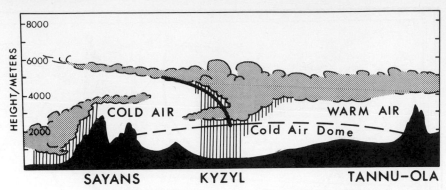

Figure 18-5 Cold front skimming across top of cold air dome in Tannu Tuva Basin. After Lydolph, *World Survey of Climatology*, Vol. 7.

contrasts are set up by land-sea differences, do significant winds occur. Here the coastal winds and seasonal reversals of direction that were mentioned along the Western Siberian coast culminate in one of the windiest areas of the country. Cape Chelyuskin, a northerly promontory of the Taymyr Peninsula and the northernmost point on the Eurasian landmass, experiences wind speeds that average 6–7 meters per second (about 15 miles per hour) throughout the year. Wind speeds of more than 15 meters per second (about 30 miles per hour) occur on 58 days of the year, and winds of gale force are often experienced, particularly during winter. Wind chill factors along this coast during winter are some of the coldest on earth, reaching values as low as −152°C. In contrast, Irkutsk in the southern part of the region has wind speeds that average 2–3 meters per second throughout the year and experiences wind speeds greater than 15 meters per second only 20 days of the year. The highest wind speeds in Irkutsk are reached during spring–summer when convective activity is greatest, rather than during winter, as is the case at Cape Chelyuskin. In between, in the center of the Central Siberian Upland, Tura averages wind speeds of only 1–2 meters per second and experiences speeds of greater than 15 meters per second only 5 days per year. Wind chill during winter at Tura reaches only −66°C.

Lake Baykal acts as a cold source during summer and a warm source during fall and early winter before it freezes over. It thus exerts considerable influence on the surface air above the lake and in the immediate shoreline areas, although these influences do not extend very far onto the upland because of the upturned edges of the mountains surrounding the lake. Particularly in early winter, both isotherms and isobars may be packed in close juxtaposition encircling the lake. During this time of year the large pressure gradients across the shoreline cause cold bora winds to descend with great force down the many short, steep river canyons leading into the lake. The best known of these winds is the sarma, named after the Sarma River, which descends the midsection of the western coast in the vicinity of Olkhon Island. Here bora winds blow on the average 113 days per year with speeds from 15–40 meters per second (30–80 miles per hour). They occur primarily from October to December before the lake freezes over, but on occasion when they blow during summer they carry great clouds of dust onto the lake. Generally these wind speeds die down no more than 10–20 kilometers from the shore. During early winter when cold air descends over the lake, dense steam fogs boil up from the relatively warm surface of the lake. Although the surface air is saturated, moisture still continues to move from the lake surface upward because there is a vapor pressure gradient directed upward from the relatively warm surface of the lake to the colder air above.

This sort of steam fog is a common phenomenon over most of the larger rivers

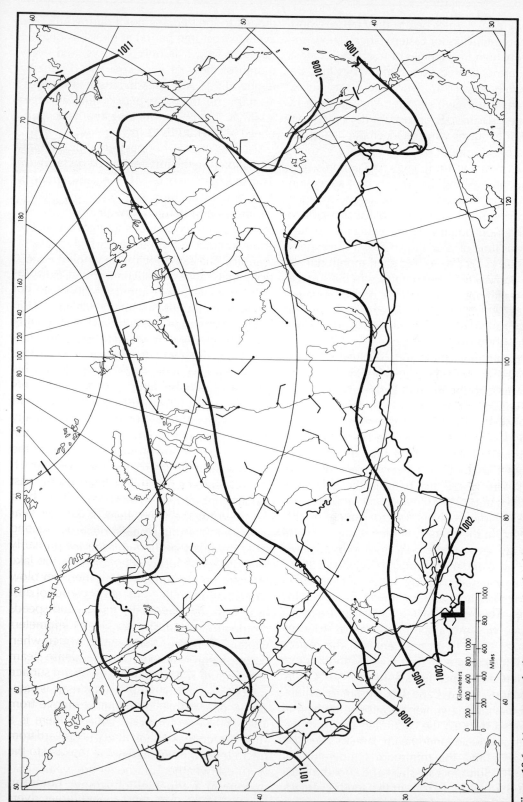

Figure 18-6 Mean atmospheric pressure at sea level in July. After Lydolph, *World Survey of Climatology, Vol. 7.*

during early winter before they freeze. Most climatic statistics for Eastern Siberia show unusually high frequencies of fog because most data are collected from major cities that are generally located in river valleys. At Irkutsk, for instance, where the Angara seldom freezes, steam fogs occur 103 days per year, primarily during winter. December has fog 23 days of the month. During summer in these valleys radiational fogs occur only infrequently. Along the Arctic coast advection fog occurs frequently during summer when it is carried inland from the cold water surface by the monsoonal winds blowing inland during this time of year. Cape Chelyuskin experiences 21–22 days of fog each month during July and August. Temperatures in the surface waters of the sea offshore during summer never rise much above freezing because of the ice floes in the water that use any excess heat for melting.

The condensation and freezing of water droplets in the surface air is a common problem throughout much of Eastern Siberia during winter. In the extremely cold air temperatures that prevail, even the breath of animals and people, as well as the by-products of combustion, will saturate the air and cause dense fogs to collect over settlements. The fogs may freeze and hang in the air as ice crystals trapped in the stagnant air below intense surface inversions for much of the winter. In the sparsely settled Arctic one can usually spot a settlement from a distance by the low cloud of fog hanging over the locality.

Temperatures during winter are severely cold throughout Eastern Siberia. Irkutsk in the south averages −21°C (−12°F) and experiences minimum temperatures as low as −50°C (−58°F). In the center of the region Tura averages −37°C in January and has experienced temperatures as low as −67°C. On the north coast Cape Chelyuskin is a little warmer during winter because some heat is derived through the Arctic ice cap from the unfrozen water underneath. January averages −31°C, and the minimum temperature is −49°C. Summers are short and cool throughout the region. Irkutsk in the south averages only 17.5°C in July, and temperatures have

dipped to the freezing point during July. The average frost-free period at Irkutsk is only 94 days. At Tura it is only 70 days, and every month of the year has experienced freezing temperatures. At Cape Chelyuskin there is essentially no frost-free period. July averages less than 1°C above freezing and has experienced temperatures as low as −6°C.

In spite of the shortness of summer, individual days in the interior can be quite warm. Tura at a latitude of 64° 10'N has experienced temperatures as high as 35°C (95°F). Interior location and relatively dry air under the effects of almost continuous sunlight causes the short summer season to reach high peaks of warmth. The same local topographic conditions that cause air stagnation and extreme cold in winter cause air stagnation and extreme heat in summer. Thus, very high annual temperature ranges are achieved. At Tura, the absolute temperature range is 102°C (184°F). This area, along with the adjacent area in the Soviet Far East, experiences the highest temperature ranges on earth.

The temperature distribution through the year is asymmetrical. Surface air temperatures during spring do not rise very much until the snow is melted, the ground is thawed, and much of the meltwater has evaporated. Therefore, the coming of spring is delayed well into the summer solstice, so that immediately after the need for the latent heat of melting and evaporation is gone, the temperature rises almost instantaneously under the influence of long daylight. During fall, the changing state of water on the surface is not involved, and when the soil finally starts to freeze, the latent heat of fusion goes into the surface air to prolong the autumn season even farther into winter. Therefore, the temperature descent during autumn is much less rapid than the temperature rise during spring.

Cold weather occupies much more of the spring period than the autumn period (Fig. 18-7). However, in many of the southern basins, the cold weather of early spring may be followed immediately by some of the warmest weather of the entire year. The maximum frequency of sunny, hot, dry weather at Krasnoyarsk occurs during May–

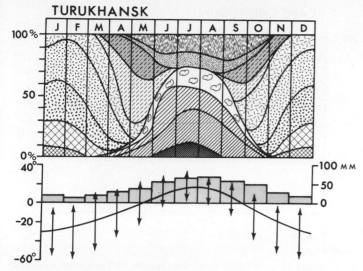

Figure 18-7   Weather types, temperature, and precipitation at Turukhansk.
For legend see page 6.

June during the height of the long days of the June solstice and low atmospheric humidities. May is generally the month of lowest relative humidity of the surface air throughout much of the interior portions of the U.S.S.R. Therefore, not only are the days long, but the sunlight is also most effective at this time of year (Fig. 18-8).

Although the greatest frequency of warm, sunny days often takes place in early summer, maximum average temperatures are generally delayed until mid- or late summer. July is the month of maximum average temperatures for most places, although along the Arctic coast the temperature maximum is delayed until August (Fig. 18-9). This temperature lag is typical of marine locations.

Drought conditions in the steppe basins in southern Siberia are generally most severe during the warm, sunny periods of late spring

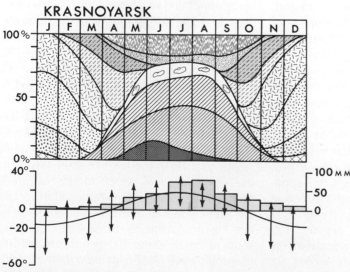

Figure 18-8   Weather types, temperature, and precipitation at Krasnoyarsk.
For legend see page 6.

CAPE CHELYUSKIN

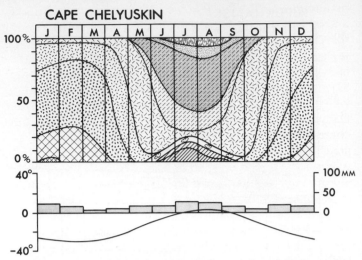

Figure 18-9 Weather types, temperature, and precipitation at Cape Chelyuskin. For legend see page 6.

and early summer. Later on, as the harvest season approaches, the rains usually come on. For instance, at Krasnoyarsk the maximum precipitation falls during August (Fig. 18-8).

The amount of precipitation throughout much of Eastern Siberia is not great. In the southwest at Krasnoyarsk the annual total is 419 millimeters (16 inches), which is a little less than the potential evaporation, and therefore the area is subhumid. In the Minusinsk Basin farther south, the annual precipitation is only 316 millimeters, and the area is semiarid. Farther east, Irkutsk has 458 millimeters per year, which is somewhat greater than the potential evaporation, so that the region is on the humid side. But in all these basins, as well as in much of the interior farther north, there are prolonged periods, particularly during early summer, when drought and sukhovey conditions may be experienced. Even in the far north, the tundra vegetation may occasionally experience leaf burn because of intense, prolonged sunlight, which causes a transpirational stress on plants even though the roots of the plants may be in water-logged soil.

Snowfall varies across the region; it is greatest in the northwest and least in the southeast. The middle Yenisey Valley accumulates some of the greatest snow depths

in the country. At Turukhansk snow accumulates to a maximum depth of 85 centimeters and lies on the ground 229 days of the year. At Chita east of Lake Baykal snow accumulates to a depth of only 11 centimeters and lies on the ground 145 days of the year. The area east of Lake Baykal receives very little winter precipitation because of the dominance of the Asiatic Maximum. Occasional winds may drift the thin snow cover in this region so that much of the land is laid bare. This facilitates deep freezing and frequent freezing and thawing at either end of winter, which is very detrimental to wintering plants. In the far north snow accumulation is not very great, but snow lies on the ground much of the year. At Cape Chelyuskin the maximum depth is 33 centimeters, and the snow cover period is 287 days.

The severe climate of Eastern Siberia has been conducive to the growth of tundra and taiga vegetation with some limited areas of steppe grasses in the intermontane basins in the south. Typical arctic tundra occupies much of the Taymyr Peninsula and fringes of the Arctic coast all along the northern part of the region. In the North Siberian Lowland south of the Byrranga Range a thin scattering of spindly trees and brush changes the tundra to forest tundra. The tundra vegetation is carried southward in the Putorana Mountains and other higher portions of the Central Siberian Upland that lies above the treeline. Tundra is also found on the high slopes of the mountains farther south. But most of the Central Siberian Upland is covered with taiga forest, which in the north consists of a thin cover of Dahurian and Siberian larch. The stand becomes denser farther south and eventually grades into a mixture of cedar, spruce, and fir with stands of pine on sandier soils. The severe climate and permafrost limit the number of species that can survive in this area. As in Western Siberia, the larch is particularly well adapted to growth over permanently frozen subsoil, because it has wide-spreading, shallow roots that can nourish the tree in the thin, active layer of soil during the melting period. During summer throughout much of the northern half of Eastern Siberia the soil never thaws much below the 1-meter level. North of about 60°N latitude the Eastern Siberia Region is underlain with continuous permafrost, while south of 60°N discontinuous permafrost continues southward all the way into Mongolia.

The forest stands generally improve southward until the climate becomes too dry in the southern steppe basins. The best stands are in Irkutsk Oblast, which usually ranks first in total wood production in the Soviet Union. In spite of the various drawbacks regarding the Eastern Siberian forests, they are better in Eastern Siberia than in Western Siberia where the land is so swampy.

In the high southern mountains, vegetation zones are arranged in vertical order, but exposure to prevailing moisture sources and sunlight may cause considerable differences on opposite sides of mountain ranges. Taiga often occupies northern slopes while steppe occupies southern slopes. In the southern Trans Baykal region steppes generally occupy the foothills up to 900–1000 meters in elevation, above which a narrow forest-steppe belt may rise to 1200 meters. Coniferous forests occupy slopes between 1000–1200 meters up to 1700–1900 meters. A narrow zone of subalpine brush generally occupies the next

zone up to perhaps 2200 meters, above which are the high mountain tundra belts. On the higher peaks perpetual snow and glaciers exist. In the mountain and basin country of Trans Baykal, forests and steppes intermingle for hundreds of kilometers as forests penetrate far southward on mountain slopes, and steppe grasses penetrate far northward in river valleys.

Soils throughout the tundra and forest zones are badly leached and not much used for agriculture. Only isolated clearings in small fields have been cultivated around cities, mining towns, and lumber camps. Crops generally consist of potatoes and other vegetables, as well as some hardy strains of small grains. Dairying is fairly highly developed around urban centers, using many natural pastures and natural haylands in river valleys. In the southern steppe basins the soils are fertile chernozems and chestnut soils that have generally been cultivated and put into grain, particularly spring wheat. Hillier sections of basins are still used for grazing. In some of the drier parts of the Tuva and Minusinsk Basins, wind erosion has carried away much of the finer soil particles and left a residue of sand that has been drifted into dune forms.

Some of the steppe basins have not yet been put into agriculture as intensively as the Soviets would like. The Tuva basin is used to a great extent for the grazing of cattle, sheep, goats, horses, reindeer, yaks, and even some camels. During winter the animals are often grazed on intermediate slopes, particularly those with southern exposures, where the temperatures in inversion layers are much warmer than they are on the basin floors. The higher temperatures keep the snow cover much thinner on the mountain slopes, which makes grazing much more possible throughout the winter than on the more deeply covered basin floors. The Soviets are eager to intensify the agriculture of these basins in order better to supply the food needs of Eastern Siberia and the Far East, which now ship in great quantities of foodstuffs from other parts of the country. In most cases this will

Figure 18-10   Sheep being driven to mountain pastures in the Buryat
A.S.S.R. east of Lake Baykal. Novosti.

entail irrigation and in some cases drainage systems. Some irrigation canals have already been built in the Minusinsk and Tuva Basins, but they are not yet very extensive.

Outside the cultivated areas in the southern quarter of the region, the agricultural use of the Eastern Siberia Region is limited primarily to reindeer herding. Reindeer collective farms have been formed in many places scattered throughout the entire area. They find ready local markets, not only for their meat, milk, and hides, but also for draft services. Many reindeer teams and drivers are rented out to geologic survey teams and other such development groups who must get into the back country where there is no other form of transportation. Geologic survey has been so active during the last couple of decades that some government bureaucrats are beginning to complain that the native reindeer herders are becoming totally dependent on the draft-service aspect of their operation and are ignoring the provision of animal products to local markets, which in the long run will be the more stable economy.

INDUSTRIAL RESOURCES AND DEVELOPMENT

Mineral Fuels

Eastern Siberia so far has not received as much development attention as Western Siberia, because it is farther removed from the main populated areas of the country. However, this vast territory with varied rock structures contains huge amounts of certain minerals and a great variety of others. It also contains the greatest hydroelectric potential of any region. During the last two decades it has begun to develop industrially in several locations, and the 15-year plan for 1976–1990 includes a comprehensive development plan for the Minusinsk area, which is to be one of the major thrusts of the plan. This development will be based primarily on the production of large quantities of cheap power, which has been the major instigator of industrial development in most of the region so far. Until now, the basis for most of the power generation has been coal mining and the construction of hydroelectric plants. The huge amounts of coal reserves in Eastern Siberia have already been mentioned. There are now statements that coal and hydropower might be joined by oil and gas in some quantities, although little has been discovered so far in Eastern Siberia.

By far the largest coal deposit in the region, and the largest in the entire country, is in the broad Tunguska Basin in the west-central portion of the Central Siberian Upland. However, this region is so remote from potential market areas that the coal has been used only locally, and production amounts are so small that statistics are not even reported for the region. Significant development probably will not take place here as long as there is adequate coal located nearer to markets in more amenable climatic conditions. Because almost inexhaustible supplies appear to be readily available along portions of the Trans Siberian Railroad, it appears that the Tunguska fields probably never will be developed.

The earliest coal production in Eastern Siberia took place in the Cheremkhovo field along the Trans Siberian Railroad northwest of Irkutsk. This basin has been producing since the 1890s and for many years was one of the major producers in the country. At present it is producing at a rate of about 20 million tons per year, mainly from strip mines. The coal is not of coking quality, but it is fairly high-grade steam coal that is used in large quantities for electrical power generation and on the Trans Siberian Railroad. Before the railroad was electrified, the firing of locomotives was the main use of the coal. Coal has also been mined for a number of years farther east at several locations in the Buryat A.S.S.R. and Chita Oblast, as well as in the west in Tuva A.S.S.R. and the Minusinsk Basin of southern Krasnoyarsk Kray. But none of these areas have produced on the scale of Cheremkhovo. The Kharanor deposit in Chita Oblast has now expanded to about 4–5 million tons per year, and the Gusinoozersk brown-coal deposit in the Buryat A.S.S.R., which began production in 1940, apparently has expanded to about 3 million tons per year.

By far the biggest coal-mining expansion

taking place at present is in the Kansk-Achinsk Basin, which stretches for about 700 kilometers along both sides of the Trans Siberian Railroad from Kansk in the east to beyond Achinsk in the west. Seams of brown coal up to 60 meters in thickness lie just below the surface and provide the cheapest coal mining in the country. Reserves are now estimated to be about 1.2 trillion tons. Production began in the area in 1950, and since then has expanded to three large open pits that now produce about 26 million tons per year. Tentative plans are to establish eight or ten open-pit mines that eventually would produce about 350 million tons per year to provide for a number of huge thermal electric plants with a combined generating capacity of 50 million kilowatts. This great amount of electricity will be transmitted westward by high-voltage transmission lines. It will also provide the basis for the industrial buildup in the Minusinsk basin to the south that is planned for the next 15 years. It is already powering the Nazarovo mine-head power plant, with a capacity of 1.4 million kilowatts, inaugurated in 1961 as one of the first large thermal electric plants in the country. If these plans are all carried out during the next 15 years, the Kansk-Achinsk Basin will become by far the largest coal-producing basin in the country.

Halfway between Kansk and Irkutsk along the Trans Siberian Railroad, the Azey brown-coal deposit came into production during the mid-1960s and is now yielding about 4 million tons per year. Mine-head thermal power stations are also planned for this area.

The Soviets are beginning to show some interest in prospecting for oil and gas in Eastern Siberia. They point out that there are thick sedimentary strata covering even larger areas than they do in the West Siberian Lowland. They also assume that the continental shelves in the Kara, Laptev, and Chukchi Seas will be promising areas. They have reported the discovery of a solidified lake of bitumen in the Olenek Valley in northeastern Siberia that stretches for about 115 kilometers and reaches depths of as much as 10–12 meters. It is estimated that billions of tons of petroleum can be derived from this reserve alone. Also, there has been a report of a newly discovered deposit of natural gas somewhere in Krasnoyarsk Kray. This may be an eastward extension of the huge gas fields in northeastern Tyumen Oblast in the West Siberian Lowland not far to the west.

As early as World War II, gasoline and other hydrocarbons were produced from coal by a hydrogenation process introduced from Germany at the new city of Angarsk just northwest of Irkutsk. This process was superseded in 1960–1961 when an oil refinery came into production at Angarsk, receiving crude oil from the Tatar-Bashkir fields of the Volga Valley by rail until a pipeline was completed to Angarsk in 1964. Now the Angarsk refinery is provided with crude oil from the West Siberian fields through the same pipeline system, and construction has started on a new oil refinery much farther west at Kritovo, just west of Achinsk, also to process West Siberian oil. The oil refining in Angarsk has prompted the construction of a major petrochemical complex that includes a plastics plant and a nitrogenous fertilizer plant. There is also a salt-based chemical industry at the town of Usolye-Sibirskoye not far from Irkutsk. This plant now produces about 12 percent of the Soviet Union's caustic chlorine. Another major complex to produce chlorine, caustic soda, and other salt derivatives is now under construction in the town of Zima ("winter") farther northwest along the Trans Siberian Railroad.

Hydroelectricity

The large volume and steep gradients in their mountain headwaters give the rivers of the Eastern Siberia Region the greatest hydroelectric potential anywhere in the country. The Yenisey-Angara River system alone is credited with a potential of at least 30 million kilowatts. Lake Baykal imparts to the lower Yenisey the largest and steadiest flow of any river in the country. So far, only a fraction of the water power potential has been realized, primarily in three large dams on the Angara and two large dams on the Yenisey River.

Many other tributaries, as well as many smaller separate streams in the Central Siberian Upland, could be tapped.

The first plant was the Irkutsk plant on the Angara, completed in 1958 with a capacity of 660,000 kilowatts. An earthen dam 2363 meters long backed up the water 70 kilometers to Lake Baykal. The second was the Bratsk plant, which began operation in 1961 and reached a capacity of 4.1 million kilowatts in 1968. At the time this was by far the largest hydroelectric plant in the world, equal to the combined Kuybyshev and Volgograd hydroelectric plants on the Volga, and more than twice the size of the Grand Coulee hydroelectric plant in northwestern United States. A concrete dam 127 meters high created the Bratsk Sea, which reached upstream more than 500 kilometers to the Irkutsk Dam. By the mid 1970s the tent city of hydroelectric workers of 20 years ago had grown into a permanent city of more than 175,000 people. Large aluminum and wood-processing industries have been established in Bratsk to use some of the hydroelectricity now being produced.

In 1975 the Ust-Ilimsk dam and hydroelectric plant were nearing completion near the mouth of the Ilim River where it joins the Angara. The workers settlement at Ust-Ilimsk, founded in 1963, had reached a population of 30,000 by 1974. The hydroelectric plant began operation in late 1974 and is to have a total capacity of 4,320,000 kilowatts when it is finally completed. A 214-kilometer-long access railroad has been built to Ust-Ilimsk from a junction on the Bratsk–Ust-Kut railroad near the iron-mining center of Zheleznogorsk, and a 250-kilometer-long highway has been built north from Bratsk. The Ust-Ilimsk station is to instigate the construction of three major industrial centers in the area. The Ust-Ilimsk center, in addition to the power station, will include a pulp plant and huge woodworking complex, which is to turn out about 500,000 tons of paper pulp per year, 1,200,000 cubic meters of sawed timber, 650,000 railroad ties, and other products such as fodder yeast for animal feed. The complex is to be built in cooperation with other COMECON countries, particularly Bul-

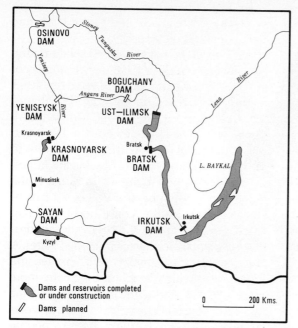

Figure 18-11 Construction projects on the Yenisey and Angara Rivers.

garia, Hungary, East Germany, Poland, and Rumania. They are to supply equipment and in return will receive wood products. The other two planned industrial centers, Rudnogorsk and Neryundinsky, are intended primarily to process local iron ores. There are long-range plans perhaps to include an aluminum-reduction plant, as well as a metal-alloys plant and an electrochemical plant.

As many as three other large power stations have been proposed for the Angara, but the only one that appears to be definite at present is the Boguchany station, which will now be built at Koda about 100 kilometers upstream from Boguchany. The Boguchany site was abandoned when it was learned that a reservoir in that area would flood newly discovered bauxite deposits. An access railroad is now being built to Boguchany, and construction is expected to start on the dam and hydroelectric plant during the next five-year plan, 1976–1980, after the Ust-Ilimsk station upstream is completed. The railroads to Ust-Ilimsk and Boguchany incidentally will open up much new timber area. The Boguchany

station when completed is planned to have a capacity of 4 million kilowatts.

At least seven huge hydroelectric plants have been planned for the Yenisey River itself. Already in operation is the Krasnoyarsk plant at Divnogorsk upstream to the west of Krasnoyarsk. The plant first went into production in late 1967 and reached its designed capacity of 6 million kilowatts on January 1, 1972. This makes it the largest hydroelectric plant in the world, almost 50 percent larger than that at Bratsk. The Krasnoyarsk Sea, 350 kilometers long and 15–20 kilometers wide, now accumulates most of the devastating floodwaters of the Yenisey that used to sweep away everything in their path. The reservoir holds more water than either the Aral or Azov Seas and made necessary the removal of 132 villages that had been in the reservoir basin. A lift has been built to carry ships over the 100-meter-high dam. This is built in the form of a giant metal tub resting on 156 wheels and traveling on rails. As it fills with water a ship sails into it and then is carried up over the dam. The presence of abundant hydro-electricity in Krasnoyarsk has prompted the

Figure 18-12 Construction of the Bratsk Dam, as of 1959. Novosti.

construction of one of the largest aluminum plants in the world.

An even larger hydroelectric station is under construction farther upstream where the Yenisey cuts through a narrow mountain gorge in the Tuva A.S.S.R. This is the Sayan Dam, 245 meters high, whose power plant when completed will have a capacity of 6.4 million kilowatts, surpassing all others in the world. This plant will be a key enterprise among the 120 major industrial complexes to be built in the Abakan region during the next 15 years.

About five other large hydroelectric stations are planned for the Yenisey River downstream from Krasnoyarsk. Apparently two of these locations will be at Yeniseysk near the mouth of the Angara River and Osinovo near the mouth of the Stony Tunguska. Wherever large right-bank tributaries enter the Yenisey, the additional volume of water causes increased downcutting, which produces rapids in a narrow gorgelike valley that provides prime sites for dams.

The huge turbines for the Yenisey and Angara Dams are built in Leningrad and shipped by sea westward through the Baltic completely around Scandinavia and along the Northern Sea Route to the mouth of the Yenisey and then up the Yenisey and Angara Rivers. The turbines, which are about 8 meters in diameter, are too large to be shipped by rail.

In the far north the Khantayka hydroelectric station on the Taymyr Peninsula began operation in 1970 and reached its full capacity of 441,000 kilowatts in late 1972. The main street in the workers' settlement of Snezhnogorsk ("snow mountain") is aptly named "68th parallel." This station, which supplies electricity to the important Norilsk nickel-copper-platinum center, was the first major construction in the far north on permafrost under the weather conditions of snowstorms lasting for days on end with winds of gale force and frost of more than −60°C. It is hoped that the experience gained there will provide the basis for building a number of hydroelectric stations on such rivers as the

Kolyma and Lena in the northern part of the Soviet Far East.

Metallurgy

The building of the huge hydroelectric plants in Eastern Siberia has sort of put the cart before the horse. The Soviets have found themselves with so much electricity in this region that they have had to cast about to see how to make use of it. For immediate purposes they have established certain industries that use large quantities of electricity without involving a great number of laborers. Ideally suited to this sort of resource utilization are aluminum-reduction plants and large wood-cullulose complexes turning out a variety of products. Consequently, three huge aluminum plants have been established at Krasnoyarsk, Shelekhov near Irkutsk, and Bratsk. These are now the largest aluminum plants in the country, and the Bratsk plant is the largest in the world. However, these too have preceded the development of adequate resource bases. Initially the plants had to ship in alumina all the way from the Urals, and after 1964 partially from Pavlodar in eastern Kazakhstan. It was only in late 1969 that production of alumina began at Achinsk within the Eastern Siberia Region, and this plant apparently only supplies the nearby Krasnoyarsk plant. Thus, it appears that the headlong building of large hydroelectric plants on the Angara and Yenisey Rivers has necessitated the establishment of large aluminum-reduction plants to utilize the electricity, and the establishment of the large aluminum-reduction plants has necessitated the establishment of alumina plants, which are finding it difficult to utilize the not-too-abundant aluminum ores other than bauxite. Also, much of the aluminum production has to be shipped back to European Russia for use. It appears that the Soviets are beginning to wonder how they got into this seemingly endless sequence of capital investment in the Eastern Siberia Region, which is not developed to the point where it can use the products of the investment. They are beginning to think that they might have done better to establish aluminum-reduction plants at sources of electricity nearer the sea coasts where alumina or bauxite or both could be imported easily from other countries. Nevertheless, the aluminum plants now exist, and the Soviets are continuing to plan for new hydroelectric stations in the Eastern Siberia Region.

The Achinsk alumina complex has been under construction since 1956. Delay after delay occurred because of difficulty in processing the local nephelite and the uncertainty about the economic feasibility of the aluminum industry in Siberia. A small pilot plant was established in 1964 to test the nephelite-to-alumina process, and finally in 1969 the main plant began operation. However, it has not yet reached full capacity. It is believed that the plant is now producing about 500,000 tons of alumina per year. Its planned capacity is 800,000 tons, which apparently is about twice the production of the plants in the Northwest Region based on Kola nephelite. But evidently it is not as big an operation as Kamensk-Uralskiy in the Urals or Pavlodar in eastern Kazakhstan, where the plants are based on bauxite ores. Achinsk gets its nephelite ore from the Belogorsk area about 240 kilometers to the southwest across the regional boundary in Kemerovo Oblast. A railroad was built from Belogorsk to Achinsk in 1968. The nephelite is calcined with limestone, and the process yields not only alumina, but also cement, soda, and potash. In fact, the cement production is about 4½ times the alumina production.

The first aluminum plant in Eastern Siberia was opened at Shelekhov in 1962. It utilizes electricity from the 660,000-kilowatt Irkutsk hydroelectric station on the Angara and apparently is now producing about 200,000 tons of aluminum metal per year. In 1964 the much larger Krasnoyarsk aluminum plant was inaugurated in association with the Krasnoyarsk hydroelectric station, which has a capacity of 6 million kilowatts. The Krasnoyarsk aluminum plant has a capacity of around 400,000 tons. The third plant at Bratsk was initiated in 1966 in conjunction with the

Bratsk hydroelectric plant, and its aluminum production has been expanding more rapidly than the earlier plant at Krasnoyarsk. It is believed now that Bratsk turns out about 480,000 tons of aluminum per year. It has been speculated that another large aluminum plant might be established at the Ust-Ilimsk dam when it is completed, but no definite plans have yet been announced. The major need for the aluminum industry in Eastern Siberia is the establishment of an adequate alumina base utilizing local resources. An aluminum plant is definitely planned at the Sayan dam, to use alumina from the Black Sea plant at Nikolayevsk.

A large metallurgical complex has developed in the far north at Norilsk, where complex ores yield nickel, copper, cobalt, iron, gold, silver, tellurium, selenium, and platinum. Development began in the late 1930s with the establishment of the new settlement of Norilsk, which since then has grown to a population of 156,000. The production of nickel began in 1942, cobalt in 1944, and copper in 1950. In the 1960s as the Norilsk ores began to become depleted, large new deposits were discovered about 25 kilometers to the northeast around the settlement of Talnakh, which has now become the major ore-producing region for the smelters in Norilsk. Also, more recently a large deposit of copper in almost pure form has been discovered farther north in the Taymyr Peninsula. It is reported that this copper ore has a copper content of more than 99 percent. A second nickel plant is under construction in Norilsk to provide enough smelter capacity for the amount of ore being produced. Previously some of the ore had to be shipped all the way to the Kola Peninsula for smelting. This new plant will recover sulfur as a by-product.

The metallurgical operation at Norilsk has been facilitated by the building of a railroad inland from the river terminal of Dudinka on the lower Yenisey, which runs about 110 kilometers eastward to Norilsk. This has now been doubletracked and electrified. Materials are transshipped to a riverboat at Dudinka. Also, two natural gas pipelines have been built to Norilsk from gas fields about 280–310 kilometers to the west. This natural gas is used in the heat and power plants as well as in the smelters at Norilsk, which originally used only locally mined coal. An additional energy source has been provided by the Khantayka hydroelectric station nearby, which has a capacity of 440,000 kilowatts. It is planned to build another hydroelectric plant of about 500,000-kilowatt capacity on the Kureyka River in the same general area.

Gold is scattered widely throughout Eastern Siberia. The richest fields occur in the Vitim Plateau where the town of Bodaybo in eastern Irkutsk Oblast has become the outfitting center for the gold workers. A major gold rush took place in 1840 that brought a flurry of prospectors to the middle Yenisey region and produced a settlement form typical of exploitive occupance — isolated shacks and small villages scattered helter-skelter in river valleys where prospectors were washing their placer deposits for the coveted gold. As the placer deposits played out, huge dredges as high as three-story buildings were floated into the middle Yenisey to work the gravels of that stream across the entire floodplain. The dredges extract the small amounts of gold found in the deposits and regurgitate the gravel in large, parallel ridges along the floodplain of the stream.

A number of iron deposits have been discovered in the southern part of Eastern Siberia. Those being mined at present are in the Khakass Autonomous Oblast near Abakan and at Zheleznogorsk east of Bratsk. These two deposits are now supplying significant portions of the iron ore used by the West Siberian Plant in Novokuznetsk. Railroads to facilitate the movement of ore to the Kuznetsk Basin have been built into the Abakan region and eastward from the Trans Siberian at Tayshet through Bratsk and on to Zheleznogorsk and farther to Ust-Kut. During the 1960s there was much talk about the building of a new large iron and steel plant at the railroad junction of Tayshet to utilize a number of small iron deposits in the surrounding region and to serve the market needs of Eastern Siberia. However, that plan never got off the ground and so far has not been revived. A small steel plant has existed for years east of Lake Baykal at the small town of Petrovsk-Zabaykalskiy. This is based on scrap metal and some pig iron from the Kuznetsk Basin. But Eastern Siberia is dependent on the Kuznetsk Basin in Western Siberia for most of its steel needs.

Smaller mining activities in Eastern Siberia include a major asbestos mining center at Ak-Dovurak in the Tuva A.S.S.R., as well as cobalt and mercury mines also in the Tuva A.S.S.R., tungsten and molybdenum mines in the Buryat A.S.S.R., and a tantalum mine in Chita Oblast. Recently there has been an announcement of the discovery of a major marble deposit on the banks of the Yenisey River in the Sayan Mountains; it rivals the quality of the famous Carrara marble in Italy.

Forestry

The large Eastern Siberia Region is credited with about 35 percent of the forest reserves of the Soviet Union, an amount larger than any other economic region. Although the forest quality generally is not as high as it is in the Northwest and Urals Economic Regions, woodworking has become a major industry in Eastern Siberia as the establishment of other industries has taken place. The Eastern Siberia Region now ranks second in total wood production, after the Northwest Economic Region. Irkutsk Oblast ranks first among all political units, and Krasnoyarsk Kray ranks third. The wood industry is scattered throughout much of the southern part of the region, and wood processing takes place in many urban centers. But outstanding is the large wood-chemical complex that has been built in conjunction with the hydroelectric plant at Bratsk. The Bratsk complex is now the Soviet Union's largest wood pulp producer, accounting for one-sixth of the national cellulose output. The Bratsk wood pulp production now amounts to about 400,000 tons annually. Bratsk also produces about 280,000 tons of paperboard, which is second only to the Archangel area in the Northwest Economic Region. An even larger wood-pulp complex is under construction at Ust-Ilimsk in conjunction with the new hydroelectric station there.

The planned capacity of the Ust-Ilimsk pulp plant is about 500,000 tons per year, with the first production to take place about 1977.

Large pulp and paperboard mills have also opened in the southern part of the Lake Baykal region. The so-called Baykalsk plant on the lake's south shore went into operation in 1966 with a designed capacity of 200,000 tons of wood pulp for the manufacture of tire cord. A second wood-pulp mill is under development at Selenginsk on the lower Selenga River that flows into the southeastern side of the lake. The completion of this plant has been held up by environmentalists who have induced the government to issue a decree to establish waste-treatment facilities before production can begin. A great deal of pollution of Lake Baykal has already been produced by logging operations and the wood-pulp mills in the vicinity. The logging operation has left a residue of sunken logs and great masses of small limbs, twigs, and chips in the river bottoms that have caused pollution of the lake and rendered about 50 streams un-

suitable for the spawning of fish. Slope denudation by logging activities has resulted in greatly speeded erosion and catastrophic mud flows such as that which destroyed part of the mica-mining town of Slyudyanka on the southwest shore of Lake Baykal in 1960.

A considerable amount of wood is shipped out of Eastern Siberia to other parts of the Soviet Union and for export primarily via the Northern Sea Route through the port of Igarka, which was established on the lower Yenisey in 1929.

TRANSPORTATION

As in Western Siberia, the Trans Siberian Railroad is the lifeline of Eastern Siberia. Most of the supplies shipped into the region come by rail and are then transshipped onto riverboats and floated downstream toward the north. Some traffic comes in from the other end along the Northern Sea Route during the short open season in summer, but generally only

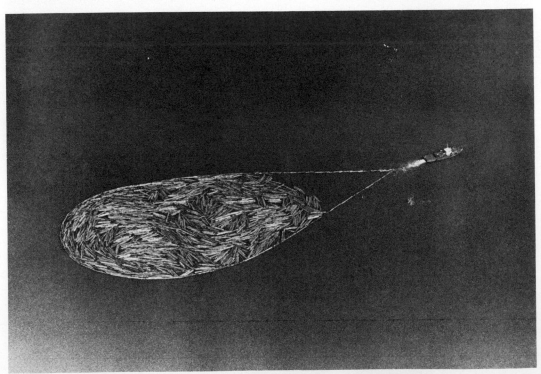

Figure 18-13 Log floating on the Yenisey. Novosti.

the lower portions of river valleys are served by this route. Occasionally very large equipment, such as the turbines for the hydroelectric plants or the gold dredges, have to be brought via the Northern Sea Route because they are too large to handle on the railroad.

The Trans Siberian Railroad, which was built through the area in the 1890s, was delayed for a number of years around the rugged southern end of Lake Baykal where a great number of tunnels and high trestles had to be built. During the interim, trains were ferried across the lake during the open-water season from about mid-May to early January, and tracks were laid across the ice from January through April. The Soviets have always wanted to construct a second rail line eastward somewhere north of the Trans Siberian to open up new territory and to provide an alternate route that is farther in the interior in case of a war involving Japan or China as an enemy. A branch line was constructed from Tayshet eastward through Bratsk and Zheleznogorsk to Ust-Kut where it connected with the Lena River traffic. But there the line was dropped. However, during the 1970s construction began on an extension of this line, which is to become the Baykal-Amur Magistral (BAM) that will eventually run all the way to the Pacific. The BAM has been announced as one of the major thrusts of the newly announced 15-year plan for 1976–1990, and a great deal of enthusiasm has been whipped up to enlist Komsomols (Young Communist League members) to organize and do much of the work on the project. Because the line will be built primarily through the Far East Region, discussion of its details will be delayed until the next chapter. But within Eastern Siberia it will, at last, provide access to the Udokan copper deposit in northern Chita Oblast, which might be the largest copper deposit in the country.

CITIES

Krasnoyarsk

The largest city in Eastern Siberia is Krasnoyarsk at the crossing of the Yenisey River by the Trans Siberian Railroad. In 1974 it had a population of 728,000. During the 1960s it was supplied with abundant electrical power from the newly constructed hydroelectric plant, and a large aluminum plant was built to utilize the electricity. In addition, its industries include machine-building, metalworking, lumbering, woodworking, paper-milling, textiles, and food-processing. It also contains a tire plant. In addition to its industries, the city serves important transport functions and is the seat of government for huge Krasnoyarsk Kray.

Irkutsk

Second in size is the regional center of Irkutsk at the mouth of the Irkut River on the upper Angara near Lake Baykal. In 1974 it had grown to a population of 497,000. Irkutsk is well supplied with energy from the Cheremkhovo coal fields and the local hydroelectric station on the Angara. It also is the eastern terminus of an oil pipeline that was laid originally from the Volga-Urals oil fields, and now is utilized to pipe West Siberian oil eastward. An oil refinery has been constructed in the nearby city of Angarsk, and a large aluminum industry has been opened in the satellite city of Shelekhov. Irkutsk has become the metropolis that has provided the core for the development of a number of satellite cities, which in addition to Angarsk and Shelekhov include the coal-mining center of Cheremkhovo and the salt-mining and chemical center of Usolye-Siberskoye. This complex of cities contains chemical industries, metalworking industries, machine-building industries, lumbering, woodworking, and food industries.

Ulan-Ude

Ulan-Ude, at the mouth of the Uda River where it joins the Selenga southeast of Lake Baykal, is the capital city of the Buryat A.S.S.R. In 1974 it had a population of 287,000. Since the coming of the Trans Siberian Railroad, Ulan-Ude has served as the main railway repair shop between the Urals and the Pacific. In addition, it has developed machine-building, woodworking, and food industries.

Chita

Chita is an oblast center that occupies an intermontane basin east of the Yablonovyy Mountains much as Ulan-Ude occupies the basin of the Buryat A.S.S.R. The two cities are very similar, being located on the Trans Siberian Railroad in steppe basins with fairly productive agriculture. In 1974 Chita had a population of 275,000.

Angarsk

Angarsk is the satellite city of Irkutsk, already mentioned as having an oil refinery. It also has chemical and other types of industries. It has grown to a 1974 population of 224,000.

Bratsk

The workers' settlement of Bratsk was established at the site of the large hydroelectric development on the Angara River. It is one of the fastest growing cities in the country. It has grown from essentially nothing in 1955 to 184,000 in 1974. Among its industries are the large aluminum and wood-processing plants already mentioned.

Norilsk

Norilsk, in the far north along the lower Yenisey, is the urban center for the large polymetallic mining district. Initiated in the 1930s, this has been a rapidly growing boom city in the wilderness; by 1974 it had grown to a population of 156,000. It is connected by a rail line westward to the Yenisey port of Dudinka.

Abakan

Abakan, the capital of the Khakass Autonomous Oblast, is the largest city in the Minu-sinsk Basin. In 1974 it had a population of 112,000. Together with the smaller city of Minusinsk nearby, it is to serve as the urban center of the huge new industrial buildup in the Sayan Region, which is to be one of the major development projects during the 15-year plan, 1976–1990. More than 100 industrial enterprises are projected to be built during that period in the vicinity of Minusinsk and Abakan. These will include a large railway wagon construction works that will build more than half of all the railroad rolling stock in the country, an aluminum plant, 12 electrical engineering enterprises, metallurgical and mining enterprises, and factories to produce light and food industries. Energy will be provided by the large Krasnoyarsk Dam to the north and the Sayan Dam to the south as well as the huge thermoelectric production that is planned for the Kansk-Achinsk coal basin to the north.

Achinsk

The development of large-scale coal mining and an alumina industry has caused the town of Achinsk to grow rapidly from 50,000 in 1959 to 109,000 in 1974.

PROSPECTS

A considerable amount of industrialization has been taking place in recent years in the southern part of the Eastern Siberia Economic Region. This development has been somewhat out of balance, being heavily oriented toward individual large enterprises that use large quantities of electrical power produced before the region is really ready for it. The retention of workers in the region has been a major problem for full development, and at present the region seems to be experiencing net out-migration into adjacent regions on either side. Perhaps the prospective buildup of a wide range of industries in the Minusinsk basin during the next 15 years has been calculated to stem this tide of population movement, but more realistic appears to be the unstated attitude of the Soviet government to limit this region primarily to exploitive industries. The construction of the BAM railroad eastward from the region may stimulate the economy somewhat because of increased traffic across the region, and it will open up new areas such as the Udokan copper deposits in northern Chita Oblast. The perfection of technology for the transmission over long distances of large amounts of electricity may further stimulate the building of hydroelectric plants on the Angara and Yenisey Rivers and the coal mining of the Kansk-Achinsk basin. If large deposits of oil and natural gas eventually are found in the thick sedimentary strata of the Central Siberian Upland, this may change the economic picture considerably. However, as in Western Siberia, any major production of oil and gas will probably be moved out of the region to markets in other parts of the country and for foreign export.

READING LIST

- Armstrong, Terence, *Russian Settlement in the North,* Cambridge University Press, Cambridge, 1965, 224 pp.

- Armstrong, Terence, *The Russians in the Arctic; Aspects of Soviet Exploration and Exploitation in the Far North, 1937–1957,* Methuen, London, 1958, 182 pp.

- *Atlas Baykala* (An Atlas of the Baykal Region), Gugk, Moscow, 1969 (in Russian).

- *Atlas Irkutskoy Oblasti* (Atlas of Irkutsk Oblast), Moscow, 1962 (in Russian).

- Barr, B.M., and J.H. Bater, "The Electrical Industry of Central Siberia," *Economic Geography,* No. 4, October 1969, pp. 349–369.

- Botvinnikov, V.I., "Concerning the Concept of the Economic Development of the Central Zone of Siberia and the Far East," *Problems of Economics,* August 1974, pp. 66–76.

- Burkhanov, V.F., "Pervyye gody planomernogo osvoeniya severa sovetskoy rossii" (The First Few Years of Planned Development of the North of Soviet Russia), *Vestnik Moskovskogo Universiteta, seriya geografiya,* No. 2, March–April 1970, pp. 34–41 (in Russian).

- "Conference on economic prospects of the Tuva ASSR (Kyzyl, 1974)," *Izvestiya Akademii Nauk SSSR, seriya geograficheskaya,* No. 1, 1975, pp. 145–147.

- Conolly, Violet, "East Siberian Oil," *Mizan,* London, No. 1, August 1971, pp. 16–21.

- Dibb, Paul, *Siberia and the Pacific: A Study of Economic Development and Trade Prospects,* Praeger, New York, 1972, 288 pp.

- Fry, V.K., "Reindeer Ranching in Northern Russia," *Professional Geographer,* No. 2, April 1971, pp. 146–151.

- Galaktionov, I.I., *Buryatiya; ocherk prirody* (The Buryat A.S.S.R.; Essay on the Natural Environment), Moscow, 1959, 90 pp. (in Russian).

- *Geografiya naseleniya Vostochnoy Sibiri* (Geography of the Population of Eastern Siberia), Nauk, Moscow, 1962 (in Russian).

- Gorbatskiy, G.V., *Fiziko-geograficheskoy rayonirovaniye Arktiki. Chast 1. Polosa materikov tundr* (The Physical Geoggraphy of the Arctic Region. Part 1. The Tundra Zone), Leningrad, 1967, 135 pp. (in Russian).

- Groves, Robert G., "Arctic Ports of the Yenisey," *Geographical Magazine,* January 1967, pp. 744–749.

- Kremnev, A., *Chitinska Oblast* (Chita Oblast), Chita, 1959, 159 pp. (in Russian).

- Micklin, Philip P., "The Baykal Controversy: A Resource Use Conflict in the USSR," *Natural Resources Journal,* No. 4, October 1967, pp. 485–498.

- Mikhaylov, N.I., "Problemy Baykala" (The Problems of Lake Baykal), *Geografiya v shkole,* No. 2, 1975, pp. 12–17.

- Mowat, Farley, *The Siberians,* Penguin Press, New York, 1972.

- Osipova, A.V., *Sibir i dalniy Vostok* (Siberia and the Far East), Uchpedgiz, Moscow, 1960, 116 pp. (in Russian).

- Shinkarev, L., *The Land Beyond the Mountains: Siberia,* Macmillan, New York, 1973, 216 pp.

- Sochuvek, Howard, "What Is it Like to Live in Siberia During Winter?" *Smithsonian,* No. 10, January 1974, pp. 44–51.

- *Voprosy geografii Zabaykalskogo Severa* (Questions of the geography of Northern Transbaykal), Nauka, Moscow, 1964, 141 pp. (in Russian).

• Vorobyev, A.A., "Problems in the Location of Transportation in the Southern Part of Eastern Siberia," *Soviet Geography: Review & Translation,* May 1964, pp. 3–12.

• Vorobyev, V.T., "Klassifikatsiya morfostruktur Pribaykalya i Zabaykalya (A Classification of Morphostructures of the Baykal Region and Transbaykalia), *Vestnik Moskovskogo Universiteta, seriya geografiya,* No. 4, 1972, pp. 100–106 (in Russian).

• Vorobyev, V.V., "The Population Dynamics of East Siberia and Problems of Prediction," *Doklady Instituta Geografii Sibiri i Dalnego Vostoka,* No. 43, 1974, pp. 34–43.

• Zubov, S.M., *Fizicheskaya geografiya SSR. Chast 3–Srednyaya i Severo–Vostochnaya Sibir; Gory Yuzhnoy Sibiri; Dalnyy Vostok* (Physical Geography of the U.S.S.R. Part 3 — Central and Northeastern Siberia; Mountains of Southern Siberia; Far East), Minsk, 1971 (in Russian).

The Far East Economic Region

	Area (km²)	Population	Persons/km²	Percent Urban
Maritime Kray	166,000	1,832,000	11.0	75
Khabarovsk Kray	825,000	1,422,000	1.7	79
Jewish Autonomous Oblast	36,000	181,000	5.0	69
Amur Oblast	364,000	841,000	2.3	64
Kamchatka Oblast	472,000	322,000	0.7	78
Koryak National Okrug	302,000	33,000	0.1	37
Magadan Oblast	1,199,000	396,000	0.3	74
Chukchi National Okrug	738,000	116,000	0.2	67
Sakhalin Oblast	87,000	640,000	7.3	81
Yakutsk A.S.S.R.	3,103,000	715,000	0.2	59
Total	6,216,000	6,168,000	1.0	73

chapter 19

the far east economic region

The Far East Economic Region, with a territory of 6,216,000 square kilometers, is by far the largest region in the Soviet Union. It contains almost 28 percent of the territory of the entire country, but it contains only 6,168,000 persons, which is less than 2.5 percent of the total population of the country. The average population density of the Far East is less than 1 person per square kilometer. Like Siberia, the Far East concentrates most of its population along the southern fringe. Huge areas in the north have practically no people at all.

Like Siberia, the Far East lies wholly within the Russian Republic. But there are small, scattered non-Russian groups who in some cases have been given political recognition. Most numerous among these are the Yakuts, a Turkic group who numbered 296,000 at the time of the 1970 census. Most of them are found within the huge Yakut A.S.S.R., which has recently been transferred from the Eastern Siberia to the Far East Economic Region. However, within the Yakut A.S.S.R., the Yakuts make up only 43 percent of the total population, while the Russians make up 47.3 percent. The Russians are even more predominant in the smaller nationality-based political units. In the Jewish Autonomous Oblast in Khabarovsk Kray the Russians make up almost 84 percent of the total population, while the Jews make up less than 7 percent. In the far northeastern part of the country the Russians make up 70 percent of the people in the

425

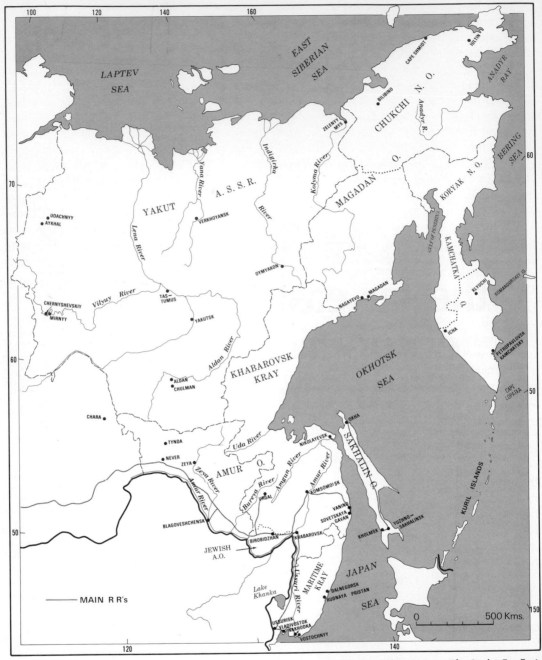

Figure 19-1   The Soviet Far East.

Chukchi National Okrug and 63 percent of the people in the Koryak National Okrug.

The Jewish Autonomous Oblast has been an unsuccessful attempt by the Soviets to provide a home for many of the Soviet Jews in a new region of the country as an alternative to Palestine. After failing in an attempt during the late 1920s and early 1930s to collectivize Jews on farms in western U.S.S.R., in 1934 the Soviets, with much fanfare, created the Jewish Autonomous Oblast in a swampy bend of the Amur River in the Far East and urged the Jews in western Russia to move out into this new country, drain the land, take up farming, and create a new Jewish community. However, this sort of life did not appeal to the Jews who were primarily artisans in the ghettos of the old Russian cities, and few of them moved eastward. In 1970 there were only 11,452 Jews in the Jewish Autonomous Oblast. Those who did move there largely set up tailoring shops much as they had in European Russia, and now the capital city, Birobidzhan, has become the clothing center for the Far East.

The Chukchi people, who numbered only 14,000 in 1970, and the Koryak, who numbered only 7,000, are two of the so-called Paleoasiatic groups of the far north.

Maritime Kray is now an anomaly in the political setup of the Soviet Union. It is the only kray without any lesser subdivision within it. It was carved out of Far East Kray in 1938 and at that time contained Maritime and Ussuri Oblasts. When these two oblasts were abolished, the term *kray* was retained. Sakhalin Oblast includes the Kuril Island chain, acquired from Japan as a result of World War II, and Kamchatka Oblast includes some islands off the east coast, including the Komandorskiye Island group, named after Commander Vitus Bering who first explored the area for Russia. The largest island in the group is named Bering.

Most of the Far East is highly urbanized, because the potential for agriculture is limited. The region as a whole is 73 percent urbanized, which is 14 percent above the national average. This varies from 81 percent in Sakhalin Oblast to 37 percent in the Koryak National Okrug.

For many years the Soviets, and the Russians before them, urged people to move to the Far East. They extolled it as the California of the Soviet Union. This area is hardly a California, particularly in terms of climate, but such government propaganda has induced a fairly steady stream of people to the Far East, in contrast to such less distinguishable places as Eastern Siberia. Therefore, the Soviet Far East has generally grown fairly rapidly in population in spite of its remote location from the more populated parts of the country. During the entire period between the 1939 and 1970 censuses, the Far East showed

a bigger percentage increase of population than any other region in the country. This has tapered off somewhat in recent years, but to a certain extent it is still going on. Between the 1959 and 1970 censuses, most of the Far East experienced a moderate percentage population growth, and the Chukchi National Okrug experienced one of the highest percentage growth rates in the country because a sudden influx of miners into recently opened gold, tin, tungsten, and mercury mines added to a very small original population base to produce a high percentage increase. This region, along with the central part of the West Siberian Lowland and the Mangyshlak Peninsula on the eastern coast of the Caspian, was one of the three regions of the country that showed the highest percentage growth rates during the 1959–1970 intercensal period. The other two regions, of course, also had low original population bases that were multiplied rapidly by influxes of oil workers. Only Sakhalin in the Far East has deviated from this consistent growth. It experienced an absolute population decrease during the 1959–1970 period. Individual years within the period show either slight increases or slight decreases. Occasionally the Jewish Autonomous Oblast has registered annual absolute decreases in population.

Of course, percentage changes are not too meaningful in huge territories that are very sparsely populated. In terms of population growth densities, only Maritime Kray exceeded the lowest category of increase. All the rest of the huge Far East Region showed only a 0–1 person per square kilometer increase during the 1959–1970 period. Sakhalin Island actually registered a decrease. The growth density in Maritime Kray, 1–5 persons per square kilometer, is not nearly as high as some growth densities in European U.S.S.R., such as in Moscow Oblast, the Moldavian S.S.R., Crimea, Kiev, and Donetsk Oblasts, as well as in the Armenian S.S.R. in Transcaucasia. Therefore, during the Soviet period the relatively rapid percentage increase of population and economic activity in the Far East has been due more to low initial base than to absolute rate of growth. At present, the population in the Far East apparently has an average birth rate significantly above the R.S.F.S.R. average, because of the youthful nature of the population of in-migrants into the Far East, and a resultant natural increase that is second highest among R.S.F.S.R. economic regions. Migration, except in Sakhalin, generally results in a modest to moderate net influx, so the population change due to both natural increase and migration generally is a modest to moderate growth, which varies from heavy growth in the far northeast to an absolute decline on Sakhalin Island.

RUSSIAN SETTLEMENT AND RUSSIAN-CHINESE CONFLICT

The Russian sweep across Siberia that took place primarily during the first half of the seventeenth century brought the Russian Empire into direct contact with the Chinese Empire in the Amur Valley. This happened during one of the strongest and most organized periods in the modern history of China. In 1689 the Chinese forced the treaty of Nerchinsk on the Russians which prevented them from navigating the Amur and established the boundary between the Russian and Manchu Empires along the Argun River and the Stanovoy Mountains far to the north. Farther east the line was never precisely determined. The Russians never really accepted this one-down position, and at the first signs of Manchu weakness, around 1840, they prepared for further expansion at the expense of China.

The Russians had already gained a foothold farther west, where as early as 1691 the northern Mongols had requested protection from the Manchu Emperor. The Russians were quick to seize the opportunity to establish relations with these people, and in the Treaty of Kyakhta in 1727 Russian traders were permitted to cross Mongolia. However, there was little activity in this region up to 1850. The opium wars of 1840–1842 clearly demonstrated the Manchu weakness, and Russia, in violation of the Treaty of Nerchinsk, in 1850 sent an expedition to explore the Amur region and to establish the Russian post of Nikolayevsk at the mouth of the Amur River. A Transbaykal army was soon organized, and military posts were established all the way to the Pacific coast and even on Sakhalin Island.

Unable to resist, the Chinese were compelled to negotiate, resulting in the Treaty of Argun in 1858, which established a new boundary along the Amur from the mouth of the Argun to the Pacific. This agreement placed the territory south of the Amur and east of the Ussuri under joint occupation, but two years later the Treaty of Peking placed the entire territory east of the Ussuri under Russian control. Other agreements between Russia and China during this same year gave Russia trade rights in Outer Mongolia, and a period of Russian economic influence in this region ensued.

The first modern Russian settlers penetrated into the Far East from Transbaykalia in 1855. These were largely discharged Cossacks who were later joined by Cossacks from the Urals and as far west as the Ukraine, generally under forced agreements, in return for which they were given relatively large segments of land extending far beyond their immediate needs. Later this small stream of Cossacks and peasants along the overland route was joined by much larger arrivals in the Ussuri region of Ukrainians brought in by the long sea route through the Suez and Singapore Straits. This mass movement by sea was stimulated by the peasant poverty and survival of serfdom in the west, and it reached its culmination in 1883–1886 when 12,700 persons arrived from Chernigov Guberniya, 3200 from Poltava, and others from Kharkov, Voronezh, Kursk Guberniyas, and Kuban Oblast.

There were a number of reasons why so many people came from the Ukrainian and North Caucasian steppe regions. First, it was felt that residents of the wooded steppe would make the most successful pioneers in the similar natural conditions of the Maritime region of the Far East. Also, the requirement that each family have at least 600 rubles upon arrival after having paid for its own voyage limited the movement primarily to middle-class landowners who could sell their land in the west to accrue the necessary capital to make

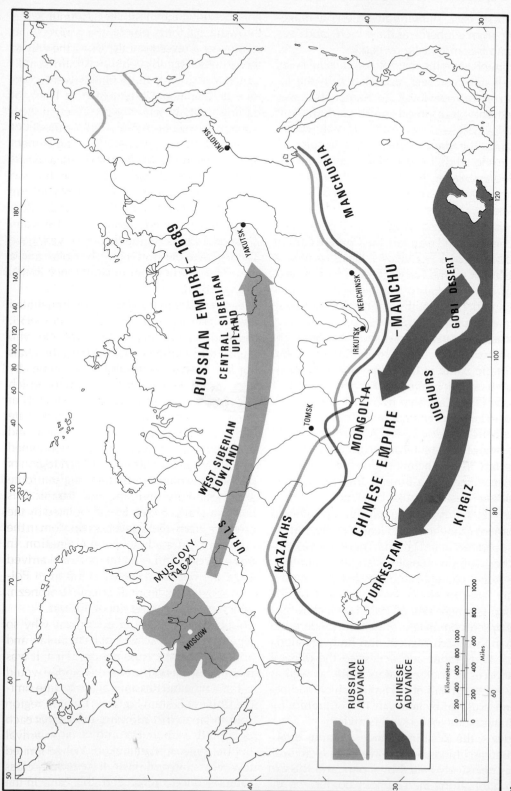

Figure 19-2 Zone of contact of Russian and Chinese Empires as of 1689.
Adapted from Jackson, *Russo-Chinese Borderlands*, 1st ed., 1962, p. 29.

the move east. This virtually ruled out movement from Guberniyas in which land was primarily communally owned.

In the Pacific the main Russian naval base, which had first been established in the far north at Petropavlovsk on Kamchatka, was repeatedly transposed southward, first to Nikolayevsk, and then finally to Vladivostok in 1872. The Manchus, in an effort to colonize the borderlands with Chinese, gave their official blessing to the Chinese settlement of northern Manchuria following 1878. But the Russians continued to press their military advantage in the area. They secured permission to construct and maintain the Chinese Eastern Railway across Manchuria that provided a direct link for the Trans Siberian running east from Lake Baykal to Vladivostok, and later they built the South Manchurian Railway leading south to Harbin.

With the completion of the Trans Siberian, Chinese Eastern, and Ussuri Railroads, the maritime traffic of Ukrainian peasants dwindled to nothing after 1900, and individual peasant families came in by rail to encroach on the large communal land holdings of the original Cossack villages. A new kind of settlement of more intensive agriculture finally evolved. The principal regions of cultivation became the Zeya-Bureya Prairie and the southern Ussuri-Khanka Lowland.

In 1897 Russia obtained mining rights in southern Manchuria and leases to the ports of Port Arthur and Dairen. These moves, together with ominous Russian penetration (in the guise of lumber concessions) along the Yalu River in North Korea, brought on the Russo-Japanese War of 1905 in which Russia collapsed completely. Russia surrendered to Japan the South Manchurian Railway, along with Port Arthur and access to the mineral resources of southern Manchuria, as well as the southern half of Sakhalin, which had become Russian by treaty in 1875 in return for Japanese title to the Kuril Islands.

Thus, the Russian takeover of lands established as Chinese by the Treaty of Nerchinsk was decisively halted by Japan, and Russian attention along the southern border was diverted farther west. In 1911 the Outer Mongols petitioned the Russian Tsar for aid in throwing off the Chinese yoke, and in the same year a revolution in Peking established the Chinese Republic. In the following years Outer Mongolia was recognized as a province of China, but Russia was to have free trading rights in the area. In 1919, after the Russian Revolution, the Chinese president canceled these agreements and Chinese troops moved into the Mongolian Region, but in 1921 the Red Army occupied Urga, and in 1924 the Mongolian People's Republic was proclaimed. Earlier, in 1921, the northwestern portion of the Mongolian Region had proclaimed itself as the independent Republic of Tannu-Tuva, but it was clearly a Soviet satellite. The Chinese protested these events strongly but could do little about them.

Farther east the collapse of the Russian Empire during World War I and the Russian Revolution afforded Japan the opportunity to invade the mainland on the pretext of protecting Japanese property and citizens. In 1918 they occupied Vladivostok, seized the Chinese Eastern Railway, and advanced along the Trans Siberian Railroad as far as Chita. They encouraged the establishment of a buffer state in Eastern Siberia called the Far East Republic, which came into existence in April 1920. This puppet state pledged itself not to admit Soviet armies into its territory, and the Japanese began a gradual withdrawal of troops under pressure from the English-speaking powers. However, immediately after all Japanese troops were off the mainland, in November 1922 the Republic voted itself into the Russian Soviet Federated Socialist Republic, which was the only recognizable Russian political entity at that time. During the following year the Buryats east of Lake Baykal were appeased by the Russians by the establishment of the Buryat-Mongol A.S.S.R.

For a time the Russians again had the use of the Chinese Eastern Railway, but it was finally sold to Japan in 1935 after the Japanese had occupied Manchuria and established the puppet state of Manchukuo. Within the next few years, World War II reversed opportunities once more, and the Soviets, just before the end of the Pacific war in 1945, entered the war against Japan with the understanding from the United States and Britain that they were again to have the dominant influence in Manchuria and control of the ports of Port Arthur and Dairen. This, in fact, took place, but the ascension of the Chinese communists in 1949, which seemed to take the Russian communists by surprise, ended the looting of Manchurian heavy industry by the Soviets and eventually induced the Soviet Union to return to China much of the equipment that had been ripped out of the factories in Manchuria. It also induced the Soviets to relinquish any claims on the Chinese Eastern Railway and the ports of Port Arthur and Dairen. As in Sinkiang, at long last Manchuria appeared to be irrevocably oriented toward China.

Located between Manchuria and Central Asia, the Mongolian People's Republic became firmly established as a semiindependent political buffer between the Soviet Union and China. The nationalist government of China in 1946 had begrudgingly recognized this independence after a plebiscite in the Mongolian People's Republic had voted almost 100 percent for independence. Because the Soviets were in complete control anyway, this was all rather meaningless, although in later years it has provided the opportunity for the communist Chinese to reopen relations with the Mongols and allowed for active trade and economic development to be carried on by Chinese workers in the Mongolian Republic. Nevertheless, Mongolia remains more oriented toward the Soviet Union than toward China. In 1947 it adopted five-year economic plans of the Soviet type and in 1949 amended its constitution to conform closely to the Soviet one. The Cyrillic alphabet was even introduced to replace the traditional Mongol script. In 1949 the Soviets constructed a railroad south from the Trans Siberian to Ulan Bator; by 1956 it had been extended to Peking. This affords the most direct railway between Moscow and Peking.

During the 1950s it appeared that at last some rapprochement, uneasy though it might be, had finally been established between the two great powers of Russia and China through the mechanism of "fraternal" communist governments. But since 1960 a great rift has developed between the two countries, as it has become clear that ancient rivalries and differences in race and customs have proved to be much more potent factors in the formation of national aspirations than the more abstract factor of governmental form. It is now quite clear that the Chinese have never accepted the boundary imposed on them by the Treaty of Peking in 1860, and they want the Soviets to admit that the acquisitions of various pieces of land stretching all the way from Central Asia and western Mongolia to the entire territories of the Amur region and Maritime Kray were made under "unequal treaties." Thus, it appears that Russo-Chinese rivalry in the Far East is a long way from being ended.

PHYSICAL LANDSCAPE

Landform and Vegetation

The huge Far East Region is occupied everywhere by mountain-basin topography. In most cases, the mountains are not very high, generally lying well below 3000 meters, but because of the high latitude of the region the higher crests of most of the mountains lie well above the tree line and either are undergoing glacial processes at present or have undergone them in the recent past. All this makes the topography look quite alpine. The broadest lowland is that occupied by the Lena-Vilyuy-Aldan River system in central Yakutia, but there are very broad lowlands along the Arctic coast through which flow the lower reaches of the Yana, Indigirka, and Kolyma Rivers, as well as many other small streams. There are also fairly broad lowlands in the south, such as the Zeya-Bureya Lowland north of the Amur River and the Ussuri-Khanka Lowland surrounding Lake Khanka and the Ussuri River Valley in the far southeast that continues northeastward along the lower Amur River. There are also extensive lowlands in the northern part of Sakhalin Island, in central and northern Kamchatka, and bordering Anadyr Bay facing the Bering Sea.

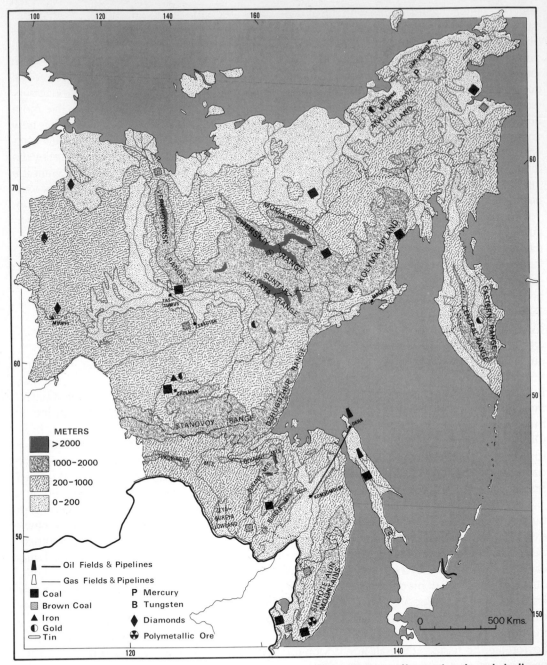

Figure 19-3   Landform, minerals, and pipelines.

In addition, there are many extensive river valleys everywhere in the region.

Moving eastward from the southwest-northeast-oriented mountain ranges in the Transbaykal region of Eastern Siberia, the mountains take a more direct turn toward the east and continue to the coast of the Sea of Okhotsk. The main range is the Stanovoy Range, which lies along the northern border of Amur Oblast and the southern border of the Yakut A.S.S.R. and forms the drainage divide between the Amur River and the Pacific to the south and the Aldan River and the Arctic to the north. These very old mountains are made up primarily of Precambrian crystalline metamorphic and volcanic rocks that have been strongly affected by long periods of erosion. The highest elevation reaches 2412 meters. The lower slopes of the mountains are covered with larch taiga, with admixtures of pine on the southern exposures. Thin forests begin at an altitude of about 1000 meters, and above 1650–1700 meters begins the stunted growth of creeping cedar, (Japanese stone pine) birch, and alder. On the summits is mountain tundra, and some of the higher peaks contain perennial snow and ice.

The southern slope of the Stanovoy Mountains is drained primarily by the headwaters of the Zeya River, which flows southward first through the Upper Zeya Plain, a flat marshy area at elevations of 400–500 meters hemmed in by the Stanovoy Mountains on the north and the lower Tukuringra and Dzhagdy Mountains on the south. On the east the Upper Zeya Plain connects across a low saddle with the upper Uda River (not to be confused with the river by the same name in the Buryat A.S.S.R.), which flows eastward through a broad marshy valley to Uda Gulf, the westernmost extension of the Sea of Okhotsk. The Uda-Zeya tectonic trough forms a corridor through which maritime air can occasionally funnel from the Sea of Okhotsk westward into the upper Zeya Valley.

The Zeya River cuts through a break between the two southern ranges and crosses an extensive rolling plain to join the Amur River at Blagoveshchensk. The southeastern portion of the plain is crossed by the Bureya River that also joins the Amur. This undulating lowland, known as the Zeya-Bureya Plain, is the most extensive lowland and most important agricultural area in the southern part of the Soviet Far East. The Zeya-Bureya Plain is primarily an alluviated plain, but the underlying planation surface rises here and there above the accumulated alluvium to heights of 60–80 meters to form rolling hills, particularly in the northern half of the plain. Also, this is the only plain in the southern part of the Far East that exhibits a continuous mantle of ground moraine, which attests to a complete sheet of ice over the region during the Pleisto-

cene that probably grew by the coalescence of glaciers descending the surrounding mountains. Also, the penetration of humid air masses up the Uda Valley into the upper Zeya Basin might have caused this area to be one of heavier snowfall, which led to ice accumulation during the Pleistocene.

East of the plain lie a number of individual low mountain ranges that generally are oriented south-southwest–north-northeast. The main ones are the Turana to the west of the upper Bureya Valley and the Bureya Mountains that lie to the east of the Bureya Valley. The headwaters of the Amgun River lie on the eastern slopes of the Bureya Mountains and flow northeastward to join the Amur shortly before it enters the sea. The various mountain ranges in this region reach their highest elevation, 2639 meters, just to the east of the upper Amgun Valley. In these mountains bald mountain relief with glacial forms dominates above an altitude of 1400–1500 meters. The lower slopes are generally covered with mixed forests of larch, jeddo spruce, Khingan fir, stone birch, Mongolian oak, and Japanese stone pine, interspersed in the flatter areas by many bogs.

East and south of this system of mountain ranges is a broad tectonic trough that extends all the way from the south coast of Maritime Kray, down the Ussuri-Khanka Plain, through northeastern Manchuria, and northeastward along much of the course of the lower Amur River. The city of Khabarovsk sits in the middle of this extensive plain at the juncture of the Ussuri and Amur Rivers. The most westerly portion of this plain within the Soviet Union is occupied by the Jewish Autonomous Oblast, where the small Bira and Bidzhan Rivers come in from the north to join the Amur on the left bank, and the Sungari River comes in from the southwest through Manchuria to join the Amur on the right bank. The capital city of the Autonomous Oblast, Birobidzhan, takes its name from the two rivers coming in on the Soviet side. In the southern part of the plain Lake Khanka partially occupies the alluviated tectonic basin of a once much larger lake that drained northward to the Amur. The area of the present lake fluctuates from 4000–4400 square kilometers, and its deepest part is only about 10 meters deep. Except on the west, it has very low, marshy banks with many smaller lakes along its sides. The valley floor in the Khanka area is subhumid, but farther north the valley gets wetter, and north of Khabarovsk the lower Amur Valley is very marshy and filled with lakes of various types. The lower Amur in many places becomes a braided stream with many intertwining channels and abandoned channels containing oxbow lakes. Dark coniferous forests and bogs cover this part of the valley.

To the east of the Ussuri and lower Amur Valleys lie the tightly folded Sikhote-Alin Mountains that parallel the coast all the way from Vladivostok on Peter the Great Bay in the south to Nikolayevsk at the mouth of the Amur River in the north. The main folding took place during the Mesozoic period, and since then the folded rock structures have been partially peneplained. During the Tertiary additional movement took place along with some volcanic activity, and during the Quaternary the whole area underwent a generally arched uplift that rejuvenated the area and caused formation of many longitudinal and transverse streams in a trellis type of drainage pattern. In most cases the drainage divide is fairly close to the sea, so that the longer streams flow westward toward the Ussuri-Amur Valley. Those flowing into the Sea of Japan are generally short and steep. During the Quaternary the narrow eastern fringe of the area was affected by outpourings of lavas that have produced lava plateau relief, which has been deeply dissected by the steep streams flowing into the sea. In some places stream valleys appear like canyons. In most cases the eastern slopes of these plateaus drop off very precipitously to the sea.

The east coast of the region parallel to the ranges has very few significant indentations, but in the south where the various folded structures trail off into the sea, deep embayments such as Peter the Great Bay have provided large sheltered harbors. Unfortunately, in some of the more enclosed embayments ice is a problem from December through May, so that ports such as Vladivostok, which

are best provided with abundant wharf areas, are the most hampered by ice during winter. Therefore, as new ports are built, there is a general movement eastward along the southern coast into more open water.

The highest elevation in the Sikhote-Alin reaches 2077 meters. The general elevation of the mountain crest lies around 1500–1800 meters. Forests climb the slopes to about 1500 meters and provide some of the best timber in the Soviet Far East. Lumbering takes place particularly on the western slopes of the ranges where the streams can be used to float the logs westward to sawmills situated along the railroad running from Vladivostok to Khabarovsk through the Ussuri Valley. There is generally a sawmill town at each rail-river crossing. Above the 1500-meter level, the mountain peaks appear as bald mountains with rock streams on their slopes.

Eastward across the Tatar Strait lies the long island of Sakhalin, which extends north-south for a distance of 948 kilometers. Its width varies from 6–160 kilometers, and it covers an area of 76,000 square kilometers, the second largest island in the Soviet Union after Novaya Zemlya in the Arctic. The island continues the fold structure of the mountains eastward. The Tatar Strait, in its narrowest portion only 7.5 kilometers wide and known as Nevelskiy Strait, is an inundated syncline, while Sakhalin Island represents two anticlinal folds with a syncline in between. The island therefore is made up of two mountain chains forming the southern two-thirds of the island separated by a longitudinal valley drained by the Poronay River to the south and the Tym River to the north. Both mountain systems consists of several individual ranges. In the west the highest peak is at 1322 meters, and in the east at 1609 meters. The longitudinal valley between varies from 5–30 kilometers in width and lies at elevations of around 150 meters. It is generally swampy with a large number of lakes, some of which are of thermokarst origin, associated with the permafrost that underlies many parts of the island. The low rolling plain that forms the northern third of the island is generally very ill drained. Hills dot the plain and rise to a maximum elevation of 538 meters. Most of the rocks on Sakhalin are of sedimentary origin and contain many coal deposits. In places these have been intruded by igneous rocks of various types. Strong earthquakes are common, and although there is no active volcanism on the island, mud volcanoes abound in several spots along the east coast in the southern half of the island.

Spruce-fir forests are typical of the Sakhalin landscape. In places they include aspen, birch, willow, poplar, elm, ash, yellow maple, and other species. Kuril bamboo undergrowths reach heights of 2 meters or more. The forests are richest in the south and grade into thin larch forests in the northern plain. The mountaintops and portions of the seacoast washed by the very cold ocean currents exhibit tundra vegetation. A belt of Japanese stone pine often occupies elevations of around 1000–1100 meters between the higher mountain tundras and lower coniferous forests. The forests on Sakhalin support a considerable lumbering industry.

Back on the mainland north of the Stanovoy Mountains, the mountain ranges once again become oriented southwest-northeast parallel to the northwestern coast of the Sea of Okhotsk. Here the mountain mass occupies a width of no more than 200 kilometers. The highest portions lie close to the Okhotsk coast in what is known as the Dzhugdzhur Range, where elevations as high as 1906 meters are reached. The drainage divide in this region lies very near the Sea of Okhotsk. Most of the streams flow northwestward into the Aldan and eventually the Lena River system and the Arctic. Only short, swift streams flow down to the Sea of Okhotsk.

North of the 60th parallel the mountains broaden and eventually occupy the entire northeastern part of the country east of the Lena River. A number of high, rugged ranges oriented in various directions lying way above the tree line in this high latitude form some of the most rugged mountain areas of the entire country. Although the mountains are not nearly as high as those in Central Asia, the high latitude puts most of them into the mountain tundra zone, and heavy mountain

glaciation, both past and present, has cut the higher ridges into cirque and horn formations.

The first range in the west, immediately east of the Lena Valley, is the Verkhoyansk Range, which reaches elevations of as much as 2389 meters. Farther east lies the Cherskiy Range and its subsidiary on the east, the Moma Range. All these ranges rise southward to coalesce into a general upland in the upper Indigirka River region known as the Yana-Oymyakon Upland. The highest peak is Mt. Pobeda ("victory peak") in the southern part of the Cherskiy Mountains at an elevation of 3147 meters. Southeast of the Verkhoyansk Range lies the Suntar-Khayata Range, which reaches its highest elevation of 2959 meters in Mt. Mus-Khaya. Considerable volcanic activity has taken place in this southernmost part of the upland, particularly in the southeast where the upland is known as the Upper Kolyma Upland, after the headwaters of the Kolyma River.

In this southern upland, sparse larch forests extend up southern slopes to altitudes of 1200–1300 meters and on northern slopes to 600–800 meters. Farther north in the Cherskiy Range the forests do not extend beyond 650 meters anywhere. Above this is a bushy, stunted forest belt of Japanese stone pine mixed with alder shrubs and low-bush lichens, and above that the mountain tundra takes over. On the higher peaks contemporary glaciers descend to 1800–2100 meters. The perpetual snow line generally runs at altitudes of 2250–2450 meters.

The northern portions of the Verkhoyansk and Cherskiy Ranges are separated by the Yana River Basin, which in its northern portion becomes coextensive with the broad, flat, alluviated Arctic Lowland that includes the lower portions of the Indigirka and Kolyma Rivers as well as many other smaller streams. This flat, marshy lowland is dotted with thousands of lakes, some of very significant size, many of which are of thermokarst origin.

East of the Kolyma River the land rises again into a broad general upland that stretches almost unbroken to the Bering Strait. Much of this upland is known as the Anyuy-Anadyr Upland, but many other names are given to local mountain ridges. In general the ranges are somewhat lower than they are farther west. Most of the highest peaks lie 1700–1850 meters above sea level. The Anadyr River flows eastward into Anadyr Gulf in the northwestern part of the Bering Sea through a broad, flat lowland that separates the Anadyr Upland in the north from the Koryak Range in the south extending onto the Kamchatka Peninsula. The highest peak in this entire eastern part of the region lies in the middle Koryak Range where Mt. Ledyanaya ("glacier") reaches an elevation of 2562 meters. The southwestern portion of the Anadyr Basin is connected through a low mountain saddle with the upper reaches of the Penzhina River, which flows southwestward into the Gulf of Penzhina, the deep embayment between Kamchatka Peninsula and the mainland. This long, narrow estuary has some of the highest tides in the world, rivaling those in the Bay of Fundy between Nova Scotia and the mainland off the east coast of North America. Differences between high and low tides in the Gulf of Penzhina reach as much as 12.9 meters.

Much of the territory in the southeastern portion of these uplands has been strongly affected by Tertiary and Quaternary volcanism, and many of the higher peaks in the area represent extinct volcanoes in various stages of destruction. The volcanic belt that rings the western Pacific extends southward through the eastern portions of Kamchatka Peninsula and the Kuril Island chain.

Huge Kamchatka Peninsula extends for a length of about 1200 kilometers and covers an area of 350,000 square kilometers. The widest part of the peninsula in the center extends for 450 kilometers. The northern end of the peninsula lies at about 60°N latitude, which is comparable to Leningrad, while Cape Lopatka on the southern tip is situated at a latitude of about 51°N, which is comparable to Kiev. However, the climate is much more rigorous than that in the western part of the Soviet Union. Kamchatka has a backbone of folded mountain ranges that extends almost the entire length of the peninsula down the central portion. These are known collectively as the Central Range. Farther east, across the broad central Kamchatka River Valley, extends another system of ranges known as the Eastern Range. To the east of this system, as well as in the Kamchatka Valley itself, lie a number of active volcanoes, some of which have formed magnificent cones. The highest of these is Mt. Klyuchevskaya, which reaches an elevation of 4,750 meters. This is truly one of the most spectacular snow-capped volcanic peaks in the world. The slightly truncated cone has a circular crater 600 meters in diameter and 100–200 meters in depth. The edges of the crater are precipitous and are covered with sheets of ice and firn. Inside this large crater is a smaller crater that is now the active vent of the volcano. About 70 subsidiary cones have formed on the slopes of Klyuchevskaya. During the last 250 years the volcano has erupted 35 times.

All told there are 120 volcanoes on Kamchatka; 23 are active, and 9 of these apparently are in the process of becoming extinct. Most of them are located on a narrow strip of volcanic plateau between the Eastern Ranges and the Pacific. This eastern volcanic plateau, which lies at elevations of 700–1300 meters, is made up of lava, tuff, volcanic sand, and ash. The volcanic cones surmount this plateau surface and spew out great amounts of ash that cover large portions of the eastern part of the peninsula and in winter cause so-called nonslip areas where the snow becomes buried by volcanic debris. Sledding, the chief mode of winter transportation, becomes impossible. Huge rivers of lava sometimes flow out of the quiet vents to cover broad areas along the lower slopes of the cones. The volcanism has broken out along major fault lines that cause abrupt dislocations in rock strata and allow the formation of many hot springs and geysers. Altogether, 22 geysers have been discovered on Kamchatka. The largest is Velikan, which ejects water 50 meters into the air for 4 minutes at a time at intervals of approximately 2 hours and 50 minutes. Some thought is being given to the possibility of using hot groundwater as a source for heating and power generating in the area. The U.S.S.R. Academy of Sciences has established the

Figure 19-4   Avachinsk volcano, Kamchatka. Novosti.

Kamchatka Volcanological Station in the settlement of Klyuchi at the base of Mt. Klyuchevskaya. This has been in operation since 1935.

Extinct volcanic cones in various stages of destruction also form the higher peaks along the Central Mountain Range where the highest peak reaches an elevation of 3621 meters. In general, the much shorter Eastern Range is considerably lower. West of the Central Mountains lies a wide, sandy, coastal plain that stretches the entire length of the peninsula. Vast areas on this plain are covered by swamps extending in the shape of narrow strips over distances of 20–50 kilometers parallel to the coast.

The Kamchatka forests do not rise higher than 380–400 meters, above which lies a thin belt of stone birch that grades through Japanese stone pine and other brushy growth into alpine meadows at an altitude of 900–1200 meters. The best forest growths are in interior valleys sheltered from the sea. Not a single tree grows on the raw, windswept, foggy, rainy exposure of Cape Lopatka at the southern tip of Kamchatka.

The belt of active volcanism in eastern Kamchatka continues southward along an underwater ridge on which are superimposed the volcanic peaks forming the Kuril Island chain, which extends for 1200 kilometers southwestward to Hokkaido in an arc that is slightly convex toward the southeast. The southern end of the ridge is divided into two parts by the South Kuril Strait just northeast of the island of Hokkaido.

The Kurils are made up of 36 large islands, more than 20 small ones, and numerous small, rocky crags sticking out of the water. The total area of all the islands is 15,600 square kilometers. The largest island, Iturup, has an area of 6725 square kilometers. Most of the larger islands are made up of several cones joined together by sedimentary materials that have been washed down from their peaks. Therefore, the larger islands are generally elongated and irregular in shape. Most of the islands have peaks rising above 1000 meters. The highest elevation is 2339 meters at the top of Alaid volcano on Atlasov Island in the northern end of the chain. Next to it, Shumshu Island has the lowest elevation with hills rising only to 188 meters. This island has no active volcanism. High, precipitous cliffs along the fog-enshrouded, smoking volcanic peaks alternate with undulant plains covered by lush growths of grasses and sedges. Extinct volcanoes with destroyed craters that have either exploded or been weathered away exhibit crater walls now transformed into grotesque shapes resembling sawteeth or picket fences. Many crater lagoons occupy old crater bottoms filled with seawater near the coast. Traces of ancient glaciation exist on some of the larger islands, and the high peak of Alaid contains some contemporary glaciers.

There are at least 100 volcanoes on the Kuril Ridge, 35 of them still active. Alaid volcano last had a major eruption in 1778. It blew off the pointed peak of the volcano and formed a truncated cone from which only smoke has been issuing since. Hot mineral springs abound, and destructive earthquakes are frequent. Tsunamis associated with earthquake activity on the ocean floor reach heights of as much as 50 meters and pound the coasts of the islands, as well as Kamchatka and other areas in the surrounding region. Such waves lash the shores with terrific force. Underwater elevations drop off very rapidly

on both sides of the Kuril Ridge, particularly toward the southeast where only 170 kilometers from the coast of Urup Island the Kuril-Kamchatka Trough plunges to a depth of 10,542 meters below sea level.

The northern islands of the Kuril chain have a very meager vegetative cover. There are no real forests. The plains and lower mountain slopes are covered with brush and Japanese stone pine, and mountain tundra takes over above 350–400 meters in elevation. Moving southward, the central islands are covered with a dense underbrush of Japanese stone pine with admixtures of mountain ash and narrow-leafed birch. In the south the islands are covered with a rich vegetation similar to that on Sakhalin and Hokkaido. Dark coniferous forests consisting of spruce and fir are dominant, while many broadleaf trees also exist, such as oak, maple, poplar, apple, and yellow birch. In general, in the southern islands broadleaf forests occupy the slopes up to 200–450 meters in elevation. Dark coniferous forests of fir and spruce extend up to 600 meters, and above that Japanese stone pine grades into upland heather and bald mountain peaks with bare rock and rock streams. Elevations of these zones vary greatly according to exposure to the raw oceanic winds that sweep the islands. Rich grass meadows and bogs occupy many of the lowlands.

The reacquisition of the Kurils and southern Sakhalin by the Soviet Union as a result of World War II has turned the Sea of Okhotsk into a Russian lake. This huge body of water covering an area of 1,590,000 square kilometers is one of the richest fishing areas in the world. The shallow northern and western parts are the richest in fish and sea mammals. Here depths average only about 100 meters. But in the deep trough along the Kuril Island chain a maximum depth of 3372 meters is reached. Much of the sea is frozen over from October to June. During the open season surface currents circulate in a counterclockwise fashion to bring cold water down the Asian coast past Sakhalin Island and produce much fog during the summer. Ice floes lodge around

Shantar Island in the western embayment of the sea northwest of the mouth of the Amur River and do not melt completely until August.

Many large streams flow through the Far East Region. Most of them are navigable at least in parts of their courses and are used extensively for travel, because much of the region is devoid of any other form of transport. Probably most significant for transport is the Amur, which has been carrying traffic from the Baykal region to the Pacific since humans occupied the area. The two largest streams in the Soviet Far East are the Amur and the Lena. The Amur with the headwaters of the Shilka has a total length of 4416 kilometers, which is second only to the Ob-Irtysh system in the Soviet Union. However, its drainage basin is much smaller than the Ob, and hence its flow is not as great. Neither is its flow as great as the Lena River, which has a total length of 4400 kilometers and is third longest in the Soviet Union. The Lena River, with its major tributaries the Vilyuy and the Aldan, drains the eastern portion of the Central Siberian Upland and the Verkhoyansk Mountain Range and has one of the largest flows of any river in the country. Like the Yenisey and the Ob farther west, its southern headwaters thaw out earlier in spring than its northern downstream portions, which causes tremendous ice jams and flooding along lower portions of the valley. The Amur River, on the other hand, drains an area little affected by spring melting, because the snow cover in much of the basin is so thin, and floods along the Amur and its tributaries are generally associated with middle and late summer rains that occur with the monsoonal inflow of maritime air during that time of year.

The rivers of the far northeastern part of the country are dwarfed in comparison to the Lena, but individual ones are still very large streams. The Kolyma has a length of 2513 kilometers, the Indigirka has a length of 1977 kilometers, and the Yana has a length of 1492 kilometers. The Olenek River west of the lower Lena has a length of 2270 kilometers. In the very northeastern part of the country the Anadyr River has a length of 1150 kilometers. All of these streams flow within the Far East Region, and all of them are included in a list of the 21 longest rivers in the Soviet Union.

Climate, Soils, and Agriculture

The continentality of the climate that was stressed in the Eastern Siberia Region reaches its culmination in the northern part of the Far East Region. Even though the landmass begins to narrow between the Okhotsk Sea and the Arctic, the fact that both of these adjacent water bodies are frozen over during the winter, plus the development of a strong monsoonal flow of air outward from the land during winter and the local stagnation of surface air in deep intermontane valleys in the northeastern part of the country, accentuates the formation of extremely cold surface air temperatures in the intermontane valleys east of the Lena River.

Even though the Arctic and the northern two-thirds of the Sea of Okhotsk are frozen right up to the coast during winter, considerable amounts of heat are still derived through the ice cover from the unfrozen water underneath, which acts to keep the air temperatures over the ice surfaces as much as 20–40°C warmer than those over the intervening landmass. Therefore, during winter the cold surface air of the interior blows both northward toward the Arctic and southward toward the Sea of Okhotsk to produce surface atmospheric divergence along a line running east-west through the center of the northeastern extension of the continent approximately along the Arctic Circle. This induces the subsidence of air from above, which maintains high pressure over the area and, combined with the extreme surface cooling over a highly radiating snow surface, produces extreme temperature inversions that begin at ground level and extend upward into the air as much as 2–3 kilometers.

Surface cooling continues to take place during the almost continuous darkness of the long polar night in the interior basins of the northeast even though snow surface temperatures are much less than air temperatures in the inversion above. The snow surface radiates heat upward almost as a perfect "black body" across the entire spectrum of wavelengths, while the warm air in the inversion radiates heat downward only selectively according to the gases in the air. Therefore, there is generally a net movement of heat upward even though the snow surface is much colder than the air in the inversion. Thus, the surface air in contact with the snow continues to lose heat throughout the winter.

A separate node of the Asiatic High generally forms over this northeastern region during the winter. It is somewhat separated from the main core of the high southwest of Lake Baykal by a saddle in the high-pressure ridge in the vicinity of the Lena-Vilyuy-Aldan Lowland. On occasion during winter cyclones follow a favored track southeastward from the Ob Gulf along the northern edge of the Putorana Mountains through the Lena-Vilyuy-Aldan Lowland, after which they have only the narrow Dzhugdzhur Mountains to cross before entering the Sea of Okhotsk and continuing on across the northern Kuril Islands and southern Kamchatka into the Aleutian Low region in the northern Pacific. A segment of the Arctic Front tends to hang along the northern Okhotsk coast during winter. This intermediate belt has greater cloudiness and somewhat higher snowfall than does either the northeastern mountain region or the lower Amur region to the south, both of which in many interior basins experience almost snowless winters.

Most of the region is usually filled up with the Asiatic High right up to the coastal mountains, and local high-pressure domes develop over Sakhalin Island and Kamchatka Peninsula as well. Thus, there are consistent high winds blowing from land to sea almost everywhere along the coastal areas during winter. The average velocities of these winds are high, and frequent gales are experienced even as far offshore as the Kuril Islands. In many places along the mainland coast, winds during winter months average 7–8 meters per second (15–20 miles per hour) and occasionally reach speeds of as much as 20–40 meters per second (40–80 miles per hour). This is particularly true along the northern and northwestern coasts of the Sea of Okhotsk where uplands right next to the coast cause the high pressure to build up and then spill over the coastal slopes and descend to the sea with great force. In some of the short, steep river valleys flowing down to the coast in this region there are almost constant bora wind conditions during winter.

Even in the very southern part of the region Vladivostok experiences average wind speeds during December and January of more than 8 meters per second. Every month of the year averages above 6 meters per second. Northerly winds funnel southward through the Ussuri-Khanka Lowland during winter, and southeasterly winds funnel northward through the lowland during summer. The average wind speed for the entire year at Vladivostok is more than 7 meters per second, and 72 days per year experience wind speeds of more than 15 meters per second. By contrast, interior locations such as Oymyakon in the northeastern part of the country have wind speeds that average little more than 1 meter per second during the year and experience winds with speeds greater than 15 meters per second only about 3 days per year. And most of the stronger winds in these interior basins occur during summer when convective activity from the rapidly heating ground causes considerable mixing of surface air. During winter from December through February Oymyakon averages wind speeds of only 0.3 meters per second (less than 1 mile per hour) and never experiences winds as high as 15 meters per second.

Thus, there is a great contrast in wind conditions between the calm, clear, stable atmosphere of interior basins and the coastal areas with their great temperature contrasts and steep pressure gradients. Although the coastal areas generally do not experience quite as cold temperatures as interior basins, their wind chill factors are much lower. Some of the lowest wind chill on earth is experienced along the northern shores of the Sea of Okhotsk and around certain promontories such as Cape Lopatka at the southern tip of the Kamchatka Peninsula where the air funnels around topographic obstructions. In such

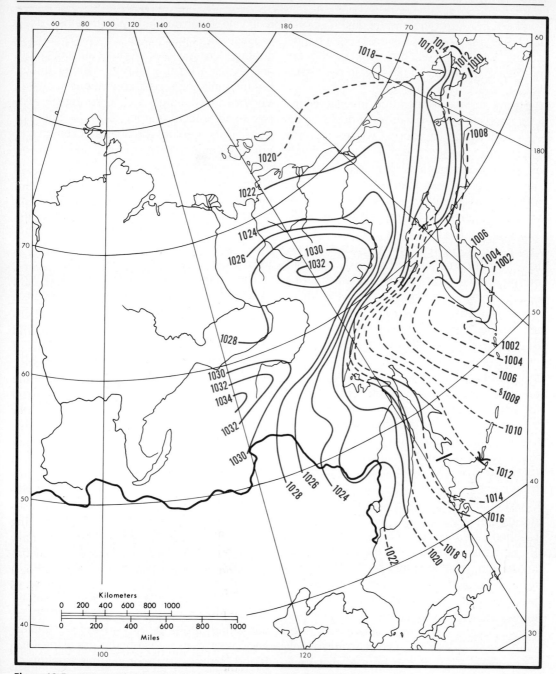

Figure 19-5 Mean sea level atmospheric pressure in January. The pressure gradient is particularly strong across the northern coast of the Sea of Okhotsk. After Lydolph, *World Survey of Climatology*, Vol. 7.

localities wind chills as low as −125°C may be experienced.

The basins along the lower Amur and Ussuri valleys during winter have the clearest skies anywhere in the Soviet Union. Blagoveshchensk in the Zeya-Bureya Lowland just north of the Amur River averages only 3.2 tenths sky cover during January and February. It has no overcast days at all from November through February. Even Vladivostok on the coast averages a sky cover of only 3.2 tenths during January. Farther north, Aldan along the southern border of the intermediate cyclone track has a sky cover of seven to eight tenths during winter. At Verkhoyansk in the far northeast, winter cloudiness again decreases to four to five tenths sky cover.

Strong surface temperature inversions are characteristic of all the valleys throughout the entire Soviet Far East during winter. It is not unusual to experience temperatures as much as 30–40°C warmer a few hundred meters up the mountain slopes than in the valley bottoms. Such conditions cause inversions in vegetation and soil characteristics as well. Many of the lowland floors in the southern basins are occupied only by such crops as hay, which can withstand the extreme cold during winter, while grain and other crops occupy the foothill regions along the lower slopes of the mountains where temperatures are warmer, the growing season is longer, and the summer is relatively free of frost hazard.

The interior valleys of the northern part of the Soviet Far East have the questionable distinction of having some of the coldest winter temperatures on earth and the greatest annual temperature ranges. The small settlement of Verkhoyansk ("upper Yana"), in the Yana River Valley between the high Verkhoyansk Mountains on the west and the Cherskiy Mountains on the east, is often cited as the "cold pole" of the earth. Temperatures here during January average −48.9°C and have reached minimums of −68°C (−90°F), which is about the temperature of dry ice. Although colder temperatures have been recorded at the surface of the earth — particularly in Antarctica — by the Soviets themselves, these temperatures have been recorded at elevations about 3 kilometers above sea level, while Verkhoyansk sits at an elevation of only 137 meters. Thus, it can be said that Verkhoyansk has the lowest recorded temperatures on earth at low elevation. Farther southeast, Oymyakon, at an elevation of 740 meters in the upper Indigirka Valley, experiences minimum temperatures as low as −71°C. Every month of the year in these valleys experiences freezing temperatures.

However, the same conditions — extreme continentality and local sites within narrow river valleys surrounded by mountains — that produce air stagnation and extreme surface cooling during winter produce air stagnation and extreme heating during summer under the influence of almost continuous sunlight. Verkhoyansk averages 15.3°C during July and has experienced temperatures as high as 35°C. Thus, Verkhoyansk has an average annual temperature range of 64°C and an absolute temperature range of 103°C (185°F). Oymyakon has an absolute temperature range of 104°C, which probably is the highest recorded anywhere on earth. The very cold winter temperatures in Antarctica are not matched with warm summer temperatures, so the annual range there is much less.

The climatic setup in summer is almost exactly the reverse of winter. A shallow low-pressure system forms over the land, and surface air generally moves inland from the sea. Local low-pressure centers with associated monsoonal flows form over the interior valleys of Sakhalin and Kamchatka. The Mongolian sector of the Polar Front becomes well established in the Amur region after April or May and a section of the Arctic Front develops in the northeastern extremity of the country between converging airflows from the sea on the north and south. The interior valleys under the influence of almost 24-hour daylight warm rapidly after the thin snow cover has melted and the surface soil has dried, and considerable convective activity causes light scattered showers producing a pronounced summer maximum of precipitation throughout the region.

Sea surface temperatures kept cold by floating ice blocks and cold northerly currents — particularly along the east sides of Kamchatka and Sakhalin, as well as both sides of the Kuril Island chain — cause prodigious amounts of low stratus clouds and fog carried inland along the coastal areas by the monsoonal surface airflows. Most of the maritime regions of the Far East experience 15–20 days per month with fog during May–July. Fog and low stratus shroud some of the volcanic slopes on the Kuril Islands almost continuously during these months. In the extreme south, Vladivostok experiences 20 days of fog in July and

16 days in June. This contrasts to only one day per month during December–February. Throughout the entire year Vladivostok experiences 81 days of fog. On the Arctic coast, Cape Shmidt experiences 96 days per year with fog, 18 of which occur in July and 18 in August. Relative humidities at Simushir in the central Kuril chain average more than 92 percent during June through August; August alone averages 96 percent. The entire year averages 85 percent. November through February is the driest time of the year, but even then the relative humidity of the surface air averages 80 percent.

These maritime conditions contrast greatly with the interior. At Yakutsk in the middle Lena Valley, fog is observed 59 days of the year, primarily during winter. December and January average 16–17 days of fog. The driest time is April–July, with less than 1 day per month of fog. Thus, while late spring and early summer are the foggiest periods on the coast, they are the clearest periods in the interior. The seasonal reversal between coastal and inland areas is due to the different processes of fog formation in the two areas. While the coastal fogs are primarily advective fogs blowing in from the sea, the interior fogs are primarily steam fogs during winter produced by the injection of moisture into the surface air from unfrozen rivers and lakes during early winter when the surface air is much colder than the underlying water bodies. Since most weather-recording stations are situated in river valleys, climatic records show unusually high occurrences of winter fogs. However, on interfluve areas this would not be the case. As has already been pointed out in the preceding chapter on Eastern Siberia, the settlements themselves may inject enough water vapor into the air to saturate the extremely cold surface air and thereby produce man-made fog that, under the influence of extremely stable air below temperature inversions, lingers over cities and towns throughout much of the winter. This usually freezes into ice-crystal fog. Dense clouds of ice crystals usually hang over herds of reindeer. On still, starry, frosty nights these crystals, settling gently to the ground, make a slight rustling sound which the Yakuts refer to as "the whisper of the stars."

In the interior basins, late spring and early summer is usually the time of lowest surface atmospheric humidity and greatest frequency of hot, dry, sunny weather (Fig. 19-6). During this time surface air temperatures rise precipitously, and early summer droughts and

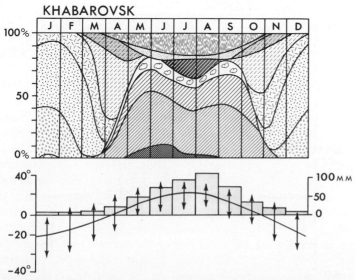

Figure 19-6 Weather types, temperature, and precipitation at Khabarovsk. For legend see page 6.

dust storms are common occurrences in the southern basins. By the beginning of July the monsoonal inflow of surface air from the Pacific up the Amur Valley and the buildup of cyclonic storms along the Mongolian Front bring on the middle and late summer monsoon rains and cloudiness, and the occurrence of hot, sunny days is less frequent. However, the average temperatures continue to rise until late July or early August, after which the gradual decrease into autumn takes place. In more marine locations the temperature lag behind insolation is even greater, and average temperatures reach a maximum in late August or early September (Fig. 19-7). In the very continental conditions of the northeast, summer weather occurs during only a short period of highly peaked frequencies and falls off very rapidly on both sides (Fig. 19-8). Winter is the longest season of the year.

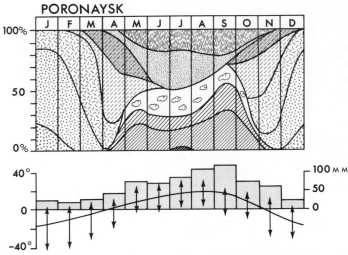

Figure 19-7   Weather types, temperature, and precipitation at Poronaysk. For legend see page 6.

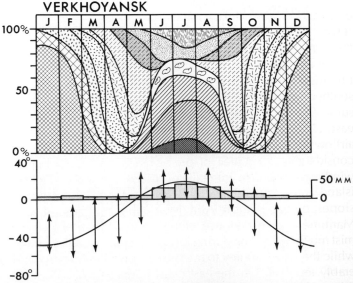

Figure 19-8   Weather types, temperature, and precipitation at Verkhoyansk. For legend see page 6.

During April–June the Mongolian Front becomes established in the Amur Region, and cyclonic storms begin to form along it. They move east-northeastward through the region out to sea across Sakhalin, the Kuril Islands, and southern Kamchatka. Rotating counterclockwise, these storms bring surface air into the region from the east in the northeastern quadrants of the storms ahead of the warm fronts. This has often led to the superficial conclusion that the monsoon rains in the Soviet Far East derive their moisture from the inflow of moist air from the Pacific at this time of year. However, the air in the warm sectors of these storms that overrides the warm fronts and provides the source of moisture for much of the precipitation has circulated completely around the western end of the high-pressure cell in the Pacific at this time of year and has entered the Asian mainland far to the south in China and then recurved northeastward in northern China, Mongolia, and Manchuria to enter the cyclonic systems from the southwest. On occasion this air is also joined by southwesterly flows that originate in the Indian Ocean and come all the way across India and China into the Amur Region. Thus, some of the moisture falling in the Soviet Far East as precipitation during the summer may have originated from as far away as the Indian Ocean. Much of the moisture originates in the western Pacific in the area around the Philippines and Taiwan. The cyclonic storms themselves, of course, move northeastward along the front.

Therefore, the primary flux of moisture that provides the basis for precipitation in the southern parts of the Soviet Far East during summer comes from the southwest, not the east, although certainly the surface easterly airflows underneath warm fronts do produce considerable quantities of precipitation on windward slopes in immediate coastal and island areas. For instance, the steep eastern slopes of the Sikhote-Alin Mountains in Maritime Kray experience clouds, fog, and mist much of the time during July and August, while the Ussuri Valley to the west is considerably less wet. On the east coast Rudnaya Pristan receives 742 millimeters of precipitation a year, much of it from June through September, while Khabarovsk at the juncture of the Ussuri and Amur Rivers west of the Sikhote-Alin receives 569 millimeters with a maximum in July and August. Farther up the slopes on the eastern side of the mountains it is estimated that annual precipitation may amount to as much as 1300 millimeters. But in interior basins the summer rain comes mainly in the form of heavy thundershowers produced by free convection in the conditionally unstable southwesterly air flowing up the surfaces of warm fronts.

The cyclonic activity along the Mongolian Front during summer reaches its height in July and August when the greatest amount of rainfall is experienced. Spring and early summer may be quite dry. This is bad for the crops, which are undergoing their greatest growth at this time. Then, as the harvest season comes on, the rains may make harvesting very difficult. This condition, which is common throughout much of the Soviet Union, is accentuated in the agricultural basins of the Soviet Far East, which generally has more pronounced regimes of rainfall than does the rest of the country.

Outside the Amur Valley, most of the summer rains in the Far East are caused by local showers set off by surface heating and weak frontal passages. Increased thunderstorm activity takes place along the segment of the Arctic Front that forms through the center of the northeastern portion of the region during summer, and many airmass thundershowers develop in southward-moving arctic air that is heating rapidly as it penetrates the landmass. Such convective activity does not produce a great deal of precipitation, but it causes frequent short bursts of showers on many days when the cloud cover consists of only scattered cumulus. Annual precipitation generally decreases northward as the cooler air temperatures reduce the air's capability to hold moisture. Yakutsk receives only 213 millimeters of precipitation per year, which falls mainly during June–September. Verkhoyansk receives even less, an annual total of 155 millimeters.

In most of the interior basins annual potential evaporation exceeds precipitation, so that drought is a constant problem. Even in the Ussuri-Khanka Lowland in Maritime Kray, where annual precipitation totals around 560–575 millimeters, potential evaporation generally exceeds that figure by a small amount, and spring and early summer droughts are common. The highest evaporation rates generally occur during early summer before the rains come on, so that the evaporation and precipitation regimes are somewhat out of phase. Therefore, these basins are drier in the early part of the growing season than annual comparisons might reveal. Farther west, in the Zeya-Bureya Lowland, annual precipitation is somewhat less than in the Ussuri-Khanka Lowland, and potential evaporation remains about the same. Therefore, early summer droughts are most severe in the westernmost basins.

Even in the far north around such centers as Yakutsk and Verkhoyansk, the results of seasonal droughts are evident. Large sectors of the Lena-Vilyuy-Aldan Lowland are vegetated by steppe grasses interspersed with clumps of trees, and the soils resemble the chernozems of the southern basins, with some alteration due to permafrost and other local peculiarities. The annual potential evaporation at Yakutsk has been estimated to be 400 millimeters, which is almost twice the annual precipitation. Potential evaporation exceeds precipitation by the greatest amounts during May–July, while there is a precipitation surplus during August–November. Again, the soil moisture conditions are out of phase with the growth needs of the crops.

Islands and peninsulas bordering on the Sea of Okhotsk are generally much cooler and much more humid during summer than the interior basins. As one leaves the mainland and proceeds eastward across this maritime region, annual precipitation generally increases, the precipitation maximum lags later and later into fall, and the precipitation becomes much more evenly spread throughout the year. In Vladivostok on the southern coast of the mainland maximum precipitation falls during August, which has 15 times as much precipitation as January. In central Sakhalin maximum precipitation falls during September, which has about nine times as much precipitation as the driest month, February. In central Kamchatka the month of maximum precipitation is December, but there is almost as strong a secondary maximum in August, and precipitation fluctuates up and down throughout the year. The driest period throughout much of the Pacific Basin is April–June, undoubtedly due to the extreme stability of the air at this time of the year when the temperature differences between the cold sea surface and the overlying air reach their greatest magnitudes. Also, this is the time of the rapid demise of the Aleutian Low and the formation of the western end of the Pacific High in the region. For a time during spring a localized high-pressure cell develops over the cold surface of the Okhotsk Sea and diminishes precipitation along most of its shores.

On the larger peninsulas and islands, annual precipitation is generally greater on the eastern coasts than on the western coasts and is least in the interior valleys. On Kamchatka Peninsula, Petropavlovsk on the east coast receives 1335 millimeters of precipitation per year. Icha on the central portion of the western coast receives 620 millimeters per year, and Klyuchi in central Kamchatka receives only 562 millimeters per year. All of these values considerably exceed potential evaporation, so that everywhere in Kamchatka the climate is very humid. In the western Pacific region, annual precipitation generally decreases northward. In the central Kuril Islands, Simushir receives 1461 millimeters of precipitation a year, while Apuka on the coast northeast of Kamchatka receives 431 millimeters, and Anadyr still farther north on the Bering Sea coast receives only 260 millimeters per year.

Precipitation usually picks up somewhat in late summer on the southeast coast of Kamchatka, the Kuril Islands, and portions of Maritime Kray due to the backwash of typhoons proceeding northeastward from the Japanese islands toward the Bering Sea. These storms hardly ever come close enough to any portion of the Soviet Far East to cause wind damage, but their widespread clouds and precipitation may significantly alter precipitation regimes on exposed southeastern fringes of coastal protrusions. Typhoons coming up from the South China Sea frequently cause regeneration of cyclonic storms moving northeastward along the Mongolian Front. In such cases the forward motion of the cyclonic storm is impeded, and prolonged rainfall results. During July–September 70–90 percent of total monthly rainfall may occur in 5–6-day periods with such occurrences. Very infrequently an aging typhoon may even wander into the Sea of Okhotsk to die.

Summers are very cool in the maritime part of the Far East. On Sakhalin July temperatures average 17°C in the southern part of the island and 15°C in the northern part. The eastern part of the island is generally 2–3°C colder than the west because of the southward drift of the cold Sakhalin Current, which carries ice floes along the area in some years as late as August. In general, the Okhotsk Sea side of peninsulas and islands is colder than the opposite side. The central part of the west coast of Kamchatka averages only 11°C during the warmest month, August, while the east coast averages more than 13°C. The center of the peninsula averages almost 15°C, and the warmest month is July. The western coast of Kamchatka remains cooler during the summer because of the late breakup of ice in the Sea of Okhotsk, even though the eastern shore of Kamchatka is washed by the cold Kamchatka Current coming from the north. On the Arctic coast, of course, average summer temperatures never get much above freezing, because there are always ice floes in the water offshore. Cape Shmidt has an average temperature of 3.6°C in July, and minimum temperatures during July fall as low as −5°C.

Thus, the coastal areas of the Soviet Far East are very cold for the latitude during winter because of the consistent winter monsoon that constantly blows from land to sea, and they are cold for the latitude during summer because of the summer monsoon that brings cool sea air into the coastal regions. During January the large port of Vladivostok in the far southern part of the region averages only

−15°C (5°F), while Boston at a similar latitude on the east coast of the United States averages 27°F.

Winter snowfall on the mainland is generally quite meager. In the southern interior basins it generally accumulates to 20–25 centimeters in depth and lies on the ground 140–150 days of the year. Because the snow is very dry in this cold region it drifts easily and lies very unevenly on the ground. Many places are blown clear of snow much of the time. This allows for deep freezing of the soil and repeated freezing and thawing during late fall and early spring, which is very detrimental to wintering crops. The snow depth does not increase much farther north, but it lies on the ground longer. At Yakutsk, it accumulates to about 30 centimeters and lies on the ground 205 days of the year. Coastal areas generally receive somewhat more snow. Cape Shmidt along the Arctic coast accumulates snow to a depth of about 50 centimeters, and snow remains on the ground 254 days of the year. Strong winds in many of the coastal areas and on some of the mountain slopes cause frequent *burans* ("blizzards"). Snow accumulation is usually much greater along the Pacific margins of the Far East. Nikolayevsk at the mouth of the Amur River accumulates snow to a depth of 89 centimeters, which is comparable to the region of greatest snow depth around the middle Yenisey in central Siberia. Farther east, the east coast of Kamchatka accumulates snow depths of more than 100 centimeters. In places on the eastern slopes of the Kamchatka Mountains it is estimated that snow accumulates to depths of 3 meters. This is probably the heaviest snowpack in the country, perhaps rivaled only by the southwestern slopes of the Great Caucasus, which bear the brunt of cyclonic storms moving inland from the Black Sea during winter. The eastern side of Kamchatka is greatly affected by the western end of the Aleutian Low during winter. Kamchatka is known for its burans.

Agriculture in the Soviet Far East is limited primarily to the southern basins where there are fertile chernozem soils and a tolerable growing season. But even in these basins, the growing season is short and fraught with oc-

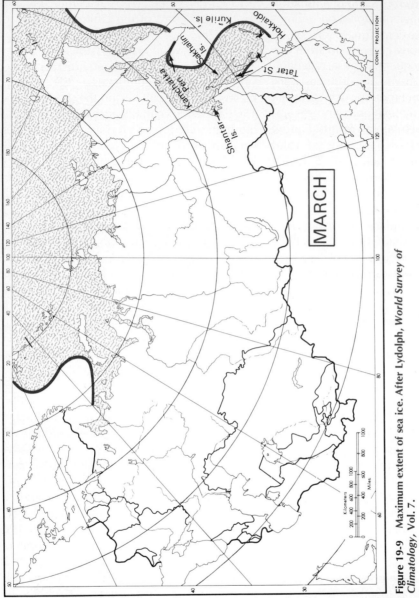

Figure 19-9 Maximum extent of sea ice. After Lydolph, *World Survey of Climatology*, Vol. 7.

casional midsummer frosts. Also, much of the land is poorly drained. On the other hand, climate is rather droughty. Therefore, for best yields, much of the land needs both irrigation and drainage systems. These have not yet been well developed. In view of all these hazards, crops must be selected with care and distributed according to the natural environment. Throughout the entire Far East Region, only 4.6 million hectares, or 2.4 percent of the total area, is considered to be in agricultural use. Of this, arable land accounts for only 2.6 million hectares. The rest is used for the grazing of dairy cattle and meat livestock. More than 80 percent of the sown acreage is situated in the Zeya-Bureya, Khanka, and Central Amur Lowlands. Grain crops — primarily spring wheat, oats, buckwheat, and barley — occupy 42 percent of the sown area, which is less than any of the other economic regions except Central Asia where cotton has displaced much of the grain. Industrial crops occupy a third of the cultivated land. These are primarily soybeans, sugar beets, flax, hemp, and sunflowers. The Far East Region accounts for 90 percent of all the soybeans in the Soviet Union. Soybeans occupy about 40 percent of the sown acreage in the Zeya-Bureya Lowland and the Birobidzhan Lowland in the Jewish Autonomous Oblast. They also cover significant acreages in the Ussuri-Khanka Lowland. The Khanka Lowland has the longest and warmest growing season in the Far East and has the greatest variety of crops. Sugar beets are limited primarily to this area, and a considerable amount of rice is grown by Chinese and Korean farmers. The Ussuri-Khanka Lowland is a meeting place for traditional Russian and Ukrainian agriculture of wheat, sunflowers, potatoes, sugar beets, and a wide variety of vegetables and fruits from European U.S.S.R. and Oriental crops such as rice, soybeans, millet, and grain sorghums.

A significant area of northern agriculture has grown up around the town of Yakutsk. This has become world famous for its development of certain strains of wheat, rye, and barley that ripen within 60 days or so after planting. Some of these strains of small grains have been adapted in central Alaska. However, at best, agriculture is marginal around Yakutsk.

Other than these pockets of cultivation, the mainland of the Far East Region is utilized agriculturally primarily only for reindeer herding. As is the case in Eastern Siberia, reindeer collective farms are scattered throughout the wilderness and raise reindeer not only for their meat, milk, and hides, but also to rent out as draft animals to supply remote districts. The Yakut reindeer drivers are well known throughout the Far East.

Small amounts of cultivation are attempted in Sakhalin and Kamchatka, primarily in the interior valleys where the summer is warmer and less affected by the cool, damp air from the sea. These regions grow some spring

Figure 19-10   Reindeer in the forest-tundra of Yakutia. Novosti.

wheat, oats, buckwheat, flax, hemp, barley, and a variety of root vegetables such as potatoes, carrots, beets, turnips, rutabagas, and radishes. Hay crops support some livestock, particularly dairy cattle. Lush natural pastures on some of the Kuril Islands are also used for grazing purposes.

INDUSTRIAL RESOURCES AND DEVELOPMENT

Minerals

Industrial resources have not been very highly developed yet in the Far East. Although many minerals probably exist in significant amounts in this far-flung area, development so far has generally been in those few high-value items that are scarce in other parts of the country and can be transported economically across the entire Soviet Union, such as gold, diamonds, and tin. Production of these is of national significance. Like Eastern Siberia, the Far East abounds in coal resources; the largest by far are the Lena coalfields in the north. However, there are many coalfields scattered throughout the southern region, and a number of these have been mined for quite a long time simply for local uses, such as power generation, heating, and firing steam locomotives on the Trans Siberian Railroad and its spurs. Usually wherever settlement has taken place to exploit some mineral, timber, or fishing resource, coal mining has been developed to serve local needs. Even in the far northeastern part of the country coal mines are dotted around to satisfy the needs of settlements concerned with the exploitation of gold, tin, mercury, and other mineral resources (Fig. 19-3).

But all of the coal mining put together in the Soviet Far East amounts to no more than 3–4 percent of the total production of the U.S.S.R. The primary producing areas are in the south near most of the population. These are the Bureya brown coalfields in eastern Amur Oblast, now producing 12 million tons of coal per year; the nearby Urgal bituminous coking coalfields in Khabarovsk Kray, now apparently producing 1 million tons per year; the

South Yakut coalfields in the Aldan Plateau, primarily around the town of Chulman, now apparently producing less than 1 million tons per year; various coalfields around the two large cities of Vladivostok and Ussuriysk in the southern part of Maritime Kray, now apparently producing about 5 million tons annually; and a number of coalfields on west-central and southern Sakhalin, now producing around 5 million tons per year. The Sakhalin coal mining has been going on for the longest time and was very important to Far East shipping when most of the ships were steamships. Now the coal is used primarily for power generation and local heating.

The biggest potential development of coal appears to be the South Yakut fields around Chulman and the new open pit being constructed at Neryungri to the southwest of Chulman. The Neryungri pit was opened in 1965 and apparently is to be expanded to an annual output capacity of 12 million tons per year. A branch railroad running north from the Trans Siberian Railroad was started in 1971 to provide access into this area. However, the present construction of the west-east Baykal-Amur Mainline will provide much greater access to coal-mining areas and probably stimulate development considerably. Total reserves of the South Yakut coalfields have been estimated to be about 40 billion tons, although recent surverys suggest they may be much larger than that. Most of this coal is of coking quality, and on many occasions the Soviets have talked seriously about using this coal as the basis for the development of an iron and steel industry in the Soviet Far East.

About 100 kilometers from Neryungri is the Aldan iron-ore area with resources estimated at around 3 billion tons. Aeromagnetic surveys for the prepartion of the building of the Baykal-Amur Railroad have revealed the probable existence of more iron ore in the general area that may total reserves of 40–50 billion tons. It was seriously considered before World War II to develop the Komsomolsk steel plant on the lower Amur River into an integrated pig iron and steel producer utilizing Urgal coking coal and Amur Oblast iron ore. However, this has never taken place, and the Komsomolsk plant still produces only steel from local scrap and pig iron shipped in all the way from the Kuznetsk Basin and the Urals. This so-called Amurstal plant, founded in 1943 during World War II, now has an annual capacity of about 1 million tons of crude steel, which serves only 30–40 percent of the needs of the Soviet Far East. It specializes in tin plate for fish canning and ship plating for local shipyards. It also produces some alloy steels in electric furnaces.

Oil has been produced in northern Sakhalin since 1923. Annual production now apparently is around 3 million tons. This provides about 40 percent of the oil needs of the Soviet Far East. The rest of the Far East needs come from the refinery at Angarsk near Irkutsk that now refines West Siberian oil. The center of the oil fields in northern Sakhalin is the city of Okha. Originally oil was moved out of this region through the western seaport of Moskalvo by barge. A pipeline was built across the narrowest part of the Tatar Strait in 1943 and extended southward to a refinery in Komsomolsk in 1953. This refinery had gone into operation in 1942. The oil moved farther southward by rail to Khabarovsk where a refinery has been in operation since 1935. A second pipeline was laid across the Tatar Strait to Komsomolsk in 1969. Although the Soviets have often mentioned the possibilities of much larger oil deposits in the Arctic coastal plain and adjacent shelf areas of the Soviet Far East, so far no development has taken place there. There are also expectations that both oil and gas may exist in the continental shelf around Sakhalin Island. Apparently both the Soviets and the Japanese are beginning exploration in this area.

It appears that the central Yakut A.S.S.R. may have considerable reserves of natural gas. The first field to be discovered there, in 1956, was the Tas-Tumus field at the juncture of the Vilyuy River with the Lena about 400 kilometers northwest of Yakutsk. A 20-inch pipeline was built from Tas-Tumus to Yakutsk in 1967, and since then it has been extended westward 190 kilometers from Tas-Tumus to tap the more recent production of the much larger Middle Vilyuy gas field, discovered in 1965. The Soviets now claim that they have proved about 1 trillion cubic meters of natural gas reserves in the Yakut A.S.S.R. and that there are probably reserves of as much as 12.8 trillion cubic meters. They plan to expand production greatly in the near future and have been trying to entice various American and Japanese companies to help develop the region. There are proposals that liquified gas be moved from this area to the west coast of the United States as well as to Japan in repayment for capital investment in equipment and personnel to get the operation moving. However, so far none of the foreign companies have been willing to come forth with any money. They are still not convinced that the Yakut gas development will become as large as the Soviets claim.

The Far East is the Soviet Union's major producer of gold. Production started in the Aldan Plateau in southern Yakutia in the 1920s, and during the early 1930s the Aldan region accounted for about 20–25 percent of the Soviet Union's total output. A road was built from Never on the Trans Siberian Railroad northward to the Aldan fields in 1931 and since then has been extended all the way to Yakutsk. During the early 1930s more gold was found in the upper Kolyma-Indigirka River valleys of the far northeast, and by 1934 this region surpassed the Aldan region in gold production. A road was built inland from Magadan on the north coast of the Sea of Okhotsk to serve this new gold-mining district. Production expanded rapidly with the use of forced labor. The region reached its peak production around 1950, after which it declined somewhat as more accessible ores played out and forced manual labor ceased.

Since the late 1950s the primary area of gold mining has shifted increasingly farther north and now lies primarily in the Chukchi National Okrug in the far northeast on either side of the Northern Sea Route port of Pevek on Chaun Bay. The first mining town, Bilibino, was founded in 1960 and rapidly developed into the principal supply center for the region. By 1967 Bilibino had grown to a population of 12,000, the largest urban center in the Chukchi National Okrug. It originally was served with electrical power from a floating coal-burning power station in the port of Zelenyy Mys ("green cape") in the mouth of the Kolyma River. But a small nuclear power plant is being completed in Bilibino itself, with the help of some COMECON countries, that will have an ultimate capacity of 48,000 kilowatts. Partial operation began in January 1974. Two newer centers of gold mining have been established northeast of Bilibino near the Arctic coast at the towns of Polyarnyy and Leningradskiy near Cape Shmidt.

To encourage the economic development of this remote region, a new political unit, Shmidt Rayon, was created in 1964. This is named after Cape Shmidt, which was named after the Russian arctic explorer Otto Shmidt. The new political unit also includes important tin and tungsten mines. Since 1959 this region has had such an influx of miners and auxiliary workers that the Chukchi National Okrug is one of the three areas in the country that has had the greatest percentage rate of population increase during the 1959–1970 intercensal period. The other two areas were the new oil-mining regions of the Khanty-Mansi National Okrug in the central portion of Western Siberia and the Mangyshlak Peninsula of western Kazakhstan on the east coast of the Caspian. Of course, all of these areas were originally almost uninhabited, so that small influxes of people made for very large percentage gains.

Although important new gold production has been opened up in other areas of the country, such as Kazakhstan, Central Asia, and the Transcaucasus, the Far East Region still remains the major producer in the Soviet Union, which is the second largest producer in the world after South Africa. This gold production is very important to the Soviet Union's foreign trade in a world that does not accept the ruble for exchange. Gold and petroleum have become the Soviet Union's stocks in trade — accepted everywhere in the world at going prices. The value of both commodities has been greatly enhanced during the past few years because prices for them around the world have increased several times.

The Far East is also the Soviet Union's primary producer of diamonds. This is a relatively recent development that has put the Soviet Union second in production only to South Africa and has provided a much-needed domestic source for industrial diamonds to provide cutting edges for all sorts of machine tools. The deposits, which were discovered in 1954–1955, are scattered throughout the northwestern portions of the Yakut A.S.S.R. The first production began in 1957 at the new town of Mirnyy ("peace"), which quickly developed into the central city for the diamond-mining operation. By 1967 Mirnyy had grown to a population of 22,000. The two other major operations are farther north at Aykhal and Udachnyy. These centers, lying north of the Arctic Circle, have presented unusual problems for development. The Soviets are in the process of constructing towns in these two areas to consist of interconnected buildings four to nine stories high made of corrugated aluminum insulated with foam plastics to give protection against temperatures of −50°C and lower. Corridors on the ground floors will connect all the buildings so that during winter people will not have to go outside at all if they do not want to. Electrical supply has also been a problem. It now seems to have been solved, for the town of Mirnyy at least, by the 312,000-kilowatt hydroelectric station opened on the upper Vilyuy River at the new town of Chernyshevskiy in 1967.

The Far East Region is also the Soviet Union's leading producer of tin and tungsten, which are often found in conjunction with one another. Production has taken place for some time in the Amur district in the south, in the Yana River Valley in the far north, and in other scattered regions, such as the Sikhote-Alin Mountains of Maritime Kray and the Jewish Autonomous Oblast of Kharbarovsk Kray. Two new developments have now arisen among the major producers of the country: the Solnechnyy tin mining and concentrating complex established in 1963 about 50 kilometers west-northwest of the city of Komsomolsk on the lower Amur River and the tin-tungsten center of Iultin in the Shmidt Rayon area of the northern Chukchi National Okrug along the Arctic. In addition to tin, the

Solnechnyy complex now turns out tungsten and copper.

The Aldan plateau region of southern Yakutia produces about 80–90 percent of the U.S.S.R.'s mica output. It is the sole producer of the valuable variety phlogopite mica since the exhaustion of older mines at Slyudyanka on the southwest tip of Lake Baykal.

Lead and zinc have been produced in the southern Sikhote-Alin Mountains since 1911 near the smelting center of Tetyukhe, which in December 1972 was renamed Dalnegorsk ("far mountain") when a number of towns of the Soviet Far East were changed from their Chinese-sounding names to Russian-sounding names. Much earlier the Chinese had produced silver in this region. The lead is smelted in Dalnegorsk, and the zinc is shipped through the small port of Tetyukhe-Pristan, now Rudnaya Pristan ("ore port"), all the way to Konstantinovka in the Donets Basin of the eastern Ukraine and Ordzhonikidze in the North Caucasus. Also, zinc concentrate moves westward by rail to Belovo in the Kuznetsk Basin of Western Siberia. The lead smelter at Dalnegorsk also produces some bismuth and silver, and recently it has been revealed that a fairly large boron industry has grown up in the vicinity. The same general area has also been producing fluorspar along with some of the tin mines since 1963.

Forestry

Although the forests throughout the Far East are generally sparse and poor in quality, the region is so huge that in total the Far East Economic Region ranks second in forest reserves, with 27.3 percent of the U.S.S.R.'s reserves, and fourth in overall wood production, with 8.3 percent of the country's production. The highest-quality timber exists on the slopes of the Sikhote-Alin Mountains in Maritime Kray and adjacent Khabarovsk Kray and on the southern two-thirds of Sakhalin Island. Khabarovsk Kray is by far the largest wood producer in the region, producing about 43 percent of the total. Adjacent Maritime Kray produces about 20 percent of the total. Sawmilling towns have been established all along

the Trans Siberian Railroad, particularly along the section running south from Khabarovsk to Vladivostok. Practically everywhere that the railroad crosses a small stream flowing down the western slopes of the Sikhote-Alin Mountains a sawmill has developed to process the logs that are floated down the streams toward the west. The southern half of Sakhalin is dotted with sawmilling towns. Sakhalin lumber has been very important to Far East shipping for many years, providing much of the wood needed for ships, piers, and auxiliary equipment. There is even some sawmilling on the lower reaches of the Kamchatka River in central Kamchatka.

The largest development in recent years has taken place at the new town of Amursk south of Komsomolsk on the lower Amur River. The town was founded in the late 1950s, and by 1974 had grown to a population of 32,000. This made it the fastest-growing town in the entire Far East Region. The Amursk Plant turns out bleached and unbleached pulp, viscose pulp, yeasts, fiberboards, and container board. The container board industry will become a very large industry in the Far East as more and more of the goods shipped along the Trans Siberian Railroad are containerized.

Fishing, Hunting, and Trapping

Since World War II the total fish catch in the Soviet Union has increased several times, and the geographic distribution has shifted until at present the seas, rivers, and lakes of the Far East yield about one-third of the country's fish catch. This makes it the most important fishing region in the Soviet Union. Fish collectives have been established all along the lower Amur River from Khabarovsk to Nikolayevsk; along the shores of Maritime Kray, especially around Peter the Great Bay in the vicinity of Vladivostok; the southern part of Khabarovsk Kray, particularly around the mouth of the Amur River; along the northern coast of the Sea of Okhotsk; around Sakhalin Island; and around Kamchatka Peninsula (Fig. 19-11).

The Sea of Okhotsk is one of the richest fishing grounds in the country. It is especially known for its salmon, which are caught in

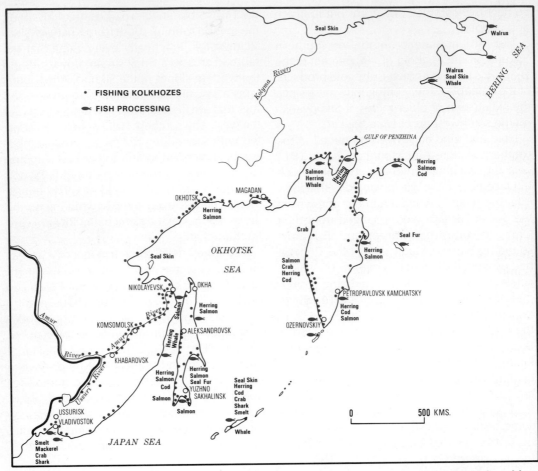

Figure 19-11 Fishing in Far Eastern waters. Adapted from *Atlas selskogo khozyaystva SSSR.*

either the lower Amur River as the fish enter for their annual spawning or in the Gulf of Penzhina next to Kamchatka. The Gulf of Penzhina, with an average difference of 14–15 meters between high and low water, has some of the greatest tides in the world. According to the Russians the salmon are so large and so numerous in this area that in shoal water during low tides seagulls stand on the backs of the salmon and peck at them. The fisheries of Kamchatka account for about 60 percent of the salmon catch of the U.S.S.R. Another product in the Kamchatka area that is of world renown is the Kamchatka crab, which the Russians claim grows to the size of a washtub.

Before World War II a large part of the

fishing in the Sea of Okhotsk was done by the Japanese, who then controlled the southern half of Sakhalin and the Kuril Island chain. Now that the Soviet Union controls all of these islands, it considers the Sea of Okhotsk to be its own private lake, and the Japanese have had difficulty negotiating fishing rights in the area. The Russians report that since the war they have arrested 1,307 Japanese fishing boats and 11,049 Japanese fishermen. At the end of 1975 they were still detaining about 480 boats and 171 fishermen.

The Amur River is populated by about 100 fish species, some of which are unique to the region. Among these is the so-called Kaluga Sturgeon, called the "Amur Queen," which is reportedly the world's largest freshwater fish.

It grows to lengths of 15–20 feet and weighs several hundred pounds. The lifespan of this giant fish is about 300 years, and females do not reach adulthood until they are about 22 years old. The fish never leaves the Amur River throughout its entire life cycle.

Far East waters also are rich in sea animals — whales, walruses, and seals. Seal rookeries are maintained on the Commander Islands off the Kamchatka coast. Although minor fishing ports exist in many places along the coast of the mainland, Kamchatka Peninsula, and Sakhalin Island, larger oceangoing fleets all are based in Vladivostok and nearby Nakhodka. The whaling ships of Vladivostok range northeastward 5000 kilometers to the Bering Strait during the Northern Hemisphere summer and southward to Antarctica during the Southern Hemisphere summer.

The quest for furs originally brought Russian colonizers to Siberia and the Far East, and fur-bearing animals are still a major resource. Furs provide valuable exports as well as major domestic needs for warm clothing in this cold region. Yakutia is the Soviet Union's leading fur-supply area, normally producing about 15 percent of the annual take by value. The leading types are squirrel, white fox, ermine, muskrat, and hare. The sable has been almost eradicated and is now protected with controlled trapping. The muskrat, which was introduced from Canada in 1930, rapidly acclimatized to the familiar swampy environment of its new home. In addition to fur-bearing animals, the expansive wilderness of the Far East Region abounds in elk, wild reindeer, and mountain sheep, which provide significant amounts of meat for the local population.

TRANSPORTATION

Transportation problems in this far-flung, sparsely populated region are colossal, to say the least. From Vladivostok in the south to the Bering Strait in the northeast the region stretches for almost 5000 kilometers, which is twice the width of European Russia from the Polish border to the Urals. Much of the area is

forest, swamp, and tundra wilderness underlain by permafrost. Huge empty distances separate local settlements and make the building of roads and railroads economically unfeasible. Only a few roads exist, and most of these are negotiable only during the winter when they are frozen. During summer they are a morass of swamps. The region is almost entirely dependent for surface travel on the eastern part of the Trans Siberian Railroad and the rivers. During summer many of the rivers are navigable, and during winter when they are frozen they are used as roads for reindeer sleighs and dogsleds. Reindeer racing on these smooth surfaces is a favorite winter sport by Yakut and Chukchi herdsmen. Along the seacoast, of course, shipping is very important and is the only mode of travel between many points. Long-range airplanes have been all-important in connecting the Far East with other parts of the country, and smaller planes and helicopters have become invaluable for getting into otherwise inaccessible areas. Not only people but also many supplies are flown across the wilderness. Peculiar problems in the recent development of all these forms of transport will be taken up individually below.

Railroads

The Trans Siberian Railroad is still the lifeline for much of the populous part of the Soviet Far East, as it is for Siberia. Much of the line was built during the 1890s, although the eastern portion was built after the Russo-Japanese War in 1905, when the Japanese took over Manchuria and the Chinese Eastern Railway. The line was laid all the way on Soviet territory just to the north of the Amur River into Kharabovsk and then southward up the Ussuri Valley to Vladivostok. In 1940 a branch line was completed northeastward from Khabarovsk down the Amur River to Komsomolsk, and in 1947 the right bank of the Amur at Komsomolsk was connected by rail eastward to the Pacific Coast at Sovetskaya Gavan ("Soviet harbor"). However, a bridge was not built until 1975 across the Amur at Komsomolsk. During summer ferries had to carry the railroad cars across the river, and during winter tracks were laid across the ice. This meant that the crossing was out of commission about 100 days per year during the freezup and breakup of the ice. In 1948 a branch line was completed from Izvestkovyy on the Trans Siberian in the northwestern part of the Jewish Autonomous Oblast northward to Urgal in the upper Bureya River region to tap the Bureya coalfields. Several branch lines were also built southward from the Trans Siberian to Amur River stations, where a few of them hooked up with lines running into Mongolia and China. The most significant of these is in the southern part of Eastern Siberia where a main line has been built southward from the Trans Siberian at Ulan-Ude, the capital of the Buryat A.S.S.R., through Ulan-Bator, the capital of the Mongolian People's Republic, and southeastward to Peking, the capital of the Chinese People's Republic.

Until World War II, the Soviets were always leery of having the Trans Siberian Railroad so close to Japanese-held territory in Manchuria, and they intended to construct a line semiparallel to the Trans Siberian farther north in Soviet territory. However, they never really got going on this project before the war. After the war the Japanese were out, and in 1949 the Chinese communists came to power; they appeared to the Soviets to present a friendly regime along the border. The Soviets did eventually build the western end of the proposed line in Eastern Siberia from the town of Tayshet eastward to Ust-Kut in order to link up with the upper Lena River so that freight moving eastward on the railroad could be transshipped to the river and carried northeastward throughout the length of the Yakut A.S.S.R. The Lena River system is still the main artery of trade for the Yakut region. The Tayshet-Ust-Kut Railroad, which was built by forced labor during the Stalin era, was opened for provisional operation in 1954 and for permanent operation in December 1958. At the same time a new river port was built at Osetrovo near Ust-Kut to handle transshipments between rail and water. Part of this line was rebuilt in the early 1960s when it became

apparent that the Bratsk Reservoir would flood part of the original route.

Some construction took place in spots at the eastern end of the proposed line, such as a tunnel driven through the divide between the upper Bureya Valley and the upper Amgun Valley in the early 1950s. But none of these scattered construction projects were ever linked up, and with the demise of the forced-labor system after the death of Stalin, the idea of a second railroad all the way to the Pacific seemed to be abandoned. The worsening of relations with the Chinese after 1960 did not seem to cause enough concern about the strategic location of the Trans Siberian Railroad to prompt remedial action.

However, economic developments in Siberia during the late 1960s and early 1970s have changed the evaluation of the need for a second railroad, and in March 1974 Leonid Brezhnev announced with great fanfare that one of the main thrusts of the new 15-year plan, 1976–1990, was to be the rapid construction of the BAM, the Baykal-Amur-Magistral, which would run eastward from Ust-Kut through Nizhneangarsk near the northern end of Lake Baykal, Chara, Tynda, and Urgal to Komsomolsk on the Amur where it would hook up with the Komsomolsk-Sovetskaya-Gavan Railroad across the new bridge completed in 1975 over the Amur River. The proposed line would be about 3150 kilometers long, and together with the already completed lines on either end would total more than 4200 kilometers. About 500 kilometers of this distance run through country underlain by permafrost. The line will have to cross seven mountain ranges and a number of big rivers such as the Lena, Olekma, Zeya, Selemdzha, and Amur. It is estimated that about 200 million cubic meters of earth will have to be moved. Four tunnels are to be dug, one more than 1500 meters long, and 140 bridges will have to be built ranging in length from 100 to more than 1000 meters. Approximately 100,000 workers eventually will be employed on the project. In addition, a great number of support personnel will have to be moved into the region. Equipment and materials will have to withstand temperature

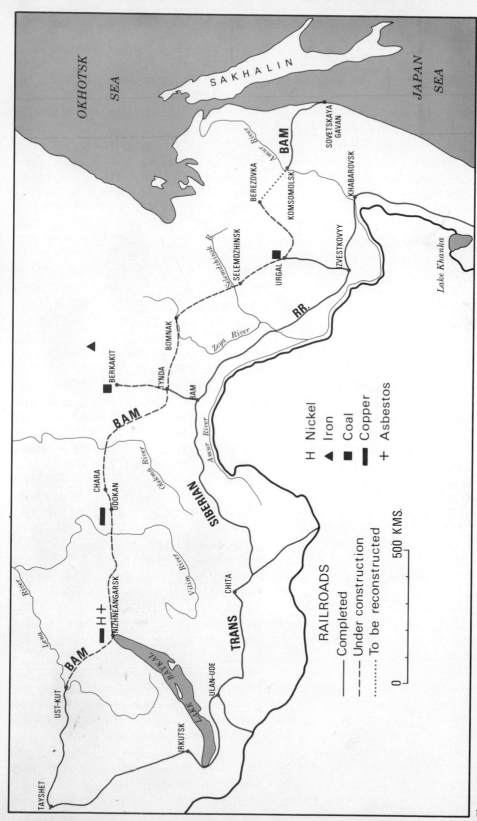

Figure 19-12 The route of the BAM. Adapted from *Soviet Geography: Review & Translation*, October, 1975, p. 504.

ranges from −60°C (−76°F) in winter to +40°C (104°F) in summer. In the horst-and-graben topography of the Baykal and Transbaykal regions the line will have to be constructed so as to withstand frequent severe earthquakes.

Immediately after the March 1974 announcement, the entire country was mobilized to support this project, and construction actually got underway at several points along the proposed route later in 1974 ahead of schedule. The main construction work is to be done between 1976 and 1980, when it is hoped that the road will begin operation, and final completion of the project is scheduled for 1983. The organization of the bulk of the work has been turned over to the Komsomol (young communist league), which is in charge of enlisting students and other recruits who are mostly in their late teens or early twenties. A pioneering fervor has taken hold of the project reminiscent of that which sparked the building of the Dnieper Dam and the Magnitogorsk steel plant in the early 1930s, the opening of the Virgin Lands in the 1950s, and the building of the Kama truck plant in the 1960s. The slogan has become "youth laughs at hardship." The young men and women who are being recruited to do manual labor on the project are issued uniforms of green overalls and battle jackets with stripes on their sleeves and bright badges on their chests to give them identity among their peers. The three-letter emblem, BAM, is sewed on their shoulders, and they are given signs to carry into the wilderness showing the cities from which they come. The Komsomol, through the various news media, has solicited work applications from youths all over the country and has published some of the enthusiastic letters from applicants giving reasons for wanting to work on the project. All newspapers posted on eastbound trains summarize the comments, such as: "I want to feel the satisfaction of being able to work on a famous project." "If I don't take the chance to see the world and to show what I can do at the age of 21, then when will I be able to?" "The toughest job in unexplored lands, in the taiga,

interests me more than the usual humdrum job of my small town."

The end of the rail line at Ust-Kut has become the jumping-off point for newcomers. The small airport at Ust-Kut is busy with helicopters arriving to airlift recruits to construction camps in the wilderness where long lines of tents and clapboard shacks have been set up as living quarters, mess halls, schools, medical centers, and recreation halls.

Unlike the pre-World War II strategic motives for building a railroad, the present BAM is being built in response to economic needs. The Trans Siberian has become badly overloaded, particularly now that the Soviets are promoting the use of the line as a "land bridge" for container traffic between Japan and Europe. The prospects of huge quantities of oil moving eastward from Western Siberia stimulated Soviet planners to contemplate how best to relieve the Trans Siberian traffic. During the early stages of development of the West Siberian oil during the late 1960s, the main planning emphasis was on a pipeline that would carry the crude oil all the way to the Pacific. But on closer examination of alternatives, Soviet economists came to the conclusion that it would be more economic and would serve more purposes to build a second railroad that would make accessible other rich mineral deposits along the way and open up an entirely new territory for development. It is now planned that crude oil will move from the West Siberian fields eastward to Tayshet by pipeline, where it will be transshipped to tankcar trains especially built for the new rail line to carry large quantities of crude oil. These trains will take the oil to Urgal, where it will be transshipped once more back to pipelines for transmission to refineries in the Far East and to port terminals for export. This will necessitate the building of a pipeline from Urgal to Komsomolsk, and perhaps other pipelines from Komsomolsk or Khabarovsk to ports on the east coast.

The proposed route of the BAM east of Lake Baykal will pass through nickel-copper deposits near Nizhneangarsk at the northern end of Lake Baykal, the large Molodezhnyy asbes-

Figure 19-13   Young Communist League members ready to board helicopters to be flown to construction sites on the BAM. Courtesy of *Soviet Life*, October, 1974, p. 3.

tos deposit in the northern part of the Buryat A.S.S.R., the huge Udokan copper deposit in the northern part of Chita Oblast — perhaps the largest copper deposit in the Soviet Union — and through the rail junction of Tynda, where it will cross a north-south railroad being built simultaneously from Bam station on the Trans Siberian Railroad north through Tynda to the Chulman coking-coal district in southern Yakutia, and perhaps eventually on to Yakutsk. The BAM will also pass near iron ore, manganese, and mica deposits in southern Yakutia as well as the operating coalfields around Urgal, where it will connect with another north-south rail line already built. The new line also will cross through regions of tremendous timber reserves and will be used to transport large quantities of this timber both westward to domestic markets and eastward to the seaports of Nakhodka (with its new outer port of Vostochnyy) and Vanino, where it will be loaded on seagoing vessels for export.

Although the main purpose for building the BAM is to facilitate the opening up of mineral resources, particularly to provide a means for transporting huge quantities of Western Siberian oil to the Pacific coast, it is also envisioned by the Soviets as a multipurpose project that will allow for the development of a whole new region that until now has been looked on as "a huge unyielding mass of land, a transit desert, culturally hopeless." Present plans call for at least 64 settlements with all essential services, most of which will be accompanied by some agricultural development in their vicinities to provide foodstuffs to the urban dwellers. The Ministry of Transport

Figure 19-14   Young Communist League members signing up for work at a BAM construction site in the taiga. Courtesy of *Soviet Life*, November, 1974, p. 8.

Construction has set up a special agency to oversee the entire project, Glavbamstroy, "the Main Administration of the Construction of the Baykal-Amur Mainline." Professional geographers have been called in to prepare recommendations on the development of the Baykal area and the Far East, and a coordinating research center for BAM has been set up by the East Siberian branch of the U.S.S.R. Academy of Sciences in Irkutsk. The Institute of Physics of the Earth has been called on to investigate the specific microseismic character of the Chara-Tynda segment of the line, and the Permafrost Institute of Yakutsk has been asked to draft recommendations for the construction of man-made structures over permafrost. The small railroad station of Shimanovsk on the Trans Siberian Railroad

Figure 19-15   A construction site on the BAM. Courtesy of the editor of *Soviet Life*.

has been chosen for transformation into a large manufacturing complex of construction materials, and repair shops have been set up in Komsomolsk and some other towns to maintain all the heavy equipment involved in the construction work. The electric power industry has a large job ahead of it to plan the provision of electricity both for the construction project and for the industries that are to be built along the rail line. Special institutes have been set up to train about 13,000 skilled workers for the Ministry of Transport Construction, and vocational training is being given to a wide range of other specialists to staff the stores, bakeries, restaurants, and

other amenities that are to be provided to the area. Wage increments of 70 percent over base pay in European U.S.S.R. have been offered to workers engaged in such auxiliary enterprises. Local municipal authorities throughout the country have been authorized to reserve the housing of skilled workers and their family members in their permanent places of residence while they are away working on the BAM project.

The construction of the BAM line should greatly enhance the prospects for trade between the Soviet Far East and Japan. Shortly after the announcement of the plans to go ahead with the BAM, the Japanese signed a contract in June 1974 to start buying coal from the Chulman district in the late 1970s at the rate of about 5 million tons per year over a 20-year period. The movement of this coal will be made possible by the Bam-Tynda-Berkakit Railroad. The BAM project will also facilitate the movement of West Siberian oil to Japan, as well as large amounts of timber from the Soviet Far East. The Soviets have decided that it might be more logical to integrate the economy of the Soviet Far East with the rest of the Far East rather than try to integrate it with the rest of the Soviet Union, whose main markets and supply areas are so far to the west.

The railroad service in the Far East was enhanced in 1973 when a ferry service began operations across the Tatar Strait from the port of Vanino on the mainland to Kholmsk on Sakhalin Island where it hooked up with the short rail system on Sakhalin. Prior to that goods had to be transshipped twice, on either side of the strait. Now railroad cars can be ferried from the railhead at Vanino to the railhead at Kholmsk. Five ferryboats of the reinforced ice breaker type maintain year-round service.

Waterways

In the huge expanses of territory that railroads do not penetrate, waterways are about the only mode of transportation. But they have many disabilities; probably the most severe, of course, is that they are frozen during long periods in this severe climatic region. Also, they do not always flow in the right direction. Many of them experience widespread flooding almost every year. Those rivers flowing north, such as the large Lena River system, as well as many others farther east along the Arctic coast, experience tremendous spring and early-summer floods when ice jams in the lower portions of the streams do not allow free flow of the water coming down from the headwaters that are already thawed farther south. In the southern part of the region where most of the population lives, the rivers generally flood during middle or late summer when the monsoon rains reach their maximum de-

velopment. The Amur and its tributaries have been of greatest concern, because it is along these streams that most of the people live. During the 1950s the Soviets and Chinese worked out a grand scheme for controlling the floods along the Amur and realizing much of its great hydroelectric potential. However, with the widening political gap between the two countries after 1960, this grand scheme has come to naught. The only construction project of any proportions accomplished so far is the Zeya River power station just north of the town of Zeya, under construction since 1965. It was hoped that the first two units of the power plant would go into operation in 1975. The construction consists of a 120-meter-high dam and a power plant with an ultimate capacity of 1.47 million kilowatts. A second dam and power station with a capacity of 2 million kilowatts has been planned for the lower Bureya River, but construction has not yet started on that project. These two dams will greatly alleviate flood conditions in the populated Zeya-Bureya Lowland, but they will not go very far in regulating the floods along the Amur River itself.

Shipping

Most of the goods moving between coastal cities in the Soviet Far East go by sea. Ports exist all along the coasts of the mainland and the many peninsulas and islands. Except for two or three of the newer ports built mainly for export-import purposes in the very southern part of the region, the ports are all severely hampered by ice for part of the year. In the far north along the Arctic coast, the Northern Sea Route is open only 2–3 months of the year, and that with great difficulty, necessitating the use of icebreakers and a wide range of support personnel and equipment to keep the convoys moving.

The primary ports for foreign connections have consistently moved southward into more open water as Russia has consolidated its control over territory farther and farther south. Before the acquisition of the maritime territory during the later part of the nineteenth century, Petropavlovsk on the east coast of Kamchatka was the primary Pacific port. This was moved southward to Nikolayevsk at the mouth of the Amur River after the 1860 takeover of what had been Chinese territory, and later it was removed again to Vladivostok on Peter the Great Bay in the very southern part of Maritime Kray. However, Vladivostok itself is hampered by ice almost every year because of its location in a very enclosed embayment.

Therefore, during the 1930s and 1940s the Soviets built the new port of Nakhodka about 90 kilometers east of Vladivostok on more open water, and the use of Vladivostok has gradually dwindled to primarily naval and fishing operations. Now another large port is being completed 20 kilometers southeast of Nakhodka in what is known as Wrangel Bay. This new port of Vostochnyy ("east") has been built with the help of Japanese investments primarily to handle containerized freight on the Transcontinental Route that the Soviets have established between Japan and Europe. It is planned that this port will soon handle about 120,000 containers per year. Some timber-loading piers have already been brought into operation, and a coal pier is now under construction that will be able to load a large ship in an hour. It is planned that a terminal for supertankers may also be built to ship oil to Japan and other parts of the Far East. It is estimated that ultimately as many as 60 piers for deep-draft vessels will be built with a total berthing length of 12 kilometers. The ultimate freight handled by Vostochnyy may be as much as five times the turnover of Nakhodka, which in 1971 had a freight turnover of 7.5 million tons — by far the largest in the Soviet Far East. When Vostochnyy expands to its ultimate size, the two ports will probably merge into one huge port.

Farther up the coast, a third large port is under construction at Vanino in the same general area as Sovietskaya Gavan ("Soviet harbor"). Vanino is being readied as the terminus of the new BAM railroad, and undoubtedly will handle much of the West Siberian oil that will be transshipped for export. It will also handle much timber and other types of mineral ores. Other important commercial ports in the Soviet Far East are Kholmsk on the southwestern coast of Sakhalin Island and Nagayevo, near Magadan on the north coast of the Sea of Okhotsk, which serves as the entrepot to the far northeastern country with its mining of gold, tin, tungsten, and mercury.

CITIES

Vladivostok

Vladivostok ("ruler of the east") is the largest city and one of the main seaports of the Soviet Far East. Founded in 1860, it soon became the main Russian seaport on the Pacific and received the transfer of the main naval base from Nikolayevsk-on-Amur. It is still one of the four main naval bases in the U.S.S.R., along with Kronshtadt near Leningrad, Sevastopol on the Crimean Peninsula, and Murmansk in the far north, and it serves as the home port for all the Soviet pelagic fishing vessels in the Pacific. The growth of the city has been rapid, and during the 1960s it surpassed Khabarovsk, the traditional metropolis of the Soviet Far East. In 1974 its population was estimated to be 495,000. The recent growth has been due to the establishment of many kinds of industries, ranging from shipbuilding and ship repairing, through fish processing, woodworking, and furniture making, to many other light industries.

Situated on a rocky, hilly peninsula at the head of Golden Horn Bay, Vladivostok is often likened to San Francisco. Its physical setting is reminiscent of San Francisco Bay. However, its climate is much more severe. During winter temperatures average only −14.7°C (5°F), and temperatures have dropped as low as −31°C, while in San Francisco winter temperatures remain above freezing all the time. Snow lies on the ground in Vladivostok about 100 days of the year and the port in the enclosed bay is hampered by ice 3 months of the winter. This has limited its value as a commercial port and has prompted the building of the ports of Nakhodka and Vostochnyy farther east.

Khabarovsk

Khabarovsk was founded in 1858 as a fortress at the important junction of the Ussuri, Sungari, and Amur Rivers. It occupies a strategic position on the rail and water transport systems where the Trans Siberian Railroad leaves the Amur River to run southward through the Ussuri-Khanka Lowland to Vladivostok. Its various industries are concentrated somewhat on machine building and metalworking, oil refining, chemicals, and lumbering and woodworking. It also has some textile and food industries to serve the Far East markets. For many years it was the largest city in the Soviet Far East, but during the 1960s it was surpassed by Vladivostok. In 1974 its population was estimated to be 488,000.

Komsomolsk-on-Amur

Komsomolsk is a Soviet city founded in 1932 in the forests along the lower Amur River to serve as the primary steel center for the Soviet Far East. In spite of its irrational location, under the auspices of the Young Communist League, Komsomolsk has prospered and grown to a city of 234,000 in 1974. When the BAM is completed through Komsomolsk its economy should be greatly enhanced, because it will be one of the main rail terminals on the line carrying oil and other important freight eastward to the port of Vanino for export. In addition to its steel industry, it has machine, metalworking, and chemical industries, the latter based largely on by-product gases from the oil refinery established in the city to refine petroleum brought in by pipeline from northern Sakhalin.

Petropavlovsk-Kamchatskiy

Petropavlovsk, with a 1974 population of 187,000, is the major city and the seat of government of Kamchatka Oblast. Located on the southeast coast of the peninsula of Kamchatka, it is one of the established seaports of the Soviet Far East, and before the acquisition of southern territories, it was the primary Russian port in the Pacific. Now its port operations are limited primarily to fish processing and movements of commodities for local consumption.

Blagoveshchensk

Blagoveshchensk, with a 1974 population of 157,000, is the major city in the important agricultural area of the Zeya-Bureya Lowland. It is a port city on the Amur River at the end of a rail spur leading southward from the Trans Siberian Railroad. At one time it was the largest Russian city on the Amur River, but it has stagnated since the Trans Siberian Railroad bypassed it to the north. Its industries are concentrated on machine building, woodworking, and food processing.

Ussuriysk

Ussuriysk, with a 1974 population of 142,000, was founded in 1866 as Nikolskoye. From 1935 to 1957 it was known as Voroshilov. It is the urban center of the rich agricultural region in the Ussuri-Khanka Lowland and is a major wood-processing center utilizing timber floated down the western slopes of the Sikhote-Alin Mountains into the Ussuri Valley. Its industries are concentrated on food processing and woodworking.

Yakutsk

Founded as an ostrog in 1632, Yakutsk early served as a center for the Russian colonization of the northern part of the Far East. In 1861 it was designated as the center of Yakutsk Region, and in 1922 it became the capital of the Yakut A.S.S.R., the second largest political unit in the entire Soviet Union, second only to the Russian Republic itself — within which it lies. By 1974 Yakutsk had grown to a population of 133,000. Located in the Lena-Vilyuy-Aldan Lowland, it has become famous around the world as the center of experimental development of arctic agriculture. However, it is far off center from the rest of the populated part of the country, and its agriculture at best is very marginal. During summer the city has contact with the outside world only via the Lena River system, and during winter it is connected by a highway southward to Never on the Trans Siberian Railroad in the far south. If a rail line ever is completed all the way from Bam station on the Trans Siberian through Tynda on the new BAM line and the Chulman coalfields of southern Yakutia eventually to the city of Yakutsk, the economy of Yakutsk will be greatly enhanced. However, the extension of the rail line into Yakutsk seems to be a dream of the future. At present Yakutsk is just an overgrown village with muddy streets and clapboard houses. Its main industries are food processing, woodworking, and machine-repair shops.

Yuzhno-Sakhalinsk

Yuzhno-Sakhalinsk ("south Sakhalin") near the southern end of Sakhalin Island is the largest city on the island. In 1974 it had a population of 124,000. It is simply a regional center with industries based on fish and food processing and woodworking.

Nakhodka

Nakhodka, the new port east of Vladivostok, has grown to a 1974 population of 121,000. At present it is the biggest commercial port in the Soviet Far East, but it will soon be surpassed by Vostochnyy just to the east. Its industries are concentrated on ship repairing, fish canning, and a tin-can factory for the fishing industry. The ports of Nakhodka and Vostochnyy will probably eventually merge.

Magadan

Magadan was founded in 1933 as the port of entry to the Kolyma goldfields inland to the north. Its population grew to 105,000 in 1974 as the result of this port function plus its role as governmental center for large Magadan Oblast.

PROSPECTS

With the decision to go ahead with the BAM railroad, the Soviets seem to have continued their practice of pouring disproportionate amounts of investment capital into the Soviet Far East. Therefore, the region is to get yet another shot in the arm that will likely keep its economy and population growing at rates above those of the national average. However, the specters of extremely long distances from the main populated part of the country and severe environmental conditions are going to continue to limit development primarily to exploitation of minerals and other resources. One cannot expect a wholesale settlement of the region. Friendly trade connections with Japan are stimulating certain industries, particularly those of the mineral fuels and timber. But in the final analysis the Far East will probably remain one of the regions where the Soviets realize some of the lowest returns on their capital investments. The region does not nearly feed itself or clothe itself or provide its own basic industrial products. So tremendous quantities of goods must be moved eastward along the Trans Siberian Railroad and eventually along the BAM. Traffic is heavily overbalanced toward the east from the Kuznetsk Basin eastward, and this overbalance intensifies toward the Pacific coast. In light of these inherent difficulties, to rationalize the economy of the Soviet Far East with the economy of the rest of the country, it would seem wise for the Soviets to reorient the economy of their Far East Region toward the general economy of the Pacific Basin, especially Japan. This is what they are now attempting to do, and the building of the BAM should greatly facilitate this effort.

READING LIST

Akhmetyeva, N.P., "O chastichnom sbrosye amurskikh vod v Tatarskiy proliv" (On the Partial Discharge of Amur River Water into the Tatar Strait), *Izvestiya Akademii Nauk SSR, seriya geografiya*, No. 2, 1974, pp. 53–57 (in Russian).

- Aleksandrov, V.A., "Rossiia na Dalnevostochnykh Rubezhakh (Utopaia Polvina XVII v.)" (Russia in the Far East Extremities — A Utopia of the Mid-Seventeenth Century), *Slavic Review,* March 1972, pp. 151–152 (in Russian).

- Armstrong, T., "Country Life in Northeast Siberia," *The Geographical Magazine,* No. 7, April 1974, pp. 344–349.

- Belenkiy, N.P., and V.S. Maslennikov, "The Baykal-Amur Mainline Railroad: Its Area of Influence and its Projected Freight Flows," *Soviet Geography: Review & Translation,* October 1975, pp. 503–513.

- Biryukov, V., "The Baykal-Amur Mainline: A Major National Construction Project," *Soviet Geography: Review & Translation,* April 1975, pp. 225–230.

- Bruner, E.F., "The Soviet Approach to Remote Area Development; The Far Eastern Example," Tenth Annual Meeting of the New York — New Jersey Division of the Association of American Geographers, *Proceedings,* 1970, pp. 147–157.

- Bruner, E.F., *The Soviet Far East: Development in a Remote Area,* Master's thesis, Syracuse University, 1969.

- *Dalnyy Vostok: Istoriya, ekonomika* (The Far East: History and Economy), Nauka, Moscow, 1974, 164 pp. (in Russian).

- Demin, L.M., *Za Tatarskim prolivom* (Beyond the Tatar Strait), Mysl, Moscow, 1965, 100 pp. (in Russian).

- Dibb, Paul, *Siberia and the Pacific; A Study of Economic Development and Trade Prospects,* Praeger, New York, 1972, 288 pp.

- Dyakonov, F.V., "Productive Forces and Productive Territorial Complexes in the Northeast of the U.S.S.R.," *Soviet Geography: Review & Translation,* January 1964, pp. 40–52.

- Gibson, James R., *Feeding the Russian Fur Trade: Provisionment of the Okhotsk Seaboard and the Kamchatka Peninsula, 1639–1856,* University of Wisconsin Press, 1969, 337 pp.

- Given, Dean W., "The Sea of Okhost: USSR's Great Lake?" United States Naval Institute, *Proceedings,* No. 9/811, September 1970, pp. 47–51.

- Gogolev, E.V., *Yakutiya na rubezhe 19-20 v.v.* (Yakutia at the Turn of the Nineteenth and Twentieth Centuries), Novosibirsk, 1970 (in Russian).

- Gurvich, I.S., and K.G. Kuzakov, *Koryakskii nationalniy okrug* (The Koryak National Okrug), Moscow, 1960, 302 pp. (in Russian).

- Jackson, W.A.D., *The Russo-Chinese Border Lands: Zone of Peaceful Contact or Potential Conflict?,* Van Nostrand, Princeton, 2nd ed., 1968, 156 pp.

- Kirby, E.S., *The Soviet Far East,* St. Martins Press, New York, 1971, 268 pp.

- Krasheninnikov, S.P., *Explorations of Kamchatka: North Pacific Scimitar,* Oregon Historical Society, Portland, 1972, 373 pp.

- Krasheninnikov, S.P., *The History of Kamchatka and the Kurilski Islands with the Countries Adjacent,* Geography Area Studies Pub., Oregon, 1973 reprint of 1764 edition.

- Krasheninnikov, V.G., "The Role of River Transport in the Development and Location of Productive Forces in the Eastern Regions of the USSR," *Soviet Geography: Review & Translation,* May 1973, pp. 295–308.

- Kravanja, Milan A., "Soviet Far East Fisheries Expansion," *Commercial Fisheries Review,* November 1964.

- Leonov, P., *Oblast na ostrovakh; kratkiy ocherk istorii razvitiya, ekonomiki i kultury Sakhalinskoy oblasti* (Oblast on Islands; a Short Essay on the History of Development, Economy, and Culture of Sakhalin Oblast), Mysl, Moscow, 1974, 318 pp. (in Russian).

- Leontov, V., *Khozyaystvo i kultura narodov Chukotski (1958–1970 gg.)* (The Economy and Culture of the Chukchi — 1958–1970), Nauka, Novosibirsk, 1973, 178 pp. (in Russian).

- Mayergoyz, I.M., "The Unique Economic-Geographic Situation of the Soviet Far East and Some Problems of Using it over the Long Term," *Soviet Geography: Review & Translation,* September 1975, pp. 428–434.

- Okladnikov, A.P., *The Soviet Far East in Antiquity: An Archaeological and Historical Study of the Maritime Region of the USSR,* University of Toronto Press, Toronto, 1965, 280 pp.

- Pokshishevskiy, V.V., "On the Geography of Pre-Revolutionary Colonization and Migration Processes in the Southern Part of the Soviet Far East," *Soviet Geography: Review & Translation,* April 1963, pp. 17–31.

- *Rossiyskaya Federatsiya. Dalniy Vostok* (The Russian Federation. The Far East), Mysl, Moscow, 1971, 399 pp. (in Russian).

- Solomon, Michael, *Magadan,* Auerbach, Princeton and London, 1971, 243 pp.

- *Soviet Geography: Review & Translation,* February 1968. (Almost the entire issue deals with Eastern Siberia and the Far East.)

- Staf, Karl, *Yakutia as I Saw It,* Foreign Languages Publishing House, Moscow, 1958, 113 pp.
- Stephan, John J., *Sakhalin: A History,* Clarendon Press, Oxford, 1971, 240 pp.
- Suvorova, A.F., "The Industry of the Soviet Far East Today and Tomorrow", *Geografiya v shkole,* No. 3, 1975.
- Thiel, Erich, *The Soviet Far East,* Praeger, 1957, 388 pp.
- Tideman, A.M., and G.S. Roukin, "Regional Planning Problems in the Soviet Far East," *Soviet Geography: Review & Translation,* February 1971, pp. 124–132.
- Treadgold, Donald L., *The Great Siberian Migration,* Princeton University Press, 1957, 278 pp.
- Udovenko, B.G., *Dalniy Vostok* (The Far East), Moscow, 1957 (in Russian).
- Zubov, S.M., *Fizicheskaya geografiya SSSR. Chast 3 — Srednyaya i Severo-Vostochnaya Sibir; Gory Yuzhnoy Sibiri; Dalnyy Vostok* (Physical Geography of the U.S.S.R. Part 3 — Central and Northeastern Siberia; Mountains of Southern Siberia; Far East), Minsk, 1971 (in Russian).

index

The author gratefully acknowledges help in indexing by
Mary Lydolph and Steven W. Lund.